Y0-ABF-140

Northeast Asia's Stunted Regionalism

Bilateral Distrust in the Shadow of Globalization

This book paints a comprehensive picture of the pursuit of regionalism across Northeast Asia in the fifteen years following the cold war. In each of six periods, it identifies the main dynamic of regionalism and the problems that slowed regionalism's advance. It examines the evolving strategies of four countries – China, Japan, South Korea, and Russia – emphasizing the importance of bilateral relations while keeping in mind the globalizing U.S. role. By focusing on debates in each country, most of which have been little covered in English, the book demonstrates how suspicious neighbors and clashing strategies have undermined aspirations for regionalism. While false starts keep giving way to fresh hopes, only by learning the lessons of this transitional era will regionalism be placed on a stable footing. These include embracing globalization more fully while using regionalism for balance, working together in integrating North Korea while recognizing South Korea's pivotal role, compromising to allow China and Japan to share leadership, and focusing on a long-term vision of Northeast Asia.

Gilbert Rozman is Musgrave Professor of Sociology at Princeton University. He is the author or editor of many books, including *Japan and Russia: The Tortuous Path to Normalization, 1949–1999* (2000).

Northeast Asia's Stunted Regionalism

Bilateral Distrust in the Shadow of Globalization

GILBERT ROZMAN
Princeton University

CAMBRIDGE
UNIVERSITY PRESS

PUBLISHED BY THE PRESS SYNDICATE OF THE UNIVERSITY OF CAMBRIDGE
The Pitt Building, Trumpington Street, Cambridge, United Kingdom

CAMBRIDGE UNIVERSITY PRESS
The Edinburgh Building, Cambridge CB2 2RU, UK
40 West 20th Street, New York, NY 10011-4211, USA
477 Williamstown Road, Port Melbourne, VIC 3207, Australia
Ruiz de Alarcón 13, 28014 Madrid, Spain
Dock House, The Waterfront, Cape Town 8001, South Africa

http://www.cambridge.org

First published 2004

Printed in the United States of America

Typeface Sabon 10/12 pt. *System* LaTeX 2ε [TB]

A catalog record for this book is available from the British Library.

Library of Congress Cataloging in Publication Data

Rozman, Gilbert.
Northeast Asia's stunted regionalism : bilateral distrust in the shadow of globalization / Gilbert Rozman.
p. cm.
Includes bibliographical references and index.
ISBN 0-521-83565-8 – ISBN 0-521-54360-6 (pb.)
1. East Asia. 2. East Asia – Relations – Russia (Federation) 3. Russia (Federation) – Relations – East Asia. 4. Regionalism (International organization) I. Title.
DS504.5.R69 2004
327.5′009′049–dc22 2003065354

ISBN 0 521 83565 8 hardback
ISBN 0 521 54360 6 paperback

Contents

Acknowledgments

There have been countless acts of kindness over the course of this decade-long project. I hope that the appearance of this book will, in some small way, serve as repayment for those who believed in the undertaking. Hundreds of academic researchers and state officials have generously shared their thinking with me and helped me to locate materials during my frequent visits to the region. Of these, I owe the greatest debt to Iwaki Shigeyuki of the National Diet Library for his unstinting support of my research on Japan and regionalism. He sets the highest standards for comprehensive research on foreign policy and has prodded me to raise my own. I am grateful also to Li Jingjie of the Chinese Academy of Social Sciences and Tamara Troyakova of the Far Eastern Branch of the Russian Academy for their repeated assistance in travel and material collection. The many others in the region who helped must go unrecognized, but not unappreciated.

Research began with grants from the Committee on Scholarly Communication with the PRC and the Chiang Ching-kuo Foundation in 1992–3. It continued with awards from the United States Institute of Peace and the Woodrow Wilson International Center for Scholars, where I was a Fellow in 1996–7. The National Council for Eurasian and Eastern European Research funded related research on Russian ties to China and Korea. I am thankful to all of these organizations for facilitating my research trips and the time I spent reading and writing. Of course, only I am responsible for the contents and the incessantly widened scope of a book that was drawn together from smaller projects.

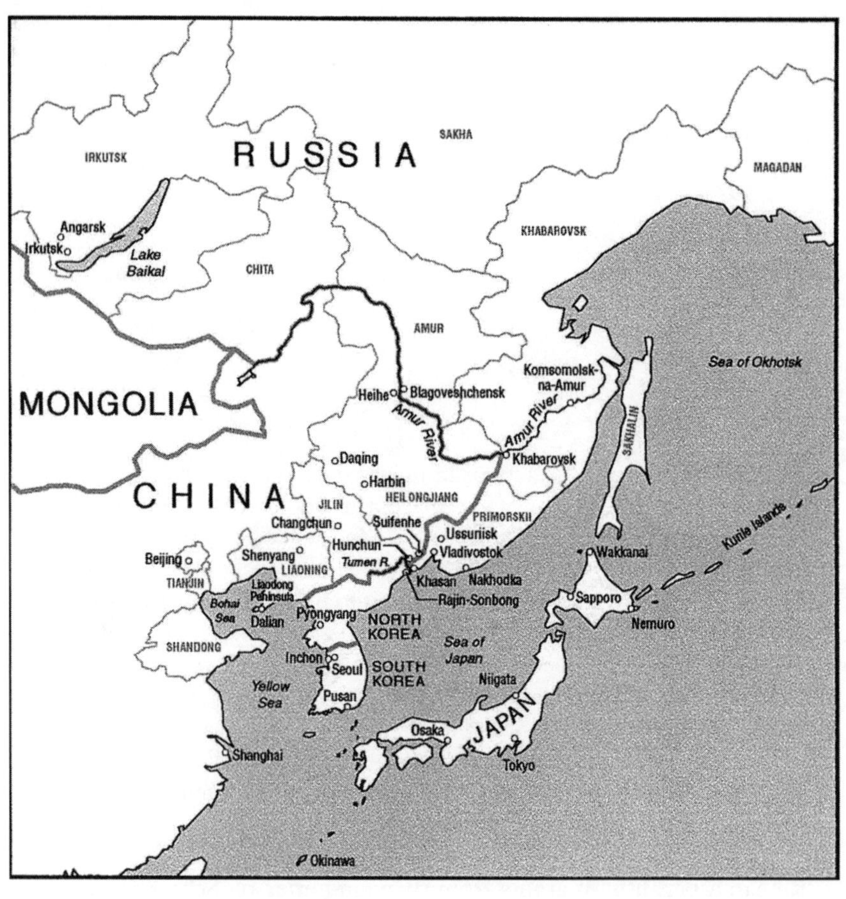

RUSSIA
SAKHA
IRKUTSK
MAGADAN
Angarsk
Irkutsk
Lake Baikal
CHITA
KHABAROVSK
AMUR
Sea of Okhotsk
Komsomolsk-na-Amur
MONGOLIA
Heihe
Blagoveshchensk
Amur River
Amur River
SAKHALIN
Daqing
Khabarovsk
Harbin
CHINA
JILIN
HEILONGJIANG
PRIMORSKII
Changchun
Suifenhe
Kurile Islands
Hunchun
Ussuriisk
Beijing
Shenyang
Tumen R.
Vladivostok
Wakkanai
LIAONING
TIANJIN
Liaodong Peninsula
Khasan
Nakhodka
Bohai Sea
Rajin-Sonbong
Sapporo
Dalian
Pyongyang
NORTH KOREA
Nemuro
SHANDONG
Sea of Japan
Inchon
Seoul
SOUTH KOREA
Niigata
Yellow Sea
Pusan
JAPAN
Osaka
Shanghai
Tokyo
Okinawa

Northeast Asia's Stunted Regionalism

Bilateral Distrust in the Shadow of Globalization

1

Introduction

The Challenge of the Northeast Asia Region

The 1990s were supposed to be the decade when the countries of Northeast Asia (NEA) coalesced into a region that is greater than the sum of its parts. Still a major center of development through the eighteenth century with the world's two largest cities (Tokyo and Beijing), it fell on hard times: first with an intensified inward-orientation in each country, then with the arrival of imperialism, and finally with impassable dividing lines lasting throughout the cold war. Suddenly, hope arose that a spirit of cooperation would turn NEA from the depths of division to the heights of integrated development. The result could be a rival for the European Union (EU) and North Atlantic Free Trade Agreement (NAFTA) and a framework for reconfiguring great power relations. Instead, the residue of the cold war suffocated the sprouts of regionalism. The potential remains; a breakthrough could be reached although further delay is likely due to reluctance to embrace regionalism by balancing globalization and nationalism.

At first glance, NEA would seem to have what it takes to establish a recognized community with its own formal organizations and regional consciousness. Parts of the area enjoy a high level of prosperity accompanied by determination to achieve economic integration with surrounding countries. The three core states of China, Japan, and South Korea have joined the World Trade Organization (WTO), committing to reduce barriers to economic ties. Intraregional trade and investment skyrocketed in the 1990s and show no letup even in the aftermath of the Asian financial crisis and the global slowdown of 2001–2. Frequent summits promised improved political ties and trust, while the theme of regionalism resurfaced as an appealing goal. Yet, it is no longer possible to take seriously the excuses of boosters that the momentum keeps building along a timetable that is not unduly long. Instead, we must ask why after fifteen years of pursuing regionalism there has been no breakthrough.

Regionalism failed when each of the six countries active in NEA succumbed to nationalism that blocked the way to trust and cooperation, but the responsibility for failure is not equally shared. At the beginning of the 1990s it was assumed that all actors in NEA were prepared to make at least the minimum sacrifice necessary in return for substantial benefits from economic integration and other regional ties. Japan was thought to have shed much of its nationalism in response to a devastating defeat and to be eager to rally its neighbors to regionalism based on respect rather than control. China and Russia would act because they were dislodging communist-inspired nationalism and awakening to the advantages of an interdependent world. South Korea would recognize that the long-sought key to reunification comes from closer ties across the region. North Korea might be the last to act, but it would be so isolated it would have no alternative. Finally, the United States was now so secure in its power and well being that it would have no problem with others, in Asia as well as Europe, joining in regional ties as long as they raised few security or economic protectionist questions. Looking back, we find these assumptions to have been incorrect. Nationalism was, indeed, the culprit along with unresolved tensions between globalization and regionalism and insufficient local vitality for decentralization to become a positive force for regionalism. The dream of a single, economically integrated region dissolved in a caldron of great-power rivalries and divided countries torn by narrow notions of national interest and distrust.

The answers suggested in the following text cast doubt on the usual targets of criticism, while acknowledging some negative impact of each on the environment for regionalism. Although U.S. opposition to NEA regionalism has been visible at times, it serves more as a myth useful to those who want to transfer the blame than as a barrier to practical region building consistent with globalization. If Japan's inability to put the history issue behind it stirs lingering resentment that plays into the hands of nationalists across NEA, the idea that this blocks regionalism conveniently diverts attention away from more compelling causes. Likewise, continued problems generated by the Communist Party's rule in China serve more as a smokescreen to deflect accusations than as the impediment to a regional community. In addition, South Korea's preoccupation to finding a path to reunification with North Korea may leave it with an instrumental approach to regionalism and Russia's anxiety over the vulnerability of its Far East may narrow its acceptance of regionalism, but neither of these factors should top our list of impediments. Finally, even though North Korea's unnerving resort to threat-based diplomacy obviously soils the atmosphere, it does not prevent the creation of a region on all sides of North Korea leaving it aside.

This book explores how regionalism was pursued, what went wrong, and who was to blame. It presents an interpretive history of relations among the countries of NEA over fifteen years and draws lessons on what is needed to restart regionalism, finding hope as well as caution in recent developments. In contrast to most studies of relations in NEA that emphasize either economics or security, this is a sociologist's story of how nations struggling with their own identities in a new era could not develop shared perceptions of the challenges before them, trustworthy networks for working together, and a common vision of what constitutes a secure and mutually advantageous environment. All sides at the national and local level were to blame as some tilted to geopolitical realism that left little room for assuring neighbors and others to a kind of economic idealism that omitted safeguards against abuse. As the decade passed, countries kept groping for a path toward regionalism through a changing mix of strategies, on a bilateral and multilateral level.

In 2003 we still do not know what kind of a region will take shape in NEA. It is difficult to say what will be its geographical range, its pattern of economic integration, its great-power balance, and even its degree of intercivilizational harmony or conflict. No other region in the world may be as confused or as significant for the coming decades of global security and integration. Yet, behind us stretches a "decade" of evidence from efforts to create a new regionalism, offering a record that can divulge a great deal about why cooperation is difficult and what seems to work best. To assess this evidence we need to avoid a United States–centered political economy that inevitably stresses globalization or a realist's deductive notion of balance-of-power politics that is bound to simplify fear of domination. Instead, we benefit by immersing ourselves in the actual views expressed within the region.[1] This means studying ties among many powers from multiple angles successively over a "decade" that reveals great variations. This book covers all of NEA for the full sweep of the 1990s (from the end of the cold war to the U.S. responses in the war against terrorism and weapons of mass destruction [WMD]), paying heed to clashing perceptions on economic, geostrategic, and civilizational aspects of regional formation.

The book argues that the prime culprit in aborted efforts to achieve regionalism is modernization with insufficient globalization. Unbalanced development dating back many decades has left domestic interests in each country unusually resistant to important manifestations of openness and trust to the outside. This fostered a prevailing worldview in each case that fixates on symbols of supposed unfairness or humiliation. The result is bilateral stumbling blocks that epitomize narrow-minded attitudes at a time when rapid change demands bold strategies. Even when many herald the benefits of regionalism in a context of globalization, preoccupation with short-term economic or political objectives, rooted in how each country rushed ahead in modernization, stands in the way.

Northeast Asia is not easy to define because it is a region still in the process of formation. At its core are China, Japan, South Korea, and, some day, emerging from its almost total isolation, North Korea. Present geographically

[1] Due to the breadth of regionalism, I have no choice but to cover some themes by concentrating on conclusions, leaving much evidence in my earlier publications. On topics less covered, I give a taste of the rich empirical evidence through listed citations.

and discussed as a factor in regionalism is the Russian Far East plus Eastern Siberia, while in the background looms Moscow. Distant geographically, but deeply engaged, is the United States, which stations more than 80,000 troops in the region, offers security guarantees to Japan and South Korea, and counts three countries of the region among its six largest trading partners outside North America. On the periphery and of little consequence yet is Mongolia. Excluded from our analysis are Taiwan and Hong Kong with their close linkages to Southeast China and beyond to Southeast Asia (SEA). This leaves North and Northeast China in the forefront, narrowing the coverage from comprehensive treatment of Chinese ties with Japan and the United States to a targeted analysis of relations most significant for the emergence of a new region including the Korean peninsula and much of Asiatic Russia. This study weighs China and Japan equally as the prime actors in regionalism, but it also takes South Korea seriously as a critical force and recognizes the significance of Russia and the United States in the meeting ground for four powers insistent on their entitlement in shaping the region's evolution.

To understand this region we must break through habitual limits on scholarship. Change accelerated to the extent that in place of patterns that typically lasted for a decade in the cold war era we observe periods of just two to three years before a strikingly new context appeared. The boundaries chosen are 1) 1989, when China chose repression over political reform, Sino-Russian relations were normalized, Russo-Japanese talks over normalization accelerated with Tokyo's decision to balance its territorial demands with support for improved economic and other ties, and U.S.-Russian ties gained a big boost from the fall of the Berlin Wall and the end of the cold war; and 2) 2003, after terrorism propelled the United States onto a new agenda that led to war in Iraq and a showdown with North Korea, Japan's foreign relations emerged from a lull to reaffirm the need for regionalism even as its economy remained stalled, China joined the WTO, Russia made a bold decision to side with the United States in the war against terrorism but drew back some after the United States occupied Iraq, and South Korea's new president took office caught between U.S. suspicions and North Korean bellicosity. At the end of 2003 the United States had consolidated its assertive global leadership with the arrest of Sadam Hussein and Libya's agreement to abandon WMD, Sino-U.S. relations had stabilized with tacit arrangements on North Korea and Taiwan, and elections in Japan and Russia had strengthened nationalist leaders who also accepted the need for cautious regionalism. Altogether this long "decade" of the 1990s is divided here into six periods, each a separate context for regionalism. The first chapter sets the context; the last chapter turns to the opening of a new era, considering lessons from the past fifteen years and clues on how regionalism is poised to change.

We can improve our understanding of NEA by concentrating on diverse sources of information, much of it little noticed in the West and published in the languages of the region. Most of the citations in this book come from publications in Japanese, Chinese, Russian, and Korean because they happen to cover the relevant themes in greatest detail.[2] Arguably, even in the age of the Internet, the knowledge gap using sources from Western countries to cover developments in NEA is not growing any smaller. Without a rich base of empirical evidence, faulty reasoning about regionalism is difficult to avoid.[3]

It behooves us to shift away from the established paradigms to an interdisciplinary examination of various dimensions of regionalism. The struggle over the future of NEA involves bilateral economic, political, and cultural relations as well as each country's domestic strategies and identities coupled with the direct effects of regionalism, all occurring in a context of globalization. The gap between what is needed to comprehend regionalism in NEA and what is offered by the standard academic disciplines has grown beyond earlier proportions. To focus on how countries struggle to work together means to emphasize international relations, but not at the expense of keeping an eye on national identities and development strategies filtered through political divisions and economic choices. Multistate relations emerge through insights found in combinations of sources from each country in the region organized with the tools of interdisciplinary studies.[4]

The following chapters treat as the four building blocks of NEA regionalism: 1) *globalization and the United States*, the world environment and U.S. relations with the major countries in the region; 2) *domestic development tied to regionalism*, including national identities, development strategies, and the balance of centralization and decentralization for the main actors within the region; 3) *bilateral relations in the region*, most importantly Sino-Japanese, Sino-Russian, and Russo-Japanese relations; and 4) *a general overview of strategies for regionalism* and how they fit together. Of these, the first is covered briefly as the starting point for each chronological chapter, and the second is reviewed quickly for each of four countries as each chapter progresses. Most coverage is given to the third building block: bilateral relations and mutual perceptions. This assumed the largest role in a decade of missed opportunities. The book focuses on the three great-power linkages

[2] I have tried for each country except North Korea to follow foreign language sources, drawing on their abundance and diversity. On Chinese studies of NEA, see Lin Chang, "Zhongguo Dongbeiya yanjiu de xianzhuang," *Dangdai Yatai*, 4 (2002), pp. 56–60.

[3] The cornerstones for research on NEA in foreign languages, ordered by the utility of sources in each language, are approximately fifteen national newspapers (Japanese, Korean, Russian, and Chinese), twenty local newspapers (Russian, Japanese, Chinese, and Korean), sixty journals (Chinese, Japanese, Russian, and Korean), and seventy-five popular and academic books annually (Japanese, Chinese, Russian, and Korean).

[4] Gilbert Rozman, "A Regional Approach to Northeast Asia," *Orbis*, 39(1) Winter 1995, pp. 65–80; Gilbert Rozman, "Spontaneity and Direction Along the Russo-Chinese Border," in Stephen Kotkin and David Wolff, eds., *Rediscovering Russia in Asia: Siberia and the Russian Far East* (Armonk, NY: M. E. Sharpe, 1995), pp. 275–89.

not involving the United States and, to a lesser degree, on South Korea's relations with its three neighboring powers in a regional context. In each case, bilateral ties are studied from the perspective of both sides, as seen in internal debates. At the beginning and end of each chapter, overviews of emergent regionalism integrate coverage of all of the countries.

Challenging Recent Idealist and Realist Thinking

Using the example of the EU as a standard sets the bar for regionalism too high. Nowhere else are countries so prepared to discard many staples of sovereignty. Using NAFTA is misleading too, since the United States dominates the region and cultural differences with Canada are slight while Mexico has been drawn closer, if still not so close, through migration quite independent of national policies and consciousness. Talk of Association of Southeast Asian Nations (ASEAN) regionalism also is deceptive, because it takes an organization long on summits and short on substance as if it signifies a process of integration.[5] Instead, we should hold regionalism in NEA to an intermediate standard measured by 1) *rapidly increasing economic ties* backed by a joint strategy of economic integration; 2) *growing political ties* nurtured by summits and organizations that set goals for collective action, regionally and globally, that have a good chance of implementation; 3) *advancing social integration* through labor migration, business networks, and a common agenda on outstanding problems; 4) *shared consciousness of regional identity* enhanced by awareness of shared culture in the face of globalization; and 5) *a widening security agenda* to resolve tensions and ensure stability. These themes have arisen often in discussions of NEA regionalism, and there is agreement on their indispensability if a threshold is to be crossed. Regionalism is a goal; its pursuit offers a lens through which to view recent developments in NEA.

Boosters of regionalism may agree on what are, in principle, some essential steps, but they differ on the order of these steps and on the degree to which they should be pursued. Most prominent are economic regionalists, who give priority to accelerating trade and investment plus the trappings of political friendship.[6] Many have a minimalist notion. Some as liberal optimists are overly hopeful about the spillover that will follow to other types of regionalism; others as nationalists, who are inherently pessimistic about cultural and strategic integration, intend to use a small dose of regionalism as a fortress against a large dose of globalization; and still others as cautious

[5] David M. Jones and Michael L. R. Smith, "ASEAN's Imitation Community," *Orbis*, 46(1) Winter 2002, pp. 93–109.

[6] Dozens of conferences have sought the least common denominator between countries and scholars. See, for example, Won Bae Kim, Burnham O. Campbell, Mark Valencia, and Lee Jay Cho, eds., *Regional Economic Cooperation in Northeast Asia: Proceedings of the Vladivostok Conference* (Vladivostok: Northeast Asian Economic Forum, 1992).

pragmatists are willing to start with topics that unite without giving much thought to the barriers ahead. Extremely rare are all-around regionalists who are willing to press for simultaneous advances in all five areas listed. Given the obstacles, many minimalists consider it prudent to seek formal approval by top leaders of some trappings of regionalism accompanied by reliance on informal mechanisms rather than the formation of strong regional institutions.[7]

Usually missing from discussions of regionalism in NEA is any strategy for tying regionalism to the other powerful forces driving the countries involved. Globalization no doubt belongs on this list.[8] Given the problems apparent in both the socialist model of development found in China, North Korea, and the Soviet Union, and the East Asian corporatist model found in Japan and South Korea, decentralization also deserves to be on the list. Another force is security stabilization and moderation of nationalism as seen in the search for a balance of great powers and confidence building where hot spots could erupt. Boosters of regionalism often misjudge the mix needed, belittling globalization, overrating localism, and underestimating the costs of nationalism and insecurity.[9]

It is essential to keep in mind that regionalism is emerging against a backdrop of rapid globalization in three most prominent respects. In 1989–93 the main impulse of globalization was the cultural claims to victory for a way of life: communism's defeat, the triumph of democracy and human rights, the information age bringing down barriers to knowledge just as the Berlin Wall had fallen, and insistence on a new world order steeped in universal ideals. By 1996–2000 financial globalization took center stage, showcasing the power of lowering barriers to the flow of capital: overwhelming the developmental state as in the Asian financial crisis and triumphantly heralding the unlimited vistas for Wall Street's way of business. Finally, in 2001–3 globalization had taken the form of the battle against terror and WMD, leading to the nuclear crisis over North Korea. This battle need not exclude either unilateralism to the tune of the U.S. administration or multilateralism in which other actors play a large role. Regionalism is rising in the shadow of both tendencies; in NEA it is the United States that is inextricably identified with globalization while images of multilateral powers endure.

At least five options for the balance of regionalism and globalization drew some attention in the 1990s. First, there is *globalization with little overt*

7 Peter J. Katzenstein and Takashi Shiraishi, eds. *Network Power: Japan and Asia* (Ithaca: Cornell University Press, 1997); Dajin Peng, "The Changing Nature of East Asia as an Economic Region," *Pacific Affairs*, 73(2) Summer 2000, pp. 171–91; Dajin Peng, "Invisible Linkages: A Regional Perspective of East Asian Political Economy," *International Studies Quarterly*, 46 (2002), pp. 423–47.

8 Samuel S. Kim, ed. *East Asia and Globalization* (Lanham, MD: Rowman and Littlefield, 2000).

9 Tsuneo Akaha, ed. *Politics and Economics in Northeast Asia: Nationalism and Regionalism in Contention* (New York: St. Martin's Press, 1999).

regionalism, as Russia accepts universal human values along the lines of the rhetoric of Mikhail Gorbachev after 1987 and Boris Yeltsin in his early days, Japan remains closely identified with the West as in the cold war, South Korea embraces global economic forces as Kim Dae-jung signaled following the Asian financial crisis in 1997, China is pressed to come aboard as some anticipated would happen after its June 4, 1989 crackdown led to global sanctions, and North Korea is left with no alternative. While most of these outcomes were doubtful, globalizers in the United States kept anticipating that the overwhelming impact of world economic forces would eventually overwhelm the weak sprouts of regionalism in NEA. Second, there is *globalization with open regionalism*, as multinational corporations from Japan and the West stand in the vanguard in the development of a "new frontier," keeping the United States fully engaged. Most dreams within the NEA region accept a vision of advancing regionalism without regarding it as a major rival of globalization. Third, there is *regionalism balanced against globalization.* In the wake of rising fears that regionalism through the EU and NAFTA would have a protectionist impact, this was the reasoning of many. It also appealed to those seeking a counterweight to limit Western values and U.S. hegemony. Fourth, there is *regionalism at the expense of globalization.* Some Chinese stalwarts of communism and both left- and right-wing nationalists in Japan contemplated an element of closed regionalism as a means for resisting globalization. Finally, we can observe *forced globalization to block regionalism and great-power balancing.* This is a kind of containment approach espoused by some U.S. conservatives who saw in challenges from China, North Korea, and Russia a replay of the cold war that requires strengthened military alliances in order to suppress any threats to their approach to globalization.

Although the actors engaged in the struggle over regionalism include advocates of all five approaches, only the second and third options were seriously pursued as means to regionalism. If the dominant tendency acknowledged was the pursuit of open regionalism consistent with globalization,[10] we would be remiss in overlooking a strong undercurrent of interest in a different type of regionalism capable of balancing globalization.

It would be a mistake to dwell only on the global and regional levels. After all, the actors deciding how much weight to give to each represented at least three other levels: the national, the local, and the domestic private sector divided between national and local, market-oriented and protectionist, legal and criminal. Central governments, sometimes swayed by nationalism, had a critical say on initiatives related to regionalism. Internal debates veered between protectionist fears of regionalism as well as globalization

[10] Peter J. Katzenstein, "Regionalism and Asia," in Shaun Breslin, Christopher W. Hughes, Nicola Phillips, and Ben Rosamond, eds., *New Regionalisms in the Global Political Economy: Theories and Cases* (London: Routledge, 2002), pp. 104–18.

and reformist support for both goals. Also claiming a voice were authorities at the local level on the frontlines of regionalism.[11] They too jostled between protectionism clothed in nationalist language and encouragement for foreign investments. Finally, business groups made decisions that shaped the course of cooperation. In favor of some regionalism, they could also scuttle broader cooperation for fear of competition. Some supporters of decentralization espoused "glocalization," forging regionalism through joint efforts of global and local forces. If the main force blocking both regionalism and globalization has been nationalism under the political leadership in the capital, both local governments and private-sector monopolists have caused obstruction too, intent on quick returns without a commitment to building a lasting foundation. Regionalism's failure has multiple causes.

Commentators on regionalism come mainly in two varieties, reflecting the narrow blinders of social science today. Neither type has done a convincing job of explaining the course of regionalism in NEA in the 1990s. In one corner sit the "liberal" political economists, who largely enumerate reasons why we should expect regionalism soon. Most of the literature on this region's efforts speaks approvingly of what is being done and optimistically about the payoff. A majority of publications are conference volumes where contributors encourage each other to more positive predictions, warning that one country or another's foot dragging is interfering with a natural process. If we may detect differences between those who look at the big picture and those with a narrower range, this should not deter us from critically scrutinizing the political economy approach in general for failing to pay adequate attention to formidable barriers in this region.

The overall economic picture of NEA does provide grounds for optimism. There is an extraordinary complementarity among the countries of the region, suggesting that everything is present for regionalism confirming economic integration. Intraregional trade climbed astronomically in fifteen years, led by China's commerce with Japan and South Korea. Indeed, the figures nearly quadrupled, approaching $250 billion a year. Serious exploration of large-scale projects, above all in energy, confirms high expectations. In a short time span South Korea embraced globalization and China entered WTO as both anticipated more impetus for regionalism.[12] Meanwhile, Japan in the midst of prolonged stagnation has focused on the region as its best hope for resuscitation. Also at the level of cross-border ties, those

[11] Glenn D. Hook, "The Japanese Role in Emerging Microregionalism: The Pan-Yellow Sea Economic Zone," and Christopher W. Hughes, "Tumen River Area Development Programme (TRADP): Frustrated Microregionalism as a Microcosm of Political Rivalries," in Shaun Breslin and Glenn D. Hook, eds., *Microregionalism and World Order* (New York: Palgrave, 2002), pp. 95–114 and 115–43.

[12] Takahara Akio, "Japan and China: New Regionalism and the Emerging Asian Order," in Hugo Dobson and Glenn D. Hook, eds., *Japan and Britain in the Contemporary World* (London: Routledge Curzon, 2003), pp. 96–112.

who praise the potential for natural economic territories have seen some expectations fulfilled for decentralized linkups and formal barriers falling. If economic conditions suffice to produce regionalism, NEA would already be noted as the world's third great regionalism. Instead, it presents a record of flawed efforts to reach beyond economics that defy standard social science explanations.

On all sides we can observe limits to economic ties that had the potential to boost regionalism. Fearful of loss of power, North Korea's leadership stymied almost every proposed opening, while Russian regional and national authorities narrowly steered most initiatives into dead-end devices for the benefit of a few. South Koreans fear dominance by Japan's economic powerhouses, but Japanese also fear damage to vested interests by farming in China and South Korea and by Chinese industry. Such tensions played out in the context of bilateral relations linked to national strategies and mutual trust, which offer the best line of vision to comprehend the limits of economic forces in regionalism. Many arguments of political economists are rooted in assumptions about what drives political leaders to make economic reforms and how changes in economic ties affect political decisions. The record of bilateral relations in NEA reveals that either leaders have resisted the economic steps that boosters of regionalism expected them to take or the economic gains failed to produce the anticipated impact on political calculations that could have made regionalism a reality. Only by placing the economic interactions in a broad bilateral context are we likely to understand why optimists should be doubted.

Optimists often extrapolate from observations of economic integration through overseas Chinese networks. In the 1980s and 1990s an extraordinary symbiosis occurred between the entrepreneurs of Hong Kong, Taiwan, and parts of SEA and the labor force opportunities in coastal China emerging from a socialist command economy and reviving traditional attitudes in a long-repressed population. There were hyperbolic claims of the emerging ASEAN region riding a wave of foreign investment, expanding exports, and political cooperation to join with Greater China on the path to regionalism. Observers made serious miscalculations in their high expectations for this new notion of East Asian regionalism focused more to the south than the north. Forces for regionalism linked to SEA and Greater China were far weaker than recognized. Informal networks of Chinese create a short-term basis for cooperation, but they do not address security questions and the larger political calculus of great-power relations and nationalism. The nations of SEA could exude confidence of shared goals as long as incoming investment flowed freely, but their blasé attitudes, political rifts, and narrow protectionist thinking were starkly exposed once the harsh facts of the Asian financial crisis interfered. The three big economies east of the Himalayas remain Japan, China, and South Korea, forming the core of regional potential. As was true in the twentieth century, the United States and Russia loom as major actors in resolving fundamental questions: security, political balance, energy, and so forth. Optimists have concentrated on a sideshow instead of reasoning broadly about the nature of regionalism, keeping in mind the presence of the two great powers of China and Japan.

Realists may claim more credit as doubters about regionalism on grounds of inadequate security in NEA. Yet, their reasoning for why security drives countries apart is not well rooted in the facts of this region. The most fundamental argument in realist theory is that a single dominant power will induce a countervailing effort by secondary powers to limit it. From 1989 to 2002 U.S. power became ever more dominant. China, the rival concerned with catching up, and Russia, the past opponent anxious about loss of status, should have joined forces. There were signs of such cooperation, but they proved quite meager. Japan, the world's second most powerful country if it chose to allocate its resources toward that end, declined to draw closer politically to either China or Russia. These facts are incompatible with the main tenets of realist theory. Some suggest that future orientation can skew reasoning about threats, and that China's rise, particularly as a regional power, trumps the U.S. rise in this era. New guidelines for U.S.-Japan defense cooperation since 1996 may be seen as a realist response to China. Yet Russia, South Korea, and North Korea are the three front-line states on China's border, and none of them have taken any clear action to find partners to limit China's power. Moreover, Japan failed to take the China threat seriously enough to curtail its own nationalist approaches to Russia and South Korea. We have no alternative but to conclude that neither U.S. nor Chinese power is producing the kinds of geopolitical reactions that realists expect.

Northeast Asia has a real threat to security from North Korea, which is developing WMD accompanied by bellicose language and no reassuring economic ties. Yet, while in 1994 the United States led a coalition to pay for an energy agreement that stopped plutonium processing, coordination to contain the North, even in 2003 as a nuclear crisis deepened, left China and Russia doubtful and South Korea hesitant. No country wants the North to develop nuclear weapons, but that does not mean there is a true joining of forces. No doubt, overall uncertainty about security limits the search for regionalism, but realist theory becomes confused if we attempt to mix together three different types of threats counteracting each other in a single region as well as the tendency for nationalist issues rooted in historical identities to trump current indicators of security threats.

Northeast Asia has conflicting territorial claims, but they have not resulted in a single military conflict or burst of casualties in the past fifteen years. China and North Korea have tested missiles in ways that were regarded as provocative, eliciting sharp rhetoric about security. Leaders have made statements that irritated public opinion in other nations. Yet, until 2003, apart from a brief U.S. buildup against North Korea in 1994, there was little fear of war. Across the Taiwan straits, where the potential for conflict brought the most concern for a time, trade and investment have flowed in huge quantity. If disputes appear to many to stand in the way of regionalism, they do so less for reasons of imminent danger than because of mutual images that interfere with trust.

The pessimists concentrating on security have trouble explaining why regionalism keeps being promoted. Simplistic assertions about barriers do little to reveal recurrent drives to reach a breakthrough in regionalism. The Chinese interpretation seems to be right that the forces of cooperation exceed the forces of competition, with the addition that each nation's calculus about the balance of the two forces has been in flux. Only a close look at evolving bilateral relations may reveal this shifting balance of forces.

Analysts find it easier to address security questions when there is an obvious threat than when there is balancing for an uncertain future or territorial reunification at stake. Among those with a pessimistic view of security are some who twist their analysis to warn against a more serious threat than really exists. At the beginning of the 1990s the lingering Soviet threat in the region was exaggerated by some Japanese, and by the late 1990s some of the same observers were warning against a rising Chinese threat as were like-minded thinkers in the United States. The North Korean nuclear crisis from the end of 2002 led to new alarm. While genuine security problems arise, instead of stymieing the search for regionalism they often stimulate more active searching for multilateral leverage.

Liberal openings and realist suspicions represent the deductive propensities of social scientists disinclined to engage in detailed research on the countries of NEA. It is not often that their ideas are presented in the form of testable theories. If realists were really interested in theories of balance of power and threat calculations, they would be weighing the three types of threats in NEA and calculating the consequences of their interface. If economic liberals were keen to prove that in NEA countries trade and investment bring broader cooperation and trust, they would be pinpointing the troubles that limit these consequences. So-called theory serves as a crutch for not preparing to do systematic research in order to bring together the extensive facts essential for evaluating what is really happening in a region. An approach that starts with the year-by-year evidence based on many nations involved in the search for regionalism is bound to be largely inductive, especially given the dearth of social science theorizing to date on regionalism.

In recent years many social scientists have turned against area studies along with cultural explanations as "unscientific." This has encouraged some to brandish a broad brush in painting as fuzzy thinkers those who point to possible causes other than the popular pantheon of choices. An unfortunate effect is to cast doubt on the utility of wide reading into how nations debate their own circumstances. Deductive arguments reenforce the authority of established ways of thinking, even in disciplines that may not have advanced far theoretically and in seeking answers to problems that may fall beyond the scope of previous mainstream scholarship. Regionalism in NEA is beyond the orbit of scholarship centered on the West, long-developed countries, and the great-power system that evolved in Europe and turned into the bipolar postwar world. Immersing ourselves in how the nations of NEA have reacted to the multisided and prolonged search for a path to regionalism has the potential to open our eyes to the deeper forces at work.

Throughout the debates of the 1990s the views of idealists clashed with those of realists, both missing a full picture of fast-changing developments. The former repeated the credo for why regionalism makes great sense, envisioning emergence of the world's third great regional entity after the EU and NAFTA through a complementary division of labor and the development of new frontiers. Their mantra combined within a single geographical area a cornucopia of natural resources and energy reserves, a vast pool of underemployed cheap labor, and great reserves of capital backed by a mix of advanced and intermediate technology. Often these upbeat views came from local administrations, which found them convenient for attracting world attention while pleading for greater support from their own national capitals.[13] In contrast, the realists were apt to reflect the reasoning of geopolitical elites, mostly in the capitals, who dismissed these dreams with warnings of unresolved hot spots and newly exacerbated great-power rivalries.[14] Some pointed to the lingering cold war on the Korean peninsula and the intensifying rivalry between China and Japan. Others blamed U.S. schemes for hegemony. All foresaw a struggle for power, scarcely limited by economic interests. The problem with viewing the decade through the lens of either the idealists or the realists is that neither side closely responded to the ups and downs of hope and disillusionment that made the 1990s a much more complicated and interesting period in this region than is usually thought. Diverse options remained open for the path regional ties might take.[15] The process is much harder than the idealists recognized, but the prospects are much closer than the realists feared.

Belatedly, idealist approaches have faced daunting questions. Mikhail Gorbachev spurred initial idealism in regionalism with his Vladivostok and Krasnoyarsk speeches in 1986 and 1988 and his 1987 program for the development of the Russian Far East and Trans-Baikal as part of the Asia-Pacific region, yet his excessive optimism about Soviet assets and neglect of many of the most pressing questions led to disillusionment evident by the beginning of the 1990s in Moscow's weak role. Japan's idealism at the beginning of

[13] *ERINA Report* (Niigata, 1994–), *Dongbeiya yanjiu* (Changchun, 1993–), and *Rossiia i ATR* (1992–) are examples of the diverse local journals for research on this region.

[14] Journals useful for views of foreign policy with relevance for regionalism include *Sekai shuho* (Tokyo), *Shijie jingji yu zhengzhi* (Beijing), and *Problemy Dal'nego Vostoka* (Moscow).

[15] Gilbert Rozman, "Northeast Asia: Regionalism, Clash of Civilizations or Strategic Quadrangle?" *Asia-Pacific Review*, 5(1) Spring/Summer 1998, pp. 105–26.

the 1990s focusing on cross-border networks to Russia appeared hopelessly naïve when investors found their assets stripped without the rule of law. China's cross-border fever of 1992–3, buttressed by proposals to create a multinational city at the mouth of the Tumen River, introduced a new element of idealism. It misjudged China's own limitations for orderly, modern commercial ties along the Russian border and the spillover from the great-power tensions welcomed by China into economic ties and trust. The United States was late to get into the act, but in 1997–8 the Clinton administration too developed an idealistic version of partnerships with China and Russia without taking adequately into account nationalist forces in both countries. Finally, in the year 2000 the idealism of Kim Dae-jung focused on North Korea, embracing all parties to regionalism. The failure of the North to do much to reciprocate did not put a stop to high hopes among South Koreans and many others in the region. These waves of rising expectations fueled the positive arguments of academic analysts, but even more persuasive were the expected effects of feverish growth in trade and investment among China, Japan, and South Korea.

Those in the realist tradition who emphasized nationalistic barriers to cooperation also kept finding their pessimism belied by events in the region. Japanese critics of South Korean nationalism, who doubted that regionalism could start with close bilateral ties between the two economically developed regional democracies, were contradicted by Kim Dae-jung's promise to put history aside in October 1998. Later the strident voices against the possibility of overriding Chinese nationalism had trouble explaining China's "smile diplomacy" toward Japan from October 1999. Finally, critics of immutable nationalism in Russia were stunned first by Vladimir Putin's shift in September 2000 toward returning two islands to Japan and then his support for the U.S. war against terrorism in September 2001. Chinese pessimists, in turn, overrated Japanese nationalism and were so negative about U.S. intentions that they failed to encourage security talks to stabilize the region. South Korean pessimists overreacted to Japanese textbook changes in 2001 as evidence of nationalism. United States pessimism in 2001, as the Bush administration took power pressing for division within the region in order to force globalization, centered on security rather than engagement through regionalism. After North Korea, Russians proved the loudest doomsayers; they had so little confidence in their own prospects in the region that they feared all parties would take advantage of them. Eventually, however, the tone of debate calmed in each country. Pessimists could not explain the sustained, rising momentum for regionalism, including increased interest in a free trade area to include part or all of NEA.

The evolving discourse on regionalism reflects repeated reassessments of how ties among the countries were unfolding. It reveals changing understanding of each country's national strengths and weaknesses, including the impact of assumptions about national identity. Even at times of hope, we detect, over and over again, clashing perceptions of what was expected from each other. The failure of regionalism testifies to the difficulty of agreeing on how to proceed, rooted in diverging preferences for what regionalism should be.[16] Its promise lies in shared views that there is no other long-term path forward.

Previous efforts to assess regionalism in NEA have been inclined to concentrate on one factor at the expense of others. The favorite choice is, of course, economics. It is customary to summarize the state of trade and other economic ties between the countries of the region, sometimes with the goal of stressing the potential in plans that have been proposed and at other times to criticize the problems that keep ties from advancing. Repeating proposals can lead us down the path of idealism. Economic linkages, however much they have grown, have yet to overcome problems that are, at their root, noneconomic in nature. We seek balance by keeping the economics coverage well below that found in most studies of regionalism. Likewise, evaluations of regionalism may concentrate on geopolitical issues. Of course, security is a major preoccupation in this region, but we would be remiss to allow that worry, rooted in realism, to eclipse other themes. It too does not occupy as large a portion of this book as one might expect in what is mostly a critical review of what went wrong. In contrast, this book covers a combination of domestic themes that fit under three broad labels: 1) each country's domestic development model – strategies of modernization, management style for business organizations, social networking pattern, and decentralization; 2) each country's national identity – confidence in one's own tradition, images of potential threats, political struggle related to openness to the outside, and acceptance of foreigners; and 3) each country's trust in critical bilateral relations – notions of victimizer and victimization, ideas about linkages in boosting ties, and acceptance of a regional or global framework for relations. Raising these themes while balancing economics and geopolitics steers the discussion that follows on a path that treads between the hazards of idealism for a region ready to soar and pessimism over a region in danger of protracted threats.

This book concentrates on the politics and perceptions of bilateral relations. Steps toward regionalism reveal a process of strategizing about how to engage other nations; negotiating to resolve barriers to improved relations; forging networks of trust and common interests; and persuading the experts and the public of the changes needed. More energy was invested in the development of bilateral relations than in the direct promotion of regionalism. In the debates over bilateral ties we see how economics, geopolitics, and domestic models, identities, and trust affected change. The story of the 1990s

[16] Gilbert Rozman, "Restarting Regionalism in Northeast Asia," *North Pacific Policy Papers* 1 (Vancouver: Program on Canada-Asia Policy Studies, Institute of Asian Research, 2000), pp. 2–21.

is told through contrasting perceptions of bilateral relations and divergent planning for regionalism, but also through signs of gradual convergence as hard choices were faced.

To achieve regionalism requires some combination of the following five conditions: 1) *national strategies for modernization* that give important weight to the contributions of neighboring countries, *recognizing* the growing need for *openness and decentralization* to diminish the role of borders and allow for a far-reaching division of labor; 2) *national identities that accept* neighboring countries as *partners* rather than threats *and orient one's own country to trusting relations* across civilizational boundaries; 3) *recognition that the dominant place of the United States does not preclude an evolving balance of powers on a regional level*, including the role of other powers in resolving hot spots, allowing for confidence in long-term relations without fear of deepening insecurity; 4) *incremental progress in bilateral relations* sufficient to put territorial disputes and other problems aside while expanding ties; and 5) *a vision of regionalism*, persuasive to elites and public opinion alike, that shows the way to substantial advantages without posing serious concerns. As countries appeared to make progress on some of the five conditions, they did not necessarily narrow the gaps among themselves. Not only did they focus on failure to overcome one or more of these hurdles, what one country perceived as its path forward on these issues contradicted what others envisioned. It proved impossible in the 1990s to develop a shared understanding of what was needed for regionalism in NEA. Moreover, repeatedly when some progress seemed to be occurring, the various parties to the negotiations had strikingly different ideas about what was happening. Such misperceptions led to new impasses and loss of trust.[17]

Because NEA ended the cold war and Sino-Soviet split without basic foundations for regionalism, the challenge ahead could take little for granted. States had to make fundamental changes in their national development strategies despite the great likelihood of intense opposition from domestic vested interests. Elites and the public as well had to rethink thoroughly their assumptions about national identity and the role of their country in the world amid repeated opportunities for a nationalist backlash. Juggling relations with the great powers active in the region might not only offer reassurances, but also rekindle fears of a threatening loss of balance in relations. Bilateral hurdles could arouse emotional reactions at both the national and local level. It would not be easy to overcome differences of opinion over visions for regionalism that joined peoples who until recently had had little contact with each other while inundated with negative stereotypes. One

[17] Gilbert Rozman, "Cross-National Integration in Northeast Asia: Geopolitical and Economic Goals in Conflict," *East Asia: An Interdisciplinary Journal*, 16(2) Spring/Summer 1997, pp. 6–43; Gilbert Rozman, "Flawed Regionalism: Reconceptualizing Northeast Asia in the 1990s," *Pacific Review*, 11(1) 1998, pp. 1–27.

often hears that the last vestiges of the cold war are found in NEA. In selecting strategies to pursue regionalism, local and national leaders often failed to confront these vestiges.

Great-Power Aspirations Face a Need for Regional Power

It is impossible to tell the story of NEA in the 1990s without discussing the great-power aspirations of four major actors and the intense desire in South and North Korea to balance the great powers. This is a region where countries are competing to reshape the global geometry of power even as they strive to resolve bilateral and regional issues. Just in the span of the past twenty years each of the three other powers of this region has taken its turn in attracting the world's attention as the presumed leading rival of the United States. First, the Soviet Union through its military juggernaut, then Japan with its industrial giants, and finally China with its rapidly rising market and assertiveness has loomed as the world's choice as the country most likely to overtake the United States. Seen through the lens of the NEA region rather than individually, these powers pose a different challenge. Clearly, they are not superpowers (after all, Russia is now an impoverished heir to the fallen Soviet Union, Japan is gasping for new life after the bursting of the bubble economy, and China remains a developing country beset with internal problems unlikely to be solved until advanced modernization is reached after many decades). Instead, they may acquire new stature as a tandem of great powers. Regionalism is not only a means to a division of labor; it is also a mechanism mixing competition and cooperation to achieve great-power goals.

The countries of NEA have been obsessed with catching up to the Western powers since the nineteenth century. Nationalism has acquired a special meaning focused on the maintenance of dignity in an ongoing competition. Even when satisfaction might have been realized after decades of rapid economic development and success in projecting a strong influence in international business, it was always possible to fixate on persistent symbols of victimization. Among the most powerful, enduring symbols are territory that needs to be recovered or may be threatened by the claims of others; history as written by others that may prettify acts that victimized your country or as written at home that may fail to reflect one's own views because of foreign pressure; and dependency obliged by circumstances that prevent full pursuit of national interests. Every country in the region considers itself, in one or another of these respects, as a victim. Regardless of the U.S. role in helping each nation, it also appears as a victimizer. Each state also believes that it has cause for grievance against some of its neighbors warranting a mood of victimization.

Perhaps no other region on the globe sustained more continuous tensions over the past century than NEA before the 1990s in the midst of so much development. Sino-Japanese relations from the time of their war in 1894–5 had rarely been upbeat until 1972, and then only with the hope that over decades memories would be gradually overcome. Russo-Japanese relations after their war in 1904–5 knew only short patches of optimism until the late 1980s, and then with the understanding that even normalization would prove a difficult challenge. A divided Korea after the war of 1950–3 had no success in moving from armistice to cooperation of any kind until the 1990s. The Sino-Soviet conflict from 1960 left the two continental powers ideological enemies until negotiations from 1982. Here the weight of Japanese imperialism, the worst cold war divisions, and the sharpest ideological schism were compounded. Regionalism has to be built on the ashes of a century of memories of multiple sorrows. Yet, the Japanese built the infrastructure for economic growth in Korea and Manchuria. Soviet assistance aided China and North Korea to develop heavy industry on the foundation that was left. Japan became an engine of postwar economic advancement in South Korea and beyond. There is also a record of genuine achievement available for boosting regionalism.

National identities were rapidly changing in the late 1980s and 1990s. Old distinctions between left and right were fading, both in Russia and China, where reform from above was finally occurring, but also in Japan and South Korea, where the left was losing past causes. Identities based on perceived threats were changing, as old enemies became new partners. Yet, alliances of convenience faced close scrutiny as well. South Koreans had less need for Japan as a political ally, and some Japanese were anticipating a different relationship with the United States after the cold war. Nationalism kept refocusing; the impact on regionalism and globalization of national strategies continued to shift from year to year.

Nations must balance regionalism, recognizing interdependency and adjustment of domestic policies and attitudes to meet the concerns of others, with nationalism, filled with charges that others interfere in one's internal affairs. On the defensive throughout the 1990s for its human-rights policies and other matters, China has been most vehement in denouncing interference in internal affairs although it champions economic integration. Normally insistent on the need for interdependence, such as environmental cooperation, the Japanese suddenly led the charge against internal interference when revised junior high textbooks caused an outcry in China and the Koreas in the first half of 2001. Nationalists on all sides drew a curtain around their country with claims that some things are "pure domestic questions" and that "foreign pressure" is an offense to national dignity.[18] Such emotionalism severely hampers a search for mutual understanding that all insist is necessary for regionalism. Seeking advantage in a presumed "competition,"

[18] "Chugoku no kentei fugokaku yokyu wa neisei kansha," *Sankei shimbun*, March 22, 2001, p. 14.

China, Japan, and Russia face the challenge of placing regionalism above strategies to best their rivals. All have shifted their thinking, accepting more globalization as well as regionalism.

Ambivalence over national interests prevails throughout NEA. Countries demand respect befitting their national strength, which they insist is underrated, while expressing the grievances of their insecurity, which they exaggerate. Often left aside are realistic expectations for opening to the outside with allowance for losses as well as gains. This leads to defining national interests as lifting one's world ranking even if it exacts a price in economic growth. Such images turn relations into a zero-sum game. Fortunately, the prevailing trend is to base national power on economic growth regionally and globally.

The potential of NEA is beyond most expectations. A united Korea not only can some day bring North Korea to the level of the South, it can add the synergy of the South connecting with adjacent areas in China and Russia. The Russian Far East can start over with geographical linkages justifying development of energy, water, wood, metals, and other resources that find ready markets in densely settled but resource-poor lands to the south. Japan can also make a fresh beginning by "reentering Asia" through regionalism. Finally, China may reach an impasse, as have its neighbors after their runs of double-digit economic growth, that will draw it to new prospects for accelerating development as part of NEA. From across the Pacific, the United States too can be a beneficiary of a regional upturn in NEA as it has been in the EU. Northeast Asia has what it takes to be a match for the EU.

In the gloomy mood of 2003, few expect the countries of NEA to overcome the obstacles of the 1990s soon.[19] Lately, it is taken for granted that Japan and Russia will continue to be bedeviled by a territorial dispute, China and Japan will intensify their rivalry, China and Russia will fail to back their rhetoric of strategic partnership with deep economic ties and trust, and North Korea will persist in thwarting the unification of Korea. In addition, many suppose that the states of NEA are too protectionist for real regionalism, so any progress in that direction must come as an offshoot of globalization. Given the clashing ambitions of great powers and the stubbornness of North Korean leaders, regionalism will be difficult to achieve. Add to this the U.S. assertive unilateralism bent on tearing down economic barriers and overriding security differences. On the offensive, the United States leaves other regional actors scrambling to react. With so many obstacles, what difference does it make that this region has great potential?

The following chapters are unsparing in their acknowledgment of the barriers to regionalism, but they also show how preconditions for regionalism are within reach. Given the rapid pace of change in the fifteen years since

[19] Nick Bisley, "The End of East Asian Regionalism?" *The Journal of East Asian Affairs*, 17(1) Spring/Summer 2003, pp. 148–72.

1989, there is reason to expect that by 2015 the threshold to regionalism will have been crossed. The road ahead will not be easy, but NEA has started on a course that is likely to enable it to join the EU and NAFTA as a region that can, despite divisions, have a major say in shaping the evolution of our globe. Breakthroughs in bilateral relations and a kickoff summit for regionalism must first be realized. In the process, advocates of regionalism will need to make clear their support for globalization. On the one hand, the path to regional integration lies in global integration. On the other, the imperative for regionalism comes from seeking leverage in the face of global divisions and seeking stability to moderate regional differences. Through six stages in the quest for regionalism progress has been fitful; even if the lessons of overexpectations are learned well, we can expect many ups and downs ahead in the search for common ground.

2

Exiting the 1980s

Cold War Logic and National Aspirations

If we consider the first stage of regionalism in NEA to be the period from the spring of 1989 to the beginning of 1991 – bracketed by the dramatic events in Beijing and the Persian Gulf War – then we should begin our story even earlier when the states that intersect in NEA were redefining their objectives while the cold war was still in progress. Long before anyone predicted that the 1990s would be free of the shadow of the Soviet-American conflict, important new currents were present. These, in turn, shaped rising hopes from 1987 and then the scrambling for a fresh start from 1989. First came national rethinking, then anticipation of regionalism, and finally a rush to seize new opportunities.

The goal of establishing an NEA region was taken seriously from the second half of the 1980s. Mikhail Gorbachev played a leading role, calling in 1986 for the integration of Russia into the Asia-Pacific region. Japanese analysts seized this opportunity, appealing for a narrow regionalism centered around the rim of the Sea of Japan,[1] at the same time offering a vision of how a breakthrough in bilateral relations with Moscow could lead to great-power ties linked to regionalism.[2] From 1990 China stood in the forefront in institutionalizing the discussion through research centers and journals devoted to NEA regionalism, a notion intermediate between Russia's broad concept and Japan's narrow one.[3] China bifurcated the analysis into heightened optimism about economic integration and a strong dosage of balance-of-power politics stressing competition in great-power relations. Neither the United States preoccupation with globalization nor South Korea's "northern

[1] Gilbert Rozman, "Backdoor Japan: The Search for a Way Out via Regionalism and Decentralization," *Journal of Japanese Studies*, 25(1) Winter 1999, pp. 3–31.

[2] Gilbert Rozman, *Japan's Response to the Gorbachev Era, 1985–1991: A Rising Superpower Views a Declining One* (Princeton: Princeton University Press, 1992).

[3] Gilbert Rozman, "Northeast China: Waiting for Regionalism," *Problems of Post-Communism*, 45(4) July–August 1998, pp. 3–13.

strategy" followed by its "sunshine policy" offered a specific framework for regionalism, yet scholars and officials in both countries were among the most influential in setting the tone of the discussion. Differing on the scale of the region and the balance of economic and geostrategic forces, voices in each of these countries debated what was needed. In the background was the reasoning that had guided each nation as the cold war was ended.

The conventional image of the final stage of the cold war omits important events in NEA that created a more complex picture than had existed previously. It correctly presents the Soviet Union as taking the offense in Asia, arousing China, Japan, and South Korea with its massive arms buildup in Siberia and the Pacific and provocative war in Afghanistan as well as support for Vietnam's invasion of Cambodia. Ruled by an aging, out-of-touch leadership and finding its economy falling into stagnation, the Soviet Union overextended itself in Asia to the anger of all but its close allies. Under these conditions, Japan drew closer to the United States and agreed to boost its military role as an "unsinkable aircraft carrier," as public opinion turned decidedly more hostile to Moscow, and leftist, pacifist thought faded before a determination to counter the growing threat. China, in turn, felt encircled by the Soviet offensive and hardened its opposition by raising the "three obstacles" to normalization, meaning withdrawal of troops from Afghanistan and Cambodia as well as removal of threatening forces in Mongolia and along the Sino-Soviet border. Later, South Korea after the downing of its civilian aircraft in 1983 drew closer to the United States and even Japan. Thus, Ronald Reagan's intensification of accusations, arms buildups, and alliances against the "evil empire" rallied a region already focused on resisting Soviet aggression. All of this is correct, but to limit ourselves to the feature story is insufficient to grasp the dynamics of a region increasingly eager to look beyond the cold war bipolar world. At work in the world's fastest rising region were deeper forces, which would shape the course of regionalism over the next decade by sharpening power interests, anxious searching for diplomatic leverage, and changing national identities.

A narrow cold war realist vision of threat and counterforce on the global stage would leave us dumbfounded to understand the roots of regional dynamics in the 1990s. None of the regional actors allowed the façade of polarization to interfere with its own pursuit of contradictory objectives. First, the United States, egged on by the Republican minority in Congress and then by an ideological Ronald Reagan at the opening of his administration, at the very time it was most alarmist about the danger of Soviet military superiority, tilted toward Taiwan, shocking the People's Republic of China (PRC). Beijing had just embraced economic reform and opened its doors while moving deliberately to dismantle its traditional communist control system, and Taiwan was not yet democratic or a champion of human rights. The move by Washington must, therefore, be explained not primarily as a principled stand of rejection of a more abhorrent system nor a renewal of an old commitment, but also in two other ways: 1) a statement of anticommunism that defies cold war logic and 2) an assertion of regional power interests independent of the global power struggle. The existence of the Soviet threat did not stop the United States from shifting toward a regional strategy that left China aware that while its rise as an economic power would be encouraged it would not be trusted as a political and military power. China's leadership rightly regarded this as refusal to accept China's Communist Party as a trusted partner, but they also had grounds to suspect it contained the seeds of rejection of any kind of nationalist power in China striving for reunification with Taiwan and increased regional and global clout.[4]

Second, Japan did not restrain its ambitions to countering a new Soviet threat. At the beginning of the 1980s it made the Soviet occupation of the "Northern Territories" the symbol of its dissatisfaction, raising the profile of this issue beyond geopolitical concerns over the balance of power in the region. This conveniently served the nationalist agenda of reinterpreting the history of the Pacific War to make Japan into a victim no less than an aggressor. Believing that they had unfairly lost territory, the Japanese could focus on undoing this injustice as the key to ending the cold war era when it was restricted from acting as a "normal" nation. The power of nationalist sentiments unrelated to any Soviet threat could be ascertained in 1982 when an attempt was made to rewrite textbooks to prettify Japan's history of occupation in Korea and invasion of China as well as the overall nature of the Pacific War. If rallying other countries against Moscow had really been foremost in Japan's reasoning, why would it have antagonized the countries on the front line? If after heated protests relayed through the sympathetic Japanese Foreign Ministry the revisions – some erroneously reported – were mostly retracted, an overarching message came increasingly into the open in subsequent years: the worldview of a large and growing number of LDP Diet members gives precedence to clearing up Japan's historical name over winning the hearts of Japan's potential regional partners. Neighbors had to wonder what kind of regionalism Japan had in mind if it was not interested in winning their trust on what mattered most for their national identities.[5]

Third, China's defection from the alliance to contain the Soviet Union should have cast the most doubt on claims of polarization and given new meaning to the concept of a "strategic triangle" that had been popular, but rather empty of content, since 1972. The new Chinese reasoning on great-power relations in 1982 would have far-reaching implications for regionalism. Having already established special economic zones in the Southeast and changed its engine of growth, China was delivering a political message as

[4] James Mann, *About Face: A History of America's Curious Relationship with China, from Nixon to Clinton* (New York: Alfred A. Knopf, 1999), pp. 115–54.

[5] Kenneth B. Pyle, *The Japanese Question: Power and Purpose in a New Era* (Washington, DC: The AEI Press, 1992).

well as an economic one. Its shift to equidistance between the United States and the Soviet Union indicated that it rejected a region dominated by the United States. If Moscow accepted Beijing's rising power in Asia, Beijing would recognize Moscow's regional importance and do its best to give it a balancing role. It welcomed an equilateral triangle that would keep the United States and its allies at bay. This outlook left room for economic integration, while aiming to constrict its political impact. In 1983 when hopes rose that Iury Andropov would put the Soviet Union on a track of "socialist reform" alongside China, internal reasoning also embraced the prospect of mutual learning in industrial reform while preserving the foundation of socialist economies. As economic openness spread northward along the coast in 1984 and was joined by urban reform, hopes arose of countering hierarchical regionalism in which China occupied a bottom rung below capitalist economies through joining with external forces of socialism.[6] China's quest to limit U.S. power was intense.

Fourth, the Soviet Union, which until the mid-1980s remained, along with North Korea, most hostile to regionalism, was already beginning new debates well before the Gorbachev era, as seen in the decision in the spring of 1982 to signal to China its interest in normalization.[7] The following ideas were raised, albeit indirectly for a long time. Maybe the enormous burden of the militarization of Soviet Asian policy could be alleviated by calming tensions in the region and shifting toward cooperation. Maybe the newly appreciated dynamism of the Asia-Pacific region could be utilized to transform the economy of Asiatic Russia, making use of the increasingly costly Baikal-Amur railroad as a Eurasian bridge. Perhaps China's economic successes offered some lessons for Soviet reform with potential for trade and joint projects between the countries. Despite censorship by a few in the old guard, Russians were opening their eyes to regionalism, but approaching it very narrowly, fearful of the spillover from one type of reform to another.[8] After 1985 glasnost reached writings on China, Japan, and Korea late, limiting the search for a realistic path to regionalism. Yet, Moscow's desire for a new security order in the region and its priority for Beijing hinted that one of its motives was overcoming diplomatic isolation and thus cutting costs.

Fifth, also shielded from open discussion were sprouts of regional thinking in South Korea that broke through cold war barriers. Beijing's turn to

[6] Gilbert Rozman, *The Chinese Debate about Soviet Socialism, 1978–1985* (Princeton: Princeton University Press, 1987); "China's Soviet-Watchers in the 1980s: A New Era in Scholarship," *World Politics*, 37(4) July 1985, pp. 435–74.

[7] Robert D. English, *Russia and the Idea of the West: Gorbachev, Intellectuals and the End of the Cold War* (New York: Columbia University Press, 2000).

[8] Gilbert Rozman, *A Mirror for Socialism: Soviet Criticisms of China* (Princeton: Princeton University Press, 1985); "Moscow's China-Watchers in the Post-Mao Era: The Response to a Changing China," *The China Quarterly*, 94 (June 1983), pp. 215–41.

reform and openness stirred some interest. After all, if Southeast China could become a magnet for investment and trade for its neighbors, why would Northeast China not follow? Once Gorbachev ventured in mid-1986 to Korea's doorstep in Vladivostok in order to deliver a speech about opening his country to Asia, minds were obviously churning in Seoul. Aspirations for regional economic integration might open an indirect route to North Korea; winning the confidence of Beijing and Moscow through regionalism would be Seoul's best bet for drawing Pyongyang into talks. No doubt, popular distrust of Japan and student-led resentment toward the United States, rising to the surface with the push for democratization in South Korea, added impetus to the interest in working with additional regional powers.[9]

Even before anticipation of regionalism began in 1987–8 we can discern nascent inclinations far different from what would be expected in cold war logic. While economic interests played a role, even more important for all countries except the Soviet Union and the United States were interests focused on regional power, national identity or unification, and a drive for reducing dependence on the United States. A confident Japan, a newly opening China, and a rapidly industrializing South Korea all were looking for new foreign policy options. Each side was frustrated by excessive limitations on its regional diplomacy. For different reasons, the Soviet Union was even more frustrated. Under Mikhail Gorbachev it opened the gates to change, allowing the pent-up desires for a new regional order to burst into the open all across Northeast Asia. With new horizons, changes in national identities could also be explored, building on the hopes and grievances that had begun to be expressed.

Mikhail Gorbachev from 1986 to 1988 sent signals that precipitated the search for regionalism.[10] While speeches at Vladivostok in July 1986 and Krasnoyarsk in September 1988 were no doubt the clearest appeals aimed directly at the region, it was his sustained message on at least five points that raised expectations the most. 1) The cold war is ending between the United States and the Union of Soviet Socialist Republics (USSR), liberating NEA as a battleground in a bipolar struggle. 2) All the military obstacles to normal relations in the region will be eliminated by Russia. 3) Moscow wants to open the Russian Far East and develop it as part of a regional economy. 4) Russia will decentralize its economy and its political system in ways that encourage regional interactions. 5) Negotiations on territorial disputes can now be pursued. Except North Korea, which was alarmed by these changes,

[9] Victor D. Cha, *Alignment Despite Antagonism: The US-Korea-Japan Security Triangle* (Stanford, CA: Stanford University Press, 1999), pp. 169–98.

[10] Gilbert Rozman, "Rising Soviet Expectations for the Asian-Pacific Region" (Ajia-taiheiyo chiiki e mukete takamaru Soren no kitai), in *Soren no kiki to Nisso kankei* (Tokyo 1991), pp. 86–96 and 243–69.

all other concerned countries responded with new strategies for regionalism or globalization. The search for a shared blueprint for regionalism had begun, albeit skeptically.

Although the Japanese were slow to awaken to the reality of Gorbachev's perestroika and glasnost, from 1988 they took the lead in looking ahead to regionalism. Think-tank experts led the way in putting together the pieces of a regional jigsaw puzzle in which maritime Japan became the focal point. While anticipation that there would be no overt United States opposition aided this pursuit, the hope was that Japan would seize this opportunity to "reenter Asia" through a combination of subregional economic spheres and great-power adjustments. As the Soviet Union fell into serious difficulty and China was left in isolation after June 1989, Japan had confidence that it could work with allies in the United States and South Korea and reach out to its troubled neighbors. North Korea deserted by its partners, the Russian Far East losing its lifeline from European Russia, and China eager for regional ties to compensate for global ones looked like easy pickings to a Japan bloated with capital in a bubble economy. Regionalism started as Japan's low-key project within a framework of United States–led globalization, but all sides had fixed preconceptions.[11]

Domestic changes also gave a huge boost to regionalism in the last years of the 1980s. In Russia these were a shift to decentralization and more open borders as well as relaxation of the command economy. In China they were great advances in economic decentralization as well as a shift in mentality after the brutal suppression of Tiananmen demonstrators away from the West toward expansion of ties with neighbors. In Japan the greatly increased value of the yen from 1985 plus the bubble economy induced the government and enterprises to look much more to Asia for production and closer ties. Although the pace of regionalism was rather slow in the three years after the Vladivostok speech, diplomatically and domestically the conditions were forming for a new intensity.

Suddenly, new debate blossomed in the periodicals and newspapers concerned with foreign affairs. It was not limited to Soviet glasnost, although that provided the most revelations. The Japanese debate on regionalism was the liveliest, anticipating an NEA at last free from postwar restrictions. The Chinese grew more serious about the rising dynamism of neighboring countries, seeing opportunities for domestic reform and new external ties. South Koreans took advantage of democratization to look at the great powers

[11] Gilbert Rozman, "Japanese Images of the Soviet and Russian Role in the Asia-Pacific Region," in Tsuyoshi Hasegawa, Jonathan Haslam, and Andrew Kuchins, eds., *Russia and Japan* (Berkeley: Institute of East Asia, University of California, 1993), pp. 101–23; Gilbert Rozman, "Japanese Views of the Great Powers in the New World Order," in David Jacobsen, ed., *Old Nations, New World: Conceptions of World Order* (Boulder, CO: Westview Press, 1994), pp. 15–35.

in a new light. If the period from 1987 to early 1989 brought a sudden flowering of speculation about prospects for regionalism, the two years that followed produced a rash of actions that actually began to shape a new region. South Korea and China led the way after Russia opened the door, but it was both the United States and Japan that created the framework. Although U.S. leaders may not have focused on regionalism, they removed the red light.

Globalization and the United States

Washington was preoccupied with outmaneuvering the Soviet Union militarily and economically through the 1980s. Under Henry Kissinger and Zbigniew Brzezinski the idea of drawing China into a long lasting "strategic entente" with the United States and its allies in Asia took hold. Given the Sino-Soviet split and the lowered U.S. profile after the Vietnam War, Washington was prepared to accept a loose political arrangement with little pressure on China while it relied on increasing Japanese economic power in a dynamic region to weave a web of economic ties in order to ensnare China over time. Despite Beijing's shift to equidistance with the Soviet Union and the United States and its opposition to a foreign strategy of overthrowing socialism through "peaceful evolution," the mainstream in both U.S. political parties was confident that the present course would continue. Only when Gorbachev reoriented Moscow's compass was it necessary to take a fresh look at these assumptions, although they were not to be seriously questioned until the mid-1990s.

In the transition from the Reagan to the Bush administration, the preoccupation with how to manage the demise of world communism remained. Pleased with the way the process was unfolding in Europe, the United States recognized more uncertainties in NEA without finding any serious cause to doubt that great-power relations there too would achieve the security conditions needed for a shift toward globalization. Amidst talk of global ideals for a new era, little attention was paid to variations for the NEA complex of multiple great powers and divided countries. Sanctions against China in 1989 were seen as a temporary necessity. Reacting to change in the Soviet Union, the United States seemed confident that it knew what to do. Despite public concern that Japan was an unfair economic rival, the Bush administration gave priority to its role as a strategic partner. If Japan advanced in linking great-power changes to regionalism, making headway with Russia, China, or even North Korea, it was assumed to be a positive contribution toward the global transition in process. Europe was the central concern; Asia could be addressed later.

The strategic triangle dragged on through 1987 as Washington used China as a "card" against the Soviet Union, and Moscow made no serious counteroffer.[12] This kind of triangle endured so long because even after emotional hostility to the Soviet Union under Mao and to China under Brezhnev had ended, Moscow's hesitation delayed efforts to rebalance the triangle. The United States beckoned to China anew with economic and security ties, while the Soviet Union alarmed it with war in Afghanistan. When after 1985 Beijing expected a new balanced triangle, it was disappointed to find Moscow more interested in winning U.S. help than in playing the China "card." It might have started regionalism on a continental track capable of balancing the maritime track of regional ties focused on Southeast China, but Moscow hesitated to join forces in economic reform and integration. Instead Beijing was dismayed to see the spread of a type of globalization that it opposed, symbolized by universal human values. Beijing was angry too at Gorbachev's comments supportive of the students at Tiananmen. Thus, bilateral ties did not get a big boost from normalization in 1989. Meanwhile, talk that dissidents would take power in China kept Russia at a distance too. The triangle would not be raised again until Moscow's foreign policy changed from 1996; U.S. global dominance and Japan's initiative in the region left no scope for regionalism as an outlet for the revival of socialist networks. With Moscow and Beijing apart, Washington was becoming oblivious to great-power issues in NEA.

At the end of the 1980s the focus remained on creating the preconditions for regionalism with few in the United States expecting progress soon. Before it could be actively pursued, much of the legacy of a half-century had to be removed. U.S.-Soviet relations, responsible for the cold war that divided the region from 1945, needed a drastic overhaul, as happened partly in 1989 with the end of the cold war but not fully until the end of 1991. Sino-Soviet relations, which for more than two decades were even more embittered than U.S.-Soviet relations, had to be normalized, as occurred in 1989 but still awaited another boost from 1992. And the isolation of South Korea and, hopefully, North Korea from regional contacts had to be ended. This process leapt forward in 1990 when both Koreas were admitted to the United Nations and the South made big strides in its ties with both Russia and China. Preoccupied with global issues, Americans were slow to notice that fundamental barriers on the path of regionalism were largely resolved.

In January 1991 the Persian Gulf War did more for NEA than secure energy supplies for the continued economic expansion of Japan, South Korea, and, by 1993, a newcomer to oil imports, China. It also reasserted the role of the United States as the guarantor of stability, able to forge a coalition of countries to repel any major threat to global security. Especially in NEA, where, along with Western Europe, the largest number of overseas U.S. troops is concentrated, this eased worries about instability. Yet, it also fueled

[12] Lowell Dittmer, *Sino-Soviet Normalization and Its International Implications, 1945–1990* (Seattle: University of Washington Press, 1992).

growing concerns in China, North Korea, and, soon, the emergent Russian state that U.S. dominance would dictate the terms of regional ties. This war raised the specter of political and military globalization, causing each country in NEA to look more within the region for balance.

At the beginning of the 1990s Americans were not very confident of the future economic competitiveness of their country. Japan, followed by South Korea, symbolized the unfair nature of international trade, dumping exports and protecting privileged sectors from imports. Proposals for regionalism in NEA or East Asia reaching down to SEA brought reminders of "Asian values" that allow assertive states to hide the manipulation of the terms of trade. If the United States offered its support for Asian Pacific Economic Cooperation (APEC) in 1989 as a mechanism for putting global interests above regional ones, it frowned on proposals that excluded the United States such as Mahathir Mohammad's 1991 East Asian Economic Caucus (EAEC). Along with revisionist critiques of Japan for unfair practices that warranted countermeasures, one could detect a groundswell of doubt that regionalism would only compound the abuse of open markets by reinforcing on a larger scale disguised protectionism. In 1990 the push for regionalism within NEA accelerated, as the United States was looking more doubtful. Japan was on the spot as the country that might cause alarm by embracing a worrisome form of regionalism in its search for a leadership role in Asia.

Americans perceived the end of the cold war as the breakthrough that would enable universal values embedded in the American dream to shine throughout the world. It meant the vindication of American exceptionalism – wide-open market competition, democracy and freedom, and states releasing control of societies.[13] If the EU might coalesce as a regional union of like-minded states posing little risk, no other region could be permitted to establish a regional grouping with military, cultural, or political potential to challenge the open world favored for U.S. interests. America's national identity had shifted from saving the "free world" to forging a unified world order in its own image.[14]

At the turn of the 1990s Japan posed a challenge to this mission in three ways. First, Americans pictured it as the foremost economic rival for leadership with its vast trade surpluses, formidable industrial giants, efficient managerial practices bolstered by social stability, and faster rates of economic growth. Second, as revisionist social science insisted, Japan, as a developmental state, championed a significantly different system – limited market competition, guided democracy with freedom sacrificed for group harmony, and state control over society. Third, the Japanese had designs

[13] Seymour Martin Lipset, *American Exceptionalism: A Double-Edged Sword* (New York: W. W. Norton, 1996).

[14] Henry R. Nau, *At Home Abroad: Identity and Power in American Foreign Policy* (Ithaca: Cornell University Press, 2002).

on establishing their own Asian economic bloc that could undermine the U.S. global architecture. Although the two sides had compromised in the creation of APEC in 1989, Japanese assertiveness to Russia and China over the next two years raised many American eyebrows as out of step with the larger blueprint. An unease could be discerned in Washington that, rather than weakened Moscow anxious for assistance or isolated Beijing fettered by sanctions, Tokyo would prove to be the most assertive advocate of a different strategy centered on its regional ambitions. Even if the United States had not been a skeptic about regionalism, Japan's strategy would have doomed it.

Japan and Regionalism

It is reasonable to divide the sixty-three-year Showa era into three periods of roughly equal length: war, resurgence, and internationalization. Whereas the first two periods are easily defined, the meaning of the last has proven difficult. When Emperor Hirohito died in 1989, reviews of the 1970s and 1980s had difficulty explaining the progression to a new era of rising global consciousness.[15] If nationalism was downplayed, sentiments about where Japan was heading still were ambivalent between emulating the West or becoming the model and host to the East. While the primary symbol of internationalization was to master English, the foremost test for regional openness was to welcome foreign students, 90 percent coming from Asia. Surveys found that the latter goal proved even more elusive than the former. Of respondents, half did not want to make friends with foreigners; far fewer desired them as workmates or marriage partners. Even East Asians, who share many traditions, were kept apart. Although enough English had been learned for regional contacts, to its neighbors Japan proved to be still largely a closed society.[16]

The Japanese were obsessed with winning respect in the world. This was demonstrated in the extraordinary attention given to how other nations, especially the United States, perceived them. All sides agreed that there was a problem, but they differed on why it existed and what to do about it. At opposite ends of the spectrum were ardent nationalists promoting "*nihonjinron*" ideology, looking to Japanese history and culture for proof of superiority now evidenced in economic development; and advocates of "internationalization," which was becoming a popular term of self-criticism so that the Japanese people could meet global expectations. Often these two camps interpreted the same concerns in opposite ways. Each was very

[15] "Senso, fukko, soshite kokusaika Showa to iu mitsu no 'jidai,'" *AERA*, January 20, 1989, p. 43.

[16] Fukami Hiroaki, "Nihon no kokusaika mondai no teihen," *21 seiki foramu*, 31 (1987), pp. 10–15.

sensitive to "Japan bashing" by Americans, the former group calling for more assertiveness toward the United States and the latter for more openness by the Japanese. Each was alarmed by the apathy of Japanese youth, with nationalists pressing for more patriotic education and internationalists for better English instruction. Both sides rejected the two prevailing orientations of the postwar era: 1) Japan as a merchant nation that speaks with a small voice in global politics while focusing on building its economic power and 2) the recommended alternative of a neutral Japan championing progressive causes that speaks loudly but carries a small stick without United States backing. Agreeing that Japan must use its economic clout to act as a political great power, neither could say how.

Narrow thinking toward two countries overshadowed realistic thinking about globalization and regionalism. If the 1980s began with relative optimism about both the United States and China, the mood in Japan had already been changing before the dramatic global events at the end of the decade. The Japanese were inclined to blame others: Americans who turned on their country over trade frictions that reflected the declining competitiveness of the United States, and Chinese who due to communist ideology became prickly about internal matters in Japan such as textbook revisions and visits to the Yasukuni shrine. Squabbles over such matters fueled doubts fed by nationalism; the number of Japanese feeling friendly to these countries dropped from three-quarters to two-thirds by 1986.[17] Despite promises to address U.S. criticisms of unfair trade and to increase trust with China based on a shared view of history, the Japanese were increasingly defensive. This diminished the potential for both globalization and regionalism, but not the hope of gaining an advantage by pursuing both by using one against the other while riding the crest of economic power.

Paradoxically, a mentality of victimization grew alongside confidence in the bubble economy, fueling growing fear of political isolation. Early summits between U.S. and Soviet leaders left the Japanese wondering if the arms race and cold war ended would they still be able to benefit as before. After all, commentary on Japan bashing in the United States warned of a rise in protectionist thinking. It was common to suggest that both the United States and Soviet Union have economic difficulties and domestic problems as if they were rushing to repair ties in order to compete with Japan.[18] Before June 1989 some also felt isolated by the rapprochement between the United States and China, worrying about romanticism toward China among Americans and an anti-Japanese strategy among Chinese. It was said that the United States and China both counted on Japanese generosity with economic support, but neither offered Japan the kind of diplomatic respect

[17] Tanaka Yozo, *Chugokujin to Nihonjin: Chugoku rikai no gokai to sakkaku* (Tokyo: Nihon keizai tsushinsha, 1987), pp. 136–7.

[18] *Yomiuri shimbun*, June 2, 1988, p. 3.

that a nation with 15 percent of the world's gross national product (GNP) deserved. As Soviet ties with the United States and China advanced, the Japanese had trouble despite the rhetoric of internationalization and regionalism, concealing their growing fear of isolation amidst distrust of what the other powers were proposing. They warned of mutual misunderstandings, not recognizing a superiority complex on their own side while faulting foreigners for overlooking Japanese values.[19] The specter of cultural conflicts, more than economic or military ones, clouded regionalism in its initial phase.

Even as Soviet-Japanese negotiations resumed in 1986–7 the United States was seen as still urging Japan to exercise self-restraint. Recalling the Japanese public's sympathy for socialism in the 1950s and early 1960s and the scare during the late 1960s and 1970s of large energy projects that could enmesh Japan in natural gas pipeline networks such as were taking shape between the Soviet Union and Western Europe, Washington preferred a cautious Japan resentful over its islands. If progress were to be made, it would be better if it occurred as an aftereffect of advances in U.S.–Soviet relations. The Japanese did not require convincing; they had found a negative image of Moscow very convenient for both domestic- and foreign-policy objectives. Hopes for regionalism started hesitantly, but as Moscow made serious strides to end the cold war and begin reforms, the U.S. position changed and so did that of the Japanese, who calculated that they would be able to condition support for Moscow's entry into the region and even the global economy on a bilateral breakthrough. Nationalism in Japan did not have to be sacrificed for regionalism.

In the late 1980s the Japanese led in debating the possibilities of regionalism.[20] This can be attributed to five factors: 1) the quest to escape dependency on the United States and flex Japan's muscles as a rising great power; 2) the eagerness to capitalize on the rise of the four little dragons and recent reforms in China; 3) the search for a new division of labor accelerated by the bubble economy, the increased value of the yen, and confidence in Japan's ability to assume leadership through economic integration; 4) the importance of a reform course in Moscow and the end of the cold war for Tokyo's suppressed foreign policy goals; and 5) desperation along the Sea of Japan to share in the dynamism and prosperity achieved along the Pacific coast. Yet, before these factors came into play it was necessary for a facilitating condition at the global level to exist. Just as in 1972 Washington ushered in a new era with its breakthrough in relations with Beijing, in 1987 and,

[19] Kobayashi Doken, "Kokusaika jidai no hikari to kage," *Jiyu*, March 1988, pp. 36–47.

[20] Gilbert Rozman, *Japan's Response to the Gorbachev Era: A Rising Superpower Views a Declining One* (Princeton: Princeton University Press, 1992); Gilbert Rozman, "Japan's Soviet-Watchers in the First Years of the Gorbachev Era: The Search for a Worldview for the Japanese Superpower," *Pacific Review*, 1(4) 1988, pp. 412–28.

more decisively, in 1989 Washington took the lead in its negotiations with Moscow. Japan's pursuit of regionalism depended on a burst of globalization; it ostensibly aimed to extend globalization, when in fact it gave Japan a long-awaited chance to turn to Asia in the hope of balancing or even challenging globalization.

The Japanese were used to walking a fine line in the postwar era between unobtrusive economic leadership along an arc from Singapore to South Korea and highly visible subordination to U.S. global leadership. At each point when caution was necessary, there was the assumption that time was on their side. Their economy was growing faster than that of the United States, and the East and SEA arc was taking shape as a natural hinterland. It was assumed that there was "a rough division of labor, with Japan mainly responsible for economic management and assistance, and the United States for regional security.... Due to severe budgetary constraints, it is getting more and more difficult for the United States to bear financial burdens."[21] Many expected that as economic power and foreign reserves kept rising, the demarcation of responsibilities would change. A struggle with the United States over regionalism might not even be necessary; it would gradually withdraw apart from basic security, while welcoming Japan's expanded role. As ties multiplied across the region, there were also concerns that, in the final analysis, the United States would be reluctant to recognize Japan's regional leadership. Sandwiched between Asian nationalism and U.S. globalization, the Japanese approached regionalism indirectly, both as a means to normalize bilateral relations and as a tactic to reduce dependency on the United States.

It had been Japan's strategy from the 1960s to assist East Asian and SEA nations in development and then ride the wave of their success to regional leadership. As one country after another achieved stunning economic growth, hopes grew stronger. The latest "economic miracle" was beginning in China, whetting Japan's appetite the most. Although the rise of a potential rival gave pause, most assumed that for decades China would remain at the bottom of a vertical production chain. Boosting regionalism in a gradual manner, Japan could guarantee its expected leadership position.

Economic conditions raised hopes for regionalism: a rapid rise in the value of the yen in 1985 fueled increased Japanese investment in manufacturing in NEA even if it was not matched by structural reforms that would have truly globalized Japan. The bubble economy gave Japan a temporary fix, using overvalued land prices and bank loans available at home to project the image of an economic superpower, but one better prepared for regional than global leadership. This image raised excessive expectations for Japanese-led

[21] Hiroyuki Kishino, "Policy Coordination between Japan and the United States Regarding Regional Conflicts and Other Sources of Threat in East Asia," *IIGP Policy Paper*, June 1990, p. 18.

regionalism. By capitalizing on these assets, Japan sought to balance the United States and direct the rise of NEA, but it failed to reassure the public on either side.

Advocates of globalization often did not trust the United States, accusing it of self-serving nationalism with elements of protectionism. Excess U.S. fears of Japan caused some backlash, but another explanation is Japanese self-doubts as the world was changing with the arrival of Microsoft Windows 1.0, CNN, the Internet, and global scorn of bureaucratism.[22] Foreign-policy debates were truncated. The political right dominated in the Soviet Union, as the political left remained preeminent in China. Each appealed to internationalization, although they differed on its meaning and were not comfortable with many of its ideals or even with genuine regionalism. Such hesitation complicated foreign-policy coordination, but it did not dim the rising consensus in favor of regionalism balancing the great powers.

For four decades the left wing had led the way in cultivating ties to China, North Korea, and Russia, always with the goal of restraining dependency on the United States. Yet, by 1990 long-established ties to all parts of the region through leftist intellectuals and politicians were in decline. It was a weakened Japan Socialist Party in 1990 that had enough energy to champion the cause of "backdoor Japan" left behind by the "Pacific megalopolis" and of a regionalism that would bring together the Soviet Union, China, and North Korea not only for economic cooperation but also for a new great-power balance in which Japan could at last distance itself from the United States.[23] The Left in Japan sought to transform initial cross-border ties aimed at economic regionalism into a platform for a reincarnated peace movement, but this had little resonance abroad. As its collapse accelerated, hopes died for a kind of peace movement regionalism. Remnants of the Left had little choice but to join with local interests focused on cross-border rather than great-power regionalism.

In 1989–90 the Japanese were debating the meaning of the collapse of communism for the world order. Many welcomed a new era, confident of their competitiveness and anxious for a fundamental realignment from the postwar era. They assumed that the military factor would diminish, led by Moscow's shift to economic priorities. Bipolarism would give way to wider integration, including Asian regionalism that would follow Europe in coordinating economies and gradually adding closer political ties. As the entire character of Europe was being transformed, the Japanese with relatively benign views of Moscow and Beijing were the most optimistic in looking ahead

[22] Kenichi Ohmae, "The Virtual Continent," *New Perspectives Quarterly*, 17(1) Winter 2000, pp. 7–14.

[23] Toma Takeo, "Tsugi no sedai e no saidai no okurimono: kaneisuru Nihonkaiken," *Gekkan shakaito*, 2 (1991), pp. 98–102.

to a new NEA region.[24] Many on the Right were also hopeful, believing that pressure tactics would now work.

A rapidly declining Soviet Union and an isolated China from 1989 created a vacuum, which beckoned Japan to extend its influence in Asia. Amidst new expectations, however, there was no consensus on how to promote regionalism. It was widely noted that "misperceptions" could lead Japan to be viewed as a threat.[25] Ties with Moscow and Beijing, as well as with Seoul and Pyongyang, did not suggest that any partner would help Tokyo find a shortcut to regionalism. The right wing preferred to keep its nationalist agenda, giving economic forces time to enhance Japan's leverage even as Japan boosted its military potential and seized new opportunities to exert political pressure.

In 1990 Japan's aspirations as a geopolitical power clashed with concern that it was being isolated as Soviet talks with the United States and Western Europe were leading the world past the cold war. Ideas were floated about building a full trilateral relationship with the United States and EU so that Japan would also have a voice in formulating security policy in Europe and elsewhere and expanding the G-7 summit agenda to cover security.[26] As they attempted to raise the territorial dispute from a bilateral to a global issue, the Japanese congratulated themselves for a diplomatic success by having it included in the July 1990 Houston G-7 summit for the first time.[27] When these hopes were dashed as the United States gave priority to aiding Moscow's transformation, regional leadership remained the best bet.

The loudest voices on behalf of regionalism were the prefectural governments along the Sea of Japan. To explain their enthusiasm we need to look back to the sense of grievance over Tokyo's earlier choice of a Pacific coast strategy of postwar development despite the emboldening pattern of national disbursements that had come from their disproportionate clout in the LDP leadership. By 1990 they were loudly boosting the idea of the "Sea of Japan rim" and insisting that the key to success would be localism backed by massive infrastructure projects funded by the central government.[28] They did not know much about their prospective partners on the other side of the sea, but that did not bother them as long as they could create public relations momentum from conferences and exchanges and keep the lobbying in Tokyo at a lively pitch. Naturally, they expected that their own area's small and middle-sized firms, low in national competitiveness, would lead

[24] "Yaruta no kabi wa kuzureta no ka?" *Sekai*, January 1990, pp. 234–47.

[25] "Posuto Maruta no sekai o tembo suru," *Chuo koron*, February 1990, pp. 166–89.

[26] *International Herald Tribune*, June 20, 1990, pp. 1–2.

[27] Eya Osamu, "Hoppo ryodo henkan no shinario," *Chishiki*, 10 (1990), p. 68.

[28] To Tsuaoen, "'Kannihonkai ken' e no teigen," *Sekai*, 1 (1991), pp. 154–69; Ikarashi Akio, "Chiho wa sekai to musubu," *Ushio*, 2 (1991), pp. 166–77.

the way to economic ties across the sea.[29] While heralding a great economic union to rival the European community by 2020, they narrowed the focus to "grassroots exchanges."[30]

Idealism ran rampant in some of the media as conferences bringing boosters together drew rapt attention. A January 1, 1991 article on the "new era of the Japan Sea rim" (*kannihonkai shinjidai*) sported the headline "Unlimited possibilities for the 21 century."[31] Yet, there were efforts to report a different reality behind the "boom" and "rush" of 1990–1. One article insisted that real conditions were still severe, including a lack of confidence in the Russian ruble and confusion in administrative organizations. It was a plea for waiting, even a decade if needed, for business to boom along the Japan Sea rim.[32] Sober voices may not have pinpointed what was wrong with the mix of assumptions raising hopes for regionalism, but they cautioned against haste. With many doubting the Soviet Union, North Korea, China, and even South Korea, spikes of euphoria did not last.

From the start, regionalism was driven by fears of competition as well as visions of cooperation. The sudden expansion of South Korean business interest in the Russian Far East gave an impetus to Japanese activities. Observers foresaw a kind of domino effect: the first to gain a foothold in Vladivostok or Nakhodka would get access to the natural resources of Siberia and the regional linkages to Northeast China and North Korea. Russians played on Japanese fear of falling behind South Korea as well as on the accusation that by insisting on the transfer of islands Japan was damaging its case.[33] Hopes rose that at last Japan would assume a leadership role. The long-arrogant Moscow that had dismissed it as a country without military might or natural resources was coming to respect its economic power. Beijing's criticisms were muffled as it looked to economic help and a bridge to end the sanctions imposed in June 1989. The United States had become reliant too in its struggle to reshape a changing world and pay for the Persian Gulf War and aid to Moscow. Regionalism promised respect to both nationalists and internationalists.

In retrospect, the best chance for regionalism before 2004 was if Japan in the late 1980s had chosen a strategy of leadership beckoning to the four little dragons, forward-looking toward the Soviet Union, and reassuring to China and the United States.[34] The afterglow of the Seoul Olympics, Gorbachev's intensification of foreign policy openness after a breakthrough

29 "Nihonkai jidai no akebono," *Nihon keizai shimbun*, April 19, 1991.

30 "'Dai keizaiken' tanjo no taido," *Sankei shimbun*, April 13, 1991.

31 "21 seiki e mugen no kanosei," *Yomiuri shimbun*, January 1, 1991.

32 "Kannihonkai keizaiken no genjitsu," *Shukan Toyo keizai*, January 26, 1991, pp. 8–14.

33 Ha Shingi, "'Kannihonkai keizaiken' ni mirai o kotozu," *Ekonomisuto*, November 6, 1990, p. 27.

34 Gilbert Rozman, "China's Changing Images of Japan 1989–2001: The Struggle to Balance Partnership and Rivalry," *International Relations of the Asia-Pacific*, Winter 2002, pp. 95–129.

with the United States, and China's isolation created a window of opportunity in 1988–9. At its peak, Japan had many levers available if it could have controlled its own narrow-minded nationalist thinking. Failing to lead, it would lose the initiative.

Looking back nostalgically to the golden days at the end of the 1980s, the Japanese spread the blame for the failure to achieve regionalism. Many agree to assign some of the responsibility to flawed domestic strategies of the bubble economy years. Japan spent too freely and ran up excessive debts. Years of overconfidence in its economy and society had produced an unjustified degree of "*nihonjinron*" thinking proclaiming the uniqueness and cultural superiority of the Japanese people. The nation had internationalized slowly, both economically and culturally. Yet, self-blame often is mixed with criticism of the United States even more than criticism of Asian neighbors for blocking Japan's options. Leaders had to settle for developing the idea for APEC behind the scenes, when what they really favored was a version of EAEC advocated by Mahathir. Only a leader who did not hesitate to thumb his nose at the United States could press for a regional grouping that excluded it. Meanwhile, a Japan afraid of invoking the wrath of its largest market had to reject the proposal. Yet, the idea of leading NEA and SEA into the post–cold war global order resonated well with elites eager for achieving the elusive goal of emerging from the shadow of U.S. dependency. It was a symbol of long-awaited "normalcy." Economic power would at last be translated into cultural and political power. Japan's abnormal identity as part of the "West" in a polarized world would be replaced by an identity as the leader of an Asian region able to bridge East and West. Tokyo sought to lead Asian economic integration to give renewed dynamism to its own economic development as well as to position itself for global power. Instead of blaming themselves for failing to win the trust of all of the countries of NEA as well as some in SEA, many recalled Washington's resistance to regionalism as the primary factor in the lost opportunity. Already in 1989–91 the Japanese were expressing their annoyance that the United States was not using its vast powers to press the Soviet Union to yield on the disputed islands and give their country its first breakthrough toward regionalism.

Japan and Russia

As Japan prospered in the postwar era, it proceeded to build linkages to East Asia and SEA largely exclusive of the closed socialist states. Economically, its approach proved highly successful; production networks enveloped one country after another in a web of imports of essential Japanese machinery and exports of items desired around the world complementary to Japan's own exports with profits flooding into Japan. If this met its aspirations as an economic great power, other objectives went unrealized. In 1973 when Tanaka Kakuei stated that Japan and Russia are "close neighbors" Japanese firms were interested in investing in Siberian resources. Seeking raw materials or energy, officials not only aimed to draw the USSR into Japan's economic web; they also had in mind political objectives. Moscow's goal also mixed economic integration with Asia and a rising political role. With Soviet relations with China on the skids and Japan having already secured the return of Okinawa from the United States, the logic of a political breakthrough had risen. However, neither side valued the economics or politics of closer ties enough to compromise. Relations deteriorated as Moscow hardened its position against the United States and its allies and Tokyo drew closer to the United States and China in opposition to the Soviet Union. Successful in energy conservation and forging economic ties across Asia, Japan had little need for Russia's economy, even twenty years later warning Moscow not to conclude wrongly that energy gives it an edge in squeezing political concessions.[35] The Soviets countered that Japan's foothold in NEA was not so secure that it could ignore a nearby great power. The nadir in relations lasted a decade until Gorbachev assumed power.

After Leonid Brezhnev's remarks at the Twenty-Sixth Party Congress in 1981 that in Japan's foreign policy "negative features had been strengthened" propaganda against Japanese militarism intensified.[36] It followed that nothing good could come from Japan's relations with its neighbors. As one Japanese diplomat asserted, "Until . . . 1985, the Soviet Union saw North-east Asia as a threat rather than an opportunity."[37] Little thought had been given to regional economic integration, although hopes survived of more trade and joint projects. Amidst complaints about Tokyo's "artificial politicization" of commerce and denial of credit, few took satisfaction in the successful completion of the first stage of the 1975 Sakhalin oil and gas project after more than twenty wells had been drilled and two deposits opened by 1984,[38] and soon development stalled.

In 1985 Nakasone Yasuhiro returned from Soviet Party Secretary Chernenko's funeral upbeat about the possibility of working with his successor Gorbachev. He was the first Japanese leader to take the possibility of a breakthrough in relations with the Soviet Union seriously, seeking to sum up the "final results of the postwar scene" and eradicate "the last trace of defeat and disgrace."[39] Japan's media started to play up even the faintest signs

35 Hiroshi Kimura, "Politics and Economics in Russo-Japanese Relations," in Ted Hopf, ed., *Understandings of Russian Foreign Policy* (College Station: Pennsylvania State University Press, 1999), pp. 214–15.

36 M. I. Ivanov, *Rost militarizma v Iaponii* (Moscow: Voenizdat, 1982), pp. 4–5.

37 Chikahito Harada, "The Relationship between Japan and Russia," *The Japan Society Proceedings*, Summer 1999, p. 33.

38 M. Maksov, "The Sakhalin Project at an Important Juncture," Argumenty i fakty, *The Current Digest of the Soviet Press*, 36(27) 1984, p. 20.

39 Hiroshi Kimura, *Distant Neighbors Volume 2: Japanese-Russian Relations under Gorbachev and Yeltsin* (Armonk, NY: M. E. Sharpe, 2000), pp. 18, 20.

of progress. Although ties were slow to improve as Gorbachev focused elsewhere, expectations soon rose among LDP bigwigs that the right connections and generosity could secure the reversion of all four islands. By 1990 personal diplomacy peaked: Abe Shintaro and Ozawa Ichiro looked for glory in the Soviet Union; Kanemaru Shin tried his hand with North Korea; and prime ministers went to each G-7 meeting with plans to leave their mark as a statesman. Blaming diplomats for passivity, LDP politicians saw the time as ripe for wooing Soviet leaders and turning Japan into a political great power.[40]

Once "new thinking" sharply diminished the clamor against the United States and China in the Soviet Union, critics of Japan remained the most vocal advocates of foreign policy continuities. After the 1988 G-7 meeting in Toronto, Japan was identified as the obstacle that prevented the international climate in the Asia-Pacific region from becoming healthy. Instead of seeking to accommodate Japan's regional leadership, Soviets charged Japan with "dangerous illusions" and pressure tactics that would preserve regional tensions.[41] The territorial issue symbolized intransigence, especially to the communist old guard.

A mismatch existed in the objective need of each country for the other. The Soviet Union craved what Japan had: the latest achievements of science and technology, mass-produced electronic goods flooding other world markets, and above all capital from a country enjoying an unprecedented balance-of-payments surplus. Moreover, Moscow increasingly wanted to be admitted as a full member of regional economic groupings. In contrast, the Japanese seemed to seek little, taking the attitude that it was the Soviets who needed their help for economic reform, entrance into the Asia-Pacific community, and even collective security. While they sought four islands, Japanese felt no need to make concessions, reasoning that now Moscow had to prove it respected them, to make Japan a high priority.[42] They waited in vain. Preoccupied with the Soviet Union as the key to ending the postwar era of low respect for their country, the Japanese failed to launch a full-fledged debate on winning respect as a champion of regionalism and internationalism. As late as mid-1988 one Soviet specialist bewailed the lack of debate in Japan about the impact of changes on the world.[43] When debate finally ensued, its scope was narrow. Nationalists warned against a repetition of illusions that made the West susceptible to "Gorbymania." Just as the debate over regionalism

[40] *Nihon keizai shimbun*, January 17, 1990.

[41] *Pravda*, July 12, 1988, p. 5.

[42] Toru Nakagawa, "Japan's Northern Territories in International Politics," *Japan Review of International Affairs*, 2(1) Spring/Summer 1988, p. 23; Togo Takehiro, "Soren shidobu no jinji ido, tainichi seisaku, nado o megutte," *Sekai keizai daiyaruru reporto*, 322 (November 1988), pp. 2–8.

[43] "'Moskuwa' igo no sekai o yomu," *Ekonomisuto*, June 21, 1988, p. 55.

in the first half of the 1990s and over the "China threat" in the second half of the 1990s would rarely challenge the nationalist position, the weakness of internationalist thinking limited debate on the Soviet Union in the 1980s. Critics branded suggestions of compromise with Moscow "traitorous."[44]

Indeed, the Japanese on the Left as well as the Right were waiting for Moscow to change its attitude. From 1986 to 1991 each high-level, bilateral meeting and each shift in Soviet thinking related to Japan led some observers to jump to the conclusion that at last significant change had begun. For instance, after ex–Prime Minister Nakasone had met Gorbachev in Moscow *Asahi shimbun* heralded the first chance of a Japanese official to present the case for the reversion of the islands on Soviet television. It assumed that after ending the Afghanistan War and improving relations with China, Moscow had shifted the priority in 1988 to Japan, as its objective turned to economic cooperation.[45] Accordingly, it would, in stages, recognize the validity of Japan's position and the wisdom of joining in regional cooperation. Rarely did discussions consider how Tokyo should change and what stakes it had in this relationship other than the islands. Simplistically, the Japanese treated the islands as the "only barrier" to a boom in bilateral ties, not anticipating that Russians would choose poverty rather than yield territory that would "smear the prestige of our great motherland and superpower." Considering their country to be the only source of cash reserves sufficient to aid the USSR significantly, the Japanese waited in vain.[46]

Few openly voiced what was really wanted from Moscow, which was the return of the islands as a symbol that would close the book on the image at home and abroad of Japan as a defeated power, and a commitment to a respected partnership that would open the way for an independent foreign policy. Soviets lacked confidence that concessions on just two islands would do any good or that abandoning all four islands would really lead to a regional balance beneficial to their country. Apart from some investment and assistance, they could not envision a place for their country in a region with three entrenched great powers. Efforts to advance through talks on a security framework based on existing Soviet military power or mutual cuts failed, however, to interest Japan as well as the United States.

In 1990 the Japanese insisted that because Moscow treated NEA differently from Europe, regionalism as well as mutual security could not take root.[47] They sought to put maximum pressure on Moscow in order to reduce its military threat, seen as inseparable from the return of the islands.

44 Gilbert Rozman, *Japan's Response to the Gorbachev Era: A Rising Superpower Views a Declining One* (Princeton: Princeton University Press, 1992), p. 103.

45 *Asahi shimbun*, July 24, 1988, p. 5.

46 Hiroshi Kimura, "Gorbachev's Japan Policy: Changes and Challenges" (Tokyo, unpublished manuscript, 1990), pp. 10, 16.

47 *Asahi shimbun*, April 4, 1990, p. 2.

Some politicians were ready to freeze economic ties with Moscow and exact a large price for its intransigence, but the official line was to mix enticements with concealed warnings of what was at stake in the hope that Moscow would yield. They saw Japan as one of the victors in the cold war against the Soviet Union, even if it failed to receive what it regarded as the just fruits of its victory. Instead of making Japan pay a high price, Soviet intransigence and high-handedness proved costly primarily to itself. They alienated the Japanese people – from the diplomatic professionals resentful at their second-class treatment to the leftist parties, which came to regard their nationalism as incompatible with a favorable view of Moscow's leadership – while cutting Russians off from critical economic assistance. Costly efforts to develop Asiatic Russia had realized meager results. Vast funds sunk into a military buildup failed to influence events in NEA. Inside Russia Japan symbolized the missed opportunities of past foreign policy. In contrast to the many Japanese who even at the end of the 1980s doubted that the Soviet Union was seriously changing, others treated the changes as a sign that Japan's assistance would soon become indispensable. They foresaw a scenario of worsening crisis, endorsement of a substantial economic reform program, and then Gorbachev visiting Japan and looking for aid.[48] This led to optimism about Japan's leverage as well as about the prospects for regionalism. Some who may have been less aware of the emerging crisis expected the Soviets to turn to Japan because it was the logical step after 1) Gorbachev's Vladivostok speech in July 1986 recognized that the Far Eastern region must become largely self-sufficient of distant Moscow and closely integrated into the Pacific region economy; 2) the Soviets announced in July 1987 a "Comprehensive Far East Plan" to the year 2000 calling for more than 230 billion rubles in investment; and 3) the Soviet Domestic Commission on Economic Cooperation with the Asian-Pacific region was established in March 1988 under Evgenii Primakov. Meanwhile, in its Fourth Nationwide Comprehensive Development Plan Japan planned to reduce concentration in the Tokyo area, promoting new industries along the Japan Sea. Advocates of regionalism saw a convergence of economic interests, a high degree of economic complementarity, drawing on Soviet timber, nonferrous metals, coal, natural gas, and petroleum. Joint ventures in shipbuilding and repair plus sightseeing were other reasons for optimism.[49] But these grand ideas on paper stumbled before any practical steps at implementation.

Despite the implicit threat to withhold assistance until a deal was reached on the islands, Japan reluctantly joined the other G-7 states in helping the Soviet Union through its economic crisis of 1990–1 and supporting the bold

48 Hasegawa Keitaro, "Sore de me Gorubachofu wa ikinokoru," *Voice*, December 1989, pp. 62–75.

49 Kanamori Hisao, "Future Prospects of Economic Relations between Soviet Far East and East Asia as well as Southeast Asian Nations" (Tokyo: unpublished manuscript, 1989).

reforms of a state in transition. As in large allocations for the Persian Gulf War, humanitarian aid was meant to demonstrate "internationalization," while showing Moscow the wisdom of flexibility. Optimistic that the impact of economic power was rising, the Japanese hoped that Moscow would calculate returning the islands as a small price to pay. Officials and even the press insisted that the public must present a rock of solidarity on the island dispute.[50] Idealizing a homogeneous nation that forges a consensus, this nationalist outlook marginalized true regionalists.

The Japanese would have welcomed the respect shown by being treated as a model for Soviet reforms. As reformers began to discuss "shock therapy," some proposed learning from postwar "Japanese style shock" (*shok po-iaponskii*).[51] Interest, however, proved too meager. Also Japan tried to soften the Soviet Union up through a cultural blitz – kabuki theater, tea ceremonies, a film festival – hoping that the fascination for Japanese culture shown by Soviet intellectuals from the 1970s would lead to new thinking about territorial claims. If economic appeals to regionalism did not work maybe cultural ones would, paving the way for informing Russians of Japan's view of the history of the islands next. The Russian people, however, had more pressing concerns, as they looked westward.

On the whole, the Japanese were skeptical of Soviet perestroika, viewing the country as a military superpower with feet of clay.[52] There was little idealism about large-scale cooperation despite interest, at times, in energy projects and cross-border ties. The Japanese insisted that the Soviet desire to conduct economic exchanges without paying the price of returning the islands was "selfishness,"[53] while Soviets saw Japan's demand for all of the islands as the entry point for serious cooperation as a threat to the inviolability of postwar frontiers that could lead to a domino effect. It was a sign of much greater suspicion than was seen in the United States.[54] Neither side viewed the other as serious about compromise.

In an interview with *Izvestiia* in June 1990 Prime Minister Kaifu Toshiki placed Japanese-Soviet relations in the context of the most dynamic region in a new world order, suggesting that ties could rise to the level of Japanese-U.S. economic ties. While noting a need for step-by-step advances toward trust, Kaifu held up a vision in which regionalism was joined closely to globalism.[55] Yet, that same week *Pravda* reported that Tokyo was shaken by Gorbachev's meeting with South Korean President Roh as much as it had been by Nixon's visit to Beijing in 1972. In contrast to Kaifu's image of a

50 *Tokyo shimbun*, September 9, 1990.

51 "Shok po-iaponski," *Literaturnaia gazeta*, August 22, 1990.

52 *Sankei shimbun*, July 18, 1990.

53 *The Japan Times Weekly International Edition*, April 15–21, 1991, p. 11.

54 Alexei Bogatourov, "U.S.S.R. – Japan," *New Times*, 32 (1989), pp. 20–2.

55 *Izvestiia*, June 15, 1990, p. 6.

regional order, this article averred that a new epoch in Asia was starting with regional security discussions, which Japan was refusing to join.[56] In short, by playing its security card and pressuring Tokyo through improved relations with China and South Korea, Moscow would shape a new regional order, not succumbing to pressure to plead for entry into Japan's order.

Japanese and Soviet mutual perceptions slowed the search for a breakthrough in relations. The Japanese showed little idealism about the reform thrust of socialism. Not taking perestroika and glasnost seriously until long after West Europeans and Americans, they narrowly viewed Moscow's foreign policy through the prism of concessions on the disputed islands. Long after the United States and Moscow were reaching strategic agreements, Japanese officials and media doubted that "new thinking" had affected the Kremlin's policies in their region. A stubborn Soviet desk in the Foreign Ministry and public opinion deeply suspicious of anything Soviet stood in the way of great-power strategists ready to seize the opportunity of rapid changes in the global environment. On the Soviet side, few appreciated Japanese economic power enough to make bilateral relations a high priority. The downfall of the hard-liners who had long disparaged Japan and the arrival of glasnost in Japan came late. Only in early 1988 was a clear rebuttal published against the thesis that Japanese militarism was on the rise.[57] Elite opinion naïvely blamed Japan's intransigence on the islands without seriously reexamining bilateral possibilities. While Japan was becoming an advocate of regionalism, including ties with the Russian Far East, a virtual stalemate in negotiations cast a dark shadow on indispensable bilateral relations.

China and Regionalism

Under the aura of communist ideology punctuated by national liberation doctrine, the Chinese interpreted the history of the twentieth century as the recovery of sovereignty as well as of regional and global standing through overcoming the insidious intent of one hegemonic power after another. In 1945 Japan withdrew its occupying forces. In 1960 Mao broke with the Soviet Union, causing it to remove its advisors. In 1982 a decision was made to stop leaning to the side of U.S. leadership. Obsessed with freeing itself from any geopolitical dependency, China's elite erected an artificial intellectual divide by combining newfound acceptance of the need for economic interdependence with old-style insistence on zero-sum great-power relations. Inclined to view wide-ranging proposals for regionalism suspiciously

56 *Pravda*, June 9, 1990, p. 7.

57 Gilbert Rozman, "Moscow's Japan-Watchers in the First Years of the Gorbachev Era: The Struggle for Realism and Respect in Foreign Affairs," *Pacific Review*, 1(3) 1988, pp. 257–75.

as disguised dependency, they were willing, nonetheless, to embrace increased economic regionalism as essential for global trade and investment.

Long before the turbulent events from the end of the 1980s, the Chinese predicted a global shift to multiple poles along with the rise of the Pacific Rim. By 1984 they wrote of three centers in the capitalist world as U.S. hegemony declined, diversification in the socialist camp as the Soviet role lessened, and the rise of the Third World. Anticipating a loosening of both military and economic hegemony, analysts saw room to maneuver for China as well as other states.[58] Thus, in the scramble ahead without a world political or economic center China would enjoy a favorable environment for extending its influence. There was a burning desire for "multipolarity" well before the term became fashionable.

From the international social scientist community China accepted modernization theory. Even before writings in the 1990s grew more sophisticated and comparative, an early wave of translations in the mid-1980s and analytical supplements established an intellectual foundation for political decisions favoring ever more economic reform and openness.[59] They gave a twist to convergence theory, not rejecting it wholesale as occurred in Soviet writings before the Gorbachev era but carving out a space to limit its range. Not only did this affirm the separate path of East Asian capitalist modernization, but it also left to be decided later a possible variant for socialist modernization. Countries would not converge on a Western model, even if all would accept basic tenets of a common blueprint for modernization that the Chinese had wrongly ignored until 1978.

In place of Mao Zedong's diplomatic strategy of "war and revolution," Deng introduced a strategy of "peace and development." The former gave rise to successive defensive alliances against the number one "hegemonic power" lasting a decade each, interrupted only by a decade of self-isolation when revolution turned inward. The latter became the bulwark of two decades of independent foreign policy, as China looked for a balance of power that would weaken all alliances and produce a new international order. In the 1990s opposition to the evolution of the world order intensified, taking the form of support for economic globalism but rejection of either political or cultural systems that lessen diversity.[60] This proved to be an uphill struggle even as it shaped regionalism.

In 1986–8 Chinese leaders could have found cause for cheer in important shifts occurring in their region and the world. Gorbachev's perestroika,

[58] Wu Yikang, "Qiantan shijie jingji de duojihua qushi – lianping weilai shi 'Taipingyang shidai' de tifa–," *Shijie jingji yu zhengzhi neican*, April 1984, pp. 12–17.

[59] See the series Shijie xiandaihua zhincheng yanjiu congshu, edited by Lo Rongqu, such as *Zhongguo he Riben de caoqi gongyehua yu guonei shichang* (Beijing: Beijng daxue chubanshe, 1999).

[60] Kokubun Ryosei, "Shuno gaiko to Chugoku," *Kokusai mondai*, January 1999, pp. 1–5.

reduction of military pressure in Asia, expanding economic cooperation with the Russian Far East, and moves away from the cold war all satisfied deep desires in China. Also Japan's rising investment in Asia amidst growing interest in economic regionalism held great promise for China's economic fortunes. After a difficult early start with the Reagan administration, relations had stabilized with U.S. expectations high for China's transition. At home reforms were proceeding well despite a wave of inflation. Then why did leaders grow more anxious? They turned against the most vocal reformers, ousting Party Secretary Hu Yaobang, warning against relaxing the country's guard against Japan and the United States, and souring on Gorbachev's leadership of the Soviet Union. Fearful of losing the clout they enjoyed from a divided and tense world and the existence of another stronghold of socialism, the leaders long before June 1989 sent mixed signals to those eager to speed regionalism and link it to globalization. They could have frightened away other states except for Deng Xiaoping's frequent intercession to accelerate the course of economic reform.

The events of June 1989 were a setback to one path toward regionalism but, at least at first, appeared to be a boon for another. By imposing sanctions against China, the United States and Japan made national coordination for regionalism more difficult. No wonder that linkages among local areas became the preferred focus by 1991. China contributed to this reorientation too. Retrenchment in its reforms left many capitalists under a cloud for two-and-a-half years until Deng's January 1992 full endorsement of market forces. In Northeast China where old-guard socialists remained entrenched it was, thus, even more difficult for business groups from other parts of China to expand. As cross-border trade grew rapidly, local peasants in collusion with corrupt officials filled the void. China's traders and joint ventures steered the first regionalism down an unsustainable path.

The Chinese foreign-policy debate of mid-1989 to early 1992 set the course for a new decade as the debate of 1979 to 1982 had ushered in the prior decade. The earlier debate under the shadow of an isolated Moscow led by Leonid Brezhnev and a resurgent Washington led by Ronald Reagan brought the goal of equidistance between the United States and the Soviet Union that was pursued but never quite realized. It had reflected a continuation of the cold war and the need for China to find maximum room to maneuver. The latter debate addressed a direr situation: the danger of a new world order with no room for triangularity. The response was a plan to await Moscow's disillusionment with the West and again find a way to limit growing U.S. arrogance. Japan figured into these debates as part of the balance of power, offering some hope because of its growing competition with the United States. It also represented a force for regionalism that could boost China's leverage as the global environment remained adverse, but China would have to be wary of Japan's pursuit of vertical regionalism. While seeking a power balance, China realized the need for economic regionalism in an era of rising international economic competition.[61]

In response to sanctions China turned to its immediate neighborhood for closer relations. This gave it the time and space to overcome its more negative international environment. This region-centered diplomacy encouraged both South Korea and Japan, tilting the balance from the strategic great-power diplomacy that had favored the United States, the Soviet Union, and even North Korea and had concentrated on military force. Beijing did not move abruptly. It kept all options open for Moscow should its diplomacy shift, and it briefed Pyongyang often in an effort to win its understanding. Also Beijing was careful to avoid anything that smacked of Gorbachev-style glasnost, for instance by refusing to acknowledge at home or abroad the truth of the Korean War's beginning. Censorship interfered with exploration of the potential for noneconomic aspects of regionalism.

A northern establishment centered in Beijing sought to limit the scope of reform, particularly political reform, and to press for nationalist causes. Southern entrepreneurial forces, meanwhile, were increasingly open to business links to the outside without regard to nationalism. Students turned against the northern establishment in 1989, but they could be moved by nationalist causes too. The second half of the 1980s brought economic reform mixed with frustrations over growing corruption and low political accountability, and the 1990s began with a search for ways to stabilize this tenuous combination.

Two subregions of China became identified with NEA regionalism: Heilongjiang and Jilin provinces and the upper part of Liaoning province in the northeast with no coastal access but potential to reach the Sea of Japan across a narrow strip of Russia and North Korea; and the Bohai rim provincial-level units of Hebei, Shandong, Beijing, Tianjin, and the Liaodong peninsula in the lower part of Liaoning. For the most part, they were not well integrated with each other, although the former area had no choice but to conduct virtually all its trade through the latter. In 1984 Dalian at the tip of the Liaodong peninsula was designated one of the earliest development zones, and it prospered with a young influential mayor who provided direct access to foreign managers. Japanese firms invested heavily, using cheap Chinese labor for export industries. While the location was terrible for access to China's domestic market by road or rail, the Japanese set up their own separate world. Dalian was in, but not of, Northeast China. As the 1990s proceeded, foreign direct investment and economic growth favored the Bohai rim over the northeast tip. Many plans for regionalism focused on China's northeast and north provinces; the imbalance between their two main parts complicated the search for regional integration.

[61] Song Yimin, "Shijie geju zhuanhuan guochengzhong de xin wenti," *Neibu ziliao suoyin, jiaoxue yanjiu ziliao*, 24 (1990), p. 7.

The provinces and cities of these areas of China vied to attract investments and forge long-term ties with firms and administrative entities in Japan, South Korea, and Russia. Until the spring of 1992 they chafed at handicaps limiting their appeal compared to the special benefits granted to the many zones established in Southeast China. Hopes were rising, however, as officials in South Korea, the Russian Far East, and Japan's prefectures along the Japan Sea sent delegations promising to boost ties.[62] The pace of contacts accelerated, and it was matched by the urgency of planning for gaining a comparative advantage as well as lobbying for Beijing to extend more privileges.

Beleaguered after June 1989, the Chinese argued that because capitalist countries were superior economically temporarily, it was necessary to make economics the central link and open more in order to expand the forces of production and absorb everything positive in capitalism. Yet, they added, because the United States and other capitalist states intended to make use of economic ties for "peaceful evolution" more would have to be done to struggle against the negative pressure from capitalism.[63] This mindset set the tone for focusing on cross-border economic ties. Local governments in China and Japan shared great enthusiasm for regionalism and gained enough support in Beijing and Tokyo to put this on the bilateral agenda. Yet, the center proved to be cautious; its economic priorities increasingly centered on the Shanghai area, and its geopolitical objectives narrowed the potential of regionalism. Even as Beijing gradually overcame its caution on globalization, it preferred open borders and lots of incoming investment with little political spillover.

In 1988–9 the Chinese began to write extensively on the four little dragons and on regional economic relations. After the suppression at Tiananmen, regional coverage expanded. Much attention turned to the differences between NEA and SEA. Two schools could be detected: the group that concentrated on the danger of Japanese hegemonism in NEA and insisted that it was premature to focus on regionalism; and those optimistic about achieving a balance through economic regionalism. A compromise was reached, supportive of limited economic integration, but wary of Japanese-led formal regionalism.

With the Soviet Union disappearing and Japan's power rising, Chinese analysts did not share in the high expectations for regionalism. They feared Japanese dominance, did not expect to gain leverage from South Korea, and were slow to anticipate Taiwan's large-scale investment in the PRC. The only backup to hopes for the Soviet Union as a balancing force was the

62 Song Shaoying, "Dongya jingji xinzhixu de jianli yu Zhongri jingji guanxi," *Dongbeiya yanjiu*, 3 (1992), pp. 3–8.

63 Zhang Xiangying, "Luohou guojia shehui zhuyi jianshe de keguan huanjing," *Lilun neican*, 12 (1990), p. 6.

image of a rivalry between the United States and Japan that would limit the latter and give China time to catch up. This thinking allowed for cautious regionalism.

Fearful of Japanese domination, China would have been difficult to entice into a major initiative for regionalism. Perhaps, an opportunity existed in 1984–5 when desire for large-scale support for new reforms left Chinese leaders eager for Japan's assistance. If leaders had chosen restraint in June 1989, regionalism might have been accepted with globalization rather than seen as a means to limit it. Lacking assurance from Japan about the balanced character of regionalism and the prospect of finding some common culture without facing new reminders of a divisive history, the Chinese could not give unqualified support to regionalism in NEA even if they had not been limited by post-Tiananmen repression.

Excitement over regionalism in 1990–1 among some groups inside China, especially in the Northeast, was not accompanied by a Chinese strategy for development or sense of national identity that would permit genuine support for regional institutions. Trust in globalization and in Japanese regional leadership was missing. Japanese regional boosters failed to appreciate the seriousness of these problems and devise strategies to try to address them. While each side found it convenient to say positive things about the desirability of moving forward to regionalism, mutual recognition of how to win the other's trust evolved slowly.

China and Japan

The Sino-Japanese rivalry took a backseat to other concerns of the two countries before the 1990s. In the 1970s China's anti-Soviet posture drove relations with Japan as with the United States. In the 1980s Japan was needed along with the United States to meet the foremost goal of joining China's economy to the global one, which proved beneficial for relations as Japan's Overseas Development Assistance (ODA) loans were welcomed and trade tripled to $20 billion by the end of the decade. Seeking integration into the emerging regional economy and opting for a wide-ranging regional diplomacy in 1989–91, Beijing again gave Tokyo cause for optimism.[64] As the regional economic leader, Japan expected to take advantage of China's relative isolation (only in 1990 was it establishing new relations with Indonesia and Singapore and only in 1992 with South Korea). After feeling obliged to impose sanctions as its international duty, Japan resumed its loans to China early and championed China as its regional responsibility while also seeing this as a means to bolster its role in a changing global environment. As the Japanese talked about "reentering Asia" and the Chinese looked to

[64] Amano Satoshi, "Nitchu kokkyo seijoka igo," *Kokusai mondai*, July 2000, pp. 64–70.

regional ties to overcome global isolation, the two nations seemed to stand side by side.

Japan and China resumed a collision course in historical consciousness and its relevance in the 1980s. Under Nakasone, the Japanese were searching for a view of the past bereft of negative historical baggage, and of the future centered on Japan's advance as a normal great power. Under Deng, the Chinese were finding that nationalism could substitute for communism and required a strong dose of historical victimization. If the Chinese joined the Japanese in accepting economic globalization, they proved more adamant against broad theories of internationalization. Even more than nationalist LDP politicians, China's communist leaders were wary of global forces. Economic linkages grew rapidly without removing fears that sacred national ideals – claims to uniqueness – would be threatened. Neither side valued regionalism enough to contemplate less nationalism.

Perhaps more than any other country, Japan was drawn into Chinese notions of "friendship" (*youhao*). For two decades this meant lots of toasts by eminent figures in many fields, especially politicians and cultural leaders, and a select group of business bigwigs. Although such linkages could smooth over troubles and even create a succession of "China booms" in Japan, they turned out to be quite superficial and difficult to sustain after the older generation left the scene.[65] The foundation proved shakier than expected.

The Japanese had misjudged the situation. Leaders had turned to China with excess hopes for regional leadership, a message present when Prime Minister Takeshita Noboru spoke in China in 1988 of opening up a new era of friendship. At home there was talk that the passage of time and changes in global international relations were nullifying the victor-aggressor relations of the postwar era that had obliged "weak-kneed" behavior; an equal framework would allow Japan's advantages to take their natural course. In contrast, when the Chinese side spoke of raising the quality of relations, they had something else in mind. Upset about huge trade deficits in 1984–6 and the slow pace of investment and technological transfer, they argued that more economic support was needed as atonement for the past.[66] Fearing Japanese hegemony, the Chinese were anxious to create more balanced economic exchange as well as politics free of economics. After they agreed on nourishing a special relationship, the two let different notions of nationalism shape clashing expectations.

Many advocates of a soft response saw this as a test of civilizations. If Japan associated itself closely with European and American civilization it

[65] Amako Satoshi, "Yuko ippendo kara no tenkan," in Amako Satoshi and Sonoda Shigeto, eds., *Nitchu koryu no shibanseiki* (Tokyo: Toyo keizai shimposha, 1998), pp. 3–17.

[66] Tomoyuki Kojima, "Prospect for Sino-Japanese Relations in the 1990s," in Dalchong Kim, ed. *Peace and Cooperation in Northeast Asia* (Seoul: Institute of East and West Studies, Yonsei University, 1990), pp. 59–79.

would be arousing doubt in Asia as well as narrowing the scope for its foreign-policy conduct. Recognizing that Gorbachev had accepted the principle of common human values, critics cited Asian political culture as a basis for a new Asianism that implies differing human values. They argued that Japan should take responsibility for promoting this, making Sino-Japanese relations the core of a new region.[67] Optimism toward China prevailed in the face of criticisms that Japanese consciousness was failing to embrace intellectual openness to the world, and that the Japanese were prone to see their country as misunderstood rather than to reexamine the closed society and narrow thinking that made it hard for them to operate on the world stage. Critics suggested that Japan must understand how to become a cultural power supportive of global values instead of succumbing to self-praise about its own culture.[68] Ironically, optimism toward China reinforced a lack of internationalism.

On the tenth anniversary of the peace treaty between China and Japan in 1988, the Japanese press wrote of a new era marked by "complete normalization."[69] China's impending normalization with the Soviet Union and expanded contacts with Korea appeared to come not at Japan's expense leading to a newly divisive region, but as precursors to relaxing political tensions and advancing economic cooperation on a regional scale. Beijing still supported Tokyo on the return of four islands from Moscow, the Japanese were told. It had reduced its criticisms of Japanese military growth and right-wing nationalism, while recognizing the indispensability of increased Japanese investment for its bold economic plans. Although the upbeat personal connection of Nakasone Yasuhiro and Hu Yaobang had been scuttled when Hu was ousted amidst charges of being too soft on Japan and the messenger who was conveying China's good intentions to Japan was none other than the hard-line prime minister Li Peng, the Japanese looked quite confidently to China as a partner in regionalism. After all, U.S.-Soviet ties and Sino-Soviet ties were improving rapidly with little sign that all would not share in the gains. Indeed, the political Left suggested that a combination of the political great-power China and the economic great-power Japan working actively together on the international arena would contribute greatly to peace, while China's acceptance would reduce suspicions of Japan in Asia.[70] Only after June 1989 did realism about China take hold in the public, stirred by human-rights concerns, but the political elite, seeing an opportunity for increased leverage in great-power relations, underestimated the resiliency of China's nationalism using the "Japan card."

[67] Yano Toru, "Tsumi o nikunde, kuni o nikumazu," *Voice*, August 1989, pp. 80–97.

[68] Irie Akira, "Ima koso shisoteki tenkan," *Shokun*, December 1987, pp. 28–37.

[69] *Asahi shimbun*, August 26, 1988, p. 1; *Asahi shimbun*, August 30, 1988, p. 2; *Yomiuri shimbun*, August 28, 1988.

[70] *Asahi shimbun*, August 25, 1988, p. 5.

In mid-1988 Chinese specialists gathered to consider Japan's place in the world in the year 2000. While many spoke of Japan capitalizing on big changes in the world economic system with its high-tech industries, the consensus was that China would overtake Japan to rank third in overall power to the United States and Soviet Union. And while some argued that conflict between Japan and the United States would outweigh their joint hegemony or that Japan would succeed in building its own regional economic sphere, most insisted that Japan would not separate very much from the United States. The majority also held that a triangular framework would not emerge involving Japan and either China or the Soviet Union. Sino-Japanese relations would strengthen, but so would frictions.[71] With this reasoning the Chinese thought about balancing Japanese power in Asia rather than working together for regionalism. While the Japanese expected gratitude for taking the lead in ending China's isolation, the Chinese feared that the end of the cold war and the relative weakness of their own country could enable Japan to gain much higher status through economic might. Periodicals were suspicious of Japanese diplomacy, warning time and again that something sinister was afoot in the drive to become a political great power.

The Chinese assessed Japanese leadership in advocating regionalism with mixed responses. They traced the growing interest in 1987–90 and concluded that it reflected: 1) the need for resources and markets to fuel Japanese economic development; 2) the pressure of competition as other regions took shape around the world or resorted to protectionism; 3) a corrective needed due to unbalanced development across Japan; and 4) a new stage in ambitious thinking since the 1970s in favor of some sort of region for Japan to lead and to use to weaken the U.S. hold on it. But they warned that Japan's limits on technological sharing as well as its priority for internationalization facing the West meant that it would approach China in a spirit of superiority rather than equality.[72] The Chinese backed regionalism to a degree, but limited its impact and reshaped its direction.

As a shared anti-Soviet stance lost relevance and China's intense commitment to fledgling economic reforms gave way to more mature economic ties, observers wondered what would be the glue for the next stage of relations. By 1990 it appeared to be mutual support for regionalism with at least two principal objectives: 1) spurring intra-Asian trade and investment and 2) balancing the forces of globalization. The two sides could agree on these objectives and, therefore, join in limited pursuit of regionalism. Yet, they

[71] Zheng Zhishi, "'2000 nian de shijie xingshi he Riben de zuoyong' zuotanhui congshu," *Riben wenti ziliao*, 7 (1988), pp. 16–19.

[72] Wang Dingyong, "Riben dui Yatai diqu 'jingjiqu' jizhong sheji de bijiao fenxi," *Riben wenti yanjiu*, 4 (1989), pp. 1–6; Ren Qingyu, "Riben dui fazhan Dongbeiya quyi jingji hezuo de shexiang yu cuoshi," *Yafei yanjiu*, 2 (1992), pp. 51–67.

had different conceptions of balance without enough acceptance of global integration.

A type of globalized thinking grew resurgent in Japan after the Tiananmen repression and breakdown of the divide between Eastern and Western Europe. It held that communism is the same the world over, China has shown its real nature by suppressing human rights, and Japan should look on it through the same lens as that used in the West.[73] This meant that the Japanese should abandon their romantic vision of China and recognize it as an authoritarian state without the rule of law. While this view came largely from the right wing in Japan and signified a rejection of regionalism that leans on China, it was not necessarily an endorsement of Western thinking on global integration. It could also be compatible with an uncompromising position by Japan's Right, based on its superior values, to assume leadership without having to compromise with China. Some analysts suggested that China's isolation put Japan's foreign policy at a crossroads.

The main thrust of China's policy toward Japan in this period was reassurance. In open forums and popular publications Chinese experts stressed the positive, encouraging mutual understanding by concentrating on what the two nations have in common and by putting differences aside. Even with regard to the sensitive subject of historical relations, it served China's purposes not to hurt Japanese feelings by dwelling on bad memories. The new atmosphere provided a favorable environment for investment, trade, and regional stability. It led others to appreciate China's deep commitment to full integration into a regional market economy. Even as late as the emperor's visit in 1992, the Chinese press was still looking for opportunities to downplay differences and advertise their country's stability, commitment to opening up, and attractiveness for investments.[74]

In 1990 the Japanese and Chinese exchanged views at conferences on what each expected of the other to establish regionalism, marked by a big boost in relations, that both claimed to favor. The Japanese emphasized the need for China to embrace a market economy with much-improved opportunities for investors. The Chinese retorted with an appeal for Japan to remove the fetters on direct investment and expand bilateral trade at an accelerated pace. Each was soon to see its wish fulfilled. The economic ties were on the verge of a dramatic upsurge. Yet, what conferences often overlooked came back to haunt relations. The deepest source of anxiety for the Japanese people was the uncertainty about where Chinese nationalism was heading after June 4, 1989 and the most profound worry in China was the nationalist direction

[73] Nakamura Shohan, "Tenanmon no daigyakusatsu koso kyosanshugi no honshitsu," *Kakushin*, 8 (1989), pp. 32–5; Nakajima Muneo, "Tenanmon jiken igo no Seio no me," *Sankei shimbun*, September 23, 1989, p. 7.

[74] Wang Yong, "Emperor's Visit Swells Optimism," *China Daily Business Weekly*, November 2, 1992, p. 1.

of Japanese notions of emerging from the cold war era with a new sense of history and new role in regional and global leadership. Such sensitive issues rarely made it onto the agenda of meetings directed at enhancing regionalism. Each side pretended that its own nationalist wing posed no problem for the future and that economics could come first and smooth the way to increased trust.

If Tokyo was fixated on the territorial issue as the hurdle to be overcome in order to unleash region-building activities with Moscow, with Beijing it was preoccupied with avoiding sensitive political and security questions in order to advance regionalism. Both ways failed: Tokyo did not succeed in building any momentum with Moscow to develop a shared vision of a cooperative future in NEA and, at the same time, it overestimated the momentum it could create on the basis of economics alone to boost the prospects of regionalism with China. As the prime advocate of NEA regionalism, Japan failed to steer its most important bilateral relations in the region on a sustainable path toward that goal. Indeed, a strategy of forging networks with the Russian Far East to win support for the return of the islands and taking advantage of China's isolation to position itself between the United States and China actually resulted in short-sighted accommodations with nationalists.

In this opening act for NEA regionalism Beijing's siege mentality under sanctions and Tokyo's cockiness from a bubble economy produced only a shallow consensus. China's leaders were fearful of Japanese economic domination and unsympathetic to increased Japanese political clout. Japan's leaders sought rapid gains that would solidify a vertical organization of production. The gap in expectations made progress toward regionalism difficult, and no other regional actor was prepared to make this a priority.

Russia and Regionalism

Moscow started the 1980s overcommitted militarily across Asia and at sharp loggerheads with the powers of NEA. It was seen as on the offensive in NEA: encircling China militarily, intimidating Japan with an arms buildup and bluster, and aiming to tie the United States down. In turn, Moscow viewed any form of cooperation among these countries as well as South Korea as part of a struggle against it. The term *Asia-Pacific* acquired conspiratorial connotations of "encirclement" and cooperation there was criticized as enrichment by a few at the expense of the majority of the people. Deep Soviet suspicions of regionalism continued to be aired in the first two years of the Gorbachev era. Even after Gorbachev on April 23, 1986 had called for a "Pacific community," giving priority to discussions of security and holding out hope for large-scale economic cooperation, Soviet academics kept warning that what

Japan and the United States were seeking was akin to imperialism.[75] They argued that Chinese leaders should be wary of joining this sort of community. Analysts kept appealing to China to slow down on economic openness and start coordinating on regional issues in order to avoid being swallowed into the designs of the capitalist powers. Insisting that Japan and the United States were fighting between themselves over rival ambitions to dominate, they warned that this division was not enough to protect other countries. After all, the United States had been pressing Japan to assume part of its burden in this region as it aimed to strengthen its military-political dominance and Japan had eagerly agreed for its own expansionist aims.[76] The last gasp of this sort of rhetoric in 1987 was accompanied by a fresh wind of glasnost. A September 1987 article by Evgenii Primakov referred to capitalism without militarism, serious problems in socialism that require new solutions, and the need for peaceful means to resolve differences between the systems.[77] Supporting regional cooperation without branding it a means of domination, the new tone took into account progress in U.S.-Soviet and Sino-Soviet relations as well as urgent Soviet needs in what was now designated a promising region for cooperation.

For decades the Russian people were told that Japan in addition to taking part in the struggle between socialism and capitalism in Asia was bent on reviving its imperialist policies.[78] It had dubious motives in expanding economic ties. Although indirect studies had begun to change this view of Japan by the early 1980s and glasnost produced direct challenges to it in the late 1980s, they could not displace prior deeply ingrained thinking. Reform circles projected a positive image of Japan as a technological great power, a rapid modernizer that retained its cultural traditions, and even a champion of economic growth without military burdens. Yet, confused on how to fit together a distant but active U.S. superpower, a still weak but rapidly rising China, and a Japan whose motives remained obscure, the Russian public did not know what to make of NEA regionalism.

For more than a decade Soviet propaganda pretended that Moscow was winning the battle for superiority in the scientific and technological revolution. Under the impact of glasnost the secret came into the open that East Asian countries led by Japan were surging ahead. In the journal *MEiMO*, published by the lead institute in international affairs of the Academy of Sciences, articles in 1988 finally pointed to socialist countries being isolated

[75] A. Senatorov, "The Pacific Community: Plans and Prospects," *Far Eastern Affairs*, 5 (1987), pp. 161–3.

[76] A. Mirov, "O skolachivanii militaristskogo 'treugol'nika' Vashington-Tokio-Seul," *Mezhdunarodnaia zhizn'*, 9 (1987), pp. 120–7.

[77] E. Primakov, "Kapitalizm vo vzaimosviazannom mire," *Kommunist*, 13 (1987), pp. 101–10.

[78] L. N. Kutakov, *Vneshniaia politika i diplomatiia Iaponii* (Moscow: Mezhdunarodnye otnosheniia, 1964).

from these advances and praised Japan's diverse achievements, even in agriculture.[79] Moscow was driven to regional cooperation more by the goal of common human science and technology than the much more publicized "common human values."

Gorbachev's Vladivostok speech signaled that both the Russian Far East was in bad shape and Moscow was interested in regionalism combining new security measures and economic ties. Russian officials were disappointed with the cautious response in Japan and the United States. Clearly the speech went too far in seeking a big say for Moscow in a new security arrangement that others were not prepared to consider even as it was too tentative in opening the Russian Far East economy. It did not make a sharp enough break between the two. The United States felt that it was doing just fine in NEA in both respects, while Japan did not find its main security and territorial interests addressed. Gorbachev tried again at Krasnoyarsk in September 1988 with a stronger appeal to Japan as a great power without a large military budget and a welcome source of investment in Asiatic Russia. The Japanese feared, however, that the Soviet military would be left with a one-sided security advantage. Not touching on the territorial issue, the speech offered too little to them.[80] Unprepared to put strategic thinking in the forefront, Tokyo missed an opportunity.

While awakening to the dynamism of East Asia, Soviet analysts failed to lay the groundwork for regionalism. First, they neglected to study Japan's role as an engine of economic development, showing what reforms allow that engine to operate and Japan's reasoning in supporting other countries. Without such analysis, Soviets still assumed that Japan needs their country as much as they need it. Second, despite welcoming normalized relations with China as a boon in great-power politics and a step toward demilitarization of Asiatic Russia, Soviets did a poor job of analyzing Chinese reforms and what could be learned from them,[81] failing to appreciate the value of free economic zones or assurances to foreign investors. Third, even as writers discovered the economic successes of the four little dragons and ties with South Korea were warmly greeted, they missed the importance of moving step by step up the production cycle through exports. They did not study Asian development well, and naturally failed to apply lessons from it in the Russian Far East despite calls from 1986 to integrate the Far East into the region. Instead, it was blithely assumed that existing industrial assets would fit into the new regional division of labor.

[79] S. Markar'ian, "Osobennosti i tendentsii razvitiia sel'skogo khoziaistva Iaponii," *MEiMO*, July 1988, pp. 122–8.

[80] *Yomiuri shimbun*, September 18, 1988, p. 3.

[81] Gilbert Rozman, "Chinese Studies in Russia and Their Impact, 1985–1992," *Asian Research Trends*, 4 (1994), pp. 143–60.

Soviets calculated that persistent divisions between China and Japan would give them a wedge to use for their great-power interests even as they followed the example of the two in joining in closer economic relations. Looking to the record of trade between China and Japan since the late 1970s, they concluded that a country could obtain great economic benefits without sacrificing its pursuit of military and political ambitions that may eventually aggravate relations.[82] Moscow had to improve relations with Beijing and Tokyo to enter this mutually advantageous exchange, but it counted on a competitive arena to keep pursuing its quest for power. Such logic mostly left regionalism aside.

As Moscow committed itself to improving relations with Beijing and Tokyo, it embraced a positive view of regional cooperation but one far removed from regionalism. This was a view of a quadrilateral power balance, which would check U.S. and Japanese power even as it required Russian retrenchment. Unlike earlier triangular conditions, the United States would not interfere each time Japan and the Soviet Union drew closer and China would join the Soviet Union in opposing Japan's inclination to boost its military power. The July 1987 program for the development of the Russian Far East would show the way to huge projects in order to develop resources and draw on each other's economic strengths,[83] enabling the existing Soviet economic apparatus to manage a kind of joint development.

In March 1988 when the staff of the new national committee on Asian-Pacific economic cooperation was selected emphasis was placed on the USSR participating deeply in the regional division of labor. It was said that the Russian Far East would open wide for cooperation. Vladimir Ivanov and Pavel Minakir explained what that meant: turning closed cities into open ones, orienting the economy to foreign trade with the region, integrating the Far East into both a national and a regional division of labor, increasing export of wood products to Japan, promoting joint ventures using foreign capital and technology, developing new ship-building and fishing complexes using foreign investments, building an economic zone at the borders with China and North Korea modeled on the Chinese experience, promoting tourism, intensively developing transportation infrastructure from ports to railroads, and so forth.[84] What was missing was any indication of how political transformation inside Russia would support these objectives. Moscow proved unable to manage these reforms without undercutting its objectives.

82 O. Ostroukhov, "Sino-Japanese Relations: Problems and Prospects," *Far Eastern Affairs*, 5 (1987), pp. 55–63.

83 M. Kapitsa, "Problemy mira i bezopasnosti na Dal'nem Vostoke," *Problemy Dal'nego Vostoka*, 5 (1987), pp. 3–12.

84 V. Ivanov and P. Minakir, "O roli vneshneekonomicheskikh sviazei v razvitii tikhookeanskikh rainov SSSR," *MEiMO*, May 1988, pp. 59–70.

Gorbachev made it clear that the Russian Far East could no longer rely on Moscow alone, and must open itself to Asia, enticing foreigners to descend as soon as possible on Vladivostok and other windows to the Pacific. His "new thinking" welcomed interdependence among countries and refocused attention to mutual security, which signaled the end of the overwhelming priority of the military-industrial complex and meant that the obstacles that others saw from Moscow's military activities in Asia would be resolved. On one occasion after another, he recognized the rising significance of the Asia-Pacific region and insisted that Russia planned to become an integral part of it. Yet, by making the United States the center of diplomacy and choosing China as Russia's primary partner in Asia, Gorbachev did little to advance prospects for regionalism under the leadership of Japan. The Russian Far East found itself in a power vacuum, not an emerging region.

China's interest in Russia was mostly geopolitical. Even after some progress was made on the Soviet occupation of Afghanistan and the huge buildup on China's northern border, China kept expressing dissatisfaction that Moscow had not addressed Vietnam's occupation of Cambodia, its primary obstacle to normalization. By 1988 when bilateral relations had overcome all "three obstacles" raised by China, differences over domestic reform strategies and political ties to the United States kept normalization from dramatically boosting relations. Meanwhile, Gorbachev's focus on China over Japan failed to impress Japanese of either Moscow's economic realism or geopolitical respect. Gorbachev's Vladivostok speech piqued interest in the region, accelerating Sino-Russian negotiations over normalization, rousing South Korea to begin its "northern strategy," and prompting an alternative view to arise in Japan with visions of regionalism. Yet, five years later not a single partnership existed that could address Moscow's economic weakness in the region or contribute to sustained growth of regionalism. Russia held a weak hand.

On the one hand, there was a powerful state with a clearly delineated vertical structure, denying a place to all other forces. On the other, informal social networks with linkages to high officials could rely on their patrons to form illicit monopolies and block competition. The experiment with perestroika gave more scope for such networks without permitting new entrepreneurs to escape the heavy hand of the state. Russia saw a rise in open debate and political reform, but little progress in building a competitive economy. Gorbachev's first inclination was to draw Japan into a global movement against nuclear weapons. Moscow wanted to end the cold war through a form of internationalism that maintained a balance of power with Washington as the arms race ended. Gorbachev mentioned Hiroshima in his speech on February 16, 1987 on abolishing nuclear weapons at the "International Forum for a Nuclear-Free World for the Survival of Humanity." In preliminary discussions of a visit to Japan Gorbachev made known his desire to go to Hiroshima and Nagasaki to take advantage of antinuclear feeling, but Japan countered with insistence that he go to Kyoto and Nara to show respect for Japanese culture.

Russians were divided on whether a foreign-policy crisis existed in their country. In 1990 glasnost had accelerated into a broad assessment of Japan and South Korea, although limits remained as relations were newly sensitive with China after Tiananmen and with North Korea angry at Moscow's changing course. Reform thinkers argued that the crisis had existed since the beginning of the 1980s and that serious mistakes had yet to be corrected despite "new political thinking."[85] Their views on Asia appeared only late in the Gorbachev era and rarely amounted to a sustained reassessment of the assumptions of Soviet foreign policy, despite hard-hitting critiques of particular mistakes such as the invasion of Afghanistan. This was not enough to shake the deeply embedded logic about why Moscow had emerged as a dominant power in NEA and what threats persisted. A competitive great-power worldview dominated over an integrative economic outlook. Russians continued to mistrust the countries of the region without making much effort to understand their territorial claims, goals for investment and trade, and hopes for forging partnerships with Russia to serve their regional aspirations. With China progress had been made on normalization and an interim territorial agreement. With Japan and South Korea negotiations were intensifying with signs of economic support for Moscow's transition and enthusiasm for opening up the Russian Far East. Yet, Russian debates demonstrated little understanding of the adjustments needed for regionalism and of the severity of the foreign-policy crisis that left their country ill-equipped for this.

The Gorbachev regime allowed a Eurocentric worldview to diminish its efforts to make NEA a centerpiece in its opening to the world. It threw its energies into superpower negotiations and talks with European powers, treating China as a secondary concern and leaving Japan behind. This occurred because of exaggerated confidence in its potential to benefit from the end of the cold war and an infusion of capital, persistent distrust and misunderstanding of China and Japan, and the lack of a realistic strategy for the Russian Far East's transformation. When Moscow had the initiative in the second half of the 1980s it hesitated to pursue regionalism. While some younger scholars challenged the prism of a bipolar world by placing Japan and China along with Western Europe among five centers of power, interest in an interdependent world led Moscow to face west.[86]

In 1990 after the cold war had ended and the so-called European problem had been resolved along with normalization with China, expectations were raised that the overall situation in Asia was next on the agenda. In June 1990 when Gorbachev met South Korean President Roh and spoke at

[85] G. Kunadze, "V poiskakh novogo myshleniia: o politike SSSR v otnoshenii Iaponii," *MEiMO*, 8 (1990), p. 51.

[86] "The Soviet Union in an Interdependent World," *International Affairs*, May 1988, pp. 130–43.

Stanford University, hope rose that Gorbachev sought not just a "European common house," but also an Asian one.[87] Yet, the Russian side found Beijing isolated and hesitant to resume reforms as well as Tokyo insistent on a deal over the islands first. No path to regionalism appeared to be within reach.

Georgy Kunadze, who was to become the deputy foreign minister responsible for Asia under Boris Yeltsin, was prescient in 1990 in recognizing the difficulty of applying new political thinking to NEA. He warned that the existence of so many contradictions impedes the development of an optimum balance of relations. He pointed to 1) the Soviet Far East, where the faults of the administrative management system were the most pronounced and the armed forces and its economic priorities played an especially large role, aggravating the isolation and psychological estrangement from the rest of the Pacific; 2) the United States, which interpreted any Soviet attempt at dialogue as "expansionism"; and 3) Japan, which so focused on the territorial question that it couldn't view relations without excessive emotionalism. In advocating a unified security system and progress on bilateral relations as the foremost goals, Kunadze demonstrated the Soviet penchant for dispensing with economic regionalism as no more than a distant dream.[88]

The first gains from regionalism came too easily in Russia, benefiting a small number of officials. Using political connections to take advantage of relaxed controls and enormous price differentials, they turned from petty beneficiaries of illicit gains through the "second economy" into avaricious dealers in the foreign trade of a handful of commodities. They benefited also from speculation in property, from the establishment of joint ventures, and the general inflow of funds from visiting foreign missions. When Nakhodka appeared on its way in 1990 to becoming Russia's first free economic zone the first party secretary reported that sixteen countries had sent proposals for about 120 joint ventures. Despite the absence of a land market and serious gaps in infrastructure – water supply, electricity supply, access to the sea, road networks, and so forth – real estate prices jumped six times.[89] Not far away the Sakhalin governor had started talking about a "Sakhalin Marshall Plan."[90] Little thought was given to how much of the existing Soviet system had to change. Instead, regional boosters called for the relaxation of controls from Moscow as if that would suffice to bring a flood of investments from Japan's biggest corporations.

Russians could not disabuse themselves of the idea that proposals for economic regionalism really had a political purpose. They depicted Japan's idea for the Sea of Japan rim and China and South Korea's enthusiasm for

[87] *Mainichi shimbun*, June 20, 1990, p. 6.

[88] Georgy Kunadze, "New Political Thinking as Practised by the USSR in the Pacific" (George Washington University, Washington, DC, unpublished manuscript, May 1990).

[89] " 'Tokku' kakegoe senko," *Asahi shimbun*, December 15, 1990.

[90] "Kannihonkai keizai," *Asahi shimbun*, December 20, 1990.

the Tumen River project not only as an economic threat, but also as a way to satisfy the political ambitions of these countries. Japan aimed to use its resources to become the regional political leader. China sought to create a new Hong Kong, which it could dominate. South Korea looked to penetrate North Korea. Only Russia had difficulty formulating a constructive aim, fearing political as well as economic consequences of a plan that came to symbolize regionalism.[91]

China and Russia

The Chinese regretted their country's mishandling of relations with the Soviet Union as they rejected much of the Mao leadership's agenda during the Cultural Revolution years. In 1979 they were poised to improve relations when the Soviets started the Afghan war and negotiations were frozen. In 1982 they urged Moscow to make new overtures, but soon found little seriousness in dealing with the main obstacles. Indeed, powerful forces in Moscow continued to depict Beijing as the enemy. After Gorbachev's Vladivostok speech of July 1986 indicated a new determination, the Chinese observed that the same high officials who had orchestrated the invectives during the split were trying to sabotage the normalization process. They let it be known that in addition to the "three obstacles" of military forces in Cambodia, Afghanistan, and Mongolia, Deng Xiaoping considered the presence of these hard-liners a fourth obstacle. Provocative new military links to North Korea in the mid-1980s were also called a potential fourth obstacle. Indeed, Kim Il-sung's 1984 visit to Moscow brought debt relief, credits for arms, and nuclear assistance that proved to be a time bomb. Right away Oleg Rakhmanin and Mikhail Kapitsa were fired from the top posts overseeing relations with China. Bilateral ties started to advance rapidly, but no sense of common purpose evolved.

The Chinese looked carefully at the Soviet Union from the end of the 1970s in the hope of finding a reform model of socialism and forging closer ties that would give China more leverage in international relations. It would have welcomed quicker normalization of relations and coordination in reform, not a return to the alliance of the 1950s but a joint role in shaping regional development. Often bemoaning the narrow thinking about socialism and thwarted by the slow pace of change in Moscow, China saw its chances of drawing the Soviet Union into regionalism as well as a great-power balance slipping away.[92]

[91] V. I. Ishaev, *Mezhdunarodnoe ekonomicheskoe sotrudnichestvo: regional'nyi aspect* (Vladivostok: Dal'nauka, 1999), pp. 78–83.

[92] Gilbert Rozman, "China's Soviet-Watchers in the 1980s: A New Era of Scholarship," *World Politics*, 37(4) July 1985, pp. 435–74; Gilbert Rozman, *The Chinese Debate about Soviet Socialism, 1978–1985* (Princeton: Princeton University Press, 1987).

Deng Xiaoping's strategy for the modernization of China not only did not have a place for the Soviet economy, but also was premised on a continuing struggle with ideologically driven domestic opponents in the communist leadership who could have used a breakthrough with Moscow against him. In addition, even after China's leaders recalculated that the Soviet Union did not necessarily pose a greater threat than the United States, they still were determined to concentrate on hegemony along their borders without letting up pressure on Moscow to retreat. It was only in 1988–9 that Moscow satisfied all of China's concerns, too late to reverse Gorbachev's worrisome path of domestic and global reform.

Four stages can be distinguished in Chinese studies of the Soviet Union during its final decade. In 1978–80 the prime purpose was to justify China's departure from the Cultural Revolution, to show that it was returning to the true path of socialism and one that promised favorable results. It was necessary to drop the term *revisionism* for Soviet socialism and to find positive ideals in the regimes and theories of Lenin, Stalin, and, to some degree, even Brezhnev. This drew thinking in the countries closer together, but Soviet ideological rigidity and foreign-policy assertiveness stymied negotiations. In 1981–5 Soviet studies focused on borrowing from the positive experiences of socialism and, to a lesser extent, pointing out its negative deviations. Soviet leadership instability and narrow-mindedness slowed the progress of ongoing normalization talks. In 1986–8 Gorbachev raised the potential for direct comparisons of the two reform processes, invigorating Chinese debates, but, to the discomfort of Chinese leaders, glasnost proved infectious as it filled in gaps on politics, culture, history, and so forth.[93] Chinese specialists were obliged to toe the line on conclusions even in this atmosphere: Stalin's achievements were at least as important as his errors, Khrushchev's role remained mostly negative in bungling reform and causing a loss of trust in communism, and soon Gorbachev could not be treated very positively for fear that his example would spread. Instead of a meeting of the minds between reform-oriented leaders in Moscow and Beijing, they were wary of each other and built no momentum toward a Sino-Soviet partnership that could have balanced growing Soviet-U.S. cooperation. In the final two years of the Gorbachev era Chinese censorship tightened, personal hostility to the Soviet leader intensified, and the international situation made it harder to explore common ground. An image spread of Gorbachev as a "traitor" to socialism who would welcome its collapse in China too.

Two mind-sets slowed Moscow's interest in pressing hard for improved relations with Beijing. Soviets had convinced themselves both that Beijing was an ideological threat and that it was a long-term foreign-policy threat. On the Left, some of China's policies appeared too heretical to be recognized

[93] "Yao jiachang Sulian Dongou guojia lishe he xianzhuang de yanjiu," *Sulian lishi wenti*, 2 (1986), p. 1.

as socialist reform. If China had posed a major ideological threat from the Left in Mao's time and even until 1982 as "Maoism without Mao," it suddenly had become a threat from the Right. In turn, the reform movement feared that any embrace of China would undercut the thrust toward the West. Although some articles on changes inside China served to alert people to the opportunity of opening to the West and breaking down the centralized economy, China still represented an ideological danger from the Left. At the same time, the border claims of China along with other foreign-policy disputes in Asia kept alive an image of a threat to national interests that stood in the way of envisioning China as a great-power balance. It proved difficult to think of China in the 1980s the way it would be seen in 1994.

Russians who understood the desperate need for both reform along lines begun in China in 1978 and normalization of bilateral ties with China found the struggle against an old guard committed to the status quo slow going. They fought through the first half of the 1980s with limited impact, although serious negotiations with China were finally begun in 1982 and the intellectual foundation was laid for the Gorbachev reform thrust.[94] One thing after another interfered with signs of a turnabout in Sino-Soviet relations. In December 1979 it was the Soviet invasion of Afghanistan coming not long after the Vietnamese invasion of Cambodia with Moscow's support. In 1984 it was rigid thinking and sickbed leadership by Konstantin Chernenko or de facto control by Rakhmanin. In 1987 Gorbachev's tilt to the West as well as his encouragement for glasnost that challenged the history of the communist movement prevented a meeting of the minds. He signaled that "further improvement and development [in Sino-Soviet relations] will undoubtedly have a salutary effect on the entire international climate and the whole system of international relations and will make it possible to resolve many issues related to the development of cooperation among the countries of the Asian and Pacific region."[95] Yet, "new thinking" disconcerted China's leaders. If some Soviets were interested in sharing the experience of building socialism with China, recognizing much in common, the majority dismissed China as a country left more impoverished than the USSR by a more radical form of socialism.[96] Despite talk of learning from China's free economic zones, Gorbachev rushed to improve relations with the West. Finally in June 1989 it was the Tiananmen repression that left Gorbachev no choice but to distance himself from China if he was to continue on a reform course at home and the opening to the West. Both Beijing and Moscow eyed bilateral ties as

[94] Gilbert Rozman, "Moscow's China-Watchers in the Post-Mao Era: The Response to a Changing China," *The China Quarterly*, 94 (June 1983), pp. 215–41; Gilbert Rozman, *A Mirror for Socialism: Soviet Criticisms of China* (Princeton: Princeton University Press, 1985).

[95] "M. S. Gorbachev Meets with K. Kaunda," *Pravda*, November 28, 1987, reprinted in the *Current Digest of the Soviet Press*, December 30, 1987, p. 13.

[96] *Pravda*, November 24, 1988, p. 5.

a means to a new balance of power, but they could not consummate their relations.

The sorry state of analysis on each other, despite valiant efforts of able scholars, contributed to delays in accurately assessing options. The most critical period occurred in 1986–8 when relations could have improved faster while shaping regional development. China's excessive distrust of Gorbachev and the Soviet elite's habit of dismissing China's reforms conspired to leave a poor atmosphere for taking each other seriously.

Chinese ideological rigidity was one of the factors that interfered with creating an atmosphere of trust at a crucial time in the political evolution of both countries. China's party elite sided with conservatives in Russia: revolution had been absolutely necessary; Stalin had followed Lenin's principles in building socialism; and Khrushchev left a negative legacy.[97] Such trite reasoning faced a huge challenge from the products of glasnost pouring forth in the Soviet Union and also could not easily withstand the reform thrust gaining ground inside China. Specialists were hamstrung – told that past studies of the Soviet Union had been too dogmatic and simplistic, yet warned to strictly observe party and state discipline. They enjoyed bursts of openness, such as in 1986 when in place of the earlier condemnation of Khrushchev's speech at the Twentieth Party Congress ("impure motives, incorrect methods, unjust evaluations, and bad effects") came the argument that the leader had to oppose the cult of personality and shake up a system in need of serious reform.[98] If for much of 1987 the spirit of inquiry stalled, Gorbachev's impact could again be strongly felt after China's Thirteenth Party Congress in the fall of 1987. If China was now recognized to be only at the initial stage of socialism, it must borrow more and break further away from dogma. This led to more attention to Gorbachev's political thought: party-state relations, democratization, glasnost, social justice, mass organizations, and the law.[99] Even as reformers won some victories on historical themes, such as that Stalin had not followed Lenin, the main battleground was shifting to assessments of Gorbachev's latest speeches and policies, namely whether his reforms were a continuation or a repudiation of the October Revolution. On the one side was party veteran Deng Liqun arguing that Gorbachev is more dangerous to the world socialist movement than the United States, and on the other scholars who championed his reform approach as able to show the superiority of socialism.[100] Despite the successive resolution of all three of

97 Ye Weizong, "Luelun Sidalin de lishi diwei," *Sulian lishi wenti*, 2 (1986), p. 1.

98 Liu Keming, "Heluxiaofu zhizheng shiqi Sulian shehuizhuyi de jige wenti," *Sulian Dongou wenti*, 1 (1986), pp. 1–11; Yuan Fenguang, "Zhongping Heluxiaofu de 'bimi' baogao," *Sulian Dongou wenti*, 2 (1986), pp. 47–52.

99 "Shenke linghui shisanda de jingshen, jinyibu jiachang dui Sulian he Dongou guojia de yanjiu," *Sulian Dongou wenti*, 1 (1988), pp. 1–2.

100 Xu Kui, "Shehuizhuyi shijian 70 nian: jinian Sulian shiyue geming 70 zhounian," *Sulian Dongou wenti*, 5 (1987), p. 4.

the obstacles raised by China, something more important was at stake: the future of international socialism. Hostility mounted. After 1989 reformers were no longer able to invoke Gorbachev's example, and in 1990–1 charges against him intensified.[101]

Decentralized ties between China and Russia became significant as China gave provinces control over border trade in 1988 and Russia transferred controls downward beginning soon thereafter. This was an unequal matchup. China's provinces were populous and experienced in decentralization after Mao's "walking on two legs" policy from 1956, the Cultural Revolution, and the reform programs since 1978. Moreover, the Chinese marginalized from the state sector were ready to swarm across the border. When Heilongjiang was allowed to open many border points and choose many firms, new and established, to cross, the traditional state controls would quickly be overwhelmed. In contrast, decentralization would allow shady alliances on the Russian side to usurp state controls in favor of new quasimonopolies suitable for trade reliant on price differentials but not for investment.

The Chinese were prone to see Russia's relations with Japan as a struggle by each side to increase its influence: Moscow needed entrance into a region where Japan stood in the way and Japan needed ties that would make it a political great power.[102] Even before the conservative swing after June 4, 1989 the Chinese placed great-power competition above economic regionalism and Russians never abandoned similar logic. In 1991 Beijing seized the opportunity of a conservative drift in Moscow to try to cement ties between the two countries, including arms deals, expecting more coordination on international relations until the collapse of the August coup. The Japanese watched with unease as Gorbachev's position on the islands hardened[103] and his April 1991 visit brought no breakthrough, but in the fall it was China looking on with alarm as communist power and the USSR collapsed.

South Korea, the Great Powers, and Regionalism

South Koreans chafed at their narrow options in the postwar era. The democracy movement in the mid-1980s brought to the fore public grievances and made it essential for politicians to look for new outlets for diplomacy as well as domestic policy. With security totally dependent on U.S. power and the economy sandwiched between Japanese hand-me-down industries and U.S. market openness, traditional nationalist urges had few outlets. As in Japan, economic success brought not only appreciation for foreign partners, but also resentment against U.S. pressure to open national markets and reduce

[101] Chen Rishan, "Gaige bulu roulin: Sulian zhengzhi jingji gaige gaiyao," *Xiboliya yanjiu*, 3 (1991), pp. 1–12.

[102] "Moscow's New Japan Policy," *Beijing Review*, May 1–7, 1989, p. 18.

[103] *Sankei shimbun*, January 24, 1991, p. 2.

trade surpluses. While many Koreans vented their own attacks on Japanese protectionism, when it came to the United States they depicted their own country as innocent. The end of the 1980s heard the same arguments that a declining United States resented fierce competition; posing as a champion of globalization, it really was turning to protectionism. At a time when worries mounted about declining trade surpluses and labor militancy making wages uncompetitive at home, some feared that SEA countries with cheaper and more docile labor would combine with the United States to leave South Korea with poor prospects.[104] Anger remained over Japan's unrepentant attitude toward the colonial era coupled with its vital current role for the South. There was a pent-up demand for new regional options.

If in the late 1980s there was much satisfaction that at last the South was making a transition to democracy to match its well-advanced economic development, the third goal of a self-confident national identity remained elusive. Koreans increasingly turned their attention to overcoming their history of dependence. Somehow, they hoped, beginning with the 1988 Seoul Olympics and its related diplomacy, to become free of a feeling that they always were under somebody else's control or protection – China over most of the past millennia, Japan during the thirty-five years of colonial rule, and the United States in the postwar era. Koreans embraced the goal of using great-power political relations and the first steps in the reunification of their peninsula to establish beyond any doubt their country's national independence. Multidirectional diplomacy became an opening wedge in regionalism.

Since the hijacking of a Chinese airliner to South Korea in 1983, talks had been taking place between Seoul and Beijing.[105] Angered by North Korea's bombing of many of South Korea's highest officials in Burma, Beijing began to recognize the inconsistency of supporting openness and a peaceful environment while remaining allied to the North. Officials who traveled to Seoul to deal with the hijacking returned with stories of rapid modernization and potential payoff from bilateral trade. Indirect trade through Hong Kong accelerated. China's participation in the Asian Games in Seoul in 1986 served as a breakthrough and it was followed by China's strong presence at the Seoul Olympics. As ties were rapidly improving between Seoul and Moscow in 1990, Seoul also used the opportunity of China's pariah status in the West to intensify its appeal, especially playing on Deng Xiaoping's eagerness to keep the momentum for economic openness going.

Building on this base and aiming to win support for direct contacts with Pyongyang and the Koreanization of peninsular relations, Seoul turned next

104 Kim Kyong-Dong and Su-Hoon Lee, eds., "Introduction," *Asia in the 21st Century: Challenges and Prospects* (Seoul: Pannum Book Co., 1990), pp. viii–ix.

105 Byung-joon Ahn, "The Soviet Union, China, and the Korean Peninsula," in Dalchoong Kim, ed., *Peace and Cooperation in Northeast Asia* (Seoul: Institute of East and West Studies, Yonsei University, 1990), pp. 83–94.

to Moscow. Quicker than Tokyo to realize the significance of Gorbachev's changes, they soon were counting on him more than China's leaders for the political breakthrough to signal the end of the cold war era.[106] The prize would not only be increased leverage on the North, but also a new regional climate transforming all great-power relations with the South.

Japanese succeeded brilliantly in integrating South Korea into their regional economic development strategy, but failed miserably in reassuring the Koreans of their remorse and understanding. Especially Nakasone Yasuhiro as prime minister through the mid-1980s was too quick to pronounce bilateral relations moving ahead to a new, easier stage, and too insensitive to the distrust of the Koreans. LDP leaders were driven not by guilt toward the victims of Japan's occupation, but by humiliation at the shame of Japan's defeat and occupation by the United States. The 1980s were wasted as a time of true reconciliation.

Anti-Americanism was widely espoused by students, whose worldviews were strongly impacted by their sense of helplessness in the face of a military-led authoritarian regime. Many had been enraged by the Kwangju massacre of demonstrators in 1980, blaming the United States for looking the other way under its joint military command and then not responding with sufficient outrage. Few gave credit to Jimmy Carter's earlier plan to withdraw U.S. troops from the South as a sign of displeasure, nor did they think much about the disastrous consequences of such a plan that could have led to an invasion by the North.

The Seoul Olympics gave a major boost to regional cooperation. It attracted lots of Japanese youth and media, who reconsidered their stereotypes of backward Korea before the physical evidence of an "economic miracle." Also it became a turning point in relations with China and Russia, transforming South Korea into an agent for bringing neighbors together. Yet, by freeing the South somewhat from its great-power dependence, it lessened the chances for Japanese leadership and altered the dynamics of regionalism.

Taking advantage of China's isolation in 1989 and the advance in trade and travel associated with the Seoul Olympics, the South moved quickly to expand ties. It offered financial support for the Asian Games in Beijing in 1990, encouraged a rise in tourism and Chinese imports, and appealed through relatives of China's leaders for Beijing to assume a larger leadership role in Asia.[107] Wooing China provided economic dividends.

Through the mid-1980s Soviet propagandists treated South Korea even more than Japan as a pawn in a United States–dominated system with stifling consequences for foreign policy and painful domestic problems gathering

106 Pae Suhan, "Namhan gwa Roshia oe gwangye pyonhwa," in So Taesuk, ed., *Hanguk gwa Roshia gwangye pyongga wa chonmang* (Seoul: Kyongnam University, 2001), pp. 357–400.

107 Chae-Jim Lee, "Seoul and Beijing: The Making of Cooperative Relations," *The Journal of Asiatic Studies*, 12 (1997), pp. 3–4.

force. Yet, they also were starting to portray in detail a remarkable record of achievement,[108] arousing curiosity that would turn to fascination once glasnost took hold. News seeped through of stunning economic success.

With North Korean communism symbolizing all that was bad and China under sanctions, South Korea and Taiwan eyed Moscow as a target of opportunity. They were ready to pay big bucks, to use backdoor channels greased by corruption, and to make lavish promises. South Korea succeeded for a time. Taiwan made inroads, but had no breakthrough. The security services of both countries kept up their efforts even after the Russian leadership and political elite reconsidered and sought to redress the balance with the North and Sino-Russian relations started on the upswing. With lots of money and junkets passed around, they could always find some takers and illusions of progress.

In the summer of 1988 Soviet experts on East Asia and economists joined forces in making the case that Moscow had to change direction in the region in order to boost perestroika. One tangible result was Gorbachev's new openness to the region in his September Krasnoyarsk speech. Another was the beginning of informal diplomacy with South Korea that fall, emphasizing economic ties. While prior to the Seoul Olympics coverage of South Korea was rare, reporters started visiting and preparing for a shift. Already in August 1988 President Roh had conveyed his "northern strategy" through secret channels. Soon Kim Young-sam had become the key figure on the Korean side. He called for a conference of six countries on Korean security, was interviewed by a Soviet reporter and invited to Moscow, and in June 1989 his visit signaled a big step forward toward normalizing relations. At this time hard-liners were attacking perestroika, sticking with North Korea as an ally, and reformers countered with a push to improve ties with the South. What started as economic ties had broadened to include politics by the end of 1989, but then as North Korea protested furiously and hard-liners had some success in Moscow, relations were set back again. South Korea wanted political ties first, expecting little from economic ones. Moscow was willing to proceed with economic ties, but it was slow on political ones. Through 1990 and early 1991 this divergence in priorities was gradually resolved in negotiations that increasingly centered on how much money would be forthcoming from Seoul. Finally in January 1991 the sum was set at $3 billion. From the summer of 1990 to early 1991 leaders in Moscow saw Korea and Japan through the lens of billions in loans and investments. Their notion of entering the region led by these countries was to play off one against the other and count success not in terms of the transfer of know-how or networks, but in dollars committed. It proved easier to abandon North Korea to satisfy the South than to return four islands as demanded

[108] B. I. Shipaev, *Iuzhnaia Koreia v sisteme mirovogo kapitalisticheskogo khoziaistva* (Moscow: Nauka, 1986).

by Japan. For Gorbachev, Seoul, not Tokyo, was to serve as a bridge to the Asia-Pacific region.[109]

The Japanese had trouble coming to grips with the depth of the Korean animosity to their country. When Emperor Hirohito died, they recognized that the symbol of "Japanese imperialist control" and an unhappy past for Korea was gone. Although blaming "anti-Japanese education" for the intensely negative feelings of Korean youth, they suggested that an entire age when memories were kept alive had ended. The fact that some Korean intellectuals sympathized with the view that the role of the emperor had been limited in the era of occupation implied that a less emotional outlook was coming.[110] Instead of coordinating with the South, Tokyo took it for granted. In 1990 Kanemaru Shin, an LDP power broker, went to North Korea with the intent to broker a deal to normalize relations. He failed but, in the process, aroused anxiety about a rush to regional leadership, which undercut South Korea and cast doubt on Japan's commitment to coordinate regionalism.

Kim Il-sung watched nervously as his country suddenly grew isolated. Unable to balance South Korea's diplomatic success with a breakthrough with the United States, he persisted in his military buildup. After a brief spurt of diplomacy in 1990–2, it was WMD that offered the most security.

Beijing opened economic ties in the 1980s with Seoul in order to boost its development, but kept political ties to Pyongyang with the aim of shaping the regional security environment. It was shifting toward a balancing act, the nature of which rested on Pyongyang's own calculations. If the North had agreed to economic reforms and to open its own free economic zones, as it hinted at the start of the 1990s, then the balance could have led to sponsorship of cross-border projects. In the absence of such interest, however, it took the form of providing limited help for the North to prop itself up even if that meant slowing regionalism. China's hesitation to pressure North Korea meant, in effect, putting geopolitical priorities above regional security and dynamism. Yet, Pyongyang's reckless behavior and anger when Beijing did not approve strained ties.

South Korean identity was changing with the pursuit of China and Russia. Until 1985, anticommunism had played an overarching role in politics and foreign relations. Taiwan had been viewed as a partner sharing the same threat. With scant preparation, the South abandoned Taiwan and accepted the PRC as the true partner for mature economic and great-power relations and pursuit of unification. China's image switched from that of a communist enemy that fought alongside the North in the Korean War to the historic power that had a big say in Korea's evolution as well as unparalleled cultural affinity. A dearth of press independence as well as concern about China's

[109] Seung-Ho Joo, "Soviet Relations with Two Koreas, 1988–1990," *Pacific Focus: The Iwha Journal of International Studies*, 15(1) Spring 2000, pp. 95–130.

[110] "Fuko na kako ga zonshita 'Nikkan' aru jidai no owari," *AERA*, January 20, 1989, p. 42.

sensitivity meant that the Korean debate over China started slowly. South Koreans were obviously not envisioning long-term regional bonds when they made their distinct "hangul" script a symbol of nationalism, sharply reducing the use of Chinese characters in the 1980s. Debates related to the great powers may have been subdued, but they propelled a fresh outlook on the world as new thoughts on national identity focused first on promoting more autonomy.

Overview of Regionalism

As North Korea stayed mainly on the sidelines, each of the five main actors in NEA twisted the goals and timing of regionalism to serve deep desires from the cold war era that acquired new urgency as it ended. Japan was the driving force for regionalism, but its priorities did not reassure either the United States of its full support for global integration or Asian neighbors of an embrace of equality. China first hesitated and then put itself into a situation where it steered regionalism onto an unsustainable path separating economics from politics and resistant to formal institutions and links to globalization. Russia was most unrealistic about what was needed, raising hopes without following through. South Korea had a narrow objective in mind, remaining reserved about other goals. Meanwhile, the United States was preoccupied with globalization, staying suspicious of regionalism. The goals across the region would have to become more mutually consistent and the major bilateral relations would need to be improved if regionalism were to have a chance to succeed.

Realistic calculations of ways to advance bilateral relations and regional goals were not the legacy of the cold war. Instead, it was a kind of ideological orientation that often failed to appreciate limits on what was possible. The realistic Japanese position on Russia would have been two islands plus alpha with negotiations to continue as relations improved, but when a few scholars broached this idea they were shouted down. The realistic approach to China would have been a more forthright apology on history accompanied by an educational campaign among the Japanese as well as early vigor to Japanese foreign direct investment encouraging reform forces. Toward South Korea new appreciation for historical realities and equal economic ties would have been a public relations success too. Instead of blaming others for a lack of trust in regionalism, Japan could have embraced a vision of NEA emphasizing balanced relations and patience for incorporating the Russian Far East and North Korea when their reforms were ready. But Tokyo was too convinced of its ability to gain a place at the head of the new region and the prospects of a quick boost in its great-power status. Only slowly from 1989 with Moscow, do we see Tokyo shifting toward a more gradual strategy. National identity, not security concerns or liberal economics, shaped Japan's view of regionalism.

China permitted nationalism to interfere as well. After an upturn in relations with Japan, it allowed strong anti-Japanese sentiments to surface at the turn of 1987 when Hu Yaobang, blamed for being too sympathetic to Japan, was ousted as party leader. At the same time its revulsion to Gorbachev's approach to reforms and foreign policy complicated the normalization of relations. And its crackdown on communist party reformers at home harmed public relations in the West and set the stage for the confrontations at Tiananmen in 1989. China could have moved more quickly in ties with South Korea and advocacy of regionalism, opening its border areas in the Northeast. After June 4, 1989 it may have embraced regional ties more, but the ideological fetters on integration only intensified. An ideological struggle to justify a decision against political reform and to prove Gorbachev's approach wrong left China's leaders unduly suspicious. It was not realist thinking about security that slowed China's embrace of regionalism.

Most idealistic was Russia's approach to the region in the second half of the 1980s. Gorbachev did not recognize the weakness of the Russian Far East in entering a new region. He did not appreciate the importance of a breakthrough in relations with Japan to build a balanced triangle with China. He agreed to ties with South Korea without a strategy for allowing the North to adjust or using the South's assistance productively. Educated on Asia when censorship was only gradually relaxed, Russians entered the new era with very unrealistic expectations and at a loss of what to do.

With Russia unable to sustain its regional security influence and China rather on the sidelines until it came roaring back in 1992 from domestic division and sanctions, the contest over NEA regionalism centered on Japanese-U.S. relations. Tokyo failed to build a foundation for persuading Washington of its commitment to international objectives that would frame its pursuit of open regionalism. It too narrowly defended protectionist interests without articulating a vision for a global community. When urged by U.S. officials to use its immense financial resources to assist Moscow's difficult transition, Tokyo acted only with reluctance while keeping its eyes focused on the nationalist cause of regaining four islands. Instead of a compromise interim agreement that would have given momentum to a special partnership with Moscow capable of boosting regionalism, bilateral relations became a drag on Japan's image as global and regional power. The time was also opportune to convey to the Chinese and Korean peoples that the Japanese truly repented the past and would sincerely strive to create trust necessary for regionalism. An isolated China was unlikely to misinterpret this offering as a sign of ulterior motive, and a newly democratic South Korea could reassure its deeply suspicious public opinion that a new multidirectional foreign policy did not need to check Japan. Japan's leaders failed to make the case for regionalism respectful of Asian nationalism and United States–led globalization. Preoccupied with drawing Russia into the West and conscious of the continued flux in NEA, the United States also did not prepare for the arrival of regionalism.

At the end of the 1980s there was a mismatch in ideas about regionalism. Each side failed to appreciate its own weaknesses and challenges in building trust in NEA. When each in turn experienced a fundamental reversal in the 1990s, the situation did not improve as some expected. The collapse of the Soviet Union and end of communism left Russia much weaker and less subject to a planned economy, but it did not make regional integration one of the priority items on an urgent agenda. After the Tiananmen political turning point, China reoriented toward Asia, separating itself from the U.S. global strategic order and speeding its rise as a great-power challenger. The sharp separation between economics and politics, however, failed to create the trust in neighbors essential for regionalism. The end of the bubble economy sharply lowered Japanese confidence, increasing the need for Asia economically but undermining the previous approach in which Japan was assured of its leading role. As the groundwork for regionalism was laid at the turn of the 1990s, not only were the interests that impeded a common agenda not being overcome, they were gaining strength from the reversals felt by political elites. In the defiance of "Cold War Logic" evident in the emergence of "National Aspirations" we can discern a shaky foundation on which to establish regionalism. Once the post–cold war transition was under way, these aspirations came further into the open.

3

1991–1993

Border Fever and Cross-Border Duplicity

In a span of a few years the most convulsive shocks since the 1940s hit the global system, striking Europe first from 1989, but not sparing NEA, which bore the brunt in 1991–3 of a second wave – if less cataclysmic still having enormous potential. Of course, the Soviet Union's collapse rocked both continents, as did Russia's flailing about in search of a new course. In NEA seismic developments shook Japan and China too. In the former, the postwar model fell from its lofty pedestal; found wanting were first the miracle economy, then the political monopoly, and finally the harmonious society. At about the same time, China turned away from economic retrenchment and the last of the 1989 sanctions to a vigorous market opening and the strut of a country crowned, perhaps prematurely, as the world's next superpower. Meanwhile, South Korea tasted for the first time the treat of multiple diplomatic options, as the North faded into economic disaster and, seemingly, diplomatic irrelevance. Reacting to the changes, a Democratic president took office in Washington intent on elevating economics and human rights. Despite the flux on all sides, old priorities were slow to fade away as adjustments kept occurring.

Dreams of NEA regionalism crescendoed to a peak at the opening of the 1990s. Above all, they targeted the Russian Far East. Russia's rapid transformation became the first driving force for regionalism; the image of a vacuum on Russia's periphery excited all of the neighboring countries except North Korea. Also arousing much interest was the overlapping momentum toward decentralization across China, Japan, and South Korea. China took the lead as the wave of free economic zones and new provincial development strategies passed from the Southeast to the Northeast. When Deng Xiaoping gave the go-ahead for a full-fledged market economy in January 1992 amidst stinging criticism of the country's "Northeast phenomenon" as the symbol of the dead weight of the past, borders opened in a trade rush to the north. Meanwhile, the collapse of the bubble economy led the Japanese to focus first on decentralization as the key to revival. Momentum peaked in 1993 with the election of a non–LDP government promising to strip Tokyo and the central bureaucracy of its crushing controls. Finally, democracy in South Korea brought the election of the first civilian administration in late 1992, pledging to revitalize local power. While dreams that decentralization would drive regionalism could still be heard into the mid-1990s, harsh realities increasingly pushed them to the sidelines.[1]

Idealism emanated from local governments on the regional frontlines as well as a vocal minority of planners and academics in the national capitals. The Japanese pressed to the forefront. Decentralized regionalism was heartily embraced by at least three types of Japanese: 1) academics of the old left, anxiously seeking an alternative to United States–dominated globalization; 2) local officials in the less developed prefectures along the Sea of Japan and Hokkaido, eyeing support from Tokyo for infrastructure to make their areas gateways to the Asian mainland; and 3) nationalists in search of an Asian sphere of influence and an independent role in balance-of-power politics. If Japanese central bureaucrats were wary from the outset and kept their hold on the purse strings, they did not stand in the way of active exploration. Enthusiasts conveyed their optimism across Japan's borders.

Local assertiveness became the driving force in the high tide of regionalism lasting through 1993. Along the Sea of Japan prefectures seized the mood of criticism against the bureaucracies in Tokyo to insist on support for their cross-border initiatives. In Northeast China interest was aroused by both central demands for more local initiative in development and a sense of injustice that other areas had long been favored through discriminatory policies. In Russia newly combative local authorities sent ultimatums to Moscow, while strikes, tax withholding, and a deep sense of unfairness toward the latest national policies stirred a search for other options. After long being silenced, local elites and administrations blamed the center for their troubles and demanded more resources.

Optimism gravitated to bottom-up regionalism in which each side persuaded its national government to loosen the reins of control. The easier it became to cross borders, the more cooperation and trust would be achieved, argued strategists seeking change at many levels: 1) central governments had to decentralize political and economic decision-making authority while generously funding the physical infrastructure for regionalism; 2) local governments had to recognize the necessity of attracting foreign investment, creating an open and transparent environment for multinational corporations from afar and for entrepreneurs from just across national borders; 3) increased ties between businesses were required to smooth the way for expanded trust in bilateral relations as a whole; and 4) a combination of these first three forces could build momentum for formal institutions of regionalism as well as

[1] Gilbert Rozman, "Decentralization in East Asia: A Reassessment of Its Background and Potential," *Development and Society*, 31(1) June 2002, pp. 1–22.

for a shared regional identity as Northeast Asians. Only slowly did a message based on reality intrude: nonmarket and criminal activities were taking over.

Even as the Japanese continued to take the lead in regionalism, on all fronts they were failing to solidify economic or political ties to prospective partners. By the end of 1993 the limits became clear in Japan's model of integration, trying to balance regionalism and globalization, while weakly embracing both. No other country filled the void. Soon, the situation worsened as political tensions exacerbated economic problems on the borders.

Neither rivalries between countries nor potential tension between globalization and regionalism loomed high in the consciousness of advocates of an era of cooperation in NEA. Japan had relented in providing more assistance to Russia. With rising interest in regionalism and Moscow's fading support for the economy of the Russian Far East, Japan was the obvious choice to fill the economic vacuum. If China and Russia had lost the shared commitment to socialism that might have drawn them together in the 1980s, they were even more determined to stabilize their border and expand economic ties across it. This could become a force for regionalism too. South Korea salivated at the opportunity to turn Northeast China and the Russian Far East in its direction and away from North Korea. These too were hopeful times for Japanese plans for Northeast China, reaching beyond the booming port of Dalian. Such "border fever" was at a high pitch from 1991 through at least the middle of 1993, leading many to argue that local economic ties would pull bilateral relations forward. As borders were bridged, trade and investment rose and strategists eagerly predicted a direct trajectory to full-fledged regionalism.

By the end of 1993 observers could no longer ignore the inherent limitations of bottom-up regionalism. In one country after another the weakness of entrepreneurship and market-oriented governance on the region's borders caused serious setbacks. Instead of small-scale transactions growing into large-scale commerce, they often degenerated into bitter disputes and dissolution of existing networks. Soon national ministries and local administrations were trading blame, while cross-border troubles were threatening harm to bilateral relations as a whole. We can trace the emergence of these troubles through the high tide of optimism that a decentralized model of regionalism was taking shape through subregional natural economic territories and a rush to the frontier.

All border areas in NEA were hobbled by a long history of stifling controls and incentives favoring the capital and other privileged areas. Conditions did not offer hope to liberal theories of starting with economic ties, advancing to civil societies, and ending with balanced democracies favoring all types of freedom. In the absence of competitive business forces, local administrations steered trade and investment toward cronies and criminal organizations distorted cross-border networks to skim away profits. The most perverse results occurred between countries burdened with the legacy of socialist planned economies. No modern forces were available to overcome the monopolistic inclinations and criminal shortcuts taken for granted in an era when markets were condemned. The legacy of the developmental state, however, was not the answer. Acceptance of a dual economy in which border areas were often sheltered from the full force of the market left front-line areas in Japan and South Korea also poorly prepared as leaders in regionalism.

Not only was bottom-up regionalism divorced from global economic engines such as U.S. capital and corporations, it was also far removed from the most dynamic business forces in the Tokyo and Seoul metropolitan areas and Southeast China. In this period the sprouts of regionalism were not planted in the fertile soil of globalization. Soon they withered from lack of nourishment and outright abuse. Americans did not welcome this result. They were eager to bring democracy and market economies to Russia and North Korea as well as China as vital steps in a kind of civilizing mission. It was with regret that they recognized Japanese and South Korean cross-border strategies were not doing the job, Sino-Russian economic ties did not strengthen modern forces, and North Korea refused to participate. Regionalism was failing to meet the needs of globalization.

Globalization and the United States

In the aftermath of the Persian Gulf War, the United States perceived its mandate as global management, emphasizing economic inducements but retaining military pressure in case of a regional flare-up. Even if time-consuming great-power transitions might be required, observers assumed the United States had sufficient clout to shape the outcome even as it pressed for more human rights compliance. Americans viewed NEA as a part of the globe with recurring danger for regional conflict and enduring challenges to progress in what had been the two great communist powers. Without denying that steps toward regionalism might alleviate both situations, the United States concentrated on global integration. It put the burden on Japan to redouble its cooperation, foregoing divisive regional policies. As in the Gulf War, Washington would forge the overall framework, leaving a supporting role for Japan. Smarting over being unappreciated despite its large financial contribution to the war, the Japanese did not fit well into the script being drafted in Washington.

When Mahathir called for an EAEC, which would exclude the United States, Canada, Australia, and New Zealand, United States Secretary of State James Baker objected, warning Japan to oppose it. Some in Japan resented strong-arm tactics to deny their regional leadership aspirations.[2] While the

[2] *The Japan Times Weekly International Edition*, January 13–19, 1992, p. 11.

United States feared that such a regional organization would be used to keep markets closed in the face of its pressure to open them, it also was negatively inclined to what could turn into a regional challenge to a new world order. In this test of wills the United States prevailed, leaving the Japanese with no choice but to give preference to globalization amidst frustration over a missed chance for regionalism, albeit not one precisely of its choice.

The January 1992 visit of George Bush to Japan underscored differences in views about transforming a regional partnership into a global one. Pressing the theme of a new world order, the United States sought to use Japan's capital (combining with that of the United States to equal 40 percent of the world's GNP) to sustain, as needed, the sort of security coalition that had won the Gulf War, to bankroll the transformation of Russia, and to press for Asia's economic globalization. Meanwhile, Tokyo dreamt of an equal partnership, at last allowing it to raise its voice as a political great power able to win support for a much-enhanced regional leadership role. The United States was thinking globally about boosting its own leadership, while Japan was focused on more independent regional leadership. Each saw the other as the main partner in meeting its objectives in NEA and, despite awareness of differences, neither seriously doubted that anything other than bilateral trade issues would, for the time being, really undermine cooperative relations on the global stage.

In the election year of 1992 Washington was distracted by domestic concerns, while differences on regional matters did not appear serious. If Tokyo was seen as moving too slowly in improving ties with Russia and too quickly with China, both responses were understood as signs of inertia based on past predispositions. The main concern was that a passive Japanese diplomacy would leave the United States with a weak regional partner. Americans presumed that they would need to keep pressuring Japan.

In fact, the clash between U.S. notions of globalization and Japanese dreams of regionalism was more serious than many assumed. From 1989 to 1992 Japan and the United States had been drifting apart. Trade relations were rife with charges and countercharges as Japan looked to its neighbors for a way out. Coordination of policies on world issues, such as relations with China and Russia, was inconsistent and not well understood by the public. Whereas in March 1989 69 percent of the American public responded that its opinion of Japan was very or mostly favorable, the figure fell to 47 percent in February 1992. The biggest decline occurred around the fiftieth anniversary of Pearl Harbor as not only did 33 percent fewer Americans regard Japan as a close ally or friend, but suddenly the ratings of the Soviet Union/CIS as an enemy or unfriendly country fell from 79 to 22 percent, while those who saw Japan in this manner grew from 7 to 17 percent.[3] If

[3] *The Japan Times Weekly International Edition*, July 27–August 2, 1992, p. 3.

most Japanese still did not openly express much anti-Americanism, they were at least more imaginative in considering ways to reduce their dependency on an untrusting partner.

Washington never worried that Tokyo would cut a deal with Beijing or Moscow that would alter the dynamics of great-power relations. When Gorbachev traveled to Tokyo, he was already the beleaguered leader of a failing state and the Japanese were obsessed with the return of four islands that limited their flexibility. Neither Beijing nor Tokyo was inclined to satisfy the other's deepest demands. While the United States saw Japan as a rising power, whose independent foreign policy might be cause for nervousness, it did not expect much diplomatic creativity. Washington could be satisfied with Japan as the dominant regional power, knowing that bilateral ties with all of its neighbors would be fragile and no new security arrangements would reduce the United States's indispensable role.

The United States completed a year that brought both victory in the Persian Gulf War and the collapse of the Soviet Union with an odd combination of omnipotence and lethargy. It was excessively confident that a favorable new world order was coming soon, but there was little preparation for addressing tough questions except by doing more of the same: throwing money at Russia to make some bold moves toward a market economy, putting pressure on China to protect human rights, and raising threats against Japan to elicit economic openness. In Bush's last year lethargy prevailed in pursuing these difficult goals. Under Clinton the mood shifted in the direction of omnipotence, downplaying security priorities and leading the world by pressing for idealist human-rights goals and hard power through financial globalization. The historical watersheds of 1991 had left Japanese on the periphery of globalization, passively trailing events, and uncertain about how to coordinate with the United States in order to achieve a more equal relationship. When U.S. notions of globalization acquired a more economic cast, intensifying pressure on Japan to disassociate itself from Asian particularism, Japan's ambivalence only grew.

Intermittently through the twentieth century, the United States championed the cause of remaking the world through strengthening international organizations, pressing for arms control, spreading democracy and self-determination, and opening markets. Although enthusiasm for these causes sometimes drew criticism under the heading "Wilsonian idealism," in fact, the idealist streak of creating an orderly, trusting global community continued. Democratic presidents usually gave greater backing to these themes. Given the absence of any great-power security threat, it should have been no surprise that Clinton eagerly embraced the goal of globalization. In 1993 hopes were highest that all aspects of globalization could be realized simultaneously. Engagement would ensnare a market-oriented China, "shock therapy" would transform a democratic Russia, and pressure to target large-scale imports of U.S. automobiles would open a protectionist Japan. All three of these globalizing causes would advance a world order in which the United States would not be fettered by "closed regionalism" or great powers set apart from international integration.

The Clinton administration defined globalization for the post–cold war era. It made engagement of Russia the highest priority, assuming that adequate leverage existed to produce a market economy as well as a democratic polity. In 1993 it placed economic competition with Japan next on the mistaken notion that the U.S. economy was declining and Japan was rising. Finally, it held relations with China hostage to progress on human rights without realizing China's ability to advance economically and diplomatically. This agenda put the United States squarely at the center, pressing in all directions. It left the other countries essentially on their own to deal with each other, searching for some balance.

Each of the signature early Clinton policies toward the globalization of countries in NEA proved to be a dead end. For the Russian Far East, U.S. hopes first centered on Japan assisting the area and investing in its economic integration, then turned to the regional work of the Gore-Chernomyrdin commission that downplayed pressure against financial chicanery in order to smooth the way to Yeltsin's reelection and continuation in power. Japan was hesitant for political and economic reasons, while the U.S. posture lacked the backbone to insist on the creation of a market economy open to foreign investment according to international standards. If on a small scale U.S. assistance did some good, it did little to create an environment for Russia's entry into the NEA market.

On Japan, Mickey Kantor, the trade representative, led the administration's charge against protectionism, but with the U.S. economy rising and Japan falling into a slump this approach had to be abandoned. Japan maintained a large trade surplus and lacked the political will to embrace a global model of fiscal reform and openness. The close partnership of thirty years was fading; Japanese blamed the United States for excessive pressure even as they neglected globalization and aired unrealistic hopes for regional leadership.

On China, the State Department under Warren Christopher and Winston Lord pressed hard on human rights until it became clear that the Clinton team had no levers to back up their tough talk as China's economy soared ahead. Congress kept voting for most-favored nation trade, and Beijing found little need to speed relaxation of its tough human-rights controls. Unfettered by economic pressure, China could turn to NEA. Top leaders resented U.S. pressure and they exaggerated their ability to find regional balance.

Although all were legitimate matters of globalization, the United States in each case lacked a sustainable strategy and acted unilaterally. Overconfident in its power, the United States did not recognize any advantage in coordinated pursuit of regionalism in NEA. Its globalization strategy, however, indirectly fueled the search for regionalism, beginning in Japan. It was not security or economic advantage as much as national identity that others sought in the face of American confidence that it could remake the world in its own image.

In 1992–3 under presidents from different parties the United States alienated each of the regional powers with lasting consequences. Its support for Yeltsin's "shock therapy" without anticipating the consequences set relations with the Russian elite and public on a course from which recovery was difficult. Its sale of fighter planes to Taiwan in August 1992 was taken as a break from the ten-year-old Shanghai communiqué that left China thinking that it would now be much harder to acquire the leverage to press Taiwan toward unification. And Japan's high hopes for raising its status in the new era were needlessly frustrated by barely disguised demands for numerical trade quotas. All sides chafed at their relative powerlessness; each looked to regionalism as a balancing force. None took the essential steps to divert U.S. demands through multilateral globalization.

Washington was not much concerned about security threats in NEA for a time. It was satisfied with the rapid demilitarization in Russia, whether intentional or a byproduct of financial collapse. Awakening to China's stunning economic success – appealing policy changes, high growth rates, attractiveness for foreign investments, expanding exports – Americans responded that this was the latest example of the East Asian model.[4] In reaction to the Fourteenth Party Congress in the fall of 1992 they largely underplayed the socialist rhetoric while concluding that China is following a tested path of development far different from the Soviet militarized economy. North Korea was noticed more for its spreading economic crisis, not for its nuclear weapons program until its refusal to allow inspections. The United States also paid little heed to talk of regionalism inside NEA. Geopolitical strategists and economists who debated policy alternatives did not take it seriously.

If at the start of the Clinton presidency the United States downplayed the significance of its military predominance in NEA, the potential remained that unilateralism centered on global financial integration and human-rights issues would be joined by an agenda of military alliances and weapons sales to press the advantages achieved after the cold war. If in Europe North Atlantic Treaty Organization (NATO) expansion would soon be added to the U.S. agenda, in 1993 warnings that North Korea surreptitiously was developing nuclear weapons left Washington on the verge of flexing its superpower military in NEA. After a compromise agreement, the nations of NEA assumed that the security dimension would stay in the background and regionalism could go forward without the United States asserting its military leadership as it enforced a global agenda. Not facing a hot spot in NEA, the United States let regional ties drift.

[4] *Heilongjiang ribao*, October 20, 1992, p. 5.

Japan and Regionalism

Japanese leaders felt increasingly confident in their country's economic and social model through the 1980s. In 1992 dismissive characterizations of American society by the prime minister and the speaker of the Lower House referred to "laziness," "illiteracy," and a "declining work ethic."[5] While ambivalent about whether neighboring East Asian countries steeped in the Confucian tradition whose economic miracles continued to show dynamism shared their model, the Japanese linked regional cooperation to the perpetuation of their special attributes. They expected this environment to showcase Japanese and Asian values within a framework of global competition, which was in danger of being twisted to allow a rising tide of protectionism at the behest of the United States. Failing to acknowledge their own protectionist ways, the Japanese branded the prospect of retaliatory U.S. actions as the real protectionism and welcomed Asian regionalism as a necessary countermeasure. Even after the stock market declined sharply, confidence remained high in 1991–2.

In the 1970s and 1980s internationalization had been the rage, while regionalism kept a low profile in Japan. Intensification of the cold war offered an approving Japan a valued position in the alliance system as it identified itself as part of the West. Economic prosperity made it attuned to modern currents of thought and consumerism transcending the era of developmentalism. Japan became a champion of causes such as foreign aid and environmentalism. Backing the Persian Gulf War in 1990–1, the Japanese faced anew the challenge of doing their share as full members of the world community. This time they were conscious of charges of not contributing to peacekeeping forces as well as more general accusations of not fostering human rights and democracy at a time when security matters were slipping from the limelight. Globalizers abroad kept pointing to the shortcomings in Japan's behavior, as nationalists at home kept finding excuses, such as the need to nurture Asian countries treated insensitively by the United States. At this stage, however, the globalizers and regionalists were largely in agreement, for instance on textbooks that conveyed Japan's historical apology more fully and mitigated fault-finding attacks by neighbors.[6] With nationalism subdued and localism on the rise, global and regional goals coexisted in rough balance. The Japanese expected to boost regionalism without challenging globalization.

Feeling pressure from the United States concerning the Gulf War and at the same time experiencing a backlash in response to U.S. resentment over the trade deficit, the Japanese grew more assertive. Spreading mutual distrust, seen in a poll on the fiftieth anniversary of the outbreak of war, cast doubt on any easy convergence between globalization and regionalism.

[5] *The Japan Times Weekly International Edition*, February 17–23, 1992, p. 10.

[6] *The Japan Times Weekly International Edition*, August 19–25, 1991, pp. 6–7.

Without discerning whether "pained feelings" were a product of clashing views over the Pacific War, resentment toward America's occupation of Japan afterward and the subsequent decades of dependence, or mounting trade disputes, the poll showed that 70 percent of Japanese thought that Americans look down on them, while their answers indicated it was they who look down on Americans as "lazy, warlike, living in a nation in decline, and blaming American economic problems on others."[7] It follows that the Japanese were prone to seek out other partners in their own region, even as Americans were becoming hesitant to trust Japan's rise as a leader. Battle lines were drawn between economic regionalism and globalization that had cultural differences at their core. Responding to criticism in the Persian Gulf War, Japan made great strides toward globalization as a "full partner" of the United States. To 2003 there was a growing maturity in security thinking and leftist pacifist irresponsibility faded. Yet, strategic thinking about foreign policy did not follow. Narrow rightist thinking became the principal barrier.

Japanese doubts about the viability of the alliance with the United States came and went over the 1990s, but they were strongest from 1992–5 before the Nye report of 1995 reaffirmed the need for keeping 100,000 U.S. troops in Asia and the April 1996 U.S.-Japan summit approved new defense guidelines. The United States had not paid enough attention to security concerns, while overemphasizing economic differences. The Japanese were prone to see the United States as self-righteous when quiet persuasion could be more effective or as too quick to criticize another great power without regard to its pride. This reasoning was applied also to U.S. treatment of China, mirrored in the apprehension that Washington's narrow, unilateral approach to globalization would put Japan in an untenable position in balancing the Sino-U.S.-Japanese triangle. In contrast to the United States, the Japanese sympathized more with Deng's "realistic" adversity to disorder than with Gorbachev's "idealistic," peripatetic reforms that brought in their wake disruptive consequences.

Academics and mass media in Japan conveyed a different image of the world in transition than that found in the other great powers. Ironically, the United States, which prides itself on theoretical sophistication in the social sciences, championed a simplistic variant of globalization that assumed the transition from traditional socialism simultaneously and without gradual stages could achieve all important objectives. It was seen in Japan and elsewhere as a radical call for instant democracy, full-scale marketization, unconditional privatization, wide-open gates for global economic forces, and abrupt transformation to a pro-Western national identity. China countered with a model of gradual economic reform under the steady hand of a dictatorship and the old communist party hierarchy gradually recruiting younger

[7] *The New York Times*, December 8, 1991, p. L26.

and more world-wise officials. In the middle were Japanese analysts, who shared with the Chinese an emphasis on state capacity and with Americans hopes for using foreign economic ties to build support for democracy. If the Chinese calculated that Russian ties to their country would facilitate a regional reform process that would serve Moscow well in balancing the disruptive elements of United States–led globalization, the Japanese estimated that regional cooperation using elements of Japan's postwar recovery model and subsequent Asian modernization models would be good for Russia and contribute to forestalling problems resulting from imitating the United States. Wary from the outset of unfettered globalization, Tokyo had regionalism in mind as one means to improve Russia's chances.

The Japanese spoke with scorn of "market fundamentalism" and "moral politics" in place of realpolitik. They saw the United States as uninformed about the problems of transition in other countries and ideologically driven. Behind such criticisms is the notion that the United States is more interested in imposing a narrow, self-serving set of changes than in globalization where Japan helps to set the rules. Washington was also faulted for its understanding of the realities in the region. The Japanese asserted that June 1989 in China was not a democracy movement with a broad base and December 1991 in Russia did not provide a mandate for democratization or marketization. A lengthy transition will be necessary in both states. If globalization proceeds as a gradual process, taking into account existing realities, the way will conveniently be open, Japanese assumed, for more regionalism along the way.

Japan positioned itself to be the indispensable great power, using its financial clout to press to limit Moscow's acceptance in 1990–3 and its diplomatic clout to limit China's isolation in 1989–92. It came to the G-7 summits with its own agenda. This was the heyday of Japan's independent great-power strategy, based on confidence in its own rise as a power and in its leverage in rapidly changing relations among the powers. If this strategy often was frustrated, the Japanese still had high hopes that their growing world clout and rising regional leadership role would reinforce each other.

It would be a mistake to think that in anticipating Gorbachev's April 1991 visit the Japanese only focused on the return of the islands. A second approach was to appeal to him to launch a new era of regional integration; the "dawn of the Asia-Pacific age." Even the conservative *Yomiuri shimbun* proposed spurring along "the Japan Sea rim age," using Soviet natural resources, Japanese and South Korean capital and technology, and Chinese labor.[8] As talk of leaving the cold war belatedly intensified, this concept gained wide currency. Yet, guided by its "balanced equilibrium" strategy to Moscow, Tokyo remained negative to big projects without a breakthrough

[8] *Yomiuri shimbun*, March 6, 1991, evening.

on territory. Meanwhile, desperate for quick results, Moscow was not inclined to seriously examine ideas that offered only a potential long-term payoff. Regionalism drew broad support in Japan, but it did not receive enough priority to become a centerpiece in foreign policy.

While the April 1991 summit ended without any momentum for Japan to expand economic ties, other events soon overtook domestic doubts. An early August summit between the United States and Soviet Union made firm progress on joint oil and natural gas exploration off Sakhalin Island. Started in 1974 by Japanese reeling from the oil shock, this project not only committed massive U.S. investments, it opened the way for Japanese firms to become partners on a large scale.[9] With the Soviet Union collapsing and Boris Yeltsin introducing shock therapy and democracy, Japan also felt obliged to join its G-7 partners in humanitarian assistance. Economic ties with promise for regional integration outpaced bilateral political progress. Problems with Moscow did not derail regionalism.

The Japanese feared being omitted from the post–cold war collective security system that seemed to be forming during and after the Persian Gulf War. In 1992 they were still struggling with the image of immobility due to factional struggles and weak leadership, only with great difficulty agreeing to send personnel to serve with the United Nations, as in Cambodia. As they strived to do something toward peacekeeping, they also looked for other arenas in order to move beyond economic superpower. Two promising claims that suited these hopeful times were to be an environmental superpower and a foreign-assistance superpower. Both of these goals readily transferred to policies in NEA: assistance to Russia for its rusting nuclear submarines, humanitarian aid to the Russian Far East, a shift to environmental ODA to China. Turning to new regional objectives, the Japanese neglected the more obvious path to trust through diminishing differences in historical memories.

Local governments led the way in a new path toward regionalism during the early 1990s. With China isolated by sanctions and the Soviet Union or the successor Russian Federation only beginning to open its borders while facing some obstacles due to Tokyo's insistence on the return of four islands, the localities seized new opportunities. Actually, they were encouraged and partially funded by central agencies carrying forward the strategy first seen in the 1950s of using "pipes" to get around diplomatic barriers. Unlike the earlier "pipes" from opposition political parties and elite cultural and business groups, the new ones came mostly from prefectural administrations eager to establish sister-city or local government relations. In addition to projects to encourage cultural, sports, and health exchanges, they endeavored to involve local business groups. These grassroots contacts were couched as citizens' exchanges, yet the funding and direction came overwhelmingly from

[9] *The Japan Times Weekly International Edition*, August 19–25, 1991, p. 17.

governments. They were supposed to induce heart-to-heart talks (communicating "honne" or the real thoughts of people), but the old "friendship" mode intruded with cheery toasts more common than the airing of concerns, and schemes for getting aboard the gravy train of travel accounts eclipsed long-term projects.

In 1990 local governments and think tanks fixed their gaze on the Russian Far East. They catalogued businessmen rushing to make contacts, companies seizing the opportunity of decentralization to form joint ventures, and a multitude of conferences and official missions exploring new frontiers.[10] Enthusiasts dreamed boldly, while skeptics had not yet focused on the pitfalls ahead. Kanamori Hisao, a leading booster, argued that while SEA regionalism had become active, NEA was forgotten despite its much greater promise: It was more compact, starting with only a tiny area around the Sea of Japan that needed to be integrated, and combined 10 percent of Asia's population with as much as 70 percent of its GNP. Given the fact that political ties had improved unexpectedly fast from 1988 to 1990, Kanamori foresaw no real barrier to regional economic integration.[11] By stressing the indispensability of the economic power of Japan and implying a vertical division of labor, he assigned a dominant role to his country. The very name chosen – the Sea of Japan rim economic sphere – left no doubt about Japan's centrality.

In the first years of the 1990s attention turned to localism not only as a means to right domestic imbalances, but also as a path to internationalization and regionalism. The national level appeared as the villain that stifled initiative for direct linkages to the world economy and grassroots ties across borders. Expectations for localism kept mounting. Cities and prefectural governments eyed new urban hierarchies, emerging both from redrawing the administrative map of Japan (*chiho bunken*) and forming cross-border, regional networks. This was a time of optimism about national power being transferred downward. Enthusiasm for regionalism became intertwined with high expectations for decentralization that would enable cities frustrated by persistent barriers and long-term decline to raise their competitiveness in order to outpace their rivals. The interruption in the LDP's grip on power in 1993–4 allowed decentralization to become a rallying cry for what was heralded as a new era. After the LDP's return to power in coalition government the hoopla survived even as the substance kept being stripped away from proposals.

Young and market-oriented Japanese were skeptical of transferring power to prefectural governments and local elites. They realized that these were the backbone of protectionism, pork barrel politics, and suspicion of

10 "Nitchi, Kan, Cho, Chu, Bei ga kono natsu satto," *Shukan daiyamondo*, July 14, 1990, pp. 22–30.

11 Kanamori Hisao, "Ugokidasu 'Nihonkai keizaiken,'" *Shukan Toyo keizai*, September 8, 1990, pp. 18–24.

internationalism. If these forces for the moment were championing regionalism, it was not because they trusted neighboring nations or were willing to see Tokyo let market forces loose. Rather, the advocates of decentralization targeted more infrastructure spending from the center and were guided by other motives rooted in old thinking. While they often couched their arguments in the language of globalization, the free market, and open regionalism, they rarely challenged nationalism. Some politicians such as Ozawa Ichiro saw a chance to reduce bureaucratic and big-business forces in the center in order to press for a more nationalist agenda. Idealists who expected localism to diminish nationalism were missing the real story.

Delegations from Northeast China and the Russian Far East called on Niigata and other Japan Sea coastal points to assist them in providing the capital and markets for the regional economy. Heilongjiang sent a group advocating a transport circle for grain and other agricultural exports from China to pass through Vladivostok by rail and on to South Korea and Japan.[12] Despite arguments about how much time and money the route would save, Niigata had neither the resources nor the interest in agricultural openness to lend its support, and Tokyo found no commitment on the Russian side to allow it to act. When it came time to pour large sums of money into cross-border regional ties, Tokyo hesitated.

Even after many in Tokyo had sobered to the barriers to regionalism, vested interests along the Sea of Japan kept pursuing the track of subregional cooperation as if it would soon produce a breakthrough. They did not candidly expose the real problems and refrained from criticizing complicating actions at home and abroad. It was more important to boost goodwill among those sought as partners than to address realistically the actual impediments to regionalism. No doubt, they feared a loss of their own national funding and local public support if they were more candid. Localism sputtered along.

If the end of the bubble economy left the prefectures along the Japan Sea aware that huge new infusions of spending by the central government were unlikely, they could still turn their sights to pork barrel projects to counter the economic slowdown. The rationale had changed and the scale diminished, but the political clout vested in these areas could still bring much desired disbursements. Niigata was used to them, having been the home prefecture of Tanaka Kakuei, who after he resigned as prime minister over the Lockheed bribery scandal remained the influential "shadow shogun." Hokkaido was also highly dependent on public-works contracts and other center allocations. Through the mid-1990s these and other areas could still plan to boost economic ties with the Asian mainland largely through spending made available through their political clout in Tokyo.

[12] *Niigata shimbun*, July 3, 1993, p. 3.

Economic relations grew rapidly between the Pacific coast industrial heartland of Japan and Shanghai and areas along the southeast coast in China or the Beijing-Tianjin area. Ties between the Japan Sea coast and Northeast China, where localism had been assumed to lead to regionalism, failed to show much dynamism. Japanese firms showed little interest in investing much beyond the Liaodong peninsula where Dalian is located. While prefectural officials and think tanks kept their eye on exchanges with the Northeast and on the Tumen project, business interests looked elsewhere. Economic ties to China were diluted in a worldwide rush of investment, failing to boost an image of regionalism. If expectations grew in 1991–2 both about the clout Japan now enjoyed and the growing dependence of Moscow and Beijing on it,[13] the contraction in Japan's economy by 1993 coupled with a sharp sale-off in stocks and property assets made the risks of regionalism more apparent. Because the LDP had hoped to use regional investments and large projects as a means to reward its supporters in and out of the construction industry, room for possible boondoggles had narrowed. Investments did not integrate Northeast China into a new region or insure vertical control over the production process, but firms began a stampede to China to lower production costs as Japan lost competitiveness.

There was a consensus in Japan that the age of decentralization had begun in the 1990s, especially with the resolution of both houses of the Diet in support of it in 1993, the law setting up a commission on it in 1995, and a new law based on the commission's report in 1999. But even as the law was being implemented in 2000 there was still talk that real decentralization (*chiho bunken*) had barely begun. Whereas early in the 1990s the emphasis was on overcoming stifling red tape, attention had turned instead to meeting crushing burdens of debts, welfare costs, and public works. Even the rich areas such as Tokyo and Osaka were talking of a financial crisis, facing new national standards for education, the police, and so forth. While expenses are borne in a ratio of nation: locality 1:2, tax revenues continue to be gathered in a ratio of 2:1. Local areas lack autonomy in raising revenue, while debts and unavoidable expenses weigh down on them.[14] The new twist on decentralization stripped it of any promise for regionalism, rendering it a failed ideal.

An advisory panel to Miyazawa Kiichi reported in December 1993 that economic prosperity in the region is heavily dependent on U.S. and European

[13] Gilbert Rozman, "Japanese Images of the Soviet and Russian Role in the Asia-Pacific Region," in Tsuyoshi Hasegawa, Jonathan Haslams, and Andrew Kuchins, eds., *Russia and Japan* (Berkeley: Institute of East Asia, University of California, 1993), pp. 101–23; Gilbert Rozman, "Japanese Views of the Great Powers in the New World Order," in David Jacobsen, ed., *Old Nations, New World: Conceptions of World Order* (Boulder, CO: Westview Press, 1994), pp. 15–35.

[14] *Hokuriku chunichi shimbun*, May 11, 2000.

markets. Despite the fact that Japan's record trade surplus may incite closed economic blocs in Europe and North America, Tokyo should turn away from any proposals for closed regionalism in Asia and use APEC to keep the United States in check.[15] Such advice offered cautious support for gradual, open regionalism in NEA, distancing the leadership from exaggerated hopes for regionalism that had spread over the past few years. Global interests took priority.

Through 1993 Japan was the driving force in NEA, but its ambivalence about globalization failed to set regionalism on a sustainable track and its lip service to localism did not challenge nationalism. The Japanese tried to steer a middle ground between Secretary of State James Baker's open and democratic Asia-Pacific policy framework and China's intent to become the leading power in an emergent region with an identity exclusive of the United States. They were naïve in weighing the responses for a cooperative approach suitable to all sides.[16] Decentralized regionalism was doomed in this region, and Japan failed to offer the leadership to leave a positive legacy for the next model of regionalism.

Japan and Russia

The breakup of the Soviet Union and an emerging vacuum in the Russian Far East beckoned to Japan as important changes opening the door to regionalism, but it greeted these changes, first and foremost, as an opportunity to recover four islands. Having been frustrated in Gorbachev's visit, the Japanese expected that dependence on foreign economic assistance would oblige Yeltsin to cut a deal. They dangled entrance into a dynamic region as a prize for the Russian people to earn. They pledged humanitarian assistance to the Russian Far East to whet local appetites and gain goodwill. At home, Japanese leaders insisted that they were ready to embrace Russia with benefits for all, but the gains were not so great as to warrant compromising on anything short of firm insistence on the return of four islands, albeit with secret flexibility over the timing of their turnover. The possibility of integrating Asiatic Russia into a new regionalism or of cooperating with Moscow to realign great-power relations paled before the lure of the islands' return.

The window of opportunity was open widest in the first six months of 1992. The Yeltsin administration secretly offered to return two islands and to continue talks on the other two after a peace treaty was signed. Tokyo could have answered as Beijing had to a similar offer in the late 1980s that it would give priority to improving relations, and it could have proposed its own timetable and conditions for negotiations on the islands that remained under

[15] *The Japan Times Weekly International Edition*, January 18–24, 1993, p. 7.

[16] *The Japan Times Weekly International Edition*, July 6–12, 1992, p. 8.

dispute. It could have pressed for an interim arrangement more favorable than Beijing received, allowing for some form of shared authority and joint development on the remaining two islands. Instead, it insisted on recognition of Japanese sovereignty over all four islands, and it kept this issue at the top of its agenda. At no point over the following decade did Moscow show any inclination to agree to this requirement, leaving Tokyo with a need to keep finding face-saving language that hinted at new momentum in relations or recognize the reality of a breakdown in relations with no alternative in sight. An opportunity was lost not only for a bilateral breakthrough, but also for a big boost toward regionalism.

Frustrated by lack of progress in bilateral talks, in the summer of 1992 Tokyo sought to elevate the territorial question from a bilateral issue to an object of international decision making at the highest level. At the Munich G-7 summit it extracted a political statement in support of solving the problem through the application of "law and justice," thus making this goal a global concern as was Japan's substantial contribution to an aid package to Russia.[17] Other nations were uneasy, however, about making policy with the globe's number two military power dependent on a few tiny islands instead of the global priorities of democratization, market reforms, and responsible cooperation with efforts to quiet hot spots and advance disarmament. Japan's priorities raised tensions with the United States at the same time as they delayed a genuine commitment to regionalism in NEA.

In the fall of 1992 Japanese opinion toward Russia fell sharply, never much recovering through the decade. After Yeltsin canceled his planned visit in September with little notice and no diplomatic niceties, there was a 10 percent drop in Japanese who said they feel friendly toward Russia and a twenty-six-point rise in those who responded that they do not feel that way.[18] While a few voices in Russia placed relations with Japan on a par with Russo-U.S. relations as critical to Russia's future in the Asia-Pacific region, a vocal minority by the summer of 1992 made resistance to an uncompromising Japan the last defense of national interests.[19] Angrily, the Russian media presented Japan as the villain, incompetently and rudely handling relations. It portrayed a nation obsessed to the point of impoliteness in contrast to South Koreans, who had made Yeltsin comfortable in his visit in October 1992.[20] Despite continued support through the International Monetary Fund (IMF) and G-7 for Russian economic reforms, the new atmosphere made it harder to discuss issues of regionalism.

[17] Hiroshi Kimura, *Distant Neighbors Volume Two: Japanese-Russian Relations under Gorbachev and Yeltsin*, pp. 120–1.

[18] Hakamada Shigeki, "Roshia ni gokai o ataeru yo na Nihonteki 'kibari gaiko' o aratameyo," *Nihon no ronten 2001* (Tokyo: Bungeishunjusha, 2000), p. 130.

[19] *Izvestiia*, August 14, 1992, p. 6.

[20] *Izvestiia*, January 30, 1993, p. 7.

For one year until Yeltsin finally visited Tokyo in October 1993 Japanese were torn between exacting revenge for the fact and manner of his rejection of their diplomacy and adjusting their approach to make progress without insisting on a breakthrough soon. They settled for the "Tokyo Declaration" that listed all four islands under dispute and accepted the language of "law and justice" for reaching a settlement. To some diplomats this was a major advance, affirming that the two parties would negotiate the four islands rather than two and would be guided by the historical record showing that Russia never had possession of any of the islands before 1945. To others it was little more than a stopgap arrangement that allowed Tokyo to move ahead with relations despite the absence of any sign that Russians were really weighing the return of all four islands. At the end of 1993 State Duma elections raised the profile of strident nationalism in Russia and spelled the end of an active internal debate on compromise with Japan.

A drumbeat of criticisms continued to echo Soviet propaganda against Japan. Leading the charge against dangerous territorial ambitions, Igor Latyshev, a *Pravda* correspondent, depicted Hokkaido as the center of Japanese revanchism.[21] While Nemuro harbored the symbol of the ultrarightist national movement against islands held by the Soviet Union, Wakkanai hoped to become the "northern gate" to Sakhalin, which was also considered to be in danger. Latyshev's message was that the Soviet Union should not trust Japan. If his voice was no longer authoritative, this message still resonated widely.

As we look back on the period through 1993, we can observe a frenzy of Japanese government activity in the formative period of the Russian Federation with little impact due to exaggerated expectations and a lack of strategic thinking about national interests. The Japanese sensed that the opportunity had come for recovering the four disputed islands and were determined to employ every diplomatic means to that end. At a minimum, five approaches were tried: 1) joining the other G-7 countries in generous economic assistance coupled with targeted humanitarian assistance in the Russian Far East to address food and medical shortages in order to create a mood of gratitude; 2) a public relations campaign centered in Moscow to present Japan's case on the history of the islands; 3) pessimism about Russia's economic reforms and prospects coupled with optimism about its growing need for regional economic ties that led to insistence on an early agreement committing Russia to the return of all four islands in order to allow Japan to maximize its advantage; 4) pressure on the United States and other G-7 countries to back Japan by treating the islands as an international as well as bilateral issue; and 5) reluctance to analyze regionalism in noneconomic terms in which Russia might turn to other options and Japan might lose great-power leverage.

[21] *Pravda*, March 23, 1987.

No approach worked because Japan did not calibrate the priorities of other nations well or question its own nationalist assumptions and interests.

Japanese national identity had become attached to the recovery of islands, three of which are visible from an observation tower in Nemuro, Hokkaido. This symbol of injustice had been artificially separated from the history of aggression and occupation in the Pacific War, as if Russia's violation of the neutrality pact with Japan in August 1945 and military advance after Japan's surrender to the Allies constituted an act of perfidy of no relation to Japan's war conduct and Russia's arrangements with the United States. In turn, the defenders of the national identity of Russia had swallowed the breakup of the Soviet Union resentfully and reacted anxiously to grave concerns over the precariousness of the Russian Federation's boundaries. Having played the Russian nationalist card as one of his paths to power while remaining vulnerable to criticisms by communists and others on this score, Yeltsin could appreciate that he was in no position to meet Japan's demands. Along with bilateral relations, regionalism was the loser in this battle of identities.

In 1991–3 local administrations on opposite sides of the Sea of Japan were encouraging trade, investment, and network building. Regardless of the fate of talks in the two capitals, local officials argued that they could proceed with regionalism. They had two very promising circumstances. First, the more than ten million Japanese in the prefectures facing Russia and the more than five million Russians in the krai and oblasts facing Japan eagerly sought foreign partners to overcome peripheralization at home and regarded each other as more modern or having less historical baggage than the Chinese and Koreans with whom they dealt, seeing a basis on which to build relations of trust. Second, newly prosperous Japanese consumers in their rush to replace older vehicles with the latest models had left a cornucopia of used cars as well as trucks at dirt-cheap prices parked in lots around the country. At the same time, Russia's fishing fleet that trawled in territorial waters rich in crabs and other marine products that fetched minimal prices on the controlled domestic market were now gaining the opportunity to sell their wares at premium prices to a seafood-loving nation. The potential existed for a billion dollars in annual revenue to the Russian side in return for a billion dollars in annual purchases of Japanese cars, trucks, and appliances. Such trade could have established a foundation for additional cross-border commercial networks and investments. While optimistic rhetoric continued, opportunities for forging lasting networks were wasted. Meetings degenerated into empty exchanges of pleasantries with no will to tackle serious problems. Criminal groups siphoned away the profits from crabs and cars. Japanese investors grew wary of deceitful partners. Russians resented the lack of follow-up in preliminary forays and studies. After a spike in cross-border trade, it declined, as did bilateral trade as a whole.

Local governments in Japan continued to spend a lot of money singing the praises of Sea of Japan regionalism. They organized cultural, sports, and academic exchanges. At their encouragement local newspapers covered stories of growing cooperation, fostering consciousness of a regional identity while often skirting the reality of disillusionment that was transpiring. Niigata led the way in its enthusiasm, even establishing a think tank, the Economic Research Institute for Northeast Asia. It chose boosterism over expertise, failing for a long time to gather evidence on troubling problems while rallying all forces in support of new projects to accelerate the pace of regional economic integration. Tokyo kept its distance. The central government provided some funds and encouraged support, but many considered such local initiatives to be just a sideshow to the determining forces of market economics and geopolitics. Sea of Japan prefectures could not persuade their small and medium-sized firms to invest, let alone sway the decisions of big corporations along the Pacific coast. They could, of course, not be expected to deal with strategic interests. Grassroots initiatives in NEA came mainly from the Japanese as trial balloons approved and funded by central ministries in the event that other factors materialized.

Decentralization was too weak in Japan to make localism viable as a path to regionalism. Even so, it could have fostered a climate conducive to increased cooperation with Russia. This was unlikely, however, given the fact that prefectures showed little interest in gaining knowledge of their counterparts and mainly targeted Tokyo in reports showing how much they were doing and requests for large infusions for infrastructure. It was even more unlikely because the Russian administrations and local elites were looking for a quick buck more often than long-term trust. Criminalization thwarted any goodwill by the Japanese. Exchanges often became junkets. Money secured from the Japanese was stripped from joint ventures and never repaid. The people of the Russian Far East showed little gratitude for humanitarian aid and commerce because few of the benefits reached them. Some targeted assistance concentrated on the disputed islands made an impact, but mostly the Japanese dealt with those whose personal aggrandizement betrayed the needs of regionalism. With prefectures competing with each other and failing to coordinate, key administrations in Vladivostok and Khabarovsk could play off one against another. Because Moscow failed to agree with them on a division of power, all should have realized that the time was not ripe for bottom-up regionalism. Russia bears more responsibility than Japan for failure. Cross-border ties did even more harm than cross-national ones.

China and Regionalism

A far-reaching debate reexamined the options for Chinese foreign policy in the rapidly changing global context of 1989–92. Responding to the end of the cold war, the collapse of international socialism, and the sanctions against their country due to the Tiananmen repression, the Chinese turned to regionalism. On the one hand, they boosted ties to Japan, South Korea, and areas in SEA, while opening borders wide. At the same time, talk turned to the rise of Eastern civilization and China's natural role as its cradle. On the other hand, compared to Tokyo, Beijing made an offer to Moscow based on great-power reasoning, while extending generous aid to North Korea as a balancing force.[22] The search continued for ways to balance regional as well as global relations. Beijing was looking in all directions to cope with a radically changed environment in NEA.

Chinese circles debated fateful changes in the international environment. The Persian Gulf War left them pondering the overwhelming predominance of U.S. military technology and power projections. The collapse of communism in the Soviet Union left a sense of isolation, followed by concern that the breakup of that country would create a power vacuum along China's northern and western borders. A mood of trepidation in 1991 left leaders little prepared for bold moves from the United States for globalization or from Japan for regionalism. Accepting the general direction of global economic integration and increased regional trade and investment, Deng encouraged more localism as a way out for areas smarting at wide inequalities at home but eyeing new cross-border opportunities.

As this important assessment of the state of the world reached its climax, the Chinese simultaneously debated the swift collapse of the Soviet Union, the meteoric rise of Japan, and the staying power of the United States with its incomparable military but now shaky economy. Rejecting warnings that China would be threatened by all three powers, Deng decided, with qualifications, to welcome economic globalization with U.S. leadership, regionalism despite Japan's high profile, and close cooperation with Russia regardless of differences in systems. In the fall of 1992 Beijing received both Emperor Akihito and President Boris Yeltsin in a stunning display of letting bygones be bygones. It thus publicized policies of noninterference in the affairs of other countries and cooperation in pursuit of regional stability and closer economic relations. Yet, it harbored intensified concern about Japan's plans for regional hegemony and made anxious pleas that Russia would shift to balanced diplomacy supportive of the struggle to keep a lid on U.S. and Japanese ambitions.

The Chinese somehow decided that the regional and world environment became more favorable in 1992 and was likely to stay positive through at least the rest of the decade.[23] They argued that the fall of the Soviet Union is likely to be balanced by a decline in U.S. hegemonism as the struggle among

[22] Gilbert Rozman, "China, Japan, and the Post-Soviet Upheaval: Global Opportunities and Regional Risks," in Karen Dawisha, ed., *The International Dimensions of Post-Communist Transitions in Russia and the New States of Eurasia* (Armonk, NY: M. E. Sharpe, 1997), pp. 147–76.

[23] Ge Insheng, "Lun Eluosi lianbang de duiwai jingji zhanlue yu woguo duice," *Shijie jingji yu zhengzhi*, 9 (1992), pp. 1–7.

capitalist powers intensifies. This will lead to an equilibrium, which buys time for China. Only gradually will Japan overtake the United States, thus China can emphasize improving relations with Japan without concentrating on counteracting its ambitions. Steeped in logic of strategic balance, Beijing expressed confidence in its ability to gain ground by economic growth and geopolitical patience.

Even as they saw one superpower collapse and the other rise triumphant, the Chinese did not discard their assumptions about a world in increasing balance. Along with the Japanese, they retained a belief that U.S. power would inevitably decline. Each nation saw itself as a rising power within a region on the upswing. Thus, globalization did not figure as a long-term force that would keep their countries weak, however objectionable it may have been as a lever to force short-term changes. It was a fact of life that had to be shaped by great-power competition and regionalism. Time was on the side of Asian powers.

Mao's reasoning on domestic and international issues had been laced with ideas about the principal contradictions. Chinese analysts revived this type of analysis even after a decade of domestic reform and the end of the cold war. In 1992–3 the mainstream argued that even as economics becomes the center of international relations China would benefit from ever-intensifying contradictions between the powers. It faces a favorable regional environment as the United States and Japan are locked in competition. A minority view insisted that the primary struggle would continue to be between capitalism and socialism with China becoming a common target or that an antihegemony united front of the south against the north would involve China on the side of the less-developed countries. They too treated regionalism more as a means to take advantage of contradictions than as an integrative force. Images of Japan challenging U.S. power and of the United States struggling in retreat to widen its hegemony showcased regionalism as a way to handle contradictions.[24]

Of all the Chinese misperceptions, those of the United States were the most pronounced and sustained. Driven by a worldview that emphasized balance-of-power politics, the Chinese had little room for the notion that globalization of economic ties enhances peace and trust in political relations. One-sided thinking was especially apparent in discussions of U.S. assistance to Russia. It was much easier to argue that the United States wanted a weak Russia and welcomed that country's economic decline and fragmentation than to suggest that U.S. idealism favored democracy as a path to prosperity and the latter as a guarantee of peace. In later years as Chinese thinking grew more nuanced on many international themes, it remained difficult to acknowledge U.S. ideals. The coming of Clinton to power only made the

[24] Yang Yunzhong, "90 niandai Riben fangwei zhanlue de zhongda zhuanbian," *Shijie jingji yu zhengzhi*, 5 (1993), pp. 33–6.

Chinese more suspicious of globalization. This, in turn, made it hard to appeal to American public opinion, even as a new approach to Japanese opinion was adopted.

The Chinese found changes in party leadership in the United States difficult to understand and rather frightening. For a nation that respects Richard Nixon more than other presidents, the arrival of a Democrat with a vocal human-rights agenda also proved disconcerting. If 1981–2, when Ronald Reagan alarmed the Chinese with plans to boost U.S. ties to Taiwan led to a major reassessment of the international environment, then 1993–4, when Bill Clinton frightened the Chinese with talk of human rights, kept the reassessment since 1989 going longer. The new U.S. leaders failed to reassure the Chinese early that they would be realistic about China's power and respect its independent outlook. Since Nixon most presidents had learned to treat China with great caution and to provide expected signs of respect, but the Chinese found these wanting at the start of the Clinton administration.

Officials recognized that deepening economic relations with Japan are critical to regionalism. While concerned about political differences and clashes over cultural issues, they expected to be able to boost economic regionalism, which would keep these sources of conflict in check.[25] Unlike enthusiasts in Northeast China, however, Beijing was wary of decentralized ties as a device that would allow Japan to gain dominance. It preferred limiting local ties to narrow economic linkages, and it insisted that the scope of the region be large enough to give the capital a role. Aware that development was concentrating to the Southeast, the central government pressed not only for Shanghai to be the dragon's head for the Yangtze River and central China but also for it to be a balance further north.

From the outset, great-power thinking and omission of the political impact of socialism and its civilizational legacy skewed Chinese reasoning about NEA. It was assumed that countries are the actors and they are driven to struggle for supremacy. Thus, Chinese analyses combined rave predictions about economic complementarity with sharp warnings about politically inspired competition. These views were cushioned by realistic assessments of economic patterns, such as the weakness of Heilongjiang in the light industry needed for trade with the Russian Far East or the primary orientation of Japan and South Korea to the U.S. market. Regionalism would have to come slowly.[26]

Desperation drove the most ardent advocates of regionalism: China's provinces of Jilin and Heilongjiang narrowly separated from the sea without any dependable access; and Japan's prefectures along the Sea of Japan, with

[25] Wang Huning, "Guoji xinzhanlue gejuxia Zhongri guanxi fazhan de qianjing," *Fudan xuebao*, 1 (1992), pp. 35–9.

[26] Xu Zhongquan, "Lun Dongbeiya qiyu jingji hezuo," *Xiboliya yanjiu*, 1 (1992), pp. 1–8.

memories dating back half a century of lively maritime commerce mixed with distress that the Pacific coast had overwhelming supremacy in postwar development. These advocates joined in exchanges and found common ground at conferences, but they were not comfortable together without drawing on partners in other countries. Each preferred ties with developed areas in the other country, where the forces of modernity were more prominent. Real power on crucial decisions lay elsewhere. Despite early hope in ties such as between Niigata and Harbin, local networking proved unsatisfactory.[27] Bottom-up regionalism had little prospect even for two countries whose economic ties had begun to grow exponentially.

As decentralization finally came to Northeast China in 1992–3, it confronted realities far bleaker than in Southeast China, already brimming with dynamism. First, the command economy remained more deeply entrenched in provinces more urbanized, more industrialized, and more integral to the military-industrial complex. Second, there were many factory towns with pronounced community powers creating high levels of citizen dependency and few prospects for economic diversification. Often they were attached to military factories or to vital natural resource extraction, becoming enmeshed in vertical organization extending from central ministries. Third, unlike the role of Hong Kong, Taiwan, and Southeast Asian capitalists in spurring small-scale entrepreneurship, South Korea and Japan brought a vertical model of organization to North and Northeast China. As reorganization of state-owned enterprises became imperative, managers, under pressure from officials and unions, could not change traditional danwei into Korean-style chaebols, let alone replicate the vibrant competitive atmosphere in Southeast China.

The Chinese in the Northeast became the most fervent advocates of regionalism, albeit in narrow economic terms. With excitement building in 1992, each province found its own hopeful twist. In Jilin talk centered on "Tumen River fever." It lavished benefits on Hunchun, the dragon's head of the Tumen River Area Development project, gaining support from Beijing to make a successful case for it to be adopted by the United Nations Development Program, attracting foreign investment and drawing neighboring countries closer. Even if North Korea and Russia were slow to embrace the project, Jilin could show the way. Hunchun made progress in the export of textiles, foodstuffs, and electrical appliances, while anticipating rapid expansion of industrial production as well as banking and other services. Eyeing the arrival of some of the world's largest firms, the Chinese pictured it as a dragon's head for regionalism.[28] Yet, as advocates tallied the tens of millions of dollars from hundreds of investors that fell far short of expectations, they

[27] Da Zhigang, "Heilongjiang sheng yu Riben de jingmao guanxi," *Longjiang shehuikexue*, 3 (1992), pp. 33–7.

[28] Sui Qingjiang and Zhu Xianping, "Hunchun," *Dongbeiya luntan*, 4 (1994), pp. 54–7.

blurred the reality of distrustful neighbors and companies weary of large commitments.

In the starry-eyed thinking of the early 1990s it seemed as if all countries with a stake in the region had only positive reasons to favor Tumen: the United States recognized that the economic impasse it faced required the dynamism of the world's emerging economic center in Asia to overcome; Japan needed a regional association after being challenged by the EU and NAFTA; and, of course, the countries of Russia and North Korea as well as China bordering on Tumen had everything to gain. Jilin sources blotted out the actual responses. For example, articles insisted that Japan welcomed the U.S. presence to dispel memories of the "East Asian Co-Prosperity Sphere."[29] Idealists used such unabashed boosterism to justify central funding to the border regions in China as in Japan.

When visitors arrived in Northeast China they not only found the strongest haven of the economic organization and thinking of the 1950s Soviet model left in China but also the physical symbols of that era. Large statues of Mao topped by slogans such as "Long Live the Great Thought of Mao Zedong" stood in front of some buildings, and Stalin Street and Stalin Park were prominently located in major cities. Yet, they were told that everything is changing; the entire area was "breaking geographic confinement" and "leaping to match the opening tide of coastal regions."[30] The sudden spurt in border trade made many overconfident, not recognizing warnings that a backlash was approaching.

At the start of the 1990s, still faced with domestic confusion and international isolation, China was not sure what model of development to follow. By the end of 1993 its confidence was more than restored. Foreign direct investment had tripled from 1990 to 1992 and was in the process of tripling again to 1994. Foreign trade doubled from 1990 to 1994. Shanghai had become the foremost engine of growth, while the dynamism of village and township enterprises spread across the Southeast. If for a time some argued that Northeast China deserved high priority for the next stage of development, success elsewhere and disillusionment with this area altered thinking about regionalism in NEA.

The provinces of Heilongjiang and Jilin failed to become magnets not only for Russians but also for Chinese businesses from the Southeast. The strategy of "opening to the north and linking to the south" through border cities and the Harbin commercial fair, the establishment of manufacturing branches for exports to NEA, and hurried attempts to introduce modern financial methods in place of barter with Russia did not work. It was not that China did not have modern, competitive firms ready to participate; rather, local firms fearing competition from the south, often blocked direct deals

[29] "Tumenjiang re," *Dongbeiya luntan*, 2 (1992).

[30] *People's Daily*, October 8, 1992.

between foreign guests and southern firms. In an effort to protect their monopolies, they did not involve China's most modern elements in cross-border ties, thereby exacerbating the damage. Without the rule of law, communist patterns of deception thrived.

The Chinese wrote extensively on regionalism in NEA and East Asia, stressing its importance by 1992 but conditioning its emergence on horizontal relations reflecting a new economic order. In contrast to some idealistic local appeals from Northeast China, Beijing analysts pointed to a dual track of joint economic openness and complementarity across borders, while aiming at developing one's own country's comprehensive national power. This meant firmly resisting the so-called flying geese model of Japanese financial circles and opening China only to a narrow version of "internationalization."[31]

Enthusiasts reasoned as follows. One, the world is being reshaped into three great regions, of which the Asia-Pacific will have the edge over the EU and NAFTA. Two, within the Asia-Pacific, NEA is emerging as the economic and trading center of the Asia-Pacific region. It was slow to take shape because of political and military tensions, but these are declining. A common consciousness is emerging, as expectations of peace and stability spread. Three, at least one major problem now needs to be solved, such as agreeing on cities that will lead the way (each country needs more internal coordination) or proclaiming a horizontal division of labor so that all sides will be committed.[32]

Awakening to the Persian Gulf War and the fading of socialist states, the Chinese affirmed that science and technology is the primary production force. Everywhere plans were announced to establish development zones for industries in the forefront in this sector. Journals such as Dalian's *Caijing luntan* paid close attention to Japan's successes. For Northeast China the lesson was not to follow the path of Guangdong by developing export-processing zones with cheap labor or of the Yangtze delta with booming village and township enterprises, but to leap into the high-tech sector using its many educational institutions long recognized within China and its solid industrial base. Cities were urged to internationalize, but Russia was in no mood to share its military-oriented technology, South Korea preferred to rush further south into Shandong for cheap labor, and Japan was more interested in Dalian's infrastructure and cooperative labor than in hiring personnel accustomed to large state-owned enterprises elsewhere. The new zones had scant success.

31 Song Shaoying, "Dongya jingji xin zhixu de jianli yu Zhongri jingji guanxi," in Jinian Zhongri bangjiao zhengchanghua 20 zhounian 90 niandai Zhongri guanxi de keti guoji xuexu taolunhui lunwen (Beijing: unpublished manuscript, September 1992), pp. 1–8.

32 Liu Zhongshan, "Lun 'neilian Dongbei, waitong Yatai' de Hunchun jingji kaifa zhanlue," *Dongbeiya luntan*, 2 (1992), pp. 1–5.

With Northeast China claiming one-quarter of China's industry and much of its strategic assets, Dalian could enter the 1990s thinking that its situation was parallel to that of Shanghai, designated the dragon's head to pull the Yangtze River delta into the modern economy. Boosted by plans to build a superhighway north through Shenyang, Changchun, and Harbin and also to expand railroad capacity, Dalian looked to transport inland as well as sealanes outward to make it a dragon's head. Yet, whereas Shanghai found a vibrant hinterland and ample transportation advantages, Dalian was stymied. Other provinces chafed at their forced dependence on extended and slow transportation routes to Dalian, and apart from the nearby Liaodong peninsula Northeast China never gelled as a common space being drawn into a larger cross-national region. Most serious was the lack of dynamism and competition generated by small and middle-sized firms.

The city of Dalian hoped to become the link that would chain China and Japan together in regionalism. It cited history as a positive factor: 200,000 Japanese lived in the city in the 1940s, many of whom – such as the economic architect Okita Saburo – had risen to prominence; a large friendship society and the highest competence in China on Japan and the Japanese language drew the two sides together; and by 1992 success in attracting more than 300 Japanese companies with over $1 billion in investment made this the logical partner. Yet, while local boosters played up the emotionalism joining the two sides and shunted to the side any negative historical legacy, there was doubt that Dalian could convert Japanese interest in cheap labor into success in surpassing other Chinese cities in the high-tech industry. Admitting the low quality of administration and management, local leaders worried that if the culture of the city was not raised to meet international standards, advantages of history, geography, and infrastructure would count for little.[33]

The Chinese noted that Japanese interest concentrated in Dalian and the nearby coast and on private rather than state leadership.[34] Yet, there was no meeting of the minds over Tumen or the scale of regionalism. Dalian as well as Liaoning province doubted the need for a new growth center at Tumen, while Beijing preferred including North as well as Northeast China in an emerging region,[35] suspecting Japan of seeking to draw parts of China into its own hinterland through the narrowly defined "Sea of Japan economic rim."

For several years the debate on regionalism in China was in full swing. Supporters insisted that fear of Japan's dominance and confidence that China

[33] Guo Yonghai, "Dalian jingji dengshang xintaijie de jidian sikao," *Riben yanjiu cankao xinxi*, September 30, 1992, pp. 1–10.

[34] Cai Mingzhe, "'Dongbeiya jingjiquan' yu Zhongguo he Nanchaoxian de jingji zhixu hezuo guanxi," *Yatai jingji*, April 1991, pp. 50–63.

[35] "Kannihonkai keizaiken to Chugoku," (Tokyo: JETRO, special economic survey report, 1990), p. 9.

can use U.S.-Japanese differences while opposing both ought not to slow pursuit of closer regional ties. They argued that 1) the tremendous role of overseas Chinese in the PRC economy gave it security through its own children; 2) small and middle-sized firms working together in subregions minimize the danger of domination; 3) Japan may try to use economic power to achieve political power, but it will not rely on military power and needs economic regionalism so much that China has maneuver room; and 4) China can benefit from Japan sharing an Eastern culture, while it must be realistic that Japan as a capitalist country with an ideology close to that of the United States is not likely to stray far from its foremost partner.[36] Together, these arguments favored regionalism, but they could not overcome a rising tide of nationalism linked to growing self-confidence in China's success and disapproval in conservative and military circles of Bill Clinton's pressure tactics to change China.

The Chinese responded to Clinton's criticisms confident that U.S. national interests – competitiveness in Asia and frictions with Japan – would keep U.S.-Chinese relations on course.[37] Even if the collapse of Soviet socialism had raised U.S. hopes that it could push China around, the Chinese concluded by 1993 that there was no need to make sacrifices for regionalism as had occurred after June 1989 when the danger of isolation was far greater. Growing assertiveness toward Japan signaled priority for nationalism over regionalism.

China and Japan

In 1989–92 the Japanese took satisfaction that they were championing the position that China must not be isolated from international society, leading the way in ending the freeze on assistance to China and winning a lot of credit from Chinese officials for pressing for China's full reentry. Simultaneously, Japan could shape the evolution of a global society with an Asian twist, build a foundation for regionalism, and serve its own nationalism as a great power with distinctive interests. Optimism about China spilled over into confidence over Japan's leverage in navigating through the end of the cold war.

On the one hand, the Japanese were more optimistic about relations with China in 1992 than at any time since 1984 when Nakasone and Hu Yaobang had forged a forward-looking partnership. Around the historic October visit of the Japanese emperor there was talk of bilateral relations entering a new stage. Especially in Japan hopes were raised that at last relations with China would turn a corner, becoming normalized in spirit as well as in name.

[36] Feng Zhaokui, "Yazhou xingshi fazhan de ruokan tedian," *Shijie jingji yu zhengzhi*, 2 (1993), pp. 22–4.

[37] Qian Wenrong, "Kelintun zhizhenghou de Zhongmei guanxi," *Shijie jingji yu zhengzhi*, 2 (1993), pp. 60–3.

Whereas in the 1980s every two to three years a dispute flared, in the early 1990s diplomatic ties proceeded quite smoothly. When matters arose, as in China's declaration of sovereignty over the Senkaku (Diaoyutai) islands, they were handled quite calmly, suggesting a new maturity in relations.[38] On the other hand, rhetoric warning against Japan's dangerous great-power ambitions intensified, leading the Japanese to grow more concerned about rising nationalism in China. Already in 1993 attention turned to China's preoccupation with comprehensive national power, including double-digit increases in military spending. Cautious optimism prevailed against a backdrop of recurrent concern.

The Japanese had confidence that economic ties through 1992 could serve as a wedge to improve bilateral ties in general, but they failed to meet Chinese expectations. Articles cast suspicion on the motives and methods of Japanese firms entering China. Compared to U.S. firms, those from Japan were seen as having excessive expectations, but offering fewer rights and more overtime to Chinese employees without high wages. Critics warned that Japanese employees did not adjust as well to Chinese society and Japanese firms found it harder to keep talented Chinese personnel, resulting in U.S. firms gaining ever-greater dominance in information-sector industries.[39] The Chinese wanted closer economic ties even as they doubted Japanese motives in bilateral and regional relations.

The Japanese had high hopes that the emperor's trip to China to mark the twentieth anniversary of normalized relations would be a watershed event, giving Tokyo a much stronger tie to Beijing and a "freer hand in pursuing future-oriented policies in Asia."[40] It would be comparable to 1972 in its impact, concluding the postwar period. When the fruits of the visit failed to materialize at the end of 1992 at the same time as a backlash arose over Boris Yeltsin's canceled visit to Japan, hopes for regionalism fell sharply.

At the time the emperor visited China, much of the coverage in Japan supported his admission that Japan "inflicted great sufferings on the people of China." It recounted approvingly the 1972 joint statement that the Japanese side "is keenly aware of Japan's responsibility for causing enormous damage in the past to the Chinese people through war and deeply reproaches itself." It was common too for the media to complain about nationalistic elements that "conspired against Japan's unflinching acknowledgment of its criminal aggression" and to warn that they are growing stronger.[41] This attitude was a building block of increased trust needed for regionalism, but it largely

[38] Tanaka Akihiko, "Tainichi kankei," in Okabe Tatsuo, ed., *Chugoku soran* (Tokyo: 1994), p. 144.

[39] "Nitchu saiko," *Sankei shimbun*, November 10, 2000.

[40] *The Japan Times Weekly International Edition*, August 24–30, 1992, p. 3.

[41] *The Japan Times Weekly International Edition*, November 9–15, 1992, p. 9.

stayed on the surface without much follow-up. Later in the decade it would be much harder to find.

In 1992–3 Chinese uneasiness toward the West led to some tilt toward Japan. Arms sales to Taiwan by the United States and France and democratization plans by the British governor in Hong Kong along with the campaign rhetoric of Bill Clinton against China's human-rights policies left Japan's quiet demeanor as a buffer. Also the Chinese calculated that Japan needs them more to balance the United States and provide a regional base. Despite warning against Japan's ambitions to become a military and political great power, China hesitated to undercut the closer ties developed in the past three years under sanctions.

By 1993 the Japanese were confident that they were forging a new Asian policy with China as the centerpiece boosting their country's political power, while the Chinese were insisting that they were blocking Japan's aspirations to become a political great power. The new Japanese success was trumpeted as "independent of the U.S. and achieved by moving ahead of the G-7 countries in resuming official economic assistance to China in the summer of 1990, sending the prime minister on an official trip to Beijing in the summer of 1991, and taking advantage of the Emperor's visit in October 1992." Despite debates over whether Japan is in a position to lead other Asian nations based on its own reasoning or must continue to be sensitive to their concerns about the past in order to be recognized as a real partner, Japanese were optimistic on China and regionalism.[42] The main thrust of China's policy toward Japan in this period was reassurance. In open forums and popular publications Chinese experts stressed the positive, encouraging mutual understanding by concentrating on what the two nations have in common and by putting differences aside. Even in regard to the sensitive subject of historical relations, it served China's purposes not to hurt Japanese feelings by dwelling on bad memories. This atmosphere created a favorable environment for investment, trade, and regional stability. It led others to appreciate China's deep commitment to full integration into a regional market economy. Assessing the results of the emperor's visit, the Chinese press saw it as an advertisement for their country's stability, commitment to opening, and attractiveness for investments.[43] If this was the main message, however, it was being slowly eclipsed.

In 1993 some Asia experts in the Japanese foreign ministry saw the time as ripe to press for regionalism, increasing Japan's commitment to work with China and showing displeasure over U.S. pressure. But the prevailing position was that Japan could not give up the world for the region. Even if it was less eager to work closely with the United States in Asia, it must keep balancing both sides. In turn, Chinese experts argued that as long as Japan

[42] *The Japan Times Weekly International Edition*, January 11–17, 1993, pp. 1, 6.

[43] *China Daily Business Weekly*, November 2, 1992, p. 1.

focused on the West, it would not be committed to regionalism on terms favorable to China. Few were satisfied with the balance between globalism and regionalism.

New Japanese guidelines for the use of ODA in 1991 began to be applied to China at the end of 1992. While giving more than $1 billion a year, Tokyo announced a shift from infrastructure development to environmental protection and other uses less likely to be helpful for China's military buildup. Japan was prepared to set the terms for regionalism. Yet, more important was the rivalry between Tokyo and Washington in the burgeoning Chinese market. Both sides appeared to be winners: Japan's bilateral trade rose 30 percent in 1993 and another 22 percent in 1994, as China rose from Japan's fifth to its second trading partner. Japan compensated for its more negative historical image by showing understanding with China's position that the Clinton administration's stress on human rights was excessive and undermined Chinese stability. Yet, after the visit of the emperor, Japanese experienced a letdown that it had not made a difference. Critical that China opposed Japan's bid for permanent membership in the Security Council and in other ways was anxious to limit Japan's rise, they doubted that real relations of friendship could be forged. In their view, China rejected a relationship of equality and trust.[44]

Some in Japan were reading developments in China pessimistically. They saw a persistent pattern of firing officials who drew closer to Japan, especially Hu Yaobang who was charged with wasting national funds and accelerating the bourgeois spiritual pollution of students and intellectuals with his invitation in the fall of 1984 to 3,000 Japanese youth. They predicted troubles ahead from China's firm intent on rising as a political and military great power, backed by stronger language since the U.S. military success in the Persian Gulf War. And they observed a new territorial push on the Senkaku islands in 1992.[45] Already they were warning that Japanese should not trust China.

Pressures were building from two sides in China to reconsider the policy toward Japan. From below, mass movements that had never accepted the 1972 decision by Mao Zedong and Zhou Enlai against seeking reparations, although thwarted from holding demonstrations during the emperor's visit by Deng Xiaoping's attitude that the matter was settled, were becoming energized. Perhaps, this was an inevitable result of having been suppressed for so long without satisfaction and now finding it possible to make use of a freer atmosphere on campuses. It may have also been a spillover from the general antiforeign mood in the post-1989 isolation and the ease with which Japan was targeted by propaganda for its ambitions. At the top, China's leadership

[44] "Chugoku no tosen tamesareru Nihon no anzen hosho senryaku," *Chuo koron*, November 1992, pp. 124–5.

[45] Okada Takahiro, "Nitchu kyoseijoka nijunen, part 2," *Toa*, June 1992, pp. 30–2.

grew more assertive in lambasting Japan for its "strategy," "plotting," and lack of goodwill. As they grew bolder in playing the "nationalist card," they cited at least three factors for distrusting Japan.

First, writings painted Japan as the only country that had forfeited the moral right to be a political or military great power because of its brutality in Asia through 1945. As talk of a new world order spread, Chinese intensified efforts to expose the lessons of history and use them to keep Japan in fetters. Japanese generosity to China over twenty years was dismissed as having little to do with morality, reflecting calculations of national interest or only paltry compensation for damages caused. The fact that Japan spends only 1 percent of its GNP on its military and has a constitutional clause barring military expansion also counted for little. Instead, its supposed ambitions, including its desire to lead the NEA region, and preparations to change national consciousness drew harsh warnings as if they would bring it dangerously close to its prewar past.[46] As the Diet was considering bills to permit limited deployment of the Self Defense Forces overseas, Chinese criticisms exaggerated the dangerous implications for militarism. At the very time Japan had become more respectable as an economic model, arguments against its right to convert economic into political power became more strident and these were reinforced by alarmism over the reemergence of militaristic ambitions.

Second, attacks targeted a world order resembling a rich countries' club with Japan leading Asia, excluding and controlling others.[47] Japan appeared to be the rising leader of capitalism. Some saw it as just another interventionist power, perhaps using softer means, intent on overthrowing socialism and spreading Westernization. If in its rivalries with the United States it was trying to enlist China's support, its overall strategy was consistent with the interests of the West and not really with China's best interests.

Third, the Chinese were bothered by the nature of economic ties with Japan, complaining that by keeping investment low and limiting the transfer of high or recent technology the Japanese want to lock China into a junior role. Analogies were made to imperialist economic methods and even the Greater East Asian Co-Prosperity Sphere. Even if we discount rumors of outrageous behavior by Japanese firms, such as dumping bad quality products, we find sustained criticism against investments limited to the short term and consciously trying to keep China from becoming a serious competitor.[48] Rarely was it mentioned that China's economy benefited substantially from Japan's ties. Even as bilateral trade soared in 1993, complaints continued that there was too little technology transfer and Japanese companies were keeping

46 Yuan Yuanzhong, "Riben zouxiang zhengzhi daguo de bufa mingxian jiakuai," *Riben wenti ziliao*, 6 (1992) pp. 15–18.

47 Lin Xiaoguang, "Shixi Riben de guoji xinzhixu gouxiang," *Riben xuekan*, 5 (1992), pp. 29–30.

48 "Yinianlai Riben xingshi huigu jiqi qianjing fenxi," *Riben wenti ziliao*, 3 (1992), pp. 15–16.

control over critical components in order to maintain a vertical pattern in the region associated with the goal of domination. Some articles charged too that Japan is lukewarm about regional cooperation as it remains wedded to the United States. Clearly, the contradictions between the two largest capitalist powers so eagerly predicted by Chinese analysts were running behind schedule. China would have been more interested in regionalism had it brought a counterforce to globalization.

The alarmist literature in China on Japan was growing as prospects were widely noted of Japan using its "economic superpower" clout. Warnings pictured economic expansionism, arrogance of a nation that considers itself special, a narrow-minded national psychology that poses a danger to others, and a threat that the Chinese would be wise not to embrace by accepting the Japanese model of regionalism.[49] The argument spread in 1992 that Japan had taken the offense against China.[50] The Chinese recalled Prime Minister Kaifu's reassuring stance in March 1990 that Japan's goals for the new order did not include pressure over human rights, placing Japan close to China in recognizing that each country drawing on its own culture should decide how to handle human rights. But they noted that in April 1991 Japan had proceeded to make foreign aid conditional on military expenses, a step aimed at China, and in the spring of 1992 it had gone further by pressuring China on human rights and raising the theme of the China threat. A debate ensued over why Japan was doing this. Was it trying to prove that it behaves like a political great power to impress the West? Does it lack a concrete enemy with the collapse of the Soviet threat? Has it become overconfident that the world situation had changed to its advantage? Perceptions of Japan's intentions and actions colored China's caution and led eventually to assertion of another model of regionalism.

Some in China feared rising Japanese independence in vying for power against the United States, using its regional base. Others warned of closer cooperation with the United States, as the two together pressed China. The most promising outcome was increased competition to a degree that gave China room to maneuver but not to the extent that actually enabled Japan to gain as a regional power. China's cautious support for regionalism sought to realize this goal, taking advantage of the tensions between regionalism and globalism in Japan's strategies.[51] Another approach was gaining as Chinese confidence grew. Many opted for Beijing taking an active role in steering globalism toward multipolarity and regionalism toward great-power balance as it replaced Tokyo as the driving force.

Already in 1992 some Chinese warned that their country might make a mistake by prematurely turning away from concentrating on economic

49 Cun Rui, "Waiguoren yanzhong de Ribenren," *Riben yanjiu*, 1 (1992), pp. 93–4.
50 Liu Jiangyong, "Riben zhengzai quanmian 'nanjin,'" *Riben wenti ziliao*, 10 (1992), pp. 1–3.
51 "Lengzhanhou Rimei guanxi zhongxin diaozheng," *Waiguo wenti yanjiu*, 3 (1992), pp. 41–4.

and technological cooperation with Japan. Although recognizing that the honeymoon era of the first twenty years after relations reopened was ending, they held out hope that by working closely with Japan for stability and development, China could still boost its national power greatly. Wary of new attention to the past, they feared that the movement to revisit the war reparations issue and revive history as a central concern could result in China paying a huge price from a downturn in public trust within Japan.[52] Clearly, they were reflecting a debate that was already in progress and would soon lead to China souring on Japan's aspirations for regionalism. The seeds had been planted for a groundswell of antipathy toward Japan. If China was not ready for regionalism, Japan's approach deserves some of the blame.

Russia and Regionalism

On the eve of the collapse of the Soviet Union, Russian analysts placed more stress on what their country needed to do to satisfy foreign partners than on blaming the outside world. They saw a need to clear away barriers: closed cities, an unconvertible ruble, excessive centralization, a poor business culture, and, at the top of the list, old-style communist leadership.[53] They also took for granted that it was within Russia's power by stripping away obstacles to realize economic cooperation between the Soviet Far East and the many suitors waiting for the opportunity. Only later did doubts surface about Russia's capacity to make use of regionalism and globalization with the legacy that remained.

For a short time radical reforms in Moscow and rampant decentralization in the Russian Far East suggested Russia was prepared to do its part for regionalism. The main barriers appeared to be insufficient infrastructure to sustain the rapidly growing trade and inevitable growing pains, as strangers grew accustomed to new ways. But the backlash inside Russia did not take long. Exports relied on sharp price differentials between the domestic and international markets with little control on how the gains were used. Imports undercut local producers at the same time as the national market was crumbling. The Russian side soured on regionalism fast even as Japan and China kept pursuing it.

In the second half of 1992 Russians concluded that the initiatives advanced by Gorbachev in Vladivostok and Krasnoyarsk had run their course.[54] While they had played a positive role in reducing tension in NEA and normalizing relations, they no longer had much to offer for a country

52 Jiang Lifeng, "Xinshidai Zhongri guanxi de zhongdian: jingji jishu hezuo," *Riben wenti ziliao*, 9 (1992), pp. 1–3.

53 A. B. Parkanskii, "Sovetskii Dal'nii Vostok i Amerikanskii Dal'nii Zapad: Vozmozhnosti ekonomicheskogo sotrudnichestva," *SShA*, May 1990, pp. 9–11.

54 Vladimir Miasnikov, "Vostok – delo tonkoe," *Nagapo*, 33 (1992), p. 4.

much weaker than the old Soviet Union, facing confident neighbors focusing on economic integration, and in danger of losing all influence in this region while becoming dangerously dependent on the West. Lowering the nation's guard and opening borders had their limits. A search for influence replaced one for integration. In the span of several months Boris Yeltsin spurned Japan by canceling a summit, visited South Korea but recognized the limits of additional economic or geopolitical support, and finally went to China to make that country Russia's principal regional partner, but not for economic reasons. While still largely pro-West, Yeltsin was not proglobalization and, even less, proregionalism, let alone accepting Japanese leadership of the latter.

Recalling the days of the Far Eastern Republic from 1920–2, local elites in 1992 seized the opportunity of the breakup of the Soviet Union to call for the formation of a state loosely linked to Moscow with control over its own resources of timber, gold, fish, oil, and so forth.[55] Neither ethnic nationalism nor trust in neighboring areas to be included in the republic drove this appeal. Instead, it was a grab for resources with little thought for the loss of support from Moscow and the dependency on Asian countries that would have followed. By 1993 the idea was fading as elites found that they could divert ample resources under existing decentralization while keeping funds flowing from Moscow. Such elite attitudes undercut efforts to forge networks of trust as a basis for regionalism.

The Russian Far East had started on the path to regionalism with an unsupportable combination: 1) the old nomenklatura elite remained in place and whetted its appetite on a foreign investment boom, a rapid succession of visiting economic missions, and the bonanza of exports taking advantage of price differentials; and 2) foreigners eagerly established joint ventures, assuming that legal and financial protections would soon be forthcoming. The Russian elite overestimated the ease with which it could make money without having to make structural changes. The scene was set for mutual disappointment.

Russian hopes of regionalism faded along with dreams of globalization. In 1993 the appeal of "Eurasianism" came at the expense not only of joining the "Western" community of nations but also of accepting regional integration through proposals such as the Tumen area project. Warning that reform and democratization are "the sword of universal values thrust into the heart of traditional Soviet nationalism," Hakamada Shigeki pointed to 1993 as the time when nationalism returned in Russia.[56] The choices had narrowed to chaos that fueled a crisis of national identity and left fertile ground for extreme nationalism or a powerful leader who was able to cloak himself in

55 *Moscow News*, 41 (1992), p. 5.

56 Shigeki Hakamada, "The Prospects for the Putin Administration and for Political Reform in Russia" (unpublished manuscript, 2000).

nationalism at the expense of globalization or regionalism. If Yeltsin had little interest in regionalism, opposition politicians were contemptuous of it. When local leaders in the Russian Far East paid lip service to it, the reason was that it still helped to attract investments.

Vested interests in the Russian Far East reacted angrily to international meetings in support of the Tumen River area project. They demanded that priority on the Russian side go to reconstructing the infrastructure from Vladivostok to Nakhodka, not diverting resources toward a new complex that would spoil with dangerous industries one of the most serene places in this part of Russia.[57] Narrow reasoning on regionalism dominated.

The Nakhodka free economic zone (FEZ) epitomized the failings of Russia's strategy for regionalism. It was the first FEZ, chosen by Gorbachev in 1986 although only given legal status by Boris Yeltsin and the Supreme Soviet of Russia in October 1990. Of eighteen areas formally designated as FEZs, it was the one with the most implementation. In 1991–4 it received domestic backing in the form of tax exemptions, customs incentives, infrastructure funds, and special measures for immigration and registration of enterprises. Moreover, through a treaty with South Korea and agreements with Korean firms, this FEZ gained important international backing. Yet, it proved to serve primarily as a financial strategy for the distribution of budget revenue within Russia and the evasion of taxes on foreign trade. After peaking in 1994 at 460 companies with foreign investments, the FEZ lost its legal status and increasingly its foreign firms, especially after Russia's default of 1998.[58] Nakhodka's failure symbolized the dead-end approach to foreign investment in the Russian Far East apart from the special case of Sakhalin oil and gas.

Meanwhile, Prime Minister Chernomyrdin was ensuring that Gazprom would control the rich oil and gas deposits off Sakhalin. After signing agreements in 1992 with an international consortium to develop two of the deposits discovered in the 1970s, he made sure that Moscow would work with a large Russian firm independent of local interests.[59] Despite requirements to purchase local equipment and supplies, through 2002 there was little spillover across the Russian Far East from the many Sakhalin projects.

Vladivostok's aspirations suggested parallels on both sides of the Pacific. Known as Russia's San Francisco, the city experienced its own mid–nineteenth century boom on the far coast of a continental power originally facing another ocean and could look with envy on what America's Pacific gateway had become. To the south it could turn also to Hong Kong as a model of prosperity demonstrating the possibilities for an open city rather

[57] *Krasnaia znamia*, July 30, 1993, p. 2.

[58] Svetlana J. Vikhoreva, "The Development of Free Economic Zones in Russia," *ERINA Report*, 38 (January 2001), pp. 1–5.

[59] *Izvestiia*, September 3, 1993, p. 2.

than a closed one. A local geographer proposed that Vladivostok be treated as the "third capital" of Russia. Just as Peter I built St. Petersburg as the second capital to open a window on the west, now a new capital is needed to join the Asia-Pacific region.[60]

When Vladivostok opened to the world at the start of 1992 just as Moscow was dismantling the command economy, it seemed obvious that the gateway to the dynamic Asia-Pacific would prosper at the expense of the headquarters of socialist centralization. But Vladivostok revealed itself to be a military-industrial outpost, whose elite was more interested in protecting the existing complex and gaining hold of the profits from marine exports than in fostering a new economy, while Moscow proved adept at seizing the reins of a monopolistic economy that was replacing the socialist one. Moscow attracted most of Russia's foreign investment and upwardly mobile people; Vladivostok grew shabbier with meager investment. The former became the sole symbol of Russian transformation, the latter the most infamous example of "wild east" criminalization.

In Vladivostok, Khabarovsk, or elsewhere in the Russian Far East, foreign investors, who had acted in good faith and fulfilled their obligations, suddenly found themselves, in effect, stripped of their high-profile property with no compensation or legal recourse. One example was the air terminal in the city of Khabarovsk. After a joint venture was established in 1990 and the Japanese paid for the construction of a new air terminal, an obligation existed to repay more than $10 million over seven years. The Japanese discovered, however, that the former party chair of Khabarovsk who had been employed as general director was siphoning funds away. As the joint venture's debts to the government mounted, the conclusion became unavoidable: the local authorities were planning to let the firm die in order to avoid repaying its debts.

Sergei Agafonov, *Izvestiia* reporter in Tokyo, in 1994 accused the leadership of Primorskii krai of stripping a reputable Japanese firm with thirteen years of experience on the Soviet-Russian market of what had been the first Soviet-Japanese joint venture in Vladivostok. Established when this was still a closed city in 1990, this classy operation combining a hotel, parking area, and tourist agency had been earning a profit. Suddenly in November 1993 the Japanese were told that controllers from Moscow found that the krai administration had not had the right to enter into a contract to become part of a joint venture and the contract was null. In an uncompromising manner krai officials proceeded to liquidate the enterprise, resume operation of the tourist business without the Japanese, and offer no compensation. Agafonov called this "divorce" Primorskii style.[61]

[60] Matvei Romanov, "Vladivostok: 'Tretii Rim' Rossii," *Dal'nevostochnyi uchenyi*, 21 (1994), p. 3.

[61] Sergei Agafonov, "Razvod po-primorski," *Izvestiia*, June 30, 1994.

Another case was a hotel known by the Chinese name "Yuan dong" (Far East), which constituted the largest enterprise in Russia with 100 percent foreign investment. After bringing the materials from China, building the complex with Chinese labor, hiring 200 Russians, and operating the hotel with all the necessary comforts, the Chinese company found that its lease for fifty years was meaningless when the central government at the end of 1993 rescinded a decree giving benefits to foreign investors. Tax inspectors descended on the company, leaving it with huge obligations and on the verge of bankruptcy.[62] Many such examples arose of the Russian authorities penalizing firms for no fault of their own. Confidence in business operations fell rapidly.

Desperate conditions are not what Russians in the Far East had been led to expect. At the beginning of the 1990s the optimism came chiefly from foreign sources, championing the prospects of a new NEA region or Japan Sea rim economic zone. Sister-city relations, energy projects, FEZs, the Tumen River project, and other initiatives were thrust before the Far Easterners with such hyperbole and from so many directions that a rosy future seemed all but assured. Anticipating Gorbachev's April 1991 summit in Tokyo, observers focused on huge investments from Japan awaiting only a compromise agreement on four islands. Then it was South Korea that was destined to play the leading role in the Russian Far East as part of a strategy for reunification with North Korea achieved on the basis of enticing all around with market-oriented prosperity and regional integration. In 1992–3 came the "China boom," "borderlessness" that promised no limit to the expansion of barter trade and joint ventures.[63] Cross-border regionalism would enable one part of Russia to capitalize on its supposedly ideal geographical situation.

Russians never had a chance to become optimistic about regionalism. Apart from a brief flurry of glasnost about opportunities in the Asia-Pacific region from 1989–91 and momentary enthusiasm for decentralization, Moscow paid little heed to this distant area and the local population grew apprehensive when they realized the enormous price they would pay in lost subsidies. By the beginning of 1993 a crisis of confidence in Primorskii krai led to the replacement of a reform governor with Evgenii Nazdratenko, head of an association of industrial managers, and in Khabarovsk krai it was seen in three times as many people distrusting Boris Yeltsin than trusting him (only about 5 percent trusted his administration) as well as local shakeups in response to negative views of government.[64] A mixture of fear of the future and apathy led to xenophobia and no hope for regionalism.

[62] Iurii Tanich, "Investor sdelal vse, chto mog dlia razvitiia goroda . . . fiskal'nye organy tozhe delaiut vse, chtoby drugim investoram nepovadno bylo," *Izvestiia tikhookeanskoi Rossii*, May 1996, p. 2.

[63] *Tikhookeanskaia zvezda*, March 2, 1993, p. 2.

[64] *Priamurskie vedomosti*, March 5, 1993, p. 2.

Demarcation became a focal point for nationalism. The two sides reached a constructive solution in 1991 to their long-standing border dispute. It set aside perhaps the three most difficult islands for a later time and established a principle grounded in international law that would lead to only small adjustments in territory, for the most part favoring China. On both sides the agreement was seen as the starting point for a new era in bilateral relations. Progress toward it had smoothed the way to the May 1989 summit normalizing relations. Ratification gave impetus to cross-border trade. Revelation of its details in 1993, however, handed an issue to nationalists, especially in Vladivostok, to rally public opinion simultaneously against Moscow's "sellout" and Beijing's ambitions. Through 1997 when the demarcation process was completed, Nazdratenko railed against it and used every means available to block it. Instead of relief that the chief focus of past recriminations was overcome, Russians were treated to a recurrent barrage of accusations that a duplicitous deal had only whetted China's deep-seated expansionist aims.

Often talk turned to economic integration of the Far Eastern economic region as a response to slackening ties to Moscow and to the danger of fragmentation before the vast economies of neighboring states. Yet, Moscow had relied on vertical integration through European Russia, leaving little room for mutual ties within this designated economic region. It extracted cheap raw materials sent in the direction of the center in return for subsidied consumer goods and energy provided at a cheap railroad fare. Both politics and economics had a colonial character, leaving the anxious local elite looking to Moscow to maintain them instead of cooperating with their neighbors and looking across the border.

By 1994 the initial opening of the Russian Far East to neighboring countries had reached an impasse. One by one, each of the early hopes for regionalism had failed. First, the boom in exports of Russian natural resources ended as Moscow recognized that price differentials were being used to make huge unreported profits sent abroad. Controls were reinstated on many products sent from inland Russia, although it would not take long for local authorities to find new ways to make money on local exports such as marine and wood products. Second, the joint venture fever ended. Seeing their properties stripped away, the Chinese, the Japanese, and other foreigners stopped investing in the Russian Far East. Also, authorization for FEZs was withdrawn before investments amounted to much. Third, the import wave from China nose-dived. Having bought cheap goods when little else was available, Russians found new suppliers and turned sharply against Chinese traders. Fourth, funds for big projects such as rebuilding the Trans-Siberian railway disappeared. With no trust in Moscow, local administrations could expect little.

Gradually a kind of regularity was achieved in the Far East. Prices rose on the domestic market after being five times lower than world ones. Barter arrangements allowed tax avoidance to prevail. The state gained more control over exports of many items even as traders in other products systematized their methods for deceiving or bribing customs inspectors. The atmosphere did not beckon those interested in building a long-term foundation for regionalism. In fact, it caused frequent frictions, none more serious than the cross-border tensions that were mounting in Sino-Russian relations. Left in a state of perpetual crisis, Russians along the border turned their anger against Chinese.

The inability of Russian leaders to establish the rule of law and market forces in the Russian Far East continued to be exposed by Nazdratenko. Only after eight years of repeated showdowns did President Vladimir Putin finally get him to agree to leave the governor's post in Primorskii krai, but at the price of appointing him head of the State Fisheries Committee. In charge now of distributing fishing quotas, half of which he demanded be allotted to the krai he had just left, Nazdratenko could continue the opaque practices that fed corruption and stood in the way of development. It took another two years before Prime Minister Mikhail Kasyanov secured Putin's approval to suspend Nazdratenko, but again a deal was made allowing him to become deputy head of the Security Council, which coordinates all organs of power.[65] To keep him away from Vladivostok has proven difficult, but even harder is the challenge of creating a central, market-based system that denies new governors the right to parcel out fishing quotas and manipulate bureaucratic red tape as a source of corruption.

China and Russia

Until the August 1991 coup failed, Beijing was taking a fresh look at Moscow as a partner. For a time it appeared as if Soviet reforms might shift back onto a politically conservative track. After the Persian Gulf War Beijing turned from awaiting Gorbachev's fall while viewing his new revisionism in ways reminiscent of how China's leaders had seen Khrushchev's revisionism in the late 1950s, to recognizing that Yeltsin was a more dangerous alternative and finding some promise in a recent conservative shift. Hoping still for a convergence of interests, Jiang Zemin spoke of two great socialist countries.[66] Interparty relations intensified amidst pledges of noninterference in internal affairs. The desire in Beijing to reward the People's Liberation Army for support at Tiananmen and the desire in Moscow to compensate its military-industrial complex for a rapid drop in orders resulted in arms sales. New alarm in 1991 about U.S. power and interference around the world led to talk of "playing the Soviet card." In May Jiang's visit to Moscow intensified contacts. With Jiang and Li Peng among the one-third of China's leadership

[65] *Gazeta.ru*, May 5, 2003.
[66] *People's Daily*, May 18, 1991, p. 1.

that had studied in the Soviet Union, a meeting of minds appeared possible. It appears that Chinese officials had hoped that the August coup would succeed and make the Soviet Union a bastion of socialism again as well as a close great-power partner. Even control over ethnic separatism and some distancing from the West would have brought relief.

The collapse of Soviet communism and then the Soviet Union at first sent shock waves across China. Some who were educated in the fifteen years before the Cultural Revolution asked in bewilderment how could their socialist god have collapsed. Others influenced by the propaganda over the following fifteen years and the sharp reduction in military pressure on their country could not avoid some self-satisfaction. China's leaders issued a string of party documents that were well reflected in publications in order to pacify emotions and alleviate doubts threatening to communist rule in China. The main aim was to draw lessons from the Soviet experience that would help China's communism to survive and prosper. One such lesson announced by Deng Xiaoping only a month after the Soviet Union's demise was to use the market economy, without reservation, both to satisfy consumer needs and to develop the forces of production.[67] Another was that any change in the status of the communist party and its guiding thought would produce confusion and lead to everything else that went wrong. Thus, leaders gave comparable weight to material forces and ideas in shaping popular attitudes, satisfying concerns at both ends of the Chinese political spectrum. On the far left there were renewed calls for vigilance against the dangers of humanistic thought and democratic socialism. For true reformers there was some satisfaction that China had avoided the chaos and decline in Russia and was now moving forward with a market economy and more openness to the outside. Warned by the fate of the Soviet Union, the Chinese became more cautious in pressing for political change. The consensus on regionalism also narrowed, valuing it as a means to boost national economic strength and solidify forces against political dangers.

Deng ensured that the response to the collapse of the Soviet Union in China was worried, but still upbeat. If it was feared that the incoming Yeltsin regime was ready to join the United States and Japan in controlling China and working with South Korea, few doubted that Russia would at least be careful to develop businesslike relations with China. Even if Japan seemed poised to become Moscow's first partner in the region, Russia would in any case turn more to NEA, narrowing the huge economic gap in its capacity to face two oceans simultaneously. It would develop its vast natural resources, seeking a long period of peace, while remaining a military great power with independent interests. Although limited Sino-Russian relations would leave China's position weak, it would benefit from

[67] Li Shugan, "Lun Lianmeng de jieti," *Waiguo wenti yanjiu*, 2 (1992), pp. 3–4.

good economic opportunities befitting the dynamic region foreseen as 1992 began.[68]

There is reason to think that Chinese authorities had second thoughts that, over a quarter century of conflict, they had helped to weaken the Soviet Union and to contribute to its collapse and the resultant loss to the forces of socialism. One author noted that the West believes that socialist countries are doomed: if there is no economic reform, they will collapse materially, and if there is, these countries will collapse spiritually. To prove the West wrong, socialist states must draw a line between trade and material exchanges on the one hand, and cultural diffusion and the spread of ideas on the other. They must stop destroying each other economically, overturning each other politically, and stirring each other up ideologically.[69] Rather than openly explore the theme "who lost the Soviet Union," the Chinese turned their attention to forging closer ties with the new Russia.

Officials were quick to dismiss Russian plans for a transition as an illusion: ignoring differences between civilizations, expecting assistance that would not come, failing to grasp the laws of reforming a traditional socialist economy, and misjudging domestic political and social forces. Driven by different notions from those in the United States of the transition from socialism and the revival of great-power contradictions, analysts saw no quick entry into any sort of new world order ahead. Many predicted quick redirection of Russian domestic and foreign policy, denying the pessimism that others had shown.

Consistently over a decade Chinese sources have posed the choice for Russia as subordinating itself to the strategy of the West, aimed at controlling and crippling the country, or allowing national interests to guide its way into closer ties with China. This view contrasts the United States's resort to pressure and threats with China's offer of genuine friendship without interference in Russia's internal affairs. Through the 1990s almost never could we find advice to Russia to accept globalization, even in a narrow economic sense, which was what China claimed to be doing. This outlook on Russia applied also to its course of action in NEA, revealing no concern about its rejection of global standards. Instead, the aim was to reinforce alarm that Russia was turning into a vassal of Western economies, producing raw materials.[70] Because open regionalism relies heavily on globalization and assumes exports of energy and other natural resources, China was, in effect, discouraging Russia from embracing regionalism. It encouraged paranoia that left Russia a poor risk.

[68] Zheng Biao, "Sulian jieti dui Dongbeiya de yingxiang," *Dongbeiya luntan*, 2 (1992), pp. 84–9.

[69] Wang Jiafu, "Lun Dongbeiya shichang de zhanlue jiegou," *Longjiang shehuikexue*, 4 (1992), p. 41.

[70] Li Xinnan, "Zai miwangzhong de Elousi jingji," *Dalian cankao xinxi*, 23 (December 1992), pp. 56–64.

On the Russian side, China was mostly an afterthought in late 1991 and most of 1992. Leading reformers sought to prove that Russia belongs in the Western community by siding firmly with human rights and other criticisms of China. A few even couched the argument in terms of rejecting Russia's "oriental" roots, while joining in "civilized" globalization.[71] However, even as Russians continued to look down on the Chinese, many lost faith in Western civilization. Having rejected the Soviet past and being skeptical of the West as the future, they could not escape reflecting on alternative scenarios in Asia.

As Russians increasingly regretted the way their country was being transformed, they took a closer look at the contrasts with China. This long-time alter ego of socialism loomed high as the alternative path in integrating into the global economy and the one great power beckoning Russia to turn its foreign policy toward great-power competition. Yet, past negativism and continued association of China with the lingering communist opposition inside Russia made it hard to evaluate Chinese reforms on their merits. If increasingly one could find comments alluding to learning from China or cooperating in development, Russians repeatedly failed to grasp the lessons of Chinese reforms or to pursue diverse bilateral economic linkages.[72] The Chinese model was not taken seriously.

In the years of supposed diplomatic isolation from mid-1989 to 1992 China made great gains in normalizing relations with its neighbors, expanding cross-border trade, and otherwise engaging in "border diplomacy," opening the way to Sinocentric regionalism. As resources flowed in, China's influence radiated out.[73] This allowed it to compete with Japanese-led regionalism, in which big corporations and the power of capital reigned. In accord with this trend, Sino-Russian trade developed quickly from 1989 to 1993 and the Chinese were optimistic that the pattern would continue. Yet, analysts drew misleading conclusions that the kind of exchange fostered through state agencies could continue despite the dramatic changes in 1992 as both countries pressed for market economies and that the main problems to be resolved were infrastructure and a shortage of capital rather than absence of market practices and corruption.[74] After rising 50 percent in 1992 and 31 percent in 1993, trade reached $7.68 billion and seemed headed for much higher totals as the decade proceeded. Dramatic growth occurred in cross-border trade as crossings opened one by one and controls were loosened. Plans for broader linkages, including West Siberia and West

71 Yegor Gaidar, *Gosudarstvo i evoliutsiia* (Moscow: Evraziia, 1995).

72 Gilbert Rozman, "Chinese Studies in Russia and Their Impact, 1985–1992," *Asian Research Trends*, 4 (1994), pp. 143–60.

73 Mori Kazuko, "Shuhen kara mita Chugoku, Chugoku kara mita shuhen," *Chugoku kenkyu*, May 1992, pp. 12, 26.

74 Song Kui, "Lun bianjie maoyi de zuoyong," *Longjiang shehuikexue*, 3 (1992), pp. 43–7.

China, and big energy projects suggested the great hopes already aroused.[75] Japanese backers of regionalism pointed to the soaring Sino-Russian border trade as a harbinger of a new era without recognizing the severe limitations that existed.[76]

While the model of a market economy based on that of the United States won the most support among Russian leaders, two rival Asian models with implications for regional integration aroused some interest too. On the one hand, there was the Japanese model championed as a means to build capitalism under a strong state. It found expression in *Japanese Experience for Russian Reform*, a periodical issued with Japanese government support by the Institute of Oriental Studies in Moscow.[77] On the other hand, there were regular reports from the Institute of the Far East brought together in 2000 in a two-volume collection entitled *Chinese Reforms in Russia*. Here the emphasis on a strong state was highlighted along with a call for self-respect for one's own people, not turning the nomenklatura into opponents or creating a "lost generation."[78] These dueling appeals to Asian models each circulated only in a few hundred copies without either gaining strong backing. Advocates of the Japanese model had no confidence in the Russian workers, managers, or state officials behaving as Japanese had, and they could not overcome the pro-West inclinations among economists. The more conservative backers of the Chinese model were quick to reject dependence on the world market, showing that they were more interested in sticking close to the old Soviet model than really finding a reform course. Even in discussions about reorienting the development of the Russian Far East, neither the Japanese nor the Chinese variant was taken seriously.

It was clear very early that Russians viewed an international city at Tumen as a threat to their own ports suffering from excess capacity. Chinese analysts knew too that Japan's interest wavered and could shift depending on a breakthrough with Russia that led to priority for the disputed islands or a breakdown leading to retaliation. Yet, the Chinese poured funds into their gateway city at Hunchun to the extent that some Japanese grew concerned that they were on the sidelines in this emergence of a new "Shenzhen,"[79] and some South Koreans looked hopefully for a spillover beneficial to opening North Korea. Without the larger Tumen project, Hunchun was isolated, and within China many favored focusing only on

75 Lu Nanquan, "Miandui 21 shiji Zhonge jingmao hezuo wenti de sikao," *Xiboliya yanjiu*, 5 (2000), pp. 3, 8.

76 Ogawa Kazuo, "Churo keizai kankei wa ima 'kakudai to tayoka no jidai,'" *Sekai shuho*, December 28, 1993, pp. 22–7.

77 *Iaponskii opyt dlia rossiiskikh reform* (Moscow: Association of Japanese Studies, 1995–).

78 Institute of the Far East, *Kitaiskie reformy i Rossiia*, Vol. 1 (Moscow: RAN, 2000), pp. 71–2.

79 Ishii Akira, "Chugoku Tohoku no 'Shenzhen' o mezashite," *Gaiko forum*, February 1993, pp. 21–7.

the Yellow Sea and Dalian.[80] The chances for the Tumen area project were not strong from the outset. Its potential for regionalism was never realized, and cross-border ties between China and Russia remained bilateral rather than regional.

In 1992 the Chinese lacked self-confidence in economic as well as political relations with Russia. In Harbin they already were resigned to the negative psychological effect in Russia from inexperienced Chinese traders flooding across the border and cognizant of the strong preference for the quality and higher technology of Japanese and South Korean products and the lure of dollars rather than bartered Chinese goods. Each side gave the other the dregs of its production. Desperate even for such fractured ties, the Chinese did little to bring the situation under control even as Russians grew increasingly resentful.

For China the boom in cross-border trade with Russia held promise of becoming a balancing force in regionalism. But they did not reckon with the discrepancy between organized Chinese communities, accustomed to working together to overcome barriers in distant cities and the decisions of bureaucrats, and individual Russians only used to dependence on officials. They also miscalculated the danger from criminal groups on both sides rushing into the vacuum of modern institutions along the border. The Chinese soon were looking down on Russians for doing little to help themselves and cheating Chinese traders along with other foreigners, while Russians were in a rage over Chinese duplicity.

Border points expected to lead the way in regionalism from below lacked contact with the commercial economy and were dominated by officials and propaganda organs mired in old ways. Most isolated was Heihe, a city of 150,000 that for a quarter century had been kept as a fortress against the Soviet threat. Articles in its journals clashed: early in 1989 some called for breaking away from stifling traditions to join in commercialism, while in 1991 they gave undiluted support to the success in 1989 of blocking capitalism at China's doorstep.[81] Rhetoric aside, material interests prevailed.

Later both sides would acknowledge that as the gates were opened wide, China's most unsavory types used the chance to rush across the border. They bribed their way onto tourist groups, paid border guards to break laws or stay longer, and traded whatever they could find in order to make a quick profit. Neither government knew how to control them. Soon Russia would resort to drastic measures. Tourist groups might have to pay a huge fine if one of their members was missing or might not be allowed to cross back.

[80] An Qingchang, "Nuli shixian Tumenjiang diqu guoji kaifa guihua shexiang," *Dongbeiya luntan*, 2 (1992) pp. 6–8.

[81] Gan Chengzhong, "Quanmian shenhua gaige yu youhua," *Heihe xuebao*, 1 (1989), pp. 1–4; Yu Wanling, "Shouxian ba women zizhi de shiqing banhao," *Heihe xuekan*, 4 (1991), p. 1.

With local ties in jeopardy, the Chinese and Russians found a modicum of stability through joint criminalization of the border. As criminal groups battled in violent turf wars for control in the Russian Far East, a local leader fended off rival Chechens (combining groups from the Caucasus) and interlopers from Moscow with the help of Chinese gangs. Because the Chinese limited their predatory behavior to traders from their own country, they proved to be a convenient ally. In the mid-1990s after the local criminal head was securely in power, he visited China and solidified the alliance, which lasted until his death in 2002 after which the Chinese boss was arrested.[82] Local ties of this sort did not bring trust.

Through the 1980s the Russian Far East and Northeast China faced off under the dominant influences of their security forces and military industries. In the 1990s these power elites did not fade away. They provided much of the new leadership, controlled entire communities and vast resources, enjoyed separate legal treatment and border and energy privileges, and found lucrative opportunities for smuggling. In the first phase of regionalism they operated quite separately, but as the border was regularized the security forces on the two sides began to cooperate more. This led to a criminalized border beyond the control of modern economic organizations and it left a poor basis for regionalism.

In 1993 Russians awakened to China's dynamism. Suddenly, the world financial organs were buzzing with a new ranking based on purchasing power that put China third. China became the "other," supposedly enjoying higher living standards as Russians tasted poverty and appearing to have a strong state as Russia fell into division.[83] If the response among many was alarm that a potential threat was developing, the prevailing geopolitical view was that Russian power had slipped so much more versus the United States that a rising China is best treated as a balancing force essential to Russia's further status as a power.

The momentum for closer Sino-Russian ties developed through the second half of 1992 and 1993. For Beijing arms sales to Taiwan and the linkage of sanctions to human-rights behavior left a negative impression of the United States after hopes had risen that sanctions over June 1989 were ending and a new market orientation of China's economic reforms would boost ties. For Moscow rifts over NATO expansion and war in Yugoslavia aroused anger toward the United States, prompting a turn to China. As talk resumed of a strategic triangle, interest in regionalism was slipping. China made its first purchase of Sukhoi interceptors in 1992, followed by agreements in 1996, 1999, and 2001. The new relationship boosted sales from a plant in

[82] "Ties between Far Eastern, Chinese Crime Groups May Be Ending," *Russian Regional Report*, 7(29) November 25, 2002.

[83] *Izvestiia*, September 3, 1993, p. 5.

Komsomolsk-na-Amur, north of Khabarovsk, making a big input in the local economy and bilateral trade. In 1994 a further uplift in geostrategic ties became the centerpiece in a search for leverage rather than for a path to regionalism.

South Korea, the Great Powers, and Regionalism

In the midst of uncertain diplomacy with the Gorbachev regime, Kanemaru Shin, a leading powerbroker of the LDP, visited Pyongyang in an effort to make an end-run around the barriers to NEA regionalism and Japan's diplomatic marginalization. His gambit in 1990 failed, but it showed the willingness of Japan's leaders to act unilaterally without the United States or South Korea. Tokyo sought a platform for converting its economic prowess into recognition as the regional power of NEA. It showed little inclination to coordinate with its closest economic partner in the region and its fellow opponent against the spread of communism over the past half century. Tokyo proceeded on its own.

Although Pyongyang feared that an opening to South Korea would delegitimate it, it eagerly sought the attention of the United States on matters of security while giving enough rhetorical support to keep its name alive in discussions of economic regionalism. Given its totalitarian grip over the North Korean nation plus the likelihood that China would provide enough food and energy assistance to prevent a collapse, Pyongyang could risk brinkmanship. In 1993–4 the threat of preemptive war against the North hung over the region. After a showdown with the United States over Pyongyang's rejection of nuclear reactor energy inspections, war was averted by the Korean Peninsula Energy Development Organization (KEDO) agreement to provide oil in the short term and build two reactors with safeguards for the long term. From the second half of 1994 many around North Korea breathed a sigh of relief, anticipating that this agreement would be followed by reform and regional cooperation along with reconciliation with the United States. Others, however, expected that the North would collapse before the reactors were built; Pyongyang would remain an obstacle to be bypassed in the search for regionalism.

Tokyo never gave serious attention to winning the trust of the South Korean people. When President Roh Tae-woo met the emperor in Tokyo in May 1990, political leaders permitted only a vague statement of the "deepest regret" over the "sufferings" inflicted by Japan,[84] far short of what was sought. South Korean public antagonism toward Japan kept being fueled by new sensations, some shared with China and others not. In 1992 when the issue arose of comfort women forced into slavery at military bases by

[84] *The Japan Times Weekly International Edition*, August 24–30, 1992, p. 3.

the Japanese occupation, the most emotional coverage stressed that even elementary students had been the victims. Little things also could inflame passions. At the Hiroshima Asian Games of 1994 when kimchi disappeared from the athletes' table, Koreans charged that the Japanese were trying to sap the strength of Koreans who considered this their source of power.[85] After one issue arose a vicious cycle often followed, as grievances were aired one by one. Instead of following the emperor's visit to China with a trip to South Korea, Japan hesitated in the absence of any consensus on assuaging the feelings of the Koreans. A decade later there has still been no visit despite anticipation that an appearance at the jointly held World Cup would offer a rare opportunity. Indeed, the outcry over Japanese textbook changes in 2001 doomed the visit; only an imperial relative was sent.

In 1993 when Kim Young-sam came to power the Japanese criticized his use of the "anti-Japan card" to boost his authority. They charged "Japan bashing," implying that South Korea was an abnormal country that stirred negative feelings in young people toward Japan to bolster an artificial national identity.[86] Perceiving their neighbors in this light, the Japanese showed little inclination to turn to them as close partners in regionalism. Their planning took Koreans for granted, assuming that they would join whatever scheme that was adopted without crediting the South Koreans with an active role in its creation.

South Koreans were looking to their continental neighbors for something other than the globalization sought in Washington and the regional integration favored in Tokyo. They had their eyes fixed on leverage to move Pyongyang to negotiate and to provide long-awaited maneuverability in great-power relations. Because the "northern strategy" meant building economic and political ties around the borders of North Korea, Seoul cast its lot with those making use of decentralization. Having high hopes for economic ties to China, the South was delighted with new market openings. In contrast, Koreans mainly saw Japan as a competitor with suspect motives, not as a partner in regionalism.

Seoul placed its hopes first in Moscow, laying the groundwork through the late 1980s for improved relations. When preparing for a new approach to NEA, Moscow had to face the threat of obstructionism from Pyongyang. After all, it had often feared that adventurist acts of the latter would drag it into conflict. Thus, one of its first aims in normalization with Seoul was to stabilize the regional environment to end this threat. Already in 1989 Moscow's decision to switch to hard-currency trade with the North was bringing a freefall in trade. The decision to normalize ties with Seoul brought a second shock to relations, but Moscow expected a big economic payoff from Seoul. It could sell the new deal at home as a turn from geopolitical

85 Kanno Tomoko, *Suki ni natte wa ikenai kuni* (Tokyo: Bungei shunju, 2000), pp. 93, 95.

86 Kanno Tomoko, *Suki ni natte wa ikenai kuni*, pp. 98–104.

confrontation to economic cooperation and entry in a dynamic region. The economic benefits, however, proved ephemeral. When the strategy for using funds proved to be deeply flawed and the loans were suspended before all of the planned funds had been released, Russians tended more to blame the South for not fulfilling its part of the agreement rather than blaming their own government and business community for creating an inhospitable environment. It was easier to find fault with others for rejecting Russia as a regional partner than to reflect on why a country, without the great-power ambitions of the United States, China, or Japan, should also be aiming to force Russia into a kind of colonialism and steal its natural resources.

South Korean ties to Russia were personalized. Even before Kim Youngsam became president, he had become a central figure in meetings with top leaders in Moscow, while the chairman of Hyundai after a January 1989 trip was the leading business figure. Their efforts, bolstered by a large economic mission and a sustained message that Seoul really needs Moscow for political reasons, helped to entice Gorbachev into the establishment of consular departments in December 1989 and later embassies. In 1992–3 when Moscow did not repay its debts, personal ties helped smooth the first political transition in Seoul. Politics stayed in the forefront. Relations hardly needed to be renewed after Kim took power in 1993, although a change in administration in 1998 following the sudden decline in Hyundai business fortunes was more serious.

Although Seoul benefited by the collapse of the Soviet Union as Moscow tilted to it, the souring of relations between Moscow and Pyongyang and the sharp deterioration in Russia's economy meant that the decision to provide $3 billion in credits was bringing little in return. If Yeltsin during his November 1992 trip to Seoul soothed concerns by announcing that Moscow would stop arming Pyongyang, by 1994 the tone had changed to brushing aside Seoul's concerns in order to gain leverage over the peninsula. At the same time, expectations from trade and investment in the Russian Far East had dimmed. Seoul had to think anew about how it fit into the great-power strategies of NEA.

Whereas Japanese exports to Russia through 1992 had been ten times those of South Korea, the South caught up quickly and in 1995 surpassed Japan's total.[87] Its direct investment also surpassed that of Japan, although both were rather paltry. The South's linkages centered on the Russian Far East, unlike other foreign states that concentrated in Moscow. Despite the criminalized environment, Seoul persisted longer than Japan or China with this localized strategy. Its "border fever" had a political imperative.

After South Korea realized that its breakthrough in relations with Russia would bring few additional economic or political benefits, it was China

[87] I Yun, "Hanguk gwa Roshia kan muyok oe tukjing gwa chonmang," in Chong Yochon, ed., *Hanro kyongje kyoryu 10 nyon e pyongga gwa Roshia kongje oe mirae* (Seoul: KIEP, 2002).

that held the key to the help it needed with the North as well as economic gains. Rediscovering China, Koreans gave vent to increasing optimism. They abruptly cut relations with Taiwan, failing to give any advance notice or to offer soothing assurances. Recalling China's place in the history of the Korean peninsula, South Koreans accentuated the positive. They credited China with an enormous positive cultural influence, while choosing not to take much notice of the fear of China at times in Korea's history or of China's role in the Korean War. Even as the decade progressed Koreans showed little concern over the possibility of a China threat.[88] This tilt to China reduced Japan's leverage in shaping regionalism.

Whereas Moscow extracted a promise of $3 billion from South Korea before agreeing to diplomatic relations, Beijing was subtler in its conditions. It took a long-term view, confident in the expansion of trade and investment as well as goodwill in the South. Instead of the sort of debate that erupted soon in Moscow about not having demanded enough money for the price it paid in its great-power standing by abandoning the North, the Chinese accepted the North's disappointment patiently while enjoying ever larger economic benefits from ties to the South. It worked hard to sustain ties with the North, sending Hu Jintao to the fortieth anniversary of the armistice and cultivating ties to Kim Jong-il before he took power. For Beijing the economic gains from regionalism did not need to be weighed against the geopolitical losses from balancing relations.

Beijing preceded Moscow in expanding trade with South Korea. Indeed, while Sino-Soviet trade rose quite rapidly to more than $1 billion in the second half of the 1980s, trade with South Korea jumped more than tenfold to nearly $6 billion in 1991. Beijing was careful, however, to let Moscow take the lead on diplomatic relations. Thus, it was able in 1990–2 to keep ties with the North from deteriorating sharply when it finally boosted political ties to the South, culminating in diplomatic relations. As the North grew more isolated, China became virtually its only economic link, accounting for most vital food and oil imports.[89] It became the pivot in a triangle with the two sides of the Korean peninsula, quietly backing gradual steps in contrast to the loud U.S. role, which took center stage as a crisis neared over nuclear weapons in 1993–4.

For a time South Koreans reacted with a mood of euphoria in 1991–2 to Russia's abandonment of the North and to the rapid growth in economic ties to China and Russia. Some spoke of a second springboard for the Korean economic miracle, a new center of which would be along a natural gas pipeline

[88] Chi Togyoku, "Hanto de kyugeki ni takamaru Chugoku no eikyo ryoku," *Sekai shuho*, August 1, 2000, pp. 33–5.

[89] Samuel S. Kim, "The Making of China's Korea Policy in the Era of Reform," in David M, Lampton, ed., *The Making of Chinese Foreign and Security Policy in the Era of Reform, 1978–2000,*" pp. 371–408.

from Siberia through the Korean peninsula.[90] After all, North Korea had given a temporary boost to regionalism when in November 1991 it designated a free-trade zone between Rajin and Sonbong close to the Tumen River and a year later agreed with China, Russia, South Korea, and Mongolia to lease some territory to foreign capital as part of the United Nations Development Program plan for the Tumen River area.[91] As late as the beginning of 1993 a high tide of regionalism occurred with Tumen at the center of calls for FEZs and decentralization linking local areas. Rhetoric aside, the North revealed no inclination for market reforms and decentralization. Above all, its leaders persisted in closing off residents from the outside world. Hostile to any form of globalization, it could not accept regionalism.

As hopes stirred for cross-border dynamism to build regionalism from the bottom, Pusan was South Korea's contender. Whereas other aspirants in Japan, China, and Russia focused on one sea, Pusan's spokesmen envisioned a two-sea region embracing both the Yellow Sea to North China and the East Sea (called the *Sea of Japan* in Japan) to the Russian Far East. Pusan would become the international business center as the most connectable city of NEA.[92] In fact, the East Sea only saw a short-term rise in trade with Russia, while the Yellow Sea became the route for labor-intensive industries such as Pusan's footwear manufacturers to be transferred to China. Along with cities facing Russia along Japan's coast, Pusan could not sustain its dreams of regionalism.

Seoul became embroiled in the enthusiasm for reducing the size of government, but, as in the case of China and Russia, calls for "small government" were belied by further increases in personnel.[93] The fusion of powerful bureaucratic offices and business interests persisted. Dreams of borderlessness through independent business interests and civil society joining hands were thwarted not only by the distrust generated in China and Russia but also by the sheer difficulty of boosting market initiatives locally. The economic boon with China accelerated, but most of South Korea was left aside.

South Koreans feared regionalism as a device for increasing their dependence on Japan even more than globalization for its potential to make harder their independence of the United States. Although a mercantile strategy had brought rapid growth with low penetration of the domestic market or foreign capital control, the South could not shake off inordinate dependence

[90] Kim Chaemyong, "Siberia kaebal un che doyak oe palpan," *Wolgan chungang*, 2 (1991), pp. 336–46.

[91] *The Japan Times Weekly International Edition*, February 15–21, 1993, p. 17.

[92] Yong-Suk Oh, "A Strategic Approach to Realizing Regional Economic Cooperation in Northeast Asia," in Kap Young Jeong and Jaewoo Choo, eds., *Towards New Dimensions of Cooperation in Northeast Asia* (Seoul: Institute of East and West Studies, Yonsei University, 1998), pp. 94–8.

[93] Park Dongsuh, "Research and Reform of Korean Public Administration: Track Adjustment," *Korean Social Science Journal*, 1 (2000), pp. 37–55.

on Japan's technology and capital goods as on the U.S. market. Growing economic interdependence within NEA seemed inevitable, but the South preferred a gradual and multilateral form of regionalism that would maximize its flexibility. The rise of China promised welcome balance. Russia provided some as well. Long-term hopes centered on the opening of North Korea and even reunification. For the moment, further economic success dulled pressures for drawing closer to Japan in an emerging region.

Overview of Regionalism

In the early 1990s regionalism heavily infused with localism was ascendant in NEA. The United States largely ignored this mood, weighing globalization far above regionalism. Japan encouraged it, even as Tokyo gave preference to globalization and saw localism as a stepping-stone for forging a region under its leadership and a means to strengthen the country's hand on a global level. Most enthusiastic were local governments and left-leaning idealists, presuming that Japanese cities would rise to the top of a vertical chain of cross-border integration or that dependence on the United States would be reduced. Also in support were Chinese local governments and, to some degree, Beijing. They assumed a horizontal pattern of natural economic territories, in which sheer numbers of traders and sojourners would determine the pattern of regionalism. Localities in the Russian Far East were eager for the attention, although cynically taking advantage of outside eagerness. In their cross-border economic forays South Koreans had narrow objectives in mind: political gains from Russia and bilateral economic integration with China. The localized option for regionalism attracted many actors, but it also revealed conflicting strategies and little readiness to pursue it fully. If globalization loomed in the distance, it seemed scarcely relevant to the ad hoc, small-scale, and often barter arrangements across long-sealed frontiers. Few recognized that nationalism had a large role in strategies for regionalism.

The strategies of 1991–3 failed for many reasons. They did not incorporate the forces of globalization that provided the glue in regionalism elsewhere. They depended on a shaky localism in countries long accustomed to overcentralization and very uneven spread of market forces. Furthermore, these strategies were sharply at variance with each other and did not take into account the forces of nationalism lurking in the background. Tokyo's strategy of regionalism plus globalization stumbled when North Korea refused to make a deal, ran into an impasse in September 1992 when Yeltsin canceled his visit, was dealt a decisive blow when Beijing not only refused to acknowledge Japan's right to political leadership but also from 1993 launched a nationalist campaign based on negative historical images of Japan to bolster the legitimacy of Communist Party rule, and failed even to consolidate its main foothold when Kim Young-sam started as president of South Korea with a more negative tone toward Japan. Meanwhile, local strategies articulated by prefectures along the Sea of Japan barely got off the ground before corrupt leaders in the Russian Far East abused their goodwill. At the end of 1993 the same local leaders dashed local strategies sought in Northeast China by nearly shutting the border to ordinary traffic and raising the specter of the "yellow peril." The United States stood by indifferent as it was never persuaded that the strategy behind regionalism served its goals of globalization.

The local areas that championed faster integration were looking back more than forward. The Russian Far East, the Chinese Northeast, and the Japan Sea coastal areas with Hokkaido all felt left behind and rather isolated by rapid transformation elsewhere in their country, while believing the political leadership in the capital owed them special treatment. Their heyday had passed – in Japan with the regional imbalance centered on the Pacific coast after 1945, in China with the priority on the Southeast coast and its special economic zones after 1978, and in Russia with the decision to stop funding the military juggernaut in 1991. Yet, they deemed themselves deserving of new largesse. They were most dependent on the old economic order, most traditional in their political and economic outlook, and they were also frustrated and persuaded that they deserved priority for their new cause. Thus, they desperately jumped on the NEA regional bandwagon, looking back to old sources of domestic support while failing to take bold steps toward external openness.

Local ties proved difficult to forge across the boundaries of NEA. There was no tradition of business networks and no historical hierarchy of cities to reestablish. Indeed, many border areas had been stripped of talent, as aging populations wrestled with dying villages and cities with little entrepreneurial spirit. Hopes for localism slipped further as initial euphoria about "local sovereignty" faded. The limited funds, power, and economic vitality of critically situated areas became more evident over the decade. A demographic time bomb was ticking, as national populations were eyeing negative growth rates, rapidly aging populations, and movement of able-bodied persons away from depressed areas. Conservative elites fortified their power, appealing to fearful populations.

In 1994 abandonment of the peripheries began. Sino-Russian cross-border trade and travel slid precipitously. The Hosokawa administration fell in Japan and with it naïve hopes of a major readjustment of center-local power. The Tumen River area development project faced the open rejection of North Korea and the barely disguised hostility of local officials in the Russian Far East. To be sure, some momentum toward decentralization would linger. National governments were prepared for political reasons to sustain the hopes of the forces of decentralization and to subsidize their localities. Shuttle traders and suitcase companies still found a niche to fill in local markets. The initial model of regionalism faded without being repudiated. While each countries' companies had a sense of failure, especially in dealings with the Russian Far East, there was no effort to draw an overall assessment. The result was another decade of trouble and criminalization.

The withdrawal of national subsidies came at different times across the region over the remainder of the decade. As new economic strategies were discussed, it was obvious that wasteful ways of the front-line localities in the search for regionalism were too costly and unwarranted by cross-border opportunities. Hokkaido banked on Sakhalin offshore oil and gas projects, but they advanced slowly and before 2003 proved of little value for nearby Japan. A worsening crisis in the Russian Far East and an unwelcoming atmosphere for Japanese businessmen produced despair when Hokkaido's Takushoku bank collapsed and with it most credit for new initiatives. Northeast China was in difficulty after China's leaders grew serious about slowing credits to debt-ridden state-owned enterprises. The Bank of China that had lent heavily to suitcase trading companies with few tangible assets found itself in particular trouble. Large cities built around natural resources discovered that the state was reluctant to pay for their services once the resources were being rapidly depleted and the operating companies forced to cut their costs. As Vladimir Putin consolidated power and launched an economic program, the Russian Far East was seen as a budget drain more than an area poised for development. One by one, each national government turned away from the NEA frontier after prospects had seemed bright. Despite residual hopes, the seeds of failure were evident by 1993.

The localities on the frontier failed to build effective horizontal linkages within their own countries or vertical alignments across borders. Vested interests in local administrations remained heavily dependent on the center and deeply suspicious of their neighbors. While talk mounted along Japan's Sea of Japan coast of an organization that would coordinate in lobbying Tokyo and pressuring Russia, it produced smoke, not fire. Similarly, proclamations of the increased clout of the Russian Far East Association were exposed as empty by the clashing policies of the various governors. There was too much pork and power available to local authorities to sacrifice for the uncertain benefits of regional leverage against distant forces. Large companies could have established branch offices and begun the vertical economic integration of NEA. This would have resulted in increased migration and mobility across borders, growing investment from financial markets, and new institutional arrangements beyond the whim of local authorities. Instead, North Korea to an extreme, Russia, despite lip service to regionalism, and other countries in NEA to a considerable degree protected their own monopolies. Such protectionism was magnified at the local level. There was no consolidation of urban networks, allowing bigger and more efficient cities and companies to reorganize the space of the region. Decentralization favored inefficient local monopolies rather than market forces. Worse, criminal groups often hijacked it to make a quick buck. Only after the 1998 Russian financial crisis did Moscow companies penetrate deeply along the Pacific. Tougher financial controls also gave established firms in Beijing and Tokyo more leverage near the NEA borders in place of the earlier, nonmarket decentralization.

However misplaced early plans were for combining localism and regionalism, they left some building blocks for substantial regionalism. The Chinese presence in the Russian Far East barely expanded over the next decade, but shuttle trade played a vital interim role before ties could be rechanneled to large energy projects that were likely to rely on Chinese labor. Links between Kyushu in Japan and Pusan in South Korea grew with expanding trade and investment, as did ties between the Seoul region and Shandong, China across the Bohai Sea. Where the economics were put on firm market footing in accord with globalization decentralization proved that it could be a boost to regionalism. Yet, regionalism stands little chance as long as Russians fear Chinese dynamism to the degree that they refuse to open a corridor to the sea while Japanese and Russians are locked into a criminalized border that defies territorial compromise. Early "border fever" faced a cold shower when it opened the way to "cross-border duplicity" on a massive scale. Distrust prevailed along national borders across NEA.

4

1994–1996

Civilizational Bridges and Historical Distrust

The year 1993 ended with the Seattle APEC summit, the first occasion when the leaders of this organization established in 1989 met to set an agenda for cooperation. This upgraded meeting conveyed the unmistakable message that a more robust organization was sought, but for what purpose? The balance between regionalism and globalization was at stake. On the one hand, Mahathir Mohammad of Malaysia had advocated creation of the EAEC to exclude non-Asians, notably all nations with white Anglo-Saxon majorities. If initially this idea had been rejected, it still resonated in some circles and talk of some sort of regional entity in NEA or together with SEA persisted. On the other hand, Bill Clinton had invited the leaders to Seattle to further institutionalize their activities within a global context, seeking a commitment to reduce trade barriers and new financial openness consistent with the U.S. global agenda. After all, the United States had greeted APEC as a mechanism for placing trans-Pacific interests over Asian ones, and in the uncertainty of 1993 after the euphoria of 1991–2 this goal required reinforcement.

In the background a transnational discussion of Samuel Huntington's provocative warning about an emerging "clash of civilizations" helped to place issues of regionalism in a context of questions of cultural disposition toward the role of the state, the place of the market, and the degree of openness to foreign ideas.[1] If APEC could be invigorated to press for rapid globalization, civilizational differences at least on the western rim of the Pacific might be submerged and more divisive regional entities would have little room to operate. While the summit gave a boost to trade liberalization, it did not manage to bridge other differences and could not preempt the search for a path toward NEA regionalism. Asian Pacific Economic Cooperation is too loose a rubric and too global to meet the needs of neighboring countries

[1] Samuel P. Huntington, "The Clash of Civilizations?" *Foreign Affairs*, Summer 1993, pp. 22–49; Samuel P. Huntington, *The Clash of Civilizations and the Remaking of World Order* (New York: Simon and Schuster, 1996).

in search of economic integration, cross-border trust, and a counterweight to U.S. power. As Washington globalizers pressed at successive summits to forge a mechanism to undercut protectionist barriers, Asian member states denied APEC a means to exert such pressure.

What civilizational bonds held promise for joining the countries of NEA? China, South Korea, Japan, and even North Korea could draw on memories of Confucianism for positive associations, contrasting harmony to Western individualism and hierarchy to the discord of a conflict of interests. They could enlarge the scope to incorporate the recently popular theme of Asian values, dramatizing a preference for the developmental state and the rejection of a human-rights agenda. If China or Russia took the initiative, the anti-Western goal of opposing the world order sought by the United States could also rise to the fore. The three civilizational themes – Confucian heritage, Asian values in development, and anti-Western diplomacy – all provided potential rallying points as regionalism in NEA shifted from the microlevel of local linkages to the macrolevel of grand designs. In the aftermath of the Seattle summit these issues drew increased attention. Already China was seen as the next challenger to the United States and a firm advocate of a multipolar world reaching across to Russia and other Asian neighbors in order to balance Western civilization.

Culture was explored most fully in the mid-1990s. With South Korea's economy riding high, China in its fastest growth spurt, and Japan still appearing to be in temporary stagnation rather than facing the collapse of its developmental model, there was talk of a common cultural foundation to the past decades of regional dynamism and the predicted Asian century ahead. Naturally, hopes turned to the uses of culture for boosting regional trust and integration. Not only on a regional level, but also in each of the countries of NEA no consensus could be reached. Vague accord on opposing U.S. cultural hegemony did not translate into shared thinking about privileging regionalism over nationalism.

If some Japanese would have welcomed a Confucian identity for regionalism, shifting attention from the half century of Japanese aggression to more than a millennium of shared heritage, most of their countrymen found the theme passé. With the LDP out of power for a year and then forced to share power with a socialist prime minister, Japan's leadership was temporarily inclined toward soothing historic grievances, but this did not lead to reaching into the past for Confucianism. The LDP was too defensive of the era of colonialism linked to Japan's unique role in leading Asia, and the socialists remained too hostile to the feudal roots of failed imperialism for either to embrace Confucianism. Also the leading corporations were too globally minded to accept a retrospective worldview that could be twisted to justify Asian values associated with protectionism. Business interests recognized Chinese and even South Korean cultural norms to be a screen for networks of corruption, doubting that if these countries did not overcome such barriers a level playing field would be possible.[2] The Japanese were attuned to civilizational differences.

No longer was the cultural rationale for regionalism centered on Tokyo. As seen in a conference on Confucianism in the fall of 1994, China used this theme to display its assertiveness in rejecting Western cultural premises, especially related to human rights.[3] Resisting "complete Westernization" and "American unlimited individualism," the Chinese interpreted modernization as absorbing traditional culture rather than erasing it, and wrote approvingly of regional commonalities creating stable societies as well as rapid economic development.[4] Yet, the Chinese rejected the idea that a "clash of civilizations" would ensue. Rather, they anticipated peaceful competition as civilizations proved their value for more development. An obvious goal was to add momentum to the decline in talk of the West being the center.[5] Such reasoning might have boosted regionalism over globalization if it had not been inextricably linked to nationalism, as seen in the worsening tenor of the Chinese reporting on Japan's history and culture. If some acknowledged that Japan had borrowed the Confucian tradition, they could not erase from their minds the image of a militarized samurai ethos wreaking devastation on their country. At the very least, they depicted the Japanese variant as a paltry imitation that needed to be refreshed by the source of Eastern civilization. In discussing cultural superiority, the Chinese were obsessed with boosting comprehensive national power for competition with the United States, not limiting the nation to regional coordination within the already confining framework of globalization.

While some were tempted to see Confucianism as a means to reconstitute a sinocentric order, far more, including guardians of socialism, were inclined to press for nationalism drawn from modern history than for a regional identity. Although insisting that ideology no longer drew them closer to the Russians, the Chinese did not hesitate to stress common values enhancing their growing partnership. Of course, Russia did not fit into a rubric of Confucianism or Asian values. Thus, resentment against U.S. hegemony and the diffusion of Western values became the essence of the shared rhetoric. This was not made easy by the clash between a Chinese tendency to accept values associated with global economic integration while opposing democracy and a new Russian habit of at least paying lip service to democratic values in the midst of suspicions about economic dependency. In fact, the Russians faced a crisis of national identity, searching in their past rather than in the West or East for a shared identity. Their distrust of regionalism and potential

[2] *Nihon keizai shimbun*, September 15, 1993, p. 9.

[3] *The Asian Wall Street Journal*, October 5, 1994, p. 1.

[4] Mo Chengzhang, "Yanjiu quantong wenhua, cujin xiandaihua jianshe," *Kongzi yanjiu*, 1995, pp. 98–100.

[5] *Renmin ribao*, June 6, 1995.

Chinese hegemony left claims of shared values little more than summit rhetoric.

Across NEA memories of historical differences overwhelmed notions of cultural commonalities. In the 1997 financial crisis it became clear that those who invoked Asian values could not be divorced from crony capitalism, antipathy to the transparency and checks and balances of democracy, and even distrust of neighboring countries. The civilizational theme was fading. Once regionalism is firmly established, culture may again be invoked to reinforce it, but we learned in the mid-1990s that culture is not likely to stimulate it to take root. The search for regionalism would turn next to great-power ties.

If the United States looked with benign neglect on regionalism associated with localism, its reaction to civilizational pretenses for regional integration was more critical. After all, its objective was to preempt exclusive regionalism confined to East Asia or SEA that might reinforce limits on free trade and eventually create a geopolitical counterweight. It sought a broad Pacific community that would facilitate global economic liberalization. After the Seattle summit APEC for a time was gaining as a venue for ambitious planning to lower trade barriers, while regional integration in NEA was left far behind. Washington seemed to have achieved its goal as the champion of an Asia-Pacific community parallel to Atlanticism. Yet, even before the Asian financial crisis brought the conflict in views more into the open, it was clear that leading Asian countries would not accept the U.S. agenda. All feared free trade on a fast track as mostly beneficial to the United States. To differing degrees, each worried about U.S. hegemonism, assuming that financially, militarily, culturally, and politically, Washington would gain a dominant position. Thus, the major parties were still searching for a vehicle separate from the Pacific community inclusive of East Asia and, in some versions, SEA states. In 1996 two venues were added: ASEAN +3, bringing China, Japan, and Korea together in the context of the annual ASEAN meeting; and Asia Europe Meeting (ASEM), allowing leaders of the Asian and European countries to meet without the United States. These loose associations gave some relief to critics of U.S. dominance. However, they did not preempt interest in a separate, substantial NEA regionalism.

In 1994 the United States and North Korea barely avoided a clash over suspected nuclear weapon development in the North. In November the Clinton administration was scarred by the success in congressional elections of the Republican right, whose rhetoric on China was often inflammatory and who criticized the compromise negotiated to halt the North Korean program in return for the establishment of KEDO to build new reactors in the North and in the interim meet some of its energy needs. In light of the new realities, Washington became more active in assuring regional security. The security dimension of globalization grew more visible. In 1995 rallying partners was not easy. That year Japan suffered one disaster after another, including the

Aum shinrikyo terrorist attack and the Kobe earthquake, while its coalition politics undermined strong leadership. Russia was mired in the first Chechen war as Yeltsin kept losing popularity and finding it necessary to bolster his nationalist credentials as a presidential election neared. Although China had joined in arranging a compromise over North Korea and, along with the United States, had entered four-party talks, its rapid arms buildup and suspected proliferation of missiles and parts for weapons of mass destruction to "rogue" states put it at loggerheads with the United States. It was China that seized the offensive, capitalizing on its growing place in the regional economy and the uncertainty in regional security. More than any other state, China was setting the terms for exploring regionalism, while Americans watched nervously.

In the mid-1990s localism was in retreat. In Russia it had turned against regionalism toward nationalism. South Korean interest in regionalism dropped now that the North loomed as a problem for great-power relations. In Japan appeals for regionalism grew fainter, apart from lingering idealism from the fading political left. Now China emerged as an equally strong advocate, but its interest shifted from the spontaneous cross-border openings of the early 1990s to a nationalist focus on shaping an environment for the rise of Chinese civilization. Confident from economic success and closer security ties with Moscow, Beijing joined Japan in placing localism low on its regional priorities.

After 1993 the initiative in regionalism was passing from Japan, troubled by both political and economic problems and at a loss to reactivate its foreign policy. Not only were there psychological barriers with each country in the region, but also unexpectedly a lack of military influence left Japan feeling weaker. If previously Russian weakness had stimulated interest around the region, it was now China's dynamism that became the driving force. Russia seized the opportunity to encourage China, although its suspicions of regionalism gave China only part of what it wanted. South Korea was growing more confident and openly critical of Japan. Even as these divergences drew attention, rapid expansion in economic integration among China, Japan, and South Korea was creating a basis for further consideration of regionalism to stabilize this process.

Globalization and the United States

Locked in bilateral struggles with China and Japan, the United States gave scant attention to a regional strategy in NEA in the first years of the Clinton administration. It fumbled for a policy as Clinton failed in his intention of linking China's human rights to most-favored nation status on trade. Many lobbies aimed to sway national policy. Before long, the growing weight of conservatives in Congress meant that even if few would object to increased trade with China, support was lacking for multilateralism involving China in new ways. This was the reality as Democrats on the left and Republicans on the right found common cause in attacks on China for one or another human-rights violation. It became more so when Republicans took the offensive in charging that China had become a security threat. Uncertain about China, the United States was inconsistent in dealing with NEA.

The first Bush presidency left a legacy of resistance to efforts to divide the Asia-Pacific with a formal organization excluding the United States. When Mahathir proposed an EAEC, there were suspicions that behind the scenes Japan was supporting a "caucus without Caucasians" as a means to become regional leader. After voicing its opposition, Washington found itself on the defensive when Japan warned that the U.S. plan for NAFTA threatens to alter bilateral relations and may force it to take like action on its side of the Pacific. Mutual doubts persisted, breaking into the open again in 1997 when nervous Americans suspected Sakakibara Eisuke of Ministry of International Trade and Industry (MITI) of being a resistor against globalization and sympathizer for Asian exclusivism, while suspicious Japanese perceived Larry Summers of the Treasury Department as a voice of U.S. domination.

In his first year in office Bill Clinton upgraded the importance of Asia, while offering a vision of a "New Pacific Community," open to global influences rather than building regional distinctiveness. He followed this call by raising the profile of APEC, turning the Seattle gathering into a summit that brought Jiang Zemin to the United States for the first meeting of Chinese and U.S. leaders since 1989. Yet, Clinton found it hard to steer a path through the thicket of tense economic negotiations with a Japan vying to overtake the United States as economic leader in NEA; a China hostile to the U.S. strategy to spread its values through globalization; a South Korea giddy with economic success based on high levels of protectionism; a prickly Russia allowing its Far East to succumb to economic chaos; and a North Korea preparing to draw attention by casting aside global safeguards in order to develop nuclear weapons. As seen in Beijing, this economically driven approach mixed with human-rights rhetoric was bound to open fissures wider and intensify competition between the United States and Japan that could be exploited by others.[6]

The Clinton foreign policy shifted in mid-term. Idealist globalization diminished as financial globalization rose, based on pressing the U.S. advantage, as did globalization focused on flexing a superpower military toward North Korea in 1994 and later toward China. Along with economics as the centerpiece, security had been boosted through a dual approach: 1) to maintain America's military presence while strengthening its alliances, especially with Japan; and 2) to develop constructive engagement with China with new attention to security while allowing human-rights issues to slip into the

[6] Jin Junhui, "An Analysis of the Clinton Administration's Foreign Policy," *CIIS International Studies*, 4–5 (1994), pp. 11–20.

background. After the scare of North Korean nuclear weapons, Washington reluctantly approved the multilateralism of KEDO as an energy trade-off, but it had no strategy for balancing diverse goals in a rapidly changing region where security issues were unsettled.

As the North Korean crisis unfolded and Sino-Russian relations started to gather momentum, the U.S. response was largely to separate the two. It was dealing with a rogue state, but not a great-power problem. Given its fading presence and dependence on international assistance, Russia might complain, but it could largely be ignored. China had to be taken more seriously, yet its agreement on KEDO allowed it only a peripheral role in propping up a collapsing regime. KEDO could prepare the way for new levels of cooperation linking security concerns to economic assistance. If heated rhetoric revealed discontent in Russia and China that slowed the pace of regionalism, the United States showed little interest as it had no vision of NEA regionalism as a positive, globalizing force.

In 1995 the U.S. approach to Japan, China, and North Korea was in flux. At last recognizing the priority of traditional security concerns in the region, the Nye Report reassured Japan that it was the "linchpin of U.S. security strategy in Asia," that the United States would keep 100,000 troops in the region, and that Japan would no longer be threatened with economic sanctions over trade disputes. No longer so idealistic in its advocacy of human rights toward China and North Korea, the United States also became more dependent on Japan. But the Japanese still felt that they were not taken seriously as a partner. In 1994 the KEDO agreement obliged Japan to pay heavily for the construction of a nuclear reactor in North Korea, in 1995 the rape of an Okinawan girl created a sensation used to question the deployment of U.S. troops, and in 1996 the move of the Seventh Fleet into the Taiwan Straits in response to Chinese missile launches nearby came without the Japanese feeling adequately consulted. Not only was an economically weakened Japan not playing the global role it had expected, a politically disheartened Japan was not satisfied with the U.S. notion of a regional partnership. U.S.-Japanese coordination was proving harder.

If the Clinton administration failed at first in pressing vigorous globalization on NEA, its adjustments in the second half of its first term placed more realistic limits on the region. Washington grew more interested in China's cooperation in the four-party talks over the Korean peninsula than in its human-rights record, and it was more concerned about Japan's agreement on security (shifting the alliance from joint defense of Japan toward support in case of emergencies outside Japanese territory) than in trade deficits. The drive for financial globalization meant that South Korea had to open its financial markets as part of a deal to gain entry into the Organization for Economic Cooperation and Development (OECD). Lingering tensions between the United States and all of the countries in NEA left ample incentive for them to pursue regionalism.

Many Republicans in Congress opposed Clinton's NEA foreign policy, rejecting compromise with China and North Korea and increasingly suspicious of Russia too. They responded with China bashing, Taiwan backing, Russia warning, and calls for North Korea containing. If Clinton's approach was lukewarm to regionalism, Congress was downright hostile. Some advocated a confrontational approach, obliging Japan and South Korea to follow the U.S. lead on globalization, in which some countries would be drawn closer and others shunted aside until they accepted a single, international agenda, which happened to be unilaterally decided in Washington. In the second half of 1996 Clinton took a conciliatory approach to Russia, feeling relieved that Yeltsin had been reelected despite dismal popularity at the beginning of the year, and to China, anxious to avoid a repeat of the showdown over Taiwan that winter. It appeared to reject unilateralism, while searching for a way to accentuate common interests with potential even for supporting regionalism. In contrast, the opposition was becoming more doubtful of multilateralism, preferring a self-righteous leadership stance regardless of its practicality. Also, nationalism in the United States complicated the environment for NEA regionalism.

By the end of 1996 the Clinton team was hopeful that it had stabilized the region. Talks with China offered hope of maintaining the status quo in the Taiwan Straits, and there was confidence that another five years of stability would be available for Russia's transition. The situation in North Korea seemed under control. Ties with Japan appeared closer. There was even hope that the new stabilization of regional relations could lead to a strategy for intensified globalization with some elements of regionalism. After winning reelection Clinton made many changes in his foreign-policy team, suggesting a fresh start with less unilateralism. China's continued rise, however, left the United States in need of its close cooperation, and China remained ambivalent in balancing regionalism and globalization.

U.S. foreign policy was threat-oriented. Memories were still fresh of the first half of the 1980s when the Soviet military threat appeared most pronounced. Early in the 1990s it was the Japanese economic threat that drew most attention. Finally, from 1996 the emerging Chinese threat to U.S. regional interests had risen to the top. It was difficult to focus on building regional cooperation involving all countries when, one after another, a threat loomed in NEA. Whereas European regionalism seemed benign because of the presence of NATO and of civilizational commonalities in countries that championed globalization, Americans could not envision regionalism in NEA without wondering about persistent security uncertainties and civilizational differences. It took a large stretch of the imagination to see regionalism as a mechanism for managing the troubles evident in the protectionism and bilateral tensions of NEA. The United States preferred globalization's clout, suspecting that regionalism would be more likely to be used against it. If early in the 1990s Japan had the initiative and failed to offer sufficient reassurance, in the mid-1990s it was China that had little interest in melding regionalism with globalization. Yet, hope for the region rose as deals were made. To Washington, regionalism was only a vague possibility to be tolerated as long as it was locked into galloping globalization. If China and Japan could both be drawn inside, the embrace might become secure.

Japan and Regionalism

At the start of the decade hopes for regionalism had been linked to assumptions that the United States was in decline while Japan was on the rise as part of an ascendant region. By the end of 1993 stories abounded on how the United States had restored its confidence while the Japanese were starting to feel unsure of themselves.[7] Even if this shift had the positive effect of Americans becoming less critical of Japan, it left the Japanese wary of their own role in globalization and even regionalism. Having struggled to approve a limited supportive role in global peacekeeping operations, the Japanese were in doubt about where they could find a real leadership role. Compounding this problem were lingering trade talks with the Clinton administration that left them feeling slighted. At the time of the APEC Osaka summit in 1995, they anxiously awaited a sense of direction in U.S. Asian policy; yet they also feared that the United States was hesitating because it objected to community consciousness in the region.[8] Indeed, some Japanese foresaw a chance for a turning point, contrasting the U.S. agenda for trade liberalization and globalization at the 1994 summit with the prospect of building a regional spirit in an agenda shaped by Japan. From this viewpoint, the United States, by concentrating its attention on human rights in China, nuclear weapons in North Korea, and selective global economic interests, had slowed regionalism and set limits on APEC's evolution.[9] Clearly, Japan was chafing for a more active role.

The Japanese in the 1990s consistently favored stable adjustments in relations without attempting to overthrow communist regimes. They lacked confidence in declarations of democracy, fearing chaos. Indeed, many feared that if they took a tough posture toward China, they would open themselves to more U.S. demands and have less likelihood of reducing dependent relations. While conservative forces in Japan gained ground in the 1990s, the United States misjudged them. In addition to economic interests, who as in the United States prefer not to antagonize China, political calculations also led to hesitancy to arouse that country if it would mean reducing Japan's diplomatic options. Aware of divisions in the United States and policy inconsistencies, the Japanese preferred to hedge their bets.

7 *Yomiuri shimbun*, November 7, 1993, pp. 6–7.
8 *Yomiuri shimbun*, November 17, 1995, p. 6.
9 *Yomiuri shimbun*, November 17, 1995, p. 3.

The Japanese grew anxious about globalization in 1993–4 for at least four reasons: 1) their own economy stagnated and LDP leadership of nearly four decades was lost, which shook confidence in the direction of their country; 2) globalization was associated with materialism and the spread of a different model for organizing society, while fears were rising about the loss of values in society as seen in school girl prostitution; 3) the United States had become more aggressive in trade negotiations, adding to a sense of vulnerability in the new era; and 4) Japan was losing leverage in great-power relations and regionalism rather than gaining as had been expected. Compounding all of these factors was the presence of another element: 5) the rise of nationalism insistent on Japan's view of the history of the region at the expense of trust by its neighbors. In May 1994 Justice Minister Nagano Shigeto called the Nanjing massacre of 1937 a "fabrication," and in August Sakurai Shin, director-general of the Environmental Agency, said that "Tokyo did not fight with the aim of waging a war of aggression, and Japan was not the only one that was wrong. . . . Although we caused trouble to Asian nations, it was thanks to us that they were able to become independent." A series of such remarks by cabinet officials aroused the rest of the region; Taipei as well as Beijing and Seoul protested.[10] Rising nationalism directed against Japan in both China and South Korea during the mid-1990s cannot be divorced from such self-defeating provocations. Lacking a global perspective, the Japanese helped to put civilizational divisions high on the agenda of a region in flux.

Falling confidence in Japan's own model for NEA was compensated by rising hopes for "neo-Asianism" as other countries of the region flourished without an obvious model. In these circumstances, it was not surprising to hear Foreign Minister Kono Yohei say that Japan is not fully "part of the West."[11] The old triangular framework of three centers of capitalism in the United States, Europe, and Japan was yielding to a new image of the West versus the East, each with its own values. Some argued that Japan should "Asianize." After all, manufacturing was moving to the mainland, cheaper Asian products were lowering domestic consumer prices, and the strong yen appeared ready to become an international currency through cooperation with nearby central banks.[12] Weakening confidence in Japanese-U.S. economic ties as well as a search for a new model for Japan's weak economy kept alive dreams of regionalism even if it was unclear what type of cultural and security ties would support regionalism that Japan could not dominate.

Japanese interest in "reentering" Asia pervades the final third of the twentieth century. There were a series of area "booms," focused in the 1960s on

[10] Virginia Sheng, "Japanese Official Chided for Remarks," *The Free China Journal*, August 19, 1994, p. 2.

[11] O. Arin, *Aziatsko-Tikhookeanskii region: mify, illiuzii i real'nost'* (Moscow: Flinta, Nauka, 1997), p. 271.

[12] *The Japan Times Weekly International Edition*, August 1–7, 1994, p. 9.

SEA for raw materials and unskilled labor, in the 1970s and early 1980s on the NIES for diligent labor and lower rungs of the production cycle, on ASEAN and Southeast China after the Plaza accord of 1985 for similar manufacturing, and from the early 1990s on East China for more varied manufacturing. As time passed, Japanese companies found that the pattern was less vertical and the competition more severe. They had lost their monopoly. Indeed, the U.S. influence exceeded that of Japan when Shanghai rose as the center of the 1990s investment boom. China increasingly defied the expected pattern in many respects. It advanced along the production ladder so fast that its exports squeezed out others from Japanese firms in SEA. Its supply of cheap labor proved limitless; so it could make use of its own internal differences to restrain rising costs. Moreover, Shanghai and Beijing advanced in some high-tech industries that began to compete with those of Japan.[13] Thoughts of Japanese-dominated regionalism faded as these realities became clear.

Diverse groups were actively discussing the nature of Japan's regional role in Asia. Each had moved beyond bilateralism in the region and with the United States to explore a regional approach. Compared to early in the decade it was recognized that countries will not consider the Japanese model of development as suitable, but that did not rule out talk of a new Japanese model or cooperation on a regional model that maintains regional values without succumbing to the Anglo-Saxon model.[14] Instead of seeing economic troubles as slowing Japan's role in the region, some argued that they were motivating corporations to advance new strategies, accelerating involvement. As before, the Japanese saw Asian countries as needing a transitional period in the shift to free market economies and democracy, arguing for slower globalization than Western leaders demand. Naturally, Japan would play a leadership role through its "soft power" and know-how as well as its dominant economy. Even those who argue that the cold war continues in Japan's vicinity often agreed that the United States cannot play the same cohesive role as before and that cohesion now must be built within the region. Taking a long-term perspective, the Japanese were discussing a regional order no longer designed by the United States and less under its hegemony. They sought more freedom of action, not a strong global order requiring a loss of much sovereignty; in other words, balance between internationalism and Asianism.[15]

In 1994–5 the security environment in NEA changed abruptly for Japan. Suddenly, North Korea loomed as a threat and steps toward unification on the Korean peninsula began to arouse concern. China's nuclear weapons

13 "Chugoku no hatten to Roshia," *Kokusai kinyu*, April 1, 2001, pp. 44–5.

14 "10th GISPRI Symposium," *GISPRI: Message from Japan*, 18 (2000), pp. 11–14.

15 Takashi Shiraishi, "Asia's Regional Order; A Two-Century Perspective," *Japan Echo*, 27(3) June 2000, pp. 9–12.

tests after the other nuclear powers had halted them aroused intense concern. Just as economic ties with China were growing rapidly, trust inside Japan was falling. In contrast to the beginning of the decade, the Japanese lost confidence in their neighbors. From 1989 through the middle of 1992 opinions of Russia had briefly become more favorable. Through the middle of 1994 opinions of China remained largely favorable. After new "shocks" from these countries, however, the public could no longer look hopefully on regionalism. Yeltsin's cancellation in September 1992 brought the favorable rating down to 15 percent, and further decline to barely 10 percent would follow. China's rating slipped below 50 percent and would soon spiral downward. Tokyo would no longer push regionalism with much enthusiasm.

Politics were also changing in Japan. The composition of the Diet shifted to favor more nationalists, a larger pro-Taiwan lobby, and fewer on the Left who sympathized with China or cultivated ties to North Korea. The mass media also was changing; newspapers on the Left moved toward the center, and those on the Right grew bolder. New journals on the Right catered to popular anxieties; alarming stories on the China threat drew readers. The bureaucracy was split into fiefdoms with clashing allegiances. The Japan Defense Agency backed strategic cooperation with the United States, necessary in order not to fall behind in developing a high-tech military. MITI promoted economic ties in NEA as elsewhere, seeing mostly gains from cooperation. The Ministry of Foreign Affairs was divided; different desks argued on behalf of different bilateral priorities. Japan spoke with many voices, leaving preferences unclear among globalization, regionalism, and nationalism.

The much-discussed collapse of Japan's political system dating from 1955 freed politicians to become more engaged in foreign affairs and right-wing LDP members from deferring to long-established groups who monopolized bilateral networks. Challenging LDP China veterans and the China desk in the Foreign Ministry as well as the Russia desk became much easier. Cabinet coordination on foreign policy also suffered. In 1996–7 the message to China became garbled. For instance, when Kato Koichi, the Secretary General of the LDP known for his engagement of China, spoke of the new defense guidelines with the United States not extending to Taiwan, Kajiyama Seiroku, the Chief Cabinet Secretary who had earlier made waves by calling for promoting trade between Okinawa and Taiwan as well as Fujian in an official public briefing,[16] responded that coverage of Taiwan could not be excluded. Diverse and conflicting messages could be heard.

The right wing felt stymied. Instead of an isolated and poor China turning to Japan for help, an assertive China riding a boom economy was taking Japan for granted. A declining Russia was not capitulating on the islands but resentfully snubbing Japan. After the nuclear weapon scare in North Korea

[16] "Media Eye Foresees New Era in Japanese Relations," *The Free China Journal*, May 9, 1997, p. 7.

Japan was left with a large bill for KEDO nuclear reactor construction but excluded from four-party talks. In South Korea the transition to civilian-ruled democracy had failed to draw the nation closer to Japan, producing instead a new wave of nationalism. All of this occurred against a reversal in fortunes as Japan's economy had fallen dormant while the United States was riding the wave of new technologies. Also humiliating was the need for coalition governments that allowed Prime Ministers Hosokawa and Murayama to speak apologetically about the past, even if they were blocked from supportive policy initiatives. Resentfully, a rising number of politicians at the national and local levels kept the rightist cause alive. They seized on U.S. trade pressure and then the rape case in Okinawa to distance Japan more from its main rival. They voted for resolutions marking the fiftieth anniversary of the Pacific War defeat that rejected apologetic wording and sometimes even offered justifications. Using the opportunity afforded by Chinese nuclear tests and renewed nationalism, they eagerly debated ways to punish China at the same time as pro-Taiwan clubs expanded. Because the left wing, driven by its nuclear allergy, agreed to suspend some ODA to China, the right wing had a chance to ride a national wave of alarm as it began to press the "China threat" argument. Losing faith in Japan's economic future, they disavowed optimism about the effects of economic interdependence. South Korea's continued dependence on Japan's economy and now a rapid increase in Sino-Japanese economic ties no longer gave hope for Japanese regional leadership. The specter of competition within NEA overtook the dream of complementarities, even if corporate decisions kept expanding economic ties.

Japan faced a crossroads in its pursuit of regionalism as it commemorated the end of the war fifty years before. It could decide that it had not achieved a real reconciliation with Asian people and redouble its efforts cognizant of the changing balance of power in NEA. Or it could hope that the ideological vacuum of the 1990s would allow it to escape from the burden of history, assuming that a need for its regional leadership would oblige its neighbors to tone down their reactions. Political parties differed in their statements on the war, but the LDP, the largest force in the Diet and the core of a coalition government, preferred to thank the spirits of the "war heroes" than to mention any aggression or make any apology.[17] When Socialist Prime Minister Murayama did apologize on August 15, opposition from the Diet majority contradicted the tenor of his message.

In early 1996 after the coalition government broke apart amidst rising tensions with China, the old Japan Socialist Party (already called the *Social Democratic Party of Japan* in English) changed its Japanese name and platform. The resurgent LDP now eyed a greater military role along with the United

[17] *The Japan Times Weekly International Edition*, August 21–7, 1995, p. 5.

States, while the Left called for an "Asia of solidarity" by nurturing regional trust.[18] This weak opposition, however, was vague in details on how to make breakthroughs on bilateral relations or anything grander. Its regionalist theme failed to win it support or to be identified as a dividing line in Japanese politics.

Critics of Japan's acceptance of capitalist, liberal ideology argued that it had failed to reposition itself for entering continental Asia. At the start of the 1990s it had hesitated to embrace the idea of an EAEC, and in 1997 it would be blocked in raising the theme of the Asian Monetary Fund (AMF). It must not keep hesitating in developing a design to bridge maritime and continental Asia through a common civilization, rejecting those who only see another version of East versus West.[19] This call to action proved insufficient in the face of rising nationalist fears along with continued pressures for globalization.

Japanese internationalism cannot be divorced from historical consciousness, which many experts agree has been filled with myths and illusions through the twentieth century.[20] Misjudgments characterized militarist thinking, Marxist thinking, and finally images of Asia in the last decades of the century. Something still seems to be missing despite widespread support for the principal tenets of internationalization. As nationalism gained ground, the Japanese made little progress in balancing regionalism and globalization.

The stagnation in Japan brought to the surface its failure to inspire respect. Its material goods had been popular, but not its ideas. If its management system had been the exception in the 1980s, the rapid loss of luster as a business innovator left the Japanese with little else. Having tried to capture both the upscale department store trade and the youth popular market, the Japanese started to find that their stores in China were losing money and their pop groups had fallen out of fashion. Asian students looked elsewhere, preferring if they had a choice not to go to Japan for study abroad. Japan's cultural leadership proved a failure, while few Japanese would consider notions of civilization from the Chinese.

Fading gradually was the ideal of "Asianism" (*Ajiashugi*) in Japan. On the Left and part of the Right it long stood as the alternative to becoming part of the West as a U.S. dependent. Through convoluted reasoning, it symbolized the path for pacifism and neutrality to one group and for overturning historical verdicts for the other. Once the USSR was a target of opportunity, then it was China and even North Korea, as seen in the Kanemaru initiative to Pyongyang in 1990. By the year 2003 South Korea, unexpectedly, became

18 *The Japan Times Weekly International Edition*, January 29–February 4, 1996, p. 4.

19 Nishiwaki Fumiaki, "Nihon gaiko: Panajiashugi e no tenkan o teichosuru," *Sekai shuho*, October 24, 2000, pp. 32–3.

20 *Yomiuri shimbun*, October 7, 1999, pp. 16–17.

the hope, however faint, for the Left. On the Right, the North Korean nuclear crisis of 2003 led to closer ties with the United States and lowered interest in "Asianism." Even as many more Japanese assumed the U.S. aims to keep NEA divided and to split China and Japan in order to ensure that the region is politically weak, they were losing faith in finding a civilizational alternative through Asia. That could not make the case for regionalism.

Japan and Russia

Russians associate resource-supplying countries with the "Third World." They comment disparagingly on the negative terms of trade that emerged in the 1960s–70s between the Soviet Union and Japan, when Asiatic Russia supplied raw materials and energy in return for Japanese industrial production and, furthermore, a trade imbalance resulted from large Soviet purchases on credit.[21] Yet, the reality of the mid-1990s was little changed: Russia exported coal, wood and wood products, fish and marine products, metals, and aluminum in return for technologically advanced products of Japanese industry. Large trading corporations such as Mitsui and Sumitomo dominated the exchange. And as plans went forward for mega projects such as the development of oil and gas deposits, most prominently offshore along the shelf of Sakhalin Island, it was the major trading companies together with the Export-Import Bank of Japan that played the leading role in conjunction with U.S. or other multinational firms. The Japanese expected more of the same, and they foresaw other Russian needs for Japan remaining high. As an example Russia's chemical industry was established with substantial assistance from Japanese companies, and now the participation of those firms rather than other foreign firms was deemed most beneficial in their modernization. Also Russia was looking to new joint ventures with Japanese firms to address three serious problems of its Far East: to develop energy supplies; to reconstruct the transportation infrastructure; and to convert the defense industry. A delegation from the business group Keidanren agreed in the summer of 1995 to assist in the construction of Khasan port, the modernization of the aging Vanino port, and the exploitation of coal deposits in Primorskii krai and Sakhalin. Such plans left the Japanese anticipating growing leverage on an increasingly poor Russia, but they overlooked both the depth of resentment and the lack of Russian commitment.

From 1994 to 1996 Russian-Japanese relations were at an impasse. The Japanese watched as Russian domestic rhetoric grew more nationalistic, doubting that they could find any signs that negotiations over the disputed islands could begin. Russians heard reports of deep distrust in Japan and saw much less interest in investment and trade than in the West, blaming the

[21] B. Afonin, "Nuzhen proryv v storonu progressa: Rossiisko-Iaponskie, torgovo-ekonomicheskie sviazi," *Rossiia i ATR*, 1 (1996), p. 5.

Japanese for holding ties hostage to territorial demands. Behind the scenes, ambassadors from the two states were quietly trying to build on the "Tokyo Declaration" of 1993, but they came to appreciate that another initiative would be needed just to break the impasse. With Yeltsin playing the nationalist card to win reelection and Japan weakened by coalition government, the timing was not propitious for an initiative.

Nationalism increasingly infused Russian foreign policy in the mid-1990s. As politicians renounced Atlanticism, the debate about national identity and priorities turned to the concept of Eurasianism. Although the impact did not bode well for globalization, the meaning of this term for NEA remained unclear. Some Japanese saw a tilt away from the West as holding promise for their relations. It was not just China that looked askance at the one-sided Western-leaning foreign policy of 1992 as unbefitting a country such as Russia. The Japanese too wanted Russia to pay more attention to diplomacy in NEA, arguing that the more it sought an influential role, the more it would value Japan's cooperation and support for full participation.[22] If most were pessimistic about bilateral relations, at least there was a basis for hope. In 1997 Prime Minister Hashimoto would appeal to this logic by presenting Japan's new approach as "Eurasian diplomacy" too. It was a stretch of imagination, however, to think that acceptance of this term could bridge the deep civilizational differences that kept being raised in explanations for stagnant relations.

The situation looked bleak in 1996 not only politically but also economically. Business ties were not progressing well. The Japanese who had formed joint ventures in Russia found it hard to make money or even to escape without losing everything. Often they could not rid themselves of bad partners until all assets had been stripped away. If the business somehow became profitable, then the Japanese partners were likely to be driven out, even by the threat or use of force. After a short-lived boom in establishing joint ventures, the number fell sharply for Japan as for Russia's other neighbors. Talks with officials in the Russian Far East and in Moscow offered little hope that the problems would be corrected. When Hashimoto promised new economic ties in return for talks on the territorial issue, it was unclear what could be achieved in this troubled atmosphere.

The local population of Sakhalin was slow to benefit from the huge investment in offshore oil and gas that was under way. Russian authorities often delayed cooperation in order to press for more funds for local companies and infrastructure, but this did not mean that they really had economic development and public welfare in mind. It was a complex problem for the multinational corporations, frustrated by local corruption and failure to adhere to promises. The one bright spot in economic regionalism was delayed

[22] Chikahito Harada, "The Relationship between Japan and Russia," *The Japan Society Proceedings*, Summer 1999, p. 35.

and was not boosting confidence that wider cooperation could be achieved, although some advances continued and became more valued as energy security rose in priority.

Moscow did not have much to offer to Japan or to the crisis-ridden economies of the Russian Far East. It was afraid to challenge nationalist critics at home or to open economic doors against the wishes of domestic interests. It did not increase centralization that could have given confidence to foreign partners bothered by arbitrary local actions; yet it also did not bolster decentralization in a way that could have raised the incentives for local authorities to make long-term decisions favorable to development. In November 1994 it proposed a free trade area covering the four islands, but Tokyo dismissed that as a ploy to accept Russian sovereignty and bail out troubled economies.[23] Through 1996 Japan remained a low priority, as did regionalism. Yet, in the hysteria over China in the Far East and the nationalistic ambivalence over China elsewhere, thoughts that Japan would be needed as a balancing influence kept percolating.

The lack of progress in Japanese-Russian relations speaks to rigidity on both sides. The Japanese kept talking about the objective of regionalism, but they were not making progress in political relations with any country in the region. If civilizational assumptions left Russia apart, they did not bring any improvement either with other nations steeped in the legacy of Confucianism. Within the Foreign Ministry great-power logic was driving officials to take a fresh look at ways to approach Moscow, while some economic circles at least deemed it advisable to build more beachheads in advance of possible openings. Skillful management of networks with Russia's new politicians and media meant that the venom of September 1992 mostly dissipated and by the presidential elections of 1996 Japan was overlooked. This made it easier to start anew.

Placing much trust in cultural ties, the Japanese never considered Russia to belong either to the advanced civilization they admired in the West nor the traditional culture they respected in East Asia. This made it unlikely that Russia could join in globalization on the basis of elections and privatization, more prized in the West, or in regionalism through entrepreneurship and informal networks expected in the East. Apart from natural resources sought by the countries of NEA, Russia held little appeal. Used to viewing rivals through the lens of national character rather than democratic symbols, the Japanese linked Russian and Soviet identity. In 2000 when Putin avowed ideals of patriotism, state power, and great-power status, one writer contrasted this identity to universal values. He warned against excessive expectations of the new leader, arguing that until order was established on the basis of

[23] Akihiko Tanaka, "The Asia-Pacific Region and Russia," in Robert D. Blackwell, Rodric Braithwaite, and Akihiko Tanaka, eds., *Engaging Russia* (New York: The Triangle Commission, 1995), p. 134.

a civil society Russia would remain a "medieval state."[24] This stress on different values reflected an inability to narrow the bilateral gap. Yet, it did not prevent Japanese leaders from seeking advantage from a breakthrough in relations.

Once Yeltsin won a second term as president, Japanese officials had reason to take a fresh look at their diplomatic options. Increasing tensions with China in 1995–6 raised the question of gaining more leverage through great-power relations. Lack of progress in ties with South Korea and pessimism over North Korea left diplomacy in NEA in a rut. The United States was eager to enlist Japan in boosting Yeltsin's standing at home after the scare of a communist challenge at the ballet box and considered the oligarchs who were working with Yeltsin worthy of international economic support. Yet, another argument was particularly persuasive in Tokyo. It was that Yeltsin in his final term had the legitimacy at home as well as the freedom from electoral considerations to agree to Japan's terms for returning four islands. Aware that Russian public opinion was not persuaded and that most politicians were strongly opposed, politicians and foreign policy officials rested all of their hopes on convincing one leader to make a bold decision. Securely in power, the LDP led by Hashimoto prepared a showy initiative to end the stagnation in relations and, simultaneously, to win acclaim for regaining the islands and transforming NEA ties and global great-power relations. They would build regionalism on the back of nationalism.

China and Regionalism

In the late 1980s many Chinese had seen the sea as the bearer of an advanced civilization that could enable China to overcome a continental orientation alleged to be responsible for backward, autocratic, inward-looking elements in its heritage. After all, global economic integration was already arriving through the Southeast coast. In the first years of the 1990s the sea also came to represent the arena of Eastern civilization, a force that created a distinct model of modernization and could be used to balance the more distant force of globalization with its more threatening Western civilization. Investments flowed into China accompanied by diaspora influences. From 1996, however, the sea rose more ominously as the site of a security challenge from Taiwan resisting appeals for unification and the United States and Japan broadening their military alliance through new guidelines. There was no easy answer to what the sea means to a nation torn between conflicting economic aspirations and expanding security interests, but China's leaders turned to nationalism rather than put their trust in shared global or regional civilization.

24 Hakamada Shigeki, "Chusei kokka toshite no Roshia," *Aoyama kokusai seikei ronshu*, 5 (June 2000), pp. 55–71.

Chinese officials made it clear that they would not tolerate efforts to sow conflict between their continental base of power and the growing maritime orientation of the national economy. While striving to bridge the gap, they embraced themes that reinforced national unity and identity. They had trouble, however, in diffusing the prosperity of the coastal areas to critical inland and border zones. In the early 1990s efforts to open borders along China's continental boundaries were aimed at multidirectional regionalism with a big role for a combined coastal and inland NEA. By the middle of the decade, however, troubles along most of the inland borders necessitated a new strategy just to calm these borders while continuing to direct energies toward the more promising coastal areas.

China's effort to quietly reposition itself at the center of at least ten neighboring states was running into difficulty. Using its infinite number of aspiring traders, abundant cheap labor, and a vast market, China had claimed to be a magnet for all around because of its stable political influence and assurances of equality between states. Indeed, its very weakness as a power and its poverty were advertised as just what was needed to join all areas in regionalism. Not the exporters of capital and technology, their main market could be the glue to hold everyone together. Rather than rich firms and powerful states pressing for control, China's upstart companies and decentralized provinces could be a basis for horizontal ties. Yet, North Korea balked at market-based economic integration, while Chinese traders with their barter methods frightened customers and businessmen in the Russian Far East. The argument that economics alone matters proved unconvincing. As China opened the many side doors along its borders, neighbors left their own open only a crack. In place of modern corporations bringing tested management and financial methods, they feared an outdated approach with reminders of China's old tribute system. Most inland neighbors had their own socialist backwardness to overcome; they were even less prepared than China to welcome modern methods. Socialist civilization cast a dark shadow on China's continental ties, while global civilization made its maritime advance.

In the start-up phase of regionalism the Chinese recognized that their country was at a disadvantage and assumed that each province or FEZ would have to make a deal to woo foreign partners. After failing to meet the competition of cheap labor in Southeast China in drawing manufacturing for global markets, Northeast provinces kept trying to lure large multinational firms to invest in resource development or high-tech industries. Many, however, feared that foreigners would take unfair advantage. Given the psychological residue from Japan's history in the region, there was special concern that it would have to accept an "equal" model of development, offering fewer benefits to its suppliers of capital and technology. Yet, those striving to convince the Japanese as well as the Koreans to choose their locale for investments often invoked history in a different manner, explaining that past ties meant familiarity and shared Confucian culture in the cooperating firms.[25]

Consistent with national goals for modernization, the cities of Northeast China targeted economic development without political reform and human resources without individualism. Their goals proved to be contradictory. If in Southeast China community traditions favored entrepreneurship, in the Northeast areas had been settled only in the twentieth century and the communist system had become most deeply implanted. At the same time as policies called for outward-looking citizens with specialized, modern skills in international cities, they also assigned to Communist Party committees the goal of rallying people to be patriotic, collectivist, and socialist. This made modernization a top-down project administered by the very people who had run old-style campaigns. Village and township enterprises were stunted, as state-owned enterprises, backed by abundant loans, retained a disproportionate presence in the Northeast provinces only to be targeted in a new wave of reforms begun in 1997.

If in the early 1990s "border fever" was driving regionalism, in the mid-1990s the capital cities of the Northeast had reasserted their primacy. As a city of 3 million with strong memories of three periods of regional leadership – developed by imperial Russia, further industrialized by imperial Japan, and heavily industrialized as the center of the Sino-Soviet socialist partnership – Harbin expected to be one of the nation's "dragon's heads." Using the underground tunnels built for defense at the end of the 1960s and then converted into subway construction before a shortage of funds interfered, Harbin claimed to have the right setting for an underground international business city. As the site for the annual fair aimed at the Soviet Union and its successor states, it expected to duplicate Guangzhou's foreign network building and contract signing that had led in that city's rise. When Harbin was authorized to form two development districts and began to regroup and change the scale of its many large and middle-sized enterprises, much was written about favorable prospects for regionalism. Yet, the dinosaurs of the state-planning era, which guzzled energy and raw materials using long-dated technology, had trouble overcoming the mentality of a planned economy. The goal of attracting Russian advanced technology and using it to capture global markets did not appeal to the Russians. The city was no longer located at the only, or even the shortest, transport axis. The Russian Far East would not tolerate making it the nexus that left them on the periphery. The second wave of local reorganization for regionalism did not result in another collapse in trade as in 1994, but it also did not raise the prospects for sustained cross-border linkages.

[25] Zhao Chuanzhun, "Guanyu zai Dongbeiya diqu jianli kuaguo qiye jituan de gouxiang," *Longjiang shehuikexue*, 1 (1992), pp. 20–5.

After winning State Council approval for the special benefits needed to achieve high-level technological and economic zones, Harbin followed with a conference in June 1993 on how to convert itself into an international economic and trade city of NEA. Papers explored ways of becoming the greatest border city by positioning itself between the newly rising small border cities and the other parts of China while linking Russia's industrial adjustment to the rising Asia-Pacific regional economy. Some papers raised big dreams such as following Shanghai and Hong Kong in striving to become one of China's first international cities or joining the ranks of Seoul and Tokyo as a Northeast Asian regional city. Others warned that proponents of a "hard" approach such as that used elsewhere to concentrate on physical infrastructure overlooked how far behind Harbin was after becoming merely a shell of what it had been, especially in its managerial thinking and culture. Plagued by economic inefficiency, it must start slowly by cultivating human resources and networks. While the former view took a campaign approach of setting the overall goal and then assigning responsibility to every office and planning unit until all chanted the same scripture, the latter hinted at the prevalence of poorly educated, corrupt leaders who prefer local protectionism rather than facilitating market competition.[26] Just at that time Beijing was curbing the investment fever across the country, dashing hopes for easy capital. Yet, until Beijing grew serious about reforming state-owned enterprises from 1997 the old ways continued in the competition to become the next dragon's head.

In 1994 Beijing seized firmer control over cross-border activities of its Northeast provinces. This strengthened the hand of Shenyang as the regional center, which was later exposed for its high level of criminal collusion between government and business. Dalian's independent leanings and pro-Japanese stance were left more isolated. The leadership of Heilongjiang wisely was replaced in early 1994 as it was considered too conservative, and new power was vested in Harbin to tighten its hold over wayward border cities. Policies toward Russia emphasized great-power partnership and military cooperation, not reestablishing economic cooperation. In particular, the Chinese soured on decentralized regionalism as causing havoc or allowing excessive foreign influence in certain areas. No strong objections were registered when the Tumen River area development planning was on the verge of dying in 1994. Although in December 1995 a new agreement for Tumen talks was signed after Beijing sided with Jilin province, this was a low priority with no realistic prospects. Beijing had recognized that Russia and North Korea were unwilling to consent to the project or to easy cross-border exchanges. It was now confident that Japan's plans for regionalism would not succeed and no counterweight would be needed in Tumen. Economic success made

[26] *Bai Haerbin jiancheng Dongbeiya zhongyao guoji jingmaoyu jingji chengshi yantaohui lunwen huibian* (Harbin: Haerbin ribaoshe, 1993).

the Chinese recognize that regional blocs in the West would not derail the overall advance of globalization.[27] A narrowly focused regionalism would not be needed. Chinese leaders gave priority to three centers – Hong Kong-Guangzhou, Shanghai, and Beijing – leaving the Northeast as a secondary interest.

Of more promise to China were South Korean ties to North China along with Japanese commercial ties across the Yellow and Bohai Seas. Economically, these could give a big boost to regionalism. Politically, however, Beijing's priority for improving relations with Moscow and patiently assisting Pyongyang furthered a different concept of regionalism. Abandoning efforts to revive local linkages aimed at regionalism, Beijing allowed nationalism to bring civilizational differences to the fore in the mid-1990s.

The Chinese worldview stressed the pursuit of national interests to divide the West. It was founded on reasoning that the principles of the world system since the nineteenth century are meant to maintain a vertical division, whether colonialism or hegemonism. In its new emphasis on human rights (another version of the long-criticized humanism) and globalization, the West is again showing a lack of respect for the nation as a unit. Japan has previously proven itself to be an imperialist power and its strategy remains to impose a vertical approach on NEA. In its peaceful evolution strategy and its policy toward Taiwan, the United States is pursuing its self-interest at the expense of China's national power. Feeling beleaguered still and determined to bind the Chinese Communist Party to the dual nationalist claims of great-power assertiveness and economic dynamism, the Chinese pressed another agenda for NEA that undermined regionalism. It was not so much an economic agenda, as increased openness and economic globalization were largely approved, as a civilizational one. Regionalism must limit cultural globalization, have an independent security dimension, and form a barrier to Western domination. This seemed unlikely as long as Japan's objective in regionalism was demeaned as both linked to U.S. manipulation of human rights and steeped in its own twisted nationalism.

China's calculations in 1994–6 drove the stake through the plans for regionalism evolving since early in the decade. All sides contributed to the reversal, but China's actions proved decisive. In important new ways they privileged: nationalism over regionalism, great-power balance over cooperation, Russian fears over reassurances to Russia through multilateral economic ties, North Korean autonomy over integration, and the "history card" against Japan over increased mutual trust. China had taken the lead in pressing for a new order, but its approach left further regionalism unattainable.

[27] Jean-Marc F. Blanchard, "The Heyday of Beijing's Participation in the Tumen River Area Development Programme, 1990–95: A Political Explanation," *Journal of Contemporary China*, 9(24), 2000, pp. 271–90.

If Japanese in the first years of the 1990s had allowed nationalism to doom their hopes for regionalism based on localism and linkages to globalization, the Chinese in the middle of the decade had even less chance of pursuing regionalism through civilizational affinities while fostering nationalism against all but economic globalization. It was now Beijing's turn to show excessive sensitivity to setbacks and allow overconfidence to blind it to the damaging impact of its foreign policies on essential partners. In 1994 nationalist remarks by officials in Japan gave added impetus to a campaign to highlight the Chinese Communist Party's role in liberating the country from the Japanese occupation and warn against a new inclination in that country to become a political and military great power. In 1995 when President Lee Teng-hui of Taiwan was allowed by the U.S. government to travel to Cornell University for a talk, Beijing perceived a big change in U.S. policy toward Taiwan and responded in ways that in fact made that outcome more likely. In 1996 its extreme reactions along with its rhetorical opposition to U.S. global power and Japanese regional power caused the sharpest downturn in the pursuit of regionalism.

China had fully emerged from the isolation it faced from 1989 and its economy was leaping ahead. Pressure from the United States was ebbing under the liberal reasoning that economic interdependence would lead to political reforms and a peaceful foreign policy. Japanese goodwill remained strong. Russia was drawing closer for security cooperation. South Korea's economic ties advanced rapidly, as its political attentiveness kept rising. The compromise reached on North Korea's nuclear program proved the indispensable role of Beijing in security matters. These circumstances gave Beijing a chance to steer regionalism forward, but it had other priorities. In 1995 a disproportionate response to the United States and Japan revealed a rising tide of nationalism that drowned out economic sprouts of regionalism and brought security questions to the forefront. If in the early 1990s Japan's overconfident leadership doomed regionalism based on opening borders to local forces, at mid-decade China's assertive nationalism made civilizational appeals divisive. Stunning economic success blinded China's leaders to the harm that could be brought by worsening images of their country in the United States and especially in Japan.

China and Japan

Consciousness inside Japan continued that Sino-Japanese relations are special. After all, Japanese had from 1972 sharply differentiated the culturally close Chinese from the distant Soviets. Many felt that the Chinese are "*dobun doshu*" (same culture, same race).[28] Along with economic and political

[28] "Chugoku no tosen tamesareru Nihon no anzen hosho senryaku," *Chuo koron*, November 1992, pp. 118–19.

exchanges, cultural awareness was anticipated as a force that could rekindle awareness of commonalities such as the "kanji cultural sphere" and smooth the way to regionalism.[29] Prepared to identify China as Confucian more than communist, Japanese were less inclined to identify themselves as part of the West in anticipation of rising regional consciousness after the end of a bipolar world.

Through 1994 Japan's leaders looked forward to becoming a bridge between China and the West, distancing themselves from claims to universal values while hinting at common regional values. Sometimes, this led to contradictory messages, telling each side what it wanted to hear. In March 1994 Prime Minister Hosokawa Morihiro said to Premier Li Peng "it is not sensible for Western countries to impose their own values of democracy upon other countries," despite saying in a briefing to reporters that he had urged China to improve its human-rights record.[30] This contradiction typifies Japan's struggle to balance regionalism and globalization. Envisioning a great-power triangle with the United States and China, opinion leaders predicted that Japan would "leave the U.S. and enter Asia" or at least that it would distance itself from the United States, drawing closer to Asia.[31] The Japanese were losing their identification with the West and aspiring to a position between two sides of the globe with economic, great-power, and even civilizational implications. For a few years, apart from Hong Kong, Japan led in investing in China. But after investments peaked in 1994, Japan was overtaken by the United States and the EU, a gap that widened as China's entrance into WTO approached. The downturn in Japan's economy was a factor. So too was the difficulty for Japan in switching from processing for exports by using cheap labor and land to producing for the Chinese market. Contrary to cultural claims, Japanese-style management does not fare well in comparison to the U.S. style in meeting the needs of Chinese employees. The Japanese are less adaptable in promoting local managers and coping with high turnover.[32] The height of competitiveness was passing as relations soured for other reasons. This result was seen too in the loss of market share to local makers, especially a decline of appliance sales for air conditioners, refrigerators, and washing machines. Only slowly did the Japanese recognize that compared to firms from the West or from overseas Chinese, their firms were slow to adapt.[33] In the mid-1990s as the Japanese began to struggle with shortcomings in management at home, they had trouble adjusting in

29 Son Byonhei, "Tohoku Ajia kyokuchiteki keizai togoron no tenkai," *Sekai keizai hyoron*, June 1992, pp. 48–55.

30 *The Japan Times Weekly International Edition*, April 4–10, 1994, p. 2.

31 *Mainichi Daily Newspaper*, November 30, 1994, p. 2.

32 Kon Kentoshi, "Nikkei kigyo no nozomashii taichu seisaku to wa," *Sekai shuho*, July 31, 2001, pp. 40–1.

33 Sha Hataaki, "Chugokujin ni keiensareru Nihonshiki keiei sutairu," *Shukan Toyo keizai*, July 28, 2001, pp. 112–13.

the newly competitive market of China. However, hopes for closer economic ties could not be suppressed at a time of stagnation in Japan and rampant growth in China. As they looked for a path to recovery, the Japanese naturally foresaw regional ties to China along with South Korea and other neighbors as essential. Before long, competitive firms were more and more persuaded by the economic case for expanding into China. Even as Japanese public opinion soured, business expectations could not be dimmed.

The Chinese pictured a battle between two rivals for cultural influence. In the early 1990s Japan was still riding the wave of global fascination as the non-Western model of modernization and the alternative to Western civilization in explanations of how a different culture could combine with development to produce a contrasting pattern of social organization and national values. The Chinese twisted these arguments to claim for Confucian societies as a whole the right to be taken most seriously as the challenger to the West, dismissing Japanese culture's special strengths and insisting that China had become the latest and already most successful modernizing alternative to the West.[34]

In one year from the fall of 1994 to that of 1995 Japanese answering that bilateral relations were not good climbed by more than 10 percent, a repeat of what had occurred in 1988–9 when the Tiananmen repression had shocked the public.[35] The "friendship mood" was fading on both sides. China's nationalism was largely responsible. It would not be easy to recover lost trust, as the public on both sides remained aroused.

The shock in Japan from the deterioration in trust with China turned assumptions about the post–cold war era topsy-turvy. Instead of passing through a long transition of learning from Japan and deferring to it, China was assertively challenging it and vying for regional leadership. Assumptions that Japan could use its vast economic superiority to keep China dependent proved false. Manufacturing firms flocked to China aware that no other place of production offered comparable attractions. If they did not move, they could not control costs to meet international competition or others might invest in China and undercut them. Because Japan's large ODA to China had become a routine and essential ingredient in relations, seen by the Chinese and others as the equivalent of war reparations, Tokyo had difficulty using it as a lever. Only in 1995–6 in response to China's defiance of world opinion to remain the last country testing nuclear weapons, conduct that resonated strongly in the only country to experience a nuclear attack, did Tokyo dare to withhold some ODA. Without other instruments to shape bilateral relations, Japan turned to the security treaty with the United States. In April

[34] Ji Genan, "Ribenren de guojiaguan yu Riben de guojia zhanlue mubiao," *Riben wenti ziliao*, 6 (1992) pp. 3–8.

[35] Amako Satoshi, "Yuko ippendo kara no tenkan," in Amako Satoshi and Sonoda Shigeto, eds., *Nitchu koryu no shiban seiki* (Tokyo: Toyo keizai shimposha, 1998), p. 22.

1996 the two allies announced a revision in their defense guidelines allowing Japan a more active role far from its shores. In the wake of the Taiwan missile crisis, controversy swirled over whether in the event of fighting between China and the United States in the Taiwan Straits Japan would supply logistical and other assistance to the United States. China's tough stance in pressuring Taiwan along with other insensitive acts soiled the climate for regionalism.

The Japanese confidence in China was eroding rapidly. Many incidents offered proof of this transformation. In the background were several prime causes: a growing disparity in security policies as China boosted its military and Japan tightened ties with the United States, shifts in domestic politics as leaders with more nationalist agendas managed relations, and a new boldness on both sides in handling sensitive historical issues.[36] In this setting the Japanese identified Chinese people and culture in a more critical way. Suddenly, the reality of communist rule of China drew much more attention. For a long time the Japanese had been prone to view Soviets as communists rather than Russians, heirs to the glorious literature of the nineteenth century, and the Chinese as the successors to the traditions that had greatly enriched Japanese civilization rather than communists. In the outrage of 1989 more Japanese saw the Chinese as communist, and, despite the decisive market opening that followed in 1992, the downturn in relations in the mid-1990s cast the Chinese as communists again. The right wing seized the opportunity to flood the bookstores and newsstands with sensational accounts of China, implying that Japan's national essence is at stake in these ties. Instead of seeking a regional bond with long-time cultural partner China, the goal had shifted to finding Japan's lost national identity by resisting the new China threat.

Why did the Chinese government grow more assertive to Japan and more negative in its presentation of that country and its history in the mid-1990s? Newfound confidence offers part of the answer. A conscious strategy to strengthen national identity and reshape foreign policy is another part. It is doubtful that the architects of this approach anticipated that the Chinese people would react so strongly that it would complicate efforts to put bilateral relations back on track. Also they may not have anticipated that the Japanese public would rally behind a more nationalist response as well as welcome closer military ties with the United States. Choosing nationalism, Beijing complicated the search for regionalism.

Chinese calculations of friction in U.S.-Japanese relations underlined an assertive regional strategy. Assuming both that a seriously hobbled U.S. economy would be driven to pour more investment into Asia and that Japan's economy would continue its advance in the region, Chinese analysts in the

[36] Michael J. Green and Benjamin L. Self, "Japan's Changing China Policy: From Commercial Liberalism to Reluctant Realism," *Survival*, 38(2) Summer 1996, pp. 35–58.

early nineties foresaw increasingly intense competition.[37] They assumed that the glue that joined the two capitalist powers as partners in security in the cold war was losing its hold. Even if Tokyo would still accept a predominant U.S. military role to contain China and North Korea, this would not suffice to limit political rivalry. In 1995–6 the same logic was used to explain why Japan's new strategy of "leaving the U.S. and entering Asia" flowed from the "flying geese model," which signified that a struggle for regional economic leadership had barely begun and created an opening favorable for China's economic development. If to 1993 the United States had been on the offensive versus Japan, in the mid-1990s, the latter, flush with capital, was supposedly taking center stage.[38]

For a time, observers appeared to be confident that U.S.-Japanese relations would unravel. In their analysis, the two allies would increasingly turn on each other after the collapse of the Soviet Union. One of the biggest differences would be Japan's goal to assume the leadership of a separate region and the U.S. determination to develop an open region under the framework of globalization. Predicting that such contradictions would not be resolved and even that a nervous United States would resort to containment efforts against Japan's economic expansion, Chinese analysts were prepared for prolonged trouble that would open the way for the rise of their own country. They also foresaw new breakout attempts by Japan to establish itself as a political and military great power in defiance of U.S. hegemonic ambitions. Such problems could not be resolved and were expected to result in serious cultural conflict. Mutual distrust for each other's culture would even turn the spotlight to a degree away from cultural clashes between China and the United States – a boon for their own country's ambitions not only as an economic and political power, but also as a civilization. Hopes were dashed, however, as Japan's decline as a cultural power amidst economic stagnation left China in the unanticipated position of facing a torrent of globalization reflecting U.S. culture. Having impeded regional identification, the Chinese were left alone to face the powerful onslaught of Western-tinged globalization.

Cultural assumptions shaped Chinese reasoning on Japan's drive to gain political power and U.S. insistence on hegemonism and power politics. Acknowledging by 1995 that Japan's economy had seriously weakened and reform would be unlikely for several years, the Chinese did not conclude that a softer line might seize this opportunity to solidify ties. Instead, they insisted that Japan's leaders would be even more assertive.[39] In the background

[37] Zhou Dongyan, "Cong Xiyatu huiyi kan Meiri de Yatai zhanlue," *Dongbeiya luntan*, 1 (1994) pp. 1–5.

[38] Yang Fan, "Yatai diqu: Meiri moca de xin zhanchang," *Shijie jingji yu zhengzhi*, 3 (1995) pp. 83–5.

[39] Li Cong, "Weilai de shijie – 2020 nian de shijie qianjing," *Taipingyang xuebao*, 1 (1995) pp. 7–10.

were assumptions about a nation unwilling to show contrition about history unreasonably pressing ahead with an agenda to impose itself on its Asian neighbors. It followed that the Japanese had not overcome the civilizational forces that had ravaged East Asia a half century earlier. Chinese analysts also depicted the U.S. imperative to dominate the region and the globe as an ideological holdover from the era of imperialism, which had been resuscitated in the cold war struggle with communism. Blaming other civilizations for aggressive motives, the Chinese failed to look forthrightly at regional divisions and what they could do to alleviate them. Claiming that they had foresworn ideology for pragmatism, China's leaders wore ideological blinders when they saw others as more ideological than they really were.

Jiang Zemin was busy consolidating political control before Deng Xiaoping died in 1997. If Deng's image was inseparably linked to economic reform and growth, Jiang's was still unsettled, and he made sure to bolster his credentials through nationalism and great-power consciousness. This boded ill for relations with Japan, seen as the main regional competitor, and eventually with the United States, which was not prepared to accept China's reasoning for sharing global power. While provincial and business leaders in the booming Southeast might have articulated different national interests, China's one-party dictatorship, reflecting conflicting interests and lingering local elites in a country divided by uneven development, allowed nationalism to prevail. As the economy roared ahead as a magnet for foreign investment, China did not seem to pay a price for its nationalism.

One Chinese analyst who followed the course of regionalism through the decade explained that through 1994 a vertical division of labor was still in existence making it difficult to achieve equal relations, which are essential as none of the great powers here is willing to accept a position of weakness. This left the national capitals wary of moving quickly. Meanwhile, Japan and South Korea needed encouragement from the Russian Far East, which they did not get, and China could not forge FEZs on its northeast borders, which prevented the model used elsewhere from working.[40] The fault was not only that of Russia and North Korea, but also that of the Northeast Chinese provinces caught between monopolistic large firms poorly prepared for external ties and a lack of vitality in small and middle enterprises. China's retreat from localism as a basis for regionalism was partly an admission that its Northeast did not have what it takes. It was also proof of distrust for opening wide in an area where Japan might reassert itself. Yet, as the pendulum swung from grassroots networks to overarching cultural themes the result was not discovery of a path to regionalism through equality, but awakening of the need to reassert great-power connections in

[40] Lu Nanquan, "Dongbeiya quyu jingji xiezuo de fazhan qushi tedian ji woguo duice," *Dongbeiya yanjiu*, 1 (1995) pp. 3–12; "Dongbeiya quyu jingji hezuo yanjiu xianzhuang he redian" (Harbin: Haerbin gongye daxue Dongbeiya jingji zhixu yanjiusuo, 1995), pp. 1–42.

order to maximize national security. Over the next years this message was to change, but it was only in December 2002 that the Japanese took notice of an entirely new, if still exceptional, message in Chinese thinking about bilateral relations, in which "Japan bashing" was repudiated and replaced by the civilizational message that its economic success represented the "pride of Asia."[41]

Russia and Regionalism

If the Chinese approached regionalism from a rush of new confidence, the Russians did so under the pale of lost bearings. They were not prepared to think seriously about economic integration because they doubted that they had assets that serve their nation well and easily succumbed to fears of how other nations would take advantage of them. The only vision that offered hope was of a recovery of enough national power to block the evil designs of others while somehow uncovering assets that would allow regionalism through equality. "The idea of a renaissance of Russia as a great power absolutely dominated in the political mentality of an overwhelming majority of Russians."[42]

After victory in the State Duma elections of December 1993 of ultranationalists and communists draped in the mantle of nationalism, the dominant national idea was belief in Russia's greatness. Only regionalism that catered to Russian power would be countenanced. This naturally led to political cooperation with China, which appealed to Russia's rightful place in a multipolar world. Such reasoning, however, left little place for Japan's leadership. Even in the case of China, Russians looked only for great-power leverage, not economic integration. The first Chechen war symbolized the nationalist thinking, while indifference to economic reforms reflected hostility toward regionalism. Blaming others, Russians found no one to trust in NEA, reasoning that: 1) others are trying to turn it into a Third World country; and 2) they want to split it and weaken it.

For Moscow it was easy to abandon a local approach to regionalism in favor of a national one. After all, the idea of regionalism never had more than a precarious hold on the governors of the Russian Far East, who had conducted cross-border diplomacy in its heyday. Leaders decided that they had to stake a national claim in the regional context. With this thinking, they found significance in the fact that Russia was not a member of APEC. Some argued that Japan was to blame, keeping Russia out as punishment for its refusal to return the islands. China catered to this psychology, joining the blame game by arguing that the United States and Japan were trying to keep

41 *Yomiuri shimbun*, December 12, 2002, p. 6.

42 Vl. F. Li, *Rossiia i Koreia v geopolitike evraziiskogo Vostoka* (XX *vek*) (Moscow: Nauchnaia kniga, 2000), p. 283.

Russia down and to exclude it, and that by strengthening ties with Beijing, Moscow could back the claim that it indeed is an Asia-Pacific country as well as a European one. Yet, Moscow did not want to rely much on Beijing. After the KEDO agreement with North Korea, in which China had joined the United States in excluding Russia, it was confirmed that China could be used, but not trusted.

Failure to be included in the KEDO agreement was a wakeup call to Russia. Holding the blueprint for construction of a nuclear power plant at the site chosen, Russia considered itself unfairly excluded from the major regional initiative to date. Moscow now turned to other means to ensure that it would not be ignored, focusing its diplomacy on Beijing. Only if security concerns became a central focus and it gained clout with at least one country in the region would it stand a chance of having its voice heard. It revived the idea of an international conference on security in the region.[43] Nobody else was interested because there was no consensus beyond a minimal accord to halt the nuclear weapons program in North Korea. Quite nettlesome was the notion that Moscow's role in coordination on the Korean peninsula was low because Beijing was cool to the idea for such a conference. One analyst contrasted its passive diplomacy with efforts by Moscow years earlier in restoring the PRC's place in the United Nations, warning that certain forces oppose a stronger geopolitical role for Russia.[44] It did not help that in Bangkok at the 1996 first meeting of ASEM with ten Asian and fifteen European states Russia was conspicuously absent, as continued to be the case at later meetings. It did not have a place on either side.

Russians talked of a region in which states decide who gets to enter on the basis of their assessment of the worthiness of other states. Signs that Russia was failing to gain a firm foothold in NEA naturally meant that others did not give it its due, ignoring what was assumed to be its key role in stability. Russians overlooked their own part in scuttling plans for economic integration and for enhancing trust. After all, they chose to put security concerns above economic openness. Frustrated when looking back over international developments since 1989, they were searching for a great-power identity that would realize so-called national interests.[45] In preparation for a difficult presidential election, Boris Yeltsin sought to convey an image of restoring Moscow's power, and NEA with its uncertain terrain provided one of the most promising sites.

Moscow turned to NEA for great-power balance, but that did not mean that Russians envisioned themselves joining Asia in the manner that they

[43] Lyudvig A. Chizhov, "Russian Ambassador's Lecture," *IIPS News*, Spring 1995, p. 3.

[44] Vl. F. Li, *Rossiia i Koreia v geopolitike evraziiskogo Vostoka (XX vek)* (Moscow: Nauchnaia kniga, 2000), pp. 275–6, 280.

[45] Dmitri Trenin, *The End of Eurasia: Russia on the Border Between Geopolitics and Globalization* (Washington, DC: Carnegie Endowment for International Peace, 2002).

viewed Europe. If they agreed that Russia was not totally a European country, they also understood that it had little in common with NEA. In 1998 one poll found 70 percent asserting that Russian culture was Western and just 17 percent that it was Eastern.[46] A mood of defending a superior Western civilization impeded trust especially in contacts with China. Nationalism was suspicious of the West, but it went further in demeaning the East. Searching for the meaning of national identity, Russians retreated to the great-power logic of the socialist era as if rejection of other civilizations somehow could produce one's own *raison d'etre*.

Russia balked at being excluded from regional issues. Moscow had given up hope for local governments to play a constructive role, fearing instead that they would damage relations with China, Japan, and even South Korea. Yet, Russians regarded Japan and the United States as inclined to ignore it on regional matters – entry into APEC, resolution of strife on the Korean peninsula, and even economic cooperation. Rather than withdrawing to focus on concerns in Europe such as the expansion of NATO or the conflict in Bosnia or concentrating on the rising instability in Central Asia, Moscow determined that it also needed to find a way to restore its influence in NEA. It turned to China, joining with it not only in pressing a global image of multipolarity but also in putting great-power security issues in the forefront of regionalism. This was its only means of inclusion, even if for Beijing a dual track of security and economics was possible with Moscow of little consequence for the buildup of economic cooperation seen in booming trade and investment ties to Tokyo and Seoul.

The situation in most of the Russian Far East was deteriorating. Even the area with the most promise, Primorskii krai, had fallen into crisis by 1996. Despite living in a country with huge oil and gas exports and the promise of more from the much-trumpeted Sakhalin shelf developments, people worried that the long winter ahead would be spent in frigid apartments with only occasional hours of electricity and hot water as well as in the tense economic state of persistent factory shutdowns. Previous winters had seen other energy crises, but this time it was worse, foreshadowed by hunger strikes by coal miners, who in protest of wage arrears shut down the area's mines, and by huge increases in energy costs imposed by Moscow and denounced by krai administrators as unbearable.[47] Eventually, Moscow bailed out the area in what would be an annual battle over resources with Governor Nazdratenko until Putin lured him away to become Minister of Fisheries.

Suffering from high railroad tariffs as well as energy costs and claiming huge unpaid debts by the central government, Primorskii krai insisted

[46] *Osennii krizis 1998 goda: rossiiskoe obshchestvo do i posle* (Moscow: PNIS: NP POSSPEN, 1998), pp. 74–5.

[47] *Krasnoe znamia*, July 5, 1996, p. 1.

that a satiated Moscow just did not understand how poor and vulnerable it is.[48] Moscow, in turn, regarded the area as a sieve for the flight of capital abroad. The struggle persisted despite political compromises, for example when Yeltsin needed local support to win reelection. During the campaign while visiting Khabarovsk on April 24, 1994 he announced a costly program for long-term development of the Far East,[49] and in a June 4 letter to residents of Primorskii krai Yeltsin recalled more than ten decisions he and his government had taken over the past three years in support of the development of the krai's economy and the social defense of its residents, which were now being accompanied by a series of new measures from payment of back wages to the go-ahead for FEZs. On the heels of these promises, in the presidential runoff election on July 3, 1996 Yeltsin won easily in the two krai of Khabarovskii and Primorskii, together half of the population of the Far East. Once again hopes had been raised, but by August again questions of blame rose to the forefront. Promises to promote the Far East through a presidential program of development were contradicted by policies that followed the election. Instead of vast new investment, the area feared that for the fourth time in a decade a national program to save it would prove to be empty rhetoric, turning promised salvation for the region into a cruel hoax. Aware that corruption doomed any initiative, Moscow had reason to turn away.

Election eve excitement about energy projects contributed to Yeltsin's strong showing. At long last Sakhalin-2 was to begin production on June 22. Two weeks earlier Sakhalin authorities presented their territory's share of the federal program for 1996–2005 unveiled by Yeltsin on April 28. It would be 48.2 trillion rubles, which would raise the percentage of this area in the total Russian Far East regional economy from 5 to 10.3 in 2005. At the same time a Khabarovsk official declared that Korea Electric and Power Corporation had agreed to invest $831 million in that city's energy stations.[50] Playing on pent-up hopes for regionalism, Yeltsin followed his April unfolding of a presidential program for the development of the entire Russian Far East and Trans-Baikal with specific bait to dangle before pockets of local residents, however unrealistic the promises. The idea that Moscow would pay a premium for boosting regionalism proved to be a fantasy.

Reform forces in Moscow had targeted Nazdratenko as one of the most serious local threats to the revitalization of Russia since the year he came to power in 1993. Apart from his demagogic interference in border demarcation

[48] *Vladivostok*, September 6, 1996, p. 8.

[49] "Vedemosti mezhregional'noi assotsiatsii 'Dal'nii Vostok i Zabaikal'e': Pasport federal'noi programmy," *Izvestiia tikhookeanskoi Rossii*, May 1996, p. 3.

[50] *Utro Rossii*, May 29, 1996, p. 29.

with China, where he cloaked himself as a nationalist defending Russian territory, the issues were largely economic such as the manner of insider privatization in the krai. Both Yegor Gaidar and Anatolyi Chubais had tangled with the governor, but Nazdratenko had powerful backers in Moscow. When Chubais emerged as the new chief of staff while Oleg Soskovets and others were ousted, the battle was renewed. This time the cause was the low energy prices in the krai, leading to indebtedness and now hunger strikes and mass walkouts. The governor was accused too of misuse of federal funds targeted earlier to pay miners' wages, and on August 14 Yeltsin issued a decree referring to the governor as not qualified and demanding a written report from him in a month. Nazdratenko backed down on energy prices and a scheduled referendum, and Yeltsin – in no health to take charge – dared not oust an elected governor on the eve of gubernatorial elections across the county. Yet, the power struggle was by no means resolved. If locals charged Moscow reformers with casting aside the interests of the region and Russia to sell themselves to foreign countries, national voices accused Nazdratenko of seeking personal riches by selling out the country and his constituents with schemes of independence.

The problems of the Russian Far East complicated regionalism. After it became clear that separatist warnings early in the decade were an empty threat, the area still symbolized four negative tendencies: 1) lawlessness and disorder verging on domination by organized crime in a region criminalized by Stalin's labor camps and the ex-convicts who had left them; 2) xenophobia expressed in paranoia about international conspiracies and even the racist notion of the "yellow peril" in what had been the front line during the Sino-Soviet dispute;[51] 3) dictatorship by local demagogues capable of arousing public animosities toward domestic and foreign conspiracies and winning popular support; and 4) desperation and even flight to avoid a miserable existence worsened by market reforms with dire warnings of mass depopulation leaving a vacuum for overpopulated China.

In place of localism in the mid-1990s local voices were joined by national ones in asserting the high priority of Far Eastern development to preserve an area essential to the country's geostrategic and geoeconomic well being. In the face of a perceived Chinese demographic threat and frayed ties to other parts of Russia due to skyrocketing transportation costs, it was assumed that Russian national interests urgently demanded a strategy to develop the Russian Far East. Many calls to action produced few concrete results.

A United States Information Agency survey in the spring of 1996 found respondents in the Vladivostok area skeptical of U.S. intentions, even in

[51] Viktor Larin, "'Yellow Peril' Again? The Chinese and the Russian Far East," in Stephen Kotkin and David Wolff, eds., *Rediscovering Russia in Asia: Siberia and the Russian Far East* (Armonk, NY: M. E. Sharpe, 1995), pp. 296–9.

comparison to the prevailing suspicions in the Moscow, St. Petersburg, and Ekaterinburg areas. While 48 to 53 percent of the sample in the other cities agreed more with the statement "the U.S. is trying to dominate the world" than with "the U.S. usually plays a constructive role in world affairs," in Vladivostok the figure was 56 percent (32 percent chose the other and 12 percent were uncertain). And while 48 to 54 percent in the other cities preferred "the U.S. is trying to reduce Russia to a second-rank power and producer of raw materials" instead of "the U.S. wants to help Russia revive, as it helped Germany and Japan revive after 1945," in Vladivostok the figure again was 56 percent (30 percent the other and 14 percent uncertain).[52] Distrust of globalization overlapped with fear of regionalism.

As suspicion of trade relations with China grew along the border of the Russian Far East in 1993–4 so did efforts to capitalize on this for political purposes. Opposition to transferring land to China in accord with the demarcation accord became a mark of nationalism. In addition, Governor Ishaev in September 1993 spoke in opposition to navigation rights already granted to the Chinese past Khabarovsk from the Ussuri onto the Amur River, charging that it worsened the border situation. Meanwhile, Nazdratenko objected to the Tumen River project in part because it would give China navigation rights to the Sea of Japan thus introducing competition to ports including Vladivostok. Through the mid-1990s demagogic rhetoric and alarmist articles reinforced these fears.

Viewed from Russia, Beijing and, especially, Heilongjiang, the principal neighbor in NEA, is driven by nationalist motives to develop cross-border ties. Repeatedly analysts pointed to some strategy or plan at work with ominous consequences. Cross-border ties appeared not as means to integration in an international or regional system, but as steps to one-sided advantage. Writing in English, Alexander Nemets typifies this psychology in his analysis of the "detailed plan of Greater Heilongjiang." Making no effort to distinguish fact from speculation, he proclaims that the goal of Northeast China is the establishment of strongholds across the border, the integration of parts of Russia into Northeast China's economic system, the formation of networks that turn officials in Moscow into Chinese "influence agents," economic expansion, and finally a new geopolitical structure with a Chinese "heartland" and a bordering "rimland."[53] Seen through a nationalist lens, measures aimed at economic cooperation in transportation and energy are twisted to signify another country's extreme nationalism, rather than being portrayed objectively with advantages for all sides of multilateral cooperation in NEA.

[52] Anatole Shub, "Four Russian Regions View the United States: a survey in spring 1996," *USIA Research Report*, Washington, DC, May 1996, p. 25.

[53] Alexander Nemets, *The Growth of China and Prospects for the Eastern Regions of the Former USSR* (Lewiston, NY: The Edwin Mellen Press, 1996), pp. 43, 49, 64, 78, 98.

China and Russia

The Chinese and Russians failed to understand American idealism or the U.S. sense of honor. They interpreted U.S. behavior as a result of other motives, agreeing that the most serious of these was a lust for power. Thus, they saw great-power hegemonism where it was not intended or may have been readily diverted. If this was just one of many images in the uncertain atmosphere of 1994–5, it grew much larger as the decade proceeded. The legacy of traditional socialist thinking about U.S. imperialism became the backdrop as the Chinese explored versions of nationalism to fill a spiritual vacuum and the Russians began a nationwide hunt for the "Russian idea" to fill the void in national identity. Joining in their rhetoric, they became civilizational as well as strategic partners of convenience.

Russia began to sell weapons to China not as part of a strategic realignment but in pursuit of military mercantilism. It needed markets after many clients had turned away or no longer could pay. In 1995–6 the economic imperative grew, but the rationale was also changing. Arms sales accelerated and began to acquire strategic significance as a means to influence a world where the United States and Japan were denying Russia influence or markets. If Russians were suspicious of China's long-term intentions and hesitated to sell the most advanced weapons and the Chinese drove a hard bargain seeking the technology to produce the weapons, the two still managed to find common ground and deliver a shared message.

In calculations of comparative power China continued to rate Russia quite high, even above Japan. Its analysts often overestimated Russia's prospects for recovery and the will of Russia's elite to sustain a challenge to U.S. power. Prime Minister Li Peng was a driving force in Chinese foreign policy at the same time as Evgenii Primakov became foreign minister in tune with the security elite who influenced Russian policy. They combined to draw Chinese and Russian nationalism closer together, a matter of embellished rhetoric that served to catch the attention of the United States and Japan and contribute to an upsurge in great-power summitry. Anti-Western nationalism forged a civilizational bond, albeit a superficial one, and raised the profile of security concerns.

The Chinese took satisfaction that security relations with Russia were completely restored. Indeed, confidence in Sino-Russian relations reshaped Chinese attitudes toward regionalism. It boosted Beijing's assertiveness to stand more firmly against the United States and Japan and to envision regionalism more as a counterweight to globalization. China made assumptions about Russia as well as appeals to South Korean nationalism that failed to encourage Japanese confidence in regionalism or reduce rising anxieties over security.

Bilateral relations between Beijing and Moscow were most plagued by local distrust in the mid-1990s. Vested interests in the Russian Far East only looked back to Moscow, not out to regional partners. They did not have any confidence in the proposed Tumen River development zone let alone the Nakhodka new FEZ wholly within Russian territory.[54] It was convenient to link their fears to charges of deviousness: by Chinese plotting covert expansion, by Moscow reformers who had acceded to Chinese demands for land, and by local reformers who weakly faced a threat. Nationalism reached a peak in Vladivostok and Khabarovsk in the mid-1990s, fueled by demagogic rhetoric.

The Chinese keep close tabs on the publications in Russia seen as hostile. From a slow start in 1992, they reached a peak in 1995, of about 150.[55] Despite a decline in the most explosive accusations in later years, the emotional legacy remained as new articles more obliquely sustained the same negative themes. During election campaigns warnings were sounded, for instance that before long Chinese armed attacks would begin and military preparations along the banks of the Amur River would be likely. Xenophobes lumped China in the Far East together with others who supposedly want Russia's extinction: the United States in the West and Turkey in the Caucasus. In the mid-1990s, the Chinese welcomed Russian anger against the West with its strong rhetoric, failing to note that Russians also blamed them. A few years later, however, the Chinese stopped accusing a few demagogues and came to attribute the problem to a hegemonic political culture with strong grassroots support. No longer justifying the new nationalism of the 1990s as a reaction to the duplicitous behavior of the West, analysts traced it to irrational psychology born in loss of national power that led to excessive fears of becoming dependent and, unlike other nations that accept Chinatowns as natural, arguments that they represent a "flood of wild animals."[56]

For a time in 1992 China was concerned about Russia siding with the United States and then the United States extending its power along China's powers from North Korea to Central Asia. Drawing lessons from the collapse of the Soviet Union, China feared that the nationality issue would spread across its borders. Yet, soon afterward, Chinese leaders determined that they would have to trust Russia to restrain Islamic fundamentalism linked to nationalism. They joined forces in Central Asia, forging a new organization named after the site of its first meeting in Shanghai. Another objective was to gain access to oil fields and begin to address the newly perceived vulnerability from rising imports.

In the 1970s Soviet experts focused on explaining what traditions in China had caused the historical abnormality of Maoism. They wrote a lot about

[54] Ludmila Zabrovskaia, "The Tumangang Project: A View from Primorie?" *Far Eastern Affairs*, 1 (1995) pp. 34–8.

[55] Li Chuanxun, "E yuandong diqu duihua yulun zhong de mouxie xiaoji qingxiang fenxi," *Xiboliya yanjiu*, 2 (2000) p. 6.

[56] Li Chuanxun, "E yuandong diqu duihua yulun zhong de mouxie xiaoji qingxiang fenxi," *Xiboliya yanjiu*, 2 (2000) pp. 7–8.

negative elements of Confucianism. By the mid-1990s some of the leading figures in the critique of Chinese civilization had transformed themselves into devotees of its positive qualities. At the Institute of the Far East, which had led the criticisms, M. L. Titarenko, the director, kept holding China up as a model for Russia. Before becoming an advisor to the International Confucian Association in Beijing, he traced Deng Xiaoping's ideas that had contributed to China's success to Confucianism. He wrote of trust, discipline, respect for authority, and other sources of stability.[57] Mostly, it was communists and those of similar outlook who used China as a positive model in Russian domestic debates, highlighting forces that preserve continuity with communism and political authoritarianism.

At the opposite end of the spectrum from Titarenko's praise of China is V. L. Larin's charge that the euphoria of rapprochement in Moscow ignores the reality of China observed in the Russian Far East. Reviewing the history of the border demarcation in the first half of the 1990s, he criticized both Moscow and leaders in the Russian Far East in this stormy process. He accused Moscow of erring in its territorial concessions of 1991 and then using Nazdratenko's tough stance as a means of pressuring Beijing. While conceding that when there was no real Chinese threat during the early 1990s Russians exaggerated what was happening, Larin warned primarily of the opposite tendency: idealizing China, humbling Russia before it, and showing weakness. He insists that the Chinese threat is coming, and Russians must be realistic about it and avoid drawing too close to a country whose civilization is incompatible with Russia's. Acknowledging the value in much of what Larin writes, Alexandr Yakovlev of the Institute of the Far East reviewed the book by concluding that the dominant factor is the common threat posed by the West, which justifies what are largely equal relations with China as opposed to the weakness in responding to the United States.[58] The Larin book and Yakovlev's response reflect the dual reasoning toward China, combining distrust with ambivalence about relations.

Sino-Russian trade dropped by 34 percent in 1994, then fluctuated between $5 and $7 billion over the following five years with Chinese exports as low as one-third of Russian ones.[59] Despite frequent references to joint efforts at overcoming trade problems, there was little mutual investment or change from commerce or barter bringing Russian fertilizers and raw materials in exchange for Chinese foodstuffs and textiles. Both sides imposed tight controls on Chinese traders and the goods they handled. It proved easier to agree on what would not be allowed than on steps to develop cooperation

57 M. L. Titarenko, *Kitai: Tsivilizatsiia i reformy* (Moscow: Respublika, 1999); *Far Eastern Affairs*, 1 (2000) pp. 78–83.

58 V. L. Larin, "Kitai i Dal'nii Vostok v pervoi polovine deviatnostiakh godakh," *Far Eastern Affairs*, 1 (2000) pp. 94–7.

59 Lu Nanquan, "Miandui 21 shiji Zhonge jingmao hezuo wenti de sikao," *Xiboliya yanjiu*, 5 (2000) pp. 3, 10.

in production and infrastructure. China kept pressing for more agricultural exports with little success.

Meanwhile, Russians had unrealistic expectations toward economic ties with China. Just as relations stagnated, they were repeating claims that economic ties were developing well and that great possibilities existed for China to use Russian machinery for modernization of factories built earlier with Russian assistance. Some imagined that firms in the Russian Far East could reorient production for export to China, while placing controls on exports of raw materials in order not to become dependent on this humiliating type of trade.[60] Fearful of a discrepancy in economic development in the two countries, their lack of realism in identifying actual problems only guaranteed that problems would not be faced. Only after Putin became president did trade finally rise rapidly.

In late 1995 a new agreement on the Tumen project was reached. Nazdratenko gave his approval in return for the promise of large infrastructure investments, but the reality of Russian antipathy to the proposed international city had not changed. A transit corridor to a Russian port offered the prospect of short-term gains without any need to allow sustained development. Meanwhile, the North Korean missile crisis awakened Russia to its loss of influence on security matters and persuaded many that, like Beijing, Moscow needed to maintain ties to Pyongyang and find advantage from security fears.

Looking back to the mid-1990s, we see Sino-Russian relations more exuberant in their claims than any other bilateral relations in NEA. Their inflated rhetoric distorted the promise of regionalism, failing to reassure the forces of globalization and raising doubts about the civilizational basis of regionalism. As Dmitri Trenin argues, the reality in the thinking of Russian elites was far more modest. They recognized that Russia needs a solid relationship with China in order to secure its territory, but they were satisfied with a narrow agenda of cooperation.[61] Lacking another agenda for regionalism, they allowed exaggerated claims of partnership versus the West to grab the limelight. Even more, the Chinese political elite trumpeted these claims in place of encouraging Russia to accept economic regionalism and of reassuring all concerned of its own embrace of regionalism.

South Korea, the Great Powers, and Regionalism

Why were ideals for regionalism less in evidence in South Korea than in China and Japan? One obvious answer is that preoccupation with North Korea was so intense that any discussion of regionalism became lost in strategies

[60] O. Davydov, "Osvaivaia novye mirovye rynki: Rossiia i Aziatsko-tikhookeanskii region," *Mezhdunarodnaia zhizn'*, 2 (1996) p. 15.

[61] Dmitri Trenin, "The China Factor: Challenge and Chance for Russia," in Sherman W. Garnett, ed., *Rapprochement or Rivalry? Russia-China Relations in a Changing Asia*, pp. 39–70.

for starting the process of reunification. In addition, the South lacks a great-power identity concerned with shaping a region that it can lead. One more factor is the weakness of decentralization in South Korea. Local areas lack the resources and even the symbols of autonomy to forge direct ties with neighboring countries, and geography is not conducive to finding obvious partners for cross-border ties except Japan, to which strong economic ties already exist and historical memories stand in the way of interest in championing other ties despite their tacit emergence. If border areas in Japan, China, and Russia have some institutional memory of earlier efforts to forge cross-border ties in the 1950s and 1960s, the South was cut off from all its neighbors except Japan until the second half of the 1980s. Finally, the South fears the dominance of others, particularly Japan; regionalism could become but one more source of dependency for a nation seeking independence at last. Only under Kim Dae-jung were there at last signs of enthusiasm for regionalism, which were magnified in 2003 by Roh Moo-hyun as the geopolitical situation was changing.

The term *globalization* (*segyehwa*) became popular in South Korea. Kim Young-sam proclaimed the "Globalization Era" and organized a "Committee for Globalization" in 1994, turning the country to financial openness in order to join the OECD and establish Korea formally as an advanced nation. In some respects this was belated recognition of the realities from the late 1980s: increased FDI to reduce production costs after rapid wage increases and currency revaluation; rising numbers of foreign workers to lower costs too; and greater openness to foreign technology to increase productivity. In the mid-1990s financial openness was expected to bring in large amounts of capital as another way to sustain high growth rates at home and allow more investment abroad, especially by chaebols now joining small and medium firms in FDI into China, but making their focus electronics, semiconductors, automobiles, and steel. Korea experienced a travel boom, as the number going overseas tripled from 1990 to 1996, and an international conference boom. But Park Sam Ock of Seoul National University concludes that much of what occurred was only "pseudo-globalization" and it failed too as regionalism. While local governments took the lead in promoting sister cities and regions, almost all other criteria related to foreign ties were overwhelmingly concentrated in and around Seoul. Unlike Greater South China, local areas in Korea were little integrated into the global economy and, later, when the economic crisis struck, they were most vulnerable and experienced much higher rates of bankruptcy. Localities lacked comparative economic advantages, kinship ties, regional identity, and other forces that helped to integrate South China with Taiwan and Hong Kong. As trade with China grew rapidly, it was essentially Seoul reaching out through individual firms, many with few linkages across Korea.[62]

[62] Park Sam Ock, "Globalization in Korea: Dream and Reality," *GeoJournal*, 45 (1), 1998, pp. 123–8.

Cross-border ties with Russia (by sea from the port of Pusan) did not lead to the same disillusionment in South Korea as elsewhere in the region. In 1994 after Sino-Russian cross-border ties had plummeted and the Japanese were deeply distrustful of Russian contacts and careful to limit their exposure north of Dalian in Northeast China, Koreans continued to be active in the Russian Far East. They too had encountered xenophobia and rapacious stripping of assets, but Hyundai working with the government in Seoul allowed political goals lingering from the "northern strategy" to guide it. This was deemed a way to keep the pressure on the North. There was also a sense of a vacuum in an area left with little support from Moscow into which Seoul could extend its weight, eventually shaping the environment for transformation in North Korea.

In 1994–6 Korea was still energetic in exploring development projects in the Russian Far East, while other countries were retreating. By early 1995 an agreement had been reached to develop a large Korean industrial park in Nakhodka providing as many as 10,000 new jobs. While Koreans were looking for an opportunity to use cheap labor (much of it from China) and to lower land costs, the Russian side never could guarantee stable conditions, providing legal protection that was approved in Moscow and financing the minimal infrastructure needed to operate. Even as the project was scaled down in later years, essential conditions were lacking to make this more than a shell of the early plan.

By the middle of 1992 Moscow had allowed relations with North Korea to slip badly. It ended military cooperation, promised to revoke the 1961 treaty of defense, and joined in pressure on the North for its nuclear program. On human rights, it began for the first time to allow lumberjacks from camps run by the North who had escaped their confinement to remain free. Economic ties to the North faded fast as Russians admitted the lousy quality of its goods. Moreover, Yeltsin transferred documents on the Korean War to the South. No wonder anti-Russian emotions ran strong in Pyongyang's elite. From the Chinese point of view and before long as seen in Russia too, this abrupt shift caused a huge loss to Russian national interests.[63] Although as early as late summer 1992 the Ministry of Foreign Affairs in Moscow began to have some success in restoring ties and by summer 1993 Russian officials had stopped using negative language about the North and begun economic normalization, the damage would be slow to heal.

Rather than acknowledging that Russia backtracked on its early commitments to South Korea, Moscow analysts reasoned that their country never received the promised flood of investments from the South; what they did get were some consumer goods of less than the best quality that could be obtained elsewhere, and few Russian exports found their way to the

[63] Zhang Wanli, "Eluosi jiachang yi Chaoxian guanxi de yitu yu yingxiang fenxi," *Dongbeiya yanjiu*, 4 (2000) pp. 37–8.

South. Analysts decided that Russia had just thrown away its assets in the North, while clumsily establishing relations with the South.[64] This justified a change in course, blaming others for not reciprocating and boosting ties to the North.

Before his arrest for leaking secrets to South Korea, Valentin Moiseev of the Foreign Ministry wrote of Russia's national interests in peace and stability rather than maintaining a balance in relations between North and South Korea. Although bemoaning the low investment by South Korean firms in the Russian economy, he noted the difficult situation on the Russian side. To be sure, Moiseev repeated Moscow's call for an international conference on the Korean peninsula, insisting that Russia could only gain from reunification. In the same journal, however, was a warning that even if trade would likely grow the period of "euphoria" in relations had ended.[65] Unlike Moiseev, others were looking for ways to boost Russia's influence through North Korea. Moscow felt compelled to build up its great-power clout before it would consider regional integration.

South Korean ties to Russia represented, above all, a means to gain leverage over North Korea. No doubt, some hoped that they would be useful in diminishing dependence on the United States, while others may have anticipated economic gains from production networks as in China and energy projects. Investments in agriculture and industry alike failed. Meanwhile, the South received marine products illegally exported from the Russian Far East, if not in the quantity going to Japan. Although the mood of optimism about Russia that had arisen from 1988 was largely gone by 1994, South Koreans kept alive a feeling of needing Russia. In June 1994 Kim Young-sam traveled to Moscow at the peak of the nuclear crisis over the North, and he showed South Korea's serious consideration of Russia's proposal for a broad conference on peace and security in NEA. Yet, in Russia the South Koreans were dismissed as ungrateful. When under U.S. pressure the South failed to buy much Russian military equipment in payment for Russian debts, some Russians felt abandoned. The cultural divide left the two sides without much trust.

In September 1994 Kim Il-sung's death came amidst Russian efforts to improve relations. Pursuit of a balance between North and South Korea could be seen in the State Duma in 1994 and in the Foreign Ministry, which offered to assist the North in rebuilding seventy Soviet-assisted factories, extended debts of more than $4 billion, and supplied fuel for rockets. But it took until 1996 for both countries to take more substantial, if still gradual

[64] Georgi Bulichev, "Russia's Korea Policy: Towards a Conceptual Framework," *Far Eastern Affairs*, 2 (2000) pp. 3–6.

[65] V. Moiseev, "Rossiia i Koreiskii poluostrov," *Mezhdunarodnaia zhizn'*, 2 (1996) pp. 45–52; O. Davydov, "Osvaivaia novye mirovye rynki. Rossiia i Aziatsko-tikhookeanskii region," *Mezhdunarodnaia zhizn'*, 2 (1996) p. 16.

measures, to improve relations. As in relations with China, Yeltsin was implementing Eurasianism to cater to popular sentiment and with little thought to regionalism.[66]

Democracy brought a downturn in South Korean attitudes toward Japan until Kim Dae-jung in 1998 boldly reversed this trend. In 1984 under 40 percent chose Japan as the country most disliked within the region, in 1988 the figure topped 50 percent, and in 1995 it was close to 70 percent.[67] Before the Asian financial crisis Koreans pragmatically placed Japan as the country from which they should learn the most, but it was also judged to be the one against which their nation most needed to guard itself. Public opinion polls showed Japan more than four times as disliked as North Korea in the mid-1990s.[68]

New confidence in relations with China and Russia may have fed a growing appetite for criticizing Japan. As in China, public criticisms of Japan mounted in the mid-1990s as an island dispute aroused a nationalist outcry (over Tokdo or Tokushima held by South Korea but newly identified by Japan in regard to 200-mile territorial boundaries at sea; as over the Sentaku or Diaoyutai islands where Japanese rightists sought to solidify Japan's hold with construction of a lighthouse to the anger of the Chinese people). In the summer of 1995 there was a campaign to contribute to one's own economy. It pressed the South Korean people not to buy Japanese tobacco, leading to *Mild Seven* no longer being displayed in stores.[69] The trade deficit with Japan was also cited as a reason for not opening Korea to Japan's mass culture. Attention to cultural differences loomed large.

A few voices in Japan argued that the key to regionalism is how other Asians view Japan, among them Koreans, who serve as a barometer testing the level of Japanese internationalization. They recognized that relations were severely unbalanced, economic ties far outpaced social ones, and an explosive situation existed whereby even a small spark could produce intense emotions. If regionalism requires balanced ties and trust and other bilateral relations in NEA are also troubled, Japan would have been wise to focus on Korea first, argued Sunobe Ryozo, former ambassador to that country.[70] Nationalists refused this counsel despite their own interest in regionalism. They did not seem to care that more Japanese liked China than South Korea, and more thought that Sino-Japanese relations were better than Japanese-South Korean relations. Failing to recognize that this outcome was largely

[66] Zhang Wanli, "Eluosi jiachang yi Chaoxian guanxi de yitu yingxiang fenxi," *Dongbeiya yanjiu*, 4 (2000) pp. 38–9.

[67] *Dong-a ilbo*, July 29, 1995, reported in Hahm Chaebong, "Remembering Japan and North Korea: The Politics of Memory in South Korea" (Seoul: unpublished manuscript, 2000).

[68] Ue Ichiro, *Rikai to gokai: tokuhain no yomu Kim Dae-jung no Kankoku* (Tokyo: Kokushokan kokai, 1998), pp. 126–41.

[69] Kanno Tomoko, *Suki ni natte wa ikenai kuni* (Tokyo: Bungei shunju, 2000), p. 64.

[70] *Ajia kara mita Nihon* (Kanazawa: Kannihonkai bunka symposium, 1993), p. 21.

Japan's own doing, many Japanese kept looking down on Koreans. They gave little thought to building regionalism through South Korea first.[71] Talk of a shared Confucian civilization made no sense when the Japanese overlooked Koreans.

Japanese leaders felt marginalized by the outcome of the Korean nuclear weapons crisis of 1994. They were inadequately consulted, left with a bill of $1 billion for the KEDO program to build a nuclear reactor in the North, and excluded from the planned four-party talks. This outcome was compounded as the Japanese watched China and Russia draw closer with geopolitical rhetoric casting Japan's notions of regional stability aside.

South Koreans were pleased with the surge of ties with China in the first half of the 1990s. The rise of trade and investment was phenomenal. By 1995 China was first as a destination for investments from the South, primarily by small and mid-sized companies. The two countries had become the third and fourth largest trading partners of each other. The mood on both sides was positive; the South took satisfaction in China's equidistance from the North and the leverage that it now had as well as in the economic benefits.[72] Despite far larger trade with the United States and Japan, one-third of the public chose China as the nation "most important to South Korea's economic well-being" – as many as named the United States and twice as many as named Japan. More also chose Japan (18 percent) than China (12 percent) as a possible threat to regional peace and stability over the next decade.[73] At this point South Korea was solidifying ties with China rather than building a bridge between China and Japan or invoking regional civilizational commonalities.

The South sought primarily two things from China: help in bringing North Korea to the negotiating table, and economic ties that allowed its firms to develop production networks in China comparable to Japanese production networks throughout much of East and Southeast Asia. Although some may have hoped for a special tie to Chinese Koreans, activating a diaspora for the benefit of the South, this was not a major goal nor was it much realized despite a rising number of Korean Chinese immigrant laborers. Moreover, the South was slow to consider how it might transform China as a future regional partner. It sufficed to picture China as posing little threat and, given the strong ties already forged with the United States and Japan, serving a positive role in balancing the South's relations.

As South Koreans took satisfaction in booming trade with China, some gravitated to the model of a linear axis to regionalism abbreviated as

71 *Yoron chosa: gaiko*, April 1994, pp. 45–7.

72 Chae-Jim Lee, "Seoul and Beijing: The Making of Cooperative Relations," *The Journal of Asiatic Studies*, 12 (1997) p. 13.

73 *Briefing paper* (Washington, DC: USIA, Office of Research and Media Reaction), November 7, 1995, p. 1.

BESETO (Beijing via Seoul to Tokyo). Flanked by Beijing and Tokyo, Seoul would become the center of the axis linking the cities that would add to their administrative centrality, leadership in high technology within their own borders, and cooperation in a new regional division of labor. Air transportation would prevail, because South Korea would remain a de facto island country and the other two cities in any case are separated by sea. As the central point, Seoul would gain new importance in air transportation and in various balancing functions. In 1997 as the nation's economic vulnerability was exposed and the pace of globalization accelerated, the idea of building a global city jointly with regional partners who could assure some balance against distant global forces spread.

South Korean idealism had a cultural twist, as did idealism in China and Japan. Each side recognized the need for some cultural component to regionalism. In Seoul there was talk of having a superior cultural mix: 1) sharing China's long-standing Confucian tradition; 2) being most familiar with Japan's twentieth-century modernization; and 3) ranking first in NEA in knowledge of Western culture. Educated Koreans prided themselves on being more open to the West than the Japanese, enabling them to combine globalization and regionalism. At times in the mid-1990s optimism of this sort could be observed, but nationalism more often found expression in negative responses to events in Japan and eagerness for improved balance in great-power relations. South Koreans were scarcely able to conceal their delight with the turn of history in the 1990s meaning that they would no longer have to be sandwiched between U.S. and Japanese power. This mattered more than serving as a civilizational bridge that could bring nations together.

In the fall of 1995 for the first time Chinese and South Korean leaders spoke together at a press conference of their criticism of Japanese historical consciousness. In contrast to a few years earlier when some Japanese were trying to get joint recognition of a shared Confucian culture as a means to regionalism, the message from Seoul suggested that regionalism should be built on a joint understanding of the history of the first half of the twentieth century.[74] Civilizational issues had taken a more threatening form for Japan.

In the mid-1990s Seoul was obliged to take some steps toward globalization and at the same time to yield to more social pressure at home, while striving to retain the core of its state-led model of development. From the global community leaders accepted the liberalization of its capital market required for joining the OECD in February 1996, and from labor and other social groups they conceded to rapid wage increases (nearly a quadrupling in one decade) and other benefits in order to win democratic elections.

[74] *Yomiuri shimbun*, November 19, 1995, p. 3.

It all seemed to be working as foreign loans flooded into Seoul and big firms invested at home and abroad at a record pace. Yet, adding rapidly to long-term and short-term indebtedness only increased Korea's vulnerability, while it was increasingly caught in a squeeze between China with its low-cost labor able to undercut traditional Korean exports and Japan with its high technology standing in the way of many new exports. Change was needed, but Koreans were not prepared for the sudden jolt that would come in 1997.

The record of the 1990s shows the acute sensitivity of South Koreans to cultural openness. Through 1998 access to television and movie theaters was barred to Japanese imports, and even after a multistage opening was announced delays followed. Only in late 2003 was the final stage reached. In addition, a bilateral investment treaty with the United States remained stalled as did any prospect of FTA negotiations by the screen quota system protective of Korean films. Cultural barriers to global and regional integration persisted.

For a time China reduced aid to North Korea, reasoning that the North had lost its strategic influence or was likely to collapse if the North's leaders did not change course. In addition, recalling that China had given aid to the North and Vietnam in the 1960s when their people were better off than the Chinese people, there was a new orientation to domestic priorities. Yet, in the second half of the 1990s China took a more favorable attitude to aid to North Korea as to Myanmar, both deemed important to regional security. Reasoning that regionalism must proceed on the foundation of the right security balance, China was in no hurry to pressure countries wary of reform to open their economies. Even as famine spread through North Korea and refugees started flooding into Northeast China, Beijing did not approve of pressure tactics to force reforms. This was reflected in an aversion to the human-rights diplomacy of the United States and claims to a different civilizational outlook about how change should be produced. China's handling of North Korea set the scene for the security problems to come.

Overview of Regionalism

By the end of 1996 economic ties among China, Japan, and South Korea had accelerated beyond expectations, but plans for regionalism had reached a dead end. Russo-Japanese relations were stagnant. Sino-Japanese relations had deteriorated sharply as measured by official rhetoric and public opinion polls. Sino-Russian relations had detoured toward great-power bravado without more than lip service to close economic ties and encouragement for others to join in economic regionalism. South Korean moves toward globalization did not bring increased trust in Japan. It was no longer persuasive to claim that economics would lead the way as the rest of the elements of regionalism fell into place. Great-power tensions and sharp cleavages in expectations would have to be addressed. Regionalism and globalization had to be better coordinated.

Explorations of civilizational commonalities proved to be a dead end at this stage of insecurity and rising nationalism. A shared Confucian identity could not represent the historic reality of East Asia when rekindled memories of Japanese imperialism blocked the view of the past. Pride in Asian values bringing faster economic growth and greater social stability slipped with Japan's stagnation and the tendency to justify human-rights abuses and excessive central power. Anti-Western thinking may have been shared, more or less, across the region, but reasons for it varied widely and its uncertain intensity could not displace even stronger reservations against neighboring nations.

Compared to Koreans, who fear being dominated by Japanese culture, the Chinese have confidence in their own identity. Not having suffered through Japanese assimilation policies or still fearing the tug of close affinity to Japanese pop culture, they were ready to give more weight to the cultural meaning of regionalism. In the 1990s cultural imports had entered from Hong Kong, Taiwan, South Korea, and the United States as well as Japan. Indeed, the Chinese welcome some balance from "Eastern civilization" with its respect for teachers and the elderly and its resistance to Western individualism. Yet, torn between clashing notions of regionalism and inclined to weigh nationalism heavily, the Chinese could not rally behind a cultural proposal with appeal to any other country.

Having realized that cultural divisions outweighed shared memories, advocates of regional cooperation decided that other reasons would have to drive formal institutional ties. Above all, security factors had to be explored, and a shared determination to face them achieved. Additionally, it would have to be clear that the principal force behind regionalism would be the political will to compete in a world headed toward WTO economic integration. Only the need for a larger scale of shared infrastructure for economic coordination and clout would bring nations together on the basis of security. The mood was changing by 1996 as security eclipsed civilization as a popular theme.

Japan's notion of "Asianism" skirted Asian concerns. China's thinking about "Eastern civilization" reverted to sinocentric assumptions. Russia's embrace of "Eurasianism" revived Soviet logic, while South Korea's belated talk of "globalization" masked hopes to cloak an unbalanced modernization model in a global mantel. The first three were blatantly antiglobal integration, and the fourth veiled long-standing resistance to globalization. The spike in cultural rhetoric that accompanied rising nationalism offered no prospect of a common denominator for a vision of regionalism against the backdrop of post–cold war American triumphalism, whose values seemed too narrowly attached to one nation to promote confidence in a diverse world. Although the multilateral emphasis in the Clinton regime provided some reassurance, lurking in the Congress were Republican fundamentalists and Democratic human-rights enthusiasts ready to impose their values.

Overconfidence across NEA had raised expectations for shaping regionalism that could not be sustained. China expected too much from its new strategic partnership with Russia and underestimated the negative fallout in Japan from its nationalist posture. With its narrow approach to civilization, it had no prospect for turning advancing economic ties in NEA into regionalism. Japan suddenly felt isolated, fearful that U.S. pursuit of China would leave it aside, angry over China's nationalistic swing, uneasy about South Korea, and at an impasse with Russia. Yet, its ambivalence about being part of the West and historic blinders toward Asia left it unable to bridge civilizational barriers. Another sharp turn in the path to regionalism could not be avoided as trust in NEA deteriorated. Those who had expected to build "Civilizational Bridges" found instead that the fiftieth anniversary of the termination of Japan's war of occupation symbolized the depth of lingering "Historical Distrust."

5

1997–1998

Strategic Partnerships and National Rivalries

In the euphoria after the end of the cold war little thought was given to great-power rivalries and balance-of-power politics. Only in 1996 did great-power relations rise to the surface again. The Taiwan missile crisis called attention to Sino-U.S. differences that could result in armed combat. Suddenly, the United States had a potential rival, whose power was growing along with determination to alter the status quo. In April Sino-Russian relations were upgraded to a strategic partnership amidst talk of how these two powers could shape a multipolar world. Now the image grew of powers cooperating to balance U.S. hegemony. The Japanese-U.S. security alliance was also strengthened with warnings that security threats loomed. This indicated that the United States was responding in NEA to build a coalition of powers. Before long Sino-U.S. negotiations accelerated with China treating them as a means to forge new strategic triangles and quadrangles. Tokyo, in turn, readied an initiative toward Moscow, suggesting that the two great powers had geopolitical as well as territorial and economic reasons to talk. A high tide of geostrategic scrambling ensued, overshadowing other aspects of regionalism. There was no imminent threat that eliminated the search for regionalism or undercut growing economic ties, but cooperation was perceived as requiring an underpinning of great-power agreement and balance.

Northeast Asia lacked a security forum, although some discussions piggybacked on the new annual ASEAN Regional Forum (ARF) in SEA. For the most part, the jockeying for great-power advantage occurred in summits between two leaders. In the exchanges on bilateral relations, each side attempted to convey that it needed the other less than the other needed it. This is China's characteristic approach so it is not surprising that as efforts proceeded to recoup from the downturn in relations with Japan in 1996 Chinese sources insisted that Japan urgently needs China due to contradictions caused by U.S. unilateralism, better opportunities through China for Asian diplomacy, and the growing significance of China for Japan's economic security amidst intensifying competition for the China market.[1] Officials placed China in the middle, pointing to Washington's newfound interest, as it turned to China for stability in the region, and to Tokyo's dead end without China.

Moscow also argued that Tokyo's push for improved bilateral relations in 1997–8 reflected its great need for Russia: as a balance in international and regional relations due to the rise of China and as a source of energy and natural resources. Aware that China had turned to it for leverage with the United States, Moscow was also laying claim to the status of pivot in great-power relations.[2] Because Tokyo was keen on enticing Moscow into serious talks it did little at first to disabuse the Russians of their lofty expectations.

Having just boosted its alliance with the United States, Tokyo was less forthright about its hopes for centrality. Yet, it noted Moscow's concerns over Beijing and proposed that the time had come when Moscow was ready to seek balance through Tokyo. Moreover, for a time it saw another opportunity to gain leverage from a falling out between Beijing and Washington. As after June 4, 1989, some Japanese anticipated a chance in 1996 for a balancing role. Later, when Tokyo grew nervous about signs of rapprochement between these two, some analysts dared to suggest that Tokyo must approach Moscow to recoup its influence.[3] Balance-of-power reasoning gained ground on all sides, although in the United States Republican critics warned that Clinton should have been concentrating more on Japan to build a strong alliance structure instead of engaging China more vigorously.

Seeking to tilt the balance, one state after another turned to great-power summitry. Yet, we should not confuse this environment for the desperate search for alliances on the eve of a great war. No side was prepared to pay a big price for changing the balance of power or really expected a sudden breakthrough. Each state understood that the overall context remained one of globalization, and increasing economic cooperation formed the backdrop for competition. Furthermore, nations were interested not only in global power, but also in the goal of regionalism. They had recognized that only the security of stable great-power relations in NEA would allow regionalism to proceed, and they were trying to find a means to that end as well as to limit growing U.S. world influence. Each assumed that its preferred balance of powers would create the desired environment.

In 1997 the Asian financial crisis shook South Korea most of all in NEA, and it was followed by the 1998 Russian financial crisis. The immediate effects were harmful to regionalism. Seoul had less capital to spend, abruptly

[1] Xu Zhixian, "Forecasting Sino-Japanese Relations in the 21st Century," *Contemporary International Relations*, September 1998, pp. 6–7.

[2] M. L. Titarenko, *Rossiia litsom k Azii* (Moscow: Respublika, 1998).

[3] Miyamoto Nobuo, "'Nichibeichuro' no shijuso no fukyowain," *Chuo koron*, 2 (1998), pp. 138–49.

curtailing investments in high-risk areas such as the Russian Far East. Its attention switched to globalization, meeting the terms of the IMF bailout and attracting capital from U.S. corporations. After sharply devaluing its currency, its market for imports declined further. Considering Japan's stagnation through much of the late 1990s, the obvious engine for the region was China's swelling economy led by exports. Investment in China in order to export beyond NEA, particularly to the United States, kept growing, but this was not sufficient to promote regionalism. With South Korea and Russia looking more doubtful for regionalism and Japan's role as leader declining, globalization moved even further ahead of regionalism. Searching for great-power leverage may have reflected doubts about regional economic leverage.

Before long, the crisis atmosphere amidst a surge of globalization actually may have given a new impulse to regionalism. In Japan many objected to the response of the United States and its rejection of regional solutions to the Asian crisis. Despite the most spending to stabilize the countries in crisis, the Japanese felt that they had been shunted aside. As U.S. triumphalism sounded across the world, the Japanese redoubled their determination to prove that the regional economy can find a distinct place in the world. Appreciative of the grave danger that a Korean meltdown would have for their country, they agreed to work more closely with the Koreans and accept more equality with China in working for economic regionalism. As some great-power stabilization was reached, the economic agenda was pushed more vigorously. By 1999 South Korea was rapidly recovering, investment and trade across the region leaped forward, and hopes for regionalism had fully revived.

The Asian financial crisis was a wake-up call to China. Enamored of Korea's model of state guidance and close state ties to large corporations in the mid-1990s, China's leaders now recognized that the separation of state and enterprise must go much further. Alarmed at the unexpected domination of the U.S. economy and United States–led global financial institutions, leaders also began to support multilateral planning for regionalism. Stronger regional economic ties could supplement a broader great-power balance in limiting U.S. control. China's deeper commitment to regionalism dates from the late 1990s.

The dynamics of regionalism changed from "Asia in Japan's embrace" to "Asia lured by the China market" even as U.S. unipolarity was consolidated. Inoguchi Takashi, a Tokyo University professor, describes this transition and Japan's combination of alarm and "multilateralizing" of its diplomatic initiatives.[4] Utilizing the more institutionalized setting of SEA, Tokyo made some progress in forging multilateral institutions for Asians alone. In addition to the ASEAN Regional Forum created in 1993 with the United States as well

4 Takashi Inoguchi, "Introduction: Japan Goes Regional," in Takashi Inoguchi, ed., *Japan's Asian Policy: Revival and Response* (New York: Palgrave, 2002), pp. 7–8.

as NEA participants, ASEAN +3 was established to bring China, Japan, and South Korea together. In 1997 Japan pressed to internationalize the yen through a new AMF. Although the idea was blocked by U.S. opposition and Chinese suspicion, before long Beijing reconsidered. Despite news headlines warning of tensions across NEA, quiet advances in regionalism were being achieved by the end of the 1990s.

The greatest change in the regional dynamic in the late 1990s came not only from the Korean financial crisis, but also from the more active Korean leadership role under Kim Dae-jung from 1998. This could be seen in both his multisided efforts to reduce tensions and his new authority as the voice of regionalism. South Korea's assumption of the middle role between China and Japan cast regionalism in a more appealing light, especially in the midst of a search for great-power balance. Also the fact that Kim Dae-jung gave the strongest endorsement of any NEA leader to the principles of globalization made this pursuit of regionalism fundamentally different from what had preceded. Instead of Japan looking to localism to carve out a separate sphere of its own or China seeking a civilizational counterpart to a Western-dominated world, South Korea was not driven by its own hunger for power nor a narrow image of a force to limit globalization. In the second half of 1999 after the war in Yugoslavia had ended, as great-power jockeying was losing momentum, the promise of Seoul's role as conciliator kept growing.

Having won the war in Yugoslavia and with Yeltsin's grudging acquiescence settled, the last obvious challenge to the extension of European regionalism to the borders of the former Soviet Union, Washington was split over how to proceed in NEA. A vocal Republican opposition objected to political engagement with China, the pursuit of North Korea along the lines set in the 1994 agreement, or even further support for Yeltsin's inconsistent efforts to reform Russia. Taking advantage of the Clinton administration's weakness at the time of the impeachment proceedings against him, it launched a steady barrage against policies of appeasement. Its views were out of touch with those inside NEA, compounding a dearth of regional strategizing in the executive branch. The result was that the United States appeared to be a bystander at the turn of the century when the most energetic wave of regionalism arose. Perceptions of its rising power from the sustained economic boom and the victory in Yugoslavia showed the futility of strategies to balance great powers, but they could not deter strategies of regionalism building on globalization.

Globalization and the United States

With the U.S. economy riding high, the Clinton administration continued its push for financial globalization. Before the Asian financial crisis and in response to it, the message remained essentially the same: globalize by opening national economies to foreign direct investment, companies to foreign shareholders, and trade to the widest range of imports. United States expectations were higher than ever. China under Prime Minister Zhu Rongji accelerated its economic reforms, especially with steps to transform the state-owned enterprises. Japan stopped appearing as a counterweight with its own management system; instead, patronizing American voices advised it to act sooner rather than later to tackle its debt burden and globalize more fully. South Korea yielded to further pressure to open its financial markets. In Russia the oligarchs now were in charge after they had found a way to get Yeltsin reelected, and he had promptly become so ill that he could not interfere with their plans even if it were his intent. Yet, amidst the good news some in the United States recognized that to make the world safe for globalization would require more than to control hot spots of potential conflict in Korea and Taiwan. It would also mean dealing with countries behaving as great powers by turning to each other to limit U.S. power.

Potentially the one great-power relationship that could challenge the United States was Sino-Russian relations. In 1997–8 the United States was relaxed about relations between China and Russia, doubting that ties would advance far or that they would, with North Korea involved, steer regionalism down a threatening path. It was not until 1999 that a kind of wake-up call came, warning that Russia was strengthening its role as engine of China's military force modernization and that bilateral ties were deepening although not to the point of an alliance. The war in Yugoslavia brought the rhetoric of strategic partnership to its highest pitch. Although some in Congress raised an alarm, the Clinton administration continued to assume that it had sufficient leverage to keep its equanimity. It did not take the scrambling for great-power leverage seriously and stuck to its basic policies.

The second potential nightmare for the United States would have been an abrupt move by Japan to look for an answer to its insecurities in the region rather than in closer ties to the United States. After the strict global conditions set by the IMF and the United States to deal with the Asian financial crisis clashed with what many Japanese deemed advisable in their own backyard, resentment of the United States intensified. This was also a time of further deterioration in the Japanese economy, when, despite strong American criticisms, the Japanese showed no alarm in comparison to the emergency felt in South Korea. Many consumers indulged themselves in luxury goods with little sense of danger.[5] If a few opposition politicians in Japan warned about insufficient globalization, they usually did not agree with U.S. impressions. For instance, opposition leader Kan Naoto said that those who associated South Korea and Japan's problems with SEA crony capitalism and corruption are mistaken. Although Japan's habit from the

[5] Kenichi Ohmae, "The Virtual Continent," *New Perspectives Quarterly*, 17(1) Winter 2000, pp. 4–6.

war era of preferentially allocating credit had proven to be a bad influence, U.S. pressure on South Korea to remove protection for its credit system in order to enter the OECD had been an error. Japan had not removed it and was better off. Kan recognized that Japan needed reforms to separate private and public and reduce the role of the center, but he was reticent to favor fundamental shifts in the system.[6] Agreement with the United States on globalization or approval of a new path for regionalism proved difficult in this atmosphere where even those politically against the LDP did not suggest an alternative. Recalling the long-time objections of the Japanese left wing to U.S. leadership in the world, Americans of all persuasions looked only to the LDP as a partner, even as nationalist voices in that party grew more critical of the United States.

In the second half of 1996 the Clinton administration was solidifying a new strategy to China – strategic engagement – after rebounding from new tensions over Taiwan. This was a time also of redoubled efforts toward Russia – more economic assistance after Yeltsin's election – despite the weakness of economic reform and state leadership. The administration had new confidence in Japan – broadened alliance – yet it did not expect much economic reform and considered the gap in power to be so great that it had little need to coordinate closely with Japan on China. Nobody responded in line with expectations: China did not compromise much on strategic matters such as export of missile technology and repaid Clinton's conciliatory remarks in Shanghai on Taiwan with a tough policy that along with its worsening human-rights atmosphere alienated U.S. public opinion. In the second half of 1998 opponents in Congress and nervous Japanese who felt bypassed by Clinton's trip increased pressure to keep Beijing at arm's length. In August 1998 Clinton's Russia policy also fell into deep trouble when Russia's economy landed in default. Even the Japan policy aroused alarm, as Republicans noted that the Japanese had lost trust in the United States and were growing more resentful of China. Without changing direction, the Clinton administration became more detached. It focused on the war in Yugoslavia and globalization, not perceiving any direct challenge in NEA. There were no ready answers when leaders in all NEA countries had their own domestic reasons for inaction on a global agenda, and there was no compelling reason why the United States would press hard to transform a region in disarray that did not pose much of a short-term threat.

Great-power maneuvering was taken calmly. The White House calculated that through subtle dialogue with Russia it could convince the Kremlin that it is not in Russia's own interest to sell advanced armaments to China, although the allure of the extra income for the Russian arms industry would be hard to resist. It assumed that Japan's ties with Russia were largely to recover

[6] Naoto Kan, "Japan: Not Enough Globalization," *New Perspectives Quarterly*, 17(1), Winter 1999, pp. 25–6.

disputed territory with little geopolitical meaning except to put pressure on China. In short, Washington was slow to recognize any challenge to U.S. leadership. The Clinton administration refused to take seriously Chinese and Russian claims that power politics had revived. Sino-Russian and Russo-Japanese relations were of little concern, as Russia did not arouse security concerns.

The nationalist upsurge associated with great-power maneuvering did, however, make some Americans nervous that the U.S. strategy was not working. Claims to "indispensability" in management of regional security issues were driving China and Russia together, as NATO expansion and interventionism along with lack of sympathy over Chechnya was riling Russia. Moscow turned more nationalistic in its foreign policy, including support for China over Taiwan. Declining confidence in U.S. management of relations with Taiwan disturbed China. The tone of criticisms against U.S. hegemonism grew quite belligerent. Sino-Russian arms deals accelerated, ranging from missile technology to fighter planes to submarines and destroyers. North Korea tested a missile over Japan and with its weapons programs and bellicose rhetoric reminded the world of its threatening posture. If some argued that the United States should ready a containment strategy, few contemplated how to shape a program of regionalism consistent with globalization.

The financial crises in countries as diverse as South Korea and Russia left many asking whether globalization demanded by "market fundamentalists" in Washington and Wall Street had not reflected "rampant arrogance, simplistic nostrums and disdain for foreign political realities...."[7] Had the Treasury Department and the IMF not forced governments into financial bubbles and premature competition among companies and then offered advice after the crisis had begun that threatened to make matters worse? While both South Korea and Russia would emerge quickly and better prepared for global and regional integration, the message conveyed to their citizens and many others in NEA was that balance had to be found in the face of unrelenting U.S. pressure to globalize. Whether the worry was "Japan passing," "Russia passing," or "China bashing," the nations of NEA reacted to the paralyzing divisions in Washington and lack of a strategy to address their needs by turning more to each other. Even as they tried great-power summit diplomacy, the goal of regionalism remained on the agenda. Unexpectedly, it was South Korea, driven by its preoccupation with the famine-ridden and bellicose North, that took the lead by capitalizing on the great-power aspirations of its neighbors, each of which was closely associated with the uncertain future of the Korean peninsula.

[7] Joseph Kahn, "Are You Better Off Now?" review of Joseph E. Stiglitz, *Globalization and Its Discontents* (New York: W. W. Norton and Company, 2002), *The New York Times Book Review Section*, June 23, 2002, p. 12.

Across SEA and NEA many decided that the financial crisis was mishandled, and the United States was largely responsible. It was faulted for viewing the problems through a global lens of one-size-fits-all rather than a regional perspective cognizant of the fundamental strengths of most of the economies in question. Belatedly, the handling improved, but not before damage was done and proof had been found for why regional management would have been more effective. Likewise, many accused the United States of being unsympathetic toward attempts within the region to act, most importantly the Japanese proposal for an AMF. While many attributed this to concern that regional financial controls would tolerate crony capitalism and other deviations from global standards, some suspected that at the root of the problem is fear of concerted regional action that would evolve into a unified voice on the global stage that would limit U.S. power. Increasingly, even Japan came to appreciate that its economy was too small to compete on the new global playing field as the huge U.S. economy added to its weight with NAFTA while the EU gained ground through a common currency and other steps. The U.S. stance on regionalism in 1997–8 remained a troubling memory not only for South Korea caught in the crisis, but also for Japan blocked in its quest for regionalism, and even for China able to exploit the fissures as it reassessed the promise of regionalism.

Japan and Regionalism

In 1996 it was obvious that Japanese foreign policy had reached an impasse. With the LDP now in control again, a determined leadership set a new course for diplomacy. Tokyo boosted security ties with the United States, somewhat repaired frayed political ties with China, and turned to Russia and South Korea for the principal diplomatic gambits to strengthen its regional standing. Yet, officials remained uneasy about unsteady relations with each of these countries. They continued to be troubled by China's assertive policies, the weakness revealed in NEA as well as SEA in the Asian financial crisis, and the depth of suspicion in South Korea. Doubts were greatest toward North Korea, even before the shock of its missile test over Japanese territory in August 1998. Losing confidence in old ways to manage a complex region, leaders grasped for new strategies. In the background rising nationalism at home limited the state's initiatives to the other countries of NEA.

It has become common to read in Japan that the postwar era has not ended. The reasoning is: 1) no peace treaty has been signed with Russia because the islands have not been returned to Japan; 2) North Korea and Japan have yet to resolve the war legacy; 3) China and South Korea still demand apologies, playing the "history card"; 4) Japan's foreign policy is still unnaturally dependent on the United States; and 5) the Japanese people have not found the confidence and national identity that will come from putting the past behind them. The political right is anxious to enter a new era. Their methods are to put pressure on Russia, China, and South Korea, reject any demands from North Korea that might interfere with the rebirth of Japanese nationalism, and proceed deliberately but cautiously toward independence from the United States. They blame weak leaders at home and campaigns of distortion and falsification abroad for lack of progress, but they focus more on boosting solidarity at home than on changing opinion abroad.[8] Accusing the main national newspapers, academic experts, and some in the Foreign Ministry of caving into foreign pressure, many warn that, through weakness, the country is in danger of taking the wrong path.[9] Their message intensified from 1996, remaining at a high pitch through 2003.

Many signs pointed to an upsurge in nationalism in 1999. Relations with China were strained, as the debate in Japan turned more pessimistic. Negotiations with Russia had stagnated. Despite new optimism about ties to South Korea, the Japanese were not confident that they would coordinate in common resistance to China with the United States. Given these varied doubts, the main tendency was to turn inward toward more reliance on Japan's own resources, including national pride and defense of national interests. At this time nationalism reasserted itself. The Diet voted to establish a joint commission on constitutional revision with the expectation that two-thirds of the members would support breaking what had been a taboo since the 1947 Constitution was adopted, and it made the Hinomaru flag and the Kimigayo anthem national institutions again to inculcate patriotic identity in schools. Also new guidelines for Japan-U.S. military cooperation were voted into law. With even half of the Democratic Party, including its leader Hatoyama Yukio, in favor of constitutional revision to boost Japan's military, it seemed as if nothing could stop the new nationalism.[10] While some on the left warned of a contest between cherished pacifism and the renewed threat of "war-ism," under pressure from globalization that was synonymous with Pax Americana,[11] others sought common ground with the right in favor of a different type of international community centered in Asia that might offer Japan a chance to bridge regions and civilizations. Nationalism was ambivalent on regionalism.

Increasingly in the second half of the 1990s momentum gathered to reassess history by rescuing the reputation of Japanese conduct during the war period and replacing approved textbooks deemed to be anti-Japanese. Critical of widespread apathy among young people, many called for a

[8] Ko Bunyu, *Tatsu o kidoru Chugoku, tora no odoshi o karu Kankoku* (Tokyo: Tokuma shoten, 2000).

[9] *Sankei shimbun*, November 11, 2000.

[10] Ishikawa Masumi, "Japan Makes a Sharp Turn to Right," *Japan – Asia Quarterly Review*, 29(2), 2000, pp. 22–5.

[11] Oda Makoto, "'Pacifism' or 'War-ism,'" *Japan – Asia Quarterly Review*, 29(2), 2000, pp. 26–8.

national history to restore self-dignity. Even as tangible results were registered in boosting national consciousness, a rise in globalization counteracted the rise in nationalism. The right wing could not be pleased at Japan's weak voice in the world arena as economic, political, and cultural forces of global integration intensified. They hardened their critique of foreign policy, targeting weak policies against China and North Korea, but not sparing the United States from criticism. At this time regionalism had failed to offer a credible vision of the future, allowing more space for nationalism. Disappointment over the state of Sino-Chinese relations left many people more receptive to scathing criticisms of China. Increasingly, the answer was sought not in reliance on the United States, but in Japan's own actions: cuts in ODA became the centerpiece of the anticipated stronger response. Preoccupation on the right with uses of history came at the expense of anticipation of future regionalism.

Many in Japan were embarrassed by the nationalist assertions of Tokyo Governor Ishihara Shintaro and other signs of backpedaling on respect for the views of Japan's Asian neighbors. They recognized that their country was sending mixed messages, adding confusion over the past without pointing the direction toward the twenty-first century. Yet, others were concerned about the quagmire of foreign-policy ineffectiveness, becoming more receptive to the clarity from Ishihara and his fellow nationalists. A false image of progress in relations with Russia as well as a breakthrough with South Korea in 1998 kept the balance on the side of the mainstream despite nationalist inroads. The United States hesitated to make common cause with the resurgent nationalists in Japan.

The debate over the direction of Japanese foreign policy was fought without much guidance from national leaders. Initiatives to boost relations with Russia or South Korea or to repair relations with China came with little reflection on global currents. Leaders even failed to convey an image of support for joining the world community. Of the prime ministers in recent decades only Nakasone Yasuhiro and Miyazawa Kiichi have spoken to a global audience. Others, including all who presided over the troubled times after the collapse of the bubble economy, seemed stiff and communicated awkwardly. Hashimoto Ryutaro showed initiative in 1997 toward Russia and strove to keep relations with China from deteriorating, but he did not become a voice to shape national or regional thinking. Only Koizumi Junichiro from 2001 offered a fresh appearance.

Many Japanese analysts bemoaned the weakness of their leaders in conducting foreign policy. For instance, one analyst compared the boldness of Kim Dae-jung, acting on his own initiative in 1998 toward Japan and bringing his fellow Koreans behind him, to the timidity of Japanese leaders, who refuse to take an initiative unless public opinion has already matured. The same person wondered why Zhu Rongji from an authoritarian country could speak in October on Japanese television in a much freer format of questions and answers than the leaders of democratic Japan.[12] What is wrong with Japan that it cannot produce an active leader in foreign policy such as Clinton or Putin? The problem extended to images of Japanese national identity, suggesting a "closed" or "stagnant" country without a commitment to principles such as refugees and democracy. Of course, those who pressed for more personal leadership differed in what they wanted to see: some favored inviting ex-president Lee Teng-Hui from Taiwan as Japanese nationalists advocated despite China's displeasure; others supported a bold deal with Russia for two islands and a treaty against the wishes of Japanese nationalists.

Japanese leaders were eager, sometimes to the point of desperation, to prove that their country deserved a voice in setting global policies. They accepted the reality of globalization, but they worried that Japan would not be granted its due place as the country with the second greatest comprehensive national power. Continuing to press for reform of the United Nations Security Council to give it a permanent role as a political power in the organization that it prized more than the United States, it also valued the G-8 sessions and when its time as host country arrived no expense was spared. One Japanese charged that in the Okinawa/Kyushu meeting of July 2000 Japan had spent almost 100 times what Germany paid for the previous year's G-8 summit. Implying that the funds were a waste, he noted that in his swan song President Clinton's heart was actually in the Mid-East talks that he had just left and in his debut Vladimir Putin came with a message on North Korea and a joint statement with China against the U.S. plan for National Missile Defense that left the prepared agenda in the shadows.[13] There was no quick fix to Japan's loss of influence.

Japan's notion of globalization is understandably more multilateral than that of the United States. It evaluates the United Nations more highly, seeking a permanent Security Council seat as a measure of economic clout and right to global leadership. It emphasizes ODA and wider ties to developing countries through assistance, believing that Japan is using its economic power as a world leader. And, until recently, it considered disarmament of nuclear weapons a priority. This leads to a different outlook on globalization, one that leaves room for regionalism. As U.S. economic, military, and cultural power grew more pronounced in the late 1990s, it was only natural for Japanese interest in regionalism to be rekindled. As nationalism gained ground, a search for a path to regionalism continued.

The Asian financial crisis led many to conclude that globalization is both a cause of trouble and a cure. If regional models of development no longer could follow their old course, it does not mean that they need to be fully

[12] Kitaoka Shinichi, "Nihon gaiko kono ichinen no tanazarashi," *Chuo koron*, December 2000, pp. 38–41.

[13] Miyamoto Nobuo, "Amasuginaika Nihon no tairoshia ninshiki," *Sekai shuho*, August 15, 2000, p. 34.

discarded. This reasoning drew Japan closer to other countries in a growing sense of shared destiny. It also forced the Japanese to think more seriously about their readiness for closer ties. In 1999 there was increased attention in Japan to the importance of English-language instruction – as the second language or even an additional official language – for both global and regional purposes. It was reported that Japan's Test of English as a Foreign Language (TOEFL) scores were the worst in East and Southeast Asia apart from North Korea.[14] Newspapers added that only Japan's government ministers, as a rule, do not communicate in English. The Japanese are still awakening to the importance of spoken English in globalization. Should English become the second language of Japan? Should conversation be stressed in school? What would be the tradeoff between loss of national culture and gain in global integration? Clearly, regionalism was also at stake. How embarrassing to claim to be the bridge between Asia and the West, while interacting with other Asians more fluent in English and often educated in Western universities! The growing economic gap with the United States made it more essential to globalize using the Internet and English as well as to regionalize with English as a means of communication.

Supporters of economic regionalism, such as the Sea of Japan rim economic sphere, kept expressing optimism. They insisted that China was focused on economic growth and would not for decades to come endanger stability. Charging that Japanese politicians are stirring up public opinion for domestic reasons, they warned that the unfortunate outcome would be more dependence on the United States, not bold advances in regional cooperation that are within Japan's grasp. Although their idealism and search for geopolitical balance to the United States was a throwback to leftist thinking, think-tank analysts and university writers made common cause with local administrations fighting for handouts from Tokyo. This was no match, however, for the geopolitical arguments on the political right or the case for globalization generated in financial circles.

The reality also left local boosterism in trouble. Even more than along the Japan Sea on Honshu, the situation in Hokkaido worsened at the end of the 1990s. Employment opportunities declined. New high school graduates gave up hope of securing a job near home and fled to Tokyo. An image spread that globalization means more concentration in Tokyo and its vicinity. At the periphery, regionalism now appeared to be just a dream with unfulfilled promises to help local areas. The debate shifted further from localism.

Worried about impending national decline due to demographic and economic reasons and calculating that U.S. unipolar hegemony would also decline and lead to the weakening of the U.S.-Japanese alliance, some analysts found another way to focus on regionalism in Northeast Asia. They

[14] Watanabe Shoichi, "Eikaiwa ni henshi, (yomi, kaki) o kirisuteru no wa kokumin kyoiku no jisatsu da," *Nihon no ronten 2001* (Tokyo: Bungei shunju, 2000), pp. 608–13.

reasoned that Russia could not rely on China alone, that North Korea would turn to international aid despite its reluctance, that South Korea and Japan from 1998 were at last forming a complete partnership, and that China was now amenable to Japan planning a positive role in security and to forging multilateralism. Especially over the first decade of the twenty-first century as U.S. national power stayed predominant and China remained weak, an opportunity existed for Japan to work toward regionalism.[15] In the background was deep concern that Japan had lost leverage in the 1990s and become too dependent on the United States and on outdated Asia-Pacific thinking based on containing communism through impairing regionalism within Asia. Japan had to cast its lot with great-power maneuvering as well as NEA regionalism.

By 1997 the Japanese government had concluded that it needed more strategic thinking, including greater academic input into its long-range forecasting and analysis of global trends. In contrast to the cold war era distrust of academics as leftist idealists, there was a new appreciation for the balanced, realist coverage by leading experts. The choice of experts did not repeat the late 1980s formula of picking those on the right who could present established diplomatic positions to the outside world. Instead a group of experts, mostly specialists on one region and many from Tokyo University but also including professors at Keio and Aoyama Gakuin, were selected for freewheeling monthly meetings with the Foreign Ministry's Policy Planning Department. Increased trust in geopolitical reasoning accompanied the new spirit of jockeying for great-power balance. When the Foreign Ministry was wracked by divisions in 2001–2 another academic advisory group was formed that met with the Cabinet Planning Office in a renewed search for strategic thinking to guide relations with Japan's principal partners.

Many groups have been discussing the nature of Japan's regional role in Asia. They have moved beyond bilateralism in the region and with the United States to explore a regional approach. Compared to early in the decade there is recognition that countries will not consider the Japanese model of development as suitable, but that has not ruled out talk of a new Japanese model or cooperation on a regional model that maintains regional values without succumbing to the Anglo-Saxon model.[16] Instead of seeing the Asian financial crisis and Japan's own economic troubles as slowing Japan's role in the region, many say they are motivating corporations to advance new business strategies, accelerating involvement. As before, the Japanese see Asian countries needing a transitional period in the shift to free economies and democracy, justifying slower globalization than Western leaders demand.

[15] Kojima Tomoyuki, "Hokuto Ajia no takoku kan anzen hosho taisei kochiku o," *Sekai shuho*, December 5, 2000, pp. 34–5.

[16] "10th GISPRI Symposium," *GISPRI: Message from Japan*, 18 (2000), pp. 11–14.

Naturally, Japan will have a special leadership role through its "soft power," know-how, and dominant economy. Herein lies a rationale for regionalism.

Fearing a massive invasion of the U. S. economic model and of American influence, the Japanese pressed to make the yen the regional currency and to protect vested interests. Elite opinion doubted the motives of the United States, seeing it as an unwanted hegemon even as it was also credited as the indispensable balancer.[17] Indeed, as Japan's economic troubles deepened through 2002 the idea spread that the United States as well as China is to blame. In 1985 Japan had faithfully agreed to strengthen its currency (then worth 240 yen to the dollar) in order to bail out the U.S. economy, and it was left with a fragile base for expanding exports, apart from a small number of industrial firms. Later China's exchange rate gave it a competitive advantage. It follows that the other two states must agree to let the exchange rate rise to 150 yen and stop holding Japan back.[18]

The Japanese placed some blame on the United States for the causes of the Asian financial crisis linked to overly rapid and excessive financial opening and on the slow recovery associated with remedies focused less on production revival than on meeting global standards. Thus, in 1997–8 the two countries were driven apart by economic events, leading the United States to demand more globalization with growing suspicion of regional approaches while Japan became more suspicious of globalization. In the cold war the foundation for the U.S.-Japan relationship was advertised as shared values – democracy, human rights, a market economy – but the United States came to doubt this, first in the early Clinton years with criticisms of Japan's commitment to transparency and economic liberalization as well as peacekeeping and then as Japan's economic stagnation grew more obvious along with concerns about Japan's adherence to globalized standards. The Japanese too grew to doubt U.S. values, at times faulting excess idealism that failed to take Asian complexities into account and at other times fearing excess realpolitik that was based on unilateralism. To counter both, nationalists too came to the conclusion that Japan needs regionalism to boost its leverage with the United States even if the way forward would not be easy, and resolution of great-power differences would be needed to open the way.

Regionalism does not spare Japan the dilemmas that have caused it to hesitate about globalization, such as agricultural protectionism. Already in the year 2000 new regulations allowed Chinese farmers to expand exports rapidly of onions, tomatoes, and sweet peppers. While Japan's domestic onion production was falling sharply, tomato imports more than doubled

[17] Takashi Inoguchi, "Japan's Foreign Policy under U.S. Unipolarity: Coping with Uncertainty and Swallowing Some Bitterness," *Asian Journal of Political Science*, 6(2) December 1998, p. 11.

[18] Hiroshi Ota, "Weaker Yen May Be Cure to Lead Nation to Fiscal Health," *Daily Yomiuri Online*, January 3, 2003.

in 2000. Local politicians appealed to the LDP, and soon trade disputes with China resembled those with the United States not many years earlier. No wonder that Tokyo hesitated to press for economic regionalism beyond cross-border ties.

The Asian financial crisis even more than Japan's own economic stagnation cast doubt on existing notions of regionalism. The very idea of Asian values, which Japanese had regarded ambivalently but largely accepted in one form or another, lost credibility. Yet differences in U.S. and Japanese responses indicated that Tokyo was determined to use the crisis as an opportunity to bolster regionalism rather than to allow globalization to advance unfettered. The Japanese were not content to open the gates to globalization. As South Korea's economy rose from the depths of crisis and memories faded of China and the United States jointly chastising Japan for slow growth, a search for regionalism resumed.

The financial crisis began a resurgence of Japanese interest in regionalism. At first the focus of Japanese efforts appeared to be SEA with an emphasis on currency. Before long Korea had risen to the forefront and the goal of a free trade area was under discussion. Especially in September 1998 the Japanese ambassador to Korea initiated the acceleration of planning for a free trade agreement. As China took steps to enter the WTO, the scope of discussions widened. Although the most dramatic development came only with the May 2000 Chiang Mai agreement for a currency swapping program, already at ASEAN +3 meetings and elsewhere the Japanese had welcomed the progress being made.

In August and September 1997 miscommunications between the U.S. Treasury Department and Japan's Foreign Ministry may have given Washington the impression that the United States would be invited to join a new grouping to be called the AMF (Asian Monetary Fund), while Tokyo thought it had the go-ahead for launching an Asian regional body. When the dust cleared after the idea came into the open and the United States made clear its opposition, many in Japan felt resentful that their pursuit of regionalism had been blocked. When Kuroda Haruhiko, Vice Minister for International Affairs of the Finance Ministry, pressed in 1999 for the Chiang Mai initiative as a more modest version of financial cooperation, both sides acted carefully; the United States was seen as taking a wait-and-see attitude. Inside the Japanese bureaucracy, the Finance Ministry had solidified around the goal of regionalism since the Asian financial crisis, but it fought a continuing battle with part of the Foreign Ministry, led by the U.S. school, and also MITI. After the 2000 agreement at Chiang Mai some wanted to press ahead with a stronger crisis-prevention mechanism close in spirit to the AMF idea and others favored bold FTA agreements. Having just served as foreign minister, Obuchi Keizo became prime minister already being familiar with the issues. He boosted support for regionalism, as the Foreign Ministry joined the Finance Ministry in making the Chiang Mai initiative possible. Later, however, the Foreign Ministry would be mired in confusion, while politicians were bombarded by small and middle-sized firms among their constituents alarmed by China's rapid rise as a competitor. It would be hard to take the next steps toward regionalism after the advances in Japanese support of 1997–2000.

The Japanese accept the process of globalization, but they balance it with approval for multipolarization and regionalism. In the search for a leadership role, they emphasize use of economic power to ameliorate the regional impact of globalization and "soft power" to increase their voice as mutual dependency grows.[19] On the positive side, officials look back to the refocusing of ODA in 1992 to gain leverage against excess military expenses and insufficient environmentalism, and they look ahead to currency stabilization and other coordination under discussion since the Asian financial crisis. On the negative side, officials warn that "soft power" is lacking a spiritual appeal, whereby Japan becomes a magnet for Asian nations. It is proving difficult to boost Japan's noneconomic image. A quick answer was sought, for instance from a breakthrough in relations with Russia.

Japan and Russia

Japan's policies toward Russia had operated in the shadow of U.S. superpower diplomacy since the end of World War II. In 1955–6 and 1973–5 as prime ministers showed signs of drawing closer to Moscow, the United States was known to have been displeased. When Tokyo considered relaxing its demand for four islands, some feared that the United States would have refused to return Okinawa. Two decades later some in Tokyo thought that the Lockheed Scandal brought down Prime Minister Tanaka Kakuei because the United States was upset over his soft stance toward Moscow and excessive investment plans in the Russian Far East. In 1991–3 when Tokyo was harder on Russia than Washington preferred, the response was less direct. The pressure to follow the U.S. lead came through intense persuasion for the use of economic assistance amidst broad discussions of geopolitics among officials. As in the mid-1950s and mid-1970s, many in Japan's Foreign Ministry eventually accepted the new logic. In the former instances, they became more anti-Soviet than the Americans, aroused by the disputed islands. By 2000 signs of their willingness to compromise for geopolitical reasons might have again aroused anxiety in the United States, now worried about rising Russian nationalism (especially just after Putin took power). Great-power differences with the United States kept arising; Japan never seemed to find the right balance to overcome its uncomfortable dependence, and Russia kept figuring in the equation.

[19] *Sangiin kokusai mondai ni kansuru chosakai kaigiroku daigogo*, Part 23, March 7, 2001, pp. 20–1.

As Japanese diplomats acknowledge, many forces led Tokyo to press for closer relations with Moscow. 1) As in the United States, there were many reasons that steps must be taken to prevent a failure to democratize or to create a market economy, each of which could lead to a challenge to the new world order. 2) "Japan's desire to play a greater role in the international arena requires it to cooperate more closely with Russia."[20] 3) Resources from the Russian Far East and Siberia are more significant now, especially energy to fuel the growing Asian economies. And 4) Japan must cooperate because potential threats have newly developed. None of these factors drew much attention, however, because officials and the media played up the single objective of regaining all four lost islands. Of course, first they had to catch Russian attention, broadening the agenda.

In 1997 Hashimoto Ryutaro framed Japan's new approach to Russia as "Eurasian diplomacy." Without emphasizing the objective of the recovery of the disputed islands, he made an appeal that resonated in Russia for a transformation in geopolitics and in the economics of a region, linking maritime and continental Asia, bridging civilizations, and setting a new course for great-power relations. While Russians had been searching for a regional framework to replace the suspect framework of joining the European community and had flirted with their own notion of Eurasianism as a continental identity, the Japanese offered a different notion of regionalism crossing Central Asia, restoring the glory of the Silk Road, and giving Russia a place in the maritime zone of Asia. For Russia it could slow the momentum of Sino-Russian ties and refocus attention on a broader regionalism. For Japan it replaced the narrow notion of a Sea of Japan economic sphere where Tokyo would dominate. This was an appeal for a grand synthesis of economic and geopolitical ties in which Japan would settle for a reduced, if still unequaled, role. Instead of a rich Japan giving an ultimatum to Russia to accept its offer or forego benefits, a subdued Japan offered a partnership to "avoid relative sidelining on the Asian continent."[21] Just a few months later Hashimoto met Yeltsin in Krasnoyarsk amidst optimism that the "countdown to the year 2000" that they initiated would produce a breakthrough.

Hashimoto's "Eurasian diplomacy" speech of July 1997 broke new ground by not only appealing to Russia to set relations on a fresh path but also by choosing a new lens for Asia. In response to the expansion of NATO, Japan proposed a broad regional context on the Asian continent.

[20] Chikahito Harada, "The Relationship between Japan and Russia," *The Japan Society Proceedings*, Summer 1999, pp. 34–5.

[21] Reinhard Drifte, "Japan's Eurasian Diplomacy: Hard-Nosed Power Politics, Resource Diplomacy, or Romanticism?" in Arne Holzhausen, ed., *Can Japan Globalize? Studies on Japan's Changing Political Economy and the Process of Globalization in Honour of Sung-Jo Park* (Springer/Physica Verlag, 2001), p. 265.

Although the idea was vague, it implied that a regionally isolated Japan would, as in the prewar era, reduce its strategic vulnerability by promoting the development of resources and markets along the old Silk Road. Bolder diplomacy along with new uses of ODA in Central Asia and new assistance for Russia would lead to closer economic ties. Surprisingly, a prime minister who had consulted little among bureaucrats floated the idea before a business group.[22] It signaled great-power diplomacy punctuated by a touch of economic regionalism, offering Russia a chance for a stake in both.

Marking an attempt to come back as prime minister as a force for shaping Japanese ties to Russia, Hashimoto wrote in late November 2000 of the real meaning of Krasnoyarsk. He recalled that in the first months of 1997 Clinton and Yeltsin had agreed in Helsinki on NATO expansion, after which Clinton had called Hashimoto asking to make Russia's membership complete in the G-8. Expecting to have to persuade the Japanese leader, Clinton may have been surprised with the answer "I am not against it." Hashimoto added one condition: Japan and Russia must strive to normalize their relations as it is odd if two of the eight countries are missing that. In June at the Denver G-8 summit when Yeltsin made clear Russia's wish to join APEC that fall, Hashimoto responded that he would be the one to introduce the resolution, causing all the leaders to smile at the turn of events. While attention to Japanese-Russian relations in 1997 focused on Japan's interest in territory and Russia's in economic relations, Hashimoto suggested the importance of great-power relations – a complete partnership in the context of global and regional organizations.[23] It was not, however, a priority he would sustain.

Russians placed the Yeltsin-Hashimoto economic cooperation plan ahead of the climate for resolving the territorial problem and reaching a peace treaty on the agenda for negotiations decided at Krasnoyarsk. They reported new planning for economic projects in 1998 as a positive achievement, neglecting to note both the loss of credibility from the default by Russia that summer and the sense of betrayal among many in Japan when in November Russia pulled back from its commitment to negotiate the fate of four islands enshrined in the 1993 Tokyo Declaration and renewed at Krasnoyarsk.[24] From this angle, progress comes neither from reassuring the Japanese on genuine improvements in the economic environment nor from following through on promises that increase Japanese trust. It requires more Japanese effort to assure Russia that it wants better relations regardless of what happens to the

[22] Michael Robert Hickok, "Japan's Eurasian Gambit: An Asian View of Eurasia," *Problems of Post-Communism*, May–June 2000, pp. 36–47.

[23] Hashimoto Ryutaro, "Krasnoyarsk no shini," *Gaiko forum*, December 2000, pp. 30–5.

[24] Victor Pavliatenko and Alexander Shlindov, "Russo-Japanese Relations: Past Achievements and Future Prospects at the Start of the 21st Century," *Far Eastern Affairs*, 4 (2000), pp. 3–32.

islands and even independent of Russian economic reforms. Russians also suggest that prior to 1996 Japan's only political goal was the islands, but afterward it turned to Russia in search of a multipolar regional policy linked to the rise of Chinese power and the uncertainty on the Korean peninsula. In these circumstances, there is no need for Russia to yield on the islands. In 1999 such talk left a bad taste on the Japanese side, dimming hopes for the final stage of the countdown.

In 1997–8 the Russians convinced themselves that Japan was pursuing their country not so much for the return of islands but for great-power reasons: new leverage in global affairs due to concern over the rise of China, new resource development needed because of a weaker domestic economy, and interest in multipolarity as dependence on the United States continued. They calculated that as long as their state did not close the door to progress on the islands, Japanese leaders could keep the fiction alive that a deal would be made while continuing to boost ties for other reasons. When Japan's pursuit continued even after Moscow's retreat on negotiations over the islands, Russian officials found these views confirmed and waited for another initiative to come from Tokyo.

A surprising development occurred in Japan's government after the Moscow summit of November 1998. Instead of registering deep disappointment at Russia's response, spokesmen expressed optimism about relations. They conveyed this to the Japanese public, many of whom continued to think that Moscow was serious about an agreement on all four islands in 2000, and to Russian leaders, who began to calculate that Tokyo was more interested in a deal than they were. Commenting in late 2000, Foreign Ministry official Togo Kazuhiko recalled the upbeat mood after the April Kawana summit when Yeltsin had responded to Japan's proposal as a "very interesting suggestion," adding that he feels "optimistic about this problem."[25] He said nothing about any letdown when the Russian side rejected the Kawana proposal. Even as Tokyo was failing to make progress on the islands and offering no justification to the public for a bold advance in relations strictly for geopolitical reasons, the media claimed that Japan was advancing to both its territorial and great-power goals. This approach obscured new flexibility on the Japanese side. By dividing an agreement on sovereignty over the islands and their actual return, Hashimoto at Kawana set a precedent for a two-stage approach.[26] LDP official Suzuki Muneo would carry that thinking further in 2000–1 when he pursued a two-stage initiative that appeared to call for the return of two islands first, but the need for it would not be understood.

[25] Togo Kazuhiko, "Puchin Ro daitoryo honichi no kekka to Nichiro kankei no zento," *Sekai keizai hyoron*, December 2000, p. 10.

[26] Toshikawa Takao and Futatsuki Hirotaka, *Muneo no iikata* (Tokyo: Asuka shinsha, 2002), pp. 50–3.

The Japanese grew to see economic involvement in the Russian Far East as taking one of two forms, each minimizing contacts. For small projects, a fleeting presence was needed to supervise training programs for managers or other support roles. And for large, long-term investments, such as the Sakhalin oil and gas project, self-sufficient, closed compounds were preferred for safety, cleanliness, and efficiency. Neither brought real integration, although they could serve a transitional role on the path to regionalism.

Incrementalism in Japanese-Russian cross-border ties proved difficult. On the one hand, the Japanese side feared that joint development of the disputed islands would be tantamount to recognizing Russian sovereignty and would relax the pressure from the locals to change the status quo. On the other hand, Russian local governments feared relinquishing any control, interfering with proposals from Moscow for joint development of the islands. Only when national leaders determined that they had to act for geopolitical as well as nationalistic reasons were cross-border troubles left behind. In the late 1990s the two nations agreed on zones and payments for Japanese fishing boats as one sign that an upbeat mood on national issues could resolve local ones, but this only led to an uneasy truce when the low points in relations spilled over into new conflicts over fishing.

Russians attribute the "lost decade" of Japanese-Russian relations to cold war inertia and old stereotypes, in short to unsuitable Japanese territorial demands in an era when big issues should be addressed. They claim that this led Russia to turn to other partners, especially China, after Japan mishandled bilateral relations early in the 1990s. Yet, they declare a preference for a multilateral approach to political relations, opposing U.S. leadership in the region and seeking Japan's help in forging a broader-based security system. As the United States recedes as a unilateral power, Russians anticipate a vacuum in the region. China will rise, posing new conditions for Japanese diplomacy. Also many Asians will still worry about Japan's rise, stirring fears of a revival of imperialism. The advice to Japan is to join with Russia in balanced quadrangular relations to stabilize the region, normalizing ties in the process without lingering over old notions of humiliations.[27]

Quadrangular great-power relations were not yet ripe for Tokyo and Moscow to feel a strong push toward each other. Each was nervous about the United States, but Tokyo never expected Clinton's flirtation with Jiang Zemin to go far and the Kremlin with Evgenii Primakov as foreign or prime minister was focused on balancing the United States, not China. Nationalism focused on each other's attitudes to the legacy of the war rather than on China's future. Many in Japan were still suspicious of Moscow's intentions in NEA. Instead of normalizing relations based on economic ties with its

[27] Andrei Kortunov, "Wareware wa otagai o hitsuyo to shiteiru no daro ka?" *Gaiko forum*, December 2000, pp. 43–7.

neighbors in Asia, Moscow saw the region as the stage for a great-power game. Thus, many viewed its actions as a ploy for extending political influence and not as a contribution to regionalism.[28]

China and Regionalism

Chinese leaders had cause to picture their country at the center of an emerging region dominated by great-power calculations. Following the agreement of 1994 China was the primary conduit between North Korea and the outside world, despite ongoing talks between the North and the United States at the United Nations. After Yeltsin called on Jiang Zemin to boost bilateral relations in April 1996, Beijing felt confident of Moscow's pursuit of it to balance U.S. power. Clinton soon decided to seek a breakthrough in ties with China, concluding from the Taiwan missile crisis not that containment was needed but that engagement must be intensified. Not to be outdone, Hashimoto had Japan pull back from the abrupt downturn in Sino-Japanese relations with renewed effort to stabilize ties. Meanwhile, South Korea became more deferential as relations grew exponentially. Not only did all economic roads lead to China as the new driving force of growth in NEA, for a time all political roads also appeared to be converging on Beijing.

China became the leader in great-power summitry and "partnership fever" in 1997–8. Building on the strategic partnership achieved with Russia and striving to block the expansion of alliances as seen in the U.S.-Japan defense guidelines, Beijing looked to equal, bilateral relations among the great powers as the core of a balanced international system favorable for China's rise. The order of pursuit was 1) solidifying new ties to Russia; 2) building a partnership with the United States; and 3) stabilizing ties with Japan. Indeed, the Chinese were prone to relegate Japan to the level of "regional power," giving less weight to its economic prowess and more to its small territory and population as well as lack of nuclear weapons. Additionally, they continued to calculate that U.S.-Japanese relations have strong currents of discord. This lent support to the prospect of balancing powers through triangular relations. The Chinese took to heart U.S. assurances in 1997–8 of China's importance. Rather than feeling isolated by the closer U.S.-Japan security alliance, they added Russia to the equation and insisted that China had gained a decisive voice.[29]

Beijing's great-power logic accepted a mixture of cooperation and competition on a regional and global scale. It posited an environment in which the United States would not be able to consolidate world hegemony because

[28] Hiraiwa Shunshi, "Chosen hanto e no kanyo o mezasu 'taikoku' Roshia," *Toa*, October 2000, pp. 35–47.

[29] Gilbert Rozman, "China's Quest for Great Power Identity," *Orbis*, 43(3) Summer 1999, pp. 383–402.

scattered states, whose sovereignty should be respected, would pose military threats by creating "hot spots" damaging to U.S. interests. Other great powers, fearful of the United States becoming too powerful, would at least assist these states in protecting their independence from U.S. pressure. Beijing's attitude toward North Korea epitomized this outlook. Pyongyang was valued as a check on U.S. power even if it would not undertake the reforms essential for it to be useful to China in other respects.

The year of energy awakening in China was 1997. Planners began casting about for secure supplies. They feared that the country's vulnerability was growing as sea-lanes could be choked. The response was not only a large investment in Central Asia with talk of a pipeline from west to east, but also joint plans with Russia to develop resources and build a pipeline from north to southeast. Energy security reinforced great-power thinking. By 2002 rivalries over which oil and gas pipelines should be built rose to the forefront in jockeying for advantage in the emergent region with China's plans under challenge.[30]

The Chinese keep suspecting a grand world strategy of the United States to dominate the globe and to control Asia. When the April 1996 defense guidelines with Japan were announced, this played into their reasoning. The key for China was whether Japan would follow the U.S. lead or move without much delay toward an independent pole in a multipolar world. The guidelines led Chinese analysts toward the former position, but efforts by both the United States and Japan to improve ties with China in late 1996 and 1997 gave new support to arguments about a great-power triangle as the regional form of multipolarity. This theme could be found for another year. In 1999 the Chinese reconsidered, acknowledging that they had exaggerated U.S.-Japanese friction and that the mainstream in Japan trusted the United States.[31] This was a sign that hopes for a great-power balance were crumbling.

If early in the 1990s Chinese identity was linked to the successes of the East Asian developmental state model, after the Asian financial crisis there was a sober assessment that this model was a temporary industrial strategy reliant on labor-intensive industries but poorly suited to a new high-tech age or rapid innovation. In response, Beijing chose to press for deeper economic reforms, committing itself to the economics of globalization. Yet, its fear of the politics of globalization also intensified. United States hegemony loomed much larger, even in China's neighborhood. Beijing would have to support regionalism more if it were to fend off the U.S. challenge. Great-power goals merged with regional ones.

30 Selig S. Harrison, "Gas and Geopolitics in Northeast Asia: Pipelines, Regional Stability, and the Korean Nuclear Crisis," *World Policy Journal*, Winter 2002–3, pp. 23–36.

31 Jin Linbo, "Japan's 'U.S.-Centered Perception' and Its Roots," *Foreign Affairs Journal*, June 1999, pp. 23–7.

There was nothing new about China's view of globalization in the wake of the Asian financial crisis. As before, the mainstream asserted that globalization is a fact, not a choice, crediting it with facilitating the flow of capital that allows rapid development. Yet, they also repeated the warning that countries become more vulnerable and must act to safeguard their autonomy. Seeing the weakness of Asian countries and the power of global financial institutions, Chinese officials grew more sympathetic to the creation of regional institutions. This drew them closer to Japanese thinking, but rivalry outweighed cooperation. When Tokyo proposed creation of an AMF, Beijing was pleased that Washington scuttled the idea. Chinese leaders were more focused on forging ties with the United States and widening divisions between the United States and Japan. It would not be until 1999 that they would reconsider their opposition to an AMF and recognize that they should give priority to Japan's value as a regional partner.[32] By that time, Tokyo had put in place the Miyazawa initiative that offered $30 billion in assistance and reaffirmed its commitment to the regional economy to which Beijing wanted to make its input.[33]

Amidst the emphasis on great-power relations, Chinese leaders faced the fallout of the Asian financial crisis in the second half of 1997. Across SEA there was resentment at the IMF's rigid approach and the slow response of the United States. Many wondered if Beijing would be struck by the crisis too, and even if it were not, would it devalue its currency, undermining the recovery effort in the worst hit countries. Through its prudent response, continued growth, and financial assistance China acquired the image of a "responsible" state. Although it rejected Japan's proposal to establish an AMF, China found itself drawn into closer cooperation with welcoming nations in ASEAN. The Asian financial crisis transformed Chinese thinking about economic security. Beijing felt newly vulnerable to foreign economic pressures. Given its large volume of nonperforming loans, China's leaders understood that they needed to work with others. China grew more supportive of regionalism and started to look more favorably on ties with Japan. The new entity ASEAN +3 was born. As Japan's trade and investment to SEA fell and resentment against the United States persisted, China found an opportunity to develop regional ties to its south and to use them for making inroads toward regionalism to its east and north.

Having failed to achieve continental regionalism as balance, China turned further toward maritime regionalism. Whereas in the first half of the 1990s there was much talk of initiatives to link the two, as through the Tumen River project, by the end of the decade the Chinese had little to say about the role

32 Gilbert Rozman, "China's Changing Images of Japan 1989–2001: The Struggle to Balance Partnership and Rivalry," *International Relations of the Asia-Pacific*, Winter 2002, pp. 95–129.

33 Koichi Hamada, "From the AMF to the Miyazawa Initiative: Observations on Japan's Currency Diplomacy," *The Journal of East Asian Affairs*, 13(1), Spring/Summer 1999, pp. 33–50.

of Russia and North Korea in regionalism. They had lost confidence in ties to the Russian Far East and expected rather slow economic reforms and openness from North Korea. Other hopes for continental projects had led to letdowns. Chinese investment in the oil fields of Kazakhstan with plans for a pipeline had been dashed by Kazakh delays in reform and the disappointing nature of the oil in quantity and quality. The second Eurasian railroad through Kazakhstan carried little traffic. Hopes for Chinatowns and lively Chinese economic ties with nearby cities such as Almaty, Khabarovsk, and Vladivostok, let alone more distant cities of Central Asia and Russia, had been thwarted too, often by blatantly anti-Chinese discrimination.[34] Even hope for large-scale military-industrial linkages to Russia had faded as Moscow tightened the transfer of sensitive technology. Just as Beijing heralded great-power balancing, it was faced with growing evidence of economic realities undercutting such plans.

China's 15th Party Congress in the fall of 1997 focused attention on refining the domestic development model to link it more closely to globalization. Although the result would be massive layoffs from state enterprises, economic growth would be sustained. The country would be poised after the fallout of the Asian financial crisis for a vast influx of foreign capital.

The Chinese do not feel that they are very much welcomed in the countries of the region. While both Russia and Japan will soon be facing large deficits in the working age population and virtually all notions of regional economic projects assume Chinese labor and entrepreneurs moving in larger numbers across borders, recent Chinese arrivals have encountered strong resistance. In Japan, Russia, and South Korea many are persecuted as illegal migrants whether they have overstayed their visas or snuck across borders. Even those legally present face inhospitable environments. Instead of preferring Russia to Japan for historical reasons, nearly all choose Japan for the superior public order as well as the economic opportunities. Russians' hostility toward the Chinese far surpasses that of the Japanese. If the Chinese concede that in the first years of border openings some Chinese behaved in an uncivilized manner, they see that as far less serious than the unfriendly and sometimes criminal treatment of the Chinese by the Russians that has continued.[35]

The geography of economic integration was changing. Reversion of Hong Kong to China without serious incident solidified China's standing. Transfer of capital from countries caught in the financial crisis to China added to the momentum of a high-flying economy. Shanghai's position in the Chinese economy continued its steep ascent of the 1990s. Instead of SEA and China's

34 Hsueh Chun-tu and Xing Guangcheng, eds., *Zhongguo yu Zhongya* (Beijing: Shehuikexue wenxian chubanshe, 1999).

35 Gilbert Rozman, "Sino-Russian Mutual Assessments" and "Turning Fortresses into Free Trade Zones," in Sherman Garnett, ed., *Rapprochement or Rivalry? Russia-China Relations in a Changing Asia* (Armonk, NY: M. E. Sharpe, 2000), pp. 147–74, 177–202.

southeast coast near Hong Kong leading in appeal, the center of gravity of economic activity moved northward. Beijing could at last be confident of its ability to balance Tokyo in NEA. Galloping globalization did not exclude the rise of regionalism, although China still had no strategy for achieving that.

China and Japan

As Beijing and Tokyo looked to bilateral relations in a regional context they each sought to maximize their assets, tangible and intangible. Beijing enjoyed two intangible strengths: the view outside Japan that the history of that country disqualified it from leadership; and the growing expectation that China's future would entitle it to primacy of place. As long as the present balance of assets was discounted, Beijing could gain the upper hand. Tokyo, in turn, called for setting the past aside and focusing on the short-term future. Its economic superiority deserved to be weighted highly in a process largely economic in nature. Assessments of national power in the debates over great-power status could not be divorced from claims related to regionalism. No middle ground was found.

China figures into three of the foremost goals facing Japan. One, more than South Korea and North Korea, it stands as the barrier to Japan's desire to put history behind it and reinvent itself in the twenty-first century as a normal country. The Japanese want the Chinese to forget and forgive the past as well as to forego the Senkaku Islands and forge future-oriented relations. Two, the Japanese see China as the indispensable country for reentering Asia. It is a partner in regionalism that can boost Japan's economy and help to balance both other regionalism around the globe and globalization with its tendency to disregard Japan's special arrangements. Thus, they want China to embrace economic regionalism and strive for multilateralism in order to institutionalize cooperation. Three, China also has acquired the image of Japan's future rival, serving as a useful symbol of the need for national unity, military preparedness, and alliance strengthening with the United States. Seeing no alternative to this rivalry, the Japanese seek to pressure China and ready their country for a struggle ahead. These goals are contradictory, leading some to appeal for closer ties to China and others to stress a new threat. Each has a different meaning for regionalism.

Sino-Japanese relations sank in the summer of 1996 to their low point since 1973. On the Chinese side the popular outcry over Japan became a focal point in resurgent mass nationalism. When Hashimoto paid an official visit as prime minister to the Yasukuni shrine, war memories were rekindled. Provocative plans by Japanese nationalist groups to build a lighthouse on the disputed Senkaku islands aroused anger. These actions occurred against the background of much criticized, new defense guidelines between Japan and the United States. Prime Minister Li Peng seemed to be steering relations with Japan on a downward spiral. Only when his term came to an end early in 1998 did it seem likely that relations would rebound, but another setback followed, despite strong efforts on both sides, when Jiang Zemin's November visit to Japan turned into a fiasco.

Before Jiang's trip leaders on both sides struggled to keep bilateral relations from any new blows. They heralded positive developments, showcasing advancing economic ties and pledging to keep improving political ones. The twenty-fifth anniversary of the reestablishment of diplomatic ties became an occasion for forward-looking rhetoric. As part of its great-power balance sheet, Beijing forecast a triangle with Japan and the United States in which its cooperative ties with Tokyo would outweigh competitive ones and give it leverage. Expectations for an independent foreign policy in Japan were one reason for Chinese optimism about achieving a multipolar world. The fact that Japan was weaker than was anticipated early in the decade offered hope that it would become reconciled to a balancing role rather than insist on hegemony in NEA, as seen in Chinese rhetoric. A visit by Hashimoto to Beijing came amidst awareness that a new era of important summitry had dawned, but the Japanese leader went without concrete proposals and only modest progress occurred in creating an upbeat mood.

Flooding in China obliged Jiang Zemin to postpone his much-anticipated visit to Japan. Meanwhile, Kim Dae-jung was continuing his postelection sweep of NEA powers, in each case to raise ties to a higher level, with a historic trip to Japan. In offering to put history behind in return for a written Japanese apology for Japan's conduct Kim set an impossible standard for Jiang to meet. On the one hand, the Japanese apology did not come with a forthright review of what the Japanese side was acknowledging as improper conduct, and it could not offer much reassurance that future incitement by officials bent on vindicating past conduct would not follow. On the other hand, the Chinese public and leadership had a nationalist worldview in which Japan's wrongdoing was so central that it could not be dismissed by a promise to let history rest. When Jiang followed Kim by a month he knew that no agreement could be reached. Unwisely, he played to his domestic audience by repeating criticisms of Japan's historical behavior and allowing headlines about the past to crowd out agreements aimed at the future. Angered Japanese lost confidence in bilateral relations, while the Chinese public was aroused to blame the Japanese more than before. Leaders on both sides quickly appealed to the media to stop the polemics and prevent further damage to mutual trust, thereby putting the brakes on what could have been a sustained downward spiral in relations.[36]

[36] Gilbert Rozman, "Japan's Images of China in the 1990s: Are They Ready for China's 'Smile Diplomacy' or Bush's 'Strong Diplomacy?' " *Japanese Journal of Political Science*, 2, pt. 1 (May 2001), pp. 97–125.

Some in Japan subscribe to the notion that the Chinese communists gained control of China through opposing Japan and continue to legitimate their power successfully by reminding the Chinese people of their actions against Japanese cruelty, real or invented.[37] By implication, they reason that as long as Chinese communism holds power, Japan will have little hope in winning over the Chinese public. In other words, the problem lies with Chinese politics, not the way the Japanese continue to deal with the historical question.

The Chinese, in turn, closely monitored growing sympathies in Japan toward Taiwan. They noted a sharp rise in the number of Japanese favoring Taiwan's independence, although most were cautious about Japan's use of anything more than diplomatic pressure in the event of trouble. In 1998 they noted political support for including Taiwan within the U.S-Japanese defense guidelines, recognizing that the traffic through the Taiwan Straits was important for the Japanese economy. In 1999 the Chinese were aware of "earthquake diplomacy" when Japanese sympathies to the victims on Taiwan went far beyond what occurs when natural disasters strike the PRC. They feared that Tokyo was moving closer to using the "Taiwan card" in its diplomacy. Yet, some who were alert to forces inside Japan that were turning to Taiwan and raising the notion of a "China threat" suggested that China could do a better job of making its case to the Japanese people.[38]

Is Japan likely to be a bridge between China and the United States or is it more likely that the United States will be the bridge? For most of the 1990s the answer seemed obvious that Japan, eager to reenter Asia and more sympathetic to China, would strive hard to be the bridge. But in 1997–8 as Clinton met twice with Jiang Zemin the Japanese feared that they were the odd nation out. Moreover, seen from three angles, the Japanese-Chinese rivalry had a more alarming quality, especially under the stewardship of a right-center coalition. First, the history question poses an obstacle at the level of public opinion that has no parallel in Sino-U.S. ties. Second, looking ahead, an arms race and struggle for regional ascendancy is more likely to pit China versus Japan than China versus the United States. Third, Japanese views of Taiwan focus on security in a way different from U.S. views.[39] After all, this was the first target of Japanese imperialism. The Japanese are coming to see Taiwan as the first line in their own defense as well as vital to their energy supplies and a link to vital interests in SEA. Finally, the Taiwanese are perhaps the Asians who like the Japanese best, because the long occupation was handled more sympathetically by the Japanese Navy than the way the Army ran Korea or the rest of China and economic ties

[37] *Sankei shimbun*, October 30, 2000.

[38] Zhou Guangrui, "Ritai guanxi de fazhan yu women de duice," *Ribenxue luntan*, 3 (2000), pp. 16–21.

[39] Nakajima Mineo, *Chugoku, Taiwan, Xianggang* (Tokyo: PHP shinsho, 1999).

have produced little friction. Also the switch from the control of the KMT, which initially treated Taiwanese and Japanese collaborators as the enemy, has boosted Japan's standing.

The Chinese observed the tension in Japanese-Russian relations in the mid-1990s and considered it Japan's worst diplomatic dilemma. As Russia turned more nationalistic, Japan saw a dead end in its relations. Given their ambition to become a political great power, the Japanese people could not welcome such an outcome. Thus, the Chinese were not surprised to see Japan in 1997 pursuing Russia in a manner that offered another chance to make progress on the territorial issue as well as great-power benefits through a positive stance by Russia on Japan's Security Council ambitions and the regional power balance.[40] They expected great-power maneuvering to persist, but nationalism on each side to limit its impact. As long as there was such maneuvering, U.S. hegemony would be checked.

The trade boom between Japan and China lasted through 1996, bringing annual increases in the two-way total of about $10 billion a year. If in the 1980s Japan exported steel, cars, and electrical appliances, running up a trade surplus, in the 1990s the surplus increasingly favored China, not only through exports of textiles but also through Japanese firms sending color televisions, electrical appliances, and motorcycles back to their home country. The Chinese trade surplus grew by about $5 billion a year from 1992,[41] a trend that persisted even as trade grew more slowly late in the decade. One of the alleged reasons for a temporary downturn was a March 1996 NHK television report on the failure of a Japanese investment in China. After charges that the coverage was extreme, NHK tried to counter it in August with a positive show on investment in China, but the damage had been done, feeding a suspicious public bombarded with negative political news.[42]

Whereas the Japanese had once viewed China as the "sick man of Asia" or a troubled hybrid of poverty and communism, by the end of the 1990s China was turning into the "giant" of Asia. After years of thinking of it as a partner, serious doubts had arisen. First, China's image had slipped in 1989 with repression, but in 1992 the number of Japanese who like China had recovered much of the lost ground. The falloff had left the figure still above 50 percent, and for a time, it was back over 60 percent. Second, after a gradual slide in 1993–4 in those who like China, the second big shift occurred in 1995 as the number who dislike China for the first time exceeded those who like it. In 1999 the gap reached 49.6 to 46.2 percent. In turn, the Japanese drew friendlier to the United States and more supportive

[40] Lin Xiaoguang, "Rie guanxi: 90 niandai ilai de fazhan yu bianhua," *Dongbeiya yanjiu*, 4 (2000), pp. 30–3.

[41] Okazaki Yuji, "Chugoku e nabiku Nihon no kigyo," in Amako Satoshi and Sonoda Shigeto, eds., *Nitchu koryu no shiban seiki*, pp. 48–55.

[42] Okazaki Yuji, "Chugoku e nabiku Nihon no kigyo," pp. 61–7.

of the alliance with it.[43] The postwar "friendship" diplomacy of Chinese and Japanese drinking together to put the past behind them was turning into more normal diplomacy focused on security. By bringing up the past, China was causing concern about the future.

By the end of 1996 more than 50,000 Chinese had come to Japan to study. Instead of becoming the new "pipes" to replace the elder generation, they did not return with the expected warm feelings. One reason is that by the time that most left for Japan feelings in China had turned more negative. From 1988 when 55 percent of Chinese in seven large cities answered that they were very friendly or more or less friendly the figure in 1995 had dropped below 20 percent. In 1996–7 it fell further as over one-third of respondents to China's youth newspaper said that they disliked Japan.[44] Once students were in Japan they were likely to face unpleasantness in various forms, which reinforced their negative expectations. Feelings of goodwill were far less than the Japanese had anticipated. Some Japanese who follow why Chinese intellectuals and students turned more negative to their country trace the deterioration to 1995–6, blaming the Chinese government. Chinese scholars working in Japan countered by blaming the Japanese side, especially some politicians insensitive to Chinese public opinion.[45] The mood stayed grim in the late 1990s.

The Japanese identify Asians with crime and disorder. Crimes by foreigners in Japan rose ten times in the 1990s to 34,000, as they became more scattered across the country and more professionalized through organized groups. Newspapers singled out crimes committed by the Chinese, 45 percent of the total and growing in 1999 alone by 48 percent.[46] This did not help the image of China, even if many realized the need for closer cooperation.

The Japanese struggled to define China. On the right they insisted it was not the China studied by sinologists in which people steeped in Confucian culture strived to become "superior men." Instead it was a place without order where manners were lacking. Above all, the Chinese had very different values from the Japanese.[47] Thus, Japan must be wary of China as a regional partner, while preparing to compete with it and guard against it. In contrast, optimists concluded that Chinese troubles are huge, generational change continues, and there will be little choice but to turn to Japan. That means that value differences will not be a major problem. At each stage some had been hopeful that the optimists would be proven right, but the number of

[43] Kojima Tomoyuki, *Chugoku no seiji shakai: fukyoku taikoku e no mosaku* (Tokyo: Hoshobo, 1999), pp. 109–13.

[44] Amako Satoshi, "Yuko ippendo kara no tenkan," in Amako Satoshi and Sonoda Shigeto, eds., *Nitchu koryu no shiban seiki*, pp. 18–24.

[45] Ryo Seiko, "Tainichi kanjo ga akkasuru Chugoku no chishikijinzo," *Ronsa*, December 2000, p. 163.

[46] *Hokuriku chunichi shimbun*, May 1, 2000.

[47] *Sankei shimbun*, October 23, 2000, p. 1.

doubters kept growing. As some on the left called for more patience, a rising chorus from the right demanded more pressure.

In 1997–8 the Japanese were bothered by what they saw as Chinese arrogance reminiscent of Soviet arrogance in the cold war. Chinese sources were saying that Japan is not the power it thinks it is, and it had become a kind of public ritual not to look weak in dealing with Japan. The Japanese were chagrined by Clinton's visit to China in the summer of 1998 because he played into this thinking rather than urging China to take Japan more seriously. Some saw the U.S. leader even encouraging the Chinese to think that China is the special partner of the United States and that it warrants a sphere of influence in Asia. Even if some Japanese understood that the United States was working on behalf of both countries in trying to draw China into a global system, conventional wisdom held that Clinton went too far.[48]

During the Asian financial crisis Japanese experts depicted a newly realistic Beijing recognizing growing national dependence on the U.S. economy and striving to sweep away the "China threat" argument that was spreading among Americans. They assumed that personal networks, drawing on many in the Chinese elite who had studied abroad in the United States, were bringing China closer to the United States, while networks that had linked China and Japan were fraying.[49] Reactions to the Clinton visit to China varied. One group saw the "strategic engagement" of the United States and China as "Japan passing," linking it to "Japan bashing" because it had become a force for joint criticism of Japanese economic behavior. They welcomed congressional criticism of Clinton and sought to make common cause with Republicans in reversing this process. Others argued that this bilateral improvement could be used to build a trilateral framework that also recognized the huge role of the Japanese economy and growing interdependence among all. Within months both sides recognized that Sino-U.S. relations were not in good shape, as China let its image in the United States as well as Japan deteriorate. Japan had new leverage, but no strategy.

A wide-ranging Chinese debate on Japan was under way at this time. Challenging existing assumptions, it suggested that Japan is in flux searching for an escape from the post–World War II system rather than remaining a status quo country and that China has little chance to drive a wedge between Japan and the United States or, if it could, the resulting independent Japan would be less in China's interest.[50] Such academic judgments were reflected in the policy shift after Jiang Zemin's flawed summit. Beijing redoubled its efforts to improve ties.

48 Inagaki Takeshi and Kaji Nobuyuki, *Nihon to Chugoku eien no gokai: imo bunka no chototsu* (Tokyo: Bungei shunju, 1999).

49 *Mainichi shimbun*, July 20, 1998, p. 8.

50 Liu Jiangyuan, *Panghuangzhong de Riben* (Tianjin: Tianjin renmin chubanshe, 2000).

While it initially seemed that China responded to the Asian financial crisis by eagerly joining the United States in criticizing Japan for not stimulating its economy to assist in recovery, the more enduring impact was a calculation that a new opportunity was presenting itself. Many South Koreans believed the United States provoked the crisis. Some Japanese thought so too; others resented the U.S. response as a mixture of gloating and dismissing Japan's role in recovery. Recognizing a new divide created by globalization versus nationalism, the Chinese spotted an opportunity to promote regionalism.[51]

Rethinking its approach to Japan, China turned its attention to how Japan looks at the world aware that it had not managed relations with Japan well in the 1990s. It had overplayed the historical and territorial issues while unproductively dwelling on Japan's interest in using its great economic power to become a political great power.[52] Instead of following its natural tendency to seek more independence of the United States and balance great-power relations, Japan had moved closer to the United States as seen in the defense guidelines first proposed in April 1996. China lacks scope to oppose U.S. hegemony directly, but it has room to maneuver in a triangular framework due to U.S. ambivalence toward China and Japanese ambivalence toward the United States. Instead of vaguely referring to the global struggle against unipolarity, Chinese analysts targeted one triangle as the key to multipolarity in the Asia-Pacific region. They believed that their better grasp of Japanese psychology would allow them to avoid repetition of past mistakes.[53] A strategy of patience was born.

The Japanese were divided. On the left some pictured Japan and China together caught in the Asian economic crisis, bringing an unstable period ahead for China when Japan could with understanding achieve a new balance in relations. By the end of 1998 the North Korean missile scare also raised China's value. From this perspective, Japan could take advantage of a triangle with the United States rather than be once again limited by a tight, unequal bilateral relationship.[54] Many find it hard to imagine the impact of abandoning engagement with China.[55]

Japanese views of China range from fear of a superpower just beyond the horizon to dismissal of a dynasty in the moral decrepitude of its inevitable decline. Those with the latter outlook see the U.S. engagement policy as too soft, Japanese media coverage as long distorted by suppressing negative information, Japanese firms as recklessly losing money through misplaced

[51] Liu Fang, "Shilun shijie maoyi zuzhi yu quyi jingji yitihua de xiangrongxing," *Shijie jingji yu zhengzhi*, 1 (1998), pp. 28–30.

[52] "Shiji zhijiao de Zhong, Mei, Ri sanguo guanxi," *Guoji zhanlue yanjiu*, 4 (2000), pp. 7–10.

[53] Jin Xide, " 'Zhongri huoban guanxi' de Beijing, shizhi ji qushi," *Riben xuekan*, 5 (2000), pp. 1–16.

[54] *Asahi shimbun*, July 8, 1999, p. 4.

[55] Reinhard Drifte, "U.S. Impact on Japanese-Chinese Security Relations," *Security Dialogue*, 31(4), 2000, p. 451.

trust in China, and the Japanese government as coddling the Chinese for no good reason. As an alternative to propping up the existing system, they propose letting China's internal contradictions mount while waiting for a democratic transition through either a soft or hard landing.[56] Such views spread widely in 1998–9.

The Japanese seem convinced that they get along with the Chinese worse than Americans and not only for reasons of history. In Japanese enterprises located in China conflict also results from stricter management supervision and wide wage differentials. Something more is involved, the Japanese often suggest. If the Chinese are prone to charge the Japanese with discriminating against them as opposed to Westerners, the retort is that the Chinese are the ones who are biased whether for historical or other reasons.

When the Japanese accused the Chinese of advocating "outdated nationalism," through patriotism artificially cultivated by a government seeking to maintain its authoritarian power, the Chinese responded that patriotism comes from below, drawn from a history of Japanese atrocities and of humiliation under great-power hegemonism. The Japanese joined Americans in discerning in 1996–9 a recklessness in Chinese foreign policy, threatening military forces toward Taiwan without paying heed to the price to be paid in economic development, demonizing both Japan and the United States with little regard to the impact on public opinion. Yet, Japanese advice was often equally contemptuous of Chinese public opinion, showing no inclination to understand its deep roots or to assuage it.

Unlike South Korea, China has not taken special measures to block an invasion of Japanese culture. After all, Japanese culture is more distant and did not penetrate through assimilation policies as in Korea. Furthermore, cultural imports from Hong Kong, Taiwan, South Korea, and the United States have all been flowing into the country, leaving Japan's role relatively unthreatening. The Chinese have a strong sense of their own identity and do not regard Japan as a cultural great power. Indeed, there is some desire to balance Western with Eastern civilization, which offers greater respect to teachers and elders as well as less individualism. China does not worry about the cultural danger of regionalism.

At the end of the 1990s an outpouring of critical books and articles on China had relabeled it first and foremost a communist country driven by ideology. It was not a friend of Japan as seen in votes against Japanese candidates for international posts such as the United Nations Educational, Scientific, and Cultural Organization (UNESCO) head in 1999. Although such critiques were increasingly noticeable, they had not persuaded the majority of Japanese. Indeed, the tendency to embellish them with right-wing crusades hurt their credibility. For instance, rejecting Chinese claims that

[56] Nakajima Mineo, "Chugoku kenkoku gojunen no sokatsu to sono horai o yomu," *Ajia jiho*, September 1999, pp. 4–47.

300,000 of their countrymen lost their lives in the "massacre of Nanjing," one author called on the Japanese to clean away the stain on their ancestors.[57] Nationalist attacks against Japan bashing over history lumped Chinese, Chinese-Americans, and Japan's Chinese-watchers. For them, the goal of nationalism surpassed both regionalism and globalization.

Russia and Regionalism

Moscow had an opportunity to start afresh after Yeltsin's election in July 1996. Indeed, some in the West expected this to happen, rationalizing the nationalist drift in foreign policy as driven by electoral politics from the time of ultranationalist Vladimir Zhirinovsky's stunning rise in the Duma elections of late 1993 to the challenge of Gennadyi Zyuganov's run for presidency as a communist. The abrupt end to the first Chechen war that accompanied Yeltsin's victory fueled hopes that nationalism would take a backseat to encouragement of foreign investment. Each of the other great powers prepared a strategy to win Moscow closer to its side. Yet, the preelection nationalism continued without serious exploration of the new offers, whether the explanation was Yeltsin's poor health, leaving Evgenii Primakov as the popular foreign minister largely in charge; the power of the oligarchs who had bankrolled the election and did not desire a competitive and open economy; the United States and IMF overgenerosity placing few conditions for good governance on assistance; or just the makeup of the top leadership. Moscow stuck to its new line with Beijing without embracing proposals for boosting diverse economic ties aimed at some kind of regionalism. When Japan followed with its 1997 initiative, including a call for large-scale economic cooperation, Moscow neither paid the political price for a deal nor created economic conditions that could have tested Tokyo's intent.

Throughout the region U.S. notions of how to accomplish Russian reform, variously called the human-rights approach or the monetarist approach, were ridiculed from the outset as naïvely optimistic. Taking much more seriously the role of the state, critics inside and outside Russia argued that the loss of a great many state functions created a crisis of chaos for which Western-inspired reforms had no answer. Hakamada Shigeki wrote that "liberalization gave birth to a criminal society and privatization actually amounted to a plundering of state assets." Pressing for reforms that added to the disorder only worsened the identity crisis of the Russian nation, leading to nostalgia for times of security. Hakamada cites a survey reported on February 9, 2000 by *Nezavisimaia gazeta,* showing, among periods of the twentieth century, the most favorable evaluation for the Brezhnev age (51 percent positive, 10 percent negative), and the least favorable for the Yeltsin age (5 percent

[57] Toyota Aritsune, *Ii kagen ni shiro Chugoku* (Tokyo: NonBook, 2000), pp. 142, 166, 186.

positive, 72 percent negative in August 1999; and 15 percent positive, 67 percent negative in January 2000 after the resignation speech) and the Gorbachev age (9 percent positive, 61 percent negative).[58] As Russians abandoned hope in globalization, the peoples of NEA lost hope in its contributions to regionalism.

Russians' mistrust of the United States climbed sharply in the second half of the 1990s.[59] By 2000, 85 percent of respondents agreed that the United States is trying to dominate the world and nearly as many that it is utilizing Russia's current weakness to reduce it to a second-rate power and producer of raw materials. The U.S. response to Russia's economic crisis and its military action against Serbia were mentioned as the causes of cooling relations. More Russians saw relations with the United States as difficult compared to views of ties with China or Japan (48 percent versus 9 and 18 percent).[60] Until Putin made a fresh start in 2000, distrust of globalization compounded fear of regionalism.

It was common in Russia to blame failures in the Asia-Pacific region on Russian weakness and the ill will of hostile powers. This meant arguing that Russia was in danger both from the U.S. desire to dominate and from the inclination of many countries to exclude Russia. Instead of asking what Russia could do to reassure the United States and others, many focused on how a weak Russia could oppose their nefarious intentions. Usually, they came down on the side of cooperation with China and against Japan. Yet they could not avoid a contradictory call for urgent economic growth of the Russian Far East and Eastern Siberia through regional integration careful to limit China's growing influence.[61]

The voice of the Russian military has usually been heard loudest in relations with the countries of NEA. When in 1983 under Iury Andropov there were discussions about improving relations with China and Japan to gain leverage on the United States, the military torpedoed talk of meeting China's "three obstacles" through pullbacks or of giving the disputed islands to Japan. Only in 1987–9 did Gorbachev overcome such opposition with regard to China, but not toward Japan. Neither Moscow nor Tokyo gave enough early priority to making an attractive offer to the other, and by 1991 Gorbachev no longer was able to challenge the military. If Yeltsin started with a window of opportunity, this did not last long. His appointment of Evgenii Primakov as foreign minister in January 1996 gave a strong

58 Shigeki Hakamada, "A Middle Ages Society: The Fundamental Problems of Russia" (unpublished manuscript, 2000).

59 Eric Shiraev and Vladislav Zubok, *Anti-Americanism in Russia: From Stalin to Putin* (New York: Palgrave, 2000).

60 "Russians' Mistrust of the U.S. at New High," *Opinion Analysis* (Washington, DC: Department of State, Office of Research, March 14, 2000), pp. 1–5.

61 Anatoly Boliatko, "Threats and Challenges to Russia in the Asia-Pacific Region," *Far Eastern Affairs*, 3 (2000) May–June, pp. 3–11.

say to the military and other nationalists. When Putin came to power, he relied heavily on his special bond with the military and his popular nationalist image. Later, he defied nationalists with some bold foreign policy moves, but uncertainty over the security situation in NEA kept the input of the military from receding.

If many in Russia were carried away with rhetoric of building a great-power coalition, exemplified by Primakov's call for Russia to join China, India, and Iran as a balancing force, others found the prospect absurd in a weak country desperate for economic development and foreign investment. They doubted that Russia could get much from China or the other countries, supposing only that they might be of use as Russia cut a deal with the West. Given the popular mood, the great-power enthusiasts held sway in the media and the pressure mounted for leaders not to look weak in dealing with the United States.

Little cause for optimism has been found in Asiatic Russia. The population of Eastern Siberia is down to 9 million and the Russian Far East had dropped to 7.3 million. Together these areas with just 11 percent of the country's population have less than one-twentieth the population density of European Russia. In their northern extremities the population has fallen by one-quarter to one-third. Workers face higher rates of mortality, and residents are subjected to worse environmental hazards. The age structure keeps deteriorating, as able-bodied workers and young professionals buck the odds to find jobs elsewhere, while pensioners are left behind. The professional level of those left behind has fallen drastically. Little remains but energy and natural resources to meet NEA needs.

While many predicted a rise of Asia's share in Russia's economic ties, the opposite happened, especially in the eastern half of Asia. Russian trade actually was becoming more European oriented, and inside Asia only Israel, Turkey, and Cyprus achieved special roles. In Northeast Asia only South Korea saw a big increase in trade after 1992, but it invested little and in 1997–8 financial crises exposed the fragility of economic ties. Chinese firms initially formed many joint ventures, investing little capital. Because Russia needs vast amounts of capital from multinational corporations, no wonder economic ties with China were not viewed optimistically under Yeltsin.[62]

Although shuttle trade across the Russian Far East's borders with China, Japan, and Korea was recovering from its falloff, it offered little perspective to the major interest groups in cities such as Khabarovsk. The military-industrial complex and other powerful organizations were looking for big projects: power plants, assembly production of large weapons systems, monopolies over the export of abundant natural resources, and so forth. Enough

[62] Wang Bingyin and Zhou Yanli, "Shiheng de Eluosi Yatai zhengce," *Guoji zhengzhi*, October 2000, pp. 80–2.

deals were struck to keep the governors of the region and their entourages living well, reducing the pressure for genuine regionalism from the top. To some degree, the shuttle trade supplied consumer goods and foodstuffs that lessened the pressure from the bottom. Yet, on the border an image persisted of contradictions exceeding mutual interests.[63]

Russians grew so cynical that they regarded notions of globalization and regionalism as illusions to screen the naked truth of grasping for power. In the mid-1990s it was common to blame naïve Gorbachev and reform intellectuals for believing myths, such as that the Asia-Pacific region would form a community to which the Soviet Union could join and benefit. Looking back, some saw the temporary cooperation of U.S.-Japan-China as an anti-Soviet grouping that was inherently unstable. Countries merely used each other, and the 1990s proved that conflicts based on the struggle for hegemony are the reality of Asia.[64] It follows that China, which was far behind the other contestants, turned to the Soviet Union and later Russia and will keep doing so in the intensified conflict ahead. This critique of the very idea of the Asia-Pacific region or of regionalism in NEA is rooted in a worldview where economic integration counts for little, while national interests articulated through traditional security reasoning explain everything.

Clearly, Russians approached regionalism with China and others incorrectly. While they established FEZs, the outcome was poor because they were abused by Russians who had bad intentions to evade taxes on exports coming from other parts of the country and imports aimed at consumption. Instead of coordinated policies under central control, Russia faced the region with internal disintegration.[65] It could not counter this situation by strengthening the two existing regional organizations – the Siberian Agreement and the Far East and Trans-Baikal Association – because the center lacked leverage over local governors. Earnings from exports were diverted instead of being used to address local socioeconomic problems: 1) declining population and professional qualifications; 2) deteriorating infrastructure; 3) negligible capacity to process what is extracted; and 4) a still inhospitable environment for investment in increasingly desired reserves of natural resources. Negative trends prevailed as natural resources on land and sea were misused, illegal immigrants formed a growing percentage of the local population, narcotics and weapons flowed into the country, and the national government failed to become an active force in support of globalization or regionalism.[66]

63 V. L. Larin, *Kitai i Dal'nii Vostok Rossii* (Vladivostok: Dal'nauka, 1998).

64 O. Arin, *Aziatsko-Tikhookeanskii region: mify, illiuzii i real'nost'* (Moscow: Flinta, Nauka, 1997), pp. 3, 13, 25, 214.

65 Judith Thornton and Charles E. Ziegler, eds., *Russia's Far East: A Region at Risk* (Seattle: University of Washington Press, 2002).

66 "Strategiia razvitiia Rossii v Aziatsko-Tikhookeanskom Raione v XXI veke," *Analisticheskii vestnik*, special issue no. 17 (Moscow: Sovet Federatsii federal'nogo Rossiiskoi Federatsii, 2000), pp. 9, 24, 29.

China and Russia

Obsessed with the world's march to multipolarity, Chinese analysts foresaw a sharp rise in the function of great-power relations. The crux of their argument was that the United States and its allies were responding to the end of the cold war with a two-track policy toward Russia, mixing support with containment, the latter aimed at limiting its recovery of great-power status. This caused dissatisfaction in both the leadership and society, eliciting a rising outcry to do exactly that.[67] In contrast, China welcomed Russia's great-power role, insisting that there is a very large degree of common interests in economics, politics, and security.[68] This reasoning brushed aside divergent interests, ignoring skepticism in Russia and even in China that prospects were, indeed, rosy.

In retrospect, the Chinese recognized that the personal role of Boris Yeltsin backed by the geopolitical logic of Evgenii Primakov as foreign minister had a lot to do with the sharp upswing in relations from 1996. If originally they had insisted that the nature of great-power relations and Russian national interests were the real forces at work, in 2000 they were changing their tune.[69] Primakov sought to orchestrate a linkage to India as a pole with Iran as another possibility, but China nixed India as a partner. No doubt, Russian concern about becoming China's junior partner motivated this approach, while China's preoccupation with favorable balances of power on all of its borders dictated its response. If for a time it seemed that a bilateral partnership could become a base for a wider group to challenge U.S. power, differences over how to achieve multipolarity soon interfered.

Although at first Chinese sources were careful not to criticize Moscow, later openness revealed the pent-up frustrations from 1997 when the Chinese had expected to consolidate the new strategic partnership. Particularly galling was the dual acceptance of NATO expansion and the U.S.-Japanese new defense guidelines. The Chinese speculated that this was payback for acceptance of Russia into the G-8. Also closely observed in China were visits by Russian political forces to Taiwan. Beijing was looking for an old-style strategic relationship that Moscow would not accept, while Moscow sought a socialist era economic relationship through trade agreements that Beijing would not permit.

Apart from young people, the Chinese and Russians understand each other quite well. They recognize that they experienced the same education,

[67] Liu Shaojun, "Eluosi waijiao zhengce de zhidao sixiang," *Shijie jingji yu zhengzhi*, 4 (1995), p. 68.

[68] Xu Kui, "Zhonge guanxi de xianzhuang he qianjing," *Dongou Zhongya yanjiu*, 6 (1996), p. 9.

[69] Li Jingjie, "Zhonge zhanlue xiezuo huoban guanxi jiqi Meiguo insu," *Dongou Zhongya yanjiu*, 3 (2000), pp. 3–14.

and they nurtured the same kind of nationalism and great-power reasoning. Indeed, even those who were most vehement in their criticisms on each side in the years of the split found in the 1990s that they shared a great deal in common. Yet, after a short period when Russians seemed to welcome Western ideas, it was the Chinese who embraced globalization much faster. While Russians equated it with Americanization and even doubted the benefits of a market economy, the Chinese perceived it as inevitable and as an opportunity. Such differences led to doubts that political ties based on shared thinking among leaders could be sustained.

The 1990s started as a time of diminished threat perceptions, but peoples accustomed to invoking threats soon found new ones or revived old ones. Russians found it easy to arouse fear of China.[70] After all, the memory of the "Mongo yoke" reinforced by alarm over the "yellow peril" from immigration long predated the hysteria over the "Chinese heresy" in the 1960s–70s. In the Russian Far East insecurity naturally rose due to the breakup of the state subsidy system that had been the area's lifeline. Moreover, the military industrial complex now wavered between continuing to have a "vested interest in maintaining fears of a Chinese threat"[71] and wanting to identify a revived threat in the West, which among other things justified selling weapons to China.

Some Chinese have come to recognize that they are special targets of Russian animosity. Various explanations are offered for this situation. One is geographical. Whereas the expansion of NATO and the rise of Iran and Turkey occur close to the heartland of Russia, Siberia and the Russian Far East are remote and in deeper social and economic crisis. With great powers nearby, there is more emphasis on a geopolitical vacuum. Another is economic. The sudden fall of Russia's economy coupled with the rise of China's and projections of further growth arouse disorientation. A third explanation is historic. After more than 1,000 years of looking to European culture and identifying with Europeans, Russians have little understanding of China. This gap is exacerbated by the two decades of the Sino-Soviet split and has been little remedied in the 1990s because news coverage of China is skimpy and often biased. Additionally, the Chinese accuse politicians in Russia of stirring negative feelings, sometimes as a means to achieve other foreign-policy goals such as closer ties to the West and at other times to deflect discontent. Finally, it is not uncommon in China to charge that foreign politicians influence Russians with their own version of the China threat.[72] Whatever the cause, the Chinese cannot trust Russia.

[70] V. G. Gel'bras, *Kitaiskaia real'nost' Rossii* (Moscow: Muravei, 2001).

[71] Alexander Lukin, *The Bear Watches the Dragon: Russia's Perceptions of China and the Evolution of Russian-Chinese Relations Since the Eighteenth Century* (Armonk, NY: M. E. Sharpe, 2003).

[72] Li Chuanxun, "E yuandong diqu duihua yulun zhong de mouxie xiaoji qingxiang fenxi," *Xiboliya yanjiu*, 2 (2000), pp. 9–11.

For a time in the mid-1990s China interpreted Russian nationalism as a justifiable response to Western hegemonism and crude power politics. Even when some nationalists in Moscow and the Russian Far East specifically directed their accusations against China, the Chinese downplayed the message. Instead, they pretended that anti-Chinese sentiments really came from pro-Western reformers, but experts were aware that it is not possible to escape the realization that Russian nationalism is also deeply worried about China and that many Russians believe that China needs Russia more than Russia needs China.

Briefly during the mid-1990s China imposed limits on the import of the raw materials that the Russian Far East sells. Firms in Heilongjiang could not get permission to import fertilizer, raw and refined oil, and other products. Russia refused multiple entry visas to Chinese farm workers. If they try to bring daily articles such as clocks with them, the Russian customs agents impose duties. No wonder border trade was slow to develop. Some recovery had begun in conjunction with the goal of boosting bilateral trade to $20 billion in a few years, but the Russian financial crisis set things back before a new spurt of economic ties occurred.[73] Leaders such as Governor Viktor Ishaev in Khabarovskii krai made some accommodation, but their outlook for regionalism made it clear that China must be contained.[74]

The extreme rhetoric of the leadership of Primorskii krai toward China was well revealed by the 1996 book *The Yellow Peril*, comprised of inflammatory writings just before and after the Russian Revolution on the threat of migration by Asians. Introducing it, K. V. Tolstoshein, the mayor of Vladivostok and associate of Governor Nazdratenko, argued that Russians want to live in peace and friendship with their neighbors, but China and Japan have too many people and cannot control migration. Lumping together illegal migration, border demarcation, relaxation of the border regime, and Japan's campaign for the return of four islands, the addition to the book pointed to a region again under siege.[75] Discussion of issues linked to regionalism eventually quieted, but nationalist writings were easier to find than sober assessments of the advantages of compromises.

The Chinese and Russian leaders trumpeted their success in completing demarcation of their common border, but the process was not easy. The severity of the resistance to the demarcation was concealed when Boris Yeltsin went to China in November 1997 and joined in an announcement of the completion of demarcation along the eastern border. First, local authorities under Nazdratenko had waged a four-year struggle against carrying out the

[73] Li Ping, "Heilongjiang duie bianjing maoyi fazhan xianzhang cunzai wenti qianyi," *Dongbeiya luntan*, 3 (2000), pp. 68–72.

[74] V. I. Ishaev, *Mezhdunarodnoe ekonomicheskoe sotrudnichestvo: regional'nyi aspect* (Vladivostok: Dal'nauka, 1999).

[75] *Zheltaia opasnost'* (Vladivostok: Voron, 1996), p. 124.

demarcation, even blocking its completion in 1997. The Nazdratenko camp kept hindering the work of the demarcation group even after Beijing changed its position to allow Russia to keep land where Soviet troops had been buried in 1938 in the battle against Japan. Second, despite statements by Russian leaders on the eve of Yeltsin's trip that all demarcation posts were in "order" and the formal announcement at the summit of the end of the process, the work actually dragged on into early 1998. Once the process was over, Nazdratenko abruptly softened his tone. The demagogic alarm about China was largely gone. Had Primakov at last made a deal to silence this thorn in his pursuit of a partnership with China? A more convincing answer emerged in trade statistics: in the year 2000 industrial production in Primorskii krai rose precipitously, as helicopters began to be exported to China. Leaders profit a lot from local ties with China, including the export of marine products and the use of Zarubino and other Russian ports. The Chinese have cut deals with leaders on the Russian side that finally quieted the tumult along the border. Yet, China's interest in large-scale development of Zarubino through a corridor to the sea aroused only fear in Russians protective of existing ports.

As post-Soviet relations matured, the Chinese pictured the vast space formerly occupied by the Soviet Union as a head and two wings. At the wings are the Russian Far East and Central Asia, of economic interest for energy and shuttle trade. With much talk of China as Russia's "latent enemy," officials took care to avoid annoying Moscow by turning directly to the wings.[76] While officials had to suppress hopes for regionalism with these areas that would give wide rein to Chinese entrepreneurship and labor migration, they found value in stabilizing borders. From the head in Moscow, China sought a great-power partnership backed by substantial cooperation in the military-industrial sector.

Chinese arms purchases from Russia climbed from about $500 million to $1 billion per year in 1993–7 and kept rising afterward. Much was not recorded in bilateral trade figures. Negotiations over purchases were not easy. On the one hand, the Chinese prefer to keep imports down, seeking the transfer of production rights. On the other, Russians try to attach conditions obliging China to buy surplus items or extraneous civilian products such as airplanes. As talk turned to joint production, it was clear that Russia is reluctant to share its best technology and China is worried about quality and bypassing market mechanisms for anything that is not strictly military in nature.

Russia's position toward China lacked consistency. On the one hand, it accepted arms sales and talk of China as Russia's number one ally. On the other, it was known to view China with suspicion, even considering it Russia's foremost enemy over the long run. Authorities both drew close to

[76] Wang Shuchu and Wang Shixin, "Zhonge guanxi qianjing zhanwang," *Dongbeiya yanjiu*, 4 (2000), p. 27.

China with appeals that it must be as angry about U.S. behavior as Russia, and cautioned China to be less confrontational over Taiwan in order not to endanger stability. The Chinese had trouble figuring out what Russia really wanted.

While some China experts in Moscow depicted China as a model and favored maximum improvement in Sino-Russian relations, Chinese officials and scholars were discerning in their judgment. They were well aware of the mixed images inside Russia and the delicate state of relations. Ambassador Li Fenglin, who after leaving Moscow became part of a small consulting group for Jiang Zemin, was known for his range of contacts and understanding of the complexities of Russian nationalism. The Chinese kept well informed and patiently persisted in seeking opportunities to stabilize and broaden ties.

China tried hard to strengthen ties with Russia in the first two years after the strategic partnership was set in April 1996. One objective was to overcome negative public opinion. Li Fenglin and his staff were eager to correct misperceptions about a migration threat, including exaggerated estimates of the number of Chinese involved. They went to the border areas to smooth the demarcation process. Inside Moscow they worked to normalize the situation of Chinese residents. Despite some improvements in public opinion and the completion of the demarcation, in the end they decided that there was not much the embassy could accomplish. As in the case of the Japanese embassy's public relations campaign earlier in the decade, a pause followed marked by more sober thinking even as new efforts were being debated.

Alarm over China's presence in the Russian Far East was hard to dispel. Some in Russia saw a quiet border not as a sign of cooperation to eliminate the problems of the early 1990s, but as evidence that Russia had lost control as Chinese through bribes co-opted border guards and local elites. When Chinese purchases of submarines, fighter planes, and other arms allowed production lines in Far Eastern cities to hum again, some Russians saw this as a takeover and resented the Chinese officers out of uniform and present in these factories. Talk of cooperation with China in the development of raw materials led to accusations of economic colonialism. Behind this hysteria was lack of confidence that Russia could manage economic ties in a way that would benefit its own people.

The earlier notion of regionalism through cross-border integration did not fare well in these years of great-power jockeying. Although China tried to implement the call by Jiang and Yeltsin at the 1996 summit for expansion of bilateral trade to $20 billion in the year 2000, they could not get the Russians to reduce the barriers on the border. In 1998 the Russian economic crisis compounded the problems of high transportation costs and low population densities in Asiatic Russia to leave the provinces of Northeast China with little hope for their exports. Big Chinese companies especially abandoned plans to become more active in Russia. They saw a population in the

Russian Far East shrinking to barely 7 million (less than one-fifth the total in Heilongjiang province alone) and losing much of its purchasing power. Trade had evolved to bypass the border.

Russia has been upset that China has not bought more of its industrial big-ticket items. Despite agreements about the purchase of Russian turbines for the Three Gorges hydroelectric project, China turned elsewhere. As a rule, China does not buy Russian civilian aircraft. When Xinjiang did buy some, it was dissatisfied. When salesmen called on China to buy 1,000 planes by 2010, the Chinese were heard to say that not even Russian airlines are willing to purchase them. Shanghai purchased German subway cars, taking advantage of loans that Russia could not extend. The Chinese government has to keep telling Russians that under market conditions it cannot tell firms to buy Russian goods.

While for many years the Chinese had found it sufficient to blame the Russians for not doing what was necessary to develop Sino-Russian economic ties, they had to acknowledge that on their side too only some top leaders and scholars had been pushing for these ties. Ministers and managers of big companies generally had no interest in Russia, along with a new generation of leaders without educational or economic links to it.[77] It took special effort to boost trade after 1999.

River transport played a small role in Sino-Russian trade. As much as railroads were criticized, they moved the bulk of goods. The infrastructure in ports and the services there proved to be far inferior, causing high costs and long delays. Although Vladivostok and nearby Russian ports were but 1,800 to 2,300 kilometers from Dalian, Tianjin, and Shanghai, the sea was little used. When on April 30, 2000 a new sea route opened using Zarubino port, south of Vladivostok, linking Jilin province to South Korea and Japan, it too failed to attract much commerce. Eager for a corridor to the sea with access as far as the United States, the Chinese raised doubts about legal conditions on the Russian side. They recalled that as early as 1986 an agreement had been reached on navigation along border rivers, but Russia kept raising obstacles. Even when Moscow agreed in 1999 to open more border points and allow passage on additional land and water routes, the improvements were very slow.[78] Given the many bottlenecks, no wonder that from 1996 air traffic between the two countries rose to fill the void. Mostly charter flights, as many as 200 planes a month, linked the two countries.

Direct flights joined Tianjin, near Beijing, to cities in Western Siberia and beyond. In 1996 Tianjin airport boosted flights to Russia to 2,600, carrying more than 10 million tons of goods, but this level was not sustained. In 1998 the number of flights dropped to 1,300 and the quantity

[77] Hsueh Chun-tu and Lu Nanquan, eds., *Xineluosi: zhengzhi, jingji, waijiao* (Beijing: Zhongguo shehuikexue chubanshe, 1997).

[78] *Xiboliya yanjiu,* 5 (2000), pp. 17–19.

carried fell faster. As Russia strove to increase its exports to China, it seemed content with a low level of imports. Chinese firms, which lost their markets and the savings left in Russian banks, were little inclined to return soon. And rising Russian exports were narrowly concentrated; little besides natural resources and arms interested buyers. A rise in trade was finally registered in 1999, but it did not signify complementary, interlocked economies.[79]

In its new watered-down version, the Tumen River area development project (TRADP) offered a transit corridor for Chinese goods through Russian territory. Even in this limited form it was a failure. China spent a great deal to upgrade infrastructure, while Russia delayed implementation of agreements. The Chinese charged that Russian transport tariffs were too high while shipments encountered repeated checks and delays. Visas were too expensive and available only at a distance. Vehicles could not operate freely. Losses caused by delays were very large. Russians saw the need to keep a military guard at the main crossing points, even forcing a wait of a few days to clear customs. The Russians argued that they would improve only if the Chinese state guarantees a fixed amount of business. Some groups appealed to the Japanese or South Koreans to compensate for these troubles by making a strong commitment,[80] but the North did not even bother to attend key meetings and the Russians were more interested in blocking China than in promoting transit. Seoul's interest switched to direct ties with North Korea across the DMZ, and Beijing tired of progress that "is as slow as glacier melt."[81]

While Beijing and Moscow have found common language in great-power rhetoric, they do not share the same thinking on economic liberalization. Russians active in dealing with the Chinese often are fearful of the kinds of economic changes that the Chinese take for granted. Some Chinese see Russia's foremost problem as ideological. This is not the ideological threat feared in 1992 from a democratizing Russia, but the failure to break away from traditional communist thinking. While the Chinese treated the United States as a cultural threat for its ideology of human rights and its irrepressible popular culture and viewed Japan as a cultural problem for its historical amnesia, only slowly did they acknowledge the cultural challenge from Russia. In doing so they reacted to the language of fear expressed by the media inside Russia, especially in the Russian Far East.

79 Qiao Guanghan, "Eluosi jingji weiji dui Zhonge jingmao de yingxiang ji duice," *Xiboliya yanjiu*, 1 (2000), pp. 9–12.

80 Tsogtsaikhan Gombo, "TRADP Transport Working Group Meeting Summary Report," *ERINA REPORT*, 38 (January 2001), pp. 26–9; Li Mao Xiang, "The Basic Issues of the Development of the Lower Reaches of the Tumen River," *ERINA REPORT*, 38 (January 2001), pp. 33–4.

81 Hisako Tsuji, "UNDP-led Tumen Region Development at the Crossroads," *ERINA REPORT*, 38 (January 2001), pp. 38–41.

As the Chinese looked ahead to regionalism, there was no reason for optimism about cross-border ties with Russia. In talks with Nazdratenko they found no interest in the economic development of his area within a regional context and even hostility to market competition, while with Ishaev the picture was hardly better. Realists in Beijing reaffirm that there is no future for the Tumen River project, as both Moscow and the Russian Far East remain opposed and even North and South Korea have lost interest. If some Chinese considered it a tragedy that the "Russian mentality" holds back the development of the Russian Far East, others kept proposing steps forward for economic gains that could create an environment for regionalism.

South Korea, the Great Powers, and Regionalism

If earlier in the decade South Korea was more cautious than Japan or China about regionalism, on the eve of its financial crisis the South was the most optimistic, although cautiously so. Koreans had more confidence in economic ties with China and continued to invest in Russia after others had pulled back. They expected their own economy to continue growing rapidly with capital and technology sufficient to lead in the integration of the Russian Far East. Idealistic writings kept anticipating the opening of the North Korean economy, while critical treatments of Russia were restrained in light of the need to keep that country's cooperation in dealing with the North. Indeed, now that Japan was weaker and China offered more balance, South Koreans were more inclined to view NEA regionalism as favorable to their interests.[82] More than others, they felt a need to shift from national competition to regional linkages in order to get Pyongyang's attention and some day to pay the projected costs of reintegration.

In 1994 under Kim Young-sam the term *globalization* (*segyehwa*) became very popular in Korea. It was filled with optimism about how a country continuing to rise in world economic ranks could benefit as one of the top-ten trading powers from global integration. In 1997 the Asian financial crisis forced Korea more than any other country in the region to reexamine its ties to the rest of the world, but the result under Kim Dae-jung was a reaffirmation of globalization. This time it came with grudging recognition that Korea was far from certain to keep its place near the top and that more borrowing of institutions would be needed. Concentration on globalization left room for regionalism.

The Asian financial crisis heated up the debate in Korea over globalization versus nationalism. In the course of the transition to the Kim Dae-jung administration, many decided that Kim Young-sam had done too little to

[82] "Tongbuka kyongjegwon oe chukmyon eso pon hanguk gwa Roshia (kuktong chiyok) kan oe kyongje kisul hyomnyok hyonhwang gwa chonmang," *Kyongyong ronsup*, December 1997, pp. 59–83.

move beyond the closed nationalism that constituted Park Jung-hee's legacy. When enthusiasm for the use of English as an official language grew, nationalists warned that it would mean the abandonment of Korean traditions and acceptance of Western hegemony. However, in December 1998 on Korea's fiftieth independence day, Kim Dae-jung proclaimed the second foundation of the nation. If the civil war of 1950 represented the first crisis for founding a nation, the 1997 IMF regime was regarded as the second crisis. But instead of capitalizing on the nationalism associated with emergency measures such as the gold-gathering movement or calls to "buy Korean," the new president proposed that the crisis could be met by a pan-nationalist movement reaching out to the North in the context of globalization. Instead of dwelling on this as a national disgrace requiring more exclusive nationalism, it could become an opportunity for open-ended acceptance of a new identity.

South Koreans, much more than the Japanese, consider themselves victims of the cold war because they have been unable to conduct an independent foreign policy. Lacking a great-power identity, they feel hemmed in by surrounding powers, less able to shape globalization, and eager for "normalcy," meaning a mixture of independence and balance-of-power maneuverability. Thus, they look back on the end of the 1980s and the decade of the 1990s not just as the coming of democracy but also as the beginning of serious diplomacy. This mind-set leaves a feeling of anxiety over the possibility that a new cold war will descend on the region. While some see China or North Korea as the likely villain, many fear that the United States prefers dominance to acceptance of a larger role for China or that Japan's ambitions will become the primary barrier to the South's struggle for breathing room. It follows that the South earns greater trust from Beijing by not siding with the United States and Japan, that efforts to improve relations with Russia require independent diplomacy, and that South Koreans take pride in achieving a more proactive and positive range of relations. The South seeks a regional order with a balance of power even if the United States is dominant for now, and it aims to become the driving force in forging it.[83]

Opinion in the South would rather see a new equilibrium emerge giving their country a balancing role in great-power relations than a return to a polarized region with dependence on the United States and Japan. They worry about the United States being too hasty to return to containment and Japan too nationalist to accept a role as one of many regional powers. Indeed, they welcome China's interest in checking the rise of Japan as a political and military power with cooperation from South Korea, while believing that China greatly wants economic help from the South. Some experts wonder how Seoul can manage these complex great-power relations,

[83] Lee Tai Hwan, "Korea's Foreign Policy in the Post-Cold War Era," *Korea Focus*, November–December 1999, pp. 1–17.

and South Koreans themselves are torn between optimism that they are leading the way to regionalism as a balancing force and pessimism that they will be forced to make choices as a country too weak to shape the course of events.

One means to regionalism would have been for Japan's Koreans to spearhead financial linkages and diaspora ties. However, the Koreans who came to Japan, unlike the Chinese who went to Southeast Asia, were driven by poverty or coercion to work in coal mines and construction, not entrepreneurs in search of commercial opportunities. Discrimination in the postwar era kept them confined to trash collection, small eating establishments, and pachinko parlors. They were excluded from both public and private enterprises. When the bubble economy contributed to a pachinko boom and labor shortages led large firms to accept Koreans with strong educational credentials, the situation seemed to be changing. Yet, the bubble burst, pachinko parlors lost one-third of their labor force and half of their land value, and most fell into the red with no buyers in sight.[84] Young Japanese turned to other luxury outlets. The Korean-Japanese community lacked the economic clout and occupational ties to contribute much to regionalism. Many were linked to North Korea and through their remittances supported a threat to regionalism.

Operating more independently of the Korean government under Kim Dae-jung, whose backing came especially from smaller chaebol linked to the China market, the big chaebol were tightening ties to Japan. Drawing near to Japan too were Southwest Korean firms with close ties to Japan's Korean community. Once subjected to a brutal purge for harboring communist sympathizers and counting many whose relatives had fled to Japan and joined pro-North organizations, this region was most eager for rapprochement with the North. Yet, Koreans were slow to feel close to Japanese. In 1999 only 10 percent said that they like Japan, while 13 percent of Japanese responded that they like South Korea. Friendship networks as a base for regionalism trailed business linkages.[85]

Conservatives in Japan have long warned of government softness toward the North. When the powerful LDP politician Kanemaru Shin went to Pyongyang in 1990 they saw it as a betrayal of the families of Japanese kidnapped by the North, which had been exposed already by 1988 in the Diet. Then in October 2000 the story broke that Prime Minister Mori Yoshiro three years before as a Diet member had proposed to the North to set the issue aside if the abductees were freed in a third country. He was accused of failing to protect Japanese sovereignty. Also the right wing charged that throughout the decade the principal newspapers

[84] Kim Chanjon, "Henbo suru zainichi Kankoku – Chosenjin shakai," *Sekai shuho*, October 17, 2000, pp. 22–5.

[85] Kanno Tomoko, *Suki ni natte wa ikenai kuni* (Tokyo: Bungei shunju, 2000), p. 52.

and television networks had maintained a taboo on this topic.[86] Despite a mood of alarm in the country over North Korean missiles, the right wing charged that top leaders were allowing a desire for normalization to drive policy.

Japanese concern for North Korea's missile program from late 1998 fueled a desire to redouble efforts to improve ties with Russia and to reinvigorate ties to China. North Korea drew center stage, and Japan was not prepared to just rely on the United States. It eventually became clear that even as the public was aroused against a growing threat, diplomats were working behind the scenes to engage Pyongyang and improve ties.

South Koreans give Japan little credit for leadership toward regionalism. They fault it for not winning the trust of its neighbors and not producing leaders such as Willy Brandt who led West Germany to take bold political initiatives to reduce tensions with the East. Worrying about economic stagnation and Japan veering to the right politically and thus making it even harder to be trusted as a leader, Koreans talk of their country having to adjust to Japan's weakness. Seoul had success with Moscow and Beijing by setting aside unification for the foreseeable future in favor of economic cooperation and reduced military tensions with Pyongyang, but it found that Tokyo and Washington are more cautious.

While some in Japan grew optimistic that a turning point was reached in 1998 in mutual understanding between the Japanese and South Korean people, others on the right insisted that Korea is just a "little China" unable to turn its gaze from the past. As China, they argued, it arouses anti-Japanese feelings in order to transfer responsibility for its own shortcomings.[87] The Japanese were too divided to build relations of trust quickly. Indeed, many felt triumphant as if the past was totally resolved, and proposals to use the momentum for genuine reconciliation were brushed aside.

Personal networks remain key to political and economic relations in the region. When the Asian financial crisis hit, one response in South Korea was to reaffirm the importance of connections in trade ties with China, but now to rely more on networks of economic experts and businessmen instead of old-fashioned bureaucrats to smooth the way to a new economy.[88] At this level progress has been considerable. At other levels more problems appear. Among the 100,000 or so Korean Chinese who work in South Korea, personal relations have not been warm. On the visitors' side the grievances are many, such as nonpayment of promised wages. Returning to China, they

[86] Nishioka Tatomu, " 'Ratchi ka kome ka' uredaga no seijika retten," *Bungei shunju*, December 2000, pp. 202–11.

[87] Koo Bunyuu, *Tatsu o kidoru Chugoku, tora no odoshi o karu Kankoku* (Tokyo: Tokuma shoten, 2000).

[88] Yoo Hee-Moon, "Excerpts: Importance of Human Connections in Trade Policy toward China," *New Asia*, Autumn 1998, pp. 169–70.

sometimes take out their wrath on Korean travelers.[89] There is no population of Chinese in the South to cushion the transition. Most Chinese were expelled, and the small numbers left behind were both discriminated against to the point of exclusion and inclined toward Taiwan, whose ties had fostered an anticommunist front line as well as a shared economic destiny in the 1960s–80s. But the South lacked a shared identity with Taiwan, compounding the distance felt toward Chinese from there. Whereas both had been Japanese colonies, the South viewed Taiwan's closeness to Japan with suspicion. A new community of Koreans from the PRC has not gained stable footing because those admitted are short-term manual laborers, who often overstay their visa or illegally switch workplaces.

South Koreans view China as a force for "external balancing" in order to escape the constraints of the "asymmetric alliance" with the United States, which has shifted to support the U.S.-Japan alliance in a possible containment of China. To the extent that the defense of South Korea is no longer at great risk from North Korea, the South faces the question of whether its notion of regionalism aimed at enticing more change in North Korea coincides with other notions focused on security and Taiwan. Because South Koreans value the rapid growth in trade with China and are troubled by dependency on the United States, hesitation over being dragged into an unplanned approach to the region is considerable. Asked in 1997 with which major powers the South should strengthen relations, 56 percent chose China, 45 percent Russia, and just 25–30 percent chose the United States and Japan. Also in 1997 Koreans gave high priority to the prevention of militarization by Japan (51 percent), favored a self-reliant defense for Korea (51 percent), and were as concerned with gradual withdrawal of U.S. forces as checking the rise of China (34 percent). In early 1999 even the media "viewed the U.S. question as more controversial than the China issue at the moment."[90]

Respecting Chinese culture more than the Japanese do, Koreans were loath to accept the cultural critique of China that spread in Japan during the late 1990s. They were willing to rely on Chinese paternalism, reverting to an old way of dealing as a small country with the huge Chinese empire. Their own identity accepted more cultural similarities with China, including a shared bias against Japanese culture and history. Moreover, confident of the United States and Japan in the background, South Koreans aspired to the role of intermediary. Seoul sees its mission more as opening a window to unification, however gradually, than shutting the door to invasion. This leads it to sympathize with China on Taiwan, not to blame Beijing for pressing for

[89] Chi Togyoku, "Hanto de kyugeki ni takamaru Chugoku no eikyo ryoku," *Sekai shuho*, August 1, 2000, p. 34.

[90] Jae Ho Chung, "The Korean-American Alliance and the 'Rise of China': A Preliminary Assessment of Perceptual Changes and Strategic Choices" (Stanford: Institute for International Studies, 1999), pp. 13–14, 26.

reunification. It does not see communism versus democracy, but nationalism overcoming division amidst instability.

Korean optimists kept predicting that an upsurge in investment in Russia would soon be forthcoming. In 1997 they grasped at the temporary economic growth in Russia and the misleading last gasp of the Korean model of development to assert that large-scale economic cooperation was on its way. More than in Japan, the upbeat mood was sustained through the mid-1990s, despite ample evidence of troubles not being addressed. A decline in trade in 1996 and continued problems with no repayment from Russia only made many writers even more eager to tout the prospects of moving into a new stage of a higher quality of cooperation, meaning increased Korean investment. Koreans seemed more eager than Japanese to develop Russian natural resources and gain access to high technology, both means to use Russia to boost Korea's regional standing.

Some in South Korea prized Russia as means to a more independent foreign policy. They observed that through the first forty years of the cold war the South had no maneuverability in relations with the Soviet Union or other major powers. It had feared jeopardizing its close ties with the United States as well as economic ties to Japan, and it was angry at Moscow for supporting the North. In 1998 trade and investment between the South and Russia fell sharply when both countries suffered financial crises at the same time. Also Moscow expelled a Korean diplomat and the South retaliated. With Russian nationalism turning again to North Korea for leverage in regional relations, there was concern that Moscow would decide that the economic gains from recognizing the South had been exhausted and it was no longer any more important than the North. But those who clung to the Russia card urged Korea to keep ties advancing by meeting Russian insistence since 1994 for the South to do more, for instance by investing in an industrial complex in Nakhodka and in a large natural gas development in Yakutsk.

Unexpectedly, military ties advanced more smoothly than political ones, which in turn were more positive than economic ties and, especially, cultural ties. High officials of the armed forces of Russia and South Korea exchanged visits in the 1990s earlier and with far greater frequency than Japanese-Russian meetings. Generals and their wives spent time together to build amity. South Korean officers trained in Russia. Sustained talks about arms purchases from Russia in repayment for its debts added another force for cooperation. At the Seoul air show of 1996 advanced aircraft were under review. There was talk of buying T-80 tanks. Naval ties advanced. If in 1997–8 economic setbacks first to South Korea and then to Russia lowered hopes, the persistence of networks of trust left open the possibility that a new Russian leader would adopt the spirit of the "sunshine policy" and offer personal leadership to make Moscow active in regional diplomacy.

This was different from playing the "Pyongyang card" to attract Seoul's investments.[91]

Kim Dae-jung set a new tone for relations with Japan that gave a major boost to regionalism. While he ambitiously sought to break down barriers with the North, he understood that it was best to start with a country that in cultural attitudes and social structure was a great deal like South Korea but in images of friendship seemed very distant.[92] Unlike Kim Young-sam's fanning of nationalism toward Japan, Kim Dae-jung gave the Japanese trust that relations would be kept on a steady keel. He worked out an agreement on joint management of fishing on strictly economic terms, setting aside the emotionalism of the dispute that had flared in 1996 when territorial waters were being redrawn. Both nations could now look ahead to sharing the 2002 World Cup as Kim's term in office ended.[93]

After a boom in the mid-1990s in novels hostile to Japan, the breakthrough of October 1998 contributed to a desire to learn what life in Japan really is like. Travel accounts became popular. In turn, a boom of Japanese writings on Korea in 1999 and especially 2000, showed confusion over what Koreans really think of Japan, some warning that hostile views continue and others suggesting that a sharp change has begun. The new writings along with increased travel contributed to a new realism in perceptions of Korea in 1999.[94] But South Koreans had their sights fixed on the United States and English-speaking countries. While 11,000 studied in Japan's institutes of higher education (compared to 22,000 Chinese), hundreds of thousands more were scrambling at all levels of education to find a spot elsewhere. Education favored globalization, not regionalism.

Falling self-confidence, a new presidential attitude, and more casual acceptance of Japanese mass culture all reshaped Korean attitudes toward Japan from 1998. A Japanese observer saw coverage change from "anti-Japan" to "know Japan,"[95] learning about real life and setting aside taboos. It helped that the Japanese seized the opportunity of a weak won and new spirit in South Korea to arrive in record numbers of two million a year as well as that they grew eager for an FTA with the South, while Koreans started to explore how to cope with an age when both globalization and regionalism required forging FTAs.[96]

[91] Vasily V. Mikheev, "Russian Policy towards Korean Peninsula after Yeltsin's Re-election as President," *The Journal of East Asian Affairs*, 11(2) Summer/Fall 1997, p. 374.

[92] Ue Ichiro, *Rikai to gokai: tokuhain no yomu Kim Dae-jung no Kankoku* (Tokyo: Kokushokan kokai, 1998), p. 216.

[93] Ue Ichiro, *Rikai to gokai: tokuhain no yomu Kim Dae-jung no Kankoku*, pp. 199–203, 216–17.

[94] Gilbert Rozman, "Japan and South Korea: Should the U.S. Be Worried about Their New Spat in 2001?" *Pacific Review*, 15(1), 2002, pp. 1–28.

[95] Kanno Tonoko, *Suki ni natte wa ikenai kuni*, pp. 113, 196.

[96] Chong Ingyo, *FTA shidae e ottoge daejohal gos inka?* (Seoul: KIEP, 2001).

Kim Dae-jung seized the opportunity after Clinton visited China in mid-1998 to raise Seoul-Beijing ties to a new level. While the Japanese were worried by the visit and Americans soon soured on China, South Koreans were building momentum with the Chinese that would carry through 2000 as a driving force for regionalism. South Korean ties with China are special despite signs of excess. Indeed, some held the view that Korea dearly needed China for its further development, as West Germany needed Eastern Europe. The embassy along with the Korean Chamber of Commerce helped lots of small and middle-sized firms with little capital benefit from a strong community in moving with great speed into China. Only later did the chaebol arrive, focusing on autos and other major industrial products, although in 1996 plans for joint production of medium-sized airplanes collapsed. If investments of other countries were largely located in Southeast China, half of Korean FDI went to Shandong, Tianjin, and Beijing. Despite the presence of more than 80 percent of Korean Chinese in Jilin (1.18 million) and Heilongjiang (450,000), fewer than 10 percent of FDI went to these Northeast provinces. The focus was the Yellow Sea rim. There was even talk of equidistance between the United States and China, but when the United States objected it was quickly denied as a personal view.[97]

Kim Dae-jung addressed the U.S. Congress in June 1998 with a ringing appeal to the principles of globalization, blaming his own country for causing a financial crisis with excess government interference, collusion, and corruption, and insufficient democracy or free market practices. He went to Japan in October 1998 to heal the wounds of history, receiving recognition in his Nobel Peace Prize two years later for this as well as for the summit in North Korea and the promotion of democracy and human rights at home. If many other Koreans hesitated to dismiss "Asian values," Kim was outspoken in rejecting them and speaking critically of any "clash of civilizations." Kim was a consensus builder, not a divider who would stir up nationalism or regionalism resistant to globalization.[98] He also was the foremost champion of bridging regional differences not only in order to win a breakthrough, but also to establish a mood of cooperation in order to integrate the North through regionalism. That was the only way to persuade Pyongyang and also served as a practical step to cover the costs of rebuilding the North over decades. By 1999 we can detect the seeds of Kim's leadership in regionalism and also of the "sunshine policy" of striving to draw all six actors in NEA together. Kim Dae-jung's consensus-building ways had something to offer each state, proving that regionalism can advance with a positive platform. Problems that had appeared so divisive at the end of

[97] Young Rok Cheong, "Prospects for South Korean-Chinese Economic Cooperation: An Institutional Appraisal," in Davison Lee and Jason Z. Yin, eds., *Comparison of Korean and Chinese Economic Development* (Seoul: Yonsei University Press, 1999), pp. 22–39.

[98] "President Kim Dae-jung's Visit," *The U.S.-Korea Review*, May/June 1998, p. 1.

1998 looked quite different in the heady days of 2000, although too many pieces of the puzzle were missing, such as North Korean reform and trust and U.S. approval of regionalism, for Kim's idealism to work for long. If he gave regionalism a jump start when both the power of globalization and the dangers of antiglobal forces were unduly discounted, it would take much more to cross the threshold when regionalism would become a self-sustaining reality.

At last, North Korea entered the picture of economic integration. The South initiated economic ties with the North with the hope that others would follow suit. Its projects began small. Among the biggest were the Unification Church's Pyongyang car repair operations, a mineral water project named for Kumgang Mountain, and an LG electronics assembly shop capable of issuing 15,000 televisions in Pyongyang. Altogether, more than 580 firms started some sort of processing, construction, or trade with few rising above the scale of several hundred thousand dollars. In each case Seoul bore a one-sided burden. Over half of the trade was in kind, the rest based on aid from the South. The biggest projects were a deal to pay for sightseeing rights at Kumgang Mountain (after December 1998 as many as 10,000 South Koreans a month went to this cordoned spot) and the supply of heavy oil and construction for a nuclear reactor as internationally agreed through KEDO. By 1999 the annual burden to the South exceeded $500 million. This gave the go-ahead to others for new overtures to the North as well.

After Kim Dae-jung took power in February 1998, South Korea quickly moved to the center stage in regionalism. While bilateral ties among the powers suffered setbacks, all sides were ready for active leadership from a country that was not a great-power rival. Kim invigorated ties with China through a November 1998 summit, made a breakthrough in relations with Japan in a historic October 1998 visit, repaired frayed ties with Russia in a May 1999 visit, and increased exchanges with North Korea. Promoting globalization, including universal values, he made an even deeper impact by leading in regionalism. As the voice for regionalism, Kim Dae-jung proposed the formation of a vision group for cooperation through ASEAN + 3 that soon would win approval. In the next period Seoul would take center stage in a very different dynamic exploring the path to regionalism.

Overview on Regionalism

Wishful thinking centered on a quick path to regionalism was yielding in the second half of the 1990s to maneuvering through bilateral relations to shape a more gradual process. Loss of confidence in security drove some of the jockeying, but it was also a recognition that economic integration does not suffice for regionalism. Spillover from new tensions over globalization as the Asian financial crisis sent shockwaves across NEA as well as SEA added to the sense of insecurity. If all sides were frustrated in their great-power strategies, they had at least taken new steps toward institutionalization of multilateral relations, most importantly the establishment of ASEAN +3. Yet, the legacy of divisive security calculations outweighed the fragility of hesitant regional cooperation.

Russia reverted to great-power maneuvering desperate to salvage some of its lost sway over global affairs. China followed in search of the strategic triangle that had been lost in 1989. Japan joined the fray after its rising hopes for global clout had been dashed. Even the United States in the hope of drawing China into a web of security cooperation tried its hand at strategic partnerships amidst the pomp of summitry. When the aftermath of the Clinton visit to China in early summer 1998 brought disillusionment and then Russo-Japanese and Sino-Japanese summits in November set back relations, the pace of bilateral strategic posturing slowed to a crawl. The U.S. war in Yugoslavia provoked one more round of joint Sino-Russian great-power chest beating, but U.S. ascendancy continued.

At the end of 1998 great-power strategies had been exposed as unrealistic. China and the United States could not agree despite the upbeat mood of Clinton's summer visit, and the U.S. Congress and public were increasingly concerned by security questions at year end. China had hoped to solidify its partnership with Russia. Japan had at last turned to Russia for a breakthrough to normalization. China and Japan had appeared on track to recoup from their downturn in relations in 1996. The United States expected to build on its 1996 upgrading of security ties to Japan. Each state was looking for leverage among the powers, expecting that the outcome after the surge of summit diplomacy would favor it. None had reason to be pleased. In the final analysis, the scramble among the powers had been little more than a sideshow before the relentless force of globalization and a distraction in the continued shuffle along the road to regionalism. Great-power maneuvers did not build trust.

By 1999 the adversity of the Asian financial crisis along with the common plight of bystanders to U.S. triumphalism had given new life to the pursuit of regionalism. All of the economic models favored just a short time earlier appeared unsustainable. Russia's oligarchic capitalism with little central control over the Far East governors and resources was at a dead end. South Korea's chaebol model had crash landed. Japan's recession had turned into long-term stagnation with no prospect of transformation without a dramatic shift that many expected to involve regionalism. Even China realized that despite its high growth rates a new round of reform must tackle its most deep-seated problems, including dismantling the state-owned enterprises and addressing their perpetual debts. A shared sense of economic adversity evoked growing recognition of the need for a joint solution.

Winding up the flurry of great-power summitry, Jiang Zemin traveled to Japan in November 1998 with a dual message suggestive of the ambivalence arising in all of the major bilateral relationships of NEA. On the one hand, he and Prime Minister Obuchi Keizo claimed to be forging a twenty-first-century partnership with numerous agreements on deepening cooperation. On the other, the summit was "haunted by the current century" as a joint declaration did not include an apology by Japan and remained unsigned.[99] Just as Japanese-Russian relations were chilled by a disappointing summit in the same month and depressed Sino-Russian economic ties cast a dark shadow on upbeat rhetoric, the key regional linkage ended 1998 struggling for signs of optimism. Euphemistic claims to be establishing "Strategic Partnerships" for close cooperation could not conceal the reality of deep-seated "National Rivalries" that required more effort if they were to be tempered.

[99] *The Japan Times Weekly International Edition*, December 7–13, 1998, p. 1.

6

1999–2000

Sunshine Policy and Security Dilemmas

Globalization swept forward as the U.S. economy reached the apex of its boom and the successful conclusion of the war over Yugoslavia confirmed the unlimited reach of U.S. military force. The futile objections of China and Russia during the war period demonstrated that great-power differences no longer could exercise a restraining force. United States triumphalism reached its peak. No rival challenged the military dominance of the world's lone superpower, and only isolationist states such as North Korea resisted its economic penetration. Cultural diffusion also intensified, to the alarm of national elites as well as the various losers in globalization. A backlash was building that found only two outlets: 1) terrorism to use destructive force surreptitiously so that retaliation would be difficult; and 2) regionalism to pool multiple national resources in order to find balance against one or another form of U.S. hegemony. Regionalism in NEA found new life both as a by-product of increased economic interaction and as expression of a desire to balance the overwhelming power of the United States. Given the ambivalence of nationalist elements, each country was tempted to take a shortcut to make regionalism appear unthreatening.

In 1999 and 2000 the United States was preoccupied with first the war in Yugoslavia, then the political struggle over Clinton's personal life, and finally a nail-biting presidential election. Apart from a late burst of talks with North Korea, it was satisfied with a holding operation in NEA, even as other countries explored new cooperation. Regionalism now advanced with the United States on the sidelines, but never far from the minds of all concerned.

In the aftermath of the Asian financial crisis, China, Japan, and South Korea were drawn into cooperation linked to ASEAN. They discussed financial issues and eventually a currency stabilization fund. Annual summit meetings gradually deepened the agenda. Recognizing that trade and investment ties in NEA were rising continuously, all three countries had a stake in institutionalizing some forms of regional cooperation. Along with nervous awareness of interdependence in a possible opening in North Korea's ties with the South, economic linkages were the driving force boosting prospects for regionalism.

If first Japan and then China led the search for regionalism in the 1990s, South Korea took the lead at decade's end. If this different kind of leadership was aimed largely at persuading North Korea to break away from isolation, it also brought the first instance of a leader firmly embracing regionalism. China's supportive position loomed in the background as a major reason for increased progress on regionalism. Beijing was looking for leverage in relations with Washington and a way to boost ties with skeptical Tokyo, and it found that Kim Dae-jung's visibility in the forefront eased the way to cooperation.

Even as rhetoric in support of regionalism spread in several countries, prospects for sustaining the momentum of 2000 were precarious. How long would an unusual combination of circumstances continue? The United States was optimistic about globalization through WTO membership for China and was participating in efforts to entice North Korea away from isolation. South Korea had a bold leader ready to take risks to appeal to the North and boost regionalism. China's eagerness to improve ties with Japan and boost regionalism was paralleled by Japan's interest in boosting ties with Russia and continued desire to reenter Asia. Yet, in late 2000 the momentum was fading. The security situation and levels of trust were still inadequate, while doubts were rising about the U.S. stance.

Leadership convergence contributed to the upbeat mood for regionalism in 2000. Ever the optimist, Kim Dae-jung displayed the activist, fence-building style that gave new life to regional integration. He could proceed because Bill Clinton did not weigh security threats heavily and looked benignly at modest measures aimed at regionalism consistent with the economic thrust of globalization that was enhancing U.S. leadership. After all, these measures appeared promising for enticing North Korea from its WMD threat posture, for engaging China still hesitant on noneconomic forms of globalization, and for opening Russia economically to advance a precarious transition. Jiang Zemin was still searching for a way to limit U.S. influence in NEA and welcomed Kim's "sunshine policy." Japanese prime ministers Obuchi Keizo and Mori Yoshiro took an incremental approach to foreign relations, valuing the breakthrough in 1998 with South Korea and eyeing Russia as another target while holding the line against nationalism toward China. No leader stood in the way of exploring with Kim Jong-il a deal that would trade security guarantees and economic assistance for a commitment to open gradually to global ties and regional integration, but many doubted that a deal could be reached.

In each nation many questioned the assumptions behind the promised scenario. Given the destabilizing impact of reform, would Pyongyang be content to lower its guard? Was Beijing's long-term goal regional dominance that could threaten Japanese and U.S. interests? Would Russia be able to defend its distant flank in a region where it had few assets? Were the Japanese too fearful of their economic decline and historical image to trust regionalism? Fundamental questions of globalization had yet to be resolved, making it difficult to be confident that the nations of NEA were ready for regionalism.

Globalization and the United States

Americans ordinarily do not give much thought to foreign policy in NEA beyond bilateral relations and alliances to guard against threats. It is generally assumed that new forms of economic integration in the Asia-Pacific will cover a broad geographical range with allowance for subregional zones – an open, if perhaps complex pattern of economic interdependence that allows room for no country in NEA to serve as a hub. This would be accompanied by decentralization and limited state dominance, not only maintaining the leverage of the United States but also helping the region to gravitate toward a new unthreatening equilibrium. Yet, with the rise of China and the uncertainty over North Korea, many in 1999–2000 feared new divisions, requiring the United States to struggle to reassert its influence in a region troubled by rivalry and hot spots. This split in thinking about prospects for NEA was mirrored in domestic politics, where the Clinton administration counted on economic ties to become the driving force for globalization above regionalism while advisors in the Republican campaign of George W. Bush stressed security threats to globalization.

Under Clinton officials and experts as well sometimes spoke of the need to create a new community in East Asia, but this was seen as an Asia-Pacific community built mostly on bilateral security ties centered on the United States. In other words, this was little more than a subset of globalization under U.S. leadership with some room for multilateralism. It incorporated elements of containment while emphasizing a strategy of engagement, seeking to preserve the status quo in most respects but also to induce North Korea to forego a military option and China to abandon or at least postpone pressure against Taiwan. It accepted Japan, still the dominant economic power in the region, as the special partner of the United States, while assuming Japan's leadership would not develop very far independently of the United States and showing little inclination to embrace Japan's nationalism, which could be divisive in the region. In the final two years of the Clinton administration there was some optimism through progress on China's entry into the WTO and on using the Perry report as a basis for working with South Korea and Japan to entice North Korea from its isolation. But there was at least as much pessimism as relations with China grew more tense, Putin's ascent to power and visit to North Korea raised new doubts about Russia's role in the region, and initiatives across NEA appeared more and more beyond the control of Washington. Sino-Japanese, South Korean-Chinese, and

Japanese-Russian relations, as well as Sino-Russian relations, unfolded without active U.S. involvement. A liberal agenda remained of extending webs of economic interdependence while patiently waiting for all to realize the benefits of lowering security threats as part of globalization.

Even the Clinton administration was noticeably uncomfortable with steps toward regionalism in 2000. South Korea's advances toward the North raced ahead of efforts to proceed cautiously on the basis of the initiative proposed to the administration by former Defense Secretary William Perry. One fear was that large cash payments from Hyundai to North Korea in connection with the Kumgang Mountain tourism groups would, along with humanitarian aid, give the North new means to boost its military threat. Another concern was that without really resolving the growing tensions in the region in the late 1990s proclamations of emerging regionalism in 2000 might allow security problems to fester and undermine U.S. leadership. Whether blame was put on the weakness of Clinton's policy or on divisions caused by Republicans overanxious to find a threat, the verdict was that a new president drawing on bipartisan support would need to reassert the indispensable U.S. role before regionalism subordinate to global forces could take hold.

After watching relations with both Russia and China deteriorate in 1999, ostensibly related to the war over Kosovo but actually based on diverse geopolitical factors, Washington had modest success in improving matters in 2000. Fear of a growing threat to attack Taiwan drove pessimism about Beijing's impact on the region, while the gnawing impression endured that Putin would assert nationalism abroad and control at home. Overall, Clinton's administration saw a messy region, not a particularly dangerous one. Sino-Russian relations were strong in rhetoric in 1999, but they lack natural affinities as the Soviet-educated generation of Chinese leaders fades from the scene and Western-educated advisors are on the rise. If advisors to George W. Bush were wary of Russia and China separately or together, experts on China minimized the significance of their ties. Michel Oksenberg reacted to the July 2001 treaty signed by Putin and Jiang, saying, "The Chinese are the ultimate realists, and they know Russia is now a third-rate country economically, technologically and politically . . . they view Russia with scorn, disdain and pity."[1] Such complacency left no reason to doubt U.S. leverage.

American triumphalism was at its peak. Not only had the Kosovo war spotlighted military supremacy, the aftermath of the Asian financial crisis proved the universality of the U.S. economic model. South Korea had been disciplined, left with no choice but to accept the model. Japan's continuing economic failure proved that it had no alternative either, however long political stubbornness postponed the inevitable. Now that China was preparing for WTO entry, it would be pushed in the same direction. Americans

[1] *The New York Times*, July 19, 2000, p. A6.

reasoned that tough global medicine dispensed to these countries was for their own good. Thank goodness that the United States runs the show; regional financial control would have failed.

The years 1999–2000 saw more Americans deciding that neither China nor Russia matter much for international security. Indeed, bringing this outlook to a head, the incoming Bush administration gave the impression that it would do less to "engage" these countries, shunning that word as well as the word *partnership*. It had reverted to cold war era thinking that what matters is security ties and economic integration on the fringes of East Asia, setting conditions for incorporating the continental Asian powers without worrying much about their hesitation. As in the previous decade, it was assumed that Beijing would be inclined to go along, given its economic priorities, and Moscow would be harder to persuade but could not stay on the sidelines indefinitely. "Russia passing" and "China passing" each assumed that neither country matters much for the global economy, the danger of military blackmail is low, and the two would not work together.

Increasingly Americans separated globalization linked to WTO with great-power discord and rogue-state threats requiring increased military preparedness. Northeast Asia became the focus of both: China's entry into WTO symbolized universalism, while North Korea's missiles and China's tough talk on Taiwan justified missile defense. Military unilateralism took precedence over economic universalism as the Bush administration took office. Already the Clinton administration had been sensitive to grumblings in Japan that its interests were being slighted. Aware of resentment over U.S. opposition to proposals for an EAEC and AMF, Washington remained neutral as the ASEAN +3 emerged. It had no problem with FTAs in NEA and was amenable as long as regional economic groupings did not undermine international regimes. If this posture may not have been reversed by Bush, the new emphasis on security left economic integration in NEA more difficult to pursue.

Bush campaigned against overoptimism in U.S. foreign policy with China, Russia, and North Korea. Some supporters favored maximum isolation of North Korea, virtual containment of China, and "realistic engagement" leaning to disengagement with Russia. Even if few expected a sharp lurch, there was little doubt that a hard-nosed foreign policy would replace what was demeaned as a "romantic" one.[2] With strong reservations against further moves toward regionalism that might strengthen China's hand should a showdown with the United States occur or ease the pressure on North Korea to abandon its blackmail tactics, the Bush administration was preparing to

[2] David Hoffman, "Russia Was Lab for Theories on Foreign Policy," *The Washington Post*, June 4, 2000.

end the benign neglect in 2000 that had allowed the most progress in regionalism during the 1990s.

The image of U.S. national identity in 2000 did not satisfy those who drafted Bush to run for president. While many in NEA were critical of an imperious America aiming to impose its brand of globalization mixing economics, security, and culture, the Clinton administration recognized the reassuring value of a gradual, voluntary process. It was content with a cautious leadership style, accepting multilateralism except when crises arose beyond U.S. control. In contrast, the Bush team favored an unambiguous identity of where America stands, having no compunctions about using its superior power to shape the world in its mold. This called for a confident, assertive leadership clear on its goals. By implication, the pursuit of regionalism in NEA in 1999–2000 reflected a leadership failure that let North Korea gain leverage through South Korean diplomacy that should not have been tolerated and let China fill a vacuum that should not have been allowed to emerge. The first step to stop this would be to boost Japan as an ally in globalization.

Japan and Regionalism

In retrospect, the rise of nationalism in 1999 set Japan on a course that would continue unabated through 2003 and probably well beyond. Influenced by such catchwords as novelist Shiba Ryotaro's "*kuni no katachi*" (the shape of the country), the number of people in favor of constitutional revision rose rapidly, not just including those in favor of modifying Article 9, renouncing war and making peacekeeping abroad a shaky undertaking, but also counting those who emphasized rights such as the right to privacy in order to produce a new citizenry.[3] In late 2003 a yearbook subtitled "*kawaru kuni no katachi*" (the shape of a changing country) highlighted nationalist themes.[4] A section on the Constitution and national security stressed the indispensability of revising Article 9, while even raising the possibility of possessing nuclear weapons. A section on the state and patriotism targeted the contradiction between following the United States and raising national consciousness. Another section pointed to new waves in Japanese politics and what is the key to Japan's revival. From 1999 domestic politics were proceeding down a new path.[5]

Other signs of an upsurge in nationalism could be found in foreign relations. Ties with China were strained, as the Japanese remained pessimistic

[3] *Hokuriku chunichi shimbun*, May 2, 2000, p. 5.

[4] Bungei shunju, ed., *Nihon no ronten 2004: kawaru kuni no katachi* (Tokyo: Bungei shunju, 2003).

[5] Oda Makoto, "'Pacifism' or 'War-ism,'" *Japan–Asia Quarterly Review*, 29(2), 2000, pp. 26–8.

after Jiang's alarming visit in late 1998. Negotiations with Russia were stagnant in 1999. New optimism about ties to South Korea brought increased confidence in joint resistance with the United States to China more than plans for regionalism. The nationalist message took advantage of a growing sense of helplessness in the face of rising Chinese nationalism, increasing American unilateral power, and unpredictable developments on the Korean peninsula. Loss of national self-confidence created a fertile soil for easy and extreme answers. The message started with an attack on the postwar intellectual elite, especially teachers, for failing to instill moral values. It followed with a condemnation of the closed-minded thinking of most Japanese, left rudderless without historical pride, and it broadened into a critique of foreign policy, apologetic to Asian states or passively following the United States, not befitting an economic great power. The answer to uncertainties about stability in the region and willpower at home was a clear "*kokkakan*" (state worldview) asserting what must be the "national interest."[6]

Textbook changes in Japan brought history to the fore just as talk of constitutional change was rising. Many Japanese accuse Chinese and South Koreans of inculcating anti-Japanese feelings through school and media coverage of history, and they appeal to these nations to forget about the history that is closely linked to their national consciousness. What they omit is that feelings about history are kept alive largely because the Japanese deny or ignore the same events in their own history, failing to accept the others' version of the past while trying to make the case that the Japanese are different today. Having refused to punish or even repudiate those guilty of historical crimes, the Japanese should understand that the victims cannot be appeased by recurrent signs of rationalization of the past.

Japanese leaders were eager, sometimes to the point of desperation, to prove that their country deserved a voice in setting global policies. They accepted the reality of globalization, but they worried that Japan would not be granted its due place as the country with the second greatest comprehensive national power. When Japan's time as host for the G-8 summit came, no effort was spared. The Mori cabinet had hoped to turn the G-8 summit of 2000 into an event to showcase Japan's Asian leadership by inviting China, India, Indonesia, and South Korea as observers and giving this event an Asian flavor.[7] When that failed, the Japanese still sought a visit by Chinese Prime Minister Zhu Rongji and an opportunity to reflect China's views.[8] A decade after leaders had seized upon China's post-Tiananmen isolation to dream of becoming a bridge between the Western powers and Asia's rising power, aspirations to work closely with China remained strong. Beijing, however, did

[6] *Sankei shimbun*, May 3, 2001, p. 1.

[7] Lu Guozhong, "Mori Yoshiro shangtaihou de Riben waijiao," *Guoji wenti yanjiu*, 6 (2000), p. 37.

[8] *Hokuriku chunichi shimbun*, May 10, 2000.

not want Tokyo to speak for it. At the summit, one Japanese asked, if Japan spent almost 100 times what Germany had paid for the previous year's G-8 summit, how could the money be well spent when in his swan song Clinton's heart was actually in Mid-East talks that he had just been hosting and in his debut Putin brought a message on North Korea and a joint statement with China against the U.S. plan for National Missile Defense that left the prepared agenda in the shadows?[9]

At the millennium summit of the United Nations Mori Yoshiro offered a view of globalization quite different from that of the United States. It was a call for strengthening the United Nations and expanding the Security Council. Added to idealism about global political cooperation was support for two initiatives: 1) to boost the "Human Security Fund" established at the United Nations in March 1999 as a pillar of diplomacy in favor of the dignity of the individual; and 2) to submit a new draft resolution on the elimination of nuclear weapons consistent with Japan's special nonnuclear status.[10] Contrasting these stands to U.S. reluctance to back the United Nations, some insisted that Japan is the true champion of global cooperation. Japan's notion of globalization is more multilateral. It emphasizes ODA to developing countries, using economic power to earn a spot as a world leader, and seeks to balance globalization with multipolarization and regionalism. In search of a leadership role, the Japanese stress use of economic power to ameliorate the regional impact of globalization and "soft power" to increase their voice as mutual dependency grows.[11] On the positive side, officials look back to the refocusing of ODA in 1992 to gain leverage against excess military expenses and insufficient environmentalism, and they look ahead to currency stabilization and other coordination under discussion since the Asian financial crisis. On the negative side, officials warn that "soft power" is lacking a spiritual appeal, whereby Japan becomes a magnet for Asian nations. They recognize that this limits Japan's regional authority.

Worrying about the coming decline of Japan's power due to demographic and economic reasons and calculating that U.S. unipolar hegemony would also decline and lead to the weakening of the U.S.-Japanese alliance, conservatives made their own case for regionalism in NEA. They reasoned that Russia could not rely on China alone, North Korea would turn to international aid despite its reluctance, South Korea and Japan from 1998 were at last forming a complete partnership, and even China was amenable at last to Japan playing a positive role in security and joining in multilateralism. In the near term as U.S. national power continues to be predominant and China

[9] Miiyamoto Nobuo, "Amasuginaika Nihon no tairoshia ninshiki," *Sekai shuho*, August 15, 2000, p. 34.

[10] "The International Community in the New Century," *Japan INFO*, October/November 2000.

[11] *Sangiin kokusai mondai ni kansuru chosakai kaigiroku daigogo*, pt. 23, March 7, 2001, pp. 20–1.

remains weak, Japan must seize the opportunity to work toward regionalism.[12] In the background is deep concern that Japan lost leverage through the 1990s, becoming too dependent on the United States.

In the uncertainty over presidential succession in the United States, the Japanese doubted U.S. leadership even more than before. Trust in a docile Japan following U.S. leadership of a new world order alternated with fear of a chaotic world in which Japan must find its own way toward multipolarization. For some this meant new willingness to make concessions to other great powers. To others it was a call to stop a pattern of weakness toward China and Russia.[13] Only a strong Japan looking after its own national interests could qualify as a pole in a multipolar world. Many bemoaned the weakness of their leaders in conducting foreign policy. For instance, one analyst compared the boldness of Kim Dae-jung, acting on his own initiative in 1998 toward Japan and bringing fellow South Koreans behind him, to the timidity of Japanese leaders, who refuse to take the lead unless public opinion has already matured. Some wondered why Zhu Rongji representing an authoritarian state could speak on Japanese television in a much freer format of questions and answers than the leaders of democratic Japan.[14] They asked what is wrong with Japan that it cannot produce an active leader in foreign policy such as Clinton or Putin? Images of national identity depicted a "closed," "stagnant," unprincipled country with no commitment to refugees and democracy. Of course, the right wing sought personal leadership to invite Taiwan's ex-president Lee Teng-Hui despite China's opposition, while some on the Left contemplated a bold deal with Russia. Even in the political center opinion was divided on regionalism drawing closer to China or finding ways to balance China. The purposes of becoming more assertive varied, but almost always one of the means was regionalism.

The situation in Hokkaido and along the Sea of Japan grew worse at the end of the decade. Employment opportunities declined. New high school graduates were giving up hope of jobs and flocking to Tokyo. The image spread that globalization meant more concentration in Tokyo, little different from the role of Seoul in the Korean economy, while regionalism was but a dream with unfulfilled promises to help local areas. Yet, supporters of economic regionalism, such as the Sea of Japan rim economic sphere, kept expressing optimism. While insisting that China is focused on economic growth and will not for decades to come endanger stability, they charged that Japanese politicians are stirring up public opinion for domestic reasons

12 Kojima Tomoyuki, "Hokuto Ajia no takoku kan anzen hosho taisei kochiku o," *Sekai shuho*, December 5, 2000, pp. 34–5.

13 Sakurai Yoshiko, "Kokueki o wasureta gaimukanryo no shittai," *Shukan shincho*, November 30, 2000, pp. 54–8.

14 Kitaoka Shinichi, "Nihon gaiko kono ichinen no tanazarashi," *Chuo koron*, December 2000, pp. 38–41.

and the unfortunate outcome is more dependence on the United States, not bold advances in regional cooperation within Japan's grasp.

In retrospect the Japanese recognized that both the end of the cold war and the acceleration of information technology had opened the way to much freer flows of money, information, technology, and services across borders. Limits of time and space are succumbing to global networks. Hard power based on territory, natural resources, population, military might, and industrial capacity is yielding to soft power reliant on technological breakthroughs and responsiveness to information. Countries will have to accept growing cultural diversity as well as promote creativity. National identities will be reshaped through globalization and the need to put more trust in international networks and justice. Recognizing that Japan lacks the needed vision, even spokesmen for the LDP speak of more structural and educational change based on an understanding of the new realities.[15] Yet, they also are quick to warn of the secondary effects of globalization, such as the spread of dangerous weapons, terror, global crime, drugs, environmental damage, poverty, infectious diseases, and nationalism. These effects require Japan to maintain close ties to the United States without committing the error of thinking that they are sufficient for prosperity and stability. Many insisted that Japan must regularize contacts in NEA too. Regional cooperation with China and Korea had gained much support by late 2000.[16]

The Asian financial crisis began a resurgence of Japanese interest in regionalism. It led many to conclude that globalization was both a cause and a cure of economic troubles; regional models of development no longer could follow their old course yet did not necessarily have to be fully discarded. This reasoning drew Japan closer to nearby countries in a growing sense of shared destiny. After the United States objected to Japan's plan to establish an AMF backed by $100 billion, attention centered mostly on currency. In September 1998 Japan's ambassador to Korea initiated planning for a free trade area. As China took steps in 2000 to enter the WTO, the scope of discussions widened. Many heralded the May 2000 Chiang Mai agreement for a currency-swapping program and the November ASEAN +3 Singapore meeting that built on this. New links to Singapore promised a free trade area that could be a precedent for South Korea and lead to a "multilevel trading policy." If earlier the Foreign Ministry preferred a low profile, this time the Cabinet was united in support of a group exclusive of the United States.

Japan welcomed steps toward economic regionalism linked to ASEAN +3, but it was wary of political and security cooperation in this framework. It

15 Fukui Nobuji, "Guroborizeshon 'chisei kokka' Nihon," *Jiyu minju*, November 2000, pp. 14–15.

16 Morimoto Satoshi, "21 seiki Nihon no kokkazo o too," *Jiyu minju*, November 2000, pp. 16–17.

recognized that the 1997 Asian financial crisis had boosted a shared sense of community and that recent momentum had come from China's new interest, but it was uncertain where things were heading. Was ASEAN being eclipsed by what had begun as a sideshow among three tag-alongs whose economic scale dwarfed the others? Did China's desire to draw ASEAN into a free trade proposal but exclude Australia lead toward open or closed regionalism? While agreeing to an information technology (IT) belt of Tokyo, Shanghai, and Kuala Lumpur, Japan remained cautious about what would follow,[17] despite talk that a turning point had been reached in acceptance of the idea of an East Asian community. Yet, Obuchi led the way in the fall of 1999 by inviting Jiang Zemin and Kim Dae-jung to a breakfast meeting that separated the NEA core of 3 from the ASEAN-10, drawing attention with a triangular table. Later, however, Japan would sow confusion with the unpopular idea of adding Australia and New Zealand.

Japan's right wing grew very assertive over China at the end of the decade. They argued that Taiwan's future should be decided by the Taiwanese, China's involvement in the Korean peninsula reflected expansionist ambitions, Japan must compete with China as Asian economies become the nucleus of the world economy, and other positions supportive of regionalism centered on Japan.[18] Right-wing journals insisted it was time for a normal power to assert its own national interests in the same manner as other states, while the Left still aimed for an autonomous state with peace diplomacy. To both extremes it seemed that only the elimination of U.S. bases would mean the true end of the "postwar."[19]

Opponents of regionalism also made their voices heard. One retired diplomat long suspicious of U.S. softness to communist states argued that the Democratic Party is China-centered and the Republican Party is Japan centered. If in the year 2000 Japan had to fend off the reckless initiatives of Kim Dae-jung made possible by soft policies of the Clinton administration, times would change. In a world marked by both economic globalization and intensifying power politics, Japan must avoid dreams of regionalism for the next five to ten years.[20] Instead it needs to remain close to the United States and respond firmly to China as well as Russia and North Korea. Opponents of regionalism welcomed Bush's victory.

After the Japanese found that they could not shape regionalism as anticipated at the beginning of the 1990s, they focused on how China would try to do so. Having once eyed Siberian resources, they drew the obvious conclusion that China would look north too. One article predicted that just as Russia

[17] *Asahi shimbun*, November 25, 2000, p. 1.

[18] *Nihon no ronten 2001* (Tokyo: Bungei shunju, 2000), pp. 96–129.

[19] *Sankei shimbun*, November 22, 2000, p. 3.

[20] Arai Hirokazu, "Toajia ni okeru Nichibeichuro kankei," *Shin kokusaku*, October 15, 2000, pp. 10–14.

moved south into Manchuria from the end of the nineteenth century, China was now readying itself to move north for resources and that exchanges with Russia would develop unexpectedly quickly.[21] Japan's approach to regionalism would need to take into account this momentum toward integration. Many debated what China wants from its new embrace of regionalism. Most were skeptical of China's motives, suggesting that Japan was being used to counter the United States. But others viewed China's goals as more moderate or found merit in ASEAN's leading role in the drive for regionalism from fear of China's growing power and share of investments, hoping to use Japan to strike a delicate balance with China.[22] Even more than Malaysia, which leaned toward closed regionalism, Singapore's preference for open regionalism appealed to Japan, as did its goal of managing a new range of ties with China.

The Japanese for a long time had been keeping track of what topics still had to be addressed to put the postwar era behind them. As prospects of intensified negotiations with Russia and North Korea were growing, it was agreed that these two topics were the main ones left, but reports spread that the Foreign Ministry was split. After the June 15 summit of the Koreas some in the media and the LDP called for bold leadership, preparing to compromise quickly in order not to be left behind in a new era. Others said that it was time to act soberly by drawing a line: Japan should threaten to stop economic cooperation with Russia and insist that North Korea resolve the issue of kidnapped Japanese and the missile threat.[23] Unpopular, Mori could not proceed with compromise policies. Shortly after Bush took office, Japan also had a new prime minister, Koizumi Junichiro, seen as a maverick who would bring bold economic reforms but unknown in foreign affairs except for his use of nationalist symbols as proof he would defend Japan's interests. After he gained power ties to Russia and North Korea deteriorated; foreign policy hit an impasse. It was not only that maverick foreign minister, Tanaka Makiko, was steering diplomacy in new directions, but also Koizumi had no clear designs for where it should be heading.[24]

Japan and Russia

Japan kept pushing for improved relations with Russia, despite the discouraging Moscow summit of November 1998. If some were saying it is time to slow down and wait, a small group led by Diet member Suzuki Muneo and

[21] "Chugoku no hatten to Roshia," *Kokusai kinyu*, April 1, 2001, p. 45.

[22] *Asahi shimbun*, November 25, 2000, p. 6.

[23] Kato Kiyotaka, "Nanika hen, saikin no Nihon gaiko," *Sekai shuho*, December 5, 2000, pp. 34–5.

[24] Gilbert Rozman, "Japan's Quest for Great Power Identity," *Orbis*, 46(1), Winter 2002, pp. 73–91.

a few Russia experts in the Foreign Ministry pressed for a breakthrough before the end of 2000. They were excited by the advent of the Putin administration and did not want to wait to see what direction he wanted to lead his country. To others it appeared that Russians were content with the status quo as it was being pursued, and the time had come to make them understand that Japan had reached its limit. They had to be shown that the Japanese people would not allow major projects to go forward without trust that Russia was also meeting Japan's interests. In defiance of this mood, a speech by LDP luminary Nonaka Hiromu on July 27, 2000 said that if one precondition was not resolved it does not mean that a friendship treaty cannot be reached. This was taken to mean that Mori was ready to sign a peace treaty without fully resolving the Northern Territories question.[25] In the shadow of the Korean summit, Tokyo was beginning to explore its own "sunshine policy."

Even after Nonaka withdrew his statement, critics warned of a sellout. There was a palpable sense of fear, undermining real signs of diplomatic progress. The media on both sides was responsible. The Russian newspaper *Kommersant* responded that peace now matters more to Japan than the Kurile Islands,[26] giving the impression that Moscow is taking Tokyo for granted and implying that Japan needs Russia for great-power or economic reasons and is "prepared to swallow the disappointment" of not getting the disputed islands.[27] Despite optimism by some in the Japanese government that Putin's September 2000 visit was "epoch making" because of his acknowledgment that the 1956 treaty was still in effect, doubters saw the new Russian position as bringing matters to an impasse and Japanese newspapers conveyed this message.

Some in Japan were openly critical of the reticence of Japan's leaders to convey clearly to the Russians that only an agreement to return four islands would lead to a peace treaty and normalization. Whether or not the Mori administration had actually decoupled the territorial issue and a treaty, many feared that Russians had begun to think so. They felt uneasy with the newfound wisdom that Japan needs Russia more than it needs Japan. In place of confused signals from Japan that apparently convinced Russians that even without progress on the islands they could count on continued Japanese cooperation, critics argued that Moscow should be told without equivocation that the only way to gain the trust of the Japanese people is to resolve the territorial impasse and without such a turnabout in public opinion no Japanese government would dare to sign a peace treaty. Only a few voices countered that the price to be paid for a breakdown in relations

[25] *Mainichi shimbun*, September 2, 2000, p. 2.

[26] *Sankei shimbun*, August 4, 2000, p. 11.

[27] Sergei Kazennov and Vladimir Kumashev, "Putin in 2001: A Burden of Choice," *Ponedelnik*, 6 (February 2001), p. 3 (as reported in www.ups.rule-index.html).

if no agreement is reached would be too great; in brief, Japan needs to use the "Russia card."[28]

On the agenda in September 2000 were not only the big-ticket items of territory, economic cooperation, and great-power concerns (this time the Korean peninsula), but also cross-border trouble areas. One newspaper listed these as drugs and guns as well as other smuggling and oil spillage from the new fields off Sakhalin and tankers leaving there.[29] Still remembered well was how Russian courts stripped Japanese owners of the Santa Hotel in Sakhalin. Until laws and taxes were clarified and administered in a fair manner, real economic cooperation as well as trust remained in doubt. Criminalization of border trade had forged strong interests opposed to a territorial agreement.[30] Despite Japanese generosity at the start of 2000 with loans of $120 million for nuclear submarine disposal in the Pacific and $20 million for a Moscow center for science and technology at a time when others were withholding funds, Russians offered little gratitude. They pointed instead to a lack of direct investment by Japanese firms compared to other countries.

Putin took new interest in some of the persistent problems of the Russian Far East. Already in his 1997 foreign intelligence post he had shown an interest in cracking down on the smuggling of marine products. Moscow did not succeed; in 1999 it was still estimated that Russia lost $700 million from smuggling to Japan. Not only did Putin seek new centralized powers to solve this problem, but he also was preparing to use satellites for controlling fishing boats.[31] Even after new procedures had gone into effect in 1998, fishing near the disputed islands remained a bone of contention. Russians continued to accuse Japanese ships of illegal acts in their territorial waters, seizing about one a month in 1999 and 2000. They called for procedural changes, warning that they might refuse to extend the agreement.[32] In response to Japanese ships acting illegally in Russian waters, there was also talk of new tough measures. And on energy needs in the Russian Far East talk had turned to an underwater cable serving as a Japan-Russia energy bridge and Japanese help in construction of an atomic reactor in the Far East. High on Russia's list of desired energy projects is a natural gas pipeline from Sakhalin to Vladivostok.[33]

In the year 2000 Japan's interest in Russian energy grew as a result of rising energy prices. There was new talk of a pipeline from Sakhalin to Japan. Development of Sakhalin energy can be traced back to the first oil

[28] Gilbert Rozman, "A Chance for a Breakthrough in Russo-Japanese Relations: Will the Logic of Great Power Relations Prevail?" *Pacific Review*, 15(3), 2002, pp. 325–57.

[29] *Hokkaido shimbun*, September 1, 2000.

[30] Brad Williams, "The Criminalization of Russo-Japanese Border Trade: Causes and Consequences," *Europe-Asia Studies*, 55(5), 2003, pp. 711–28.

[31] *Hokkaido shimbun*, September 3, 2000, p. 3.

[32] *Hokkaido shimbun*, September 3, 2000, p. 3.

[33] *Hokkaido shimbun*, September 3, 2000, p. 3.

crisis of 1973, as Japan showed an interest in freeing itself of dependence on the Middle East. In the 1990s changes in Russia breathed new life into this interest, and production from one project had begun. But in 2000 additional enthusiasm could be detected as world and regional demand for natural gas was expected to rise sharply. Zhu Rongji spoke of using liquid natural gas (LNG) in Shanghai and Beijing. Guangdong province was preparing to do so. Taiwan stopped construction of a nuclear reactor in anticipation of using LNG. In this competitive environment Japan seeks a new supply, and Russia beckons, able, some say, to play the "energy card."[34] With strong international consortia moving ahead on Sakhalin-1 and Sakhalin-2 and talk about as many as six other projects under way, it seemed likely that Sakhalin's enormous energy potential would give a boost to regionalism. But Tokyo would have to decide that its relations with Russia justified the huge infrastructure costs to build a pipeline to transmit natural gas to Honshu Island and simultaneously invest heavily in a national system for distributing the gas to consumers. It would also need assurance that Russia would create the legal and political conditions for investors to be confident of a solid return for their money. Finally, deregulation inside Japan would need to proceed, taking advantage of new pressures to reduce utility rates, create a competitive business climate, and resist nuclear power-plant construction. As long as Japan relied heavily on oil without making a transition to gas,[35] and Putin hesitated to make Japan a priority or to make essential reforms, interest in using natural gas to boost the three Es (economic growth, environmental pollution reductions, and energy security) remained secondary.[36]

The Japanese recognized the desirability of boosting relations with Russia to gain leverage on China, and they perceived some quick results, as exchanges of military leaders with China started soon after negotiations with Russia grew serious. Military ties between Russia and Japan and Russia and South Korea played a strong supporting role in improving the atmosphere in relations in the late 1990s, as they had in Sino-Russian relations over the middle of the decade. Further confirmation of this came in a meeting of Russian and Japanese defense ministers in late November 2000, where Russia announced a 20 percent cut in troops in the Russian Far East as part of an overall cutback and a decision to concentrate on a few areas, especially Central Asia. It drew attention to the strategic nature of relations. When the arrest of a Russian spy threatened to set back relations in the fall of 2000,

[34] Igarashi Taku, "Senryaku naki Nihon no 'Saharinoki kaihatsu,'" *Foresight*, November 2000, pp. 80–1.

[35] *Izvestiia*, January 17, 2001.

[36] Al Troney, "Japan and the Russian Far East: The Economic and Competitive Impact of Least Cost Gas Imports," *Japanese Energy Security and Changing Global Energy Markets: An Analysis of Northeast Asia Energy Cooperation and Japan's Evolving Leading Role in the Region* (Houston: The James A. Baker III Institute for Public Policy, 2000).

it was easier to overcome this threat due to the goodwill generated by military ties. Some charged that it was a step by Japanese rightists to interfere with the momentum of relations generated by the September summit, but in fact the Japanese may have uncovered the spying earlier and held back for the summit.[37] When bilateral talks lagged, military ties were less significant. After all, many argued that Japan does not need to play the "Russia card," and some insisted that more important in influencing China was the breakthrough in Japanese ties with South Korea in 1998.[38]

As the backlash intensified against the compromise under discussion by Mori and Putin, former Deputy Foreign Minister Georgy Kunadze asked the Japanese to consider what really matters, the islands or bilateral relations with their large latent potential. He stressed that both states could use closer relations to contain China and gain leverage on the Korean peninsula. Adding that the U.S. superpower could not avoid isolating itself, Kunadze appealed to Japan to recognize that it has room to use relations with Russia also in its ties with the United States.[39] As before, Russia's case for regionalism centered on security.

The Russian people clung to the reasoning that territories sought by neighboring states were just war prizes or sources of pride gained through past achievements. Their loss would leave Russia exposed, it was assumed, not build trust that enabled Russia to become part of a new region. There was no confidence in regionalism or globalization. A mood of insecurity left people recalling old notions of security, at least until economic growth resumed and Putin restored confidence in leadership and in ties with the United States.

Many of the arguments on how to deal with Russia were buttressed by assertions about the nation's psychology. This led to arguments about wounded pride and what measures and timing can restore it. The Japanese, including officials who explored parallel talks on two sets of islands, spoke of the need to assuage Russian concerns, differentiating their strategy from that of the young Americans who pressed Yeltsin to undertake abrupt reforms heedless of national psychology and, implicitly, from Japanese past pressure that proved counterproductive.[40] Rival analysis, however, insisted that Soviet thinking still operated and any weakness on Japan's part would only fuel more one-sided demands.

Russians insist that Japan must first change the views of the Russian people before concessions can be made on the disputed islands. This means

[37] Hakamada Shigeki, "'Tairo fushin' o seikaku ni Roshia ni tsutaeyo," *Foresight*, September 16–October 20, 2000, p. 9.

[38] Hakamada Shigeki, "Puchin seiken no naigai seisaku o doo miru ka?" *Ajia jiho*, September 2000, p. 49.

[39] Georgy Kunadze, "Interview," *Sekai shuho*, April 24, 2001, p. 21.

[40] Togo Kazuhiko, "Roshia no zentaizo o yomidoku," *Gaiko forum*, December 2000, pp. 20–1.

that Japan should offer economic assistance and find ways to win credit for as long as may be necessary before expecting the Russian government to reach a final stage of negotiations. Japan responds that Russia cannot expect dramatic advances in economic ties without persuading the Japanese public that it is doing all it can to meet their concerns about territory. Each side accuses the other of using public opinion as an excuse, not doing enough to try to change attitudes. In turn, each presses the other to build trust to transform the atmosphere. They have agreed on the importance of cultivating personal trust between top leaders, but they have not linked the symbols of such trust to the realities of national interests.

After nine years of "no visa" travel to the islands, a peak of 1,129 persons participated in 2000. But instead of friendly ties leading to mutual understanding and then to support by the Russian islanders for Japan's "civilian diplomacy," the response was that the territorial question is for the center to decide. The Japanese noticed a sense of fatigue as the current islanders avoided talking about the dispute. Meanwhile, among the visitors from Japan the percentage of former islanders and their family members slipped from 50 in 1992 to just 23. Disillusionment was present among the former inhabitants already over age 70 and no longer able to handle the rigors of the group visits.[41]

The Japanese counted on Moscow sharply reducing its support of the islanders, their increasing anger, then public opinion shifting to support for transferring the islands to Japan, and finally pressure on Moscow to do just that. Through most of the 1990s this was, indeed, the pattern, although the pressure scarcely registered on a leadership more concerned about nationalist voices such as Governor Igor Farkhutdinov in Sakhalin warning against concessions to Japan. At the end of the decade matters changed. A businessman from Moscow moved to Etorofu, where 8,000 people or 40 percent of the total on the four islands live, bought state-owned enterprises and fishing boats, and built a successful business starting with a catch of 300 tons a day. He expanded into financing, a hotel, and port reconstruction, hiring workers with wages three times those in Russia. Hiring soon spread to Shikotan Island. As all of the islands were falling under the spell of the "king of the islands" and trade with Alaska expanded, instead of helpless islanders begging Japan for humanitarian aid, local support intensified for keeping the islands Russian.[42]

In mid-2000 Farkhutdinov called on Russia to make the Sea of Okhotsk an internal waterway. While international law allows countries to make such a declaration if geographical, historical, economic, and other preconditions are met, they must get the agreement of nearby states. As the only other

[41] *Hokkaido shimbun*, October 28, 2000.

[42] "Hoppo ryodo no tomin wa kokorogawari kigyo katsudo no seiko de henkan hantai ni," *EL NEOS*, September 2000, pp. 84–5.

bordering country, Japan could be expected to oppose this move and be incensed by its inflammatory nature covering disputed territory. One Japanese paper observed that this effort to monopolize a sea rich in natural resources would damage relations.[43] Shortly afterward, accompanying Putin to Tokyo, Farkhutdinov sat with Governor Hori Tatsuya of Hokkaido and joined in a joint call for expanded local exchanges, as the Japanese tried to overlook his nationalist rhetoric.

Looking back over a decade of visits between their prefecture and the localities of the Russian Far East, a Niigata journalist charged that one reason for no improvement in economic relations is the visa problem. Tokyo authorities oblige Russians invited by the Japanese side to wait a month or more for a visa and in 1999 Russia retaliated with visa delays of its own. In addition Russian customs officials arbitrarily decide that a visitor has too much luggage or, suspecting intent to conduct commerce, they limit the stay to only a few days. Unlike the days of the "bubble" when local areas energetically pursued their own foreign exchanges, those trained for this have nothing to do now that tougher times have come. The newspaper appealed that as the only local city with a high image as a pipe to the Russian Far East and North Korea, Niigata must not be forgotten.[44]

If negotiations were to break down the Japanese speculated about the consequences. One, the original islanders and their descendants in Japan are preparing to seek Japanese compensation for the property left behind as well as the fishing losses they have suffered. A newspaper estimated the value of marine resources alone at $1 to $1.5 billion a year.[45] That would turn the problem into a Japanese domestic issue. Two, Japan might try to rally international opinion to condemn Russia, but this was unlikely to work after failing in 1990–2. Three, Japan could cut economic ties with the islands and Sakhalin, yet when Putin was in Tokyo the governors of Hokkaido and Sakhalin signed a plan to expand ties, on which the Hokkaido economy was already dependent. None of the options had appeal.

In the new atmosphere of 2000 people wondered if Nemuro and other parts of Hokkaido were growing angrier at Russian intransigence over the islands and demanding more curbs on aid to them as a form of pressure or were becoming more economically dependent on the Russian Far East and relaxing their conditions.[46] On October 29 the first flights began from Nemuro to Kunashiri. Previously, travel to the disputed islands had been limited to ships during the warm months of the year and an occasional emergency flight, but when Japan agreed to help rebuild the electrical network on the island it insisted on regular flights. The charter flight that inaugurated the new route

[43] *Niigata nippo*, July 7, 2000, p. 3.

[44] *Niigata nippo*, July 3, 2000, p. 3.

[45] *Hokkaido shimbun*, September 5, 2000, p. 1.

[46] *Hokkaido shimbun*, October 30, 2000.

was led by politician Suzuki Muneo and carried a donation of drugs and medical equipment.

Memories lingered of the 1970s when Japan had been the Soviet Union's biggest capitalist trading partner apart from West Germany and huge development projects in Siberia and the Russian Far East had been seriously explored. By 1999 Japan's exports to Russia had tumbled to $480 million, just one-sixth the $3.1 billion level of 1989 and one-fiftieth the level of exports to China. Because most of Japan's exports had been directed at Russian industry, the collapse of investment in machinery had caused much of the loss, as had the import substitution owing to Russia's financial crisis that cost Japan half of its exports. Joint ventures in marine and timber products as well as services in electronic sales, hotels, and restaurants faded fast after their startup phase in 1989–92. A 1995 agreement for Japan to assist Russia in building a diesel engine plant for Kama trucks was scuttled by unresolved debts and the bad state of the Russian economy. Yet, unreported in official data are the large numbers of Japanese goods entering Russia through Finland, the Middle East, and Singapore. One estimate put the number of Japanese color television sets sold from 1994–7 at 10 million and suggested that electronic goods and cars arrive in large numbers as well. Such purchases declined after August 1998 but rose again in 2000. Also significant were the shops in Hokkaido that depended on Russian crews.

More important to economic relations are exports from Russia to Japan. In 1995 they peaked at $4.7 billion, with 70 percent of the total consisting of marine and lumber products, coal, aluminum, and other metals. The total remained at $3.8 billion in 1999. With Sakhalin oil and gas starting production in 1999, that figure was likely to rise. But the key to long-term economic ties, according to the head of Japan's trade office in Moscow, is trust. Ahead of problems of infrastructure or political reservations in Japan, he placed cultural problems, singling out local governments east of the Urals. For the Japanese to overcome their view of Russia as a "dangerous country," they must be matched with "trusted partners" and have available reliable ways to resolve problems.[47]

A divided Japanese government could not make up its mind about Russia as a geopolitical partner and energy supplier in the midst of uncertainty over national identity and relations with North Korea and China. In turn, Russia was not ready to commit itself to globalization, leaving its regional strategy and approach to Japan in abeyance. With the end of the countdown to 2000 the two faced a crossroads with tough decisions ahead. The Mori administration was under attack, leaving it to Koizumi to handle mutual accusations over who was responsible for the failure of one attempted shortcut to regionalism. If, at first, he let negotiations slip, new circumstances in

[47] Okada Kunio, "Nichiro keizai kankei," *Gaiko forum*, December 2000, pp. 56–61.

2001–2 led to a reassessment. The logic of improving bilateral ties to shape the NEA region could not be ignored.

China and Regionalism

Is China on the verge of becoming a near superpower second only to the United States in comprehensive power and first in overall GDP as an economic great power or is its future marred by many difficulties that for several decades justify a low profile among the great powers? Many writings on great-power relations assume the former. Yet, it is not hard to find strong rebuttals citing contradictions between economics and politics still burdened with centralization; severe poverty and income inequality; a shortage of natural resources (arable land, water, forests, energy, etc.) second only to Japan among the great powers; environmental dangers; and unemployment threats. Many pointed to uneven development both in West China, where priority was placed in 2000, and in Northeast China, which in August 2003 was belatedly seen as equally critical. China also faced severe challenges in joining WTO, fearing a trade-off between great-power and economic interests. Different answers on what kind of a power China is becoming lead to divisions in reasoning on regionalism. Pragmatism about problems ahead leads to support for regional integration.

The Chinese had consistently tried to put the best light possible on great-power relations in the 1990s, but in 1999 their hopes frayed. United States unipolarity exceeded anything that had been acknowledged, Japan as well as the EU was closer to the United States than had been anticipated, and Russia was less powerful and less reliable than many had assumed. By fall 1999 the group of Jiang Zemin, Zhu Rongji, and Qian Qizhen had fully replaced Li Peng in managing relations. Greater pragmatism drove China to a new strategy.[48]

When relations with the United States deteriorated in 1999, China acted as it had a decade earlier after sanctions were imposed over Tiananmen. It turned to its Asian neighbors. Already in 1996 when the ASEM meetings began bringing together Asian and European heads of state, Asians were concerned that the Europeans enjoyed greater coordination. In 1998 after the Asian financial crisis had changed the context of regionalism – weakening ASEAN and raising joint alarm about excessive dependence on U.S. and global financial institutions – meetings had begun with leaders of China, Japan, and South Korea joining the ASEAN heads. In 1999 at Manila an informal breakfast began among the three non-ASEAN countries. In Singapore in 2000 the gathering grew more formal, and the agenda was broadened. This showed increased trust in Japan as well as in Kim Dae-jung as a

[48] Gilbert Rozman, "China's Quest for Great Power Identity," *Orbis*, 43(3), Summer 1999, pp. 383–402.

balancing figure. There was talk of a free trade area with Singapore, as the countries emphasized macroeconomic coordination, investment, energy, environment, and trade.

Debates centered on globalization and its links to regionalism, while in the background the struggle for succession to political power was unfolding. Zhu Rongji pressed ahead with WTO membership, regionalism, and the argument that the age of IT means that China's stage of reform in 1980–2000 must yield to a more externally oriented strategy. Optimistically, fourth-generation circles predicted that if no war over Taiwan and no trade war occurred China's regional and global standing would be much elevated.

In 2000 Chinese recognized that 1) multipolarization is not the main recent tendency; it comes second after the rise of U.S. hegemonism and the scientific and technological dominance of the West; 2) the role of military elements in international relations has declined in relative terms but has a greater impact than expected due to the unchallenged power of the United States; and 3) globalization is accelerating and is not limited to economics; through information technology and nongovernmental organizations (NGOs) it is far reaching despite drawing a backlash. On this basis, scholars concluded that although almost all countries would be ambivalent about U.S. power, the world would revolve around relations with the United States.[49] Clearly this left regionalism as a secondary force unable to counteract the dominant one, even if it was deemed imperative for shaping globalization and boosting multilateralism. Warning that China is one of the few major economies not in a free trade association, they insisted that a historic change toward an East Asian system had begun in May with the Chiang Mai currency agreement,[50] followed in the fall with strong support for ASEAN+3 summitry. China was at last in the forefront of region building.

Having hesitated in accepting Japan as a partner, China waited before becoming serious about regionalism. It had been comfortable with a weak APEC, recognizing that it was not a vehicle for genuine regionalism. Only in 2000 did Beijing set aside its fears of Japan taking the leading role to embrace East Asian regionalism eagerly. Paying close attention to the regionalization of the world economy, many argued that it both stimulates globalization and intensifies international economic competition. Articles left little doubt that China must do more to foster its own regional community.[51] There was movement in accepting Japan, the only developed country in the region (South Korea and Singapore are seen as less so), in financial assistance,

49 Song Yimin, "Jingji quanqiuhua he Meiguo de zouxiang," *Guoji wenti yanjiu*, 6 (2000), pp. 13–18.

50 Wang Yi, "Quanqiuhua beijing xiade duojihua jincheng," *Guoji wenti yanjiu*, 6 (2000), pp. 1–6.

51 Zhou Zhonglin and Peng Shaozong, "Shijie jingji quyi jiduanhua ji qi yuanin yu yingxiang," *Shijie jingji*, October 1999, pp. 74–7.

investment, currency, and trade. If a year before the Chinese had been obsessed with the U.S.-Japanese military alliance and the Japanese with China's use of the "history" card, shared interest in regionalism generated fresh hope.

After replacing the ideology of class struggle with a worldview centered on the development of the forces of production, the Chinese have kept adapting that perspective to changes in the world. As entry into WTO was nearing completion, analysts argued that in the emerging stage of history the lone state is too small to facilitate growth in production forces. Instead both globalization and regionalization are essential. Of the top thirty countries in the world in gross domestic product (GDP) only China, Japan, and South Korea are missing a regional platform.[52] It follows that China must remedy this situation. This perspective views China as still in the stage of industrialization, while Japan is a very successful industrializer and boasts research and development funding twenty times that of China. In the information age, Japan's high-tech exports still constitute 11.9 percent of its total (trailing the United States at 19.2 percent) as opposed to China's at 1.8 percent. China has much to gain from Japan.

Local representatives at the end of the 1990s were freed to vent more grievances against the center. While acknowledging that the backward thinking of managers accustomed to a command economy was partially responsible, many in Northeast China charged that government had not actually transferred much power to these enterprises and that many foreigners who showed an interest in investing were delayed and then gave up from frustration. They accused the central government of turning its back on the region: first in the second half of the 1960s with the decision to invest in the interior due to the Sino-Soviet conflict, then in the late 1970s with the preference for Southeast China and light industry. In fact, price controls were kept on this region more than elsewhere. In some cities as much as 90 percent of industry operated under the limits of the old system. As a result, the Northeast has paid a huge price in support of other regions. Losing hope that the center would come to the rescue, locals appealed for more economic autonomy as an improvement over the status quo.[53] Renewed reform of state-owned enterprises brought a surge in unemployment. Difficulty in addressing problems of Northeast China left regional ties with South Korea, Russia, and Japan geographically skewed.

While some supposed that Northeast China had finally joined coastal China in sustained economic growth by the mid-1990s, the situation was direr. After slowing economically from the mid-1960s and then falling well behind from the end of the 1970s, the area had been branded as the

[52] Feng Zhaokui, "Guanyu Zhongri guanxi de zhanlue sikao," *Shijie jingji yu zhengzhi,* November 2000, pp. 11–16.

[53] "Dongbei canyu dongbeiya jingji hezuo de 'ying' huanjing fenxi," *Dongbeiya luntan*, 3 (2000), pp. 61–2.

"Northeast phenomenon" when in 1990 Heilongjiang, Jilin, and Liaoning ranked second, fourth, and fifth from last in industrial growth. Especially worrisome was the overwhelming dependence on large and middle-sized state-owned enterprises, with Liaoning alone sporting 1,367 or one-tenth of the total in China. In Harbin there were 188 such firms, almost half in serious debt. What had been the pride of the region had become its burden. Instead of solving their problems through switching to contracts or renting out facilities, these enterprises only exhibited short-term behavior, yielding to corruption and "eating" state property. Despite a large number of scientists and technicians (3.2 million in 1993 with half in Liaoning, which ranked second in China), there was little technological improvement. Train tracks remained clogged with loads of grain, lumber, coal, and iron moving laboriously over long distances, leaving no capacity for new products. Energy and water were in short and uneven supply. Despite ambitious plans in each of the major cities to attract foreign investment, little is forthcoming. One article made clear in 2000 that this region still was plagued by the "Northeast phenomenon," a "hard environment" that hampers participation in regionalism.[54]

Heilongjiang shifted its expectations for regionalism to agricultural production and processing for the Japanese and South Korean markets. A new governor arrived from Shandong with a long record of cooperation with South Korea. Concerned about inefficient agriculture in the transition to the WTO, Beijing could look to Heilongjiang as the area with the largest tracts of farming land and the most extensive methods. With help, it might become a force in serving domestic and regional markets. Rising exports to Russia and trade wars launched in 2000 and 2001 by South Korea and Japan against Chinese farm products showed that even before FTA talks Chinese agricultural successes were becoming a major theme in discussions of the prospective regional division of labor.

With entry into WTO on the horizon, Chinese firms showed a new inclination to go out to the world. But the stress was on market ties, making it difficult to advance into the "red" belt. Caught between the relatively prosperous East and the newly prioritized West of China, the Northeast still was having trouble making expected inroads into Russia. It was easier for the Chinese to invest in Africa, for instance through oil companies active in the Sudan, than in Russia. As for transportation ties to Russia, the routinization of charter flights had lessened the risk of losses en route. Tianjin took the lead, but Beijing, Shenyang, Taiyuan, and Jinan were also active. Moscow was the prime destination, followed by Irkutsk, Novosibirsk, and Krasnoyarsk. The air corridor approach allowed customs duties to be simplified by planeload. Yet, there was risk, because Chinese goods lacked separate

[54] "Dongbei canyu dongbeiya jingji hezuo de 'ying' huanjing fenxi," *Dongbeiya luntan*, 3 (2000), pp. 58–60.

documentation when they reached the market. While customs had received its money, tax offices had not. In 1999 they organized raids, forcing their way into Chinese complexes, demanding papers that were unavailable, even beating, stealing, and arresting as they saw fit. The air corridor, intended to provide large quantities of Chinese goods at reasonable prices, failed to fix troubled trade relations.

Chinese leaders so feared United States–led internationalism that they appealed to one type of nationalism after another, at home and abroad. From 1992 they encouraged Russian nationalism. At the end of the 1990s they reluctantly relied on Japanese nationalism. And in 2000 Korean nationalism in both North and South was welcomed as a force that could limit U.S. power. Little thought was given to the possibility that nationalism in Russia could turn against China, as it did. Despite concern about Japanese nationalism, Chinese leaders appeared to calculate that it was the lesser of two evils, as U.S. hegemonism became more ominous. If Korean nationalism remained in the shadows for a time, in 2002–3 officials were forced to face first South Korean anti-Americanism that was destabilizing to the region and then North Korean belligerence that put China on the spot with the United States. Until 1999 support for regionalism may have been more of an extension for China to boost nationalism collectively than a vote of confidence in regionalism as such. By 2003 the dangers of nationalism undermining regionalism were apparent on all sides.

Chinese sources have taken great pains to calculate what is the nature of China's great-power standing. They concur that China is a regional great power and has some of the attributes of a global great power, such as Security Council veto power, but analysts warn that it is far from having all that is required, such as the ability to project its power abroad. Acknowledging that the Chinese have for a century desperately sought such a global voice for self-respect and reduction of the pressure and humiliation they have felt, these analysts also agree that a gradual approach is needed. If the ultimate aim is to change the situation where Western nations led by the United States enjoy world superiority, the immediate aims must include improving Sino-Japanese relations, forging a broad security system in NEA that can contend with the U.S.-Japanese and U.S.-South Korean alliances, and, by extension, using regionalism to smooth acceptance of China's rise as a great power.[55]

China and Japan

Prime Minister Obuchi visited China in July 1999 after Chinese public opinion had begun to quiet down from the anger aroused by Jiang's visit to Japan and then by the U.S. bombing of the Chinese embassy in Belgrade.

[55] Shi Yinhong, "Guanyu Zhongguo de daguo diwei ji qi xingxiang de sikao," *Guoji jingji pinglun*, 9–10 (1999), pp. 43–4.

Overlooked elements of partnership approved during Jiang's visit could now take concrete form. With his support level falling and a need for reelection as LDP head, Obuchi aimed to prove that he could strongly defend the national interest and make progress in foreign policy. Understanding the situation, Jiang Zemin went out of his way to ensure the success of the summit, remarking that he values a stable Japanese political situation. Some Japanese detected an ulterior motive. One paper remarked that Jiang was swaggering in 1998 with confidence in a China-U.S. strategic partnership after Clinton's visit, but after a downturn in relations with the United States and on the eve of China's fiftieth anniversary celebration, Jiang found it expedient to stress smooth relations.[56] To reduce risk, Obuchi kept his visit short.

In 1999 experts in both China and Japan were telling their governments that the two countries need each other and must not allow the public opinion downturn to set back relations. Awareness of economic and social problems at home buttressed this thinking in both countries. So too did alarm over the United States after the embassy bombing, uncertainty over Russia after its financial collapse, and concern about overseas Chinese hurt by the Asian financial crisis. Japanese experts argued that these conditions gave Tokyo more leverage, interpreting signs of more Chinese cooperation on North Korea from mid-1999 positively. They pinned their hopes on the next generation of leaders, such as technocrats in Southeast China, who did not carry the war memories of Jiang Zemin's generation. Agreeing to China's WTO entry at the 1999 summit, Japan boosted its image in China and left the United States to press for concessions on issues still not satisfactorily resolved.

One Japanese equated the turnabout in Chinese attitudes toward regionalism in 1997 and the establishment of the annual ASEAN +3 summit to the initiative of Mahathir to form an EAEC, and then traced China's 1999 agreement to solidify the trilateral side of the summit to new appreciation for East Asian interdependence. Japan changed in 1999 to favor FTAs with Singapore and South Korea, and China followed close behind.[57]

The downturn in Sino-Japanese relations at the end of 1998 raised concerns in China about emotionalism interfering with the pursuit of national interests. The Japanese were starting to see China as communist, while the Chinese seemed to see Japan as a reincarnation of militarism. Warning that a growing number in China reacted by insisting that China does not need Japan's ODA and technology, advocates of closer relations said that China could fall back in history again, missing a big opportunity. Even when Japanese rightists take an emotional approach to history, China must be calm. After all, they calculated (differing from U.S. figures that count

[56] *Asahi shimbun*, July 9, 1999, p. 3.

[57] Akio Takahara, "The Shift in China's Regional Policy in the Latter Half of the 1990s," *Rikkyo hogaku*, 61 (2002), pp. 150–7.

re-exports through Hong Kong), Japan is China's largest market and China Japan's second-largest market. Relations must focus on the future.[58]

Chinese analysts of Japan refuted the assertion that Japan was likely to become a military great power in the foreseeable future, deciding that the parliamentary democratic system was secure. They added that an economic great power with interests all over the world and a small island dependent on others for resources must realize that it has too much to lose by turning to military power. It must rely on the strength of the United States. Only an abrupt, severe threat might produce a different outcome.[59] After insisting since the early 1990s that China now looked on foreign affairs strictly through the lens of national interests, Chinese scholars finally acknowledged in 2000 that at last they were switching from emotionalism to strategic thinking by focusing on Japan as a normal great power that is a partner for the future. One reason was new economic awareness in the wake of the Asian financial crisis in support of multilateral ties with priority on currency and technological cooperation. Recognizing the danger of a bottleneck in development ahead for China, experts pointed to the significance of Japan. Cynics detected another reason, tactical rather than strategic. After the U.S. bombing of Serbia, concern over rising Japanese power diminished, and the need for balance against the United States grew appreciably.

In deciding on their strategy toward regionalism, the Chinese have long relied on estimates of the evolution of U.S.-Japanese relations. While recognizing past tendencies to exaggerate the degree of conflict, they continued to stress that elements of conflict are increasing.[60] Growing awareness that shared concerns over a "China threat" had driven the two powers closer together, however, led leaders to switch to reassuring the Japanese, including playing to Japan's desire for regional power. In 2000 officials made that appeal repeatedly, breaking from years of warning about the danger of growing Japanese power.

While Beijing beckoned to Tokyo for closer economic cooperation, it was not ready for direct political cooperation on Taiwan, the Korean peninsula, and security questions. Some in the relatively realistic middle generation born between the 1949 founding of the PRC and the Cultural Revolution in the mid-1960s, including many who studied in the West, distance themselves from the more emotional older generations. The compromise is to steer Japan toward economic interdependence in a regional context, while moving from all-around restraint to selective restraint of Japan. Eventually, as its

58 Feng Zhaokui, "Guanyu Zhongri guanxi de zhanlue sikao," *Shijie jingji yu zhengzhi*, November 2000, pp. 11–16.

59 Li Hanmei, et al., *Yazhou wenti yanjiu congshu: 21 shiji Riben de guojia zhanlue* (Beijing: Sheke wenxuan chubanshe, 2000), pp. 120–2.

60 Xu Wansheng, "Lengzhanhou Rimei tongmeng guanxi de sanda qushi," *Dangdai Yatai*, October 2000, p. 49.

influence grows in the region, Japan will grow more independent of the United States.

China's dilemma over Japan was whether to encourage greater independence of the United States with the danger of it becoming a military great power and a stronger regional rival or to welcome its closer bonds with the United States, which could enhance American power and a tighter alliance leaving less room for China to maneuver. Although always keen on finding a middle way, analyses shifted toward approval of Japanese independence. This can be explained by a new appreciation of the growing power of the United States and reduced expectations of Japan's economic, cultural, and political power. Analysts took a fresh look at Japan's desire to become a political great power and found it in many ways not incompatible with China's own great-power strategy. After all, Japan took pride in championing the causes of Asian countries and offering relatively large ODA. Given the consistency with multilateralism of these views, it was not surprising that a September 2000 conference on Sino-Japanese relations stressed the need to boost ties.[61] Along with the goal of urging more independence of the United States came a second goal: hurrying the pace of multilateral regionalism in East Asia in order to provide another form of integration to Japan. One test of the limits of rethinking was whether China would back Japan's entry as a permanent member of the United Nations Security Council. Would it truly accept Japan as a political great power? After all, Japan is more positive than the United States toward the role of the United Nations in world peace and less supportive of "humanitarian interventionism." Beijing hesitated, fearful that an emboldened Japan will raise its political voice in Asia.

On May 20, 2000, the day that Chen Hsui-bian was being inaugurated in Taipei to Beijing's consternation, Jiang Zemin sent a message to Japan by meeting representatives of a 5,000-person Japanese cultural-exchange group and stressing his support for friendly relations. The Japanese were told that Chinese leaders recognize that by appealing to anti-Japanese feelings, China cannot solve its serious problems. Now they are trying to control these sentiments.[62] It follows that Japan should also use restraint in stirring up passions anew. In August when Foreign Minister Kono visited, statements were made that China would not use the history card and would be careful not to provoke another negative reaction among the Japanese people. In response to recent Japanese concerns about Chinese naval vessels, officials promised additional confidence-building measures.

Prior to traveling to Tokyo in October Zhu Rongji held a news conference for Japanese reporters. He emphasized a new priority on relations with Japan, preparing since the spring for the success of this visit. Treating Japan

[61] Lu Guozhong, "Mori Yoshihiro shangtaihou de Riben waijiao," *Guoji wenti yanjiu*, 6 (2000), p. 40.

[62] *Asahi shimbun*, March 20, 2001, p. 3.

as independent of the United States, Zhu made it clear that regional stability in East Asia depended on multipolarity rather than U.S. unipolarity. Zhu stressed the importance of Japan's prior ODA and China's deep gratitude, acknowledging that Beijing had not done enough to publicize Japan's role.[63] He also allayed fears by saying that history is not a suitable card to be used by China to seek benefit from Japan. To counter the retirement diplomacy by Lee Teng-Hui in Japan and Chen Hsui-bian's independence strategy as well as to attract Japan's support for the new priority development of West China, Zhu offered lots of reassurance.

Zhu appeared on television, charming many Japanese with his humor and openness as well as his clear commitment to improving relations. The effect seemed to reverse the pattern of unfriendly feelings toward China, although the Japanese warned that such a reversal was not occurring in anti-Japanese feelings across China.[64] While China had recognized a crisis of trust in bilateral relations and changed its strategy by reporting at home its gratitude for economic assistance, the Japanese remained wary that a fundamental shift had occurred, continuing to call Beijing intransigent for allegedly repeating that the historical question is the political foundation of bilateral relations.[65] Some pointed to two sharply conflicting images of Japan. One, as expressed by Zhu, held that postwar Japan had followed the path of peace and development, achieving tremendous success. The other insisted that militarism was being revived. Rightists in Japan found Zhu's message insincere, a tactical response with little chance of overturning the effects of a campaign that had loudly spread the negative image. Others said that it was a significant change.[66]

Zhu also responded to the U.S. presidential elections by meeting with Japanese reporters and expressing China's hope for Japan to play a larger role in Asia and the world. Moreover, he linked the need to reduce tensions on the Korean peninsula to strengthening relations in NEA, thereby appealing to Japan for patience and support in dealing with North Korea. This message both conveyed a deepening of concern about changes to come in U.S. policy and an intensified appeal to the Japanese.[67] While it was too late to block the consensus forming in Japan in favor of a broad cut in ODA, China's friendly face in 2000 helped to limit the damage. Despite the vocal role of a group in the LDP deemed anti-China, the change was structured to be across-the-board and to reflect Japanese fiscal realities rather than any shift in foreign policy. The mood in Chinese ruling circles was to

63 *Asahi shimbun,* October 9, 2000.

64 "Zhu Rongji no 'biso' no imi," *Sentaku*, November 2000, p. 32.

65 "Chugoku gaisho 'Nihon seifu ni sekinin,'" *Nihon keizai shimbun*, March 7, 2001.

66 "'Nihonjin ga kokan' Chugoku wa hodosezu," *Yomiuri shimbun*, evening, November 7, 2000.

67 "Nihon e no kitai fumikomu," *Asahi shimbun*, November 10, 2000.

accept the reduction without much fuss rather than to stimulate a new debate that could further damage China's image in Japan and lead to deeper cuts.

In 1999 a consensus was forming in Japan to get tougher on China. For the right wing this was the opportunity of the decade after years of unrealized expectations. At last Japan could play power politics while boosting domestic nationalism as a means of changing the nation's direction. They were in no mood to join China in putting the disastrous Jiang Zemin visit to Japan behind them. As Sino-U.S. ties worsened, they saw an opportunity to press China harder, rather than to return to the bridge strategy of the early 1990s. Although the national mood shifted by 2000, the right wing had gained confidence that it could win public sympathy and boost Japan's great-power role.

Many Japanese observed that China had erred in its policy toward Japan, warning that it would be hard to turn things around.[68] China had riled a "peace state," contributing to a change in its course and squandering deeply rooted pro-Chinese sentiment that had been a big plus for China. If in 1972 China could use moral superiority to its advantage, in 2000 repetition of criticisms only rallied the Japanese people and media to see China in a different way. Meanwhile, Taiwan had been realizing its distinct identity, and the Japanese were sympathizing with it more. China would have to face these realities. Many Japanese were ill disposed to China by 1999, reacting suspiciously. They assumed that newfound pressure on China from the threat to cut ODA had forced China's hand. The right wing focused on what they perceived as a growing consensus in responding to China. When the Chinese foreign minister visited on May 10–11, 2000, newspapers declared that China was shocked that Japan had made cuts in ODA the biggest theme of the visit, obliging the Chinese at last to take the views of the Japanese public into account. The hope was that Japan now had the leverage to control Chinese defense expenditures through ODA threats and could after years of frustrating restraint speak its true feelings (*honne*) to China.[69]

The Japanese approached regional relations as a challenge of networking, using politicians as "pipes." Former prime ministers or LDP power brokers are ideal for this role. After the death of Takeshita Noboru, there was talk of reconnecting the pipes, which had been suddenly weakening. But in contrast to earlier ways, this time the focus turned to young leaders. In mid-September 2000 a seven-member delegation of LDP "youth" joined a group of Chinese Communist Party cadres at a hot springs to thrash out contentious issues such as historical consciousness, the Taiwan question, and economic cooperation. Noting the spirited exchanges, one newspaper said a chillier atmosphere

[68] Okabe Tatsumi, "21 seiki no Toajia," *Kokusai mondai*, September 2000, pp. 58–70.
[69] *Hokuriku chunichi shimbun*, May 13, 2000, p. 5.

meant that close to thirty years of "special bilateral relations" should be yielding to "normal" relations.[70]

Responding to signs that the Japanese public was warming to Zhu Rongji's "smile diplomacy," Japanese sources charged that the real problem is the Chinese public's contempt for Japan. One professor in Japan from China reported after a return visit that the feelings of intellectuals since the mid-1990s have turned much more negative. As evidence, he cited the response to a ground-breaking article at the beginning of 2000 in *Shijie zhishi* by Feng Zhaokui. Letters pored into the journal lambasting the author's reasoning behind a more positive understanding of Japan. Polls show that young people in China overwhelmingly rate Japan as the country they like least. Readers of the Internet note strong criticisms of China's soft diplomacy. Teachers report that it is hard to teach about Japan because students dislike it so much. Unlike nationalism directed against the United States there is a qualitatively different character to the emotionalism focused on Japan.[71]

The Japanese quickly noticed the positive message to the Chinese public about Japan of January 2000 in *Shijie zhishi*, regarded as a voice of the Chinese Foreign Ministry. Some, however, gave it little significance. One expert charged that Chinese government leaders bear a large responsibility for anti-Japanese patriotic campaigns turning Chinese opinion very negative and that other articles in the same journal and elsewhere contradict the new message. He claimed that Japanese pressure to lower ODA has had an effect that must not be relaxed. Refuting the argument that countries that trade a lot do not go to war with each other, the author insisted that first must come a change in Chinese opinion.[72]

If Japan used ODA as leverage on China, China more than reciprocated by dangling lucrative contracts as rewards for correct conduct. The very Japanese minister who offended China on August 15 by visiting the Yasukuni shrine appeared in Beijing in September to present China's case for the $1.5 billion contract to build a rapid train to Shanghai. China enjoyed playing off competing countries for such prizes. Yet, as Chinese leaders in 2003 weighed proposals from France, Germany, and Japan for construction of the railway, an Internet campaign against choosing Japan left a strong impression.[73]

The debate on China intensified in Japan. As the campaign for reducing ODA to China accelerated in 2000, *Sankei shimbun* unveiled its list in favor of sharp cuts. First, it charged that no major city around the world had been so dependent on a single country's assistance as Beijing was on

70 "'Futsu no kankei' o mosaku," *Nihon keizai shimbun*, October 7, 2000.

71 Ryo Seiko, "Tainichi kanjo ga akka suru Chugoku no chishikijinso," *Ronsa*, December 2000, pp. 155–65.

72 Okabe Tatsumi, "Nitchu kankei to 'yoron,'" *Toa*, September 2000, pp. 2–3.

73 Mo Banfu, "Intanetto de hirogara han nichi," *Sekai shuho*, August 19–26, 2003, pp. 48–9.

Japan. Its airport terminal, subway system, electrical generators, hospitals, and so forth were built with vast amounts of Japanese funds over twenty years, and now Beijing is using this infrastructure as proof that it should be awarded the 2008 Olympics rather than Osaka. Then it argued that most Japanese assistance to China is not through ODA but rather through more shadowy accounts independent of diplomatic strategy. The Japanese people are in the dark about the true scale of loans. Finally came accusations that much Japanese assistance actually goes for infrastructure that serves military purposes.

On the other side were academics and business leaders who argued that such cooperation was in Japan's interest in fostering both peace and prosperity in a developing country such as China, while serving as a replacement for reparations. Moreover, in the Sino-U.S.-Japanese triangle ODA contributes to multilateralism.[74] Defenders of ODA made the following arguments: 1) it is proportional, as Indonesia is first with 20 percent and China second with 14 percent until 1999 when Indonesian circumstances changed and, for the most part, it has to be repaid; 2) since 1998 China has expressed its appreciation often, including a panel in front of the domestic counters at the new Beijing airport terminal; 3) Sino-Japanese talks on the disputed Chinese ships are progressing; 4) China's per capita GDP below $1,000 still reflects a developing country; and 5) ODA serves to stabilize China's development and to make it into a responsible great power.[75]

Some conveyed a sense of hopelessness about public opinion in China toward Japan. The message was that the Chinese people really hate Japan, the Japanese in the postwar era are not at all responsible for this, and there is little that the Japanese can do about it except to show their displeasure by withholding assistance and other strong signals. To back up this line of reasoning articles reported ethnic slurs widely used in China, such as *xiao riben*, comparable to the English "Jap." They also reviewed Chinese textbooks and media, even in October 2000 when China was heralding its "smile diplomacy," for their sustained coverage of the war period rather than postwar Japan. And they link the media blitz to the patriotic campaign launched in 1994 under Jiang Zemin's direct leadership. Reinforcing Japanese alarm about anti-Japanese emotions in China were reports of a *Time* Internet survey of Chinese youth between 18 and 30 years old that revealed that 65 percent chose Japan as the country most disliked.[76] This news was reported in the midst of Zhu Rongji's "smile diplomacy" with the charge that the leadership after realizing that the authority of communist ideology had faded had turned to the "last ideology" to garner support, building

[74] *Asahi shimbun*, January 31, 2001, p. 13.

[75] Kojima Tomoyuki, "Chugoku o 'sekinin aru daikoku' ni suru tame ni," *Gaiko forum*, 2 (2001), pp. 38–45.

[76] *Mainichi shimbun*, October 16, 2000.

on the legitimacy it had won in the anti-Japanese war and pouring oil on still smoldering anti-Japanese feelings nurtured whenever it was useful after 1949.[77]

As China was striving to assuage rumpled Japanese feelings in 2000, the Japanese right insisted that the real problem is heightened dislike of Japan in China as a result of "mind control."[78] Blaming the Chinese government, these Japanese regarded the belated acknowledgment of gratitude for Japanese ODA and of sharp differences between present-day and wartime Japan as a paltry effort. The Japanese left, a mere shadow of its once feisty self, also bemoaned the state of Chinese opinion toward Japan. While citing examples of more sympathetic media coverage, such as praise for Japan's women's marathon gold medalist at the Sydney Olympics as the "pride of Asia," it too pointed to many of the tens of millions of educated young people on the Internet airing their hostility toward Japan and even calling Zhu Rongji a traitor for his assertion to Japanese reporters that on the historical question China does not want to hurt Japanese feelings. Two years after Jiang Zemin's dismal visit, Chinese public opinion was not softening.[79]

In early 2001 Makida Kunihiko, head of the Asia continental department of the Foreign Ministry, with the understanding of Foreign Minister Kono Yohei, opposed a visa to Lee Teng-Hui, who had cited medical reasons for coming to Japan. A media outcry followed. At first the Ministry courted disbelief when it claimed that no application had been filed. Then a majority in the Diet made known their support for Lee as the public drew to their side; the argument that a visit would damage Japan's national interest was overcome.[80] Whereas some argued that this was a victory for humanitarian diplomacy, others realized that it signified an important change of direction in policy. As in the case of relations with Russia and textbook revisions opposed by South Korea and China, the Foreign Ministry found itself under fire and isolated, as nationalists grew emboldened.

From the right came the charge that Japanese politicians were bending to China's "invitation diplomacy." In 1999 about 170 Diet members had visited China, and in just a three-week period in late summer 2000 eight groups with fifty-one Diet members joined the "rush" to Beijing, attention not bestowed on any other foreign city. Critics charge that these visitors, such as Nonaka Hiromu in May 2000, fail to raise issues of concern to Japan such as Chinese ships in Japanese waters or the rise of the Chinese military. China pays for the trips and controls the agenda, filled with advocacy of friendship. Charging that U.S. congressmen in China refuse Chinese funding and insist on meeting

77 "Nitchu saiko," *Sankei shimbun*, October 24, 28–9, 2000.

78 "Sekai wa Nihon ni kanshajo o," *Sankei shimbun*, October 30, 2000.

79 Banto Kenji, "Chugoku no tainichi kanjo," *Mainichi shimbun*, November 2, 2000.

80 Sakurai Yoshiko, "Opinion," *Shukan daiyamondo*, April 21, 2001, p. 175.

high-tech figures and intellectuals, *Sankei shimbun* called the Japanese visitors "birds in a cage."[81]

Sankei shimbun led in the fall of 2000 in covering foreign diplomatic pressure and Japanese textbooks. Arguing that it is time for Japan to prepare textbooks without foreign interference, *Sankei* said that Japan must deal in its own way with oft-criticized conduct of Japan's military, such as the "Nanjing incident" and comfort women.[82] Capitalizing on the mood of historical justification seen in the best-selling manga *Sensoron* (*War Theory*), the Japanese right was emboldened. At stake was their view that Japan's national identity should be as a normal country past and present and that the basis of its regional cooperation should be as a country with no future need to apologize and no past that needs to be explained.

Japan had limited confidence in Northeast China. Reports on Shenyang in mid-1999 noted 600,000 unemployed in a workforce of four million and another 1.1 million with wage arrears. The result was demonstrations in front of government buildings and low consumer demand. This market did not tempt many Japanese firms.[83] Nearby, in Dalian, where Japanese firms made their earliest and most concentrated advance into China, DITIC (Dalian International Trust Investment Corporation) essentially went bankrupt, leaving enormous debts, 40 percent of which Japanese negotiators were obliged to write off.[84]

Japanese trade with China was increasing in the second half of the 1990s largely due to Chinese exports, many the products of Japanese firms. Finding solace in good economic results despite the idea that relations had slipped, some argued that entry into WTO would accelerate ties and give Japan much more access to the Chinese market. This, in turn, should smooth relations. One Chinese educated in Japan argued, if many in the United States wanted the collapse of "socialist" China, the Japanese should find it easier to understand the advance of "open" China.[85] Japan's investment in China had dropped from a peak in 1994 of 432 billion yen to 84 billion yen in 1999, and the number of projects had fallen from 770 to 67. Yet, as China was rising, first to the tenth trading country in the world and then to the fourth or fifth exporter with \$40–\$50 billion a year in direct foreign investment, the Japanese interest revived. Investment rose rapidly from 2000, complementing a total ODA of close to 2.5 trillion yen over twenty years from

81 "Nitchu saiko," *Sankei shimbun*, October 26, 2000.

82 *Sankei shimbun*, October 16, 2000, p. 1; *Sankei shimbun*, October 30, 2000, p. 1.

83 *Asahi shimbun*, July 9, 1999, p. 14.

84 *Sankei shimbun*, November 11, 2000, p. 3.

85 Ka Ryu, "Nitchu kankei wa honto ni akka shiteiru ka?" *Sekai shuho*, November 28, 2000, pp. 22–5.

1979–98.[86] Soon marquee firms were unveiling far-reaching plans for bulk manufacturing in China. Again, economic ties were driving closer bilateral integration and debates on regionalism.

The Japanese complained about the trade deficit with China, suggesting that unfair practices were responsible despite the image of a "vast market." In 1999 bilateral trade equaled $66 billion, making China Japan's second trading partner and Japan China's first partner (according to the accounting used in both countries that excludes U.S. imports of Chinese goods through Hong Kong). The deficit had climbed to $20 billion.[87] Yet, on the whole, the movement of trade and people helped to keep ties with China advancing even after the idea that China is special was fading. The number of Japanese going to China annually reached about 1 million, and the number of Chinese rose sharply from 50,000 in 1996 to 230,000 in 1999, many in long-term stays as students, industrial trainees, and so forth.[88] Even as relations were tested, they stayed on track. Japan's inclination to escape from the roller coaster of U.S.-Chinese relations by strengthening ties to China was made easier by a belief that China's priority is modernization and economic cooperation, not Taiwan.

In May 2000 there was talk of a cultural gap due to a controversy over Toshiba, which had sold 200,000 notebook personal computers in China, but was blamed for unfair treatment to Chinese customers when it refused compensation after paying a billion dollars in the United States in response to a lawsuit over a latent defect. When the news reached China by Internet, users demanded similar treatment. In response, Toshiba said that China's laws are different, reminding the Chinese that over the past thirty years it had invested heavily in China. Although in 1989 Toshiba's president had led in opposing sanctions on China, the company was accused in 2000 of hurting the feelings of the Chinese people.[89]

Countering the upturn in relations in 2000 were stories of Chinese naval research vessels exploring the East China Sea near Okinawa. They painted a picture of a country ambitious to take hold of seabed natural resources in waters claimed by Japan.[90] No wonder some eagerly anticipated the arrival of the Bush administration and a stronger alliance with the United States to balance China. After years of concern that the United States was stressing China more than Japan and indirectly fueling China's assertive position

86 Yamaguchi Shigeru, "Kokusai shakai ni okeru Chugoku," *Kaigai jijo*, September 2000, pp. 21–3.

87 *Sankei shimbun*, November 10, 2000.

88 Amako Satoshi, "Nitchu kokkyo seijoka igo," *Kokusai mondai*, July 2000, pp. 64–7.

89 *Sankei shimbun*, November 9, 2000.

90 Teruya Kenkichi, "Chugoku ga nerau Higashishinakai no kaitei shigen," *Foresight*, October 2000, pp. 80–3.

toward Japan, many Japanese awaited new U.S. attention, but not necessarily a close embrace.[91]

Russia and Regionalism

In 1999 the Russian public was angry about internationalization, after suffering from the financial crisis of 1998 and being aroused about the United States–led war in Yugoslavia, and mostly treading water on regionalism. Relations with Japan were on hold. Ties with China were mostly rhetorical. Efforts to repair relations with South Korea and to restore ties to North Korea needed time as well as new leadership in the Kremlin. Russian policy was adrift. At the end of 2000 after Vladimir Putin had been president for one year the role of Russia was reinvigorated. Putin's vigorous diplomatic activity and his country's new economic vitality raised Russia's profile despite a weak hand in regional trade.

Instead of calling for more openness, Russian officials were increasingly relying on the state as organizer and protector. The lesson that some drew from the recovery in the two years after the crisis of August 1998 was that Russia could now manage without foreign loans or investments through reliance on increased energy exports, a global cartel to keep oil and gas prices high, and a devalued ruble to protect domestic industry. Putin's vertical consolidation led to plans for developing the state as a stronger force at home and in regional and global circles. On November 22, 2002 the new State Council received the Ishaev report on the strategy for the development of the state in the period to 2010. While mention was made of the Chinese state's role in development and the urgency of boosting the Russian Far East for its strategic importance, nothing in the lengthy report suggested a need to win the trust of foreign investors as China had done. Instead it offered support to the state's dominance in the military-industrial complex, the agrarian-industrial complex, and infrastructure. While generally favoring concentration of production as efficient, the report did warn against excessive concentration in a few regions of Russia, leaving others such as the Far East noncompetitive. It suggested that while some now favored a state policy to promote growth in competitive areas and leave aside for the time being the others, this would not serve the social consolidation needed. The state should allow regions able to boost revenues to keep 70 percent of their gains.[92]

Russians continued to be torn between two conflicting models of development: state mobilization emphasizing domestic industry for consumption at home and global integration relying on foreign investment

91 Michael Richardson, "Japan and Australia Expect Gains in Asia-Pacific Security," *The International Herald Tribune*, December 18, 2000.

92 *Strategiia razvitiia gosudarstva na period do 2010 goda* (Moscow: Report to the State Council, 2000).

in natural resources for export. Those eager to build a strong Russian state feared the centrifugal effects of globalization or regionalism and proposed economic mobilization. Ishaev, who from his post in Khabarovsk long had feared disastrous consequences from the Russian Far East being absorbed in economic regionalism, spoke for this agenda. The Ishaev Report was placed before the State Duma as the alternative to the liberal program under discussion.[93] Clearly, those fearful of global forces do not see regionalism as better; they hark back to more economic self-sufficiency and more state direction of the economy rather than trust in regional ties.

Preoccupied with its geopolitical identity as well as state revenue objectives, Russia under Putin turned to centralization. In the first months of the new presidential representatives it was unclear how much power they would obtain over the oblast and krai. Again Primorskii krai became a test case. Its energy crisis in the winter of 2000–1 exceeded anything seen earlier in the decade, creating an emergency that left little alternative to central intervention. The quarrel between Konstantin Pulikovskii, Putin's representative in Khabarovsk, and Evgenii Nazdratenko, the perennial target of Moscow officials, acquired a personal character, ending even the appearance of cooperation. Each blamed the other, the local media accusing Pulikovsky of seeking to gain control over properties, and the governor withdrew the man he had sent to assist the president's representative. Again regionalism had to wait until Russia settled its power struggles.

Putin squandered many opportunities to show sustained interest in regionalism. After forcing Nazdratenko's ouster as governor in February 2001 he not only did not arrange for huge fishing fleet profits from unrecorded trade to be fully recorded and used for the benefit of the local Russian population, he even appointed Nazdratenko to head the State Fisheries Committee. Looking back on dramatic economic gains from a year of 7.7 percent growth in GNP and 47 percent growth in foreign trade, observers wondered where was the regional economic investment plan to reflect this turnaround. Because one essential step for preparing the Russian Far East for regional integration was to break down protectionism even against domestic companies, Nazdratenko's departure did at least serve the goal of enabling national firms to make inroads into the local economy.

While forces in Moscow bemoaned his behavior repeatedly over Nazdratenko's eight-year tenure as governor, leaders always cut a deal with him hoping to moderate his excesses without ousting him. Rumors swirled that he had strong protectors among top figures first in the Yeltsin and then in the Putin administration. He survived despite his negative impact on border demarcation and relations with China, smuggling and income to Moscow,

93 Jonathan Tennembaum, "The Ishaev Report: An Economic Mobilization Plan for Russia," *Executive Intelligence Review*, March 2, 2001, reported in the Johnson Russia Report, February 25, 2001.

energy supplies and the well being of the local population, and criminality and the possibility of economic development and foreign investment. Always he shifted the blame to others, clothing himself as defender of local and national interests.

Long in the background to Nazdratenko but similarly vehement about China, Governor Ishaev assumed a more prominent role. Negotiations had resumed over territory, but this time the focus was an island on the outskirts of Khabarovsk. Vague references in statements after high-level meetings mentioned continued negotiations on nonresolved border issues without alerting outsiders to the challenge. There is no reason to think Russia will yield. The only possibility is a trade, offering China something else. What China wants most is access to the sea through Tumen or further north at Zarudino. This brings Primorskii krai back into the picture, where fear reigns that even the lease of a corridor to the coast would serve only Chinese interests while existing Russian ports would atrophy.

In 2000 Putin shored up ties with Europe first, even stressing Russian integration into the West, but his message soon shifted to warnings about ways to create a balance of power, punctuated by new concepts of national security in January and of foreign policy in July. At the same time his message at home focused on building the power of the state, reinforced by brutal handling of the war in Chechnya. Thus, nationalism prevailed over globalization, accompanied by dire warnings about Russia's need to survive as a nation and a civilization. This view sees United States–led action as unilateralism and globalization of the world economy as producing mixed results such as increasing dependence.[94] If Putin also appeared to be a pragmatist, the meaning of this remained elusive in his first year.

The prevailing view of Russia's role in NEA in late 2000 combined increased nationalism, cautious exploration of regionalism, and limited resistance to globalization. This view recognized that globalization and regionalism are two tendencies of world development, and Russia is too weak to oppose both. Thus, it needs a strategy to shape both or even to use one against the other. Foremost in this thinking is not how to attract investment to help Russia enter the global economy, but how to serve some geopolitical interests. Economic, financial, and scientific and technological integration with the countries of NEA, including their investment in the Russian Far East and Eastern Siberia, were cast, at best, as means to bolster national security. In September 2000 the Baikal Economic Forum in Irkutsk combined a call for actively and deeply participating in the integration of NEA with an intensified orientation to security, the former through an attractive investment climate for foreign investors made possible through a special economic regime under central control, and the latter requiring Russian steering of the process of regionalization – strengthening the Russian national side, making

94 *Rossiiskaia gazeta*, July 17, 2000.

sure that Russia acquires a balancing role in the region, and driving regionalism to limit globalization. At the same time as Putin pursued European countries extending natural gas exports, he was intensifying discussion of the development of resources as the key to integration in Asia. Unlike earlier discussions, this time there was frank recognition of the need to attract workers from neighboring countries and of the need to make long-term arrangements suitable for investors. The question remained, as in annual conferences since 1995 of the Northeast Asian Gas and Pipeline Forum and in summit declarations, of Russian follow-up and of coordination between Moscow and the Russian Far East.[95]

A report to the Federation Union drawing on the results of the Baikal Economic Forum suggested four functions for Russia in a region still in formation in contrast to Russia's role in Europe where it is relegated to the role of an outsider in a region already set.[96] 1) It can serve as a Eurasian bridge through its transportation potential, despite the fact that some are actively against the proposal for a Northern Silk Road through the Korean peninsula as a threat to Russia's seaports. 2) Russia should become the centerpiece in a regional energy system, including creating a strategic reserve oil fund for energy security in the region, perhaps, in accord with China's wishes, and an oil pipeline through Chita and Daqing in Heilongjiang province. 3) Russia must maintain its military strength and create zones of technology based on its military-industrial complex in order to enter the region with military parity and military-political partnerships. 4) It must strive for a region based on strong states, in which increased central authority at home keeps it an equal partner.[97]

Russians are inclined to broaden the concept of region into two main units for the world, leaving some areas on the periphery. In the West is the Euro-Atlantic region. In the East is the Asia-Pacific region. The United States has a major role in both regions, but Russia also is present in both and has possibilities for securing a larger status. It follows that NEA is a subregion of the Asia-Pacific region, as the EU is a subregion of the Euro-Atlantic region. By solidifying ties with nearby subregions, Russia can gain some balance versus the United States and limit globalization as well as shape regionalism that raises its stature. Analysts warn that Russia lacks influence on globalization, facing asymmetrical dependency. They reject the old euphoria toward globalization, saying it does both good and harm. The harm comes from threats to sovereignty: technological dependency as trade

95 Vladimir I. Ivanov, "The Baikal Economic Forum in Irkutsk: Good Intentions and Modest Outcomes," *ERINA Report*, 37 (December 2000), pp. 51–3.

96 "Strategiia razvitiia Rossii v Aziatsko-Tikhookeanskom Raione v XXI veke," *Analisticheskii vestnik*, special issue 17 (Moscow: Sovet Federatsii Federal'nogo Rossiiskoi Federatsii, 2000).

97 "Strategiia razvitiia Rossii v Aziatsko-Tikhookeanskom Raione v XXI veke," *Analisticheskii vestnik* (Moscow: Sovet Federatsii Federal'nogo Rossiiskoi Federatsii, 2000), pp. 1–8, 14, 19.

barriers fall; global cultural diffusion as images of the norms and values of a few countries are spread through propaganda; and even exploitation as the resources of one country are used largely for the benefit of the leading countries. Russia by itself may have little leverage, but strategic thinking under Putin treated regionalism as a means for balance.[98]

Dimitry Rogozin, chairman of the Duma foreign affairs committee, asserted in an assessment of the year 2000 what many great-power Russian nationalists think: while Europe is integrating without leaving Russia any promising prospects, foreign policy must concentrate on the Far East in which the promise for Russia is greatest. Rogozin applauded Putin's trips to China, Japan, and North Korea, suggesting that some combined approach to the countries of the region offers the best prospect for benefits. In contrast, Vladimir Lukin, the former chairman, insisted that while Russia should develop relations with both China and Japan, it should never forget that its main interests are in Europe.[99] Yet, even mainstream Eurocentric thinking takes NEA seriously as an arena where Russia has major stakes, which it cannot afford to lose.

In 1999 and 2000, Russian rhetoric stressed Asian great-power linkages to counter the dominance of the United States and its allies. Instead of Asian regionalism appearing as a means for Russian domestic economic development, it loomed as a device to balance Euro-Atlantic strategic power. This was the outcome of a way of thinking that had been gaining ground over most of the decade after being deeply rooted in the 1980s. By the end of the decade it had taken three new forms: 1) negotiations for a friendship treaty between Russia and China, pledging each to defend the other and harking back to the 1950s although the word *alliance* was unlikely to be used; 2) more serious talk of a long-term agreement among Russia, China, and India versus the hegemony of the West, in which Russia hoped to be the lever holding the Asian great-power triangle together; and 3) desire for close Russian relations with North Korea to use its threat to regional security as a source of pressure against the United States, Japan, and South Korea. Yet, Putin's conflicting interest in economic growth linked to the West could not be ignored.

Russian coverage vacillated between dreams and harsh realities. In the former category are proposals for tunnels from Alaska to Chukotka and Hokkaido to Sakhalin. Rarely is there mention of who would pay and under what conditions, despite hints that the start of the project could be in the near future. In the category of realism are estimates for population decline in the Russian Far East to 6.3 million in 2016. The distribution continues to

[98] "Strategiia razvitiia Rossii v Aziatsko-Tikhookeanskom Raione v XXI veke," *Analisticheskii vestnik*, special issue 17 (Moscow: Sovet Federatsii Federal'nogo Rossiiskoi Federatsii, 2000), pp. 12–15.

[99] *Segodnya*, December 28, 2000.

change too. Already the far north of Chukotka and Magadan had lost 48 and 35 percent respectively, and the sea-wrapped elongations of Kamchatka and Sakhalin had dropped by 17 to 18 percent.[100] Concentration along the Amur and Ussuri rivers is proceeding, putting a higher percentage of people by the Chinese border.

Many problems trouble Russia's economic partners. Often countries in the region must export through Moscow using specified organizations with duty-free rights, even if the goods are destined for the Russian Far East. This is the opposite of FEZs. Fragmentation among competing areas in the Far East with small populations interferes with the coherence desired through a regional approach. Border crossings are difficult, for instance on the border of Heilongjiang and Primorskii krai one may be subjected to two stages of passport control and customs clearance and then two more by the military.

In 1999 Sakhalin rose to first in Russia in volume of direct foreign investment, exceeding $1 billion. Elsewhere in the Russian Far East, Japanese investment in timber logging continued to do quite well, but investments in hotels and the service sector were a disaster. Russian partners forcibly took these joint ventures over, leaving no appetite by Japanese or Koreans to persist.[101] Wherever Putin travels in NEA he is reminded of the dismal business climate, and he responds with promises of change.

Even as the differences over foreign policy narrowed under Putin, there is still no clear idea of the priority to be given to regionalism. Putin needs a strategy for NEA for three goals: 1) economic revival in which Moscow and Western Siberian oil and gas are not alone as engines of growth; 2) entry into the Asia-Pacific region, allowing two-headed Russia to balance Europe and Asia and, within Asia, to gain leverage in dealing with the great powers; and 3) reassertion of Russian national identity as a strong, centralized state without the danger of separatism. With so much at stake, Putin's interest in the region showed no signs of flagging.

Increasingly, the message spread that Russians give preference to what they call "respect" from the world over trust. As doubters warned that the first year of the Putin era had been largely squandered as a negative image of Russia spread, the elite and media took satisfaction from a new sense of Russia standing up and forcing others to take notice. They harkened back to the "respect" once shown to the Soviet Union, arguing that again Moscow's voice must be heeded. In this view, globalization is not a competition for investment dollars or creditworthiness, but a new stage in the old game of great powers vying for influence and states directing the flow of trade and assistance accordingly. Putin rose to power and made the thrust

100 "Russia's Population Predicted to Continue Decline," Interfax, reprinted in *Johnson's Russia List*, January 2, 2000.

101 Kyoji Komachi, "Investing in the Russian Far East," *ERINA Report*, 37 (December 2000), p. 47.

of his early efforts at vertical control as a savior who would overcome national weakness. Obsessed with centralization and national power, Russians had trouble focusing on regional integration. First Putin would need to restore trust in their own promise along with confidence in the gains from globalization.

China and Russia

In the spring of 1999 in response to shared outrage over NATO conduct in the Yugoslav war, Jiang Zemin and Boris Yeltsin agreed to closer relations, leading some in both countries to use the word *alliance*, although with qualifications. The focus turned to more military and industrial cooperation, as well as to energy security for China through ties to Russia. Arms sales to China were increasing from roughly $1 to $1.5 billion a year. A contract was signed to sell 40 SU-30MKK fighter jets made in Komsomolsk-na-Amur in Khabarovskii krai. Talk advanced on coproduction of a fifth-generation fighter that neither could afford to build on its own. Progress in economic relations took the form of an agreement for joint production of electricity. After years of stagnation in economic relations, possibilities existed for some important advances.

Later that spring when Russia acquiesced to NATO's presence in Kosovo and cooperated in ending the conflict, the Chinese felt let down. They started to reassess Russian weakness and the likelihood of concessions not only to the West but also to Japan.[102] Even before Vladimir Putin became prime minister in late 1999 a reassessment of foreign policy was under way. With Evgenii Primakov no longer foreign minister or prime minister, his great-power maneuvering over more than three years drew scrutiny. Emerging from the financial crisis of August 1998, Russian leaders gave thought to how they again could attract foreign capital. Concerned about "Russian passing," Russia needed to catch the attention of Americans again. Meanwhile, China was beckoning to solidify the partnership that had angrily denounced U.S. and NATO conduct in Yugoslavia, and Japan was pressing to accelerate the "countdown to the year 2000" that had stalled. A process was set in motion that would culminate early in 2000 when Putin as president would adjust foreign policy in at least three directions: 1) to reemphasize ties to the West, especially by expanding personal ties to leaders in Europe; 2) to make Russia's voice heard on more issues, including rebuilding ties with North Korea; and 3) to put relations with China on hold while exploring Japan's initiative.[103]

[102] Lin Xiaoguang, "Rie guanxi: 90 niandai yilai de fazhan yu bianhua," *Dongbeiya yanjiu*, 4 (2000), p. 32.

[103] *Novoe vremia*, 37 (September 1999), pp. 17–18.

Putin started off on the wrong foot with China by writing on December 30, 1999 that on the edge of the twenty-first century Russia should focus on returning to Europe. Having relied on Yeltsin's personal diplomacy and knowing little of Putin, the Chinese were shocked. One possible cause of the letdown was Putin's decision to suspend the transfer of some sensitive military technology to China promised by Yeltsin.[104] The Chinese were also disappointed that Putin chose to emphasize relations with the West in his first official statements. They had expected an early visit to China, but he only came in July en route to the Okinawa G-8 summit featuring the West. In turn, Russians were more open in their complaints, such as that when China's leaders visited other major countries such as France they brought as gifts contracts for big export items, but not with Russia. Hard negotiations were straining relations. When Russian civilian planes did appear in China, it was the result of a contraband deal for irregular use, not because China yielded to crude negotiating tactics to force such purchases if China wanted to buy military craft.[105]

Only when Putin finally came to Beijing did the clamor diminish. The Chinese reasoned that at least Putin is a strategic thinker, whose foremost goal is to balance "all-sided relations." If bilateral coordination might recede, Russia's assertive stance as a pole in a multipolar world would remain. Yet, observers understood that, while Russian geostrategic assertions often waxed more enthusiastic about Sino-Russian relations than did those of China, targeting the United States more forcefully and warning more unambiguously of an alliance, their ardor is less deeply rooted, appearing more as a short-term emotional reaction or tactic. In fact, the Russians trust China even less than the Chinese trust Russia. The tone of relations changed even before Putin supported the United States in September 2001.

When Putin met Jiang Zemin first at the Shanghai-5 meeting in Tajikistan on July 5 and then on July 17, 2000 in Beijing, the Chinese saw him as Western-centered. While many in the West feared Putin as a great-power nationalist, the Chinese determined that he was an economic realist, which, after all, is the foundation for nationalism. This led them to conclude even more clearly that he would boost ties to the West, especially with the EU.[106] Instead of coordination, the Russian text of the Beijing summit downplayed any reference to opposition to theater missile defense while the Chinese text highlighted it. The Chinese do not expect Russian assistance in the event of a military clash over Taiwan and realistically assess

104 Vinay Shukla, "Russian Eagle Unfolds Wings in the Year of Putin," Press Trust of India, December 25, 2000, reprinted in *Johnson's Russia List*, December 26, 2000.

105 *Renmin ribao*, December 1, 2000.

106 Peng Liping, "21 shiji chuzhong Zhonge guanxi zhanwang," *Jinri Dongou Zhongya*, 4 (2000), p. 31.

the conditionality of bilateralism, depending on the state of U.S.-Russian ties.[107]

The Chinese well understood Putin's preoccupation with restoring Moscow's great-power standing coupled with his intent to achieve sustained economic growth, but that did not necessarily mean they expected him to work hard to link the two as a foundation for a bilateral partnership. Analysts noted that economic ties had evolved independently of political ones: in 1989–93 when political ties were often shaky, trade grew fastest; whereas in 1994, 1997, and 1998 when leaders were in a very cooperative mood trade fell sharply. As of 1999 recorded bilateral trade revealed the following weaknesses: 1) the total was only $5.7 billion, below the level of 1992, let alone the $7.7 billion of 1993; 2) China's exports had fallen below $1.5 billion, mostly limited to foodstuffs and textiles rather than much desired value-added items; 3) mutual investment was next to nothing, averaging $200–$300 million each over eight years, as science and technology cooperation was also slight; 4) existing trade was unstable and its mechanisms such as arbitration and credit failed to meet international standards; and 5) the Russian side under Yeltsin did not pay much attention to these troubles. Yet, from 2000 trade at last was rising sharply,[108] while energy exports and joint development of natural resources were being taken more seriously. This partly reflected Beijing's push to get firms to buy Russian exports, which reinforced the nonmarket nature of bilateral ties, but it also signified the impact of Putin beginning to bring economic relations into the forefront. Trade appeared to be focused on the two extremes: border trade, which was recovering in 2000, and mega projects such as energy. The former involves shuttle traders dealing in small volumes with little need for modern economic mechanisms. The latter depends on state planners with some role for multinational corporations. Arms sales also are decided by the top, limiting the role of the private sector. While negotiations in 2000 paid a lot of attention to how to make intermediate-level ties easier, including changed banking procedures, the Chinese doubted that Russia would be able to build a "civilized economy" for many years.

As hopes rose for an oil pipeline from Angarsk to Daqing, a feasibility study and a cost-sharing agreement seemed to move a project for the Kovyktinskoye gas fields along.[109] Seoul gave its blessing to it and encouraged the Korean firm Kogas to participate. China's goal is a continental supply of resources to lower dependence on vulnerable sea-lanes as energy dependence rises rapidly. China has the infrastructure for oil piped from Russia through

[107] Iwashita Akihiro, "Kankei zaikochiku no ura ni shimiku Churo sorezore no omowaku," *Sekai shuho*, September 5, 2000, pp. 6–8.

[108] Lu Nanquan, "Xintiaojian xia tuijin Zhonge jingmao hezuo de zhongyaoxing yu silu" (Beijing: unpublished manuscript, 2000).

[109] Felix K. Chang, "Chinese Energy and Asian Security," *Orbis*, Spring 2001, pp. 23–4.

the Daqing fields in Heilongjiang and is eager to involve foreign companies studying projects in Eastern Siberia or the Russian Far East to lend outside support.[110] In 2003 Japanese competition cast doubt on the route to Daqing.

The Chinese in the year 2000 tried to assess what Russia really wants from Asia. They concluded that its goals are becoming more specific. It seeks the development of Asiatic Russia both through natural resources as other global resources are diminished and as a Eurasian bridge – pipelines, railroads, electricity grids, and so forth. This means Russia will need capital and technology, not a formula for China's influence to grow, as well as labor. But Russia also looks to all parts of Asia as arms markets, a reason for close ties to China. Moscow needs such ties to China also because of fear of lingering separatist tendencies in the Russian Far East. The Chinese use the label *emotionalism* to describe the feelings in that area, which no longer are expected to be dispelled in the near future. Russia needs to impress diplomats in the West that despite its weak national strength it deserves a voice on international issues.[111] This leaves China as a tool to be discarded, not a friend to be prized.

Not only did the Chinese conclude that economic necessity will drive Russia to the West, they decided that cultural and political ties lead there as well. Putting aside figures that show two-thirds of Russian territory in Asia and an even higher percentage of its natural resources, analysts point to 80 percent of its population living in Europe, even more of its historical identity there, and finally its predominant strategic focus there. In 1997 when Yeltsin made his number one priority Russia's full entrance into the G-8 "club," it was seen in China as a sign that foreign relations with Asia are secondary. Some suggested that Russia uses the East when it wants to frighten the West, but that it is not at all inclined to a new cold war. In these circumstances, China cannot compete.[112]

In 2000 the question of India rose noticeably in Sino-Russian relations. Although in 1999 China had contracted to buy additional fighters from Russia, India made a larger deal, including production rights for the jets (the technology would be transferred to China only in 2010) and amenities not offered to China. Many perceived a Russian tilt to India. If Russians spoke of three-way opposition to U.S. unipolarity, the Chinese were wary due to rivalry in SEA and a border dispute.[113] Russia preferred a distant partner in

110 Xia Yishan, "Zhonge youqi hezuo xianzhuang qianjing he yingxiang," *Guoji wenti yanjiu*, 6 (2000), pp. 31–6.

111 Ding Fenghua, "Luelun Eluosi Yazhou waijiao," *Ouya guancha*, 3 (2000), pp. 7–10.

112 Wang Bingyin and Zhou Yanli, "Shiheng de Eluosi Yatai zhengce," *Guoji zhengzhi*, October 2000, pp. 79–82.

113 Komagata Testsuya, "'Kokubo sangyo to gunji gijutsu iten," *Chugoku soran 2000* (Tokyo: Kasankai, 2000), p. 124.

India with no aspirations for regionalism, against a beckoning China with a close embrace.

As Moscow was recalibrating its Asian relations with less emphasis on Beijing, the Chinese perceived increasing interest in Japan as a balance and in North Korea, not in coordination with China, but to give Russia a voice of its own. For some, the loss of momentum in relations with Russia was a recent shock second only to that a year earlier from the deterioration of Sino-U.S. ties. In this context, certain experts decided that Japan must be elevated above Russia as China's main partner. Economic considerations dictate this assessment, as does China's preoccupation with Taiwan that requires more attention to keeping the mood in Japan under control than catering to Russian rhetorical backing.

Japanese-Russian relations were now seen less as a threat to the balance of great-power relations, and more as a means to boost economic regionalism. Recognizing that some in the two countries see bilateral normalization as a response to the "China threat," Chinese analysts offer assurances that no short-term improvement could proceed far. For domestic reasons on each side, the degree of rapprochement will be limited with the State Duma refusing to return all four islands and the Japanese people remaining distrustful. And the presence of four great powers and six bilateral relations produces a situation of mutual restraint. Adding an improved Japanese-Russian pairing to the mix will mainly have the effect of giving each of the two more leverage on the United States.[114]

The Chinese underscored the fundamental reasoning behind bilateral relations in estimates of comprehensive national power. Some regarded Russia as still in the front ranks of the world (indeed, ahead of China) and its latent power as considerable too,[115] and they took for granted the need to borrow Russian power in confronting U.S. hegemonism. Others already put Russian national power below that of China and assumed that the two will proceed with separate efforts to increase their power, including renewed Russian concern for restoring economic power, while relying on each other in global strategic competition. While Chinese calls for common struggle against the West appealed to those driven by a geopolitical agenda, they never "succeeded in persuading the most active and dynamic part of the Russian population that the PRC is developing a market economy free of an ideological agenda, and that cooperation with it can bring real profit."[116]

[114] Lin Xiaoguang, "Rie guanxi: 90 niandai yilai de fazhan yu bianhua," *Dongbeiya yanjiu*, 4 (2000), pp. 34–6.

[115] Ding Fenghua, "Luelun Eluosi Yazhou waijiao," *Ouya guancha*, 3 (2000), p. 10.

[116] Alexander Lukin, "Perceptions of China Threat in Russia and Russian-Chinese Relations" (unpublished paper for conference "China Threat Perceptions from Different Continents," Hong Kong, January, 2001, p. 16).

In 1999 incidents in Moscow damaged bilateral relations. Tax police targeted Chinese businessmen and conducted massive raids on their quarters; and, after a period of racist street beatings of Asians, a number of Chinese and at least one diplomat were attacked. Along with foreigners leaving due to the Russian financial crisis, many Chinese departed. Talk of a special friendship between China and Russia seemed empty.

On the front line of regionalism, Heilongjiang kept looking for a new approach to its neighbors in Russia. A new governor in 2000 was the latest to try to boost trade and look for a way to entice foreign investment linked to cross-border ties. On the bright side, he could point to the increased success of the border town of Suifenhe, now boasting 2,000 visitors a day and an annual trade volume of $1 billion. As Russian incomes rose in 2000, more visitors lugged away two big suitcases back to Primorskii krai, paying only modest taxes per bag and feeling positive toward Chinese products carefully inspected for quality. Yet, Heilongjiang was losing its role as middleman in trade between Southeast China and Russia. While Shenzhen held a conference with Russians, Guangdong and Fujian also expanded their direct dealings. New troubles for the air corridor charter flights from Tianjin and Beijing related to lawlessness in Moscow, not to any advantages in Northeast China. Also threatening to regionalism is the tendency to bypass both the Russian Far East and Northeast China for direct links between Southeast China and European Russia. Early in 2001 the ouster of Nazdratenko in Primorskii krai raised hopes in Heilongjiang. Yet, problems went beyond individual leaders; for example, however much it made economic sense, nobody broached the idea that Vladivostok could save 1700 km. by a rail route through the province to Eastern Siberia rather than traversing the entire Trans-Siberian.

Chinese analyses grew increasingly negative on the Russian "economic and social sickness." As Russia's economy began to recover from the second half of 1999, analysts foresaw a slow process and a high degree of dependency on foreign investment. No longer praising the successor of the Soviet Union as a science and technology great power, they recognized an outdated base that would be slow to advance. Economic growth would be unlikely to average as much as 5 percent a year over the next decade.[117]

In Putin's first year China and Russia made a fresh start on economic relations. Having learned that when governments act to boost trade the results are bad, China made it clear that this must be through companies making market decisions. In contrast to the chaotic conditions of 1992–3, the Chinese insisted that they now had tight controls over the quality of people and goods. They pointed to two big Chinese markets in Moscow, which opened in 1998 and 2000, where quality was maintained, even if

[117] Lu Nanquan, "Dui Eluosi jingji fazhan qianjing de fenxi," *Dongbeiya yanjiu*, 4 (2000), pp. 3–8.

little could be done with Russian shuttle traders who come to China to buy the cheapest items available and leave wearing multiple layers of clothes. Officials also echoed the complaints of other foreign governments that excess taxes, rents, and payoffs leave little incentive to invest. They are aware that something is abnormal when even restaurants are not dispersed and cheap, as elsewhere in the world, but concentrated in Moscow and too costly for ordinary Russians.

One Chinese expert asserted that Sino-Russian relations under Yeltsin neglected economic ties in favor of political ones, but Putin would take a realistic approach to building up Russia as a great power by stressing the economy and Sino-Russian political relations would weaken. Simultaneously, China's shift to WTO compatibility would turn China away from Russia's economy. Special countermeasures ought to be taken, he added: 1) to recognize the serious bottlenecks, especially on the Russian side, including banking services, the arbitration mechanism, and the lack of export credits and insurance; 2) to devise a long-term strategy, including a new high-tech cooperation center in Harbin and direct cross-border partnerships of oblast and provinces; and 3) to link the development of West China and Western Siberia. Ultimately, China needs natural resource security, as it will by 2010 rely on foreign supplies for twenty-four of forty-five items and by 2020 for thirty-nine of them.[118] Both countries will turn to each other for market diversification and to sell goods of lesser quality and technical standards without a large market in the West. This is a call for Chinese patience until Russia is ready. In contrast to claims in 1996–8 that China and Russia have a special bond that makes it easier for them to develop trade relations, the new position is that they have special barriers that make it harder. China must therefore approach Russia as the West does with investments and other incentives, while conveying a credible message that Russia can boost production of resources on a large scale as China meets rising import requirements by directing its companies to Russia. The development of the two should become intertwined through pipelines and export of electric power generated by hydroelectricity.

On April 29, 2000 a conference at the Chinese Academy of Social Sciences was devoted to Vladimir Putin. The result was an outpouring of realism in sharp contrast to much that had been written previously. Unlike prior claims that Yeltsin's foreign policy and Sino-Russian relations reflect stable national interests, talk centered on the start of a new age, in which at last Russia was groping for its own model and adjusting its foreign policy in line with the gravity of its economic needs. This means more dependence on foreign capital and technology, including repayment of debts. Given its national interests, Russia has no way to balance the United States, and it remains

[118] Lu Nanquan, "Miandui 21 shiji Zhonge jingmao hezuo wenti de sikao," *Xiboliya yanjiu*, 5 (2000), pp. 1–9.

deeply influenced by its past. As part of Western culture, it has accepted Europe, and will not necessarily exclude entrance into NATO, discussants warned. Taking exception to earlier Chinese views, the summary noted that the United States does not want a Russia that is too weak. A summary noted that Putin could be expected to maintain Sino-Russian relations, but he had little scope to act.[119]

Chinese disappointment in Russia was registered in new assessments of Russia's real interests. In place of earlier analyses applauding the wisdom of Russia's decision in the second half of 1992 to balance East and West, observers concluded that Russia had abandoned this approach and was leaning to the West. Given that its political, economic, and cultural center is in Europe, Russia was merely recognizing its real national interests. The Chinese stopped categorizing Asia-Pacific great-power relations as a quadrangle, instead placing Russia as a European great power that used China to fill a vacuum in Eastern diplomacy, while yearning for closer ties to the West. In contrast to earlier claims that Russians had recognized the folly of expecting to be accepted in the West, the new assessments insisted that they felt gratified to have entered the G-8 and continue to aspire to return to Europe, where the only capital and technology to save their economy are available. In this thinking, Sino-Russian relations are an offshoot of the entire system of great-power relations rather than having a strong momentum of their own. Suggesting that contradictions between Russia and Western powers are controllable, the Chinese refer to pro-Western attitudes as restraining Sino-Russian relations. Consistent with this argument is the reassessment of the Sino-U.S.-Russian triangle as unbalanced because both China and Russia are dependent on the United States but have little leverage on U.S. policy. Reflecting new distrust, the possibility was raised that Russia might cut a deal allowing NATO to expand to the China border and that the United States is managing Japan's effort to lure Russia.[120]

After years of trying to solve economic problems quietly, the Chinese in 2000 stated bluntly that what had occurred was "mutual vilification" (*dihui*) of each other's firms. The city of Harbin that had long claimed to be the indisputable center of bilateral economic ties acknowledged that it was getting nowhere. Exports to Russia remained miniscule – less than one-tenth of its imports. Russian merchants were bypassing it,[121] traveling directly to cities in Southeast China from which better quality goods originated or buying from traders in border cities such as Suifenhe. Yet, Harbin still dreamed of

[119] Wen Dong, "'Shijie zhijiao de Eluosi' xuexu yanjiu taohui jiyao," *Guoji zhengzhi*, 10 (2000), pp. 167–8.

[120] Wang Shuchu and Wang Shixin, "Zhonge guanxi qianjing zhanwang," *Dongbeiya yanjiu*, 4 (2000), pp. 23–7.

[121] Xia Huanxin, "Eluosi jingji fazhan zoushi ji Haerbin shi tonge jingmao hezuo de duice jianyi," *Xiboliya yanjiu*, 5 (2000), pp. 24–7.

becoming the processing center for Russian raw materials such as lumber and marine products.

Despite much fanfare for the Shanghai Cooperative Organization, traffic through Central Asia was acquiring an even more lawless reputation than across the Russian Far East. Commerce and investment fell far short of expectations. Heroin trade from Afghanistan through Tajikistan and Kirgistan passed close to the Chinese border before veering west and on to Russia. Islamic groups threatening to secularism were among the traders. No wonder regionalism turned inward in Asia had lost its appeal even before the U.S. war against the Taliban turned Central Asia's foreign relations topsy-turvy. The Shanghai Cooperative Organization bringing China and Russia together with Central Asia except Turkmenistan facilitated security talks, but it had no value for regionalism.

South Korea, the Great Powers, and Regionalism

In 2000 as ties between North Korea and both China and Russia improved, South Korea saw an opportunity for weaving a web of regionalism to ensnare the North. After all Pyongyang had no reason to expect that Moscow, which had abandoned it earlier, or Beijing, whose hegemonistic tendencies it feared, would meet its needs. Because Pyongyang favored a deal with Washington followed by one with Tokyo, bringing an infusion of assistance and investment for economic recovery, and feared direct economic dependence on South Korea, only a regional approach would work. Kim Dae-jung seized this chance to raise hopes, symbolized by the Nobel Peace Prize that he was granted late that year.

Kim Dae-jung's regionalism in the year 2000 elicited a chain reaction. The June North-South summit helped to spur Russia, the United States, Japan, and China to redouble their efforts to improve ties with the North. It may also be linked to Japan's decision in July to soften its approach to Russia in order to speed the normalization of relations. Within months there was a new impetus toward regionalism centered on railroad construction and energy pipelines through the North. At the very time the United States was on the sidelines except for bilateral talks with the North, China was newly excited over multilateralism in Asia, Japan was more prepared than at any prior time since 1992 to press for regionalism, and even the North was poking its head from its shell. Seoul was leading the way.

Kim Dae-jung was in a hurry to achieve an irreversible process of reunification along with regionalism, goals that became inextricably linked. Precariously balanced between four great powers and a "rogue state," the South had a mission to limit sources of tension while developing a vision for cooperation. The ASEAN +3 breakfast meeting of the +3 in 1999 discussed forming an NEA cooperative body,[122] and in November 2000 it made further progress, including support for joint efforts in information technology as a promising step toward a single community. At that time Kim led in the creation of an "East Asian vision group." While academic drafters may have been too visionary, their 2001 statement may eventually be useful for a later round of regionalism. Meanwhile, ASEAN felt threatened by the group of three stealing the spotlight. When the Korean prime minister proposed the wording "towards the East Asian Community" the use of *an* instead of *the* and a lowercase *c* for *community* were among the steps to calm concerns. Kim was trying in vain to complete his mission before his presidential term ended, but he was not alone. South Koreans are striving not only for the unity of their country, but also for a more independent foreign policy. After all, if the North is known for its fierce struggle, even at great sacrifice, for the highest degree of independence possible, why should it be strange that the South shares some of the same aspirations? Koreans foresee competition between China and Japan, leaving them as the balancer.

Conscious of an incomplete national goal and a history of frustrated nationalism, Koreans have reason to be ambivalent about regionalism and globalization. Elderly Koreans harbor strong resentment against the Japanese that is shared to a degree by all generations. Students most resent the United States, and that too resonates broadly. Indeed, while students are also the most avid consumers of U.S. culture and embrace the Internet, which brings them into the era of globalization, less vocal but more deeply rooted doubts about the United States are found in the least modern sectors. Resentful of further dependence in Korean history, many are searching for a way out. As residents of a small country among great powers, Koreans look to regional and global balances of power for leverage. They see the best hope for stability and leverage as coming from a developed system of regional cooperation among the powers. Concerned about Japanese militarism or vertical dominance, few are critical of China's rise while many are doubtful about U.S. power.

Putin's visit to Pyongyang in February 2000 started the rapid pace of change in 2000. It was a breakthrough in Russian Asian policy, stimulating North Korea to a more active diplomacy too. In the following months not only did the North-South summit occur, but also both Koreas accelerated their contacts with China, China made new overtures to Japan, and Japan changed course with a bolder initiative to Russia. Each side had a message for the United States too: Russia saying "respect us, we are a player"; China saying "in this region, you are not the only indispensable nation"; and Japan saying "don't take us for granted; we can proceed with an

[122] *South-North Reconciliation and Active Diplomacy for Peace* (Seoul: The Korean Information Service Policy Series, October 2000), p. 10.

independent foreign policy." Moscow's opening to Pyongyang was a critical step in unleashing this burst of diplomat strutting.

After a few years of little success in relations with the North, Moscow made real progress in 1999–2000. No doubt, its more strident anti-Americanism at the time of the war over Kosovo made it clear to the North that it would be a reliable force to check U.S. pressure on the North. In addition Russia renewed oil supplies in 1999. When Putin became the first foreign leader to visit Kim Jong-il, the symbolism signified a qualitative change in security relations. To Chinese analysts Moscow's reasoning made sense. After all, it had been squeezed out of the region with the KEDO agreement to build a nuclear reactor and the four-party talks on Korea and now could gain a wedge against the United States and a means for more great-power balance.[123]

Commentators in Moscow agreed that Russia's national interests are strongly represented in Korea. An outcome on the peninsula leading either to a strengthening of the U.S. position or a powerful united Korea with territorial claims against the Russian Far East would be dangerous. Some openly suggested that Russian interests are best served by the status quo, warning that only the United States would see its geopolitical agenda advanced by unification. Thus, the visit of Russia's foreign minister to Pyongyang in February 2000 along with claims of warmer relations with the North drew strong praise. Earlier it was assumed that Kim Dae-jung's sunshine policy would fail and Moscow had no reason to support it strongly. After all, the South had less to offer since its financial crisis and was too dependent on the United States to serve Russia's geopolitical needs. Even after Kim Dae-jung had visited Moscow in May 1999 and worked to boost relations, many in Russia wondered if it would do any good.[124] They were more excited by the improvement in ties with the North and the prospect of security talks including Russia.

Seoul found renewed military ties between Moscow and Pyongyang disturbing, including secret trips and deliveries. Russia justified this by saying that it was helping to restore the military balance with defensive weapons and also creating a mood that would lead to the repayment of the North's debts to it, but the supply of spare parts and new weapons seemed more aimed at increasing Russian influence, and Seoul's early efforts quietly to get Moscow to desist proved of no avail. Having learned about how actively Moscow had supported the aggression of the North in 1950 and resenting that no apology had been forthcoming for that or for shooting down KAL 007 in 1983, some worried that Moscow was reverting to geopolitical

[123] Zhang Wanli, "Eluosi jiachang yi Chaoxian guanxi de yitu yu yingxiang fenxi," *Dongbeiya yanjiu*, 4 (2000), pp. 40–2.

[124] Georgi Bulichev, "Russia's Korea Policy: Towards a Conceptual Framework," *Far Eastern Affairs*, 2 (2000), pp. 3–12.

priorities. Yet, leaders downplayed any strategic objectives in using North Korea in favor of the notion that Russia wants progress in inter-Korean relations because "peace on the peninsula would make it possible for Moscow to concentrate on rebuilding its economy."[125] The official line was that construction of the Iron Silk Road would bring immense economic benefits to all involved. After Putin and Kim Dae-jung met it was assumed that they could easily reach agreement because they had developed close relations based on trust. Idealism at the top was echoed in the press.

At the end of a year of redefining center-local relations Russia had still not decided to accept FEZs. The primary test case remained Nakhodka. After agreeing in May 2000 to a new version of an industrial park to be developed jointly with South Korea, Moscow changed its approach again. Instead of tax-free imports of goods and labor and exports from the zone, the Tax Ministry agreed only that the goods produced in the zone should receive tax and customs exemptions. Fearing that the original plan would open Russia's borders unduly, spilling beyond the zone in unpredictable ways, Moscow chose to reopen negotiations after the South Korean parliament had already approved the deal. Again protection of domestic interests trumped openness to investment. Even after the scale of the Nakhodka zone had slipped from 330 to 20 hectares and the focus on foreign ties had narrowed to South Korea, there was no mandate to proceed.[126]

North Korea sent workers to the Russian Far East to fell lumber, can fish, and erect buildings. This was welcomed by the local leadership despite the human-rights violations caused by guards accompanying the workers. It brought cheap labor, and it kept alive a different notion of regionalism with nationalist appeal. By 2001 teams of North Korean workers roamed Vladivostok, offering their construction services.[127]

At last on April 30, 2000 the Zarubino shipping route was opened, fulfilling a dream of the decade by linking Northeast China through the Russian Far East to the sea at a distance of just 648 kilometers to Pusan in South Korea. Now Korean Chinese in Yanbian could be just a day's travel by boat from Korean markets and Korean tourists could visit legendary Changbaek mountain without having to brave the complicated route through Shenyang. But the route proved to be one more dud on the path to regionalism. Koreans had lost their enthusiasm for investment in the Yanbian area, tourism had fallen to Kumgang mountain in North Korea and economic conditions did not favor it to a more distant spot, and travel through Russia conjured up inconvenience rather than the mystique of a European enclave in Asia.

[125] *The Korea Herald*, September 10, 2000, p. 1.

[126] "Fate of Nakhodka Park Still Uncertain," *EWI Russian Regional Investor*, 3(1), January 10, 2001.

[127] *Vladivostok*, June 11, 2002, p. 7.

The periphery in South Korea was poorly prepared for decentralization and internationalization. Only on the number of sister cities or regions did the Southwest rank high with 13.5 percent of the total in Korea. Its FDI firms, foreign trade firms, and international conferences were negligible, on most measures less than 1 percent of the total and on firms investing in China just 3.5 percent. In contrast, Seoul and nearby Inchon plus Kyonggi reached 79 percent, while the Southeast region added another 14 percent of firms investing in China.[128] There was no prospect for cross-border decentralization apart from modest linkages favoring the Southeast and Japan.

With the Hyundai group in the lead, Seoul used quasistate enterprises or guaranteed state funds to take economic risks for political gain. In Primorskii krai and Yanbian autonomous region bordering North Korea on two sides and then directly in the North, Seoul encouraged eye-catching investments to break down political barriers. This gave a personal touch to inter-Korean economic cooperation, which rested on approval by Kim Jong-il and risky, deficit-ridden projects started first by Chung Ju-yung, patriarch of Hyundai, and then by his son Chung Mong-hun, the head of Hyundai Asan. In the midst of widely reported scandals and interrogations by prosecutors in Seoul, the son committed suicide on August 4, 2003.[129] The old ways of mixing politics and business in intra-Korean relations could no longer be concealed.

In 2000 Seoul and Beijing boosted their relations to a full-scale cooperative partnership, claiming that they now could work closely together in every field, including military relations. The South foresaw a massive increase of investment in China and trade, much of it in high-technology and IT sectors such as mobile phones, but some in automobile production and other traditional manufacturing. While the big firms in the South were still far from overcoming the Asian financial crisis and were not reaping much profit from past investments in China, South Koreans wishfully assumed that a shift to smaller and IT firms using some newly expanding foreign currency reserves could take advantage of China's entry into WTO and a new level of goodwill. Whereas before personal deals between chaebol chairmen and Chinese government leaders had led to some misguided investments such as Daewoo's automobile factory in Guilin, small firms had been more careful and could be expected to lead the way in the new era. The large trade surplus maintained with China contrasted to the huge deficit with Japan. In the midst of the dramatic acceleration of relations with North Korea and active pursuit of improved ties with China, Seoul abruptly declared increased tariffs for Chinese garlic. Reducing its long-standing agricultural protectionism, Seoul had allowed more imports before awakening to a backlash among farmers upset at the flood of garlic from China. Beijing's response to a modest

[128] Park Sam Ock, "Globalization in Korea: Dream and Reality," *GeoJournal*, 45(1), 1998, p. 125.

[129] *The New York Times*, August 7, 2003, pp. W1, W7.

increase in tariffs from 30 to 35 percent was fast and far-reaching. It halted imports of mobile telephones and polyethylene, the former accounting for $470 million in 1999 and the latter $41 million (but this was expected to rise rapidly). If a similar trade war had begun with Japan, the South Korean media would have been incensed at such a disproportionate response from a powerful neighbor, but the media no less than the government retreated under the impact of the "China complex." Indeed, unlike the earlier heated coverage of Japanese fishing boats operating in disputed waters, Koreans pay scant attention to Chinese boats illegally fishing in Korean areas of the Yellow Sea. The Japanese noticed this special consciousness toward China,[130] yet also were aware that a bad aftertaste was left by China appearing to be a bully.

The significance of South Korea for China rose in 2000 because of both the new diplomacy on the Korean peninsula and China's new interest in cooperation with Japan and regionalism. While reassuring the North of its opposition to any scenario that would force its reform and might cause a collapse, China strengthened ties to the South.

China must be careful not to overplay its hand. Ambassador Wu Dawei annoyed some South Koreans when he discussed forced repatriation of North Koreans and used the term *escapees*, not *refugees*. When it appeared that the Dalai Lama might be invited to South Korea and when airlines aimed to reestablish direct flights to Taipei, Wu relayed China's message that the South should do nothing that might be construed as abetting separatism. Such moments of insensitivity showed the arrogance of a heavyweight, but the Chinese usually spoke cautiously.

China is in danger of taking South Korea for granted. Whereas the South sought Chinese help in bringing the North to the negotiating table and getting it to compromise, the Chinese insisted that the North will not accept pressure until the nuclear crisis in 2003 changed all calculations.

Korea was being pulled closer to China through the 1990s, but the most dramatic changes occurred in 2000. One analysis sums up developments as "consummating a 'full-scale cooperative partnership.'"[131] Not only did Kim Dae-jung turn to China for political reasons as part of his "sunshine diplomacy," Korean business was boosting trade and investment rapidly and tourism was growing apace. Bilateral trade soared, travelers to China approached 1 million or nearly the total going to Japan, and companies set their sights on markets for semiconductors and communications opening wide with China's entry into the WTO. Seoul's pull toward China became a driving force for regionalism.

130 Chi Togyoku, "Hanto de kyugeki ni takamaru Chugoku no eikyo ryoku," *Sekai shuho*, August 1, 2000, pp. 32–5.

131 Scott Snyder, "Consummating a 'Full-Scale Cooperative Partnership,'" *Pacific Forum CSIS: Comparative Connections*, 2(4), January 2001.

In 1999 public opinion in South Korea changed rapidly. Over the course of twelve months those seeing U.S. forces in Korea as very important for Korea's security fell from 44 to 25 percent (the number seeing this as fairly important rose almost correspondingly). From April 1998 to May 2000 South Koreans grew more favorable toward China, picking it by 55 percent rather than 45 percent to be the South's closest economic partner in 5–10 years, expecting it to be the most influential nation in East Asia in the next 5–10 years by 59 percent compared to 46 percent in June 1999, and leaning slightly more to China than the United States in evaluating relations as good or poor (79:19 versus 77:21).[132] This mood swing set the tone for high hopes with North Korea in 2000 and disappointment with the United States in 2001–2 as Seoul's diplomacy reached a dead end.

Following Kim Dae-jung's declaration on Japanese-Korean relations, both governments strongly backed joint projects. With an eye to the World Cup to be jointly held in 2002, they increased art, music, sports, and other cooperation. In addition to the central governments, local ties developed, especially in Kyushu and the Japan Sea coastal areas facing Korea. While current political concerns were largely left aside, a wide range of interests included the environment and the status of women. Quickly airplanes filled with travelers, especially Japanese shoppers. Young people found that they have leisure, fashion, and other trendy interests in common. Soon more Japanese were for the first time saying that they like Koreans than dislike them. While views of China remained quite negative, the Japanese looked to South Korea as a partner in regionalism. Yet, nervousness related to the Korean peninsula remained. While high electricity rates at home kept Internet use down, South Korea in 2000 was rushing ahead into the information age. Internet cafes numbered more than 12,000; housewives and the elderly in Seoul were taking lessons; and children were enthusiastically embracing the new technology. The Japanese warned that domestic protection aimed at avoiding the anger from a sharp rise in unemployment was causing their country to fall behind in Asia.[133] More seriously, fears rose that Japan alone was out of the loop on Korea; it was slow to learn of the Korean summit set for June. As China, South Korea, and the United States all began to send large shipments of grain to the North, Japan's "grain card" had lost its value.[134]

As many in Japan basked in relief that history had been overcome in relations with South Korea, some on the right warned that the mass media of the South had resumed a campaign of criticism over textbook revisions in Japan.

132 "Little Change in South Korean Public's Positive Views of the U.S.," "South Korean Public's Positive Views of China," Office of Research, Department of State, Washington, DC, February 11, 2000; June 1, 2000.

133 "Nihon o oinuita Kankoku no IT kakumei," *Sekai shuho*, November 14, 2000, pp. 38–9.

134 Maeda Yasushiro, "Nanboku shuno kaidan to kongo no Toajia josei," *Shinpo to kaikaku*, August 2000, p. 56.

It was not only China that was pressuring Japan on historical education, the Korean press was also greatly exercised about the matter supposedly with encouragement from Kim Dae-jung.[135] The right wing opposed paying the price of abandoning plans to revise textbooks to lessen war guilt. For them, nationalist goals easily took precedence over regionalism.

Advocates of textbook revisions defined the mass media criticisms in South Korea as well as China and North Korea as an anti-Japanese campaign. They could not blame the South's response on communists nor could they link it to political differences because the conservative *Chosun ilbo,* which fervently opposes the overtures to North Korea, and the rival newspaper *Hangyore,* which is most supportive, take the same stance. In contrast, the Korean media have been quick to note the sharp differences inside Japan, especially between the stridently conservative *Sankei shimbun* and the still progressive *Asahi shimbun,* called the "conscience of Japan." Japan's advocates insist that what is at stake is overcoming the "crisis mentality in Japanese society," struggling for the spirit of Japan, its historical consciousness and national will for the future. They think that only by creating a rock of agreement over history can the Japanese move beyond the postwar era.[136]

In anger over the Japanese junior high textbook revisions, Koreans contemplated drastic measures. Over a quarter of respondents called for severing relations. Young political leaders were reported to be seeking a new government stance against Japan's entry as a permanent member of the Security Council. Others insisted on a boycott of Japanese goods or suspension of the opening to Japanese culture. There was a mood of solidarity with the Chinese, who were similarly outraged. The honeymoon after Kim Dae-jung's visit of Ocober 1998 had ended,[137] but prospects for improved ties with North Korea had deteriorated and it was no time to take a firm stance toward Japan. Pursuing his sunshine policy, Kim Dae-jung did as little as possible to pander to such nationalism.

The debate in Japan had intensified over how to treat foreigners with permanent status, the vast majority of whom descended from Korean Japanese left behind in 1945. On the one side are those on the right, including Tokyo Governor Ishihara known for his derogatory language, who oppose relaxation of discriminatory standards as dangerous weakening of the state. On the other are those who point to the coming decline of Japan's population and the need to welcome foreigners and forge a multinational state.[138] Even as the image of South Korea improved following Kim Dae-jung's 1998 visit,

[135] Takahashi Shiro, "Matashitemo 'gochushinya' ga masukomi kosaku," *Shokun*, December 2000, pp. 48–59.

[136] *Sankei shimbun*, March 14, 2001, p. 4.

[137] *Yomiuri shimbun*, April 10, 2001, p. 3.

[138] *Asahi shimbun*, November 25, 2000, p. 15.

Japan's internal impasse continued over the need for social heterogeneity as part of a regional development strategy.

With South Korea hopeful about ties to the North, Japan was left to ponder the possibility that it would be left behind. There was speculation that Clinton would wind up his presidency with a trip to Pyongyang, Kim Jong-il was planning to go to Russia and Jiang Zemin to North Korea, and capping the process would be Kim Jong-il's dramatic visit to Seoul, supposedly by mid-year. The memory of 1972 lingers, when the "Nixon shock" in rebuilding ties to China left Japan scrambling to catch up. Meanwhile, four-party talks, involving the United States and China, would presumably make headway on a peace regime for the Korean peninsula while Japan would remain on the sidelines, a situation reminiscent of 1988–92 when Japan was slow to engage Moscow only to be pressed by its partners. Did this mean Japan should relax its principles, ignoring its abducted citizens and the North's missiles? Whatever the concerns, the Japanese felt confident that they had a strong hand. No one else was expected to fund the rebuilding of the North Korean economy.[139]

Japan's negotiations with North Korea were the most doubtful move in the search for regionalism. If successful, they could give a powerful jolt to the process. Seeing the progress in North-South talks and in the North's efforts to end global isolation, Japanese leaders sent 500,000 tons of rice and countenanced talk of $9 or $10 billion in assistance, equivalent in current currency value to that offered to South Korea in 1965.[140] But each side set conditions that threatened to doom this bilateral relationship to lag behind others. Japan put priority on its citizens thought to have been kidnapped as well as medium-range missiles that could target its cities. The North sought true repentance for the colonial era. Only in September 2002 was a compromise reached, leading to a summit in Pyongyang, but within weeks the nuclear crisis scuttled any chance of follow-up.[141]

The right-wing pictures North Korea as a new threat to the foundation of their worldview. Perhaps more serious than the missile threat or the economic burden, they fear the historical challenge from insistence that Japan declare invalid the 1910 treaty that allowed it to annex Korea. This would mean not just an apology, but a full repudiation, supported by the South, of the occupation of Korea as illegal and of Japan's Asian policy as imperialistic.[142] Many were alarmed by events in 2000 on the Korean peninsula

139 Okonogi Kisao, "Kurinton hocho de kyushinten suru hokuto Ajia no detanto," *Sekai shuho*, November 14, 2000, pp. 6–9.

140 Victor D. Cha, "Ending 2000 with a Whimper Not a Bang," *Pacific Forum CSIS: Comparative Connections*, 2(4), January 2001.

141 Gilbert Rozman, "Japan's North Korean Initiative and U.S.-Japanese Relations," *Orbis*, 47(3), Summer 2003, pp. 527–39.

142 *Sankei shimbun*, November 29, 2000, p. 2.

as well as more upbeat talks with China and Russia. Whereas a year earlier they had thought that these fronts were coalescing to create a sense of alarm in the Japanese public, now they had to face the diplomacy of temptation. In March 2000 in Berlin Kim Dae-jung called for large-scale aid to North Korea, preferring to lure it from its seclusion rather than to intensify pressure against it. As symbols of reconciliation increased amid calls for Japan to apologize and offer aid, the right warned that this was a challenge to the United States–led Asian order and the result would be to strengthen a Stalinist system.[143] Yet, they wrapped their goals in the mantle of noninterference in Japan's internal affairs, accusing diplomats of denying that Chinese and Korean criticisms are "textbook bashing" and of forgetting the national interest. One journal said that Kono Yohei is not Japan's man, but "the foreign minister of foreign countries." It called on Japan to become an "independent country."[144] When Pyongyang appeared in 2002 to be willing to trade away its historical demands for Japanese economic assistance, some on the right breathed a sigh of relief, while others feared a slippery slope of compromise that would interrupt the buildup of Japanese nationalism. They were relieved that this initiative quickly failed.

Responding to the changing diplomatic environment as North Korea opened and China looked for support in countering U.S. plans for TMD and NMD, many Japanese insisted that only close ties with the United States and South Korea would give Japan leverage. After all, they argued, Beijing's real goal is to split the United States and Japan, and Tokyo can take its time holding its "economic card" until North Korea meets its principles. Such warnings drew attention to the danger of following Kim Dae-jung by drawing down Japan's capital hastily without long-term strategic thinking.[145] Newfound uncertainty added to reliance on the United States and led to calls for South Korea to slow down for more coordination. Worries abounded that the Japanese media as well as diplomats would be too soft on the North or that Japan's specific human-rights concerns linked to abducted citizens would be seen as strictly a bilateral matter by the United States, preoccupied by security in its pursuit of the North. The Japanese were hesitant about the march to regionalism linked to the sunshine policy, and they waited for the next U.S. administration to show its hand.

Critics of Kim Dae-jung charged that his sunshine policy shores up a regime in Pyongyang that is still bent on conquering the South, misjudges the true intent of China and Russia in propping up the North instead of

143 Arai Hirokazu, "Toajia ni okeru Nichibeichuro kankei," *Shin kokusaku*, October 15, 2000, pp. 8–10.

144 Hirasawa Katsuei, "Kore ga naisei kansha de nakute naninanda!" *Shokun*, May 2001, pp. 107–8.

145 Ina Hisyoshi, "Taichugoku Kitachosen gaiko wa kakuarubeshi," *Foresight*, October 2000, pp. 58–61.

supporting unification on terms that could be acceptable to the South, weakens the resolve of the population of the South, and splits the South from its supporters in the United States and Japan. This is not a strategy for regionalism. Supporters saw him as a visionary, leading a skeptical Pyongyang and also the four great powers as well as many doubtful South Koreans along the first steps in a complex transition. When the Bush administration rejected Kim's approach, however, support grew.

Overview of Regionalism

The year 1999 was a slow year and 2000 was a fast year. The number of summits fell in 1999. No country was vigorously pursuing another until the end of the year. It was not only that all eyes were on Yugoslavia and the impact of the war there on U.S. global leadership. Also the deterioration in Japanese-Russian and Sino-Japanese relations at the end of 1998 left an aftertaste that took time to overcome. In 2000, however, there was a sharp rise in intraregional trade centered on China as well as a spike in intraregional diplomacy. As Sino-Japanese trade climbed by more than a quarter to $83 billion, exports and imports rose in tandem. Trade between China and South Korea rose even faster, climbing beyond $34 billion and raising Korean's trade surplus to $11 billion.[146] Such growth spurred talk of the objective necessity of institutionalizing ties through regionalism. Meanwhile, the pursuit of North Korea under Kim Dae-jung aroused even broader interest in cooperation.

Singapore in the year 2000 played an important role in promoting regionalism. After witnessing the collapse of ASEAN dreams with the Asian financial crisis and losing Beijing's support for a huge project to modernize an area of Jiangsu province through its investments and tutelage, a wounded Singapore turned to NEA for another approach to regionalism. Its leaders urged Japan to join an FTA. Because Singapore has few agricultural exports or even much manufacturing to threaten Japan's vested interests, this proposal was easy to accept. With China embracing regionalism and South Korea welcoming the idea, the Singapore initiative started a chain reaction. A late November 2000 meeting in Singapore of the leaders of China, Japan, and South Korea at the time of ASEAN +3 held out hope of a takeoff in regionalism. Along with a broad agreement in favor of cooperation, the three agreed to make 2002 the year of people's exchanges and to hold annual trilateral summits. Giving the appearance of broad East Asian regionalism inclusive of SEA, the three NEA core states nudged closer together on a joint vision. Academics, including China's Zhang Yunling, intensified their joint efforts.

[146] Chun-tu Hsueh and Lu Nanquan, eds., *Eluosi Xiboliya yu Yuandong: guoji zhengzhi jingji guanxi de fazhan* (Beijing: Shijie zhishi chubanshe, 2002), p. 110.

Both ASEAN and China were losing investment in 1999, but in 2000 China turned things around with a huge boost in investment and also an image as a country about to enter WTO and make a dramatic mark on globalization. Worried that China is becoming a giant and even that Japan's focus would shift away from ASEAN to China, some states of SEA endorsed a new image of East Asian regionalism to draw Japan closer and place relations with China in a more multilateral framework. Instead of an expanding, confident organization allowing three NEA countries to sit alongside, the shell of the old ASEAN was left without a core as Indonesia floundered. The prospect of an East Asian entity became a lone source of hope.[147]

South Korea is the natural leader for reasons of history, geography, and level of economic development in regionalism drawing China and Japan together. In 2000 Kim Dae-jung's eagerness to improve ties with the North created a promising environment for cooperation with these countries. If at times concentration on the North led to increased nationalism, such as a giddy mood in the summer of 2000 when the June summit was followed by the first family reunion in August, the pace of direct unification only briefly seemed hopeful, leaving regionalism as the most realistic means to make it possible.

There were many new reasons for optimism about regionalism by late 2000. Seoul had assumed a leadership role more appealing to the region than previous claims to lead the way. Beijing was supportive and eager to encourage Tokyo. If uncertain about its balance between the United States and Asia, Tokyo was newly encouraging to Moscow and ready to draw closer to Seoul, even if it answered Kim Dae-jung's appeal for triangular economic integration with insistence that China was not ready for an FTA. At last, Pyongyang was beginning to draw NEA states together. Through ASEAN +3, formal institutions and even a regional vision were beginning to materialize. Meanwhile, economic ties among most countries of NEA accelerated. Although the momentum would slow in 2001, the foundation already built could be applicable to a new wave of regionalism. The "sunshine policy" attempted to break the ice jam, although it soon became clear that "security dilemmas" could not so simply be brushed aside.

[147] Fujino Fumiaki, "WTO kameigo no Chugoku o yosokusuru," *Gaiko forum*, 2 (2001), p. 36.

7

2001–2003

Unilateralism and Irrepressible Regionalism

The balance shifted in 2001 to greater globalization, interpreted as priority for security and insistence on active U.S. leadership. The change began when the Bush administration took office and accelerated after the September 11 attack on the United States. This shift altered the environment for regionalism, which was squeezed between new U.S. assertiveness and resurgent nuclear blackmail by North Korea. By 2003 Japan's growing military activism and South Korea's reinforced soft posture toward the North aroused doubts that could have complicated the search for regionalism. If it seemed that divisive forces would overwhelm integrative ones, we can also find reminders that the main actors continued to pursue regionalism and now had additional reasons to work together.

Looking ahead to the year 2002, boosters of regionalism in early 2001 had seen the possibility of a breakthrough. Japan and South Korea would jointly hold the World Cup, drawing close together in this shared experience. Power in China would pass to a younger generation of better-educated leaders at the 16th Party Congress just as China would be implementing its WTO commitment to openness. Moving pragmatically closer to the West, Vladimir Putin would become a more reliable partner in Asia too as well as an energy supplier with a need for Asian markets. A new style of leadership in Japan by Koizumi Junichiro, who took office in April, would at last accelerate economic reforms and raise that country's leadership profile. Only the election of George W. Bush clouded this hopeful scenario, suggesting aggressive pursuit of a wide geopolitical agenda. Given the storm clouds still hovering over the region, Bush's impact could slow the search for regionalism. Left unsettled was whether Japan's relations with the Bush administration would make it a leader or a laggard in regionalism. Even more of a question mark was North Korea's stark choices on reform or blackmail. Also uncertain was whether as the world economy slowed from 2001, it would drive the countries of the region to redouble their economic cooperation or make South Korean and Japanese firms cautious. Even optimists paused to await the lead of the United States as the momentum of 2000 slowed.

The year 2001 initially brought bad news for regionalism even as it transformed globalization. On nearly all fronts regional ties in NEA beat a retreat. Sino-Japanese relations deteriorated despite sharply increasing trade and Japanese investment. Japanese-South Korean ties were strained largely over the issue of history. Hopes for North Korean openness to regional and global ties faded. Japan's relations with Russia also suffered a setback as Koizumi rejected the compromises being explored. There were bright spots, to be sure, such as Russia's decision to draw closer to the United States and China's entry into WTO. Beijing, Tokyo, and Seoul all espoused new, if little noticed, ideas for regionalism; however, in the changed security context NEA countries had to search harder for cooperation. Maybe regionalism had been unsustainable along the path taken in 2000 and the shakeup that followed had some promise to put it on more solid ground, but first the force of U.S. unilateralism and the North Korean resort to nuclear intimidation had to run their course.

In the first months of 2001 a downward spiral occurred in regional relations. Bush's policies alienated North Korea, China, and, for a time, Russia, downgrading relations with each. They also left South Korea's leadership in limbo, unable to sustain the "sunshine policy" as North Korea limited contacts. New Japanese textbooks infuriated China, South Korea, and North Korea. China's nationalist response to a collision of one of its planes with a U.S. surveillance flight exacerbated Sino-U.S. relations. By spring tensions had risen beyond any level seen recently. As the summer progressed no signs of a turnaround were visible. Within the Bush team a struggle arose over the balance of unilateral pressure versus multilateral persuasion to overcome shared misgivings in NEA.

As long as foreign policy revolved around the United States, regionalism had scant hope. By withholding support to South Korea's opening to the North and giving at least the impression of wanting to contain China, Bush showed skepticism of regional initiatives. No leader in NEA had found a way to bypass the United States, but Chinese officials were taking regionalism more seriously and Japanese officials were growing more frustrated about their deepening dependence on the United States. A regional backlash might have ensued if the shock of 9/11 had not refocused global attention on Washington. Having already decided to put security in the forefront, the Bush administration launched a war against terror that eclipsed regional initiatives. Washington was the hub, spokes extended to each capital in NEA, and the flurry of activity along regional crossroads seen in 2000 virtually ground to a halt except when Koizumi went to Pyongyang in September 2002. Koizumi insisted on regular visits to the Yasukuni shrine that led the Chinese to suspend formal summits. The momentum fell so sharply that one author wondered if it was the end of regionalism.[1]

The U.S. strategy, however, had little promise of blocking regionalism for long. It did not offer genuine globalization in which great powers defer to each other, signaling a multilateral framework. Instead, it imposed a unilateral U.S. vision on proud states still striving for a larger voice in international and regional affairs. Frustration intensified at the narrow range of options under U.S. hegemony, driving each country's search for new leverage. It was only a matter of time before the accelerated globalization would rebound in more active interest in regionalism, but first the United States would have to overplay its hand. Because North Korea responded by creating a security crisis for NEA, others had no choice but to work closely with the United States for as long as was necessary to resolve the crisis. They bandwagoned with Washington, while debating how they could draw NEA closer.

In 2000 Japan had pursued Russia, China beckoned to Japan, and South Korea did its utmost to appeal to China. At a distance, the Clinton administration reacted benignly, favoring engagement despite worries about strained relations with China and Russia and only partial gains in talks with North Korea. At the start of 2001 the Bush administration changed the dynamics of great-power relations and regional ties. It became the pursuer, focusing on upgrading relations with Japan. With Kim Jong-il's trip to China hinting that an economic reform dimension would be added to North Korean-Chinese ties and the Bush team unclear on its approach to the Korean peninsula, Kim Dae-jung pressed for an early meeting in Washington. Now he would have to concentrate on the United States if his plans for improving ties with the North were to be realized. Meanwhile, China and Russia gave the appearance of finding increased common ground. Some Russians at first calculated that Bush's greater priority for geopolitics would be a welcome departure from human-rights and economic themes under Clinton, with the possibility even of returning relations between Moscow and Washington to the cold war themes that had given Moscow much of its clout. In contrast, the Chinese feared a U.S. tilt toward Taiwan, downgrading relations. Moscow and Beijing pressed together against missile defense and for multilateralism.

After September 11 the Bush administration had cause to impose its security agenda on the world. By January 2002 Bush had named North Korea in the "axis of evil." Although East Asia was not a priority compared to South and Southwest Asia, the region strained under the limbo of the U.S. warning without any prospect of imminent follow-up. As the United States moved closer to launching a war to overthrow the government of Iraq, the backlash in NEA finally began a year after terrorists had struck. Regional diplomacy revived with North Korea again at the vortex of activity. Beijing

[1] Nick Bisley, "The End of East Asian Regionalism?" *The Journal of East Asian Affairs*, 17(1) Spring/Summer 2003, pp. 148–72.

was forced to exert its power. Moscow made its most concerted effort to bring the Russian Far East under control, while positioning itself to be the go-between as problems with North Korea arose. Most dramatically, Tokyo reasserted its voice. Although China and South Korea were engaged in leadership transitions, signs of new regional activism were emerging.

In September 2002 while the Bush administration was preoccupied with plans for a war against Iraq, alienating much of the world with its unilateral bent, four events raised the prospects for regionalism in NEA. The month began with Kim Jong-il meeting with Putin in the Russian Far East and then the Russian president extending his visit to discuss center-local relations with the governors in the area. The result not only was renewed focus on North Korea's central role in regionalism, but also the most serious attention in a decade to coordination within Russia related to NEA. At mid-month Koizumi went to Pyongyang to meet Kim Jong-il, arousing hopes for the first time in a decade that a sharp turnabout would occur in bilateral relations, leading to large-scale Japanese economic aid in lieu of war reparations but conditioned on a series of changes in North Korean conduct beginning with an apology for kidnapping Japanese citizens in the past. Later Pyongyang announced the establishment of a special economic zone on the border with the Liaodong peninsula in China, suggesting its most dramatic economic reform following summertime moves to end rationing and raise prices. Finally, at month's end Koizumi traveled to China to mark the thirtieth anniversary of the 1972 establishment of diplomatic relations in the most upbeat meeting of Chinese and Japanese leaders in recent years. It seemed that the sudden spurt in regionalism could be a rebuff to U.S. hegemony before the security crisis stopped regionalism in its tracks.

In October 2002 after confronting North Korean officials with evidence of a new uranium enrichment program, the Bush administration drew the line against cooperation with Pyongyang until it abandoned nuclear weapons. This sent a message to China, Japan, Russia, and South Korea that they would now be judged as participants on a WMD battlefield in the ongoing war. As 2002 drew to a close, Pyongyang responded that the United States had breached the KEDO agreement and proceeded to remove all barriers to its development of nuclear weapons. Although Bush decided to play down the confrontation while he was preoccupied with Iraq, a diplomatic shuffle began. South Korea's newly elected leader Roh Moo-hyun offered to mediate between the two adversaries, infuriating Washington with the neutral middle ground he was taking and his implicit message blaming it for the crisis. Putin and Jiang Zemin showed no inclination to impose economic sanctions on the North, as many publications in their countries not only accused the United States of causing the crisis but implied that the only way out of it is for Washington to guarantee the security of the North while leading in a massive investment effort to rebuild its economy without it having to change its totalitarian system. The Japanese grew nervous at the danger they faced; many criticized U.S. handling of the North and even expected help from Russia and China in persuading the North to desist. Regional multilateral security cooperation was now the first public concern. Worry about Pyongyang's nuclear plans that could unravel the fragile security equilibrium in the region mixed with dismay at U.S. diplomacy that had failed to prevent the crisis and offered no promising solutions for overcoming it. Yet, as the reality of the crisis grew more alarming and Pyongyang relied on brinkmanship rather than public relations, some objectives of the Bush administration were realized. Japan was frightened into tightening its alliance with the United States. China was put on notice that the time had come to choose on which side it stands in the war against WMD and security globalization, and it showed signs of making a nuclear-free Korea its priority. Finally, South Koreans sobered to the message that however much their mood had turned to anti-Americanism they had no option but to join their ally. If the front-line states had believed that they had much in common in seeking a soft landing, they learned that in a showdown environment only accommodation with the United States stands in the path of regional panic.

Even as the nuclear crisis intensified, conditions favorable to regionalism could be discerned. Sino-U.S. relations had moved well away from their nadir in 2001. Japan's nationalism calmed toward South Korea, China, Russia, and the United States, concentrating attention on a genuine threat and raising awareness of global and regional cooperation. Worries about energy security drove China and Japan to make offers to Russia for energy pipelines that could boost regionalism. China appreciated regional ties more as a means to global balance. At his inauguration Roh Moo-hyun made promotion of a NEA community for peace and prosperity the centerpiece of his leadership. Most of all, the frontline states recognized that, however the crisis may be resolved, only cooperation to integrate North Korea would give them the necessary security for their own future. If these factors gave new reason for hope, they still could not erase the negative legacy of more than a decade of false starts and the wrenching U.S.-North Korean confrontation. In August agreement was reached for six-party talks that would bring all of these states to the table to try to reconcile the differences between the United States and North Korea, raising the possibility that further security talks coupled with joint economic plans for the North could become a springboard for regionalism once the crisis was resolved.

Globalization and the United States

The United States continued to view NEA as an area where no regional hegemon should be allowed to emerge or, even more, to deny U.S. access or build a base to challenge at the global level. The Bush administration that took power was concerned that China may pose such a threat and determined to reorganize foreign relations to minimize the risk. The United States took the driver's seat, despite differences between the Department of Defense's inclination to unilateral pressure and the Department of State's nod toward multilateral compromise. If the message was not coherent, it was at least forceful and insistent. Even when the focus after September 11 changed away from the rise of China, insistence on U.S. leadership remained combined with a firmer direction as the Department of Defense gained ground.

Advisors to the Bush campaign judged Clinton's foreign policy to Russia, China, Japan, and North Korea a failure. They saw it as inconsistent and based on the wrong priorities, damaging U.S. interests in NEA. Instead, they came into office with a warning that the United States would not allow fear of Russia, China, or North Korea to deter it from pursuing its goals for globalization and regional security. At the outset, they created the impression that they would treat North Korea as a threat, China as more competitor than partner, Japan and South Korea as allies to be drawn together into a regional shield, and Russia as insignificant. This strategy implied cutting off rising regionalism as a danger to U.S. interests. It switched from the desire in the first half of the 1990s to use Japan as a bridge to China and Russia to a strong determination to buttress Japan as a stronghold resistant to those countries. It moved from the Perry process of supporting the South Korean sunshine policy toward North Korea to negating that policy in favor of pressure. Reckoning that the West and Japan enjoyed a preponderance of power and that they could rally support from allies, policy makers aimed to pursue security with warnings for each potential rival. Some contended that China and Russia stood to lose far more if relations deteriorated. This view of globalization dismissed regionalism in NEA as, if not empty rhetoric, a potential threat. It was premised on the assumption that the United States had become uniquely invulnerable and could secure the future against the likes of North Korea through missile defense. There would be no need to negotiate with rogue states or to defer to great-power partners. The way was cleared for a unilateral, preemptive approach to national security.

South Korea was not trusted as the champion of regionalism. It was deferential to China and so eager to cut a deal with North Korea that it might not maintain the pressure envisioned to keep it under control in the Perry process. With Putin wooing Kim Jong-il, Beijing unwilling to pressure the North, and Japan not wary enough to curb smuggling to the North, many working under Clinton as well as under Bush hesitated to let Seoul take the lead in both the North Korean transition and a balanced approach to regionalism with assurances that Washington would have its interests met. Japan was preferred as a leader within the region.

The Bush team challenged the Clinton team's benign neglect of regionalism. Whereas in 2000 the United States did not seriously question the assumptions that economic integration at both the global and regional levels would be positive for the evolution of China and that North Korea would survive and should be integrated into a region, in 2001 the U.S. position hardened. Now Washington feared that regionalism would boost China, while propping up a very fragile North. Security trumped economics; it would be better to face the security threat early than to allow economic gains to generate a greater threat.

The Bush administration came to power with many vestiges of the mind-set of the 1980s. It was skeptical of multilateralism, preferring bilateralism. After some progress in NEA multilateralism in 2000, it was telling its allies Japan and South Korea to change direction and rely more on the United States to handle China, Russia, and North Korea as potential threats that needed to hear a single message. The idea of economic security was viewed again with suspicion; the only true measure of security is geopolitics, especially military power, which must be the determining factor in forging regional as well as global ties. It followed that allies should defer to the United States to manage the larger strategic issues without diluting the essential message or, worse, bolstering the position of potential adversaries.

Leading figures in the Bush administration were known to argue that the path into which the Russians had put themselves with the Chinese is fundamentally insane. From many Russians they heard that Russians are scared about the rise of China; so they had trouble understanding what motivated Russia. They calculated that pressure would force Putin's hand, bringing him closer to the West and reinforcing hesitancy toward China.

Americans paid little attention to growing economic regionalism, while warning of "a volatile arc surrounding Japan" threatening to status quo powers.[2] This justified an appeal for a shift in regional diplomacy, based on a strengthened military and political alliance with Japan. Even as North Korea appeared to open its door to other states and China became more positive toward regionalism, U.S. analysts perceived a dangerous area. Instead of rising regionalism in cooperation with dominant internationalism, they saw a region where no one was in charge. If the United States is to play its desired role it must draw Japan and South Korea together into closer ties based on common goals, they reasoned.

Apart from bilateralism focused on alliance building and streaks of containment, it was not clear what critics offered as a substitute. Emphasizing United States–centered relations, they lacked any positive message about regionalism. To other countries that had forged bilateral ties except Japan and South Korea, the message was to downgrade them and rely on the United States to steer ties from afar. South Korea's opening to China and Russia as well as North Korea, Japan's initiative to Russia, China's efforts to develop close bilateral ties throughout the region, and incipient regionalism too were to be put on hold, as far as the Bush team was concerned. The United States

[2] Kent E. Calder, "The New Face of Northeast Asia," *Foreign Affairs*, January/February 2001, p. 106.

would have to take the lead, setting the framework before others would be given their chance to fill in the spaces under a watchful eye.

Redefining globalization, Bush put security at the center, indicating that the world revolves around the United States. Its overwhelming influence starts with hard power relying on military muscle, continues with intermediate financial power, and embraces soft power by shaping culture generally and moral ideals such as human rights and democracy. The Bush team did not make a big deal of economic challenges from other countries, despite disappointment that Japan's weak growth put a drag on the American economy and that China's undervalued currency pegged to the dollar undercut U.S. manufacturing. It was much more worried about security threats. Its thinking was typical of the cold war, where the state is a more prominent actor, limiting the flow of technology for political reasons and preparing to use economics as a tool for security. Little interest was shown in how others perceive America's actions or in multilateral reassurances to persuade them. From this perspective, regionalism loomed as a potential threat to the security objectives of pressuring China and North Korea and also as a challenge to United States–led globalization. To win approval, China would have to go a long way to addressing security concerns, and North Korea needed, at a minimum, to start afresh through inspections and reductions in border forces.

The Clinton administration had placed economic, especially financial, globalization at the top of the agenda while seeking to keep security matters on a steady course, addressing "hot spots" as they arose without an overall strategy. The goal was global interdependence through a technologically driven process that is largely beyond government control. The main task of governments is to promote greater economic interdependence, anticipating that it will bring mostly positive results for global security despite some need to be alert to negative effects as regional hot spots continue to flare. If NEA regionalism were to enhance China's economic integration and provide a context for enticing North Korea from its isolation, Clinton may well have given his approval. In contrast, Bush put security centered on the United States first. Although this left regionalism in a doubtful light, the fact that economics are secondary could leave room for progress on regionalism that was seen as nonthreatening to security. If nations in the aftermath of the North Korean crisis could reassure the United States on this, they might not encounter strong resistance to limited forms of regionalism. Yet, such a shift remained hypothetical, because the security imperative would continue to appear, at least in Washington's eyes, as of overarching importance.

Bush came to office intent on raising the profile of security issues while adhering to the course of economic globalization. From the outset his staff had in mind a closer security relationship with Japan and a tougher stance against both China and North Korea. This had the effect of altering the balance in regionalism as well as globalization. After 9/11 the shift became more pronounced; economic issues faded before the urgency of global security. When in his State of the Union address Bush identified North Korea as part of an "axis of evil" along with Iraq and Iran, the shift was complete. Northeast Asia regionalism now had to proceed under the shadow of a potential showdown between the United States and North Korea. The assumptions were sharply different from those of Clinton.

While the impact of 9/11 reinforced the priority on security under Bush, it created a new sense of vulnerability. No longer was defense by deterrence possible. United States forces would watch vigilantly for potential threats, threatening preemptive action and relying on other states to participate or, at least, to pressure transgressors. The dynamics of relations with Russia changed abruptly in the fall of 2001, and over the following year it became clear that a partnership in favor of stability also was taking shape with China. The initial thrust to solidify the triangle with Japan and South Korea faded into the background, as a broader regional coalition was needed to ensure UN Security Council votes as well as to contain North Korea's nuclear weapons programs. Instead of pressuring Tokyo to join an alliance targeted mostly at Beijing, Washington appealed for a global front in which the two East Asian capitals would not be opposed. This transformed the security context for NEA. Yet, Washington had made itself the security hub, bypassed the United Nations when it went to war in March 2003 with Iraq, and continued to give priority to Tokyo's military role with no regard to Beijing's views. Security globalization placed U.S. forces at the center.

On the one hand, the Bush administration practiced preemptive globalization with no room for regionalism except in the EU, where it was a fait accompli and had to be tolerated, if to a lesser degree than before. In its first eight months it had shown little sympathy with the steps toward regionalism under way, welcoming the setbacks across the region. Even after 9/11 it seemed to be undertaking an all-encompassing push for security globalization, not only placing itself at the head of NEA security in all respects (containing North Korea, fortifying Taiwan's ability to balance the PRC, strengthening alliances with Japan and South Korea, and developing a missile shield after renouncing the antiballistic missile [ABM] treaty), but also linking economic ties to security. Clearly, Washington became the driving force in NEA. In September 2002 the new U.S. National Security Strategy, or the Bush doctrine, presented the rationale for preemptive war and prevention of China's rise as a military rival, while targeting Iraq as the first state obliged to abandon WMD.

On the other hand, fall 2002 produced a crisis over North Korea's admission that it was enriching uranium to make nuclear weapons and later its announcement that it would restart the nuclear reactor mothballed since 1994 as part of the KEDO agreement that was now collapsing. Without an obvious military response, the United States soon gave NEA multilateralism a new look. This atmosphere led to increased solicitude to China, sudden determination to stop Taipei from destabilizing relations with Beijing, and, after the Iraq war, success in drawing both Japan and South Korea closer in facing the crisis. Repeating the mantra of multilateral talks in opposition to North Korea's demand for bilateral ones, the United States took satisfaction when Chinese pressure on the North finally led it to accept six-way talks in August 2003. Secretary of State Colin Powell's visit to Beijing in February 2003 was a turning point in coordination toward the North, and the visits in May of Koizumi and Roh to the United States solidified triangular cooperation with economic pressure.

When George W. Bush went to St. Petersburg in late 2002 to thank Putin for putting no resistance in the path of NATO expansion and agreeing to a United Nations Security Council resolution tightening the screws on Iraq, he was greeted with satisfaction that Russia and the United States were coordinating their positions. Russia's elite felt gratified that Moscow had reemerged as a global partner. One newspaper went so far as to argue that "Neither NATO, nor the European Union has such international authority and geopolitical opportunities as Russia . . . and this is why the sole superpower needs it."[3] It would not be long, however, before the two would split over going to war in Iraq and Russia would try its hand unsuccessfully at finding its own diplomatic solution with North Korea. Even if Russia seemed marginalized for a time, it reemerged in August 2003 as a force accepted by both Washington and Pyongyang.

Many U.S. officials now had broader concerns about trouble ahead in NEA. Five assumptions drove the most serious concerns: 1) North Korea would remain a threat for WMD blackmail, even if the current crisis were mitigated; 2) China's development of missiles and purchase of Russian weapons coupled with impatience on Taiwan, even if that seemed more under control, are destabilizing forces; 3) Russia would be positioning itself as a force for mischief as well as influence by building ties to North Korea; 4) new South Korean anti-Americanism will cast doubt on the U.S. troop presence there; and 5) frustrations about uncertain relations are becoming exacerbated in Japan. If bilateral ties from Washington may prove inadequate to manage this complex region, regionalism in which the United States is not the hub appeared more likely to defy U.S. security objectives.

The Bush administration came to power wary of those who back regionalism. Kim Dae-jung had won the Nobel Prize for his soft appeals to North Korea and appeared to have been overeager to lure the Clinton administration into relaxing its guard. Chinese interest in regionalism was suspect as a tactic to split Japan and the United States. Also Japan's leadership that in 2000–2 was, at times, pressing for conciliatory measures to Beijing, Pyongyang, and Moscow was seen as unduly influenced by a coalition

[3] *Nezavisimaia gazeta*, November 25, 2002.

including the pacifist Komeito party and the powerful LDP politician Nonaka Hiromu.[4] The October 2000 report by Richard Armitage and Joseph Nye favored closer security ties with Japan, and Armitage took the second spot in the State Department positioned to press for multilateralism in the face of pressures from others in the administration, including John Bolton who joined him at the State Department, to draw a firmer line between good and evil and get Japan to concur.

The new administration broke with both the "chrysanthemum club" of veteran Japan experts, whose long-standing ties to left-leaning academics made them wary of a resurgent right wing and prone to accept a cautious security role for Japan, and the "panda huggers" of veteran China experts, whose links to academic reformers made them hopeful about gradual reform and engagement of China. It blamed hesitancy in Japan in strengthening the alliance with the United States on the Clinton administration's neglect of that country and bombast in China in opposing the United States on that administration's coddling. With more strategic clarity and insistence from the United States it expected to bring NEA more in line with globalization while creating a security environment that would stop or at least delay regionalism until it stood little chance of posing a threat to U.S. leadership.

Some in the United States, including leading advisors to George Bush in his campaign for president, were convinced that Japan was turning to the right and ready to strengthen its alliance with the United States. Observing the negative reaction to China of late 1998–9 and the rising nationalism associated with Diet decisions over a national flag and anthem as well as constitutional revision, they anticipated a new meeting of the minds that the Clinton administration, with its record of taking Japan for granted, was failing to exploit. Yet, when some of these advisors made their views known to Japanese officials and foreign affairs experts in the spring of 2000 they found little enthusiasm.[5] They had misjudged the nature of Japanese nationalism, both by dissociating it from extremism frightening to Asians and failing to appreciate its natural inclination to reduce dependency on the United States.

The Armitage report of the fall of 2000 left many Japanese worried that a Bush presidency could pressure Tokyo into tougher measures toward China and North Korea. Current thinking focused on diplomacy more than the military and on balanced relations in the region rather than reliance on a closer U.S. alliance. The United States of late had begun to cultivate direct ties with politicians and parliamentarians rather than working through the Japanese Foreign Ministry, which through its monopoly on information had long kept the prime minister largely at its mercy. Providing U.S. intelligence selectively to a wider set of actors may seem like a good way to bypass lingering pacifist

[4] Michael Green, "Preparing for New Teams in Tokyo and Washington . . . and a Muddy Field in Both Capitals," *Pacific Forum CSIS: Comparative Connections*, 2(4), 2001.

[5] *Sekai shuho*, April 14, 2000, p. 3.

inclinations, but it also alienates some bureaucrats. Because of the strong political forces seeking more independence of the United States and feeling emboldened by diplomatic trends in 2000, it divided the politicians. The Taiwan lobby had gained ground in Japan, but it was still not a deciding force. The immediate response to the Armitage report was not actively to oppose it, but to brush it aside. The Bush administration had its work cut out to forge a consensus in Japan until the war on terror added to the pressure and then the North Korean nuclear crisis fostered a new sense of alarm. The Japanese right was drawing closer to the United States.

On December 29, 2000 the *Yomiuri shimbun* reported on the latest joint U.S.-Japanese poll focused on bilateral relations. While American views of relations were firmly positive, far fewer Japanese believed that relations were good or very good. A similar gap could be seen in the pattern of about two-thirds of Americans and one-half of Japanese expressing trust in the other.[6] The findings were consistent with Americans' sense that there are no longer any serious problems between the two countries and the alliance with Japan is the equivalent of NATO in East Asia, compared to Japanese views.

As fear of a global recession rose in early 2001, plans to concentrate on winning Japan's cooperation as a military partner with emphasis on TMD and NMD were being compromised by pressure to prod Japan to stimulate its economy. But this time the focus was not on government spending, but on allowing more competition, especially through increased imports. If new tensions might have followed, the abrupt shift in U.S. priorities after 9/11 left Washington disinclined to divert efforts to economic pressure.

After the 9/11 terrorist attack, the United States sought a closer alliance to draw Japan deeper into a global agenda. If many in Japan found this option too limiting and looked to other options within NEA involving varying degrees of regionalism, the United States could point to tensions over North Korea, China's posture to Taiwan, and China's general military buildup as well as to dangers from terrorism across Southwest, South, and Southeast Asia. This offered a welcome opportunity to Koizumi to pass new laws allowing more forward-deployment of Japanese forces and to meet nationalist demands. Many sought duality: retaining the U.S. alliance while gaining independence in Asia. While Japanese leaders had become ambivalent in regional relations aware that the United States and especially Republicans doubted the efficacy of such steps, they were pleased that Bush values Japan more than China.[7] Indeed, after a period of decrying "Japan passing" and a loss of leverage, many welcomed a competition for Japan's favor.

Distracted by urgent priorities elsewhere, Washington was content to wait as NEA countries responded hesitantly. Although hopes for Japan were greatest, backed by an image of Koizumi as both the best prospect for economic

[6] *Yomiuri shimbun*, December 29, 2000.

[7] Inoguchi Takeshi, "Kommei Beidaitoryosen," *Asahi shimbun*, November 29, 2000.

reform and a firm supporter of strengthened alliance, the United States lost confidence in his stewardship of domestic reform while finding no great merit in his early chaotic handling of foreign relations. The wait toward South Korea had begun earlier with optimism that the opposition would wrest power from Kim Dae-jung's party in the December 2002 elections and work closer with the United States to contain North Korea, to strengthen the security triangle with Japan, and even to reduce public sympathy toward China. The wait for new leadership extended to China as the United States wanted to keep its options open until after the 16th Party Congress in the fall. Yet, even without much confidence in leaders – Koizumi, who had started chaotically; Roh, who had stirred anti-Americanism; and Hu, who could not break much with the old-guard communism and Jiang's continued stewardship of some security matters – the United States used the North Korean crisis and an antinuclear consensus in 2003 to keep all sides following its orchestration in preparation for multilateral talks.

American policy makers had no easy answers to the trade-offs required in NEA. They favored the LDP as good for security relations with Japan, but they deplored its ostrich-like approach to economic reform. Preferring to woo Japan rather than pressure it or bypass it, the Bush administration did not know how to overcome the realities of a nation fearful of opening its gates to American firms that would grab assets in a fire sale. Assertive elsewhere, the administration left the Japanese pondering how they could find their own place independent of the United States. In 2002 Japan's search focused on North Korea.

In December 2003 when China's Premier Wen Jiabao came to Washington, progress occurred in coordinating positions on North Korea and Taiwan. Yet, it was insufficient to eliminate the danger of a showdown over plans for a referendum during the Taiwan elections in March 2004. Differences between the United States and China had not been narrowed to the point that globalization could coexist with regionalism. As new six-party talks formed, Beijing pressed the United States on Taiwan.

American leaders showed little patience with the mix of forces transforming the region: the balance of globalization and regionalism, the power of public opinion limiting leaders' choices, and the lack of trust in the balance of power that was emerging. Many were confident that the United States had at its disposal the means to shape the evolution of NEA, but much depended on Japan, the indispensable ally expected to reinforce U.S. leadership. For a time Koizumi's support for the war against terror raised hopes in Washington, but in September 2002 his trip to Pyongyang amidst talk of reservations about U.S. plans for war in Iraq made it clear that Japan would contemplate a separate regional strategy. If Washington was not pleased with this independent diplomacy, it soon was eclipsed by the outcry over stories of abductees and then by the nuclear crisis. As the Japanese public grew more upset, Koizumi decided that he would have to bandwagon in order to put maximum pressure on the North and have some hope of shaping U.S. policy.[8] The nuclear crisis rewarded the Bush administration with an ally more committed to security cooperation, as seen in searches of North Korean ships arriving in Japanese ports. Yet, no matter how many consultations took place (most including South Korea) and how often America's leaders used the word *multilateralism,* the Japanese shared with others in NEA the image of the United States calling the shots. They would have to wait for the end of the crisis to gain leverage and resume the search for regionalism. By that time, the Japanese people as well as the region would be accustomed to Japan's new military role.

Japan and Regionalism

In 2001 Japan lost more of its luster as a regional leader due to economic decline and diplomatic weakness. Economic stagnation turned into outright decline mixed with danger signals that without drastic reforms no turnaround was in sight. More of Japan's industries relocated to China as part of what was seen as the "hollowing out of Japanese manufacturing" and the rise of China as the "world's factory." Although it retained many economic assets – a huge trade surplus, ample funds for investments sought by China and South Korea, and potential for huge projects with Russia – an image of decline undercut Japan's clout. With Bush in office expecting more from the alliance and Jiang continuing China's "smile diplomacy," Japan would not be spared new entreaties for its support.

In the spring of 2001 as Sino-U.S. relations grew tense, there was talk in Japan of a new cold war developing. On the one side was U.S. unipolarity, while on the other was China, but not necessarily alone. Many thought that Russia was drawing closer to China, and the EU was also opposed to unipolarity. What path would Japan take? Analysts noted that it did its best to keep a low profile, "hiding like a frog at the bottom of a well" during the standoff over the U.S. spy plane that had to land on Hainan Island after a Chinese jet collided with it. While few suggested that Japan should stick close to the United States, the idea of joining a league of other great powers to counter the United States did not win support either.[9] It was much easier to envision a bridging role and to renew efforts aimed at regionalism. However, first growing nationalist momentum in Japan would have to be addressed.

Bush's victory and frustration with Japanese foreign policy intensified efforts by the right wing to transform their country. An open, sharp exchange between newspapers on the Right and Left engulfed Japan in the last week of February 2001 over the textbook issue. It was a sign of the growing

[8] Tanaka Akihiko, "Sekai wa kesshite 'jyanguru' ni wa naranai," *Chuo koron*, June 2003, pp. 72–80.

[9] "Rochu rengo vs. Beikoku no kozu," *Sapio*, May 9, 2001, p. 13.

aggressiveness of the Right, led by *Sankei shimbun* and a growing number of monthly journals as well as books aimed at a mass audience. After *Asahi shimbun* editorialized on both February 21st and 22nd critical of a report on textbooks, *Sankei* answered by challenging its outlook, calling the existing historical worldview in textbooks "self-destructive."[10] If from 1945 to 1980 the Japanese Left held the upper hand in such discussions and from 1980 to 2000 the two sides had, more or less, been in balance, the new struggle suggested that the Right was expecting to become ascendant. Just when progress toward regionalism was most pronounced and Japanese leadership could have created a barrier against the assertive globalization of the incoming Bush team, renewed nationalism set back relations with South Korea, China, and Russia.

In March 2001 Japanese politicians expressed their views of the proposed textbook revisions. On the Left Minshuto's Hatoyama Yukio insisted that massive revisions are needed because there are discrepancies with historical facts. On the Right Jiyuto's Ozawa Ichiro said that it is time for South Korea and China to stop talking only about the past and to look to the future. Now the burden is on them, not on the Japanese side.[11] The LDP was divided, but, mostly, it hesitated to challenge the rising nationalist tone. Indeed, Koizumi pressed his case for becoming prime minister not only with a maverick reform image, but also with promises that he would visit Yasukuni shrine over the objections of the nations that had been the victims of Japanese aggression.

The public had lost confidence in the future of Japan. Sections of book stores once filled with volumes extolling the uniqueness of nihonjinron had been converted into shelves replete with doomsday coverage, cataloging unmanageable problems, reviewing ten lost years, fingering who is to blame, and warning of bad news to come. Yet, these works narrowly treated Japan's real problems and only timidly, if at all, raised far-reaching solutions. They failed to name names until compelling events had already exposed people. More discussion of blame focused on foreign behavior or threats than on the actual domestic impediments. The Japanese debate on domestic and foreign policy reforms largely reflected a right-wing agenda with the old left virtually silent and centrist. Both proregionalism and proglobalization thinking were only presented hesitantly.

In early 2001 Tokyo Governor Ishihara and Russian Security Council head Sergei Ivanov spoke forcefully at the World Economic Forum in Davos against globalization. Ishihara accused the United States of intentionally provoking the Asian financial crisis to damage Asian economies, using the idea of "global standards" as a means of Americanization to block Japanese influence. Ishihara's notion of regional influence obviously is not to win the trust of neighboring countries but to use economic clout to bypass global

[10] *Sankei shimbun*, February 23, 2001, p. 2; *Tokyo shimbun*, March 8, 2001, pp. 16–17.

[11] *Sankei shimbun*, March 8, 2001, p. 2.

pressures and assert Japan's dominance. This is an extension of the notion that Japan is unique, justifying its historic aggression as saving Asia, its economic model as suitable to Asia, and its future leadership as best for Asia. Ivanov's message was that further expansion of NATO, unilateral security measures without taking Russian interests into account, and even pressure to pay Russia's debts would lead to a sharp response. It suggested a kind of regional security framework aimed at blocking United States–led global and regional integration. If neither Ishihara nor Ivanov spoke for Koizumi and Putin as they lent support to Bush's war against terror, the views they voiced continued to resonate in their countries and even suggest some common ground. Koizumi avoided Ishihara's extremism, but he too sought avenues for raising Japan's independent voice in a way that would not be ignored.

For a time the Japanese proved that their national identity was too rooted in the past to make progress on regionalism. They remained apathetic to articulating new objectives, while a vocal minority showed itself to be obsessed with the past. It became impossible to relinquish the symbol of Japanese victimization at the hands of the Russians in return for a compromise agreement that did not justify the nationalist cause. Likewise, there was no stopping the forces bent on revising textbooks and filling the media with assertions that essentially justified Japan's regional conduct in the decades to 1945. Spats with China and South Korea were framed in narrow nationalist terms. Even when diplomatic efforts managed to overcome the setbacks in bilateral relations, the Japanese did not draw lessons from these experiences helpful for moving forward. Unable to resolve its past identity, the Japanese nation made little progress in reaching consensus on a future identity.

Inconsistencies abound in use of the "history" card across the region. Japan presses Russia to apologize for its treatment of Japanese captured in 1945 and return the islands symbolizing Japan's victimization in the final stage of the war, yet Japan tells South Korea and China to stop using the "history" card and focus on the future. China, in turn, renews ties with Cambodia, but when Jiang Zemin is accused during his visit there of abetting genocide by its allies, instead of apologizing he responds that relations should focus on the future. The Japanese found irony in this.[12] It remains for the Japanese, first of all, to find a strategy to bring closure to the shadow of history on the region, and this is likely to begin with resolution of the unresolved claims of North Korea. When Koizumi went to Pyongyang in September 2002 he offered the standard apology, and few doubted that this was but the first step in negotiations to decide how much assistance would suffice to convince the North Korean government to drop its demands for a full reckoning.

[12] *Sankei shimbun*, December 9, 2000, p. 15.

Japanese foreign policy toward China, Russia, North Korea, and South Korea was in shambles in 2001. Even before Koizumi took office at the end of April an outcry erupted over the way the Foreign Ministry was handling policies to Russia and China, and shortly afterward as the uproar continued the two Koreas were added to the list. It had been a half century since such discord existed among bureaucrats compounded by indecision among politicians. Already in March an uproar had greeted the upbeat results of the Mori-Putin summit in Irkutsk that seemed to be leading to a territorial agreement and peace treaty that would not bring "four islands in one batch" as expected. The head of the Russian desk was transferred unexpectedly in late March in a move that was dissected in the media for revelations of sharp conflicts over policy or insubordination against the official government negotiating posture, and the decision was reversed in May when Tokyo abandoned its negotiating strategy without suggesting an alternative. In April stories of Foreign Ministry discord centered on efforts to block a visa to former Taiwan President Lee Teng-Hui, traveling ostensibly for medical reasons. The press charged a pro-China inclination in the Foreign Ministry led by Makida Kunihiko, head of the Asia Pacific Department, and suggested that Nonaka, then considered a possible candidate for prime minister in the turnover just ahead, operated in the background behind Makida along with the Hashimoto faction, heir to the Tanaka faction's pro-Chinese focus.[13] By the time Lee arrived on April 22 a Diet group called for Makida's transfer amidst charges that the disarray had damaged ties with China and Taiwan.[14] In the background was a trade war with China begun by Japan to protect its agricultural sector and the history textbooks that badly offended both South Koreans and Chinese.

When Tanaka Makiko became foreign minister many suspected she would go further to boost ties to China policy, harking back to her father's days as prime minister in the 1970s. In fact, over less than a year in office she was at constant loggerheads with the professionals in the ministry, leaving a scene of chaos in Japanese foreign policy. Instead of rebuilding ties in NEA, the new administration exacerbated them both by its actions and by its poor coordination. Tanaka's position toward Moscow was tougher than that of the Mori administration, causing an impasse by rejecting the Irkutsk summit approach. It was not until six months later that Koizumi made an effort to reinvigorate ties, although Tanaka did not show any signs of pursuing the matter. In contrast, in policies toward Beijing she took a more positive line than others in the leadership. In December 2001 she was seen as suggesting that Taiwan was equivalent to Hong Kong, a position similar to that in Beijing but anathema to that of the majority in the LDP party. Given the struggle with the professionals as well as the freewheeling style of the foreign

[13] "Kankai," *Foresight*, April 2001, p. 116.

[14] *Sankei shimbun*, April 22, 2001, p. 1.

minister, pursuit of regionalism was difficult because of Japan as well as the United States.

In the midst of repeated tensions with each of the countries of NEA, experts did not lose sight of rapid advances in many indicators of regionalism. Reviewing substantial survey data, Tokyo University professor Inoguchi Takashi concluded that ties were developing faster than expected, as seen in manufacturing, the service sector, and even fads for products from around the region, such as Korean kimchi in Japan and Japanese animation shows in many countries. Even political ties, reflected in the frequency of meetings of heads of state, had risen sharply in 2000. Concerned that more is needed to recognize each other's merits and build a stable foundation, the professor called for academic exchanges, mostly in the social sciences, in pursuit of an intellectual strategy for the region as a whole.[15]

After 9/11 Koizumi took three steps to reinvigorate Japanese diplomacy. First, if not as dramatically as Tony Blair and Vladimir Putin, he championed the U.S. cause in the war against terror. By pushing legislation to authorize Japanese logistical support far from the country's borders, Koizumi boosted Japan's security profile. It followed that he was prepared to give security a greater role in the pursuit of regionalism, while attaching Japan closer to United States–led globalization. Second, Koizumi patched up relations with China, Japan, and Russia in October. Clearly, he did not want recent bilateral problems to get in the way of urgent needs for security cooperation. Third, in a trip through SEA in January 2002 Koizumi began to articulate a renewed vision for regionalism with implications for NEA too. He still had no new strategy for NEA when he replaced Tanaka at the end of January, but his vision for including SEA offered some clues. When Bush visited Japan in February the balance between globalization and regionalism was left unexplored.

Fear of isolation drove Japanese interest in FTAs. Despite strong opposition to agricultural openness, interest in FTA ties with South Korea, ASEAN, and China was growing. Having signed an agreement with Singapore, Japan turned to South Korea next; in July 2002 a study group began to meet, anticipating a report in two years. Some spoke of signing an agreement in 2005. Yet, the government was divided: the Keisansho (the successor to MITI) was in favor, but the Agriculture and Fishing Ministry remained in doubt. No overall strategy had yet evolved. The momentum keeps building toward regionalism based on FTAs even if difficult political choices lie ahead. Meanwhile, South Korea is the pivot pursued by Japan but still seeks to keep a balance with China. In wooing Seoul Tokyo knows that Beijing, also aware that NEA is an FTA vacuum, is watching.[16]

[15] Inoguchi Takashi, "Ajia parometa no seiritsu o mezase," *Chuo koron*, July 2002, pp. 150–5.
[16] *Asahi shimbun*, July 3, 2002, p. 9.

When the Japanese discussed foreign policy in 2002 many kept pointing to the need to restore a sovereign state (*shuken kokka*), blaming those in China and South Korea who criticize Japan's right to prepare its own textbooks as it pleases for denying sovereign rights. China's infringement on the territory of the Shenyang consulate to take North Korean refugees away in May was reported over the following months as a serious violation of sovereign rights. The media charged that Foreign Ministry officials were failing to uphold their state. Even more, they insisted, diplomacy is a mirror of a deformed society without the resolve to enforce standards. While some sympathized with this argument as criticism of insufficient globalization or weak defense of human rights in China and beyond, others saw it as the vanguard of a nationalist backlash to global as well as regional integration. Politicians who criticized the prime minister's visit to Yasukuni or tried to reassure the Chinese or Koreans in other ways were accused by the right-wing media of playing into the hands of those who besmirch Japanese sovereignty.[17]

In September 2002 Koizumi's visit to North Korea won wide praise except from a portion of the right wing. It was seen as a bold move that would invigorate Japanese diplomacy with all of the states active in regionalism. Suddenly, Koizumi's visit to the United States prior to the Pyongyang summit acquired new significance and his planned trips to China and Russia assumed new meaning. Above all, Seoul would take note and redouble its efforts to coordinate with Tokyo in its own newly accelerated talks with Pyongyang. Before long, however, the sad stories of the abducted Japanese coupled with the nuclear weapons scare following U.S. accusations and North Korean admissions sent relations on a tailspin. The North took a tough stance toward Japan in the talks that followed, driving Japan to seek increased security cooperation with the United States in the development of missile defenses and in NEA with the countries on all sides of North Korea. There was reluctance to admit failure, however, as Tokyo gained prominence in U.S. efforts to end the crisis.

At the end of 2002 the think-tank NIRA devoted an issue of its journal to a comprehensive regional development plan for NEA. This grand design optimistically looked ahead to an area "expected to grow by leaps and bounds." It called for a "trade corridor," an "energy community," a NEA development bank, and a vision for a frontier that, freed from the spell of military conflicts, will adopt Asian-style growth methods.[18] A growing clamor for regionalism was reflected in this blueprint. As bad as Japan's security environment had become amidst concerns over North Korean WMD and the rise of China's military, its economic troubles remained the top concern. As young people there as in South Korea lost trust in U.S. leadership, economic

[17] *Sankei shimbun*, July 4, 2002, p. 1.

[18] "Hokuto Ajia chiiki no gurando dezain," *NIRA*, 15(11), 2002.

regionalism drew support. Now regionalism had a dual focus: to reestablish security and to revive economic prospects.

In November 2002 a private "foreign relations taskforce" appointed by Koizumi issued a report arguing that the national interest is to base foreign policy on a strategic foundation. It challenged U.S. unilateralism, proposing to use the United Nations to contain it and warning that America's tolerance is weak for conflicting opinions and differing value systems. The report declared that Japan's goal is for no rapid system reversal in North Korea, indirectly challenging U.S. hard-line tactics.[19] Such logic became the springboard of a renewed search for regional partners, not excluding Russia for energy security.

In the spring of 2003 after the war in Iraq ended, Koizumi was on the spot as the United States insisted that only a united front would pressure Pyongyang to abandon its nuclear weapons program. The Japanese decided that they could have the most leverage by drawing closer to the United States and agreed on inspections of North Korean ships visiting Japanese ports as part of an economic squeeze. While Koizumi's inconclusive meetings with Putin in January focused on energy cooperation and with Roh in June drew attention to the pursuit of an FTA with the South, it was the visit with Bush in May, concentrating on North Korea, that set the overall tone. The LDP was moving to the right and becoming more supportive of the United States, and Koizumi was assuring his reelection as party president as a strong leader in a foreign-policy emergency. Japan would wait for Russia and South Korea to respond to its initiatives, while relying on the United States first in the nuclear crisis.

As a populist, Koizumi played to rising nationalist sentiments. He took advantage of the downturn in idealism with the collapse of the left wing. This was a healthy corrective, allowing Japan to become a more responsible partner of the United States. In 2003 a new security consciousness rapidly matured. Yet, it was accompanied by a rising threat to strategic thinking from the right wing. Riding the emotionalism of North Korean abductions, the Japanese put off discussion of issues critical to a balanced foreign policy.

Of the various postwar legacies that encumber Japanese foreign policy, only the elimination of Article 9 of the Constitution is gaining ground. This has been the first goal of the right wing, but it also is a goal of U.S. administrations, eager to share global and regional security burdens. In 1991 during the Gulf War Japan's image as a partner in global security suffered a setback, when it could not do much more than send cash. In 1996–8 the Taiwan missile crisis gave it a chance to broaden alliance ties with the United States by agreeing to extend logistical support in the region. The nuclear crisis of 2003 was one more step in watering down Article 9. By contrast, the

[19] *Asahi shimbun*, December 4, 2002, p. 4.

postwar legacy most disturbing to the left wing – the failure to take clear responsibility for the war – is not being addressed. This slows regionalism. The legacies of no diplomatic relations with North Korea and no peace treaty with Russia likewise delay regionalism. Although in March 2001 hopes rose for Russian normalization and in September 2002 for North Korean ties, problems proved too complex. Energy security and WMD security will have to come first before bilateral breakthroughs are likely. Finally, the legacy of protectionism for the Japanese economy, especially agriculture, has also not been adequately faced so far. It holds back Japan's globalization and is a barrier in regionalism with China and also with South Korea.

A new ODA charter added a nationalist cast to regional ties just as China was accelerating its cooperation with SEA nations. At the ASEAN +3 and APEC meetings in the fall of 2003, China and even India drew closer to those nations, while Japan hesitated. Anxious to keep up, Koizumi called a hasty December summit in Tokyo with the ASEAN leaders and made his own plea for an "East Asian Community" as part of a "Tokyo Declaration."

Japan and Russia

Having artificially raised expectations for a breakthrough in relations in 1997–8 and again in 2000–1, the Japanese government and media were hard-pressed to deal with the disillusionment that came later in 2001 and 2002. Instead of renewing hope, they contributed to a frenzy of finger pointing. Although much of the blame went to a handful of officials and politicians, especially Suzuki Muneo, the anger toward Russia was also palpable. Never having read much about Russia as a desirable partner, most were in no mood to move beyond their obsession with the territorial question. Relations were put on hold once again.

Russians watched the spectacle of bilateral relations crashing against the wall of Japanese insistence on the return of four islands, bemoaning that Koizumi was showing virtually no desire to improve bilateral relations. After uncompromisingly halting the negotiations, Japan, it was said, had left relations in an ice age.[20] Instead of optimism that a breakthrough could be reached by continuing along the path followed in 2000–1, Russians were left despairing of Japan's interest in anything except recovering the four islands. Both nations gave the impression that they did not need normalization.

Especially in Japan the right wing seized the opportunity to lambaste past errors in dealing with Russia. On the tenth anniversary of the visa-free travel regime in April 2001 *Sankei shimbun* charged that it was not fulfilling its purpose. It had been intended to increase mutual understanding and contribute to resolving the territorial dispute. Instead, the Russian islanders were

[20] *Asahi shimbun*, May 31, 2002, p. 2.

enjoying tourism, staying longer, and traveling farther around Japan, even to Okinawa, and the former Japanese islanders were not finding Russians interested in discussing the territorial question during their visits.[21] Some voices in Japan appeared ready to shift from engagement to containment, ending these exchanges and hoping that isolation along with impoverishment would change Russian thinking. Yet, Russia was in no danger of isolation and its economy by 2001 had resumed growing.

After 9/11 Putin's response to the terrorist attacks against the United States changed the geopolitical environment of relations with Japan. Instead of raising the specter of close cooperation with China to deny U.S. global supremacy, he opted to join the United States against the forces that backed terrorism and to accede to U.S. missile defense plans. Now Japan and Russia were allies in the main global struggle. Koizumi did not take long to reassert Tokyo's interest in improving relations, even if it took over a year for follow-up to bring hope of new momentum, leaving aside the territorial question. Moscow awaited a diplomatic initiative from Tokyo that would demonstrate why the two capitals had to solidify their relations. It was aware that some in Japan fretted that the new era of Russo-American relations left Japan outside, further adding to the sense of diplomatic isolation in that country.[22] In July 2002 reports surfaced that Tokyo was reviving negotiations with Moscow, accepting economic cooperation as the focus and no longer emphasizing the territorial issue. The two countries had at last agreed to work together to control the smuggling of crabs, fish, and other goods that long marred cross-border economic ties.[23]

Monopolies and red tape complicated ties between neighbors. After Sino-Russian border trade started rising again and transportation costs between Pusan and the Russian port of Vostochnyi fell with the introduction of competition, it was movement between Japan and Russia that was seen to be most cumbersome. Infrequent, costly, and tightly controlled shipping compounded the slow processing at Russian customs.[24] Cross-border economic relations still did not give confidence to those trying to boost ties.

It was Koizumi's decision to go to Pyongyang that showed the logic of closer cooperation. After all, after Putin took office as president, he had championed the cause of multilateral diplomacy to realize a soft landing in North Korea, and in the summer of 2002 he had encouraged Kim Jong-il to meet with Koizumi. Both sides welcomed energy pipelines and train routes that could include North Korea. Plans for accelerated Russo-Japanese talks on economic ties preceded Koizumi's January 2003 trip

[21] *Sankei shimbun*, April 23, 2001, p. 34.

[22] "'Beiro shinjidai' wa Nihon o okizari ni suru," *THEMIS*, August 2002, pp. 98–9.

[23] *Nihon keizai shimbun*, July 11, 2002, p. 2; July 21, 2002, p. 2.

[24] Hisako Tsuji, "Growing International Use of the Trans-Siberian Railway: Japan Is Being Left Out of the Loop," *ERINA Report*, 52 (June 2003), pp. 22–6.

to Moscow. As the initial optimism over Russo-American ties in the war against terrorism subsided when Bush pressed for a unilateral approach to Iraq, Putin naturally looked to Japan as one of the states also uncomfortable with U.S. policies. Quickly, however, all such calculations were set aside as the nuclear weapons standoff between Pyongyang and Washington made security the first concern and obliged Koizumi to emphasize the U.S. alliance.

A joint action plan emerged as the centerpiece in bilateral relations on the eve of the Koizumi visit to Moscow. It went further than any previous agreement in allowing economic relations that are not held hostage to conclusion of a peace treaty following resolution of the territorial question. The Japanese were reconciled to slow progress on the latter before the presidential elections in 2004, but they had determined that their best chance is to tighten ties with Putin and create an environment that will boost their nation in the eyes of the Russian people before focusing on the most contentious issue. Such pragmatism increased the chances for cooperation in regionalism.

A delegation from the LDP visited China in August 2002 in conjunction with the thirtieth anniversary of normalized relations and considered bilateral relations from the standpoint of economic security. Surprisingly, its findings had as much to say about Russia as China. A member of the delegation wrote that Russia is the key to resolving problems through cooperative relations and warned about the danger of competition from rising consumption as China's energy needs doubled by 2020 and South Korea pursued a strategy of shifting from oil to gas. Noting that Putin and Bush in May had agreed to stabilize oil supplies through Russian exports to the United States, he stressed the importance of large-scale projects in NEA that would impact Japan's security. The analysis called for a new strategic scenario to result from Koizumi's January 2003 visit to Russia that would minimize the risk not only for Japan, but also for the United States, China, and South Korea.[25] Thinking in terms of overall, long-term strategic policies, the Japanese eyed Russian energy. New concern about energy security arose not only from developments in the Middle East, but also from a nuclear power scandal at home that led to many plants closing over falsified safety records. Seen from China, however, Japan's motives were suspect for its late effort to replace the planned pipeline from Eastern Siberia to Daqing with a roundabout route to Nakhodka that leaves China out.

As the Japanese were becoming reconciled to China's rising great-power clout, some decided that they would have to use this force, not deny it. A few talked of a G-9 ahead, adding China to the elite group of industrialized powers that Russia had already entered. Others spoke anew of an AMF to steer investments in infrastructure for large energy and transportation

[25] Obi Mineo, "Isogareru Hokuto Ajia no keizai anzen hosho koso," *Gekkan jiyu minshu*, December 2002, pp. 58–63.

projects that would give NEA a driving force for regionalism. If a buoyant Japan a decade earlier had calculated that it needs a region to stand on par with the United States, a subdued Japan was becoming aware that it has no less need of it to gain the scale of economic operations in order to keep U.S. dominance in check. Attention turned to a big region to dilute China's clout, requiring Russia. If the U.S. role in security is taken for granted in this region, its economic role is less so. The key uncertainty was whether Japan could count on China's transformation through economic reform and integration, along lines traversed by other Asian nations, or Chinese nationalism would not be tempered by regionalism. Fearful of becoming helpless before the global economy, the Japanese became more willing to bet on regional integration. What began in 2000 with plans for bilateral currency swaps to take full effect in 2003, if needed, would grow into coordination of macroeconomic policies and cooperation in exchange rates, and some day into a full regional common market. A new realism toward Russia and its energy followed.

It would be premature, however, to credit Japan with strategic thinking toward Russia. In the summer of 1988, the spring of 1992, and the spring of 2001 a lack of such thinking had led to deterioration in relations. If Hashimoto's July 1997 "Eurasian speech" and Koizumi's January 2003 energy-centered initiative suggested otherwise, these were but hints of change that was not yet grasped by many in the LDP or the public. First, the Russians would have to decide on the pipeline route and the North Korean crisis would have to be resolved, and then Koizumi and Putin, after winning new terms, would need to clarify their strategic thinking and decide how far the logic brings them together.[26]

Distrust persists. Japanese fear that Russia wants economic benefits without concern for long-term trust, and Russians suspect that Japan wants to contain China with no plan for a lasting partnership. Writing from prison at the end of 2003, Suzuki Muneo warned that the only realistic path to trust is parallel talks on the two sets of two islands, as contemplated in March 2001.[27]

China and Regionalism

Beijing's images of Washington kept changing in 2001 and 2002, setting the stage for new approaches to regionalism. The prevailing theme was increased hegemonism and a rising tendency toward unilateralism tinged with containment of China. Yet, upbeat moments grew more numerous: in August 2001

[26] Gilbert Rozman, "A Chance for a Breakthrough in Russo-Japanese Relations: Will the Logic of Great Power Relations Prevail?" *Pacific Review*, 15(3) 2002, pp. 325–57.

[27] Kamisaka Fuyuko vs. Suzuki Muneo, "Gekitotsu! Hoppo ryod," *Shokun*, 11 (2003), pp. 148–61.

when Colin Powell asserted that the United States should not oppose China as a challenger, in September when Jiang threw his support behind the war against terror, in October when Bush went to Shanghai for the APEC meeting, and again in February when he went to Beijing for a bilateral summit. The Chinese insisted that the United States should recognize that their country poses absolutely no challenge to the existing international order, and on the contrary is extremely satisfied with the benefits it receives.[28] Indeed, the foreign-policy elite drew the conclusion in response to U.S. efforts to build a coalition after 9/11 that "the main purpose of the United States in organizing and promoting this coalition is to oppose terrorism, and is not to seek hegemony at least for a period of time to come."[29]

As the new Bush administration took a harsher position toward China and displayed a more unilateral approach on global issues, the Chinese analysts responded by exploring multilateralism. Formerly they had calculated that multilateral organizations were generally controlled by the United States and its allies and served as tools to interfere in the internal affairs of other countries. Now they decided that the United States was abandoning the restraint of international society, leaving the majority of countries resentful. Because China remains only a weak great power, it can best press its interests by working with others. The previous doctrine of multipolarity in which great powers, one by one, would use bilateral relations in defense of their natural interests was yielding to approval for multilateral organizations in which the EU, Russia, China, Japan, and other rising powers such as ASEAN and India would work in tandem with smaller states to limit the willful actions of the one hegemonic power.[30] In 2001 such rethinking gained much ground.

Carrying the argument for multilateralism further, the Chinese argued that economic globalization means increased interdependency and the inevitable rise of multilateral organizations. With entry into WTO China increasingly needs to participate in these and to show its influence through them. It also must reconsider its attitude toward regional organizations. Because most Asian states object to interference in internal matters, Beijing should be able to work with them. In this way it can take the lead in shaping WTO to reflect Asian demands. The new doctrine places regionalism at the center of multilateral ties and even suggests shifting the center of Chinese diplomacy from great-power relations centered on the United States, the West, and Russia to Asian diplomacy.[31]

[28] Zhu Feng, "Bushi fanghua yu Zhongmei guanxi," *Heping yu fazhan*, 2 (2002), p. 5.

[29] Song Yimin, "The U.S. Security Strategy and Foreign Relations Have Entered a New Stage of Readjustment," *International Studies*, 1–3 (2002), p. 17.

[30] Shen Jiru, "Duobian waijiao he duoji shijie," *Shijie jingji yu zhengzhi*, October 2001, pp. 20–4.

[31] Pang Zhongying, "Zhongguo de Yazhou zhanlue: linghuo de duobian zhuyi," *Shijie jingji yu zhengzhi*, October 2001, pp. 30–5.

The Chinese calculated that the United States in its war against terror was anxious to win multilateral backing including China's support and that Bush's APEC summit visit to Shanghai in October when he expressed gratitude for full support in the antiterror effort really set relations on a constructive track in which mutual economic ties would play a large role.[32] This means he will limit his unilateralist posture and improve relations with the other great powers, creating a positive atmosphere for China. After two visits in four months by Bush labeled successes and in the midst of growing FDI from the United States, the Chinese wrote of reengagement and relations back on track.[33]

One conference on Sino-U.S. relations in February 2002 noted that some scholars are cautiously optimistic that shared thinking is on the rise as economic ties expand, China no longer rejects Western civilization, and China seeks dialogue on human rights and democracy. Yet, it concluded that the large gap in comprehensive national strength and China's greater dependency on the United States creates a disequilibrium not advantageous for the development of relations.[34] Wariness remains on both sides. In the Iraq war and Korean nuclear crisis differences of approach created new strains, but Washington needed Beijing to advance a diplomatic track with North Korea and was appreciative when it hosted trilateral talks in April and six-way talks in late summer.

The new logic explored at the time of 9/11 was as follows. For a long time to come the United States will remain the only superpower. Its strategy toward China will combine Westernization, fragmentation, and containment.[35] China needs multilateralism to check U.S. power. It must enter Asia, encourage a rising Asian consciousness, and use regionalism to extend its own limited power.[36] Yet, China also should draw closer to the United States as part of the global consensus against a common enemy. Now that America's focus is homeland defense, China need not be depicted as a threat. With its entry into WTO, its preparations to host the 2008 Olympics, and its antiterror role, China can proceed with reengagement in relations with the United States. Analysts also suggested that in Bush's two visits to China in just four months (the second for a bilateral summit that marked the thirtieth anniversary

32 Qin Xuanren, "'9/11 shijian' hou de daguo guanxi geju," *Waiguo wenti yanjiu*, 1 (2002), pp. 1–6.

33 Yin Chengde, "Diedang qifu, jiwang kailai: qianxi Zhongmei guanxi jiqi qianjing," *Guoji wenti yanjiu*, 3 (2002), pp. 13–17.

34 Cui Zhiying, "'Zhongmei guanxi huigu yu zhanwang' guoji xueshu taolunhui congshu," *Guoji guancha*, 2 (2002), p. 64.

35 Meng Xiangqing, "Canyu duobian anquan hezuo: jishi taozhan, yeshi jiyu," *Shijie jingji yu zhengzhi*, October 2001, p. 27.

36 Wang Yizhou, "Zhongguo yu duobian waijiao," *Shijie jingji yu zhengzhi*, October 2001, pp. 4–5; Pang Zhongying, "Zhongguo de Yazhou zhanlue: linghuo de duobian zhuyi," *Shijie jingji yu zhengzhi*, October 2001, pp. 33–4.

of the historic Nixon visit) a new era of constructive cooperative relations is replacing the turbulent period from June 1989 to September 2001.[37]

In discussions of regional issues new realism was displayed to the predominance of U.S. power – military, economic, technological, and cultural – accompanied by renewed concern about the U.S. appetite to lead the world. The Chinese insisted that the majority of countries in NEA would be suspicious, recognizing that a different approach is needed for regional peace and stability.[38] Thus, Beijing would have to wait patiently for divisions to widen while making the case for regionalism and accepting global ties while drawing a line against unilateralism.[39]

Changes in globalization left the Chinese ambivalent about their country's options. On the one hand, the United States in the name of combating terror was extending its reach ever closer to China's borders while changing the rules of the international order. Free to develop a national missile defense after Russia's concessions on the ABM treaty, the United States enjoyed a more favorable military balance. On the other hand, its model of economic success was losing stature with a wave of scandalous disclosures about financial wrongdoing. The U.S. economic slowdown in 2001 coming on the heels of Japan's stagnation had left China as the engine of Asian economic growth. Beijing had an opportunity to continue to prove that it is a "responsible great power," reinforcing the term used by Zhu Rongji after China's image improved in the Asian financial crisis.

China's growing interest in regionalism came also on the back of increasing acceptance of globalization. Entry into WTO left China more open to the outside in any case. When global growth slowed down as in 2001, regionalism supplemented China's options. Indeed, in the spring of 2001 Chinese scholars began to explore regionalism as a force for domestic reform as well as foreign relations. They put a positive spin on it, and as foreign relations ameliorated in the following year this message prevailed.

In December 2001 a conference in Beijing found reasons for optimism in the new political environment.[40] Noting that the United States had turned its strategic focus from China to other parts of Asia and that in spite of the qualitative change in Russian-U.S. relations no alliance could be reached, the conference summary took heart from SEA countries facing added domestic anti-American pressure and strengthening ties with China. They would leave a gap in the U.S. attempt to draw a circle containing China. Adding the

37 Yin Chengde, "Diedang qifu, jiwang kailai: qianxi Zhongmei guanxi jiqi qianjing," *Guoji wenti yanjiu*, 3 (2002), pp. 13–17.

38 Wang Chuanjian, "Luan Dongbeiya zhanlue geju yu Chaoxian bandao wenti," *Dongbeiya yanjiu*, 2 (2002), p. 9.

39 Ding Shichuan, "Guanyu '9/11' shijianhou guoji jushi de jidian sikao," *Guoji guancha*, 2 (2002), p. 3.

40 "2001 nian Yatai diqu zhengzhi jingji xingshi yantaohui zaijing juxing," *Dangdai Yatai*, 1 (2002), p. 63.

economic news of growing regional cooperation, especially as China entered WTO, the discussion suggested an overall rationale for China's emphasis on regionalism drawing on SEA. Yet, the discussion was laced with gloom: U.S. encirclement, loss of Russian and Central Asian support, Japan's growing great-power ambitions, and doubts about U.S. economic recovery. Elsewhere one could still read in late 2001 that NEA was at a crossroads as the United States plotted to drag Japan and South Korea as its security partners into containment of China and North Korea that could lead the region into a new round of geopolitical confrontation.[41] The search for regionalism stemmed as much from desperation against the U.S. style of globalization as from a spirit of cooperation with its many dimensions.

Already at the Singapore ASEAN +3 meeting in November 2000 leaders had agreed to establish research on a free-trade investment area and all-around economic cooperation, while formalizing the structure of Sino-Korean-Japanese consultations. At the November 2001 Brunei meeting the Chinese noted further progress. Under the impact of 9/11 and the war against terror as well as the worsening U.S. and regional economic situation, the three NEA leaders resolutely strengthened their cooperation, agreeing on new ministerial meetings, and China and ASEAN declared their intent to establish an FTA in ten years. Although the leaders did not approve a vision statement drafted by a small group formed for that purpose, they largely reached a common understanding on accelerating regional integration. Welcoming these advances, the Chinese side noted that China had moved ahead of Japan and South Korea in establishing an FTA with ASEAN and indicated that the goal was to advance East Asian regionalism to stand with the EU and NAFTA as one of three great regions. Systematizing cooperation requires more time than in Europe, but it is a necessary choice. With ASEAN still not fully recovered from the Asian financial crisis, Japan mired in economic slowdown, and Kim Dae-jung tied down by domestic politics, China has become the driving force. Unable to resolve the question of regional leadership with Japan and beset with other nations' suspicions, China has to move slowly. Yet, its competitive pressure and vast market as well as the compelling case for regionalism offer optimism that regionalism will be successful.[42]

Initially, the Chinese desire for regionalism rested narrowly on economics rather than on a fundamental rethinking of global and regional geopolitical and cultural matters. It was a measured embrace, not full-fledged acceptance, to be accompanied by ample reassurance to partners. Having calculated that entry into WTO could boost China's GDP 2.0 to 2.5 percent per year, analysts added that this could become the locomotive for regional economic

41 Wu Xinbo, "Dongbeiya de jueze: diyuan zhengzhi yu diyuan jingji," *Guoji jingji pinglun*, p. 20.

42 Zhang Yunling, "Dongya hezuo yu Zhongguo – Dongmeng ziyou maoyiqu de jianshe," *Dangdai Yatai*, 1 (2002), pp. 6–11.

development too and, if accompanied by an East Asian FTA, could make China the nexus of a region-wide development framework, adding a half percent or more to everyone's growth rate.[43] The economics are compelling, but clearly not enough.

Beijing's former strategy of regional balances along its borders fell apart after 9/11. In South Asia it had relied on Pakistan, now turning to the United States and losing leverage versus India. In Central Asia it had depended on Russia and championed the Shanghai Cooperation Organization, but U.S. bases were approved by all of the states that supposedly had shared China's objectives. In SEA it emerged quite unscathed in comparison to Japan in 1997–8, which had been counting on Indonesia to anchor its regional presence, although China's tendency to favor misfits such as Myanmar and Cambodia remained in many minds. In NEA Beijing had counted on playing Japan against the United States, and it had been adjusting its policies since the late 1990s as these countries kept drawing closer in their security alliance. Analysts reasoned that it was time for a decisive shift from balances within each region to regionalization.

The Chinese remain preoccupied with great-power relations, and after first Japan and then Russia tilted unexpectedly to the United States they have been left to contemplate Sino-U.S. relations at the center of multisided great-power ties. This elevation of a weak China without close partners as the global challenger to the United States poses difficult problems for analysis that is always supposed to highlight a bright future for China. If in 2000 Russia could be dragged into the equation as China's triangular balance,[44] the situation was much grimmer in 2002. Now regionalism was desperately added to the equation, and the economics driving it were given more explanatory power to salvage China's situation. Yet, the Chinese emphasized the importance of a positive foreign policy, boosting bilateral ties with the United States politically, economically, militarily, and culturally. This was a message of approval for multilateral participation, not of openly challenging United States–entrenched interests. Entering WTO, preparing for the Olympics, and joining in the antiterror effort at the outset, China could remain positive while relying on its economy above all.

Previous Chinese notions that stood in the way of regionalism lose their priority in the new logic. These include focusing relations with Russia on great-power opposition to the United States, playing up rivalry with Japan for regional leadership, allowing the goal of a security balance in Korea to slow regional cooperation, and concentrating on bilateral relations at the expense

[43] Zhang Weijun, "2001 nian woguo xueshu qikan Yatai yanjiu congshu," *Dangdai Yatai*, 2 (2002), p. 64.

[44] Wang Jincun, "Shijie daguo guanxi dongxiang," in Li Shenming and Wang Yizhou, eds., *2001 nian: quanqiu zhengzhi yu anquan baogao* (Beijing: Shehui kexue wenxian chubanshe, 2001), p. 50.

of multilateralism. At last, the necessity of regionalism along the lines of the EU from both a geopolitical and an economic point of view was undeniable.

Reduced in its foreign-policy options, China rescued its partnership with Russia if in a narrower purview, reduced its expectations for North Korea while supporting its minimal survival, expanded its regional cooperation with South Korea, recommitted itself to improving ties with Japan, and looked for ways to lessen tensions with the United States. The first necessity was to block U.S. plans to tighten the noose of globalization on the region, and the second was to boost regionalism to balance, if only gradually, global pressure. Sandwiched between the U.S. desire for globalization without regionalism and North Korea's mind-set to avoid both, China targeted South Korea, Japan, and Russia as well as ASEAN for varying degrees of support in combining and balancing the two.

The spotlight returned to Northeast China in September 2002 when Pyongyang announced a plan to create a special autonomous zone managed by a Chinese at Shinuiju on the border with China next to the Liaodong peninsula. This spot had the most promise to attract Chinese as well as South Korean and Japanese capital. Rather than the Sea of Japan, the Bohai and Yellow Seas would get a boost as the meeting place of regional commerce. In only weeks the idea had been eclipsed, however, by Beijing's arrest of the Chinese businessman named to head the zone and the crisis over nuclear weapons. After all, North Korea was not serious about reform.

The Chinese appreciated the need to lead the pursuit of regionalism indirectly, biding their time while envisioning an ever-growing geographical range. Without openly setting forth a long-term strategy, they seemed to look ahead to a coastal axis centered in Shanghai with Hong Kong and Guangzhou at one end and Beijing and Tianjin at the other. Nearby South Korea and Taiwan form the two wings, each running a huge trade surplus while investing heavily in mainland enterprises. Further out Japan is one leg, and ASEAN could comprise another leg. North Korea and the Russian Far East with Eastern Siberia, although weak economically, can along with areas of inland China round out the skeleton of this evolving region, which may be called East Asia.[45]

Chinese analysts were groping for a strategy to achieve regionalism. First, they had to minimize U.S. opposition, agreeing to more cooperation and greater congruity between global and regional goals. Second, they had to overcome Japanese hesitation, both by healthy competition to establish FTAs with ASEAN countries and by deeper forward-looking cooperation. The Chinese paid closer attention to the lessons of the EU in economics gradually creating closer bonds, in security gradually reducing fears of mutual threats, and in culture gradually building on historical roots. Having failed to nourish

[45] Yang Guiyan, "Dongya gainian bianzhe," *Dangdai Yatai*, 2 (2002), p. 21.

the strong roots of shared culture in the late imperial era and the nineteenth and twentieth centuries, East Asian nations had a long way to go to catch up to the Europeans who, even in most periods of sharp interstate rivalry, had kept developing their cultural linkages.

In 2000 the Chinese began to acknowledge the importance of Japan for the Russian economy, especially that of the Far East. And they went further to argue that as Moscow strives to restore its great-power status it is turning increasingly to Japan for East-West balance after new contradictions with the United States and the West arose in the late 1990s. Already in 1997 Japan's support had enabled Russia to become a full member of the G-8 and APEC, but Russia still recognized that the fact its relations with Japan continued to be the weakest great-power link hurt its standing in the Asia-Pacific and its ability to balance East and West. One Chinese analysis made it clear that Russia will be a big winner if there is a breakthrough in ties to Japan. Japan too, the argument continues, recognized by 1996 that the dead end with Russia was its worst diplomatic dilemma. It seeks a regional great-power balance for dealing with North Korea, the South China Sea, and China. No longer does Japan regard ties with the United States as sufficient; it plans to use the Russia card to control China.[46] Regionalism suggested a way for China to manage this reality.

In the first months of 2003 China faced four new challenges to its more subtle strategy of gradual regionalism without arousing alarm over its gradual ascent. First came Japan's new eagerness to develop an energy partnership with Russia that would lead to construction of a pipeline around Heilongjiang province to Nakhodka, bypassing China. Suddenly, the Chinese grew fearful of a Russo-Japanese deal with geopolitical as well as economic consequences.[47] Second, the North Korean decision to abandon all restraints on the development of nuclear weapons caused a crisis in which China feared spiraling decisions in favor of nuclear arms in Japan and South Korea and U.S. pressure for China to impose economic sanctions on the North. The security situation was unraveling in NEA, and China was forced to consider a more active role, beginning with three-party talks in Beijing involving the United States and the North. Third, the rapid victory of U.S. forces in Iraq without United Nations Security Council approval emboldened Washington in its global leadership while raising more doubt about what might be done for balance. Japan's approval and Russia's more strident objections than China left more uncertainty over any regional consensus on global security. Finally, the Severe Acute Respiratory Syndrome (SARS) epidemic not only cast China's cover-up and failure to contain the virus in a bad light, it also

[46] Lin Xiaoguang, "Rie guanxi: 90 niandai yilai de fazhan yu bianhua," *Dongbeiya yanjiu*, 4 (2000), pp. 28–36.

[47] Yoshida Susumu, "Koizumi shusho horo (2003 nen 1 gatsu) to enerugi mondai," *ERINA Report*, 51 (April 2003), pp. 6–9.

drastically reduced travel in the region. China's cross-border traffic with the Russian Far East was briefly interrupted. Clearly, Beijing could not lead NEA to regionalism until its leadership faced the North Korean crisis.

Beijing had wanted to keep security concerns alive in order to block globalization of economic ties from spreading to all-around globalization. Yet, when security took center stage, Beijing found that it could not resist more globalization. In 1999 it was left isolated at the end of the Kosovo War, in 2001 it found Russia siding closely with the United States, and in 2003 Japan drew closer to the United States. While the North Korean nuclear crisis continued, China was on the spot with little optimism that it could balance U.S. power. For some, this offered an opportunity to abandon wishful thinking and rethink the cult of victimization, taking advantage of successful modernization to accept regionalism along with globalization.[48] For others, it put China in even more danger from globalization.

If the 15th Party Congress moved China away from an East Asian model of state-centered development, the 16th Congress called for a more balanced approach as social modernization and even political reform gained some support. In addition to a pragmatic foreign policy highlighting stability in surrounding areas, it laid the groundwork for new steps to reduce the vast inequalities across the country, such as in urban-rural differences. Soon there was talk of increased priority to Northeast China, where social problems are severe and integration into global and regional economies trails expectations. This adds to Chinese interest in resolving the North Korean crisis and accelerating regionalism.

China and Japan

Sobered by the broad strategic picture, China proceeded with restraint even as Japan, under increased nationalist pressure, kept arousing Chinese public opinion. There were sound economic reasons for cooling passions: Tokyo was preparing cuts in ODA amidst calls that all ODA to China be halted; and Japanese firms were accelerating investment in China that could be jeopardized. Also, the problematic state of relations with the United States in 2001 left China anxious to keep Japan from joining in a containment strategy. Moreover, as the Chinese assessed the nationalist drift in Japanese politics and the loss of former bastions of political support for steady bilateral ties, they appreciated that a downward spiral could be hard to stop. Finally, the Chinese side calculated that it needed Japan for regionalism, and, given the requirements of a troubled Japanese economy and the disarray in foreign policy, even in Japan forces of regionalism would likely prevail.

48 *Huanqiu ribao*, September 2, 2002, p. 4.

For China and Japan the crux of the concern over regionalism boils down to leadership. In the first half of the 1990s the Chinese were skeptical about it because they assumed that it meant Japanese leadership, which was unacceptable. Of late, the Japanese argue that the Chinese think that China will become the nucleus of the region, and most Japanese are reluctant to accept this. Increasingly, however, many acknowledge that regionalism will sooner or later lead to this outcome and to China's superior position. One analyst warned that as China opens up with WTO mostly in areas where the United States is strong, such as agriculture, the Internet, automobiles, and information, it is bound to find other ways to eclipse Japan. Moreover, linkages between the American Chinese and China will also leave Japan on the sidelines.[49] Insecurity about their own economic prospects drives Japanese fear of either integrating too much with China and enabling it to gain regional superiority or staying aloof and allowing the United States and China to prosper together.

Giving confidence to the Chinese in 2000–2 was the upsurge of investment by large Japanese companies, including auto and electronics giants, bringing more high technology. Facing fierce competition for the Chinese market from the United States and EU, whose big-name firms had been coming earlier, Japanese firms also moved beyond an export orientation. The Chinese state worked hard to restrain public opinion in order to keep relations on an even keel centered on economic ties. They took credit for a calming effect even as bombshells kept appearing in the news from Japan. Yet, they were chagrined that on the Japanese side the soothing voices of experts were few and far between and even the business lobby paled before its U.S. counterpart, while rightists were monopolizing the discourse. It appeared that the Chinese debate had decided that economic development, not historical justice, is the principal national interest. The Chinese looked, to little avail, for comparable strategic thinking on the Japanese side.

As Japanese expectations for leadership receded, Chinese experts found it easier to accept Japan as a partner in regionalism. Step by step, Japan abandoned its notions of superiority, such as the flying geese model of manufacturing division of labor, as high-tech firms were stampeding into China. When Chinese exports overtook the U.S. total to Japan, the Chinese grew newly confident that Japan was becoming dependent on China's development and regionalism could be achieved without China's subordination.

After years of overrating Japan's economy, the Chinese had generally grown doubtful by 2002, arguing that Japan has lost not only one decade, but also is facing a second lost decade.[50] Accompanying this assessment were

49 Fujino Fumiaki and Fujimura Takayoshi, "WTO no kameigo no Chugoku o yosokusuru," *Gaiko forum*, 2 (2001), pp. 36–7.

50 Lu Jianren, "Shijie he Dongya jingji de xianzhuang yu qianjing," *Dangdai Yatai*, 2 (2002), p. 23.

arguments that Japan on its own could not escape long-term stagnation. It would have to seek all-around economic cooperation with China, which is becoming the center of a regional development framework as the only way to achieve new growth.[51] Regional hopes see China as an economic magnet.

After the leaders of Japan and South Korea launched a study group in September 2000 aimed at an FTA and China followed in 2001 with an appeal for an FTA with ASEAN states in ten years, the question of Sino-Japanese agreement on an FTA loomed in the background. The main bottleneck is agriculture.[52] Chinese exports of labor-intensive farm products including vegetables, fruits, and flowers already appear threatening and could grow very fast. In addition, recent hollowing out of manufacturing leaves the Japanese fearful that their country will be less competitive than China after barriers have fallen. Nervous about globalization because of the power of vested interests, the Japanese have reservations over regionalism too.

Beijing faces the challenge of getting Tokyo's attention in order to boost regionalism. The fact that Japan hastily countered with an FTA proposal of its own to ASEAN proved to the Chinese that competition works. The Chinese are also removing the barrier in their minds between economics and security, recognizing that one influences the other. They must make progress simultaneously on both fronts to create a climate for regionalism. If this was easier for a time with SEA, then Beijing's attention turned there, but the primary goal is to convince Japan that it needs to forge a multilateral regional grouping. The North Korean nuclear crisis put NEA security on the agenda too.

Since June 1989 China's central concern has been isolation. In a regional as well as a global context it feared that it lacked allies and would be pressured to accept what others demanded. Its change of heart toward regionalism can be attributed to greater self-confidence after relations had improved with many countries and China's economy had kept growing faster than other economies, but it also should be linked to desperation that other options were disappearing. The key to regionalism, of course, is Japan; just as the key to great-power relations favored through 1999 had been Russia. Having failed to improve relations with Japan significantly through "smile diplomacy" in 1999–2001 and through formalization of the triangle with South Korea linked to ASEAN +3 summits, the Chinese groped for a new approach. It has to appeal to Japan's economic interests as that country struggles to escape from its slump. It must reassure Japan on security now that the Japanese public has grown nervous about that. And China needs to manage the triangle with the United States, which has become a more

51 Zhang Weijun, "2001 nian woguo xueshu qikan Yatai yanjiu congshu," *Dangdai Yatai*, 2 (2002), p. 64.

52 Obi Mineo, "Isogareru Hokuto Ajia no keizai anzen hosho koso," *Gekkan jiyu minshu*, December 2002, p. 62.

assertive driving force. Perhaps, the Sino-U.S.-Japanese triangle will even displace the "strategic" Sino-U.S.-Russian triangle at the center of Beijing's attention.

The Chinese intensified calls for strengthening ties to Japan, exploring ways to reach this goal. Much of the emphasis centers on economics and cultural exchanges, for instance building on exchanges of young leaders to find successors to the old guard that had played an instrumental role in the 1970s and 1980s. But there was also increasing talk of solidifying bilateral ties as part of a regional community and trying to get the public to understand the ambivalence of Japan's need for alliance with the United States and resistance to the United States.[53] The message is that the Chinese must appeal to Japan in new ways, while showing more patience toward Japan's enduring close ties to the United States. Yet, the Chinese also spoke of the need to be patient in the face of the assertiveness of Japanese hardliners. They must avoid tit-for-tat exchanges. Although smile diplomacy has limited effect, a harder line could further unbalance public opinion.[54] This reasoning is buttressed by assessments that Japan's right wing is quite limited, while the large business class narrowly concentrates on economic matters and proceeds without serious bias against China.

Beijing's decision to intensify cooperation with Japan and brush aside to the extent possible Japanese dalliance with nationalist causes came well before 9/11. It agreed to a currency swap, adding finances to trade, investment, and ODA as economic linkages. It fretted at the way global currents in 2001 affected regional and national ones, deciding that a stronger region is needed as China becomes ever more globalized. At the same time, the Chinese calculated that the Japanese elite had abandoned its view that China should not grow very fast by accepting the inevitability of China's economic ascension and began focusing primarily on what will help Japan's economic turnabout. Both sides have decided that they cannot leave each other and their shared region. China's peace and development group is in the majority and it is now intent on regionalism. It intends to prod Japan forward by appealing more to potential partners. Fear of losing the region may force Japan's hand, just as fear of isolation has been forcing China's hand.

Chinese experts carefully trace debates in Japan on the direction of foreign policy. They have followed thinking about "Asianism," including the interest in riding the rise of Asian economies while shedding dependence on the United States, that only somewhat faded with the Asian financial crisis. Lately, they detected instead a tendency to hitch a ride with U.S. military power in order to expand military options and to revise the constitution, reserving the option of later escaping from U.S. control. After 9/11 the Chinese

[53] Jin Xide, "21 shijichu Zhongri guanxi de tezheng yu keti," *Riben xuekan*, 4 (2002), pp. 60–2.

[54] Gilbert Rozman, "China's Changing Images of Japan 1989–2001: The Struggle to Balance Partnership and Rivalry," *International Relations of the Asia-Pacific*, Winter 2002, pp. 95–129.

noted that hawks became more active, suggesting that under the slogan of internationalism neo-nationalism is intensifying.[55] Such analysis is sobering for regionalism, but other arguments counter it.

When the textbook issue arose in late 2000 and early 2001 Chinese comments showed restraint, but after Diet members made provocative statements such as that the Greater East Asian War ended colonialism in Asia and the Japanese government made clear that this time proposed revisions from abroad would not be a political concern, the Chinese attitude changed. On February 27, 2001 *Jiefang junbao* asked how a country that lacked the courage to look squarely at its history could win the trust of its neighbors.[56] The mood in China was hardening after more than a year of "smile diplomacy." Yet, the state did not allow occasional flashes of outrage to detract it from renewed pursuit of Japan in an atmosphere where alarm over U.S. hegemonism eclipsed all other issues.

Sino-Japanese relations soured in the first months of 2001 due not only to textbook revisions in Japan but also to what the Chinese called discrimination by Japanese firms and the Japanese called the "bashing of Japanese companies." Some Chinese media demanded an apology from both JAL and ANA for forcing Chinese passengers to spend the night in Japanese airports while treating other passengers differently. After Mitsubishi Motors recalled cars in the United States but refused to recall similar models in China an outcry arose. Matsushita refused to honor consumer claims over defective cellular phones in China in a similar manner.[57] Even as the Chinese government was striving to quiet criticism of Japan, consumer consciousness offered fertile soil for complaints.[58]

The Chinese media painted a picture in the spring of 2001 of a country repeatedly beleaguered by the United States and Japan. While the greatest alarm was reserved for the new Bush administration – its spy plane accident, missile plans, and added support for Taiwan topped the list –, Japan drew comparable criticisms whenever the United States slipped from the headlines. The problems ranged from Japanese textbook revisions and the visit of Lee Teng-Hui from Taiwan to an agricultural trade war and the election of a prime minister promising to visit the Yasukuni shrine on August 15. Sino-Japanese relations had cooled noticeably.[59] Yet, Chinese leaders showed restraint and, after the global political climate changed in September 2001, resumed their efforts at strengthening relations with Japan.

55 Jin Xide, "Lengzhanhou Riben duiwai zhanlue lunzheng," *Shijie jingji yu zhengzhi*, 11 (2001), pp. 61–5.

56 *Tokyo shimbun*, February 28, 2001, p. 3.

57 "Chugoku de hirogaru Nihon kigyo basshingu wa Chugoku seifu no hannichi seisaku no tsuge," *Zaikai tempo*, 5 (2001), pp. 17–18.

58 *Yomiuri shimbun*, February 24, 2001, p. 6.

59 *Mainichi shimbun*, April 21, 2001, p. 7.

There was a curious ambivalence to Chinese coverage of Japan. On the one hand, one report after another discussed Japan's drift to the right, linking the rise of nationalism to a loss of self-confidence. They depicted growing internal debates on a China threat and increasing inclinations to use Taiwan and the Senkaku Islands to contain China. When before 9/11 Japan joined the United States in warnings about North Korea, the Chinese attributed it to a desire to increase its influence on the Korean peninsula relative to China. On the other hand, the Chinese kept warning that they must not panic at Japan's drift and must avoid arousing public opinion in Japan. Instead they should develop mature relations. This means future-oriented ties, accepting Japan's existing economic strength, and even spiritually preparing the Chinese to accept a Japan with stronger political power.[60] After 9/11 when the Chinese feared that the United States would extend its crusade to North Korea and Japan would seize the opportunity to boost its military as well as political power, writers warned that the stability of all of NEA could be disrupted. If Japan's conduct appeared threatening, the cautious advice that followed was to boost great-power coordination with Japan and Russia and build on shared thinking about Korea.[61] Despite many troubles, the Chinese recognized that common interests predominate in bilateral ties. Rather than again imagining that China could somehow get either Japan or the United States to draw closer and create balanced triangular relations, Beijing had decided that one key to ties with Tokyo lies in the way it manages ties to Washington.[62]

Japanese conservatives were divided on China. A vocal group went increasingly on the offensive, denouncing China as a threat and abandoning hope for regionalism. Also suspicious of South Korea for its worldview, they could not anticipate a form of regionalism that might work. In contrast, most of the old establishment, led by former prime ministers such as Hashimoto Ryutaro and Nakasone Yasuhiro, kept trying to repair relations with China. In July 2002 Nakasone gave an interview to a Chinese newspaper that called for Tokyo to adopt a realistic, independent, multisided diplomacy that did not brand China as a threat. It gave a positive cast to Chinese motives, aimed at continued peace and development, and objected only at being humiliated. Nakasone called on Japan to forego development of nuclear weapons, and now, after a decade of drift, to formulate a future-oriented strategic diplomacy with priority to China as well as the United States but assuring that Japan speaks with its own voice. Praising the currency swap agreement, he appealed for joining with China in developing an East Asian economic

60 Shen Haitao, "Koizumi neikaku de zhengce quxiang yu Zhongri guanxi de qianjing," *Dongbeiya luntan*, 3 (2001), pp. 64–8.

61 Gao Ke, "'9/11 shijian' yu Dongbeiya diqujian de daguo guanxi," *Dongbeiya luntan*, 1 (2002), p. 61.

62 Qiu Xiuhua, "Xin shiji Zhongri guanxi fazhan de jiben qushi," *Dongbeiya luntan*, 2 (2002), p. 18.

sphere coupled with greater security cooperation.[63] Regionalism focused on China and South Korea remained a goal among many conservatives as well as across the rest of the Japanese political spectrum.

The Japanese ambassador to China, Taniya Sadaro, faulted Chinese education for not teaching about postwar Japan and said that if the Japanese side keeps apologizing to the Chinese it demeans the Japanese people. He and others also accused China of saying that Japan's defense expenditures are several times those of China, while omitting much of its own budget. Yet, unlike the right wing, diplomats call for constructive relations: mature, stable, not excessively emotional ones. They also take note of improvements. In 2000 when coverage of Japan notably improved, many Japanese politicians visited China.[64] Accused at home of being soft on China, the "China school" of diplomats worked with a silent majority of politicians to keep both sides from overreacting to perceived slights.[65]

Some China experts in Japan found the demonization of that country excessive. In the midst of a new peak in tension Kokubun Ryosei bucked the tide, reporting that the reality was that the Chinese were most concerned with globalization and regime stability on the eve of entrance into the WTO. Considering the defense burden of the Soviet Union in the arms race with the United States to have been a cause of its breakup, they do not relish a similar race. Kokubun warned that Japan was becoming too isolated in its relations with East Asia, defending new textbooks that are offensive to China and Korea, initiating safeguards against Chinese goods, and issuing a visa to Taiwan's former president.[66]

Articles in the journal *Sekai* made the case for sustaining Sino-Japanese relations in 2001. One author argued: 1) some people are exaggerating the bad atmosphere, leading to misperceptions; 2) China is entering international society, and the Japanese are losing sight of what ODA has accomplished for its modernization and continues to do, including environmental changes good also for Japan; 3) a suffering Japanese economy benefits from China becoming an economic great power, while not needing to fear a low per capita GNP, a very unequal income distribution across the country, and still severe poverty of less than a dollar a day among more than 200 million people; and 4) China's military budget is less than Japan's and a smaller part of the national income than in Western Europe.[67] Takemi Keizo, a Diet member and subcommittee chair on the Asia-Pacific, stressed China's positive shift

[63] *Huanqiu shibao*, July 4, 2002, p. 2.

[64] *Sankei shimbun*, December 8, 2000.

[65] Gilbert Rozman, "Japan's Images of China in the 1990s: Are They Ready for China's 'Smile Diplomacy' or Bush's 'Strong Diplomacy'?" *Japanese Journal of Political Science*, 2, pt. 1 (May 2001), pp. 97–125.

[66] *Asahi shimbun*, April 18, 2001, p. 13.

[67] Miyazaki Isamu, "Watakushitachi wa Chugoku no ima o," *Sekai*, March 2001, pp. 81–7.

toward recognizing Japan's role as a partner. He urged that Japan redouble its efforts to improve relations independent of politicians, using economic ties following international rules and cultural ties especially by reaching the younger generation. Takemi also noted his regret that Chinese youth are learning about the world through the United States because Beijing bookstores display the history of invasion in the Japan corner and MBA and TOEFL test materials in the U.S. corner.[68]

On Hainan Island the founding session of the Asian Boao Forum occurred in late February 2001, intended to parallel the Davos Forum at which global leaders gather. When former Prime Minister Nakasone Yasuhiro met Jiang Zemin the talk turned to 2002 when China and Japan would celebrate the thirtieth anniversary of normalization. With a vicious cycle of negative mutual images unfolding again, observers asked whether the two sides would find a way to use the anniversary to turn things around and if Nakasone, who had formed ties with Hu Yaobang, is the only politician left who is remembered for building up relations. Ironically, one of the charges when Hu had been purged was that he had grown too close to Nakasone.[69] A year later Koizumi attended the forum, legitimating its regional thrust and reinforcing the message that China is not a threat and more effort must be made to improve relations. Nakasone had paved the way, but many worried that no younger politician was positioned to play a similar role.

Which politicians would step up as the new "pipes" for relations with China? Given the hereditary character of Japanese electoral politics, offspring of prime ministers were waiting in the wings. In 1997 Sato Shinji, son of Sato Eisaku, who built close ties with the Kuomintang in the 1960s, led a seventeen-member Diet delegation to Taipei just before entering the Hashimoto cabinet as Minister of International Trade and Industry.[70] In 2001 Tanaka Makiko, daughter of Tanaka Kakuei, who normalized relations with Beijing, became Foreign Minister amidst expectations that she could draw on a special bond with China. Even before her fortunes faded quickly she faced a rival in Fukuda Yasuo, the son of Fukuda Takeo, her father's chief opponent, who as Cabinet Secretary under Koizumi was wresting control over foreign relations from the divided and discredited Foreign Ministry. In 2003 Abe Shinzo, son of Abe Shintaro who had attempted a breakthrough with Moscow, rode a hard-line position on North Korea to eclipse Fukuda.

Some in Japan detected in China's cooperation with the United States in the war against terror and in later meetings of leaders of the two states a warming trend not altogether favorable for Japan.[71] Again Japanese

[68] Takemi Keizo, "Shinrai kankei o do kochiku suruka?" *Sekai*, March 2001, pp. 88–93.

[69] *Asahi shimbun*, March 1, 2001, p. 14.

[70] "Media Eye Foresees New Era in Japanese Relations," *The Free China Journal*, May 9, 1997, p. 7.

[71] Shu Kenei, "Hu Yaobang hobei de kyusekkinsuru Chugoku to Amerika," *Ronza*, August 2002, pp. 144–9.

diplomacy appeared to be on the sidelines, while low self-confidence contributed to a fear of the consequences of a China not focused on balancing U.S. power. Yet, most attention turned to U.S. unilateralism and the limits it placed on Japanese policy options. Aware of this frustration, the Chinese posted at the end of 2002 their first unequivocal self-critique of the habit of criticizing Japan. It insisted that Japan has become a reliable partner for the future; reminders of its past no longer served a constructive purpose.[72] Coming on the heels of an upturn in relations with the United States, this appeal to put the "history card" to rest reinforced a strategy for regionalism along with globalization, downplaying overt moves to forge a balance of power to check any rival.

A conference in Beijing on July 8, 2003 discussed "new thinking" on the occasion of the twenty-fifth anniversary of the peace treaty between China and Japan. It pointed to new diplomatic logic in China from the 16th Party Congress, a new era of the United States as the sole superpower, and the urgency of new regional economic integration that is testing the two countries. Many presentations stressed how important it is to achieve a breakthrough, offering diverse approaches.[73] Through the autumn the influential newspaper *Huanqiu shibao* carried many articles on Japan, stressing that Koizumi also needs a peaceful international environment and FTAs, as seen at the Bali ASEAN +3 meeting, despite the nationalist tone increasingly prevalent in Japan.[74] If China is meeting with some success in cooperation with SEA, its weakness in NEA has only become more apparent, for which Japan's role is vital. Having decided to give greater priority to surrounding areas, Beijing naturally redoubled efforts to improve relations with Japan. Yet, it also sought to correct the simplistic response to recent Chinese reassessments of past mistakes toward Japan by arguing that both sides would have to give ground. The Japanese need "new thinking" too.

New issues almost every month were proof that hypersensitive bilateral relations are prone to easy misunderstandings. Long-buried Japanese chemical weapons were uncovered with loss of life; group prostitution in Zhuhai caused an uproar; Japanese exchange students performed a risqué skit that drove Chinese students to demonstrate; and Toyota used poor judgment in an ad that showed Chinese stone lions bowing to a Japanese SUV. Only both countries working together in what Kokubun Ryosei calls "grownup" relations could make headway in breaking this vicious cycle.[75] A looming crisis over a Taiwan election-day referendum in March 2004 on top of the crisis over North Korea could serve as a wake-up call to Japan as it remains

72 Ma Licheng, "A New Mode of Thinking on China's Relations with Japan," *Strategy and Management*, 6 (2002), pp. 41–7.

73 Wang Yizhou, "Zhongri guanxi de shige wenti," *Shijie jingji yu zhengzhi*, September 2003, pp. 8–9.

74 *Huanqiu shibao*, September 12, 2003, p. 15, and October 13, 2003, p. 2.

75 *Nihon keizai shimbun*, November 28, 2003, p. 21.

ambivalent over China. China needs to sustain the active diplomacy of 2003 that drew the United States closer.

China's pursuit of economic ties was not interrupted by the nuclear weapons crisis over North Korea. With security in the forefront, relations with the United States again became the backdrop for regionalism, as did improving ties with Russia. Yet, in the first half of 2003 more articles by experts on strategic relations insisted that China should no longer view Japan through the historical lens, but instead should regard it as essential for future economic, political, and even military objectives. It should be a strategic partner, even if many Chinese citizens are not ready to think that way. After joining in June on the sidelines of the Evian G-8 summit, China appeared to show new interest in becoming part of an expanded G-9, overcoming the fear of being humiliated as a weak member of a group that could undermine the United Nations Security Council where China carries a veto. Now there was hope that it could join Japan as Asian representatives in the G-9 and use that forum to strengthen a partnership of regional leaders. While Japan was far from dropping its opposition, even the conservative *Yomiuri shimbun* had credited China for its handling of North Korea and other foreign policies as a "responsible great-power" increasingly entering international society.[76] Japan's need for China's cooperation was growing.

The North Korean nuclear crisis loomed as the biggest test for China's value in creating a security community. The United States dominated the group of five countries preparing for negotiations with the North, but China and Japan also had a large say in working out the terms of any deal. In the geopolitics of the crisis, their influence and money as well as their vision of the future of the Korean peninsula play a significant role.[77] Sino-Japanese relations may be strained by increased military activism on both sides, but they are also given new impetus from a sense of shared problems and increased interdependence.[78]

Russia and Regionalism

Vladimir Putin firmly established his leadership in Russia, leaving his mark on foreign as well as domestic policy. Yet, his strategy in NEA remained unclear through 2003. Articulating a strategy should prove important for three of his important goals: 1) economic revival of Russia, in which Moscow and Western Siberian oil and gas sent to Europe are not alone as engines of

[76] *Yomiuri shimbun*, June 2, 2003, p. 1.

[77] Gilbert Rozman, "The Geopolitics of the North Korean Nuclear Crisis," in Richard J. Ellings and Aaron L. Friedberg, eds., *Strategic Asia 2003–04: Fragility and Crisis* (Seattle: The National Bureau of Asian Research, 2003), pp. 245–61.

[78] Gilbert Rozman, "Sino-Japanese Relations: Mutual Images and the Balance between Globalization and Regionalism," *Woodrow Wilson International Center, Asia Program Special Report* 113, July 2003, pp. 8–13.

growth; 2) entry into the Asia-Pacific region, allowing two-headed Russia to balance Europe and Asia and, within Asia, to deal with other great powers with clout; and 3) reassertion of Russian national identity as a strong, centralized state without danger of separatism or peripheral regions in crisis. Through adjusting policies toward the other five actors in NEA Putin aimed to boost Russia's role in the region after a decade of lesser significance. Yet, downgrading China, harnessing North Korea, normalizing with Japan, and finding common ground with the United States while using South Korea's initiatives for the peninsula and the region proved to be a tall order.[79]

Russia emerged as an energy heavyweight, in 2002 becoming the largest producer of oil as well as gas and searching for additional markets for anticipated, vast production increases. The Russian Far East stood poised to enhance Russia's energy clout both from its own offshore production and through pipelines from Siberia. A test for the center's commitment to regionalism was the degree to which it would encourage Russian producers to invest the new profits from energy exports in the Far East as well and assure foreign companies of the safety of long-term costly projects. Once the capital was approved, it would be essential also to arrange for young physical labor to lay the pipelines and construct the additional infrastructure for energy-led development. Giving the aging and declining population of the Russian Far East, much of the labor would have to be imported, presumably from nearby China or even North Korea. Through the flow of capital and labor connected to energy, the Russian Far East stood a chance of becoming an indispensable part of regionalism if Putin and the governors agreed on a strategy.

Before opening the Far East to regionalism, Putin faced the challenge of bringing it more fully under Moscow's supervision and cleaning up its wild reputation for abusing foreign investors and misusing export revenues. At first, he did not have a determining voice over affairs in the area. Efforts to elect trustworthy governors and to impose strong controls over illegality did not fare well. Battles continued over both diamonds and crabs, exports of which topped $1 billion each at times. In the fall of 2002 the formula was changed for diamonds, raising the federal share from 32 to 37 percent of the revenue, as a foundation for veterans that had kept its 5 percent share mostly for its own members was dissolved. Another 30 percent went to the Sakha Republic and 8 percent was split among eight local governments. In the case of crabs, however, the criminals were still fighting over the spoils, as seen in a December 2002 gun battle in Pusan harbor in South Korea between crab-catching ships linked to Sergei Darkin, the current governor of Primorskii krai, and those tied to former governor Nazdratenko, then serving as head of the Russian State Fisheries Committee. Russia still lacked a promising environment.

[79] Gilbert Rozman, "Russian Foreign Policy in Northeast Asia," in Sam Kim, ed., *The International Relations of Northeast Asia* (Rowman and Littlefield, 2003), pp. 201–24.

All of Russia's neighbors in NEA welcomed Putin's centralizing tendencies. They saw these tendencies both as a means to improve top-level relations through a leader who could deliver and as a necessity for disciplining nettlesome local leaders in the Russian Far East. Yet, some of their ideas were slow to inspire confidence in Russia. China's notion of a natural economic territory, reverting to the pre-Stalin days when Chinese small businessmen operated in large numbers across the border, was now changing to recognize the essential role of large, stable business firms. If the Japanese could draw some inspiration from the 1960s when large projects to develop and export natural resources received firm Russian government support, they too were adjusting to the fact that a multinational consortium would be needed in which Japan did not have a dominant voice. In the case of China, the switch in Russo-U.S. relations after 9/11 made it clear that regionalism would not stress bilateralism. After 9/11, it was obvious that these ties no longer represent something special for Russian foreign policy.[80] Putin was steering ties toward NEA regionalism, accepting globalization as a balancing force and waiting for agreement on the Korean peninsula.[81]

Putin made his greatest mark on thinking about regionalism in NEA in 2001–2 not through ties with the three principal actors within the region, but through relations with the United States and North Korea. His pronounced shift toward strategic cooperation with the Bush administration impressed on others, particularly the Chinese, that globalization encompasses security as well as WTO. It stimulated more realistic thinking about the nexus between regionalism and globalization. Moreover, discussions with Washington about cooperation for energy security boosted Moscow's influence not only as a global force, but also as the bridge to NEA in a position to provide for long-term energy security should the countries of the region agree on a massive investment program. Sino-Russian, Korean-Russian, and Japanese-Russian meetings all featured talks about such a program. China and Japan competed, and pipeline construction seemed to be coming soon.

There was little consensus among foreign-policy experts on the impact of rising U.S. assertiveness after 9/11 on Russian strategy in NEA.[82] The importance of a security system in the region drew heightened attention, as did the increasing prospect of working with the United States toward this end. With various powers searching for new answers to security questions, Russia could expect to raise its profile while obtaining more understanding of

[80] Wang Bingyin and Zhou Yanli, "Shiheng de Eluosi Yatai zhengce," *Guoji zhengzhi*, 10 (2000), pp. 79–82.

[81] V. V. Mikheev, *Globalizatsiia i Aziatskii regionalism: vyzovy dlia Rossii* (Moscow: Institut Dal'nego Vostoka, RAN, 2001).

[82] V. Kuznetsova, "Sobytiia 11 Sentabria i problemy bezopasnosti v ATR," *MEiMO*, 12 (2002), pp. 93–7.

its positions from the states of the region.[83] Yet, wishful thinking about riding the North Korean threat clouded most reasoning about Russia's chances for gaining influence.

When the North Korean nuclear crisis occurred, the spotlight also included Russia as the country with the closest ties to the North. South Korea sent diplomats to Russia as well as China in search of help in bringing the North to the negotiating table. Japan saw Putin as a factor in dealing with the North as it prepared for a summit meeting. With new concern about security as an essential foundation for regionalism, Russia's stock rose in discussion about long-term arrangements for NEA. Keen on establishing its own base of power independent of the United States, Russia had good reason to look hopefully to this region. After an unsuccessful diplomatic gambit in January 2003 when a Russian official went to Pyongyang to restart negotiations, Moscow was left on the sidelines for six months. It had helped the North become overconfident, becoming the "lawyer to the devil," without anticipating how dangerous the trial would become.[84] In August, however, when China pressed North Korea to join multilateral talks, it was the North that insisted that Russia be one of the six parties and even enabled Russia to announce its agreement to talk. Moscow was still depending on Pyongyang to keep it fully involved in resolving the crisis, but it also gained credit in Washington by standing firmly against a nuclear North.

In the 1990s world elite gathered at Davos used to worry about the uncertain state of Russian reforms and globalization. Russia did not have to face such scrutiny after 9/11 and years of sustained economic growth. Yet, uncertainties about Russia persisted, not the least in NEA where Russia's energy supplies, balance of partnerships, and handling of the quest for regional security were still in flux. Despite widespread acknowledgment of the rise of regions in foreign affairs, Russians have to clarify how this can become a "belt of good neighborliness" in contrast to U.S. polemics about an "axis of evil."[85] For some, including Evgenii Primakov, this meant drawing countries of the region together to resist U.S. unilateralism at the same time as Russia eliminates barriers to investment.[86] To others, it meant accepting as part of accelerated globalization a diminished role for power balances and efforts to limit U.S. leadership. If the Iraq war showed Russia and the United States in disagreement with the former careful to align itself with others opposed to the U.S. invasion without a United Nations mandate, the North Korean crisis revealed an

83 A. V. Boliatko, "Strategicheskaia situatsiia v Aziatsko-Tikhookeanskom regione i antiterroristicheskaia kampaniia," in *Rossiia i ATR: bezopasnost', sotrudnichestvo, razvitie* (Moscow: Institut Dal'nego Vostoka, RAN, 2002), p. 14.

84 Georgii Kunadze, "V poze agressivnogo nishchego," *Novoe vremia*, 4 (2003), p. 26.

85 *Nezavisimaia gazeta*, January 23, 2003, p. 3.

86 *Rossiiskaia gazeta*, January 23, 2003, p. 4.

unobtrusive Russia waiting for a negotiated endgame in which it could gain some influence.

Russia's objectives for a gradual process of Korean reintegration as the central project of regionalism became increasingly clear under Putin's leadership. They had many dimensions: 1) security: the North would rely on Russia as a guarantor of any agreement; 2) transportation: the North would become a corridor for an extension of the Trans-Siberian railway, reviving Vladivostok and the coastal strip of the Russian Far East instead of being bypassed by routes through China; 3) energy: the North would become a corridor allowing pipelines to Nakhodka from Eastern Siberia and Sakhalin to fuel the region; and 4) balance: Russia would use both South and North Korea to deny China a dominant regional role and improve its position with Japan. When six-way talks began, much was at stake for Russia's emerging strategy in NEA.

With the crackdown on oligarchs started in the summer of 2003, the election of a compliant and nationalist State Duma in December, and consolidation of power over the media and other forces by a president on his way to reelection in March 2004, Russia was poised to assert a new development model with implications for regionalism. Putin could be expected to gain greater control over the Russian Far East, ending the fiefdoms of personal rule and its "lost decade." A candidate's dissertation in 2002 warned that Russia could be excluded from the emerging region without reorganization at home and active leadership abroad.[87] The way forward is to rely on South Korea as a natural partner, keep the United States involved, and find balance between China and Japan. No doubt, Putin would press to reallocate the resources of the area as well as new energy revenues. While reaffirming Russia's military presence, he would champion its economic interests. Saving the Far East had become a rationale for supporting open regionalism without China's control.

China and Russia

Beijing follows U.S.-Russian relations with rapt attention. It watched each step of the way as Putin responded first to Bush's increased unilateralism, including a tougher stance toward China, and then to the war against terror.[88] Masking its disappointment at the sudden loss of the pillar in its multipolar strategy, China's official voice changed direction in order to draw optimistic predictions for the new environment as well. This meant breaking down the artificial separation of economic globalization and great-power competition

[87] S. V. Sevast'ianov, *Modeli mezhdunarodnogo sotrudnichestva v Severo-Vostochnoi Azii: rol' mezhpravitel'stvennykh i nepravitel'stvennykh organizatsii* (Moscow: dissertation, MGIMO, 2002).

[88] Mei Zi, ed. *Meie guanxi dashi shilu (1991–2001)*, 2 (Beijing: Shishi chubanshe, 2002).

that had characterized Chinese writings in the 1990s. The Chinese switched their argument that Russia's declining national strength put it at such a disadvantage with the United States that it needed a close partnership with China to insist that national weakness makes it incumbent to turn to the United States and the West for help.[89] In the former logic, the United States was viewed as committed to making Russia even weaker. In the latter, it was seen as ready to help Russia. Economics replaced great-power reasoning. Diminished hopes for a Sino-Russian strategic partnership refocused China's calculations for regionalism.

To interpret Russia's actions, the Chinese upgraded the concept of economic security, while acknowledging that national interests dictate great-power cooperation in order to achieve stability for economic priorities. For its overall security, according to this logic, Russia has to concentrate on economics first, persuading foreign investors. The economic security argument also became the focus in discussions of energy projects that would in a new way make Russia a vital support to China's security. Now Russia was depicted as realistically giving preference to the United States and the West for a long time to come as the only means available to build up its comprehensive national power.[90] Because it is in China's long-term interest for that power to grow as a balance in world affairs, this is treated not as a blow to China's short-term need to forge a balance while it catches up and can rival the United States on its own but as a contribution to an eventual global balance. A long-term outlook on global power makes the case for regionalism more compelling.

A Japanese scholar best revealed the diversity of local interests in the Russian Far East and Eastern Siberia in dealing with China. Iwashita Akihiro divided areas into those concerned about territorial pretensions, those worried about immigration, and those that concentrated on economic gains.[91] After the demarcation process was completed in 1997, Khabarovsk continued to focus on the territorial issue, aware that two islands remain in dispute, while Amur oblast was still concerned about immigration. In contrast, the two areas with the major railroad lines into China, Chita and Primorskii krai, devoted their attention to boosting economic ties. Instead of viewing the Russian Far East as a monolith, he demonstrated that it is diverse and economic interests matter.

The overall Chinese trade deficit with Russia reached $17.5 billion from 1992 to 1999 and was growing faster as trade expanded from 2000.

[89] Su Ge, "Lun Zhongmeie guanxi," *Guoji wenti yanjiu,* 3 (2002), pp. 3–4.

[90] Tian Yungpan, "Eluosi diaozheng duimei zhengce de zhanlue yitu," *Dangdai shijie*, June 2002, pp. 10–11.

[91] Akihiro Iwashita, "The Influence of Local Russian Initiatives on Relations with China: Border Demarcation and Regional Partnership," *Acta Slavica Iaponica*, 19 (2002), pp. 1–18.

Although much shuttle trade reliant on Chinese exports went unrecorded, the Chinese complained about the cheap, low-quality goods that they primarily sold and the absence of their big-name companies. A few border points, especially Suifenhe in Heilongjiang near Primorskii krai, are booming with Russian consumers, but they do not serve China's goal of reaching high-income Russians and putting economic ties on the same solid footing that exists elsewhere.[92]

Some efforts were finally made to clean up the lawlessness in Sino-Russian cross-border ties with their attendant costs. One example came from Chita, where logs crossed into China. The Chinese reported that Russian authorities had decided to limit exports after smuggling had grown so enormously that various areas near railroad tracks were denuded and Russian lumber-processing companies had been bankrupted. Authorities had been overwhelmed by a combination of rapidly rising demand on the Chinese side after tighter environmental controls went into effect for domestic logging and ineffective control on the Russian side in the face of payoffs.[93] The challenge ahead remains considerable.

The Chinese migration into Russia continued to arouse concern in some circles even as it became more necessary. Through survey research and a review of Russian debates V. G. Gel'bras revealed the ambivalence in Russian attitudes.[94] Above all, across the Russian Far East there was a lack of confidence in how to cope with both migrants and the rising power of their neighboring country. Putin appeared concerned as well.

Zhu Rongji's visit to Russia on September 7–12, 2001 brought a set of agreements to intensify economic cooperation. In April a Russian business delegation visited China's economic centers, as the Chinese eagerly displayed quality products and pressed for direct ties between major firms. Uncertain of uninterrupted growth for exports to the West, China sought as well to expand in the Russian market. It wants to diversify exports, which are mostly foodstuffs and light textiles, whose value added is small and are not a priority in China's export development strategy. It also wants to prepare for reduced exports of fertilizers, steel, and minerals, whose production potential is limited and may soon be shifted to meet rising demand inside Russia. Aware that Putin is making economic interests the center in Russia's foreign policy, the Chinese realize that they must prove their worth in a new way. If Russia presses forward to enter WTO, it will turn increasingly to opening Siberia and the Far East as well as to strengthening its place in NEA, giving China a chance to ride the wave of globalization to strengthen its ties to Russia. Above

[92] Chi Qinglin, "Zhonge bianjing maoyi xunqiu xin tupo," *Dongbeiya luntan*, 3 (2001), pp. 34–8.

[93] Deng Hongkai, "E jiang xianzhi yuanmu chukou," *Heilongjiang duiwai jingmao*, 2 (2001), p. 59.

[94] V. G. Gel'bras, *Kitaiskaia real'nost' Rossii* (Moscow: Izdatel'skii Dom "Muravei," 2001).

all, China is aiming for future-oriented economic integration to replace unstable, short-term dealings.

After failing from 1994 to 1999 to reverse the slump in economic ties with Russia, Beijing took a more determined position once it recognized that Putin had given priority to economic development. Soon the two countries had at least three reasons to cast economic ties in a more positive light. First, in 2000–2 officially recorded trade had risen rapidly, nearly doubling to roughly $12 billion. Second, when other trade is recorded, as many openly reported, the real total approached $20 billion, including shuttle trade in excess of $5 billion, hidden weapons sales, and unlabeled products from China imported through third countries. Third, plans for boosting cooperation in many spheres were being taken more seriously. Trade could rise substantially when energy pipelines are built, military-industrial cooperation continues to expand, science and technology cooperation agreements are implemented, and Russia opens to Chinese investments and exports. One article estimated that China would be importing $10 billion of Russian oil each year.[95] It follows that Russia's entry into WTO amidst globalization offers a guarantee that China will become a close economic partner with that country.

Talk increasingly turned to building two-legged relations with Russia by boosting economic ties along with strategic ones. Zhu Rongji's visit was the turning point for diverse planning, not only for energy. An unprecedented gathering of specialists gave a big push in November to preparations. From Russia's viewpoint, China invests too little and does not buy many Russian nonmilitary industrial products, such as civilian aircraft. From China's perspective, Russians purchase few Chinese exports, resulting in a trade deficit of as much as $5.5 billion in 2001. Both sides aim to resolve recurrent frictions by setting common standards of modern business. Behind Chinese thinking is concern over excess dependency for 80 percent of export markets on three areas: the United States, Japan, and the EU. The Russian market promises, even if only a little at first, to reduce this dependence. Of course, should Chinese fears of new restrictions on exports to the West materialize, Russia hardly could compensate. Developing business connections will not be easy: Russians still talk as if the Chinese government can dictate purchases and investments and market forces count for little, while Chinese firms are reticent to venture into such an insecure environment. Yet, leaders in Beijing seem determined for reasons of security more than economy to make these economic ties a success. If trade rises 20 percent or more a year, cooperation spreads to high-tech areas and mutual investments, and border areas solidify their place at the center of business networks, then China can prove that ties with Russia have strong substance as well as rhetoric.

[95] Qin Xuanren, "'9/11 shijian' hou de daguo guanxi geju," *Waiguo wenti yanjiu*, 1 (2002), p. 4.

China deliberately set about building stronger economic ties, sending delegations of successful firms such as an electronics delegation to inspect Russian enterprises and pressing provincial governments to solidify new economic partnerships with krai and oblast administrations. In one high-power delegation reflecting this national priority 400 businessmen went to Moscow in June 2002. Much of the gain in trade is from existing mechanisms, even if they fail to meet modern standards. One method is chartered airplanes, numbering over 2,000 a year, under Russian control, which carry Chinese exports without assessing each item and then lead to clashes over whether taxes had been paid on an estimated $3 billion in trade. Some Chinese proposed ending this route, but vested interests in Russia objected.[96]

Beijing and Moscow tried to establish a baseline for relations before 9/11. Both sides praised the Treaty on Good-Neighborliness, Friendship, and Cooperation of July 16, 2001,[97] heralding a historic agreement that raised bilateral relations to a qualitatively new level.[98] Yet, it was mainly a ploy to signal the United States, which was exposed after 9/11 much to Chinese disappointment. Even those ready to concede the priority of U.S. relations in both countries were startled at the abrupt change after 9/11. The treaty had not saved the partnership focused on multipolar relations. The reality of economic globalization was at last being recognized in Russia and of security globalization in China.

By supporting Putin's decision to draw close to the United States and back the war on terror, China undercut the large opposition inside Russia to this shift in direction. Many Russians had pressed for closer ties as well as for a "Chinese model of development," but the Chinese understood that they were not true friends as their main goal was to turn Russia back toward its closed form of communism and Soviet superpower diplomacy. Indeed, they feared precisely the kinds of economic reforms that China had undertaken, and they were inclined to the narrow nationalism that prompted the Sino-Soviet split. The Chinese mainstream approved Putin's pragmatic globalization, noting that voices in some countries that called on China to assume the mantle of the fallen Soviet Union delude themselves in thinking that they have an answer to the powerful global transformation in progress. Cooperation with the United States is first, despite the search for ways to balance it.

As Russians debated what really constitute the security threats to their country, the Chinese also raised these issues. There, too, many warned that the legacy of thinking about great powers and separatism might be obscuring awareness of new types of threats. It was suggested that strategic shortages would soon be among the greatest dangers facing China, namely shortages of

[96] Hu Renxia, "Jilinsheng duie bianmao qianli fenxi," *Xiboliya yanjiu*, 2 (2002), pp. 27–30.

[97] Igor Rogachev, "Russian-Chinese Relations: New Treaty," *Far Eastern Affairs*, 5 (2001), pp. 1–5.

[98] L. Deliusin, *Kitai: Polveka – dve epokhi* (Moscow: IV RAN, 2001), p. 292.

oil, water, and grain. In comparison to the substantial U.S. oil reserve, China has just a one-week supply. Soon ambitious plans to divert rivers to meet water shortages in North China highlighted the severity of the problem. Rich in natural resources, Russia is acquiring increased value for China's security, broadly seen.

China was overtaking Japan as the foremost oil importer in Asia. Secure energy supplies became an urgent concern, especially as the United States extended forward positioning in oil-rich areas, culminating in the occupation of Iraq. In 2001 Beijing and Moscow signed an agreement to transport oil through Eastern Siberia and Inner Mongolia into Heilongjiang province, reaching China's main oil complex at Daqing. Work was to begin in 2003 with oil to be pumped in 2005. Plans for gas pipelines, an eastern line from Kovyktinskoe (to be supplemented by Sakha supplies) in Irkutsk oblast and a western line through Xinjiang province, were nearing completion. Additional interest has been given to liquid supplies of Sakhalin gas, especially if Japan hesitates to develop a pipeline for it and a second pipeline competition between China and Japan ensues. In 2001 Putin's businesslike attitude, profitable Russian companies flush with cash and eager to dispose of surplus energy, and growing security and economic concerns in China all converged. Above all, Beijing thought it had a deal for an oil pipeline from Angarsk to Daqing, guaranteeing a stable supply replenishing the depleted oil supplies of Northeast China's refineries. Yet, Japan made a last-minute bid for an alternate, if costlier, pipeline to the sea at Nakhodka. The competition for Siberian oil was joined, reflecting narrow national interests rather than a joint regional plan. In December 2002 Beijing seemed to have the upper hand, but Tokyo countered, making energy the centerpiece of the January 2003 summit. In May Hu Jintao and Putin appeared to agree on a final plan for a pipeline to Daqing, and again Japan made a counteroffer and the decision was delayed. For strategic as well as economic goals, Russia tries to maximize its limited leverage in NEA.

The foundation for stability along the once-disputed borders between the former Soviet Union and China was the border agreement essentially reached in 1989 followed by the Shanghai Cooperative Organization. In 2003 new problems appeared when a dam was erected along with construction of a new railway bridge across the Amur River by Khabarovsk. New tensions with Governor Ishaev followed Chinese accusations that the Russian side had violated its commitment not to alter the status quo on the border. Losing clout in Russia in his role as head of the Russian Far Eastern Association because that group was fading before new centralizing forces and the presence of Pulikovskii as Putin's representative, Ishaev was again championing national sovereignty. Failure of Central Asian parliaments to ratify border agreements with China also added to doubts about how successful the Shanghai Cooperative Organization was in stabilizing borders. Mongolia's absence from the organization, despite entreaties from China and Russia, indicated that its interest had not dimmed in finding balanced ties with other great powers even after it had reached agreement with Russia on debt repayment.

Even if Moscow keeps giving priority to relations with Washington, Beijing calculates that it can keep Moscow's attention by cultivating solid economic interests. This shifts the emphasis from great-power relations to regional integration. While bilateral security concerns, including arms sales and technological sharing, are salient, it is understood that multilateral regionalism according to global standards must be a priority. Yet, Russians feared that easy transportation from China to the Pacific would leave its ports to wither, and they rejected the idea of either developing Zarubino for easy access or leasing this undeveloped port for a lengthy period.[99] Russians look to a reintegration process on the Korean peninsula and to Japan as means to shape economic regionalism.

Since 1992 China had been a quiet suitor of Russia that insisted that Russia was more eager to improve relations, but from 1997 China was clearly more eager, and in 2001–3 the discrepancy came into the open. If in May 2003 Putin hosted Hu Jintao in his inaugural foreign visit as China's president and helped Hu emerge from Jiang Zemin's shadow in foreign policy, Putin's hesitancy after appearing to commit to an energy pipeline favored by Beijing and the weakness of their joint voices on the North Korean nuclear crisis left in doubt whether there was much substance to a special relationship. In regionalism Sino-Russian ties matter, but they have a secondary role.

South Korea and the Great Powers

Seoul was hard-pressed to sustain its "sunshine policy" of simultaneously drawing closer to both Washington and Beijing while drawing Pyongyang closer. The Bush administration undercut the policy by insisting on a prolonged review of the U.S. approach to North Korea, well before it went further by branding the North part of the "axis of evil." South Korea was left with no alternative but to wait for the United States or North Korea to shift direction, and it reacted with frustration when matters worsened. As Kim Dae-jung's stature slipped, regionalism also could not be vigorously pursued.

The junior high textbook revisions in Japan posed a new barrier to regionalism of mounting attention from the fall of 2000 through the spring of 2001. They angered public opinion in South Korea and China, putting pressure on leaders who had moved well ahead of their nations in improving relations. In Korea the goodwill of October 1998 that had energized two years of increased trust was damaged. Along with Bush's rebuff, Jiang Zemin's

[99] *Sankei shimbun*, April 19, 2003, p. 15.

endorsement of a nationalist outcry after the crash of one of China's fighters with a U.S. surveillance flight undermined any prospect of Seoul bridging the gap, and Kim Jong-il's cutback in contacts after being spurned by the United States left South Korea's leader nowhere to turn. After being heralded as the winner of the Nobel Peace Prize, Kim Dae-jung stood isolated both at home and abroad. The Japanese watched with apprehension about the growing negativism toward their country, but with little sign of self-reproach.[100] The United States paid little heed until the startling developments in North Korea in the fall of 2002 and a wave of anti-Americanism among South Koreans shocked it to attention.

If U.S. conservatives were overly optimistic about drawing Japan closer in an alliance to constrain, if not contain, China, they also misjudged South Korea, which sent as its envoy to Beijing a former ambassador to the United States and foreign minister. Pressure for it to solidify a three-way alliance with the United States and Japan failed to comprehend the South's improved ties to China and revived suspicions of dependency on Japan.[101] The Bush administration failed to heed warnings of discontent in the South. Only in 2003 did a crisis atmosphere leave South Koreans little choice but to close ranks with the United States.

The rise of China has been largely welcomed in South Korea, especially among younger generations. While the elite remains ambivalent about China and strongly favors preserving close security ties with the United States, it uncomfortably sits on the sidelines when Sino-U.S. ties deteriorate.[102] Economic bilateralism with China not only makes sense for a country rapidly expanding trade and running a large surplus, it also serves as a kind of balance to the security alliance with the United States. In 2001–2 when it was tugged from both sides, Seoul neither embraced the U.S. global agenda, including missile defense, nor could do much to assist China in its newfound emphasis on regionalism. Yet, explosive growth in economic ties and a growing backlash against U.S. policies led to a tilt toward China. Demonstrations mounted against the U.S. troop presence when in late 2002 the crisis over North Korean nuclear programs unfolded at the same time as a U.S. military court acquitted two American soldiers charged with running over two Korean girls with their military vehicle. The December election of Roh Moo-hyun as president distanced Seoul further from Washington, but a drop in foreign investment and in economic growth as well as the danger of the nuclear crisis led Roh quickly to mend ties with Washington.

[100] *Yomiuri shimbun*, March 1, 2001, p. 6.

[101] Mochida Naotage, "Hokuto Ajia ni miru takokukan anpo no kanosei," *Sekai shuho*, August 8, 2000, pp. 10–13.

[102] Jae Ho Chung, "South Korea between Eagle and Dragon: Perceptual Ambivalence and Strategic Dilemma," *Asian Survey*, 41(5), September–October, 2001 pp. 777–96.

South Koreans largely looked benignly on China's role in the Korean peninsula and in regionalism. They saw Hu Jintao as inclined to cooperate with the United States and responsible in helping the North find a way out of the nuclear crisis while saving some face.[103] Optimism for regionalism did not diminish even as the crisis deepened.

The Chinese described the economic integration occurring with South Korea in similar terms to what was happening with Taiwan. Investments were pouring into China, whose growth had become essential to the other economies. China absorbed huge trade deficits, serving for South Korea to balance its deficit with Japan. Key sectors such as Korean telecommunications relied on the Chinese market. To Beijing this high level of economic integration had political significance and created more momentum for regionalism. By boosting its domestic purchasing power and training more educated workers, China insured the transfer of more technology. It was confident that this strategy would avoid vertical regionalism primarily reliant on China's cheap labor. When South Korean views of the United States deteriorated in late 2002, the Chinese could take satisfaction over their image. Yet, political and business elites in the South prefer to play China against Japan and, increasingly, to draw on the two together as they navigate carefully the limited path left by U.S. unilateralism. In turn, however indispensable the South is to China, sinocentrism remains strong and allows little trust for South Korea becoming the regional center. For regionalism, it will take a globally minded and transparent China, accepting a special relationship between South Korea and the United States and able to allay fears of dependency.

If Beijing had generally been comfortable with the status quo on the Korean peninsula, its thinking shifted in 2003. For economic development and security in surrounding areas unification suddenly seemed appealing. It no longer feared that South Korea would lean to the United States, and it was anxious to rid itself of the headaches caused by the North, including the heavy burden of economic assistance and refugees. Above all, reassessment of what is China's national interest for regional goals has led to a sharp turn in policy.[104] Over the year Beijing played the central diplomatic role in trying to resolve differences between the United States and North Korea, but even though its ties with the former were improving and with the latter deteriorating it favored an endgame that would not bring the region to the verge of war or leave the United States dominant over the region.

103 Pak Chongchil, "2003 nyon hanbando chongse chinmang," *Pukhan*, January 2003, pp. 65–72; I Samok, "21 segi Hanguk oe Chungguk gwa Roshia oegyo chongchaek oe panghyang," *Chibang chuchi yongu*, 8, pp. 91–110.

104 Moon Il-hyon, "Kitachosen ni sei o mukeru Chugoku," *Sekai shuho*, November 4, 2003, pp. 6–11.

One Seoul professor appealed to the Japanese in April 2001 to recognize the dark shadow that their distorted textbooks cast on shared cultural identity of China, Korea, and Japan as well as on joint economic development of natural resources. At the very time that these countries are discussing establishment of a community to rival the EU, Japan's message threatens to shatter the cooperative spirit. To justify Japanese armed annexation of Korea as voluntary and its war across East Asia as a sacred act to liberate nations is inauspicious, coming when emotions were cooling and both nations were hoping that cohosting the World Cup would enhance trust.[105] Yet, similar to China's leaders, Kim Dae-jung did not want this problem to sidetrack gains in relations. While he could not look weak in responding to Japan's textbook revisions, the response was much shallower than previous bouts of anger such as the 1996 uproar over the prospect that Japan was pressing a claim to Tokdo (Takeshima) Island. It seemed staged for domestic consumption, tempered by more familiarity with Japan and more alarm with the Bush administration.

Japanese optimism about relations with South Korea rose sharply in 2002. From their vantage point, the World Cup joint hosting had been a stunning success. If Koreans had started the games in a competitive mood anxious to do better as hosts and as a team, they ended it with pride in their unexpected success and goodwill to the Japanese people for sharing in it and rooting for the South Korean team after Japan's defeat. Also proud were the Japanese who believed that together the two nations had projected a fresh image to the world of individualist athletes, normal nationalism that overcomes differences among nations, and even "soft power" that boosts a country's popularity.[106] Soon there were calls for politicians in Japan not to squander this "World Cup consciousness" that signifies a new era in bilateral relations.[107] While some observers looked ahead to South Korea completing the cultural opening suspended in 2001 by allowing Japanese TV shows or anticipated a visit by Japan's emperor, others identified coordination in dealing with North Korea and progress in talks on an FTA as the critical tests that lie ahead.

After the World Cup had raised hopes in Japan that a new era had dawned in relations with South Korea, skeptics on the right warned that anti-Japanese attitudes remained deeply attached to Korean nationalism.[108] More than Korean attitudes, they feared a softening of Japanese nationalism in the search for common ground. Yet, the North Korean crisis and Roh Moo-hyun's early cultivation of closer ties aroused more sympathy with

105 *Asahi shimbun*, April 10, 2001, p. 13.

106 *Asahi shimbun*, July 3, 2002, p. 1.

107 *Mainichi shimbun*, July 2, 2001, p. 3.

108 "'Hakkin' no ue 'kokunai nankin' sareta 'Nikkan heigo raisan hon' no Kankokujin sakka," *Shukan bunshun*, July 18, 2002, pp. 158–9.

the South. The most complete switch occurred in the Japanese left wing, which abandoned the North and embraced South Korea as a force for peace in NEA.[109]

Enthusiasm in Japan for an FTA with South Korea was reinforced by arguments that the advanced firms in that country were eager for it too. After all, sales of semiconductors could rise sharply with unrestricted access to Japan's much larger market. Also the Japanese calculated that the South was awakening to the Chinese economic threat, realizing that its best position would not be in the middle between China and Japan but linked closely with Japan. Thus, economic realities were contributing to Koreans resolving their complex toward Japan. In turn, the Japanese started using the traditional term *kyodotai* (community) to suggest what an FTA would bring. Already they had witnessed a "sports kyodotai," and new exchanges could lead to an "academic kyodotai." Fearful of large numbers of migrants from China or elsewhere in Asia, some Japanese suggested that only South Koreans would be acceptable. Aware of concerns in the South that the FTA would be unbalanced, they insisted that Korean energy in developing the IT sector had shocked the Japanese into new respect and expectations of an equal partnership.

When Kim Jong-nam, the first son of Kim Jong-il, was stopped in May 2001 entering Japan with a false passport, the Japanese right wing was outraged with his rapid expulsion from the country. They charged that the best opportunity for resolving the problem of abducted Japanese in North Korea had been squandered. Recalling that since 1995 Japan had assisted the North with 1.7 million tons of rice without any change in bilateral relations, they called for tougher measures linked to more nationalism.[110] Yet, leaders continued to seek a diplomatic solution to the kidnappings, waiting for the North to decide that it could not do without a large dose of Japanese aid in lieu of reparations.

While secret talks proceeded to achieve a breakthrough with North Korea, the Japanese public grew increasingly aroused by media stories about citizens who had been abducted in the 1970s and 1980s. Many demanded that until this issue was resolved the government must deny humanitarian grain assistance and crack down further on Korean groups sending pachinko money or credit union funds to the North.[111] After five surviving abductees were allowed to come to Japan, the focus turned to releasing their family members too. Over the following year, one negative story followed another. An image arose of Japan over a decade looking the other way as the North smuggled its way to survival.[112]

[109] *Asahi shimbun*, June 5, 2003, p. 2, and issues of the monthly, *Sekai*.

[110] *Sankei shimbun*, May 11, 2001, p. 12.

[111] Yayama Taro, "Nihonjin ratchi mondai," *THE21*, July 2002, pp. 54–5.

[112] *Yomiuri shimbun*, June 5, 2003, p. 1.

Japan's relationship with North Korea became the subject of intense scrutiny in the fall of 2002 as Koizumi traveled to Pyongyang and talks to normalize relations began amidst debates over the North's nuclear weapons programs and Japanese abductees. On the one hand, discussion turned to forward-looking ways to boost economic ties, building on the promise in 1990 of LDP bigwig Kanemaru Shin to offer roughly $8 billion in assistance, which became the touchstone for later talks.[113] On the other, Kim Jong-il's admission that the North had kidnapped Japanese citizens sent shockwaves through the community of Korean Japanese loyal to Pyongyang, contributing to revelations of how vital had been their role in keeping the North afloat. One Japanese source estimated that $3 billion in cash and kind had been sent from Niigata to Wonson on one boat that makes thirty trips a year, keeping the regime afloat. After an investigation from the end of 2001 began looking into the records of the bankrupt "North Korean bank" in Japan, disturbing findings led the Japanese to charge that it was their own money that had paid for the missiles fired over their islands.[114] For Japanese North Korea was now the center of concern over security and of what would be needed for a regional breakthrough.

Koizumi's visit to Pyongyang sent a message to Seoul that Japan was working to support the South's renewed "sunshine policy." If Japanese had been noticeably nervous in June 2000 when the summit of the Koreas occurred, they were now proving that they would pursue the same aims in coordination with the South. This had special meaning at a time when both countries were anxious about U.S. unilateralism toward North Korea as well as Iraq. If at the end of 2002 the two sides split in reacting to the North's nuclear weapons programs, by June 2003 they had, under U.S. leadership, found a common position as they awaited what would become six-way negotiations with North Korea.

As South Koreans respond to the growing power of the United States and a rising interest in regionalism, ties with Japan grow in significance. In 2003 as Japanese leaders joined the United States in pressuring North Korea, Roh wooed Koizumi. He well understood that only by raising Japanese trust in South Korea would he gain some leverage with the United States and create an environment in which regionalism could be pursued. His June visit to Tokyo produced the desired public relations bonanza in Japan, but the media in Seoul warned that the Japanese side was showing little sensitivity to Korean concerns. Hostile to Roh, the major newspapers played on negative views of Japan for domestic political purposes.

Before Japan can count on a real breakthrough with South Korea it must counter the surge of concern in 2001, including the reaction to Koizumi's

113 Shigemura Toshimitsu, "Koizumi shusho hocho no shinso," *Ajia jiho*, 11 (2002), pp. 4–19.

114 "'Mangyonbon' go de Kita ni 3000 oku en okotta," *Shukan posuto*, December 13, 2002, pp. 26–33.

response to the U.S. war on terror, about a rise in Japanese nationalism and military activity.[115] Amidst the energetic debate on forming FTAs and accelerating cooperation in the region in a time of globalization,[116] there is still a need to build trust with the South Korean public. In 2003 differences in dealing with the abduction issue reopened old wounds, as South Koreans associated Japan's resurgent rightists with a history of abuses to their nation, such as the kidnapping of comfort women.[117]

Japanese-South Korean relations were put to the test by each side's approach to North Korea. In June 2003 Roh and Koizumi papered over differences on Japan's approval for joining the United States in coupling pressure with negotiations, which helped the Japanese public overcome its suspicions that the South Koreans were too soft on the North. Yet, it would take more to overcome the mutual distrust, including the frustration of the South Korean media at insults from LDP politicians that accompanied the summit, including a speech by Aso Taro arguing that Koreans under Japan's rule voluntarily switched to Japanese names. In an effort to keep Japan from embracing the U.S. hard-line on the North and to draw much needed investment, South Koreans had little choice but to temper their response. Moreover, anxious for more investment from Japan and exports to reduce the large trade imbalance with it, South Koreans gave priority to Japan over China for an FTA. On the Left, which had long criticized the South, there were calls for a regional vision to build trust with South Korea first.[118] On the Right, it was easier to accept an FTA with the South because agricultural imports would not be high.

South Korea figures more in regional energy discussions than many are aware. While the South is twenty-fifth in the world in population and twelfth in its economy, its energy consumption places it tenth, its oil consumption moves it to sixth, and its dependence on oil imports raises it to fourth in the world even as its liquid natural gas (LNG) imports are second only to Japan. Per capita levels of consumption are similar to those in Japan, caused by the importance of heavy and chemical industries in the Korean economy and by the shift to bigger cars, houses, and electric appliances as part of a modern lifestyle. While energy consumption fell by 8 percent in 1998, it roared back in 1999 with a rise of 9 percent. Energy imports of about $35 billion a year mean that Korea may soon owe $1,000 per person to oil producers. A new energy-saving drive is not likely to diminish concern, heightened by

[115] Cho Kihyun and Ho Chunggyung, *Koizumi oe Ilbon odiro kanunka?* (Seoul: Yoido, 2001).

[116] Chong Ingyo, *FTA sidae e otoge daejohal goshinka?* (Seoul: KIEP, 2001); Kim Kisu and Wang Yuncong, *Kukje tonghwa cheje wa tongasia tonghwa hyopryok* (Seoul: Sejong Institute, 2001).

[117] Ichigawa Hayami, "Ratchikan, Kitachosenkan Nichikan no rakusa," *Ronza*, December 2003, pp. 120–7.

[118] *Asahi shimbun*, June 4, 2003, p. 13.

steeply rising energy prices in 2000, that the NEA region, namely Russia, is important for meeting South Korea's needs.[119]

Russia repositioned itself in 2000–2 for leverage on Korean reconciliation. Seoul accepted Putin's wooing of Kim Jong-il, recognizing that this made Russia a more active force in the region, as it moved from words to deeds.[120] Only in 2003 when Moscow could not sway Pyongyang as the crisis intensified did the South lower its expectations.[121] North Korea went too far with its nuclear threat, altering regional dynamics.

Russians treat diplomacy with North Korea as a test of multipolar diplomacy. They warn that isolating the North is dangerous, justifying their support for the North as responsible conduct that reassures its leaders and makes negotiations easier.[122] As long as the North is looking for multilateral leverage and the South wants a regional solution not dictated by the United States, Russia serves a useful purpose. Its significance too for long-term economic programs integrating the North and the NEA region also makes its voice heard. Even if the United States single-mindedly views North Korea as a security problem, other actors in the region are eyeing economic and cultural issues along with security for a lasting outcome.[123]

By the end of 2003 South Korea had lost most of its leverage in the region. A credit card scandal left its economic mood unsettled. Roh continued to press forward with North Korea on economic projects and assistance, but revelations about a large payoff to the North under Kim Dae-jung and the stalemate as the North confronted the United States left little room for flexibility. With little domestic support he could only cling to his office. Yet, he escaped foreign criticism. Beijing took satisfaction in ever closer economic integration. Japanese tourism and popular interest kept expanding. Even the United States, as it made plans to relocate bases, kept expressing confidence in the hapless Roh, who acceded to repeated calls for coordination. Until the nuclear weapons crisis was settled, the South would not be able to reassert itself as a major player in regional dynamics.

Overview of Regionalism

In 2001–2 the world economy lost momentum, as U.S. growth fell. With Japan mired in its deep slump, China became the engine of NEA economic dynamism. Pulling industry and investment from South Korea and Japan, it

119 *The Korea Herald*, November 23, 2000.

120 Kim Yonsu, "Roshia oe shinampo junryaku gwa Tongbuka," *Ampo haksul ronju*, 12(1), 2001, p. 299.

121 Chong Taeik, "Pukhan haekmunje e taehan Roshia oe ipjang mit shisajom," *Oegyo*, 4 (2003), pp. 26–63.

122 Georgy Kunadze, "Nichirochukan de tai Kitachosen kanyo seisaku o," *Sekai shuho*, April 17, 2001, pp. 6–9.

123 Gilbert Rozman, "The Geopolitics of the North Korean Nuclear Crisis," pp. 245–61.

bolstered plans for regionalism. With fear mounting that security problems in the Middle East could threaten oil supplies, interest in Russian oil and gas also fueled hopes for regionalism. As the impact of WTO was growing, the economic case for regional integration advanced, as it had continuously since 1989. Yet, there was an interruption in the momentum that was recently building.

The security case for regionalism posed the greatest uncertainty. The need to address security rose first because the Bush administration raised its priority, then due to the new atmosphere after 9/11, and finally because of North Korean WMD development. South Korea's soft "sunshine policy" had done little to alleviate the potential of WMD blackmail or even of massive conventional attack on Seoul emanating from Pyongyang. Under the shadow of a nuclear crisis, U.S.-Japanese-South Korean trilateralism began to intensify coupled with mounting pressure on China and Russia to throw their weight behind a joint position toward the North. Yet, others were left out as U.S. unilateralism and North Korean nuclear blackmail became locked in confrontation. This gave fresh urgency to discussion of regional coordination involving China in South Korea and Japan. In addition to Washington's leadership becoming the indispensable force bringing the weight of a global solution to the regional environment of NEA, coordination in a deal to end the standoff could be a powerful precedent for broad-based regionalism.

There was some progress on the cultural front toward NEA regionalism. Despite a resurgence of name calling in 2001, primarily associated with Japan's new textbooks, the year 2002 brought notable progress. The World Cup succeeded in drawing Japan and South Korea closer, particularly by improving attitudes in Japan. At year end a prominent Chinese source offered the boldest statement yet in support of respect for Japan's record. Momentary progress in September in Japanese-North Korean mutual apologies gave a hint of what is possible. Despite the long road ahead in building trust in many troubled bilateral pairings, we should acknowledge some substantial advances already achieved.

Four initiatives of 2000 needed to be realigned to boost regionalism. All seemed for a time to be conducive to regional cooperation, but then proved to be too limited or even shortsighted to achieve their goals. In 2001–2 each reached an impasse. Japan's pursuit of Russia had mixed narrow nationalist territorial goals with broad geopolitical and economic ambition. It became clear that this was an unsustainable combination. A letdown came when the countdown to the year 2000 ended in failure. At the end of 2002 bilateral relations appeared to be recovering, but they had yet to make a breakthrough.

South Korea's opening to Japan counted on Japanese nationalism to decline in allowing for cultural ties to expand along with economic ones. Instead, new nationalist affronts shocked Koreans, and the pursuit of regionalism only began again when "World Cup" fever engulfed both nations and demonstrated how much they had in common. If in the fall of 2002 the two sides appeared to share an aversion to U.S. unilateralism toward North Korea, the deepening nuclear crisis posed a difficult test. They appeared to work together at a summit in June 2003, but South Korean nervousness was seen in hesitation on FTA talks, a new round of cultural opening, and economic pressure on the North. By late 2003 progress had resumed, but Seoul was consumed by political chaos.

China's pursuit of Russia likewise did not stand the test of time. Geopolitical interests suddenly divided the two states, and there were too few economic bonds to keep ties close; China scrambled for a new economic strategy to rekindle Russian interest in partnership within a regional context. Plans for an energy pipeline or cooperation in dealing with the North Korean crisis could draw them closer as each sought leverage on U.S. unilateralism, but the momentum under Putin generally limited genuine partnership.

Finally, China's upgraded smile diplomacy to Japan can be considered the fourth example of support for regionalism that needed reinforcement. The Japanese saw a lack of substance in China's approach, suggesting a forced smile rather than sincere desire for close regional relations. Yet, as China took regionalism more seriously, it redoubled its appeal to Japan in a way that at last may have been seen by many as credible for forging enduring trust. China's cooperation to get North Korea to multilateral talks and a series of articles in its journals repeating the call to accept Japan as it is reinforced rising economic interdependence.

In 2002 these pairs of countries began to consider anew how to put relations on a firmer footing and on this basis to build a solid foundation for regionalism. It cannot be said that the most serious obstacles were overcome, but the results were impressive in comparison to what was achieved through most of the 1990s. Crises served to bring the countries of NEA closer together in the shadow of U.S. pressure. After the Asian financial crisis with ASEAN adrift and China and Japan competing for influence, they also cooperated to link NEA to SEA. Not only did they join with South Korea in forging ASEAN +3 and vie with each other in planning FTA ties that were dubbed ASEAN +1, they also gave the impression that economic ties in SEA could jump-start regionalism in NEA. If in the past Japan had regarded SEA as its economic sphere of influence, it was China at the summits of both 2001 and 2002 that took the lead in pressing for an FTA agreement. Yet, as much as linkages to SEA helped to keep the rhetoric of regionalism alive, the reality of political and economic problems in SEA is such that ties there will do little to solve the problems of NEA. There is no shortcut to boosting direct integration among China, Japan, and South Korea, with Russia likely to be added while the United States cannot be excluded from a large voice even if it is not formally part of regionalism.

The North Korean nuclear crisis on the heels of troubling U.S. pressure to steer the world into a single front against terror and WMD also jolted the countries of NEA to appreciate their common interests. Branding North

Korea part of the "axis of evil" and delaying negotiations with it, the Bush administration alienated South Koreans as well as many others in the region. Whatever they thought of Pyongyang's tactics, they calculated that only by working closer together would they have much chance of influencing them.

Shortcuts failed to build a foundation for regionalism. Japan's countdown to the year 2000 with Russia, South Korea's "sunshine policy" to the North, China's smile diplomacy toward Japan, and Russia's multidirectional political opening including North Korea all treated regional goals as secondary to other objectives. Despite a flurry of talk about regionalism, it still appeared quite empty in the troubled days of 2001. From 2002 the search for regionalism resumed, sandwiched between U.S. and North Korean moves that left the other four actors adjusting their strategies and renewing their bilateral ties.

Well in advance there was talk of the special significance of the year 2002 for cooperation in East Asia. The combination of the thirtieth anniversary of Sino-Japanese normalization, the tenth anniversary of diplomatic relations between China and South Korea, and the World Cup shared by Japan and South Korea promised to bring a boom in ceremonial occasions and exchanges. What could not be foreseen was that the bilateral relationship foremost in people's minds would be the United States and North Korea. Along with booming economic ties, deepening security anxieties boosted the case for regionalism. By turning attention away from intraregional issues toward a common global threat and a leader insistent on addressing it, the United States transformed the dynamics of regionalism.

For regionalism to occur, there still has to be a shift in the focus of nationalism. Japan is one key. It would have to avoid two extremes: one is reversing historical verdicts and challenging the region by vindicating much of the country's conduct in the first half of the twentieth century; the other is accepting U.S. hegemony as in the cold war and using it as a means to contain China and North Korea. Either of these approaches could encourage Japan to go nuclear. Instead, Japan would have to look to its own region for balance, giving priority to strategic reconciliation with Russia, closer ties to South Korea, and a joint initiative with North Korea, assuming that country forsakes blackmail. As a champion of regionalism, it would need to define becoming a "normal power" cautiously, seeking flexibility in its diplomacy but not military muscle that may alarm its neighbors.

China, in turn, would have to meet Japan part way, further toning down rhetoric against Japanese nationalism and restraining its military pressure on Taiwan and its support for states developing WMD. If it really sought an effective strategy to limit U.S. hegemony, it would reassure its neighbors about its own intentions. Instead of posing as a victim intent on remaking the world order, China would have to accept the status of a normal country patiently rising in power and aware of the need to achieve a balance of power to ease that transition. In addition, Beijing would need to be patient as Putin sustained the course of cooperation with the United States he took after 9/11, waiting for new determination to search simultaneously for leverage on the United States in conjunction with other great powers. As the state most threatened by U.S. unilateralism besides North Korea, China has to become the most adroit champion of regionalism without alienating supporters of globalization or confronting the United States directly. It must accept a more nationalist Japan, including a military buildup that was condemned earlier. Also, its active diplomacy of 2003, including pressure on North Korea, needs to continue.

South Korea remains in a pivotal position both in the tripartite core of economic regionalism and as the country that shares a nation with North Korea. It cannot allow anti-Americanism to keep building without turning regionalism against globalization. Delicate balancing of relations with four great powers will be required if it is to play the indispensable role of facilitator in economic and security ties for NEA. Yet, Roh started with the strongest endorsement yet of regionalism, establishing a task force on making Korea the center of Northeast Asia, conveying to Japan that it is first among priorities, and reassuring Bush by accepting the U.S. lead on North Korea despite differences.

The ASEAN +3 summit in November 2002 brought a repeat of the Sino-Japanese competition for free trade agreements with ASEAN countries of a year earlier. Beijing again took the lead in promising to move ahead and Tokyo, held back by its agricultural interests, scrambled to keep up. The tone was changing, however, from one-upmanship to finding a way to accomplish this goal together. Political interests in Japan still vilified China, now as an economic threat as much as a political or military threat, but economic interests were recognizing that there is no alternative. The Chinese redoubled their efforts to reassure Japanese public opinion, debating whether to end use of the "history card" and appealing for regionalism. Economics showed increased promise of drawing the region together, while security still faced an uncharted and difficult road to resolution. A year later the Bali ASEAN +3 summit saw China again more forthcoming and Tokyo scrambling to catch up at its own summit ending in a "Tokyo Declaration."

A series of summit meetings in the aftermath of the Iraq war in May to July 2003 set the stage for deeper exploration of regionalism, despite delay due to the tough stands of the United States and North Korea. They left no doubt about the U.S. role as the driving force, while showing how Japanese-South Korean, South Korean-Chinese, and Sino-Russian ties were adjusting. Washington responded to the crisis with an emphasis on multilateral ties in the region, conceding that it lacks all but the crudest tools to shape the behavior of the North. Without defying the United States, the others were striving to shape the joint message even as they explored long-term questions. Although Roh's call for regionalism was not ready to be answered, the dearth of coordination apart from the United States was a growing concern.

First deciding in favor of regionalism in general, each state in NEA faces the further challenge of accepting balanced relations in a region that will not be easy to control. Although Japan was the first to press for regionalism, South Korea has taken the lead in supporting regionalism for the new era. In 1998 Kim Dae-jung moved in this direction, and in 2003 Roh made this his goal. China shows signs of taking this position, but its domestic politics leave doubts. Russia under Putin is looking for regional balance, but that does not equate to trust in regionalism. Japan now holds the fate of regionalism in its hands. It has been slow to make up its mind. The most serious holdout is North Korea, whose actions along with those of the United States have put regionalism on hold. We should be watching the way Japan positions itself in the aftermath of the North Korean nuclear crisis to see if it decides to offer more support for the new regionalism and how China steers between the United States and the North while trying to improve ties with Japan.

8

Conclusion

Lessons for Constructing Regionalism in Northeast Asia

Combining China, Japan, and South Korea at the core with eventual inclusion of other areas, from the eastern edge of Russia to North Korea, regionalism is taking shape in NEA after a rough decade of false starts and uncoordinated, if repeatedly refreshed, hopes. The process has been arduous because of the historical legacy in the region, the difficulty in building on truncated forces of globalization and localism, and domestic uncertainties in defining priorities at a time of resurgent nationalism. Examining the record of failure to realize regional goals in the transitional decade after the cold war, we can draw useful lessons on how regionalism in NEA can be fully realized. From the chronology of past efforts we discern that a drive for regionalism is likely to come from: 1) **the extraordinary pace of intraregional trade and investment,** driven of late by the dynamism of coastal China as well as the spillover from increased openness with entry into the WTO; 2) **a backlash from assertive unilateralism by the United States,** pressing down on nations anxious to gain foreign-policy leverage; 3) **a common interest in stabilizing systemic change in North Korea and Sino-Japanese volatility;** and 4) **a shared competitive streak that recognizes** the limited influence of each of their separate economies, along with the compelling **benefits to be achieved from the larger scale and international recognition of a regional voice on economics first of all.**

Why does regionalism matter to the nations of NEA? Obviously, it offers a means to stabilize security and establish an environment for peace and development. After the cold war this area of competing powers and divided countries still needs a framework to override its differences. Accelerating commercial linkages put pressure on policy makers to regularize ties that link their economies and enable them to work together smoothly. Yet, there is more to the case for the NEA region. The drive to regionalism is both a realistic response to the rise in U.S. unipolarity in financial markets, military power, information flow, high technology, and pop culture, and a plausible answer to a sudden eclipse of accustomed models of development. At a loss due to the collapse of socialism, the decline of the old left, or the downfall of the Asian developmental state, many are grasping for another ideal. Nationalism has gained ground, but it does not serve national interests well. Regional integration offers an essential antitoxin to nationalism, creating the potential for transformation of national identity not just to idealistic global citizenry that still comes as a jolt to most communities but also to something closer at hand with roots familiar to nationalist boosters. In a world of overwhelming U.S. power, regionalism increases leverage, by pooling national interests. Moreover, regionalism offers a chance to restart decentralization, helping peripheral areas work together across national borders. Rather than localism becoming a driving force for regionalism, the opposite is likely.

Why had regionalism failed in the 1990s? In order of responsibility, we can find all countries at fault to varying degrees. One, North Korea has scorned any loss of control, playing WMD blackmail with reckless abandon. Two, Russia has feared economic integration, for which it was unprepared, and has treated most foreign investment badly. Grouped together at three through five, the order of which changes over time, China long put objectives linked to multipolarity above regionalism, raising suspicions; South Korea took a long time to appreciate how regionalism can shape the evolution of North Korea, while remaining suspicious of globalization; and Japan narrowly defined its pursuit of regional leadership and, when disappointed, became more cautious without winning Chinese or U.S. trust in its goals. Six, the United States suspected a potential brake on globalization, sending mixed signals. None of the six countries boosted trust in regionalism through its primary foreign-policy priorities. North Korea, Russia, and the United States to varying degrees, feared it, and the core countries, South Korea, China, and Japan, that must coordinate their support, were slow to work together, each suspecting that others would be at an advantage and all doubting globalization. If by 2003 China had become more supportive of regionalism and U.S. unilateralism gave new reason for backlash regionalism, the negative impact of North Korea was at its peak.

Globalization is a continuous process, but we can appreciate its acceptance most clearly by pointing to a series of challenges that faced all of the countries of NEA. Four snapshots of the past two decades reveal the multiple dimensions of the challenge. First, in the 1980s modernization models were widely debated in NEA with an emphasis on reforming the traditional socialist model and the developmental state model. Looming before this discussion was a standard of globalization calling for liberating individuals as consumers and economic organizations as competitors from the heavy hand of the state with the possibility of forging many links to the outside world. Important successes were achieved, starting with Deng Xiaoping's open door and household responsibility systems, Mikhail Gorbachev's glasnost and perestroika, South Korea's democratization, and Japan's embrace of the concept of internationalization if not all of its substance. Yet, each stopped far short of transforming an unbalanced model of modernization into sustained convergence with a global standard. Political reforms often strengthened interest groups defensive of elements of the old model. Ideologically charged backlashes rejected "spiritually polluting" elements of a perceived new model. There was no sustained commitment to carrying the transformation to its logical endpoint. Japan's confidence in the "bubble economy" and South Korea's image as the latest "economic miracle" now boosted by successful democratic transition relieved the pressure for change. Meanwhile, compromises with existing elites in China and the Soviet Union demanded limits on globalization. Old models were deeply embedded, posing lasting barriers to globalization.

Second, the end of the cold war and collapse of the communist bloc at the turn of the 1990s left globalization triumphant, prodding NEA states with some success (except North Korea) to embrace it further. Under U.S. leadership, the standard had shifted to human rights and international responsibilities. For Japan and even South Korea one test was how much of a leadership role would be assumed in integrating China and Russia into the global community. Not only did they fail to make substantial reforms in their developmental states to accelerate globalization, they also downplayed the human-rights objectives of enticing China in its post–June 4, 1989 isolation and Russia in its start-up amidst the wreckage of the Soviet collapse. Despite the fact in the mid-1990s Seoul trumpeted "globalization" to prove its coming of age as a new member of the OECD club and Tokyo announced the "big bang" reforms, neither challenged vested interests to aspire to global standards. Beijing and Moscow took opposite trajectories, as each one-sidedly advanced in one direction of globalization while anxiously building a dam to block other outside forces. The former forswore genuine democratic reform, while suspiciously dismissing global pressures on sovereign states beyond the economic sphere. The latter was even more fearful, protecting its deteriorating economy while denying the goodwill of global human-rights enforcement such as in the former Yugoslavia. Resisting global forces, the countries of NEA were also complicating their quest for regionalism.

Third, the Asian financial crisis brought a new wave of globalization that engulfed NEA but left many resentful and resistant to its full implications. Under duress, South Korea made the biggest leap forward. China also accelerated reforms of large enterprises, trying to divest many from state ownership. Japan's reforms, however, came very slowly, and Russia's default boosted protectionism more than openness. While old models were fully discredited, backing for new models came haltingly. Nonetheless, the burst of globalization that arose in NEA from the crisis of 1997–8 spurred regionalism forward. More conscious of the power of globalization, nations recognized how regional integration could both complement it and provide some balance.

Fourth, the war against terror was brought home to NEA first by the proximity of Central Asian operations and then by the nuclear standoff with North Korea. Russia took a sharp turn in foreign policy to support the United States, although in 2003 differences arose over Iraq and North Korea. Fearful of isolation and sharing a common enemy in Islamic radicals, China gave its assent to the war and then actively facilitated U.S.-North Korean talks, lowering its profile against strategic globalization. Especially, Japan opted to draw closer to the United States in 2003, finding that in the face of a nuclear threat gaining independent leverage could not be a primary concern. The new South Korean president Roh Moo-hyun also edged closer to the United States after riding a wave of anti-Americanism to victory that threatened to leave his country exposed to a sharp drop in foreign investment and grave concerns about security. Yet, all were disturbed by the unilateral way the United States had led the region into the crisis. The rising tide of globalization on security came with strong signs of a backlash as soon as the nuclear standoff is resolved. World integration is not enough for nations steeped in the logic of boosting national influence and limiting dependency.

National Identities Prevail over Economics and Security

By now it is clear that globalization exacerbates feelings of insecurity, especially in countries and among groups that fear substantial losses. All of the countries of NEA face wrenching changes to the model of development with which they succeeded in the postwar and began the 1990s. South Korea kept its model producing high growth rates longer than Japan, and China fared dramatically better than Russia and North Korea, but even these two countries are deeply alarmed about the economic and cultural impact of globalization. Accelerated global integration with more to come has fueled insecurity, driving nations toward regionalism but keeping them from finding a joint path toward it. After all, exclusive nationalism leads only to regionalism hostile toward globalization, which is not a viable option in a region of such cultural distrust, so dependent on export-led growth focused on the United States, and desperate for massive injections of foreign capital to advance the projects that symbolize its integration. In order to proceed regionalism must steer a narrow path between the crossing swords of nationalism and globalization.

History has not been favorable for regional integration in NEA. China did not have an expansionist outlook, remaining content as the "central kingdom" with a system of bilateral relations called *tributary*, but in fact limited to ritual expressions of respect and exchanges of prize items. Instead of capitalizing, as in Europe, on advances in urbanization and national markets with an impulse for trade and migration across national borders, China, Japan, and Korea attempted to seal their borders against regular contacts. When the Western powers pried open these borders in the mid–nineteenth century, they found three nations steeped in the same Confucian elite culture but separated in their own relatively isolated economies. These same powers forced each country to face them, often at the expense of regional ties. If the era of imperialism erased domestic barriers, it left a stain on images of regionalism. First forces from afar overwhelmed regional ties in trade and borrowing, undercutting what little regional identity existed. Then Japan's reign as regional hegemon created a residue of anger and distrust. Finally, the cold war era that replaced Japanese rule bifurcated the region into two antagonistic blocs. When China broke with the Soviet bloc it was left with communist rule hostile to regional or global integration. Apart from a cold accommodation between Japan and South Korea, both U.S. allies and close trading partners, borders in NEA remained fortresses obstructing contact.

Despite progress through the 1980s that was achieved in economic cooperation and diplomatic intercourse, levels of trust remained low in NEA. Each nation had its own symbols for why compromise would be an unprincipled abandonment of cherished national dignity and goals. Japanese public opinion grew more incensed about Moscow's 1945 seizure of four disputed islands. Democratization fueled by mass movements drew the Korean public more openly into parading their loathing of Japan's occupation. After being long suppressed, the Chinese public also vented its resentment of Japan's stained history. Unable to exert leadership commensurate with its economic prowess, Japan chose to pursue economic ties without addressing popular grievances. Contrary to expectations, growing economic networks and ritualized friendship toasts did not suppress anxieties about regional ties. The first stage of regionalism bore the burden of Japan's high expectations for progress mixed with its low preparedness to win trust.

Domestic priorities privileged goals that stood in the way of regionalism. Each nation was anxious to achieve a "normal" national identity after feeling frustrated by foreign relations. The Japanese eyed an escape from the abnormality of being labeled a "defeated power," remaining a dependency of the United States without a full set of levers to be used in external relations. The Chinese had been constantly reminded of being humiliated by foreign powers, and after June 4, 1989 came to associate the isolation they faced with past abnormality. South Koreans dispensed blame in many directions for their divided country and the resulting dependency on the United States. Russians responded to the collapse of the Soviet Union with alarm about their sudden exposure to nefarious foreign schemes. Whatever the label – defeated, humiliated, divided, or fallen – in each state political forces seized on a psychology of victimization to thwart steps that would have increased trust and smoothed the way to regionalism. Meanwhile, the abrupt economic troubles of Russia and Japan as well as South Korea's financial crisis buttressed warnings of interest groups fearful of development strategies that favor regionalism as well as globalization.

Realists are wrong to assume that security concerns have been decisive in limiting regionalism in NEA. North Korea became a security threat in 1993–4, reappeared as one in Japan in 1998, and entered a standoff with the United States in 2002 with paralyzing regional effects. Yet, it was peripheral to the regional economy and could have been bypassed, particularly if others were anxious to solidify ties that could have diminished the threat. The security challenge of the past between the United States and the Soviet Union faded away, and the challenge anticipated for the future between the United States and China or China and Japan remains far on the horizon. The absence of a long-term sense of regional security counts, but it is not the principal barrier to trust.

Idealists who believe in the power of economic integration are also incorrect in their assumptions, predicting that sustained trade and investment ties lead directly to regionalism. Despite the extraordinary pace of economic integration, resentments have not diminished nor trust been achieved. Increased economic ties create bonds, but they are not enough. Looking back, we find an odd disjuncture between the most upbeat years of bilateral political relations and declining economic ties. Sino-Russian political ties improved sharply in 1994–6 as the economic peak of 1993 was being quickly lost, and even in 1996 when the two sides targeted economics as vital to solidifying their political ties the plans were for naught. Japan decided to pursue better relations with Russia in 1996 just as economic ties plunged from a peak of $5.9 billion in trade in 1995, and after trumpeting new plans to strengthen relations including economic ties in the fall of 1997 trade slid further to $3.8 billion in 1998, according to Russian figures.[1] Of course, regionalism is sought as a means to boost economies; a breakthrough can some day bring a real payoff.

Clashing national identities linked to problems in bilateral relations played the primary role in delaying regionalism. The situation keeps changing because the focus of these identities continues to shift in a fast-evolving global environment. Recent changes suggest that the core countries will draw closer in their views of regionalism, learning to avoid a repeat of the failures in the search for regionalism over the past decade. Yet, we cannot be confident that nations will act soon, even if their national interests are at stake. This may be the verdict on North Korea as it allowed millions of its people to suffer from famine while refusing to open its border or transfer resources from a bloated military budget. It is the consensus on Russia, which long disappointed each of its neighbors with policies unfriendly to entrepreneurship, economic cooperation, or mutual trust. Some would level the same accusations against China for its impatience over Taiwan or strident tone toward Japan and against Japan for its insistence

[1] Viktor Pavliatenko and Alexander Shlindov, "Russo-Japanese Relations: Past Achievements and Future Prospects at the Start of the 21st Century," *Far Eastern Affairs*, 4 (2000), pp. 20–1.

on four small islands at the price of progress with Russia. Critics of foreign policy across the region warned that failure to take into account the psychology of the other side has skewed notions of national interest. This record should draw our attention to national identities that obstruct the quest for regionalism.

After the momentum in 2000 had raised hopes, Koreans took the lead in voicing the cultural implications of regionalism. Some foresaw the arrival of a time when competition would ensue between the European-American cultural sphere and the sphere where Chinese characters have been used.[2] They had become optimistic that South Korea would bring China and Japan together, enhancing its own role as a moderating force between two great powers not as an economic bridge but as a cultural balance. While hesitant about criticizing Chinese nationalism, they reacted with alarm when Japanese textbook revisions in 2001 suggested that divisive views of the first half of the twentieth century would better define the cultural memories of the region than potentially shared views of the previous two millennia. Japan's nationalism threatened the cultural requirements for regionalism. The peoples of NEA may have hesitated to accept the idea that a clash of civilizations was unfolding on a global scale when they responded with fascination but also criticism to Samuel Huntington's thesis.[3] Yet, assessing each other they often resorted to accusations of deep-seated conflict rooted in cultural rather than strategic or economic thinking. Russian views of China, Chinese and Korean views of Japan, and Japanese views of Russia had long been steeped in such assumptions. At the end of the 1990s they were joined by a growing literature in Japan on China and sometimes on Korea too, charging that historical arrogance is too entrenched to be changed. In this view, the real problem is a Chinese sense of superiority (passed on to Koreans). This means that the Japanese can do little to assuage an excessively narrow-minded people and instead must brace themselves for a real clash of civilizations.[4] What follows is not a call for globalization through close ties to the United States, but talk of a regional struggle against the "greater Chinese co-prosperity sphere," even reviving the goal of bringing Taiwan into Japan's "co-prosperity sphere."

As leaders across the region keep calling for trust in relations, we need to look beyond the banality of the message to the reality of the situation. Given the history of vitriolic rhetoric linked to Japan's occupation, the Sino-Soviet dispute, the division of Korea, and the Japanese-Russian territorial dispute, there really is a special problem of forging trust. The idea that contentious

[2] *Asahi shimbun*, April 10, 2001, p. 13.

[3] Samuel P. Huntington, *The Clash of Civilizations and the Remaking of World Order* (New York: Simon and Schuster, 1996).

[4] Ko Bunyu, *Tsukeagaru na Chugokujin, urotaeru na Nihonjin: 21 seiki Nitchu bunmei no chototsu* (Tokyo: Tokuma shoten, 2000).

issues should be set aside in order to build trust gradually through concrete acts of cooperation may misjudge the severity of the problem. In this region everyone is a victim of someone else. None has high moral authority. In particular, Japan has failed to bolster its claims to leadership by 1) setting a high moral tone in its treatment of history; 2) forming networks and exchanges where moral issues are addressed; and 3) developing a vision of regionalism capable of winning confidence from others. Instead of gradually building trust, Japan has failed to communicate its own trust in regionalism. Yet, Japanese dissatisfaction with the abnormal state that endures long after the end of the cold war keeps reviving the goal of regionalism, if only they could be confident that it would allow them to be at ease with history while symbolizing the long-sought beginning of a new era of "reentering Asia" without leaving the West.

Experts in NEA have increasingly faulted excessively emotional coverage in their own country toward one or more of the other regional countries. It is not only China and Russia, where traditions of censorship and narrow nationalism in reporting are difficult to displace. Kokubun Ryosei criticizes the extreme vacillations in Japanese coverage of China,[5] Hakamada Shigeki bemoans Japanese misperceptions of Russia, and Ezra Vogel warns against America's failure to understand or appeal to Chinese public opinion.[6] Old stereotypes endure. Empathy for other nations is not conveyed. One's insecurities when one's identity is in doubt act as a prism through which others are viewed.

Images of untrustworthy negotiating partners loom large throughout the region. Nationalists charge that any softness in negotiations will only whet the appetite of the other country. This message rang loud in countries with a lively press: in Japan toward China, Russia, and North Korea; in Russia toward Japan and China; and since 2000 in South Korea toward the North. In 2000 when Japan's government was turning more conciliatory, the right wing stepped up its attacks, charging for instance that China continued to score a great success while attacking Japan.[7] No matter how anti-Japan its policies, China supposedly was rewarded with continued investment, tourist visits, and ODA as if nothing were the matter. Reports claimed that in place of television shows and dramas of the 1980s showing a realistic image, in the 1990s the Chinese were offered a negative historical image, and proclamations of "friendship" were only an illusion.[8] Worries

[5] Kokubun Ryosei, "Nihon no Chugoku kenkyu kaizen subeki yotsu no mujun," *Sekai*, March 2001, pp. 117–21.

[6] Ezra Vogel, "Courting the People of China," *The Washington Post*, May 14, 2001, p. A21.

[7] Gilbert Rozman, "Japan's Images of China in the 1990s: Are They Ready for China's 'Smile Diplomacy' or Bush's 'Strong Diplomacy?' " *Japanese Journal of Political Science*, 2, pt. 1 (May 2001), pp. 97–125.

[8] "Nitchu saiko," *Sankei shimbun*, October 30, 2000, p. 1; October 24, p. 1; October 25, p. 1.

about the atmosphere for various bilateral talks left little room to consider what is needed for true regionalism. This has been the record of the 1990s, but as the case for regionalism builds it is gradually fading. Since the early 1990s each stage has witnessed further buildup on the path that leads to regionalism.

The Dynamics of a "Decade" of Transition

From 1989 to 2003 all nations of NEA had difficulty calibrating the relative influence of globalization, localism, and nationalism in pursuit of regionalism. The first of these forces in its economic, strategic, and cultural dimensions proved far more powerful than any state in the region understood through most of this period. Too often regionalism was seen as a counterweight to a rather limited international community, rather than as a complementary force feeding off the enormous momentum of a single world becoming increasingly integrated. In contrast, localism in most of NEA was much weaker than anticipated in the early push toward regionalism. Even when they demanded to be at the forefront of regional advocacy, border areas, burdened by criminalization, lacked the market forces and global networks needed to bring credibility to modern economic integration. The nexus of nationalism and regionalism also confounded optimists. The former was growing in significance nearly everywhere in NEA and would not easily yield to the latter. Instead of a transitional time of roughly one decade for a breakthrough to full-fledged regionalism, advocates should have prepared for roughly a quarter century of ups and downs as a modest degree of regional integration and consciousness was achieved riding the wave of globalization. Only the force of globalization could gradually overcome nationalism, calibrating with regionalism and bolstering localism. Neither regionalism nor localism stood a chance against entrenched nationalism until they could utilize the power of surging globalization, while also gaining ground by taking advantage of the deepening resentments against unilateralism that accompany it.

Over fifteen years, each stage had a different dynamic. In 1989 to 1990 the cold war continued to cast its shadow, as states sought leverage between the United States and Soviet Union, relying on "national aspirations" that had been percolating throughout the 1980s that defied "cold war logic." The end of an era divided the United States, which equated its "exceptionalism" with globalization, and the nations of a fractured region, which pursued deep-seated strains of nationalism under the guise of achieving normalcy. All except North Korea had good words to say about regionalism. However, it represented a means to old nationalist ends that only gradually would be tempered by new, global realities.

The period 1991–3 constituted the high water mark of localism, as Japan as well as China and South Korea linked decentralization to regionalism.

If trust at the national level did not suffice to promote regionalism, each side calculated that it could gain an advantage by unleashing local forces along at least one of its borders. "Border fever" captured the fancy of many, but by the end of 1993 all that was left was a cold sweat as the Russian Far East seethed against Chinese traders' "cross-border duplicity," while the ideals of the "Japan Sea rim economic sphere" and South Korea's "northern strategy" crumbled before realities such as Russian criminal groups linked to local administrations.

At mid-decade nations turned to building "civilizational bridges," viewing the rise of Northeast Asia as a challenge to boost a shared cultural legacy. Through various guises they explored the rise of "Eastern civilization" in contrast to U.S. individualistic models. This opened old wounds in NEA. In August 1995 on the fiftieth anniversary of the end of Japan's war occupation "historical distrust" exposed this approach as Japanese legislators provocatively defended historical conduct, Chinese leaders energetically played the "history card" to bolster their nationalist image, and Korean nationalism also grew more pronounced. Hints that a kind of civilizational bond could bring China and Russia back together against the United States and others who aimed to "contain" them looked feeble in the midst of xenophobic charges in the Russian Far East and even in Moscow against the "quiet expansionism" of the "yellow peril." Security issues rose to the fore. The United States and North Korea had a showdown over the North's nuclear program, China prepared its military against a more independence-minded Taiwan, and the United States reassured Japan that its troops would stay put in the region. The search for regionalism had to take questions of power more seriously, abandoning the counterproductive goal of narrowing the cultural gap in ways driven by rising nationalism.

Next regionalism shifted to great-power nationalist maneuvering to resolve doubts on security now at the crux of stunted progress. A frenzy of bilateral summits highlighted "strategic partnerships," but by 1999 most were exposed as "national rivalries." Sino-Japanese ties took a nosedive when Jiang Zemin came calling, recalling history rather than putting it to rest, and thus sparking growing fears on each side that the other was seeking dominance. Russo-Japanese relations were given a boost in 1997 with mutual assurances that a turning point had been reached, but the November 1998 summit in Moscow brought Japanese hopes, still obsessed with the islands, crashing down. As Sino-U.S. ties deteriorated with the domestic backlash in the United States following Clinton's summer visit to China and Sino-Russian economic relations contradicted rosy promises, summitry became identified as high-sounding ritual with little basis in reality. Bombastic rhetoric about balances of power sounded hollow against the divisive forces at work in NEA and the inexorable globalization of the world economy coupled with a near U.S. monopoly of power.

At the end of the decade hope of progress intensified without reconciling the rise of regionalism with the ever-accelerating pace of globalization. China had increased its backing of regionalism after the Asian financial crisis gave evidence of an opportunity for leadership while U.S. victory in Yugoslavia revealed the futility of multipolarity on a global scale. The summer of 2000 saw the apogee of the "sunshine policy," led by South Korea's outreach to the North. Seoul championed regionalism through ASEAN +3 meetings as well as through its energetic diplomacy. At year-end, however, cloudy days had returned as what looked good for the Nobel Prize failed to pass muster before those obsessed with "security dilemmas." Pyongyang refused to commit to rapprochement, because its real target was a U.S. guarantee of its security. China's "smile diplomacy" to Japan was not making much of an impression. Although Japanese leaders were wooing Russia's new president, they miscalculated that their compromise ideas could win approval at home. The Japanese were too insecure about the rise of China and their isolation from talks about North Korea to have confidence in regionalism. China was nervous about the mood in the United States as well as about Putin's failure to sustain Yeltsin's special ties. Critics of the Clinton administration insisted on reasserting U.S. leadership through more containment of China, support of Japan, tough conditions for Russia, and resistance to North Korea, simplistically believing that such clarity could resolve the complexities of the region. At the center remained South Korea intent on using ad hoc arrangements with the North and growing economic ties to achieve regional goals, and succeeding in the waning Clinton years in keeping U.S. backing for its newly active role.

Finally, the war against terror offered a chance for a new administration in the United States to redefine globalization in a manner that sharply changed the context for regional integration. A tide of "unilateralism" suppressed regionalism, first through a strong posture to tighten alliances with friends and raise the threat of containment for North Korea and even China, and after 9/11 through an appeal for all to join the coalition against terror. The North scrambled to escape the tightening vise, playing on Japan's desire for the return of its abducted citizens, South Korea's fear of a dark fate once the sunshine policy was blocked, and Chinese and Russian efforts to prevent a hard landing that could reduce their security. A backlash burst into the open in September 2002, proving that "irrepressible regionalism" will not wait for the U.S. security strategy for the region to unfold. Japan started talks with the North as Prime Minister Koizumi traveled to Pyongyang, but progress quickly halted as the United States and North Korea faced off. Smarting at Bush's tough line that branded it part of the "axis of evil," North Korea raised the security stakes by admitting to a nuclear program and announcing the reopening of its nuclear reactor. The United States had reclaimed center stage after a decade, altering the environment in which regionalism would be decided but not necessarily dimming its prospects. By electing Roh Moo-hyun president at the end of 2002 the South snubbed the United States and rededicated its energies to a regional strategy for transforming the North. It was frustrated, however, by the North's rigid position. As signs of crisis deepened, Roh had no choice but to draw closer to Bush. Regionalism was put on hold.

In all six periods conflicting strategies prevailed amidst irreconcilable notions of globalization and regionalism as well as nationalism and localism. The search for a path to regionalism proved fundamentally flawed even if inexorable momentum in economic relations as well as the reality of global power kept the goal alive despite all shortsighted thinking. Looking back at these periods, we can draw lessons about the priorities needed to achieve regionalism. Early in the 1990s when localism took center stage the Japanese led in assuming that administrative and cultural exchanges could become the driving force, overcoming distrust. In the period of most intense great-power jockeying, the Chinese were particularly keen on forging a security balance as a limit on regionalism. These were exceptions to the prevailing obsession with economics as the engine that would pull all nations onto a regional track. Indeed, advocates of region building repeatedly urged caution in raising sensitive issues linked to culture or security, while idealistically arguing that growing economic ties would create the necessary climate for all aspects of regionalism to come together. Such logic proved insufficient to overcome divisive tendencies that thwarted any breakthrough. The forces of narrowness outweighed those approaching regionalism broadly. A dearth of long-term, strategic thinking left room only for shortsighted ideas.

In the 1980s the cold war atmosphere could not contain nationalistic impulses that suggested support for regionalism, but, in fact, would work against it once unleashed. Japan sought to establish its own hinterland region. China aimed to thwart Japan's power and take over leadership in NEA. In the early 1990s the mistake was made by both Japan and South Korea to treat localism as a driving force for regionalism, when in NEA it could only be a necessary aftereffect and means to deepen it at a later stage. Local areas lacked vitality, market orientation, and vibrant elites capable of forming modern networks. By the mid-1990s the search for regionalism had turned toward nationalist claims in a civilizational veneer. China led with rising nationalism against the spread of Western civilization, warning Russia and offering succor to North Korea in resisting much of noneconomic globalization. South Korea and Japan were still insistent on resisting the U.S. model of capitalism, while also acknowledging that they would have to borrow more of it. Aiming to redefine national identities, states failed to give globalization enough weight and made no progress toward a regional identity. Twentieth-century divisive themes crowded out unifying ones, whether reminders of earlier shared traditions or visions of the fruits of cooperation. Confucianism remained largely the bailiwick of narrow nationalists rather than being redefined to lend support to globalization and in pursuit of regionalism.[9] When during the second half of the decade countries turned to balance-of-power maneuvering, they again were denying globalization and accentuating divisions within NEA. At the turn of the century, various nations with South Korea at the center explored a new path to regionalism, but their reasoning proved porous in dealing with fundamental divisions and the fact that the United States was on the sidelines.

Over the course of fifteen years the driving forces for regionalism changed often, and none had staying power. Japanese leadership through gaining equality with the United States in the cold war and economic clout faltered as the cold war ended abruptly and the bubble economy came crashing to the ground soon afterward. Even without these developments Japanese failure to build trust in NEA dimmed its prospects. Decentralization could not draw the nations of NEA together when areas on the frontlines of cross-border contacts lacked the market forces and anticorruption mechanisms to forge modern networks that could last. When national administrations proved incapable of reforms, and when security problems rose to the fore, more central leadership was needed.

After 9/11 the nation-state acquired added significance. The Asian financial crisis revealed another reality that had been obscured in China's nationalist binge of the mid-1990s, the lingering confidence of South Korea as its "economic miracle" continued, and the pride of Japan even after it had finished. In an age of globalization protected national economies are an anachronism. Not only do borderless trade and investment activities matter, so too do large-scale economic arenas to balance the influence of the United States through NAFTA and the EU. Both China and Japan awakened from 1997 to the limits of their economic voices and the potential of regionalism as a means to amplify their economic influence. The notion that pursuit of great-power leverage would somehow enhance one's standing in the jockeying for regionalism also fell victim to glaring realities. In 1999 the overwhelming power of the United States became clear in the war in Yugoslavia and Russia's acquiescence to its endgame, and first the assertive policies of the Bush administration and then its aggressive conduct of the war against terrorism left behind all prospect of traditional balancing. All powers recognized that regionalism could only be based on a unified field of global security. Even the United States recognized in the WMD danger from North Korea that it wanted help, preferably in concert, from the other countries of NEA.

As the decade ended, levels of public distrust were much higher than early in the 1990s. Americans trusted China and Russia much less than in 1992–4. The Chinese and Russians had turned more negative toward the United States

9 Gilbert Rozman, "Can Confucianism Survive in an Age of Universalism and Globalization?" *Pacific Affairs*, 75(1) Spring 2002, pp. 11–37.

in 1999–2000. Sino-Japanese mutual images had deteriorated sharply into 1999. Although Japanese-Russian images had ameliorated some since 1997, they were built on a fragile foundation that could collapse at any time after the negotiating deadline of the end of 2000. Even South Korean trust of Russia was narrowly linked to progress in relations with North Korea, which could be reversed at any moment. The pattern of the decade was one of illusions. When positive images spiked, it was usually due to false expectations. No shared dream of regionalism offered reasonable prospects for success to skeptics. No careful weighing of actual difficulties tempered the misplaced hopes of idealists and political opportunists. Some wildly exaggerated dreams of regionalism. Fears of regional cooperation caused others to lose sight of what might be achieved. Buffeted by such extremes, few developed a balanced picture of how hard regionalism would be and how valuable it could be.

In 1991–3 the United States was under the illusion that Russia had changed much more than it in fact had, allowing the two ideals of democracy and free market capitalism to blind people to realities far removed from them. In 1997–8 the Clinton administration, albeit to a lesser extent, encouraged a favorable view of China's role in international relations that was belied by great-power maneuvering and rogue-state contacts. In 1991–3 Japan was overly optimistic about China's interest in cooperation toward regionalism, expecting to use this to become a bridge between China and the United States as well. And in 1997–8 Japan raised hopes unduly for a breakthrough in relations with Russia, reasoning that not only would this solve the territorial problem, it would also give Japan leverage with China and boost regionalism. China's illusions were no less extreme. Among them, probably the most serious was the belief in 1994–9 that it could reestablish something akin to the strategic triangle of cold war days by developing a special partnership with Russia. Throughout the post-Soviet years, the wildest illusions existed in Russia. Blaming everyone but themselves and expecting benefits from new negotiations with one or another of the countries in the region, Russians imagined without any basis that they could make progress on their problems and on one or another conception of regionalism. The harm in illusions is not only that countries pursue the wrong strategy of regionalism, delaying the process. It also is that public opinion becomes confused, making necessary compromises difficult.

Reviewing the fifteen years of clashing strategies and perceptions, I suggest that the order of determinants for successful regionalism be redrawn as follows: national identity, national security, economic interests, and cultural exchange. National identity is the foundation of state power and foreign policy. To accept regionalism means to redefine one's country's identity in contrast to nationalist attempts to buttress old notions of identity by twisting regionalism to favor one's own leadership and narrow interests. In all countries except North Korea signs of such a redefinition can be found, but none has crossed a threshold of acceptance. National security also trumps economic interests in building a basis for regionalism. Alarm about threats to territorial integrity, sea-lanes, continued autonomy, and balance of power sets off warning bells that push economic ties to the side. Successive perceptions of threat set back regionalism from 1989 to 2003 and remain engraved in people's minds. Yet, some progress has been made, and the war against terrorism raises hope that a common enemy will alter the security environment. Of course, economic gains are essential to aspirations for regionalism, even if they are not sufficient to remove barriers in national identity and national security. As integration has deepened in NEA and plans have accelerated for showcase projects that bind nations together, the economic dimension promises to play a much more positive role. Finally, the soft power of cultural exchanges and mutual images can be harnessed to assist regionalism. This has been tried repeatedly in the past fifteen years with mixed results and is likely to expand as visits to neighboring countries become ever more numerous and information attracts greater interest even as some of it warns of greater competition.

Around the globe states on the front row of development have decided that our new era demands both entry into WTO and achievement of FTAs through regionalism. One Chinese source noted that among such states only China, Japan, and South Korea have failed to enter an FTA or join others in regionalism.[10] This not only puts them at a disadvantage in the economic competition, but also leaves them less protected in the global political competition, where for a very long time to come the United States will reign alone as the only superpower. The Chinese consider their country to be the center of Asia and its natural leader, and they realize now that reassuring dexterity is the only way to achieve the multilateralism needed to gain some leverage on surrounding areas.[11] NEA, of course, was the overwhelming priority in China's search in 2001–2 for a regional base to extend its economic and political influence. If Japan's wariness of China's rising power leaves it not quite as enthusiastic for regionalism, frustration with its economic and political options drives it to overcome such reticence.

From his inaugural address in February to his trips to Tokyo in June and Beijing in July Roh became the voice of the forthcoming "NEA era." He spoke of regionalism as the path to peace and prosperity, converting NEA into one of three world economic axes. His travel around the region brought attention to the "Korea fads" in Japan and China, including rapid acceleration in visits for business, study, and tourism. Roh was careful to assert that the region must keep pace with a rapidly globalizing world.[12] Although

[10] "10 + 3: zouxiang Dongya ziyou maoyiqu zhilu," *Shijie jingji yu zhengzhi*, 3 (2002), p. 23.

[11] Pang Zhongying, "Zhongguo de Yazhou zhanlue: linghua de duobianzhuyi," *Shijie jingji yu zhengzhi*, 10 (2001), p. 31.

[12] Beijing Xinhua Domestic Service, July 9, 2003.

the nuclear crisis overshadowed promotion of regionalism, the enthusiasm of the Japanese and Chinese receptions for Roh testify to the vitality of his message in 2003. Even if Roh is seen as a failure at home, his message is likely to be sustained.

Lessons for Successful Regionalism

Assessing fifteen years of flawed regionalism, we identify eleven steps with promise to put development on a stable track. Progress has been made on each of them, but none is yet firmly resolved in a manner that should give us confidence that the course of regional integration in NEA is yet secure. These steps are 1) **embracing globalization** as a force for trade, investment, access by foreign firms, and sound and transparent financial operations, but also as a foundation for shared security and common cultural concerns; 2) joint resolve for **steering North Korea** toward a transition that gives its leaders a way to move forward without succumbing to its WMD blackmail; 3) **finding an accord between China and Japan over security** concerns inclusive of Taiwan and handling of the "history card"; 4) **building U.S. support for regionalism** as a positive force for stability, offering assistance in the battle with terrorists and the proliferation of WMD; 5) **recognizing South Korea's critical position** in bringing China and Japan together in the triangular core of regionalism and in promoting multilateral approaches to North Korea with four great powers; 6) **encouraging Russia's active involvement** in regional security as a whole and energy security in particular; 7) **fostering a regional identity**, combining a shared vision for the region's role in the world and invocation of the region's Confucian traditions in ways compatible with the needs of the new era; 8) **compromising on territorial disputes**, one by one or through trade-offs, that allows improved bilateral relations across the region; 9) **nurturing engines of regionalism,** including energy pipelines, transportation corridors, and urban networks; 10) **accepting a gradual timetable** for achieving long-term goals; and 11) **establishing organizations** that allow regionalism to be nurtured from above, however cautiously.

(1) Embracing globalization is essential for a region whose economic growth has been driven by exports and where uncertain geographical limits are likely to continue to leave doubts about the scope of regionalism. Instead of boosting narrow interests, states must approach regionalism by putting limits on nationalism and accepting the overall force of globalization. Northeast Asia requires regionalism with a high level of openness to global economic, security, and cultural integration. Moreover, unlike early proposals to start with a small cross-border region or later suggestions to concentrate on the three strongest economies of Japan, South Korea, and China, the geographical range needs to be broad, allowing for different levels of involvement within a single country. Russia with its energy cache and Pacific ports is an important player, which may consider facing both EU integration

in the West and NEA integration in the East. As a unit, ASEAN is too diverse and holds too many nonmarket economies to become integrated with NEA in the near future, but parts of ASEAN can play a valuable role as partners, especially in early stages of regionalism when China and Japan look to it to prevent the other from having the advantage. The geography must avoid countries hesitant to globalize, while reaching to countries on the borders of the core triangle that would draw China and Japan together.

Regionalism is unlikely to advance far without a heavy dose of globalization. The internal dynamic of NEA has been found to be too weak to lead far without a powerful external accelerant. Through identification with the global community or international society regional consciousness can also be fostered. Only the broadest shared identity appears capable of diminishing nationalism and fostering an identity open to regionalism too. Similarly, only a global security framework dominated by the United States appears likely to provide adequate confidence in national security. The pillar of regional security remains the U.S. forward deployment, marked by bases and alliances in Japan and South Korea, control of the sea by the Seventh Fleet, and the might of U.S. forces worldwide in reserve. This freezes North Korean forces behind the thirty-eighth parallel, warns China against using force to reunite with Taiwan, and enlists as many countries as possible in the war against terrorism. Even in economics as trade and investment within the region grow rapidly, the global impact of WTO forms the background for regionalism. Each country looks ahead to more openness and better institutions for economic transactions as other countries in NEA fulfill commitments to WTO. In cultural exchanges too, as the World Cup soccer matches in Japan and South Korea demonstrated, global standards lead to regional trust.

Few people investigated the inner workings of criminal regionalism closely. It could be dangerous. Foreign diplomats reported on the general picture, but they either found it too dangerous to delve deeply or confined their remarks to the secret pouches. A South Korean council who took seriously the challenge of learning what North Koreans were doing in Primorskii krai, including links to counterfeiting and drugs, was murdered, and little could be done when local authorities made no progress in determining whether it was the North Koreans or Russian organized crime that did it. Yakuza in Japan are closely linked with far-right politicians and causes, including the recovery of four islands from Russia, slogans for which are often splashed across their trucks and blared on their loudspeakers. Chinese criminal groups sometimes linked to military smugglers who long were exempt from customs control have shaped relations with Russia more than with most other states. Part of globalization is to attack the criminality and corruption plaguing cross-border connections and often distorting the operations of government.

In each of the core countries of NEA a consensus exists in favor of globalization, but the debate on how to proceed underestimates the barriers and the costs of their presence. Japan's embrace of internationalization in the

1980s proved insufficient and its reforms of the 1990s were slow to address the problem. Although it has recently made major strides toward the security posture of a responsible U.S. partner, new consciousness on economic openness and cultural integration still falls far short of global standards. Right-wing nationalism casts doubt on international as well as regional trust. Of late, China's academic debate on globalization has become increasingly favorable, expanding from economic to security themes. The Chinese accommodation with the United States in 2003 bodes well for its standing as a responsible great power, even if the challenge remains of embracing universal values in a way that is reassuring to regional partners. South Korea is so bifurcated between left and right that centrist support for globalization is left under a shadow. New FTA talks are a test for global as well as regional integration. Across the region a legacy of communism or the developmental state along with a holdover political elite takes time to resolve. United States management of globalization can shape the transition.

Another lesson of the past decade is the need to find the right geographical range, avoiding both narrow and broad notions of region. Targeting areas too narrow such as the Sea of Japan rim ignores the weak basis for decentralization, while expecting much from the wide-ranging Asia-Pacific expanse and APEC defies the logic of basing regionalism on a core group of neighboring countries. If the question of ties with ASEAN remains unsettled as both China and Japan have begun a quest for FTAs, the former agreeing within a decade to form an FTA of ASEAN +1 and the latter joining with Singapore in an FTA, the reality is that nonmarket states such as Laos, Cambodia, and Myanmar or even chaotic Indonesia are not promising partners. It is NEA where countries that, in essential respects, embrace globalization will determine the destiny of regionalism.

(2) Steering North Korea toward regionalism without further crises over its WMD stockpile and development has become a shared concern in NEA. In 2003 it looms as the most urgent challenge as the standoff grows between the United States, vigorously ridding the world of potential dangers from the spread of WMD, and North Korea, determined to retain its totalitarian system through the threat of developing and spreading WMD. The United States has turned to China and Russia, seeking their support in dealing with the North, while redoubling efforts at coordination with South Korea and Japan. Newly engaged in its own diplomacy with Pyongyang and targeted by its missiles, Tokyo has reason to seek Russian and Chinese assistance too. With all of the nations on the frontline nervous about the Bush administration's "axis of evil" label and its long delay in engaging the North, the case for closer regional cooperation on security is becoming stronger. A common threat appears to be bringing the region together, even if its existence stalls regionalism.

At issue is more than an immediate crisis between the world's policeman and its most dangerous outlaw. The weapons of North Korea endanger its neighbors' security most of all. In case of a meltdown refugees could overwhelm these nations. The costs of reviving the North's economy as well as of making it a central link in transportation and energy networks would pose a heavy burden on any one country. Seen broadly, the security of NEA depends on a regional approach to the crisis over North Korea, and the aftermath of the crisis is likely to foster mutual awareness of the need to work together.

(3) Finding an accord between China and Japan over security. A balance must be struck between the security aspirations of China and Japan, which neither sees as giving the other a one-sided advantage. If the Chinese calculate that time is on their side, they should have the confidence to be patient as the balance is shifting. The Japanese, in turn, may have to accept the rise of China with an understanding that they have leverage over how it occurs.

This must be a region without a leader. The Japanese in the early 1990s, Chinese in the late 1990s, and the Bush administration from 2001 all aimed to put themselves at the center of NEA. In fact, the highest hopes for regionalism came when a country not feared for its desire for dominance became the most fervent advocate: the Soviet Union as it faded in 1988–9 and South Korea in 2000. Unless the triangle of the U.S.-China-Japan can be stabilized, there will be no easy path to regionalism. Balancing the triangle depends not only on the United States, but also on what Beijing and Tokyo decide, weighing cooperation against competition. If they can resolve questions of leadership for now, they may jointly regain the initiative in the region. The presence of the United States, South Korea, and Russia helps to achieve balance.

There are no status quo powers in NEA. All have unfinished agendas and fear that they will lose vital steps toward normalcy if regionalism is not done right. China fears loss of Taiwan and a region under joint U.S.-Japanese stewardship. It seeks the fluidity of a region that can accommodate a rising power. Japan fears China's rise and the prospect of a U.S.-Chinese condominium. Caught between the security allergy left by the postwar veto of the left wing and the suspended agenda of the right wing, Japan has been relatively immobilized despite desperate breakout attempts with each potential regional partner. Each tries to use Russia's fear of being peripheralized in NEA and South Korea's desperation to find a path toward reunification. If the United States tips the balance in its relations with China and Japan, the two find it harder to find common ground for regionalism. The North Korean threat is leading toward more balance by the United States, while also heightening awareness in China and Japan of their security as well as economic interdependence.

(4) Building U.S. support for regionalism. After the United States turned to APEC as a means to press for globalization to overturn protectionist practices, countries in NEA and SEA confirmed their doubts about its value for their regional needs. It may serve a useful purpose as a forum for summitry, raising the stature of leaders who meet with the U.S. president; yet, it cannot

bridge the diversity of views in Asia as well as the U.S. position. Growing interest in a narrower approach to regionalism appears to conflict with the new unilateralism in the United States in molding a single global community. Only by accepting the main contours of globalization can U.S. resistance be lowered.

We can discern three contrasting, but also overlapping, views of globalization in the United States. The dominant paradigm shared by most Democrats and Republicans is economic liberalism. It was the consensus in the 1980s to China in the early stages of its economic reforms and openness and to first the Soviet Union and then Russia in its initial years. It also was the leading perspective on Japan. The more these countries became free market economies, the more they would change in their domestic and international behavior. Entry into WTO, idealists assumed, would drive other changes. On the Right, approval for free market policies was qualified by a very high priority on settling security questions early, not trusting economic forces to work at least for a long time. George W. Bush took power pressing for stronger global cooperation on security issues, preparing to isolate countries that resisted. This notion of globalization focused on a new security order to accompany a new economic order, including more unilateral U.S. actions with the assumption that allies and eventually other countries would fall in line. On the Left, qualifications centered instead on the need to temper economic freedom with social and environmental programs to create a just and sustainable world. This led to support for a less vertical world order and more multilateralism. Since 9/11 the Bush position prevails, not that of the Left.

George Bush and his advisors warned in 2000 that the Clinton administration was mismanaging the region. At the outset, they created an impression that they would treat North Korea as a threat, China and Russia as more competitors than partners, and Japan and South Korea as allies to be drawn together into a regional unity. This was a strategy to cut off rising regionalism as a danger to U.S. interests. Implicitly, it disapproved of the reduced role of the United States as South Korea pressed ahead in talks with the North and China boosted its regional standing. The new posture constituted an abrupt switch from the desire at the beginning of the 1990s to use Japan as a bridge to China and to Russia. Now Republicans were determined to make Japan a stronghold resistant to those countries. They rejected the Perry process in support of the South Korean sunshine policy in favor of pressure tactics and delay. Such abrupt swings in U.S. policy compounded by struggles between unilateralists and multilateralists leave the United States with an image of obstruction.

Nations look to regionalism as an escape from dependence. Once having viewed globalization as a path to equality with the United States, the Japanese too are increasingly worried that it also carries the threat of dependence. Even if they are inclined to nationalism, the new twist on globalization makes them receptive to a dose of regionalism. Koreans are especially anxious to lower their dependency on the United States for security and on Japan for economics. Regionalism means strengthening ties with China and Russia and developing economic and geostrategic frameworks with them to achieve balance. As the Chinese lose confidence in other ways to balance U.S. power, they too turn to regionalism. These forces show no signs of receding after the Bush administration converted globalization into a unilateral mission dismissive of regional dynamics. The United States is bound to fail if it does not accommodate these yearnings. Yet, the United States retains great leverage as these countries increasingly recognize that for both security and economic reasons regionalism must not stray far from global economic integration and cooperation against terrorism.

The United States should accept that China is not on the verge of becoming an economic and military power capable of dominating NEA. Its internal problems are mounting as entry into WTO proceeds, including rural unrest over corruption and excess taxes and urban dislocation from troubled reforms of state-owned enterprises. As long as the pursuit of Taiwan's independence is kept in abeyance, the United States can work with China to define regionalism in NEA with the goal of exerting a positive influence. This has been the trend since 9/11, and it did not abate with the North Korean crisis. There is reason to expect that the new generation of leaders under Hu Jintao will be inclined to sustain it.

On the one hand, for regionalism to be realized on the back of globalization U.S. involvement needs to be greater than it was through the 1990s. On the other, U.S. power must not become so overwhelming that it stifles regionalism in pursuit of a unilateral type of globalization. The United States has done little to lead the nations of NEA toward regionalism, by giving its blessing to relative autonomy within a global framework. It has not steered a steady course combining economic integration and security confidence building, instead flitting from excess confidence in global economic integration to excess alarm over security threats. Both approaches and the way they are supported by the foreign-policy establishment and the political elite appear crudely U.S.-centric. Local observers find the United States prone to oversimplification and disregard for the dynamics in the region. While inside the region one hears mostly about aspirations for national autonomy, and a balance of powers, the message from the United States is overwhelmingly centered on the goals of increased security for the United States and openness for U.S. and other global financial interests. Sensitivities are aroused, and the United States will find it hard to strike a balance. Yet, the United States has not been as much to blame for stunted regionalism as each of the countries within the region, and only a new surge in unilateralism might make it the prime inhibiting force.

At the end of 2003 the United States faced the dual danger of North Korean WMD beyond control and China pressed by Taiwan independence moves to use the threat of force. It also stared at trade deficits from NEA, led by China, on a scale never seen before. Yet, the leaders of Japan and South Korea had agreed to send troops to Iraq in support of the United States, reliance had risen on China as the critical intermediary with North Korea, and the prospects were high for compromises to cool passions over Taiwan and to accelerate trade openings. United States need for NEA cooperation had never been higher, raising the chances for acceptance of some forms of regionalism, however contentious the process.

(5) Recognizing South Korea's critical position. Regionalism must start with a core group of countries. The old superpowers are both too far from the region's center and too enamored of one type of international logic or another to be part of this core. North Korea may be close geographically, but it is at an even greater distance ideologically due to its obsession with self-reliance and neglect of reforms. That leaves China, Japan, and South Korea. Only from late 1999 did the forces coalesce drawing them together in the search for regionalism: 1) a South Korean leadership intent on reunification to the extent that it would take major strides to improve ties with both Japan and China and be eager not to divide them but to bridge their differences; 2) a Chinese leadership nervous about U.S. relations and eager for South Korea to take the initiative as it worked to undo the damage that had occurred to its image in Japan; and 3) Japanese leadership still intent in "reentering Asia" and dissatisfied with its excessive dependence on the United States and inadequate leverage in great-power relations, while looking to South Korea for an FTA and other help in regionalism.

South Korea, despite its smaller population and economy, has a disproportionate say in the region, and should Korea unite that will be even more the case despite the burdens of transition. A situation of two great rivals – the United States and China or Japan and China – uneasily eyeing each other invites a third party to be a balance. A third party closely tied to each of them can calm a region with wary economic powerhouses.

The successive failure of unbalanced strategies should be instructive for future attempts at regionalism. Japan's interest in leading East Asia to regionalism without sufficient safeguards on its vertical control or coordination with globalization hit an impasse in 1996–7. China's ambition to combine regionalism with great-power balances came undone in 2001–2 when Russia recognized that it is not a pole after all and other attempts to limit U.S. power also failed. South and North Korea played their own games of looking for combinations of great powers to support their reunification strategies, the former coming closest to backing balanced regionalism. Russia showed little interest in regionalism in its preoccupation with the threat of globalization, while the United States also dismissed regionalism in its determination to boost globalization. Although in 2002–3 China was more committed to regionalism, it realized that a new strategy is required.

This is a region where leadership is problematic. If China or Japan takes the lead, the other will be suspicious. The United States' motives are inevitably suspect as all others seek some balance against unilateral globalization. Powerful business sectors in each country fear FTAs that reach beyond WTO timetables. Japanese and South Korean agricultural lobbies and Chinese manufacturing have a large say in domestic politics. Given these complexities, indirect leadership and roundabout paths are likely. Ties to ASEAN give China and Japan additional options. Pressures from WTO negotiations and the United States can reverberate in regional progress. For some years facilitation of economic ties within the core triangle may be easier than FTA agreements as states standardize their regulations, ease customs procedures, and reduce bureaucratic red tape. Coordinated research teams are already in place to lead the way. South Korea holds the key as the leg of the NEA core triangle with superior relations with China and Japan.

(6) Encouraging Russia's active involvement. Russia's motives have often been suspect, given its history as a divisive force in NEA. At first China's leaders feared that Yeltsin was too close to the West. Soon Japanese leaders observed Russia tilting to China. In his first years Putin somewhat distanced Russia from China and responded hopefully to Japan's initiatives. He has moved Russia closer to the United States in both economic policy and strategic cooperation. With its surplus of oil and gas resources, Russia attracts interest in the countries of NEA, where energy security is a growing concern. By making energy projects and management of North Korea the central themes in the start-up phases of regionalism, the other countries are likely to offer Russia a large role in their plans. As long as Russia meets tough conditions for WTO compliance and is obliged to clean up the lawlessness in its Far East, Russia should not be excluded from a NEA community.

(7) Fostering a regional identity. Unlike many recommendations to solve little problems first, NEA must satisfy deep reservations at the outset. This means it needs a grand vision to override narrow national identities constructed in the twentieth century that mainly take notice of divisions. It will require a beacon for a bright future without sacrificing sound judgment about how hard nations must keep working to achieve it.

The period from 1989 is filled with an extraordinary degree of inconsistency in foreign policy and in strategizing about national interests. Changes in national leaders account for some variation, but China's relative leadership continuity did not prevent many of the most glaring examples of reversing course. For example, at first Beijing urged Putin to stand against U.S. power as the way to boost Russian power, but after 9/11 it argued that his decision to draw close to the United States was the only strategy to create an environment for economic growth, even equating this choice to Deng Xiaoping's strategy in the 1980s to open China to investment. The states of NEA must take a more consistent long-term view of their national interests if they are to reassure each other that regionalism is lasting.

From time to time in the 1990s the idea was floated that regionalism could be based on shared traditions. Japanese idealists championed this cause early with calls for a cultural sphere based on the use of Chinese characters. Koreans picked it up, ignoring the written language because they rarely use characters, but highlighting lifestyle traditions, in which they are most prominent.[13] The Chinese may become the main standard-bearers now that they have embraced regionalism. The search for a shared history is bound to be revived, especially when U.S. pressures draw attention to some discrepancy in values.

The region faces what one Japanese journal calls the "dangerous atmosphere" of media differences.[14] Telling splits in coverage occurred in 1) 1994 between China and Russia over contrasting views of recently opened cross-border trade and transit; 2) 1995 between China and Japan at the fiftieth anniversary of the end of the Pacific War; and 3) 1997 between Japan and Russia at the moment of a negotiating breakthrough at Krasnoyarsk. None of these issues came without prior misperceptions that contributed to a new level of distrust, and none led to a rapid reversal in the downward tide of images. The precipitating events were varied, but the outcomes were similarly bleak in damaging the basis for mutual understanding. A vision of regionalism can temper repetition of such outbursts.

Despite past preference for labels such as "socialism with Chinese characteristics" and Japan's "nihonjinron," there is much agreement on the sources of pride that are special in NEA and can be traced to the past. All parties recognize their own people's educational orientation, diligence, thrift, and entrepreneurship or industrial management. The three countries also emerged from the Asian financial crisis with new and shared appreciation for their interdependence and distance from the West. Each, in one form or another, favors an AMF. They have long agreed that they live in a region with complementary resources. As they recognize common challenges, they are reaching the point of agreement on a need for broader and more institutionalized cooperation.

By 2002 the words *East Asian community* were being taken seriously. While APEC and ASEAN had lost significance since 1997, ASEAN +3 was suddenly drawing more attention with some suggesting it is the growing ties of the "3" with only a weak presence of ASEAN that really matter. The process looks different from various angles, but one way of drawing the chronology is to start in early 1999 with Japan's interest in developing an FTA with Korea, Korea's desire to bring China into the plan, and China's enthusiasm from 2000. Roh Moo-hyun in 2003 became the champion of regionalism, but he was being eclipsed by China's efforts.

[13] *Hanguk Chongguk Ilbon kukmin uishik chosa paekso* (Seoul: Yonsei University, 1996).

[14] Kamimura Koji, "Chugoku hodo," *Sekai*, March 2001, p. 112.

At Beijing's initiative an East Asian think-tank network was established in 2003 with Zhang Yunling the general coordinator. Its first gathering in October followed a signed declaration of the leaders of China, Japan, and South Korea to expand the areas of cooperation through ASEAN +3 and to support an East Asian process, which all expected to lead to a formal East Asian summit. Because it is harder to establish a NEA community, the looser framework of East Asia must do. While Seoul, with reunification in mind, may seek to rush ahead to NEA, Beijing has its eye set mainly on Tokyo and its cautious, but growing, interest in promoting a wider framework for regionalism. So far, Tokyo is too wary of Moscow and too uncertain about Pyongyang to forego an emphasis on SEA, and Beijing has made use of that context to draw Tokyo further into plans for regionalism. Zhang has moved from involvement in a vision group to work further with academics of Japan, South Korea, Singapore, and other states to achieve a common NEA worldview.

(8) Compromising on territorial disputes. Territorial disputes cannot simply be set aside as if they will magically be addressed after economic integration has been reached. Interim solutions linked to regionalism can calm disputes over the division of Korea, Taiwan separatism, the islands that keep Japan from signing a peace treaty with Russia, and other unresolved issues less threatening to regionalism, but capable of arousing passions. For instance, compromises over the rocks known as Tokdo/Takeshima and Senkaku/Diaoyutai would be a small price for all to pay in order to set China, Japan, and South Korea on a track of shared confidence in the prospects of cooperation.

Instead of soft regionalism bypassing tough questions, our era calls for hard choices involving those usually identified as staunch defenders of national interests. The foreign ministries became targets: in Russia during Yeltsin's first term for being too soft on the United States and briefly also on Japan; in China and the United States for being too soft on each other, especially as policies hardened in 1999–2001; in South Korea in 2001 for being too soft on the United States; and in Japan for having nearly everything wrong as criticisms mounted over softness to China, South Korea, and the United States. For regionalism to work it has to enlist the big corporations and the security establishment. They played a secondary role in the 1990s although at times promoting steps toward improved ties. If the most symbolic challenges to the soft voices of the foreign ministries are handled at an early point, calls for compromise will have to be taken more seriously in the years ahead.

Negotiators must strike a balance capable of persuading public opinion and reassuring those most concerned about security. Many accused Kim Dae-jung of stepping over the line toward North Korea in the first half of 2000, when he won agreements that were not fulfilled. Likewise, Mori may have raced too far ahead of public opinion in his appeals to Putin in the second half of the year.[15] All sides must make the case on behalf of the advantages for strategic stability and a future-oriented economy, while seeking reciprocity on concessions over key matters.[16] There is no shortcut to relations based on trust drawing long-term public support and sustained by continued gains for all parties. The public must look ahead to goals that bind nations together for a long time ahead. This means that symbols of victimization cannot be left to fester.

(9) Nurturing engines of regionalism. Even if regionalism must rest on a solid foundation of globalization, it also requires some engines within NEA to pull it forward. Still useful is Japanese ODA, perceived in China as a substitute for war reparations even as Japanese nationalists and budget constraints are challenging it as never before.[17] Another engine is Seoul's desire to draw all of the region's great powers into its strategy to persuade Pyongyang to turn from threat to reconciliation. A third is the growing importance of Russian energy to fuel regional economic dynamism and to provide a measure of security should supplies from the Middle East be interrupted. Finally, we should not forget the significance of the new calculation by China that over the next decade or two in what will remain a unipolar world regionalism displaces multipolarity as the best foreign-policy tool available. Gradually in recent years more forces have been added to the regional drive for increased integration, and they will need to be nurtured in what remains an uncertain environment of nationalist identities and security uncertainties.

Regionalism will gain visibility through big, joint projects, all the better if they are packaged as answers to serious security questions. Cooperation over North Korea satisfies that criterion, posing extraordinary financial burdens and problems of trust, but also constituting a shared project to calm fears by cooperating on confidence-building measures and integrating the North into the regional economy. Also high on the list of attractions would be an institutionalized mechanism for turning a growing rivalry between China and Japan into a full-scale partnership even if quarrels will remain.

Five economic programs may showcase cross-border integration over the next decade. An energy grid may be divided into oil pipelines, gas pipelines, and tanker routes as well as power lines to hydroelectric stations. Russia plays the key role; regionalism will entail overcoming the competition for its oil between Japan and China with a joint strategy that produces a compromise. Transport routes will also shape regionalism. In this case, Russia may maneuver to make its Trans-Siberian railway the principal artery, but China has the edge with short, direct routes to Western Siberia from the Koreas

[15] Hakamada Shigeki, "Hakamada Shigeki no me," *Hokkaido shimbun*, September 1, 2000.
[16] Hakamada Shigeki, "Hakamada Shigeki no me," *Hokkaido shimbun*, September 5–6, 2000.
[17] Komori Yoshihisa, "Taichu ODA o zenpatsuseyo," *Voice*, July 2002, pp. 64–71.

and even Vladivostok. Urban hubs are likely to be reshaped too. Whereas for China as a whole Shanghai is the obvious winner, for the areas of Japan, the Northeast and even parts of North China, the Koreas, and the Russian Far East, a corridor passing through Seoul may give South Korea the edge. It has the advantage of centrality and a neutral site for China and Japan. Recent monetary cooperation is likely to be extended, playing to Japan's financial supremacy in the region. A multiplicity of programs for region building can promote many centers. Working out FTAs first between Japan and South Korea and then including China with hopes for further expansion would spread the economic gains.

(10) Accepting a gradual timetable. Past timetables expressed by boosters of regionalism have erred on the side of excessive optimism. A breakthrough usually seemed to be just around the corner. Nationalism still makes caution essential. It will take time to overcome flare-ups of nationalism as well as the doubts raised by a "decade" of flawed regionalism. In 2002–3 the North Korean nuclear crisis stalled the search for regional stability. Quick agreements without demonstrating the advantages to the public would not provide an answer. Even if there is agreement on the mutual benefits, the first pronouncements should temper expectations with warnings of a transition ahead.

If politics and economics converge, as seems possible once the endgame for North Korea's crisis helps to restart regionalism on a more solid foundation, we may expect an emerging agenda to favor security, new steps to build trust, and consensus on an alluring vision tempered by caution to allow for gradual accommodations. By 2015 a threshold proving the merits of regional integration can realistically be crossed.

(11) Establishing a new organization. The right organizational framework for considering regional problems in NEA has been slow to evolve. At the start of the 1990s the G-7 remained the primary venue for the industrial powers to discuss major global issues, including those of NEA. Japan took problems to this forum and expected to serve as spokesman for its neighborhood, while China and South Korea stayed on the sidelines. After Bill Clinton upgraded the APEC meeting into an annual summit at the end of 1993, this venue vied with what was soon to become the G-8 (adding Russia) as the showcase for high-level exchanges of views related to NEA. Side meetings such as the October 2002 talks on North Korea's nuclear weapons program occur; yet, the size of the APEC gathering is large, and many countries soon soured on its ability to get things done. From 1997 ASEAN +3 offered a new venue, minus the United States, to bring the leaders of China, Japan, and South Korea together. By 2001 the "3" had upgraded an informal breakfast chat into their own annual summit. This evolution has brought the region closer to a core organization small enough to address the needs of regionalism. The basis of a formal organization exists, even if its evolution remains far from complete.

In 2003 questions about global organization spread across the region. Would Japan support China's entry, now that China's leader had come to Evian, France to be at the sidelines of the annual meeting, converting the G-8 to the G-9? As multilateral talks over the North Korean crisis were under debate, the questions arose as to whether China would support Japan's inclusion in political talks, and would it favor Japan's permanent entry into the Security Council, as Japan has sought? At the root of these questions was uncertainty as to whether Beijing and Tokyo would agree to share leadership within their common region and on behalf of the region in global organizations. This is the key to a new regional organization as well.

An organization advocating regional identity and nurturing engines of regionalism will likely rest on three firmaments if it is to become the vehicle for full-blown regional integration over a gradual timetable. Success will depend on how soon clear answers can be offered to the following questions. One, will there be general acceptance of the unitary nature of the global economy, world civilization, and international security, as claims of regional distinctiveness are balanced with assurances to the United States and others in the world community? Divisive expectations of the 1990s such as sharp competition ahead among relatively closed regional economies, protracted separation into clashing civilizations, and intensified struggle among great powers no longer drive the pursuit of regionalism. Yet, this does not mean that regionalism will not be balanced against forces of globalization in some situations, particularly when the United States is most unilateral, or that we can yet expect a clear pathway to regionalism becoming complementary of globalization. Two, is a balance of countries to be achieved with Korea assuming a pivotal position between China and Japan and others gaining a role without fear that China or Japan will dictate the approach to regionalism? All are reassured by putting the initiative in the hands of a country that does not seek regional leadership, but are either China or Japan prepared to abandon their ambitions to make this a reality? Is the president of South Korea able to juggle the challenges of dealing with North Korea and the responsibilities of regional leadership? Three, are countries ready to abandon the myth that regionalism can progress on the basis of economics alone and allow all-around regionalists to gain the upper hand? This depends on relations of trust still slow to develop. A breakthrough Sino-Japanese meeting is needed to build confidence for a multisided summit that would formally launch regionalism. Despite voices in China that visits by a Japanese prime minister to the Yasukuni shrine should not stand in the way of formal summits and in Japan against exaggerated fears of China, in 2003 a bilateral breakthrough is not in sight.

Is there a shared will to move forward? Bold thinking is needed for an approach that will draw China, Japan, and South Korea together. China may now be ready to find such an approach, as may South Korea. If Japan seems doubtful, its leaders are driven by economic concerns as well as the

North Korean danger to continue to seek a new level of integration. Further progress depends mostly on these leaders, who, as they struggle to lift Japan's economy from stagnation and to convey a national identity that serves the country's future well, must navigate between U.S. appeals to draw closer in a global partnership and the calls of neighbors to join together for regional strength. Indecisiveness over how to proceed may make Japan the laggard that delays regionalism the most over the next decade. If China and South Korea at last recognize its value, they will have to make a compelling case to Japan to go forward. The United States may find it difficult to accept NEA regionalism, but it has many levers available both through bilateralism and its own multilateralism that could help to steer such regionalism onto a less confrontational track. Adjustments will be easier if all recognize that the issue is not whether there will be NEA regionalism, but how quickly and with what accommodation to forces of globalization it will go forward. Although the United States cannot expect to be part of the new regional organization, it must be reassured that it can position itself as a partner with no less standing than in the EU and must agree to temper recent unilateralism.

The NEA community or East Asian community, as it may be called, is likely to be based on openness to globalization, a shared program for North Korean integration with South Korea in a pivotal role, a path-breaking accord between China and Japan, and special arrangements for Russia so that it has some membership standing and the United States so that it does not grow nervous over exclusion. There is a need for gradual integration, fostering a regional identity that can deepen as a select number of engines of cooperation draw nations together and lingering territorial and historic disputes can be addressed in a spirit of compromise. It is a substantial agenda for the coming decade just to cross the threshold of regionalism. What is not needed is another wave of optimism that pays little heed to the stark lessons of 1989–2003.

Index